# *Colonial Families of*
# ***Surry***
# ***and***
# ***Isle of Wight Counties, Virginia***

Volume 11

# *Colonial Families of*
# ***Surry***
# ***and***
# ***Isle of Wight Counties, Virginia***

Volume 11

*Transcription of*
Isle of Wight, Virginia
Deed Book 1
1688-1705

*compiled by*
John Anderson Brayton
Memphis, Tennessee

**Copies may be obtained from the author:**
1900 Central Avenue
Memphis, TN 38104

Published for the author by Otter Bay Books
Baltimore, Maryland

Library of Congress Control Number 2011924630
ISBN 978-0-8063-5529-0

*Made in the United States of America*

# Table of Contents

Introduction....................vii

**Text:**
Original Index....................1
Deed Book 1....................11

**Indices:**
Names....................397

Locations....................433

Slaves....................437

Ages....................439

**Previous Publications**....................441

## Introduction and Acknowledgements

History sometimes indulges in jokes of questionable taste, a remark I wish I could take credit for, but which appeared in the introduction to a marvelous send-up of Mormon manners [if you will permit the oxymoron] entitled *Utah, Gateway to Nevada*. It is now out of print—the pamphlet, that is, not Utah. Let us mention a couple of these jokes. The first, and the one most pertinent to this study, is the notion that colonial Virginia was peopled entirely by Cavaliers and other persons of the *haute noblesse*, whose behavior always reflected their aristocratic background and high-minded vision. This long held prejudice on the part of the old Dominion's historians and genealogists has been as difficult to uproot from Virginia's imaginary garden of earthly delights as ground elder from an herbaceous border. Let me help. Enter Samuel Cohoon [item **128**], aghast at the demonstration of seventeenth century *moeurs* with which he is forced to contend, and which have already destroyed his plans for relationship-building with the hapless Frances Meacom. All because of the dastardly deeds of one Thomas Norsworthy. Well! In a modern setting, Cohoon would have gone into therapy and perhaps signed up for a anger management course. I suppose he could have texted Frances Meacom....

To continue along this line of reasoning, one will easily see that there are not many indications of aristocratic behavior in these pages. There is an amusing list of fines for what passed as local obscenities [see item **58**], although these oaths pale in comparison with the Anglo-Saxon epithets reported by Mrs. Drake or uttered by Mr. Cohoon. Of course, one will readily admit that the clerk had enormous discretion as to what would pass for material worthy of consignment to the "record." Does one imagine that he enjoyed immortalizing these episodes just a little bit too much?

This Deed Book contains a little of everything, although there are mostly deeds, depositions, and a few wills scattered throughout. It seems, finally, to be a companion to the will books which were now fully dedicated to probate information. Why this volume contains a few wills is puzzling, unless there is a completely mundane reason for their inclusion—the clerk couldn't find the will book, someone else had it, who knows?

The pleasure of transcribing an entire record book from the late sixteen hundreds lies in that every word must be rendered verbatim. In other words, the loaded revolver of authenticity was pointed directly at my head and I was forced to write down everything that I saw, no matter how x-rated. And so it goes. The depositions were particularly valuable in providing ages and personal information not often contained in the land transfers.

Readers will have to deal with what they consider obscenity in whatever way that they will. The examples from early Norfolk are, if not "worse," then much more plentiful, and much more given to precise geography. Alice Granbury Walter tastefully excluded these from her own transcriptions, but it is my hope to resurrect these early Norfolk record books at some decent point in the future. They are simply too interesting to let someone else's sense of decorum eliminate them from the public record.

Apart from the collection of administrations from the middle of the seventeenth century, this work completes the transcriptions of all the seventeenth-century records of Isle of Wight Co., VA.

John Anderson Brayton
Memphis, Tennessee
February, 2011

Isle of Wight Co., VA, Deed Book 1

## INDEX

**[a]**

ADAMS, GILBERT his pattent & acck$^{t}$ to JN$^{O}$ GOODRICH 37
ALLEN ARTHUR Maj$^{r}$ his Convey$^{nc}$ to ROB$^{T}$ FFLAKE 44
ALLEN ARTHUR his Convey$^{nc}$ to EDWARD BOYKIN 45
ATLMAN's inventory 120
ASKEW's bond to ASKEW 131
APPLEWHAITE Capt deed to his Children 315
ARRINGTON & ux Deed & release to BODY 392
ALLEN ARTHUR Deed to BOYKIN 381
ALESBUREYs Deed to PAGE 420

**[b]**

BRANCH GEO his Counvey$^{nc}$ to FRANCIS BRANCH 2
BRANCH GEORGE his Convey$^{c}$ to JOHN BRANCH 3
BRANCH GEORGE his Convey$^{c}$ to JAMES LUPO 4
BRANCH SUSANNA Let$^{r}$ of atturny 5
BRANCH GEO: his Convey$^{c}$ to JN$^{O}$ GOODRICH 7 & 8
BRONDSON ROBT Lt$^{r}$ att$^{r}$. to M$^{r}$ FEBUARY 9
BRANCH GEORGE his Convey$^{r}$ to JN$^{O}$ MOORE 10 & 11
BRANCH GEORGE his Con$^{r}$: to ANNE BRANCH 11
BREWER THOMAS his Convy to M$^{r}$ HOLLIDAY 16
BRIAN LEWIS his bond to HEN: GAY 16
BEVAN THOMAS THO: WARD Convey 19
BODDIE W$^{M}$ his Convey to JOHN DARKE 21
BRIDLE FFRANCIS his guift to THO: HAMPTON 23
BROWNE JOHN Convey to WM SCOT 33
BROWNE JOHN Convey to RICHARD SHEWELL 33 & 4
BROWNE JOHN his pat$^{t}$ & Convey to THO: REEVE 34 & 5
BRANCH ANNE yo$^{r}$ sale to ROGER RAWLINS 49
BOOTHS deed to MAN 53
BUCKNELL's gift 55
BALDWIN deed to CARRELL 58 &c
BODDIE's deed to CASEY 64
BREED RICH$^{D}$ his estate 66
BARNFIELD's attorny 66
BAKER's wive's attorny 99
BAKER's deed to WICKINS 100
BAYNTON's deed to HAVEILD 104

BARAN's deed to WOODLEY 108 &c
BODDIE's deed to CASEY 111
BATEMAN's estate valued 118
BELL exempt from levys 4
BRIDGER Col vs TURNER 4
BATEMANs estate valued 118
BAKER to WILSON Bond 264
BALDWINs deposition 265
BALLANGE deed to NOSWORTHY 214
BRIDGER HESTERs Bond to BRIDGER 276
BRETT JN[O] his Deed to PORTIS 277
BENNETT's deed to BENNETT 292
BELANGE Deed to Coll[o] NORSWORTHY 212
BURROWS power to [ ] FFURABANT 310
BAKER HEN: deed to EDMOND WICKINS 325
BRESSY M[rs] SU: deed to MAT: JORDAN 347
BRESSY M[rs] SU: deed to W[M] JONES 348
BOURNE OWEN deed to THO: MANDUE 351
BLAKE THO: & Ux deed to JN[O]. PRIME 364
BODDY W[M]. & Ux deed JAMES MERCER 364
BODDY W[M] Deed to JN[O] MARKUM bill 366
BODDY W[M] & Ux Deed to THO: CUTCHIN 374
BODY W[M] & Ux Deed to NICO CASEY 398
BODY W[M] & Ux Deed to BRAGG 394
BODDY ad WILLIAMS Deed 422
BRANTLEY EDWARD Dep[o] 395
BROWNE W[M] Deed to RICHARD BRACEWELL 401
BROWNE W[M] Deed to THOMAS BROWNE 401
BLAKEs deed to his sonne W[M] BLAKE 413
BODDY & Ux deed to GEO: WILLIAMS 422 &c
BEST PETER †Will 147
BEEL to NORSWORTHY asssignem[t] 220

**[c]**

COB PHAROAH his Convey to JN[O] HOLE 8
COLE M[rs] BETHIALL L[re] attur[n] to JN[O] FFENERYEARE 10
CAMPBELL JN[O] his acc[t] of land to W[M] CAMPBELL 15
CODIN PHILLIP his guift to THO GREENE 17
COUNCELL HODGES 2 Conveyces 30
COBB EDWARD sale of Land to ANDREW WOODLY 42 & 3

CULLEY CORNELIUS his deed to JAMES TULLAGH 43
COBB NICO: his lease to JOHN JONES 44
CARVER W$^{M}$ his Conveyce to W$^{M}$ CRUMPLER 46
CARVER W$^{M}$ his assinement to W$^{M}$ CRUMPLER 47
CAMPBELL's discharge to CARVER 79
CASEY's deed to BELLANGE 82:83:
COLEMAN's relinq: our mark 87
CARVER's deed to RAYFORD 89
CHAMBER's deed to MOOR 92 &c
CORLE's deed to KERBY 103
COLEMAN's power to GILES 111
COLEMAN's power to GILES 118
COLEMAN's power to GILES 118
COLEMAN vs HAWLY rep$^{o}$. 127
CHAMPION power to WATTS 130
CAMPBELLs deed to BURNE 262
CAMPBELLs deed to WILL JOLLY 259
CLERKE THOMAS Bond 264
CREWES to BLUNT deed Guift 267
COBBs Deed to M$^{r}$ WOODLY 297
COBBs power to COBB 298
CARVERs patent & Assignm$^{t}$ to CRUMPLAR 318 & 318
CRUMPLERs deed to CARVER 320
CARTERs deed to CARTER 324
CUTCHIN THO: Bill sale to W$^{M}$ BUDDY 373
COOK THOMAS & ux deed to SHERRER 383
CAMPBELL's HUGH patent 380 acrs 258


**[d]**


DUKE JOHN his Convey to JOHN BURNETT 25
DAVIS FRANCIS his patent Convey to HODGES COUNCELL 26
DRIVER ROBT his Convey to CHAS DRIVER 48
DAVIS HUGH receipt for records 51
Dep$^{o}$. APPLEWHAITE & STURDY 52
Dep$^{o}$. WILKINSON & PITT 56: 57
Dep$^{o}$ inter TULLAGH & WEST 60 &c
Dep$^{o}$. inter ALTMAN & BAGNAL 62
DURDEN & WALTERs agreem$^{t}$ 102
Dep$^{o}$. RANDOLPH & WILSON 113 &c
Dep$^{o}$. NORSWORTHY vs COHOON 128: 9:&c
DRYVER CHARLES power Attorney 261
DARDEN JACOB Deed to POPE 264

DOUGHTIEs Conveyance to ELLY 279
DEBERRY vs THOMAS 419
DAWSON's power to DAWSON 235

**[e]**
ENGLISH THOMAS his Convey to FFULLERTON 18
EDWARDS her deed to THROPP 119
EDWARDS's estate D^r: 131
EDWARDS her deed to BRAGG 274
ELIXONs power to DEBERRY 313
EDWARDS JUDITH deed to JAMES BRAGG 346
EDWARDS W^M. deed to W^M. KINCHIN 356
EVANS W^M. deed to GEO: BENN 361

**[f]**
FENERYEARE EDMOND L^re of atturney 12
FULLERTON ROB^T his Convey to W^M SCOTT 28
FLAKE ROB^T Deed to THO: SMITH 227
FYRABANTs power to GILES 261
FFLAKEs Conveyance &^c 301
FOWLER W^M. & Ux^r. Deed to BENJ^A. BEAL 357
[ ] Town Lands Deed to W^M SMITH 385

**[g]**
GAY HENRY his bond to LEWIS BRIAN 17
GREEN THOMAS his deed to M^C CODIN 17
GREENE BARTHOLOMEW L^re of atturny 18
Governors Lett^r to the Court 29
GARDNER's deed to WALTERS 51
GODWIN's deed to GRIFFIN 52
Grand jury prsentm^t. 58
GREEN's Negroes valued 69
Grand jury prsentm^ts 90
GREEN's acco^tt. of his ffather's esta: 95
GROSSE his pet^n. 124
GROSSE & PITT's Deed 124
GREEN's power to GILES 125
Grand jury prsentm^t 132
GRIFFIN JN^O. his † will 133
GOODRICH Deed to his son CHARLES 252
GOODRICH's Gleab Depo^t 269
GILES deed to DRIVER 270

GRIFFENs Deed to SANBORNE 271
GOODRICH Cap$^{t}$ Bills Outcry 292
GILES JN$^{O}$. & Ux Deed to WILLIAMS 334
Gleeb dep$^{o}$ 269
GREEN GEORGE Deed to WILKINSON 154
GARDNER JAMES patent assigned to WALTER WALTERS 51
GODWIN to GRIFFIN Assigm$^{t}$ 52

**[h]**
HEARNE HENRY his assignment to TH$^{O}$ PAGE 51 & 6
HILL M$^{rs}$ SILVESTRA receipt 24
HEARNE HENRY his assignement of C[ ] to MAN 32
HARRIS THOMAS Convey to W$^{M}$ CRUMPLAR 46
HOOKES ROBERT Convey to JACOB DARDEN 48
HAMPTON's oath 57
HOLLADAY vs MARSHALL audite 69
HUTCHINS deed to Col: SMITH 85 &c
HUTCHINS deed to REYNOLDS 90 &c
HAWLY's power to GILES 95
HYINGTON's receipt to BEN 110
HAWKINS Assignemt to NEVELL 233
JN$^{O}$ HALLS Indenture to W$^{M}$: GREEN 251
HOOKES Deed to BOAZMAN 222
HALL POOL's Deed to JN$^{O}$. WATTS 285
HILL SIVESTRA Agreem$^{t}$ w$^{th}$ THOMAS 335
HAVEILD Cap$^{t}$. Deed to M$^{r}$ NATH$^{A}$ RIDLY 352
HAYES THOMAS power Attorney 368
HAYES THOMAS & Ux$^{r}$ deed to THO: BEVAN 369
HAYES THOMAS to CLERKe Deed &c 370
HALL JN$^{O}$ & Ux$^{r}$ deed to JOSEPH BUCK 403
HOLMES XTOP$^{R}$ to NICH$^{O}$. CASEY Deed 81
HARDY GEO: 182

**[j]**
JOHNSON ROBERT Convey to W$^{M}$ BUSH 48
JOHNSON's deed to KENT 50
IRBY's power to FFOWLER 92
IRBY's power to ARTHER 125
JOHNSONS W$^{M}$ Deposicon 266
JOLLY's power to JOLLY 270
JOHNSONs power to CAMPBELL 280
JOYNER THOMAS Deed to PURSELL 282

JOYNERs deed to JOYNER 304
JOYNERs deed to TURNER 305
JOHNSON Doctors deed to NEVILL Jun$^{r}$ 312
JOHNSON JOHN to LUKE KENT ass$^{t}$. 73
JENNINGS JOHN his †Will 201

**[k]**
KITCHIN ROB$^{T}$ L$^{re}$ of attorny to M$^{r}$ FFENERYEAR 9
KEELL W$^{M}$ rec$^{o}$. HODGES COUNCELL & MANs Convey [ ] 40
KENTS deed to TULLAGH 72,73 &c
KING's leather viewed 81
KAE's obligacon to WRENN 243
KERBY's Deed to UNDERWOOD 411
KENT LUKE to JAMES TULLOUGH Assignm$^{t}$. 72

**[l]**
LINSCOTT GILES rec$^{o}$ his Convey to M$^{r}$ BAKER 1
LEWIS RICHARD rec$^{o}$ his Conv to JN$^{O}$ CAMPBELL 15
LEAR Col power to EDW$^{DS}$ 79
LUCKE's power to GILES 79
LUTHER's deed to MERCER 80
LONGs deed to SCOTT 233
WILLIAMS GEORGE exec Lycence 251
LUTHERs deed to NORSWORTHY 322
Lott in Towne to W$^{M}$ SMYTH 385
LEWIS ANNE L$^{re}$ Atturney to MEAKHOM 388
LUTHER JN$^{O}$ to ROB$^{T}$ MERCER deed 80
LUTHER JN$^{O}$. to BEAL Deed 172

**[m]**
Militia's Warrant vs M$^{r}$ THOMAS 13
MAN THOMAS Convey to HENRY HEARNE 24
MANDUE THOMAS Convey & pattent to HEARNE 36 & 7
MOOREs JN$^{O}$. Convey to JN$^{O}$. BARNES 40
MATHEWES ANNE L$^{tr}$. of atturny to JAMES BACON 48
MARHSALL ꝑ towne land 71
MAYO's deed to LEWIS 77:78
MAYO's wives l$^{re}$ attorny 78
MERCER's deed to JONES 117
MOOR's wives attorny 117
MOOR's [*sic*] deed to DAVIS his wife 120
MANs deed to CURLEY 121

MANs deed to DUCKE 122
MARSHALL's audite 126
MARTYNs Lease to THOMAS 228
MARTY's Lease to JONES 232
MARTYN's pattent & assignem[t] to BUTLER 234
MILESs Gleeb dep[o] 269
MARTYN's deed to JONES 273
MOORes deed to REEKS 275
MACKYes Power to TUCKER 276
MARTINs deed to ROB[T] BROCK 281
MURFREY's deed to NOLIBOY 216
MURFREY's deed to NOLIBOY 220
MARSHALls Deed to M[r] WEST 290
MARTYN & Ux Deed to APPLEWHAIT 191
MACKUNHILLs Deed to COTTON 333
MACKYs assignm[t] to FFOWLER 335
MACKQUINNYs Deed to EXUM 341
MADUS THOMAS ux[r]. deed to REEKS 332
MOORs M[r] ROBT: Lett[r]. Att[o]. to M: BAKER 345
MACKRISTY REBECKA deed to JOLLY 350
MANDUS Deed to TYNER 218
MANDEWEs Deed to PARKER 421
MARSHALL HUMPHRY Lott of Town Land 71
MAYO WILLIAM patent 77

**[n]**
NEVILL JOHN deed to BENJ[A] BEAL 22
NEVILL JN[O] Deed to JN[O] JOHNSON 253
NOSWORTHY THO: Deed to GYLES JOHN 399

**[o]**
OLTMANs inventory 120

**[p]**
POOLE THOMAS his pattent 21
PITT JOHN vs WILKINSON 27 & 28
POPE JOHN L[re] of atturney 29
PIERCE GEO: his Convey to W[M] JOHNSON 31
PERICE THO & KATHERINE Convey to JAMES BENN 38 &9
PIERCE GEO his Convey to JOHN SURBER 39 & 40
PITT Col deed for towne land 54
PORTIS sen[r]. his gift 59

PORTIS his gift 65
POWELL's deed to ALLEN 67
PARKER's deed to PARKER 84
PITT & FFULGHAM pow$^{r}$ to GILES 113
POWER ANTHO: to secure 1
PEIRCE her attorny 124
PURVIS his attorney to WYNN 245
PARKES note to APPLEWHAITE 268
PALMERs deed to MARTIN 280
A Proclamatiopn Continueing Co$^{rts}$ &$^{c}$ 283
PORTIS Deed to JN$^{O}$ BRETT 198
POLEGREENs power Attorney 229
PARDOEs Deed to THO: WOOD 308
PITT Coll JN$^{O}$s Power to GILES 310
PRICE THO: & Uxor deed to JORDAN 320
POWLL JN$^{O}$. & Ux$^{r}$. deed to Cap$^{t}$: JORDAN 337
POWELL JN$^{O}$ Bond to Cap$^{t}$. THO: JORDAN 339
PORTIS JOHN Deed to his Sonne JOHN 390
PITT & FFULGHAM vs GREEN 56
PARDOEs Deed to Cap$^{t}$ ROBT KAE 394
PITTs Deed for Town land 54
PORTIS JOHN to SUSAN THOMAS Deed of Gift 65
POWEL STEPHEN et Uxor to HENRY ALLEN Deed of Gift 66
PENNY W$^{M}$ †Will 174
[ ]

**[r]**
REEVES HENRY his Convey to Cap$^{t}$ GODWIN 13
see y$^{e}$ letter of atturney 14
RUTTER WALTER his Convey to DANIELL LONGE 14
REYNOLDS RICHARD Sen$^{r}$ & JN$^{O}$. NEVILL y$^{e}$ Sumons 25
ROADS JOHN deed to RICH$^{D}$ MATHEWS 49
REYFORD's power to GILES 94
RUTTERs deed of gift 107
RICHARDSON's estate deb: SHERRER 128
RUTTER Deed to JO: BRIDGER 238
RUTTERs Deed to JO: BRIDGER 240
RUTTERs deed to JO BRIDGER 241
RUTTERs Bond to JOS BRIDGER 242
RANDOLPH power Attur to R: REYNOLDS 243
RANDALL power Attorn to TOOKER 246
REYNOLDS deposition about Coll BRIDGER 252

REYNOLDS Deed to REYNOLDS 254
REYNOLDS Deed to REYNOLDS 254
REYNOLDS Deed to REYNOLDS 256
RANDALL ROB^T Assignemen^t to NICH^O WILSON 268
REYNOLDS Deed to BATLER 309
REEVES Dep^o for MACKQUINNYs Lands 339
REGANS Pattent assignd to CASEY 230

[s]
SENIOR JOSEPH Lt^r of atturny 19
SMITH JOHN his deed to JN^O MICHNIELL 22
SHIPLY JONATHAN Lt^r to JACOB GREENE 23
SHEARER JN^O his Convey to JOHN BRITT 27
SOMERVELL JOHN and wifes Confession 29
SOJORNER JOHN rec^o a pattent and
assignment to JOHN DOLL 32
SMELLY LEWIS Deed to SMELLY 246
SMELLY ROBERT to SMELLY 247
SMYTHs Deed to GOODMAN 248
SMYTH power Attorney 249
SMYTH Deed to BROCK 255
SYMES power to SKELTON 260
SANDERS Conveyance to COOPER 287
SMITHs Deed to Coll^o NOSWORTHY 237
STRICKLANDs Deed to his Brother 302
STRICKLAND Deed to M^r BAKER 208
STRICKLANDs deed to WHITHEEAD 311
SHELLY PHILLIP & Ux^r. deed to LEE 314
SHERRER JN^O. Sen^r. deed to THO: SHERRER &c 349
SMITH Cap^t. AR: deed to GEORGE FFLY 349
SMELLY ROB^T. THO. GIBS &^ca Patent 375
SMELLY ROB^T &c: assignem^t. to Maj^r. THOMAS SWANN 377
STRICKLANDEs Deed to WHITEHEAD 386
SPURWAYs power Attorney & attestaco to FRAZER & als 396
STRICKLANDs Deed to BOONE 398
SMITH Cap^t & Ux^r. deed to ROBT EDWARDS 405
SKELTONs Deed to Gift to her Children 422
STREETRs Deed to HUNTER 409
SMITH to NORSWORTHY Deed 226
SMITH NICHOLAS †Will 199

[t]

THORNE WA: yo[r] deed to yo[r] wife 1
THOMAS ROBT Lt[r] of atturny to M[r] CAMPBELL 19
THOMAS ROBT L[t] of atturny to M[r] FFORD 31
TOWELLs estate Valued 133
TYRRELL BLACKABY to JONES 266

[v]
VASSER PETER & Uxo[rs] deed to JN[O]. BELL 316

[w]
WATKINS JOHN his guift to THO INGLES 15
WARD THOMAS THO: BEVANS Convy 20
WILLIAMSON GEORGE Convey to SOJOURNER 36
VICKs JOSEPH M[r] COUNCELs deed to you 45
WRIGHT & WRIGHT award 63
WILKINSON to PITT audite 68
WILKINSON & Towne land 70
WILSON's discharge to RAND 75:76
WARDS power to GILES 94
WILSON's power to his wife 95
WESTs deed to HERRING 96
WICKINS deed to BAKER 97 &c
WILLIAMS her gift 105
WHITFEILDS power to CAMPBLL. 111
WILSON's power to ARTHER 113
WADEs payments 127
WHITLY THOMAS deposicon 266
WILLIAM GODERD to REYNOLDS 306:307
WICKINS EDM[D] deed Maj[r]. HEN: BAKER 326
WILLY JN[O]. his deed to WHITBY 327
WILLIAMSON L[r] attor to RIDLEY 344
WILLIAMSON GEO: & Ux Deed to RAYFORD 389
WILLIAMSON & U[x] Deed to CRUMPLER 389
WOOTTEN RICH[D] & Ux[r]. deed to BAKER 409
WILLIAMS Deed to KERBY 412
WILLIAMS W[M] Deed to BARNES 413
WILLIAMS Deed to JOHN WILLIAMS 414
WILLIAMS W[M] Deed to RICHARD WILLIAMS 410
WILLIAMS W[M] Deed to THOMAS BOONE 417
WILKENSON RICH[D]. jun[r] his [ ] 70

**TEXT**

**[1]**

This Indenture made the tenth day of May & in the third yeare of the reigne of our Soveraigne Lord / James the second by the grace of God of great Bryttane ffrrance & Ireland Kinge & Betwene GYLES / LINSCOTT of the County of the Isle of Weight Shoemaker of the one part and HENRY BAKER M^r^chant / of the Same County and the other part Wittnesseth, that I the said GYLES LINSCOTT for and in Conside / ration of the Sume of nine hundred pounds of good porke to him before the Sealeinge and delivery / of these presents by the said HENRY BAKER well and truely paid the receipt whereof he the said / LINSCOTT doe acknowledge and himselfe there with fully Satisfied and paid and thereof doe clearly / accquitt and discharge the said BAKER his heyers Exequetors & administrators for Ever have bargained / sold and Confirmed and by these presents doe Allien Bargaine Sell infeoffe & Confirme, unto the / Said HENRY BAKER his heires or assignes For Ever one hundred acres of land Lyinge and beinge upon / the maine blacke Water in the aforesaid County of the Isle of Weight begininge at a marked / Beech Standinge uppon the banke of the maine blacke water runinge thence South 33^d^: E:^ly^ to the / mouth of a branch, then up the Said branch by Various Courses to a red oake Standinge by the / side thence North ninty two Chaine to a Locus Stake thence South West by west eighty Chaine / Joyneinge upon JOHN LAWRANCEs line to the first Station beinge part of a pattent of the aforesaid / LINSCOTTs for fourteene hundred acres of Land with all its rights members Jurisdictions, & appurtena / ncies to the said premises, or any part or parcell thereof belonginge or in any wise appertaineinge / and alsoe all the Estate right, in the intrest use possesion property Claime and demand, whatsoever / of him the said LINSCOTT of in or to the same: To Have & to Hold the said hundred acres of Land and / all and Singular the premises hereby bargained & Sould w^th^: theire and Every of theire rights numbers / and appurtenanties what Soever unto the said HEN: BAKER his heyres and assignes for Ever, to the / only proper Use & behoofe of the Said BAKER his heires and assignes For ever and the said LINSCOTT / For himselfe his heires the said hundred acres of land and all and Singular the premises before / granted & bargained & Sould with the appurtenanties unto the said BAKER doth bind himselfe his / heires and assignes to pay Unto the said LINSCOTT his heires or assignes yearely quit rents for the said / one hundred acres of Land in wittnesse whereof the party first above named Unto this present / Indenture interchangeably have putt theire hands and Seales the day and yeare first above written / Anno Domini 1688

Signed Sealed & delivered GILES LINSCOTT seale
in the p^r^nce of us
THOMAS WILLIAMSON

Acknowledged in open Court held for / the Isle of Weight County aug^st^ the 9^th^. 1688 / by GILES LINSCOTT to be his free act and deed

Test JOHN: PITT C[l] C[ur]

To all Christian people to whome this present wrightinge shall Come I WILLIAM THORNE of the / upper parish of the Isle of Weight County send greetinge in our Lord God Everlastinge Know yee that / I the said WILLIAM THORNE as well for and in Consideration of the true love and affection that I have / and bare Unto my welbeloved Wife GRACE THORNE as alsoe for divers other good Causes and Considera / tions me at this present especially moveinge have given and granted and by these presents doe / give grante and Confirme Unto my loveinge Wife GRACE THORNE all and Singular my goods Cattels / Chatles Utensils brasse pewter bedinge and all other my Substance whatsoever Moveable and / immoveable quicke and dead Exceptinge and only reservinge Unto My Selfe and Unto my owne / disposinge out of the Same my horsse bridle and Sadle one Small feather Bed & boulster blanket / and rugge and my Chest, all the rest residue and remainder: To Have and to Hould Unto my / Sayd Loveinge wife GRACE THORNE Unto her owne proper use and behoofe for Ever thereof and / therewith to doe use and dispose of at her owne will and pleasure freelie and quickly without / any maner of Claime Challinge or demand of mee the Sayd WILLIAM THORNE or of any other person / or persons whatsoever for me in my name Cause or procurement in wittnesse whereof I the s[d] / WILLIAM THORNE Unto this present deed of guift have hereunto putt my hand and Seale the / 9[th] day of august 1688
Signed sealed and delivered by the within named
WILLIAM THORNE Unto his wife GRACE THORNE in the
Sight and presence of Us
THO: MOORE — WILLIAM **W** THORNE seale
THO: CLARKE — marke
WILL EVANS

Acknowledged by WILLIAM THORNE in open Court held for the Isle / of Weight County aug[st] y[e] 9[th] 1688 to be his act and deed
Test JOHN: PITT Cl Cur

**[2]**

This Indenture made the fourth day of august in the fourth yeare of the raigne of our Sovereigne / Lord James the Second over England Scotland france Ireland and Virginia Kinge defender of the / faith &c and in the yeare of our Lord God 1688 betweene GEORGE BRANCH of the Upper parish of Surry / County and SUSANNA his wife on the one partie and FFRANCIS BRANCH of the upper parish of y[e] / Isle of Weight County one the other partie Wittnesseth that the said GEORGE BRANCH and SUSANNA / his wife for and in Consideration of the Sume of three thousand pounds of tobacco and Caske to take / in hand payd or Secured to be paid at or before the Sealeing and delivery of these presents by / the said FFRANCIS BRANCH the receipt whereof, the Said GEORGE BRANCH and SUSANNA his wife doe / hereby acknowledge themselves fully satisfied and payd and thereof and of Every part and parcell / thereof doe clearely acquit exonerate and dischardge the sayd FFRANCIS BRANCH his heyres Exequeto[rs] / and administrators and Every of them, by these presents doe fully Clerly and absolutely give grant / Alien Bargaine Sell Enfeoffe and Confirme unto the said FFRANCIS BRANCH his heyres and assignes / for Ever all that plantation and Tract of Land whereon he doth now live beinge bounded (viz[t]) / begininge on the bever dam soe runinge up the bever dam branch to a marked poplar thereunto / alonge WILLIAM MILES Side line Unto JOHN BRANCH his land Soe downe his line of marked trees / to a branch that runs downe to the Second Swampe Soe downe the Second Swampe to the bever / dams branch Contayneinge about ffifty acres be it more or lesse Scituate lyinge and beinge in y[e] / upper parish of the Isle of Weight County on the Eastward Side of the Second Swampe on the / blackwater togather with all houses Edificies buildings fences woods Underwoods waters prive / ledges wayes Easements profitts Comodities hereditaments and apurtenancies whatsoever to y[e] / Said messuage or tenement and premisses or to any part or parcell thereof belonginge or in any / wise appertayneinge To Have & to Hould the above said plantation and tract of land togather / with all hoes Edificies buildings fences woods Underwoods waters and all and Singular other / the premises hereby granted bargained and Sould with all their and Every of theire rights / members and appurtenancies whatsoever Unto the Said FFRANCIS BRANCH his heyres and assignes / to the only proper Use and behoofe of the Said FFRANCIS BRANCH his heires and assignes for Ever / against them the Said GEORGE BRANCH and SUSANNA his Wife theire heires Executors adminsitrat[rs] / or assignes and all and Every person or persons whatsoever Claimeinge from by or Under them / or any of them Shall and Will warrant and for Ever defend by these presents and the Said / GEORGE BRANCH and SUSANNA his Wife doe Covenant and grant to and with the said FFRANCIS BRANCH / his heires Executors administrators and assignes and Every of them by these presents that all and / Singular the before recited land with all the houses fences profits and Comodities there unto / belonginge by these presents Sould and all and Singular theire appurtenancies now and before / Ever hereafter Shalbe stand and Continue Unto the said FFRANCIS BRANCH and his heires cleerly / and freely discharged and accquitted or other wise From time to time and at all times hereafter shall / be well and Sufficiently Saved harmelesse by the Said GEORGE BRANCH and SUSANNA his Wife theire heires / Executors administrators or assignes of and from all and Singular former bargaines Sales Joyntures / dowers gifts grants leases annuities Charges Estates titles and incumbrances whatsoever In / wittnesse whereof the said GEORGE BRANCH and SUSANNA his wife have here unto putt theire hands / and sealed the day and yeare and reigne above written GEORGE BRANCH seale

Signed Sealed and delivered as the acts and deeds SUSANNA BRANCH seale
of the within named GEORGE BRANCH and SUSANNA
his wife in the presence of
THO: MATHER
CHARLES SAVIDGE

WILL EVANS

Acknowledged in open Court held for the Isle of Weight County / aug$^{st}$ 4$^{th}$ 1688 by GEORGE BRANCH and M$^{r}$ W$^{M}$ EVANS atturney in the / behalfe of SUSANNA BRANCH to be theire free act and deed

Test JOHN PITT Cl Cur

Memorandum that full and peaceable possession and Seisen / of and in all and Singular the within plantation and land with theire and Every / of theire appurtenancies was delivered by the within named GEORGE BRANCH / and SUSANNA his wife unto the within named FFRANCIS BRANCH to the use and behoofe / within limitts & accordinge to the tenor and Effect of the present writinge the fourth day / of august 1688 in Sighte and presence of us

| | | |
|---|---|---|
| RICHARD BUIGHTON | JAMES **L** LUPO<br>marke | JONE **I** COOKE<br>marke |
| WM **M** COOKE<br>marke | JOHN **W** BRANCH<br>marke | LUCIE **LB** BYTON<br>marke |
| GEORGE **G** TETHER<br>marke | ANNE **A** TETHER<br>marke | ROSAMUND **RB** BYTON<br>marke |

**[3]**

This Indenture made the fourth day of august in the fourth yeare of the reign of our Sovereigne Lord / James the Second over England Scotland ffrance Ireland and Virginia King & defender of the faith &c Betweene GEORGE / BRANCH of the upper parish of Surry County and SUSANNA his wife on the one parte and JOHN BRANCH of the upper parish / of the Isle of Weight County on the other partie Wittnesseth that the Said GEORGE BRANCH and SUSANNA his wife for and in / Consideration of the Sume of three thousand pounds of tobacco and Caske to them in hand paid & or Secured to be paid / at or before the Sealeinge and delivery of these presents by the said JOHN BRANCH the receipt whereof the said / GEORGE BRANCH and SUSANNA his wife doe hereby accknowledged themselves fully Satisfied and paid and thereof and / of Every part and parcell thereof doe clearely accquit exonerate and dischardge the Sayd JOHN BRANCH his heires / Executors and administrators and Every of them by these presents have given greanted Aliened bargained & sould / Enfeoffed and Confirmed and by these presents doe fully Clearely and absolutely give grant Alien Bargaine sell / Enfeoffe and Confirme Unto the Said JOHN BRANCH his heyres and assignes for Ever a certaine Tract of land Scituate / lyinge and beinge on the Eastward Side of the Second Swampe of the blackwater in the upper parish of the Isle of / Weight County the same beinge already layd out Setled and bounded (viz$^{t}$) begininge at the mouth of a branch Caled / the knave tree branch that Comes out of the pinie poynt dam in the Second Swampe Soe up that branch to a marked / red oak thence Easterly alonge a line of marked trees to W$^{M}$ MILES

Side line Soe downe the Second Swampe for breadth / unto a branch runinge out of the Second Swampe Soe up that branch to a white oake marked at the head of the said / Branch thence Northeast alonge a line of marked trees to W$^{M}$ MILES his side line Contayneinge by Estimation about / fourty and five acres be it more or lesse To Have and to Hould the aforesaid tract of land togather with all woods / under woods wayes waters previledges and appurtenancies whatsoever unto the said JOHN BRANCH his heires and assig / =nes to the only use and behofe of the said JOHN BRANCH his heires and assignes for Ever against them the said GEORGE / BRANCH and SUSANN his wife theire heires Executors administrators and assignes and all and Every other person / and persons whatsoever Claimeinge from by or under them or any of them Shall and will warrant and forever / defend by these presents and the said GEORGE BRANCH and SUSANNA his wife doe Covenant and grant to and with / the Sayd JOHN BRANCH his heires Executors and administrators and Every of them by these presents that all and singular / the said Tract of land Contayneinge forty five acres more or lesse by these presents Sould with all and Singular / their appurttenancies: now be and Ever here after Shalbe Stand and Continue to the said JOHN BRANCH his heires Executo$^{rs}$ / and administrators, Cleerly and freely discharged and accquitted or other wise from time to time and at all times / here after Shalbe well and Suffisently Saved harmelesse by the said GEORGE BRANCH and SUSANNA his wife theire heires / Executors and administrators of and from all and Singular former bargaines and Sales Joyntures Dowers gifts grants / leases annuities Charges Estates tithes and incumbrances whatsoever In Wittnesse whereof of the said GEORGE BRANCH and / SUSANNA his wife have here unto putt theire hands and Seales the day yeare and reigne above written

Signed Sealed and delivered as the acts and deeds of the within named GEORGE BRANCH and SUSANNA his Wife in the presence of
THO: MATHER
CHARLES SAVIDGE
WILL EVANS

GEORGE BRANCH Seale
SUSANNA BRANCH Seale

Acknowledged by M$^{r}$ GEORGE BRANCH and / M$^{r}$ W$^{M}$ EVANS Atturny of SUSANNA BRANCH at / a Court held for the Isle of Weight Country / augst y$^{e}$ 9$^{th}$ 1688 to be theire free act and deed

Test JOHN: PITT Cl Cur

Memorandum that full and peaceable possession of seisen of and in all / and Singular the forty and five Acres of Land more or lesse with theire / appurtenancies within written was delivered by the within named / GEORGE BRANCH and SUSANNA his wife to the within named JOHN BRANCH / to the Use and behoofe within limitted & accordinge to the tenor and Effect / of this present writinge the fourth day of august 1688 in ꝑsence of us

RICHARD BUIGHTON
WILLIAM **A** COOKE
marke
GEORGE **GL** TETHER
marke
FFRANCIS **E** BRANCH
JAMES **E** LUPOE
marke
ANNE **A** TETHER
marke

JONE **I** COOKE
marke
LUCIE **LB** BEIGHTON
marke
ROSAMUND **RB** BEIGHTON
marke

**[4]**

This Indenture made the fourth day of August in the fourth yeare of the reigne of our Sovereigne Lord / James the Second over England Scotland france Ireland and Virginia Kinge defender of the faith &c betweene / GEORGE BRANCH of the upper parish of Surry County and SUSANNA his wife on the one part and JAMES LUPOE of / the upper parish of the Isle of Weight County of the other parte Wittnesseth that the said GEORGE BRANCH / and SUSANNA his wife for and in Consideration of the Sume of three thousand pounds of tobacco and Caske to / them in hand paid or Secured to be paid at or before the Sealeinge and delivery of these presents by the / said JAMES LUPOE the receipt whereof the Said GEORGE BRANCH and SUSANNA his wife doe hereby acknowledge / themselves fully satisfied and payd and thereof and of Every part and parcell thereof doe Cleerely acquit / exonerate and dischardge the sayd JAMES LUPOE his heires Exequetors and administrators for Ever by these / presents have given granted Aliened bargained Sould Enfeoffed and Confirmed and by these presents / doe fully cleerly and absolutely give grant Alien bargain Sell Enfeoffe and Confirme unto the said JAMES / LUPOE his heyres and assignes for Ever all that plantation and tract of Land whereon he doth now live / beinge already laid out and bounded between us (viz[t]) / begininge at a line of trees Called DAVISes line / in the Second Swampe on the blackwater thence down the Sayd Swamp to marked Elme in the said / Swampe thence South South East alonge a line of Marked trees unto WILLIAM MILESes Side line soe / alonge MILESes line Unto DAVISes line, and along DAVISes line unto the Second Swampe to the first / Station Contayninge by Estimation about fourty five acres be it more or less, Scituate lyinge and beinge / within the Upper parish of the Isle of Weight County on the Eastward side of the Second Swampe of y[e] / blackwater togather with all houses Edificies buildings fences woods waters priveledges ways Easements / profitts Comodities hereditaments and apurtenancies whatsoever to the Said messuage or tenement and / premisses or to any part or parcell thereof belonginge or in any wise appertayneinge To Have & to / hould the above said plantation and Tract of land togather with all houses Edificies buildings fenceings / and all and Singular other the premises hereby granted bargained and Sould with their and Every / theire rights members and appurtenancies whatsoever Unto the Said JAMES LUPOE his heyres and assignes / to the only proper Use and behoofe of the Said JAMES LUPOE his heires and assignes for Ever against y[m] / the Said GEORGE BRANCH and SUSANNA his Wife theire heires Executors adminsitrat[rs] or assignes and / all and Every person or persons whatsoever Claimeinge from by or Under them or any of them Shall / and Will warrant and for Ever defend by these presents and the Said / GEORGE BRANCH and SUSANNA / his Wife doe Covenant and grant to and with the said JAMES LUPOE his heyres Executors administrato[rs] / and assignes and Every of them by these presents that all and Singular the before recited land with / all the houseinge fenceinge profitts and Comodities there unto belonginge by these presents Sould & / all and Singular theire appurtenancies now be and fore Ever hereafter Shalbe stand and Continue Unto / the said JAMES LUPOE & his heires Cleerly and freely discharged and accquitted or other wise from / time to time and at all times hereafter shalbe well and Sufficiently Saved harmelesse by the Said GEORGE / BRANCH and SUSANNA his wife, theire heires Executors Administrators or assignes of and from all and / Singular former bargaines Sales Joyntures dowers gifts grants leases annuities Charges Estates titles / and incumbrances whatsoever In / wittnesse whereof the said GEORGE BRANCH and SUSANNA his wife have here / unto putt theire hands and seales the day yeare and reigne above written

GEORGE BRANCH seale
SUSANNA BRANCH seale

Signed Sealed and delivered as the acts and deeds of the within named GEORGE BRANCH and SUSANNA his wife in the presence of
THO: MATHER
CHARLES SAVIDGE
WILL EVANS

Acknowledged in open Court / held for the Isle of Weight County / aug[st] 9[th] 1688 by M[r] GEORGE BRANCH / and M[r] W[M] EVANS atturney of SUSANNA BRANCH / to be theire free act and Deeds: Test JOHN PITT C[l] C[ur]

Memorandum that full and peaceable possession and Seisen of and in all and Singular the within / plantation and land with theire and Every of theire appurtenancies was delivered by the / within named GEORGE BRANCH / and SUSANNA his wife unto the within named JAMES LUPOE / to the Use and behoofe / within limitted accordinge to the tenour and Effect of the present / wrightinge the fourth day of august 1688 in Sighte and presence of us

RICHARD BUIGHTON
WM **M** COOKE
marke
GEORGE **G** TETHER
marke
FFRANCIS **F** BRANCH

JOHN CLARKE
ROBERT **RH** HODGES
marke
ANNE **A** TETHER
marke
JANE **I** COOKE

LUCIE **LB** BEIGHTON
Marke
ROSAMUND **RB** BEIGHTON
Marke

marke her mark
JOHN **B** BRANCH
marke

**[5]**

Know all men by these presents that I SUSANNA BRANCH the wife of GEORGE BRANCH of the upper parish / of Surry County of my owne Volontary free will and likeinge have nominated Constituted and appointed / my Loveinge freind W^M^ EVANS of the upper parish of the Isle of Wight County by reason of my nonabi / lity to travell to a Court held for the Isle of Weight County the 9^th^ day of august instant to accknow / ledge three severall Conveyances: one unto JAMES LUPOE of the upper parish of the Isle of Weight County / for a plantation where on he now lives and forty five acres of land More or lesse the other to / JOHN BRANCH of the said parish and county for fortie five acres of Land more or lesse the other / to FFRANCIS BRANCH For the plantation where on he now lives and fifty acres of land more or lesse / the which lands weere by my husband and my selfe unto the above said persons sould and Conveyed / by these severall deeds or Conveyances beareinge date the fourth day of this present august ratifieinge / allowinge and houldinge firme and shalbe all and whatsoever my Said attorny doth accknowledge / for me to be as firme and Stable in the law as I had beene personally present there to have accknow / ledged the Same myselfe in wittnesse where of I have hereunto putt my hand and Seale this fourth day / of august 1688
Signed Sealed and delivered
in ꝑsence of SUSANA: BRANCH Seal
CHARLES SAVIDGE
TH^O^ MATHER

Proved in Court held the 9^th^ of / augst 1688 by CHARLES SAVIDGE & / THO: MATHER to be the hand and / seale of SUSANNA BRANCH
Test JOHN PITT C^l^C^ur^

To all to Whome these presents shall Come I FFRANCIS Lord Howard Baron / of Effingham his Ma^ties^ Lieu^t^: and Governor Gen^ll^ of Virginia Send gretinge in our / Lord God Everlastinge whereas his Ma^ties^ hath beene gratiously pleased by his / Royall letters pattents under the greate seale of England bearinge date at West / =minster the tenth day of october in the Eight and twentieth yeare of his reigne / amonge other things in the said letters pattents Contained, to Continue and Con / firme the ancient previledges, and power of grantinge fivety acres of Land for / Every person imported into this his Ma^ties^ Collony of Virginia Now know yee that I / FRANCIS Lord Howard Gove^r^no: &c doe with the advice and Consent of the Councell / of State accordingly give and grant unto HENRY HENRY HEARND [*sic*] one hundred / and thirty three acres of Land lyinge and being in the upper parish of Nansa / mond in the Isle of Weight County boundinge and buttinge betwixt the land of / SYMON: SYMONDS and ANTHONY BRANCH dec^d^. the said land being formerly granted / to ANTHONY BRANCH by pattent, beareinge date the two and twentieth day of Aprill / one thousand Sixe hundred and Seventy and deserted for want of sealeinge and issue / to the Said HENRY HEARNE; by and For the transportation of these persons into / this Collony accordinge to an order of the Generall Court the 15th of Aprill 1684 / whose names are in the record mentioned under this pattent: To have and to / hould the said land with his due Share of all mines and mineralls there in Contai / ned with rights and previledges, of huntinge hawkinge fishing and fowlinge / with woods waters waters and Rivers, with all profitts Comodities and heredita / ments whatsoever belongeinge to the Said Land to him the said HENRY HEARNE / his heyres and assignes For ever, in as large and ample maner to all intents / and purposes as hath bene used and allowed Since the first plantation to / be held of our Sovereigne Lord the Kinge his heyres and Successors of his Manor / of Easte Greenewich in free and Common Soccage not *in Capite* nor Knights / Service yeldinge and payinge to our Sovereigne Lord the Kinge his heyres and / and Successors For every fivety acres of Land hereby granted at the Feast / of Saint Michael the Archangle the fee rent of one Shillinge which payment / is to be made yearely, from yeare to yeares, accordinge to his Maties instructions / turne over

**[6]**
of the 12th of September 1662 provided that if the said HENRY HEARNE his heyres / or assignes, doe not seate or plant or Cause to be Seated or planted uppon the Sd / Land with in these three yeares next Ensueinge the date hereof that then it shall / and may be Lawfull for any adventurer or planter to make Choice there of and / seate thereon given Under my hand and the Seale of the Collony this thirtieth / day of october Anno: Dom 1686 Effingham
Recordatur / Test E CHILTON Cl

Know all men by these presents that wee HENRY HEARNE and ELIZABETH HEARNE / of Nansemond County, doe for Us, our heyres Executors & admisrs and assignes Sett / over Unto THOMAS PAGE his heyres executors Administrators or Assignes allow right / title and intrest that wee or Either of us have or hereafter may have of in and unto / one hundred thirty three acres of Land Mentioned in the pattent on the other side, in / Wittnesse whereof wee the Said HENRY HEARNE and ELIZABETH HEARNE have hereunto / sett our hands and Seales this tenth day of September in the yeares of our Lord God / one thousand and six hundred Eighty and Eight

Signed Sealed and ded
in the presence of
JAMES DOUGHTIE
FFRANCIS **B** BRIDLE
hir marke
ROGER **R** TARLETON
hir marke

the marke of
HENRY □ HEARNE Seale
ELIZABETH **E** HEARNE Seale
her marke

Acknowledged in open Court / held for the Isle of Weight County octob$^{r}$ y$^{e}$ 9$^{th}$ 1688 / by HENRY HEARNE and ELIZABETH his wife, to be theire / free act and deed: and ordered to bee recorded

Test JOHN:PITT C$^{l}$C$^{ur}$

This Indenture made the Eight day of october in the fourth yeare of the / Raigne of our Sovereigne Lord James the Second over England Scotland france / Ireland and Virginia Kinge defender of the faith &c and in the yeare of our / Lord God one thousand Sixe hundred Eighty and Eight Betweene GEORGE BRANCH / of the upper parish of Surry County and SUSANNA his wife, of the one partie / and JOHN GOODRICH Junior of the upper parish of the Isle of Weight County / on the other partie Witnesseth, that the said GEORGE BRANCH and SUSANNA / his wife for and in Consideration of the Some of two thousand pounds of / tobacco and Caske to them in hand paid or Secured to be paid at or before / the Sealeinge and delivery of these presents by the said JOHN GOODRICH the / receipt whereof the Said GEORGE BRANCH and SUSANNA his wife doe hereby / acknowledge them selves Fully Satisfied and payd, and thereof and of Every / part and parcell thereof doe fully Cleerely and absolutley accquit Exonerate / and dischardge the sayd JOHN GOODRICH his heires Execetors and administrators / and every of them, by these presents have given granted Aliened bargained / Sould Enfeoffed and Confirmed and by these presents doe firmely clerely and / absolutely give grant Alien Bargaine Sell Enfeoffe and Confirme unto the S$^{d}$ / JOHN GOODRICH his heires and assignes for Ever all that plantation and tract of / Land whereon THOMAS SMITH doth now live lyinge and beinge in the upper parish / of the Isle of Weight County Scituate on the East Side of the First Swampe on the / blacke water, runinge Easterly out into the woods for length and for breadth / bounded between two branches on the South side with a branch Called by the

[7]
The name of DAVISes branch Joyninge on the land that was lately GEORGE CRISPSes / and formerly FFRANCIS ENGLANDs and on the north side with a branch that did forme / rly divide a parcell of land that the said FFRANCIS ENGLAND did Sell unto one / JAMES PILAND all which land was by my grandfather FFRANCIS ENGLAND given / with my Mother, Unto my ffather, in franke Marriage Containeinge by Estimation / one hundred acres be it more or lesse togather with all houses Edificies buildings / fences orchards gardens Woods Under woods wayes priveledges Easements profitts / Comodities hereditaments and apurtenancies whatsoever unto the sayd plan / tation and premisses or any part, or parcell thereof belonginge or in any wise / appertayneinge and further for and in Consideration aforesaid they the Said GEORGE / BRANCH and SUSANNA his Wife, have given granted aliened bargained / Sould Enfeoffed and Confirmed and by these presents doe give grant Alien Bar / gaine Sell Enfeoffe and Confirme unto the Said JOHN GOODRICH Junior his heires and / assignes for Ever all

that plantation and tract of Land whereon I the said / GEORGE BRANCH and SUSANNA My Wife did formerly live Scituate lyinge and beinge on y[e] / first Swampe on the blackwater bounded on Capt PEERCEs marked trees and runing / for length west into the woods and for bredth Sixty two poles and a halfe to the before / mentioned land that was formerly FFRANCIS ENGLANDs land Containeinge / one hundred twenty five acres, it beinge land formerly Sould and Convayed / by the Said FFRANCIS ENGLAND Unto one JAMES PILAND as by a Conveyance bearing / date the Last day of September 1648 more at large it doth and may appeare / and by the said JAMES PILAND assigned over to my ffather GEORGE BRANCH / as by his assignement on the backe of the Conveyance bearinge date y[e] / 22[th] of January 1661 as by the Conveyance and assignement thereon doth / appeare togather with all houses Edificies buildings fences orchards gardens / woods underwoods wayes: waters previledges comodities hereditaments and / appurtenancies whatsoever unto the said plantation and tract of land or / and part or parcell thereof belonginge or in any wayes appertaining To / have and to hould both the aforesaid plantations and Land thereunto / belonginge togather with all houses Edificies buildings fences Orchards / gardens Woods wayes waters Comons profits and Comodities and all and Singu / =lar, other the premisses hereby granted bargained Enfeoffed and sould with all / theire, and Every of theire rights members and appurtenancies whatsoever / unto the Said JOHN GOODRICH his heires and assignes, to the only proper use / and behoofe of the said JOHN GOODRICH his heyres and asignes / For Ever, against them the said GEORGE BRANCH and SUSANNA his wife theire / heires Executors administrators or assignes and Every of them by these / presents, that all and Singular the fore recited lands with all and Singular / the houseinge Fences profitts and appurtenances thereunto belonging by these / presents granted and sould Now be and For ever hereafter Shalbe Stand and / Continue unto the Said JOHN GOODRICH, and his heires and assignes For Ever Clerely / accquited Exonerated and discharged or other wise, From tyme to tyme and at all / times hereafter Shalbe wel and Sufficiently Saved harmelesse by the Said GEORGE / BRANCH and SUSANNA his wife theire heires Executors administrators and assignes / of and From all and Singular Former bargaines Sales Joyntures dowers gifts grants / Leases anuities Charges Estates titles and in Cumbrances whatsoever has made

**[8]**

Made Committed Suffered or don by the Said GEORGE BRANCH and SUSANNA his wife / or Either of them In Wittnesse whereof The Said GEORGE BRANCH and SUSANNA his wife / have hereunto putt theire hands and Seales the day yeares and Reigne above written

GEORGE BRANCH Seale
SUSANNA BRANCH seale

Sealed and delivered as the free and Voluntary act and deeds of the within named GEORGE BRANCH and SUSANNA his wife in presence of

JAMES Ɨ LUPOE
marke

WILL EVANS
THOMAS SMITH

Accknowledged in open Court held for the Isle of Weight / County by GEORGE BRANCH and SUSANNA his wife to be theire / Free and voluntary act and deed and ordered to be recorded

Test JOHN PITT C$^{l}$C$^{ur}$

Memorandum that full and peceable possesion and Seisen of & in all and Singular the w$^{th}$in / plantations and lands with theire and Every of theire appurtenancies was delivered by / the within named GEORGE BRANCH and SUSANNA his Wife, Unto the within named JOHN / GOODRICH Junior to the Use and behoofe within limitted accordinge to the tenoure and / Effect of this present wrightinge the Eight day of october 1688 in the Sight and psence / of Us

THOMAS SMITH: JOANE -|-|- SMITH: JAMES I LUPOE WILL EVANS
marke marke

Know all Men by these presents that I PHAROAH COB of the Isle of Weight County planter for / and in Consideration of Eleven thousand pounds merchantible Tobacco and Caske already by me received / of JOHN HOLE of Devon: Gen$^{t}$: doe sett over Sell and alienate from me my heires Executors admis$^{tr}$ / assignes Unto the Said JOHN HOLE his heires and assignes for ninety nine yeares to Come from the date / of these presents a Tract of parcell of Land Contayneinge about one hundred and thirty acres be / it more or Lesse, lyinge in the Isle of Weight County: begininge at a Small red oake Saplin Standinge / in Coll SMITHs line of Marked trees alsoe of my line, and From thence to a white oake Standinge / Close by a Cart path: and soe North Something Easterly to a red oake Saplin Standinge by a Cart / path Called M$^{r}$ COBs Cart path a Corner tree a straight line and so downe the said cart path / north east or there about, to another red oake Saplin Standinge by the Side of the Same Cartpath / and Soe downe the Said Cart path north Easterly or thereabout to another white oake Saplin / a marked tree and Soe downe the Said Cart path north or thereabout to a pine saplin a Marked / tree and Soe downe the Said Cart path North or thereabout to a pine Saplin a marked / tree and Soe a straite line to the Westward of the north to a White oake a marked tree Standing / on the head of a branch: and Soe downe the Said branch to the Creeke and Soe up the Said Creeke / to a branch which parts M$^{rs}$ HARDENs and the Said COBs Land and soe up the Said branch to / a springe Called M$^{rs}$ HARDENs Springe and Soe up the Said Valley to a red oake a marked tree Stand / inge uppon the brow of a hill: by the Said Valley and Soe up the Same Valley to a hickory a m$^{r}$ked / tree Said to be M$^{rs}$ HARDINs marked tree and likewise agreed Uppon to be a Corner tree betwixt / us: the Saide COB and HOLE and soe runninge up South West or there aboute to a poplar an ould / marked tree betwixt M$^{rs}$ HARDIN and the said COBB and soe to a red oake M$^{rs}$ HARDINs Corner / tree, and soe South Easterly to a Corner tree beinge as hickory of the said COBs

& Coll ARTHUR / SMITHs to the first station: To have and to hould the Said land and Every part and parcell / thereof with in the above Specified limits to him the said JOHN HOLE, his heires or assignes / with all the previledges or profits whatsoever in as large a maner as I my Selfe might or Could / injoy it, and if any part or parcell thereof be by any legall Claime from any other person or / persons, taken from him the said HOLE his heyres or assignes that then the said COB his heires / or assignes, shall and doe hereby obleidge them selves For soe much as shall thus by a legal Course / uppon the Said line above first mentioned alwaise provided that the said JOHN HOLE his heires / or assignes yeild and pay Unto the said COB his heires or assignes Every yeare on the First of / January two Capons and peceably deliver up to PHAROAH COB his heires or assignes the land

**[9]**
In Condition as he the said HOLE his heires or assignes Shall make his or theire last Cropp in Witnesse / hereof I have hereunto Sett my hand and Seale this one and twentieth of february one thousand sixe / hundred Eighty sixe and Seaven
Signed Sealed and Delivered                                        Signed
in ꝑsence of Us                                        PHAROAH: & COB
ARTH: SMITH
JOHN GILES

Ackhowledged in open Court held for the Isle of Weight / County October the 9th 1688 by PHAROAH COB to be his reall / act and deed and ordered to be Recorded
Test: JOHN PITT ClCur

Be it knowne unto all by these presents that I ROBERT KITCHEN of The Towne of Salem: in the / County of Essex with in his Majesties Teritory and dominion of New England mercht. have assigned ordained / and made, and in my Stead and place by these presents, putt and Constituted, my Trusty and wel be / loved Freind EDMUND FFENERYEAR, of the Towne of Salem, in the same County of Essex within his / Majesties Teritory and dominion of New England aforesd. Marinr. to be my true and lawfull Atturn / ny for me and in my name and to my Use to aske Sue for Levy Require Recover and Receive all / and Every Such debts and sumes of Mony which are now due Unto me by any maner of wayes or means / whatsoever from any Maner of person or persons what Ever in and through out any or all the / Capes or Courts of Virginia giveinge and granteinge to my Said Atturny my whole power strength / and authority in and about the premises, and uppon the receipt of any Such debts or Sums of Mony / aforesaid, accquittances or other discharges, for me and in my name to make Seale and deliver, and all / and Every Such act and Acts thinge and thinges devise and devises whatsoever in the law for the / recovery of all or any Such debts or Sums of Mony as aforesaid for me and in my name to doe Execute / and performe as Fully largely and amply in Every respect to all intents. Constructions & purposes / as I my Selfe might or

Could doe if I were there in my own person present: and alsoe doe by these / ꝑsents grant unto my Said Atturny full power to make Constitute and ordaine any other atturny / or atturnyes as he shall thinke fitt in order to the Execution of the premises ratifieinge allowigne / and houldinge firme and stable all and whatsoever my Said atturny or his attuurneys shall lawfully / doe or Cause to be done in or about the Execution of any or all the afores[d] premises by vertue of these / presents In wittnesse whereof I have hereunto Sett my hand & Seale this twentieth day of September Anno / Domini 1688 Anno[q] Regis Jacobi Secundi & Quarto

Signed Sealed and delivered ROB[T] KITCHEN Seale
in ꝑsence of Us
JONATHAN VERY
JAMES COX

Proved in open Court held for the / Isle of Weight County Novemb[r] y[e] 1[st] 1688 / by the oath of JONATHAN VERY: and / JAMES COX and ordered to be recorded
Test JOHN PITT C[l] C[ur]

Know all Men by these presents that I ROBERT BRONSDON of Boston in New England merchant have / and hereby doe Constitute ordaine depute appoint and Make my much respected freind Cap[t] EDMUND / FEBUARY of Salem Marriner, my true and lawfull atturny for me and in my name and Stead and For my / Use to aske demand require receive and to Use all lawfull meanes to recover out of the hands of whome / Soever it may Concerne all Such sume or Sumes of Mony debts goods or other Estate as now is or hereafter / may be Come due owinge or payable to me the Constituant by bill bond booke account or other demand / or my any other waies or meanes what Soever, and in perticular to use all lawfull meanes to recover / out of the hands of any that is debt to me: giveinge and hereby grantinge to my Said atturny full / power and authority to Sue arrest implead & prosecute to Effect in any Court and Courts and in my / behalfe appearance to make and any action or actions to defend and if neede be into prisson to Cast / and there to deliver releases or other discharges uppon payment to give and Signe Composition if he / see cause to make atturnies one or more to Substitute and them at pleasure to revoke and Every / other way to act Execute and performe in my behalfe to all intents and purposes in as full and / ample maner measure and degree as I might or Could doe if I were presonally present To performe the Same / alwaies and in all thinges ratifieinge allowinge and Confirmeinge what my Said atturny Shall lawfully act / or Cause to be don in persuance of the premisses firmely by these presents in Wittnesse whereof I the said ROBERT / BRONSDON have hereunto Sett my hand and Seale the twenty Sixt of September Anno Domini one thousand / sixe hundred Eighty & Eighty 1688

Signed Sealed and delivered in the presence ROBERT BRONSDON Seale
of Us
JONATHAN VERY

JAMES COX

Proved in open Court held for / the Isle of Weight County N$^{o}$: y$^{e}$ 1$^{st}$ 1688 / by the oaths of JONATHAN VERY and JAMES COX / and ordered to be recorded

Test JOHN PITT C$^{l}$ C$^{ur}$

**[10]**

Know all Men by these presents That I BETHIALL COLE *alias* BETHIALL HILL late Widdow / relique and administratrixe to my deceased husband M$^{r}$ ALLEXANDER COLE of the towne of Salem in / the Countie of Esex in New England Marriner have assigned ordained and made and in my stead and / place by these presents doe putt and Constitute my trustie Freind M$^{r}$ EDMUND FFENERYEAR of the / Towne of Salem in the Countie of Essex in New England Shipp master to be my True and lawfull / atturny for me and in my name and to my Use to aske Sue for levie require recover and receive of / all and Every person and persons whatsoever inhabitinge or resideinge in Virginia or Maryland all / and Every Such debt and debts: Sume and Sumes of Mony bills bonds accknowledgements goods wards Merch /antdize: or any estate whatsoever which is or hereafter Shalbe due to my deceased husband M$^{r}$ ALLEXAN / DER COLE: by any maner of wayes or wayes whatsoever & for default of payment to Sue arrest attach / implead imprisson and Condem: his and theire bodies Lands Tenements Goods and Chattles in execution / to take and out of Execution to Deliver: and uppon the receipt of any Such debts bills bonds or accknow / ledgements & to give and grant accquittances and discharges For mee and in my name in as Full large / and ample for me and manner as I might or Could doe if personally present, giveinge and by these / presents grantinge Unto my said Atturney my full and whole power Streingth and authoritie to doe / say conclude and performe & Finish all and Every Such act & acts thinge and thinges devise and devises / in the law whatsoever needfull to be done in and about and Concerninge the premisses in as full / Large ample Maner and forme as I might or Could doe if I were personally present one or more / atturneys Under him my s$^{d}$ atturny to make and Substitute and at pleasure revoke ratifieinge allowinge and / houldinge firme and stable all and what soever my aturny or his Substitute shall lawfully doe or / Cause to be done in and about and Convereinge the premisses as if I were personally present in / wittnesse whereof I have hereunto Sett my hand and Seale this twentie ninth day of September 1688 / one thousand Six hundred Eightie Eight

Signed Sealed & delivered
in the presence of Us
JONATHAN: VERY
JAMES COX

her
BETHIALL **x** COLE Seale
mark

Proved in open Court held for / the Isle of Weight Countie N$^{o}$: y$^{e}$ 1$^{st}$ 1688 / by the oaths of JONATHAN VERY and / JAMES COX and ordered to be recorded

Test JOHN PITT C$^{l}$ C$^{ur}$

To all People to whome this present Wrightinge Shall Come I GEORGE BRANCH of y[e] / parish of Southwarke in the County of Surry in Virginia planter Son and heire of GEO: / BRANCH and ANNE his wife the only daughter and heire at law of FFRANCIS ENGLAND late / of blacke water in the Isle of Weight County dec[d] Send greetinge, whereas the Said FFRAN / CIS ENGLAND my grandfather was at this death Seized of Certaine lands and plantations / Containeinge about thirteene hundred acres Scituate att blackewater aforesaid and by / his last Will and Testament in wrightinge dated the 13[th] of May A[o]: 1677 did give all / his Estate reall and personall to JOYCE his wife whoe afterwards Married with one / GEORGE CRIPPS and in the tyme of her Coverture by Will she gave the Said land to her Said [*torn*] / CRIPPS, which Will is invallid in law, For that a woman can not give land to her husband / and she haveinge made noe other lawfull Conveyance or disposeal of the Said land the / same is descended and Come to me as heires at law to my Said grandfather his will giveinge / it to her only for Life & to be disposed by her Which She never legally did Now know yee / that I the Said GEORGE BRANCH as heire aforesaid For and in Consideration of three thousand / pounds of Tobacco and Caske to me in hand paid by GEORGE MOORE of the Said County / of the Isle of Weight with which I am fully Satyisfied and Contented have bargained / Sould assigned Conveyed and Sett over to the Said GEORGE MOORE all my Estate right / title & intrest of in and to the Said lands and plantations of which my Said grandfather / died seized at blackewater aforesaid with all Woods howses orchards profitts and / appurtenances whatsoever thereto belongeinge to have and to hould the same to the Said / GEORGE MOORE, his heires and assignes For Ever with warrantie against me and all persons / Claimeinge Under mee and I doe hereby Coevnant and agree for me my heires Execut[rs]

**[11]**

and my wife Shall at any time here after on demand make and give Such further [*torn*] / of all our rights and intrest of and in the Said land to him the said GEORGE MOORE [*torn*] / heires as by him or his Councell learned in the law shalbe required and perticularly / Said GEORGE BRANCH Shall and Will appeare at the next Court to be held for the [Isle] / of Weight County and at the Costs and Chardges in the lawe of the Said GEORGE MOORE / Will vouch him the said GEORGE CRIPPS, for a Supposed trespasse on the Said lands in / Some part the rest and for true performance hereof I binde me my heyres Execut[rs] & / administrators in the penaltie of Ten thousand pounds of tobacco and Caske in witnesse / whereof I have hereto Sett my hand and Seale the 26[th] day of March: A[o] Dom 1687

Sealed and delivered in prsence of W[M] SHERWOOD
THO: BINNS
THO: MOORE

GEORGE BRANCH Seale
SUSANNA BRANCH

Acknowledged in open Court / held for the Isle of Weight County / N$^{o}$ the first 1688 by GEORGE BRANCH / and SUSANNA his Wife to be theire free act and deed

Test JOHN PITT C$^{l}$ C$^{ur}$

This Indenture made the last day of october in the fourth yeare of the Raigne of our Sovereigne / Lord James the Second over England Scotland france Ireland and Virginia Kinge defender / and in the yeare of our / Lord God 1688 Betweene GEORGE BRANCH of the upper parish of Surry [and] / SUSANNA his wife one the one partie and ANN BRANCH of the upper parish of the Isle of Weight / on the other partie Witnesseth that the said GEORGE BRANCH and SUSANNA his wife for and in Cons[ideration] / of the sume of Sixe thousand five hundred pounds of tobacco and Caske to them in hand paid [or Secured to] / be paid at or before the Sealeinge and delivery of these presents by the said ANN BRANCH [the receipt] / whereof wee the Said GEORGE BRANCH and SUSANNA my wife doe hereby acknowledge our Selves [Fully] / Satisfied and Contented & payd, and thereof and of Every / part and parcell thereof Clearely [and absolutley] / accquit Exonerate and dischardge the sayd ANN BRANCH her heires Execetors and administrators and [every of] / them by these presents, have given granted & Aliened bargained Sould Enfeoffed and Confirmed [and by these] / presents doe fully Cleerely and absolutely give grant Alien Bargaine Sell Enfeoffe and Confirme [unto] / the Said ANN BRANCH her heires and assignes for Ever all that plantation and [Tract of Land whereon] / JOHN BRANCH doth now live beinge bounded (viz$^{t}$) on the Southard side with a line of marked [trees which] / devided JOHN BRANCHes land on the Westward Side with the Second Swampe of the blackwa[ter Swamp] [*torn*] / north side with JAMES LUPOEs line of marked trees and on the East side with WILLIAM MILES [*torn*] / trees Contayneing fivety Acres be it more or lesse Scituate lyinge and being in the upp[er parish of] / the Isle of Weight County togather with all houses Edificies buildings, barnes orchards [*torn*] / fences Woods Underwoods wayes Waters priveledges Easements profitts Comodities hered[itaments and] / apurtenancies whatsoever, unto the sayd plantation and tract of land or to any part or parcell there / of belonginge or in any wise appertayneinge To have and to hould the foresaid plantations / of Land togather with all houses Edificies buildings barnes orchards Stables gardens fences und / er Woods wayes waters previledges and apurtenancies whatsoever and all and singular [*torn*] / ꝑmises hereby granted bargained & Sould with all and Every theire rights members and appurtene / ncies whatSoever unto the said ANNE BRANCH her heires and assignes to the only proper [use and] / behoofe of the said ANNE BRANCH her heires and assignes For Ever against them the Said G[EORGE] / BRANCH and SUSANNA his Wife theire heires Executors admis$^{rs}$, or asignes and all and Ev[ery person] / or persons whatsoever Claimeinge for by or under them or any of them Shall and Will [*torn*] / and for Ever defend by these presents: and the Said GEORGE BRANCH and SUSANNA his wife [doe] / Covenant and grant to and with the said ANNE BRANCH her heires Exec$^{rs}$ adms$^{rs}$ and assignes / and appurtenancies thereunto belonginge by these presents Sould Now be and for Ever / shalbe Stand and Continue unto the Said ANNE BRANCH her heires

Clerely and Freely [*torn*] / and accquitted or otherwise From tyme to tyme and at all tymes hereafter Shalbe well [and tru] / ly Saved harmelesse by the Sayd GEORGE BRANCH and SUSANNA his wife theire heires Exec[rs] / adms[rs] or assignes of and from all and Singular former bargaines Sales Joyntures do[wers] / grants leases annuities Charges Estates titles and incumbrances whatsoever In Wittn[esse whereof we] / the said GEORGE BRANCH and SUSANNA his wife have hereunto putt theire hands and Seales [the] / Day yeare and reigne above written

GEORGE BRANCH
SUSANNA BRANCH

**[12]**

Signed Sealed and delivered as the [act]
and deed of the within named GEORGE
BRANCH and SUSANNA his wife in the ꝑsence of
JAMES I LUPOE
marke
JOHN 3 BRANCH
marke
WILL EVANS

Accknowledged in open Court held For the Isle of Weight / County N[o] the 1[t]: 1688 by GEORGE BRANCH and SUSANNA his Wife / to be theire free act and deed & ordered to be recorded

Test: JOHN PITT C[l] C[ur]

Memorandum that Full and peaceable possession and Seisen of and in all and Singular / the within plantation and land with theire and every of theire appurtenancies was delivered / by the within named GEORGE BRANCH and SUSANNA his Wife Unto the within named ANNE / BRANCH to the use and behoofe within limited, according to the tenor and effect of this / present wrightinge the last day of october 1688 in the Sight and ꝑsence of Us

JAMES I LUPOE marke    JOHN 3 BRANCH marke    SARAH I BRANCH marke

KATHERINE + BRANCH marke    WILL EVANS

Virginia In James River in pagan Creeke

Bee it Knowne unto all by these ꝑsents that I EDMOND FFENERYEARE of the Towne of / Salem in the County of Essex within his Majesties teritories and dominions of New England / Marriner have assigned and ordained & made and in my place by these presents put & / Constituted my true and welbeloved freind M[r] RICHARD

SHARPE of the County of the / Isle of Weight in Warrisqueake in Virginia in James River and in his Ma[ties] teretories / and dominions aforesaid planter to be my true and lawfull atturny for me and in / name and to my Use: to aske Sue for Levie require receive & Receive all and Every / Such debts and Sums of Mony which are now due unto me by any maner of waies and / meanes whatsoever from any Maner of persons or persons what soever in and / throughout any or all the Capes or Coast of Virginia given and grantinge to my / sayd atturny my hole power Streingth authority in and about the premises and / uppon the receipt of any Such: debts or Sums of Mony afore Said accquitance or / other dischardges for me and in my Name to make seale and deliver: and all and / Every Such act and acts thinge and things devise and devises whatsoever in the law / For the recovery of all or any Such debts or Sums of Mony as afores said for me and / in my name to doe and Execute and ꝑForme as Fully largly and amply in Every respect / to all intents Constructions and purposes as I my Selfe might or Could doe if I weare there / in my owne persons, present: and alsoe doe by these presents grant Unto my atturney Full / power to make Constitute and ordaine any other atturny or Atturnys as he shall thinke / Fitt in order to the Execution of the premisses Ratifieing and allowinge and houldinge Firme / and Stable all and whatsoever my Sayd Atturny or his Atturnys Shall lawfully doe / or Cause to be done in or about the Execution of any or all the afore said ꝑmises / by vertue of these ꝑsents in wittnesse whereof I have hereunto sett to my hand and Seale / this 2[d] of January Anno Domini 168⁸/₉

Wittnesse his EDMOND FFENERYEARE Seale
EDWARD **S** GOODSON
marke
WILLIAM **M** DANIELL
marke

Proved in open Court held for the Isle of Weight County / Jan[rij] y[e] 9[th] 168⁸/₉ by EDWARD GOODSON & WILLIAM DANIELL to / be the act of M[r] EDMOND FFENERYEARE & ordered to be recorded

Test JOHN: PITT C[l] C[ur]

**[13]**

Att a Generall Muster held in the Isle of Weight County October the 2[d]: 1688 / It is there ordered by us here under neath Subscribed that the Sherriffe doe forth with / presse Some Men to gaurd [*sic*] M[r] ROBERT THOMAS to his house he beinge in a distracted / Condition and Suppose that he may doe Some mischeife in the feild by his misbehavior / Either in rayseinge a Tumult or otherwise to Some private person given Under our / hands this ꝑsent

ARTH: SMITH
HEN: APPLEWHAITE
GEO: MOORE
HEN: BAKER

JA: DAY

To all Cristian people to whome these ꝑsents shall Come I HENRY REEVES of Rappahan / =nocke in Virginia planter Send greetinge Now [*sic*] yee that I the Said HENRY REEVES for diverse / good Causes and Considerations me there unto moveinge more espetially for and in Conside / ration of the Sume of twenty five pounds sterlinge Money to me in hand paid before the / Signeinge and delivery hereof have given granted alienated Enfeoffed bargained Sold and Con / firmed and doe by these ꝑsents ffreely and absolutely give grant allientate Enfeoffe gran / ted bargaine Sell and Confirme Unto THOMAS GODWINE of Chuckatucke one parcell of Land / lyinge in the Isle of Weight County beinge part of a pattent of Sixe hundred acres of land / formerly granted to M$^{r}$ GODFRY HUNT, and by the Said HUNT Lawfully Conveyed by an / authenticke deed of Sale Under his hand and Seale to my dec$^{d}$ ffather HENRY REEVES, and is / scituate lyinge and beinge on the South west side of the head Chuckatucke Creeke comonly / knowne by the name of the Bever dams, which said parcell of land begeining at a marked pine / Standing neare a A wolfe pitt in the forke of a Swampe knowne by the name of the Indian Branch / soe runinge Southardly to a markt Gum standinge at the lower End of a Thickett by the / side of a grate meadow Soe downe the meadow branch Containeinge the breadth of / fower hundred and fifty acres of land buttinge on the land of THO: OGLETHORPE and from / there with its due proportion runinge to the head of the Springe branch and soe run / inge downe y$^{e}$ said Springe Branch to the Extent thereof Containeinge by Estimation two / hundred Acers, be it more or lesse which Said land was lately in possession and occu / pation of one BRIDGETT ASKWE Widdow to have and to hould the said parcell of land / togather with all houses orchards Edificies and buildings with all benifitts previledges / Commodities and hereditaments thereon or there Unto belongeinge or in any wise apper / taineinge to him the said THOMAS GODWIN his heires Executors and administrators & / assignes for Ever, without the lett hinderance Molestation Eviction or Evictions of / me the said HENRY REEVES my heires Executors administrators and assignes For ever / free and freely accquited of and from all Men all maner of person or persons Claime / inge or pretendinge to Claime any right title or Intrest to the demissed premisses w$^{th}$ / the appurtenancies or any part or parcell thereof Shall and doe warrant and defend / for Ever In wittnesse whereof I have here unto Sett my hand and Seale the nynteenth / day of december Anno: do: 1688

Sighned Sealed and delivered in the ꝑsents<br>
of Us EDMOND GODWIN<br>
THO EXUM<br>
JOHN **IP** PILKINGTON<br>
his marke

HENRY **H** REEVES<br>
his marke Seale

Acknowledged in Court held for the Isle of Weight County / Jan$^{rij}$ the 9$^{th}$ 168$^{8}/_{9}$ and ordered to be recorded

Test JOHN PITT C$^{l}$ C$^{ur}$

Turne over

**[14]**

Knowe all Men by these presents that I HENRY REEVES of Rappahanocke County / in Virginia planter doe hereby Constitute ordaine and appoint my well and truly beloved / freind M^r^ JAMES BAGNALL of the Isle of Weight County planter to by [*sic*] my Lawfull atturny / for mee and in my Name and behoofe to accknowledge a deed of Sale bareinge date with / these ꝑsents for two hundred acres of land be it more or lesse as the said deed Expresses / unto Cap^t^ THOMAS GODWIN of Chuckatuck hereby giveinge and grantinge my Said atturney / full power: and lawfull Authority to accknowledge the Said deed of Sale in my name / and whatsoever my Said atturny shall doe to be as authenticke in law to all intents and / purposes as though I my Selfe was personnally present to accknowledge the same In / wittnesse whereof I have hereunto sett my hand and Seale y^e^ 19^th^ day of Decemb^r^ anno d^o^: 1688

Signed Sealed and Delivered in the ꝑsents of Us — HENRY **H** REEVES his marke — Seale

EDMOND GODWIN
the marke of
JOHN **IP** PILKINSON

Proved by Cap^t^ GODWIN to be th / L^tr^ of atturny of HENRY REEVES in / Court held for the Isle of Weight / County Jan^rij^ the 9^th^. 168^8^/~9~

Test JOHN PITT C^l^ C^ur^

This Indenture made this 29^th^ of 9^ber^ and in the yeare of lord Lord Goe one thousand sixe / hundred Eighty & Eight: betweene WALTER RUTTER of the Isle of Weight County in Virginia / of the one part and DANIELL LONGE of the place aforesaid of the other part Wittneseth that / the said WALTER RUTTER doth accknowledge himselfe to be fully Contented Satisfied and paid have / granted demissed bargained and Sould and by these presents doe fully clerely and absolutely / grant demise bargaine Sell allienate and Confirme and make over Unto the Said DANIELL / LONGE he his heyres Executors administrators or assignesse [*sic*] for ever a parcell of land of / about thirty Acres More or lesse lyinge and beinge in the aforesaid County beinge part / of a pattent of one hundred and fivety acres granted Unto the Said WALTER RUTTER bareinge / date the 30^th^ of october anno: dni: 1686 the said parcell of Land beinge bounded as followeth / (viz^t^) begininge at the boyleinge Springe branch & soe up the branch to a marked white Oke / and Soe to a greate white Oake by the bushy pond: from thence to a red Oake marked / 3 wayes: from thence to two white Oakes by the Island pond: and from thence to a Cor / ner tree, Joyneinge Uppon THOMAS POOLE: The said WALTER RUTTER doth for himselfe his / heires Execut^rs^ admins^rs^ or assignes Shall from the day of the date hereof for / Ever hereafter have hould occupy posses and quietly injoy the said parcell of land before / demissed: with all rights and profitts Comodities and hereditaments whatsoever / Molistation incumbrance trouble or Contradiction of him the Said WALTER RUTTER he his / heires Exect[rs] admis[rs] or assignes or by any other person or persons whatsoever by theire / knowledge Consent or procuration without any maner of Condition or limitation of / use or uses rent or rents, the Kings only Excepted the Said deed of Sale beinge a Conclusion / of all differences of Land betweene y[e] two aforesaid parties from the begininge Untill this / present and for the better and more authenticke Confirmation of the before dmist pmisses / the said WALTER RUTTER doth hereby obleidge himselfe to accknowledge this deed of Sale in / open Court when thereunto required to be his free and Voluntary act and deed & y[t] his / wife Shall doe the Same alsoe in wittnesse whereof the s[d] WALTER RUTTER and MARTHA his wife / have hereunto Sett theire hands and Seales the day and yeare first above written

WALTER RUTTER Seale
MARTHA **M** RUTTER Seale

Signed Sealed and delivered in psents of us
JOHN BROWNE
WILLIAM WEST Jun[r]

accknowledged in open Court held for / the Isle of Weight County Jan[rij] y[e] 9[th] / 168[8]/9 by WALTER RUTTER and MARTHA his Wife to be y[e] act & deed

Test JN[O] PITT C[l] C[ur]

**[15]**

To all &[c] whereas &[c] Now know yee y[t] I the said S[r]: W[M] BERKELY Kn[t]: Gov[r]: &[c] doe with the Consent / of the Councell of state accordingly give and grant Unto MILES and RICHARD LEWIS [--] RICHARD LEWIS / dec[d]. [--] hundred acres of land lyinge in the parish of Chuckatuck Begininge at a marked / red oake and runinge Southwest two hundred poles Joyneinge [--] of THOMAS JORDAN / to a marked [--] oake Standinge by [--] white marsh and Soe north west three hundred and / twenty pole to a marked red oake, Soe north east two hundred poles buttinge on the Land / of JEREMY RUTTER and Soe South East three hundred and twenty poles; Joyneinge to the Land / of JEREMY RUTTER and THOMAS JORDANs Land to the first Station the Said land being due / by and for the transportation of Eight persons into this Collony whose names are in the / records mentioned Under this pattent. To have and to hould &[c] to be held &[c] yeilding and pay / inge &[c] with payment &[c] provided &[c] dated this 29[th] of January 1667
MILES and RICHARD LEWIS theire pattent [--]
for 400 acres of land in Nanzemond County

Recordatur / PHILL LUDWELL C[l] off / Recorded by order of the generall Court dated octob[r] y[e] 19[th] 1687 / Test W: EDWARD C[l] gen[ll]: Cur / Vera Cop: Test W: EDWARD C[l] genr[ll] C[ur]

Know all Men by these psents that I RICHARD LEWIS now of lower Norfolke County doe accknow / ledge that I have received a Valuerable Consideration of JOHN

CAMPBELL of Nansemond County for / the price of my proportionable part of the pattent in the other Side and discharged the said / CAMPBELL his heires and Executors thereof from me my heires and Executors / for Ever for which Cause and reason before Expressed I doe by these presents sell and / make over all my right title & intrest from me my heyres and Executors to the foresaid JOHN / CAMPBELL his heyres Executors and assignes of the within pattent for Ever and doe / by these presents obleidge my selfe to warrant my foresaid right to the within written pattent / to be good and Sufficient to the saide JOHN CAMPBELL, from all and Every other person whatsoever / and I doe further obleidge my Selfe to Signe and Seale any other right to the within written pattent / which the said JOHN CAMPBELL by his learned Councell Shall advise him to wright or draw up when / the Said CAMPBELL Shall require ther Same alsoe I doe by these presents Constitute and appoint / trusty and welbeloved freind HUGH CAMPBELL to be my lawfull atturny for me and in my name / to accknowledge in Isle of Weight Court, this my deed of Sale, to the foresaid JOHN CAMPBELL / that the Same may be recorded in the Court bookes of that County I have Signed & Sealed these / presence this 17th of ffebrij 168⁷/₈

RICHARD **R** LEWIS Seale
his marke

Testes PETER SMITH
LAW: SANDEOR

Lower Norfolke accknowledged / in Court 17th febrij 168⁷/₈ and recorded
Test WM PORTEN ClCur

Accknowledged by Mr HUGH CAMPBELL atturny of RICHARD LEWIS in Court held for the Isle of / Weight County aprill the 9th 1689 to JOHN CAMPBELL.

JOHN CAMPBELL: doe for himselfe and his heyres in Court accknowledge his right and title to his brother / WILLIAM CAMPBELL and his heires for Ever that he have in the foresaid land now accknowledged to him by / Mr HUGH CAMPBELL atturny of RICHARD LEWIS and ordered to be recorded aprill the 9th 1689
Test JOHN: PITT Cl Cur

Be it knowne unto all men by these presents yt I JOHN WATKINS and MARY WATKINS of the Isle of Weight / Countie in the lower parish doth freely give unto THOMAS INGLISH & ELIANOR INGLES a hundred acres of Land / and that with MARY my wifes Consent, Unto them and the heyres of her body for ever, and if it Should please / the almighty God that the aforesaid ELLIANOR Should depart this life without a heyre then the afore / Sd THOMAS INGLES, is to kepe & to hould the above Said hundred acres of land dureinge his life tyme after / wards, to returne to the next heires without any trouble or Molestation, the above Mentioned / hundred acres of land lyinge and boundinge uppon Bowes and arrows Swampe of the South side / runinge to the head of the line: & NICHOLAS TINNER of the other side: the land beinge Called the poke courte / necke whereunto wee have Interchangeabley Sett our hands and Seales in the yeare of our Lord God one / thousand Sixteen hundred Eighty Eight the 3[d] day of octob[r] 1688 before these wittnesses

his

Testes JAMES BROWNE JOHN I WATKINS Seale

ROBERT WORGAR hand & marke

MARIE 3 WATKINS Seale

hand marke

Accknowledged by JOHN WATKINS and MARY WATKINS / in open Court held for the Isle of Weight County / aprill y[e] 9[th] 1689 to bee theire free act and deed / and ordered to be recorded

Test JOHN PITT C[l] C[ur]

**[16]**

Know all Men by these presents that I THOMAS BREWER of the Isle of Weight County in / Virginia doe for a Valuable Consideration of twenty pounds starlinge already received in hand / have bargained Sould given and granted and by these presents doe fully Clearely asnd absolutely / bargain Sell, give and grant make over and alienate Unto ANTHONY HOLLIDAY of the same / County his heires and assignes for Ever a parcell of land of thirty acres lyinge of the farthest / Side of the Clame Swampe be it more or lesse boundeing as followeth beinge part of the land / of M[r] JOHN BREWER dec[d], begininge at a red oake the Corner tree of JOHN VALLENTINE now in / the possession of the Said HOLLIDAY and the Corner tree of the said BREWER Jun[r]: and soe / runinge North East by severall markt trees to a white oake beinge the Corner tree of the / devideinge line of M[r] THOMAS PITT and the Said BREWER Soe downe the Said devideinge / line to a branch Called the Clam Swampe and Soe downe the said Branch as the branch / runs, to the Creeke and Soe Up the Creeke to the first station, beinge a red oake stand / inge on the Creeke Side and the Corner tree, to have and to hould the Sayd thirty acres / of Land be it more or lesse accordinge to the bounds above Expressed with all previledges / Royalties, profitts and Emolements marshes: & pastures woods and Under woods as in pattents / is Expressed to him the Sayd HOLLIDAY his heires and assignes For Ever, with a generall / warrantie against all persons or person that Can or Shall lay any Just Claime or claimes / to all or any part of the Said thirty acres of land, be there more or Lesse as in the bounds / as is above Expressed: and for the further Confirmation heare of, I doe bind my Selfe my / heires Executors, in the Sume of fivety pounds Starlinge Mony of England, that the / above Said HOLLIDAY shall hould the Said land accordinge to the bounds above Expressed / be it thirty acres More or lesse and to give the Said HOLLIDAY a further assurance and / insurance, as the Said HOLLIDAY,or his learned Councell in the law shall thinke fitt in / wittnesse wheare of I have heare unto Sett and afixed my hand and Seale dated this 1[st] day / of february 168$^{8}/_{9}$

Signed Sealed and delivered

in the presence of us THOMAS BREWER Seale

RALFE FRISSELL

NICKLES **N** KASY
hir marke
MARY **M** PENNY
her Marke

Accknowledged by THOMAS BREWER in open Court / held for the Isle of Weight County aprill the 9th. 1689 / to Mr ANTHONY HOLLIDAY
Test: JOHN PITT Cl Cur

Know all Men by these presents that I LEWES BRIAN of Nansamund County doe owe and stand / justly indebted Unto HENRY GAY of the Isle of Weight County his heires Executors administrators / or assignes the full and just Sume of ten thousand pounds of good Sound Merchantible tobacco & / Caske to be paid unto the Said HENRY GAY his heyres or assignes Convenient in Nansamund County / to which payment, well and truly to be made I bind my Selfe my heires Executrs and administrators / firmely by these presents In Wittnessse whereof I have hereunto Sett my hand and Seale this first / day of febrij one thousand Sixe hundred Eighty and Eight

The Condition of this obligation is Such that if the above bound LEWIS BRIAN his heires Executors / and admisrs: Shall not trouble or Molest the above named HENRY GAY his heyres Executors admisrs / or assignes in the quiett and peaceable possesion of the land and houses whereon Mr ROBERT LAWRE / =NCE now liveth, and formerly belonginge Unto Mr HENRY GAY deceased from the Maine run up / the burnt house Branch to the head line, but that the Said HENRY GAY his heires &c shall & may / quietly and peaceably have hould and injoy the Said land with the houseinge and all other pro / fitts Comodities and advantages to the Same belongeinge with out the lett trouble Molestation / Eviction or interuption of him the Said LEWIS BRIAN his heyres Executrs admisrs or assignes or any / person or persons: from by or Under him that then this present obligation to be Void and of None / Effect or Else to stand above and remaine in full force power and Vertue

Signed Sealed and delivered
in the presence of Us
JNO BRIAN
JAMES DOUGHTIE

LEWIS **L** BRIAN Seale
his marke

Accknowledged by LEWIS BRIAN / to be his act and deed in Court held / for the Isle of Weight County / May ye 1st 1689
Test JOHN PITT Cl Cur

**[17]**

Know all Men by these presents that I HENRY GAY of the Isle of Weight County doe owe and stand / Justly indebted Unto LEWIS BRIAN of Nansamond county his heyres Executors admisrs or assignes the full & / Just Sume of tenn Thousand pounds of good Sound Merchantible Tobacco and Caske to be paid unto / the Said LEWIS BRIAN his heyres or assignes Convenient in Nansemond County to which payment / well and truly to be made I bind my Selfe Execut[rs]. administrators firmely by these ꝑsents / In Wittnesse where of I have hereunto Sett my hand and Seale this first day of february one thousand / six hundred Eighty & Eight

The Condition of this obligation is Such that if the above Named HENRY GAY his heires Execut[rs]. admis[rs] / or assignes Shall not trouble or Molest the above named LEWIS BRIAN his heires Execut[rs]. admis[rs] / or assignes in the quiett and peaceable possesion of a parcell of land Joyneinge uppon the land of M[r] / JOHN BRIAN Sen[r]. alonge the maine runn and soe up the burnt house branch up to the head line beinge / part of a parcell of Land formerly belongeinge Unto M[r] HENRY GAY deceased but that the Said LEWES / BRIAN his heires &c Shall and may quietly and peaceably have hould and injoy the Said land with all / profitts priveldges Comodities and advantages to the Same belongeinge, without the lett trouble / Molestation Eviction or interuption of him the Said HENRY GAY his heires Execut[rs]. admis[rs] or assignes / or any person or ꝑsons from by or Under him that then this present obligation to be Void and of / none Effect or Elce to stand abide and remaine in Full force power & Vertue

Signed Sealed and delivered
in the psence of Us
JOHN BRIAN
JAMES DOUGHTIE

HENRY **H** GAY Seale
his marke

Accknowledged in Court held for the / Isle of Weight County May y[e] 1[st] 1689 / by HENRY GAY to be his act & deed

Test JOHN PITT C[l] C[ur]

Know all Men by these presents: that I PHILLIPE CODIN of the lower parish of the Isle of Weight / County doe with the Consent and likeinge of MARY: my now wife freely give and grant Unto / THOMAS GREENE, Sonne to my now wife, all our right Title and intrest, which wee have in the / Bricke howse and plantation whereon wee now live which formerly did belonge to Mr THO / =MAS GREENE: dec[d]: doe give to him the Said THOMAS GREENE & his heyres for Ever: it beinge in Con / sideration of the red point plantation given by the sayd THOMAS GREENE to Us for the tearme / of our naturall lives: which Said Bricke house and plantation wee doe bind our Selves / firmely by these presents to make delivery and give full and free possesion of the premisses / with in the tearme of two or three yeares after the date hereof or Sooner if I can remove / to the red point plantation Warrantinge this our guift or Exchange to him the Said THO / MAS GREENE: his heyres or Executors from the Claime Molestation and trouble of Us the S[d] / PHILLIPE CODIN and MARY my Now Wife or Either of Us: or by any other by our: or Either of our / procurement: from or Under Us in performance hereof wee have hereunto sett to our handes & / Seales this day of Aprill beinge the 24[th] 1689
Testis

THOMAS MOSTYN
JOHN **I** LINKIN
his marke

PHILLIPE **P** CODIN Seale
his marke
MARY **N** CODIN Seale
her Marke

Accknowledged in open Court held / for the Isle of Weight County June y^e^ 10^th^ / 1689 by PHILLIPE CODIN and MARY his wife / to THOMAS GREENE, to be theire free act / and deed and ordered to be recorded

Test JOHN PITT C^l^ C^ur^

Know all Men by these presents that I THOMAS GREENE of the lower parish of the Isle of Weight County / doe For divers good Causes me thereunto Moveinge doe give and graunt Unto my ffather in law / M^r^ PHILLIPE CODIN and My Mother, MARY his now wife all that plantation at theire apoint: where / on formerly MALLACKE HOWLY lived to them, for and duringe the full tearme of theire Naturall / lives: and after the Expiration of theire Naturall lives then the Said plantation to returne to / mee and my heyres accordinge as is Exprest in the Will of my dec^d^ ffather M^r^ THOMAS GREENE / Warrantinge this my deed of guift from any Molestation or disturbance of me my heyres or assignes / or any other from by or Under me or by my procurement: unto the said M^r^ PHILLIPE CODDIN and / My Mother MARY his now wife, dureinge the full tearme & date of theire Naturall lives as is / before Exprest to the true performance hereof I bind my Selfe my heyres & Execut^rs^ as Wittnesse my / hand and Seale this day of aprill beinge the 24^th^ 1689

Testis
THOMAS MESTYN
JOHN **I** LINCKIN
his Marke

THOMAS GREENE Seale

Accknowledged in open Court held for / the Isle of Weight County June y^e^ 10^th^ 1689 / by THOMAS GREENE to be his act and deed / and ordered to be recorded

Test JOHN PITT C^l^ C^ur^

**[18]**

Bee it Knowne Unto all Men by these presents that I FFRANCIS HUTCHINS & MARY his Wife for / a valuable Consideration in hand already received have bargained lett to Sale and delivered over / unto THOMAS ENGLISH one parcell of land full out one hundred acres of land lyeinge and beinge / in the lower parish of the Isle of Weight County uppon the head of a Swampe commonly / Called powel Swampe uppon the Westerne branch bindeinge uppon the line of THOMAS GALE / THOMAS POWELL & me the Said FFRANCIS HUTCHINS and in Confirmation hereof wee the Said / FFRANCIS & MARY his Wife doe bind our Selves our heires Executors administrators to and with / the Said THOMAS ENGLISH his heires Executors administrators to warrant and Maintaine the / Sale of the above Said pcell of land for Ever togather with all its previledges thereunto / belonginge in as Stronge and firme a maner as may or can be Expressed notwithstand / inge anythinge to the Contrary: in Confirmation hereof wee have hereunto Subscribed our / hands & Seales this third day of Sep[t]. 1686

the marke & Seale of

Wittnesse — FFRANCIS HUTCHINS **FH** Seale

THOMAS **TA** GALE — MARY + HUTCHINS Seale

his marke — her marke / & Seale

the marke **K** of KATHERINE / RICKSIS

accknowledged by FFRANCIS HUTCHINS in open Court held for the Isle of Weight County to be his / act and deed this 9[th] of december 1686 Test JOHN PITT C[l]C[ur]

I Under written doe accknowledge to have assigned Over unto ROBERT FULLERTON all my right / title and intrest of this with in mentioned deed of Conveyance and Unto his heyres for Ever / as Wittnesse my hand this 10[th] day of Sept 1688 Wittnesse

Signum

JS RICKSES — THOMAS **TE** ENGLISH

KATHERINE **K** RICKSIS — ELLIONER **EE** ENGLISH

her marke

this is indosed [*sic*] one the backe / Side of the above written / Conveyance

Accknowledged July the 9[th] 1689 in open Court by THOMAS ENGLISH and ELLIONER his wife / to be theire free act and deed

Test JOHN PITT C[l] C[ur]

Know all Men by these presents that BARTHOLOMEW GREENE of Charles towne / in New England Marriner have and hereby doe Constitute ordaine depute appoint / and make my much respected freind Maj[r]: THOMAS TABERER of the Isle of Weight County / in Virginia my true and lawfull atturny for me and in my name and Steed and for / my Use to aske demand require receive and to use all lawfull meanes to recover / out of the hands of whome Soever it may Concerne all Such Sume or Sums of Mony debts / goods or other Estate as now is or hereafter may become due owinge or payable to me / the Constitutant by bill bond booke account or other demand or by any other waise / or meanes whatsoever, and in perticular to use all lawfull meanes to recover out of y[e] / hands of any that is in debt to mee giveinge and hereby grantinge to my Said atturney full / power and authority, to Sue arrest impleade and presecute to [ ]ect in any Court or Courts / and in my behalfe appearance to make and any action or actions to defend and if neede / be, into prisson to Cast and thereto deliver releases or other discharges: uppon payment to / give and Sine Compotition if he see cause to make and atturnies one or more to Substitute / and them at pleasure to revoke and every other way to act Execute and performe in my / behalfe to all intents and purposes in as full and ample maner measure and degree as I / might or Could doe, if I were personally present to performe the Same alwaise and in all / things ratifieinge allowinge and Confirmeinge what my Said atturny Shall lawfully act / or Cause to be acted in persuance of the premisses firmely by these presents in wittnesse where / of I the said BARTHOLOMEW GREENE have hereunto Sett my hand and Seale this 8th. day of aprill / 1689

Signed Sealed and delivered BARTHO GREENE Seale
in ꝑsence of us
JA: DAY
JOHN PITT

Proved in open Court held for the / Isle of Weight County to be the act / of Mr BARTHOLOMEW GREENE by the oaths / of JAMES DAY and JOHN PITT augst ye 9th 1689

Test JOHN PITT Cl Cur

**[19]**

Mr JOSEPH SENIOR Mechant [*sic*] of Barbados his letter of Atturney to Major THOMAS TABERER is recor / ded in the greate Booke of Wills and testaments on follio 297[1]

---

[1] Isle of Wight Co., VA, Will & Deed Book 2, p. 297: Barbados / To all to whome this present Writeinge shall Come I Joseph Senior of the Island above Said Merchante / Send greetinge in our Lord God Everlastinge: Know yee that I the said Joseph Senior: doe by these ꝑsent / Authorize & Constitute my trusty & welbeloved Majr Thomas Taberer of James River in Virginia / Merchant: to bee on this behalfe my true and lawfull atturny: for me and in my name and Stead to / aske demand Levie Sue for recover and receive from Mr Robert Thomas in said James River in Virginia Merchant / all Such Sumes of tobacco: monies goods; Merchandizes, debts, demands dues of what nature quallity or Condition / soever: as now are or hereafter shalbe due Comeinge or belongeinge Unto mee: by or from the above said Mr / Robert Thomas or any other person or persons what soever his or theire heires Executors administrators & / assignes be it Either by Bill, Booke, Bond, letter, acompt, reconinge Noate: Ticket or any other wayes or / or [*sic*] meanes whatsoever: None Excepted or reserved and Generally: to doe, Manage and follow all my / affaires & Bussinesses what soever: in Said Virginia that Shalbe meete or requisite to be done / Giveinge & by these presents grantinge unto my Sayd Atturny my full and whole power and authority / touchinge the premisses: or any part thereof: by all lawfull wayes and Meanes: what soever: for me and / in my Name & Stead: and to my use to doe say: sue implead ꝑsent: persue Seaze Sequester Arrest / Attache imprison: & to Condemne: and out of prisson to deliver and to recover: receive, Compound agree / release accquit and dischardge one atturny or Moore, for him or Under him to substitute & at his plea / =sure to revoke: & further, to doe performe, Execute & at pleasure to revoke & determine, all and / Every other act, Matter: thing & things: what

Know all Men by these presents that I the subscriber doe Constitute and appoint HUGH CAMPBELL / to bee my lawfull atturny for me to appeare in all Causes I am or shalbe Concernd in at Isle of Weight / County Court Either as plantife or defendent and for my behofe to make any Such Motions to the fore / Said Court as he shall judge fitt or Convenient in Testimony whereof I have Sined these presents / this 6$^{th}$ day of decemb$^{r}$. 1688 ROBERT THOMAS

This is owned in open Court by M$^{r}$ ROBERT / THOMAS to be his act Octob$^{r}$ y$^{e}$ 9$^{th}$. 1689 & / ordered to be recorded Test JOHN PITT C$^{l}$ C$^{ur}$

Know all Men by these presents that I THOMAS WARD of the lower parish of the Isle of Weight Coun / ty planter doe for the love and good Will which I beare to THOMAS BEVAN: of the same parish & County / doe freely give and graunt and Confirme Unto the said THOMAS BEVAN: all my right title and intrest / which I now have or hereafter Shall or may have of the one Moitie or halfe of the land whereon I / now live adjoyneinge one Virgoes Creeke, the which Land was given and granted Unto mere by Vertue / of an Escheate pattent for two hundred and two acres of Land that is to say the innermost part of the / land from Virgoes Crekee buttinge northerly on Warrisqueke back bay Creeke, accordinge to a devidinge / line formerly laid out and made by Maj$^{r}$ ARTHUR ALLEN Surveyor, only with this alteration that the / partition line be now to be betwene us by a locust tree which stands in the ould field very neare / the Said devideinge lines beinge by Survey about one hundred acres of land togather with all houses Edi / ficies buildings fences orchards: which is or shalbe thereon Erected with all Woods Underwoods waters / previledges Comodities hereditaments and appurtenances what Soever Unto the Said plantation or tract / of land or any part or parcell thereof belongeinge or in any wise appertaineinge alwaise / reserveinge a good roade trough [*sic*] the Sayd land to my owne house and plantation To have & to hould / the foresaid plantation and land thereunto belongeinge togather with all houses Edifices

---

Soever that shalbe meete nedefull, or Expedient / to be done ꝑformed or Executed or Expedient in or about the premisses or any part thereof / as amply in Every respect to all intents and purposes as I my selfe might or Could doe / the Same if I were or should be then and there personally present did the Same personally [p. 298] Ratifieinge & firmeinge & allowinge for good and Effectuall all and what soever my said atturny shall love [*sic*] / fully doe & Execute or Cause to be done or Executed in or about the premisses or any part their of In Witnessese / whereof I have hereunto putt my hand and Seale this 19$^{th}$ of March 168$^{8}$/$_{9}$ Signed Sealed & delivered / Joseph: Senior Seale / in presence of Edmund Ffeneryeare John Thompson / This Lett$^{r}$ of atturny is provd & by the oath / of M$^{r}$ Edmund Ffeneryeare May the first 1689 / and M$^{r}$ John Thompsons oath october the 9$^{th}$ 1689 / in open Court held for the Isle of Wight County / Test John Pitt C$^{l}$ C$^{ur}$

buildinges / fences Orchards gardens woods wayes Waters: Commons profits and Comodities and all and Singuler / other the premisses hereby given and granted with all theire rights members and appurtenancies / whatsoever Unto the Said THOMAS BEVAN: his heire and assignes to the only proper use & behoofe / of the Said THOMAS BEVAN his heires & assignes For Ever against me the Said THOMAS WARD my heirs / Executors administrators or assignes and all and Every person or persons: whatsoever Claimeing / From by or Under mee or any of them Shall and Will Warrant and defend by these presents & / I the said THOMAS WARD doe Covenant grant and agree to and With the Said THOMAS BEVAN / his heires Executors & assignes & Every of them by these presents that all and Singular the forereci / ted lands with all and Singular the houseinge fences profits and appurtenancies there unto belong / inge: only a roade as before Exprest Excepted by these presents given and granted now be and / for Ever hereafter Shalbe Stand and Continue Unto the Said THOMAS BEVAN his heires Executors / and assignes for Ever from the Claime and Molestation of me my heires Executors or assignes / For Ever the Said land to ly in Common for range of pasturage betwene us without puttinge up / of any fence hgedge: ditch or other wise to be a hinderance of the Common range or any parcell there / of with out the Consent of both parties dureinge our Naturall lives and further I doe bind my / Selfe that if it Should happen that I am minded to part with that part of land which I now hould / to lett THOMAS BEVAN have the refuseall uppon reasonable tearmes as Wittnesse my hand and / Seale this 18th day of September 1689

Signed Sealed and delivered
in the presence of us
NICHOLAS FFULGHAM
RICH WILKISSON
JOHN PITT

THOMAS **T** WARD Seale
his marke

Livery and Seizen was made and given of all / the before recited premises in presence of Us / the 18th day of Sept^r^. 1689

NICHOLAS FFULGHAM
RICH WILKISSON
JOHN PITT

Accknowledged in open Court held for / the Isle of Weight County octob^r^ y^e^ 9th 1689 / by THOMAS WARD to be his free act and / deed and ordered to be recorded

Test JOHN: PITT C^l^ C^ur^

**[20]**

Know all Men by these presents that I THOMAS BEVAN of the lower Isle of Weight / County Carpenter, doe for the love and good Will which I beare to THOMAS WARD of the Same parish / and County: doe freely give grant and Confirme Unto the Said THOMAS WARD all my right title and / Intrest: which I now have or hereafter may have of the one Moitie of halfe of the land or dividend / of land which did formerly belonge to my Uncle PETER HAYES and by him given to mee as by his / last Will doe

appeare lyinge on the West Side of Virgoes Creeke and buttinge northerly on Warisqueke / backe bay Creeke Containeinge in the whole two hundred and two acres: that is to Say the lower most / part of the Tract of land Joyneinge on Virgoes Creeke accordinge to a devideinge line formerly laid / out and Made by Maj[r] ARTHUR ALLEN Surveyor only with this alteration that the partition line / be now to be betwene Us by a locust Tree, which Stands in the ould feild very neare the Said / divideinge line beinge by Survey about one hundred acres of Land Togather with all houses Edi / ficies buildeings fences orchards which is or shalbe thereon Erected: with all Woods Underwoods / Waters previledges Comodities heridatements and appurtenancies whatsoever unto the Said / plantation or tract of land or any part or parcell thereof belongeinge or in any waise apper / taininge To have and to hould the foresaid plantation and land thereUnto belongeinge to / gather with all houses: Edificies buildings fences orchards gardens Woods wayes Waters Com / =mons profits and Comodities: and all and Singular other the premisses hereby given and granted / with all theire rights members and appurtenancies whatsoever Unto the Said THOMAS / WARD his heires and assignes to the only proper Use and behoofe of the Said THOMAS WARD / for Ever: against me the Said THOMAS BEVAN my heires Executors: administrators and assignes / and all and Every person or persons Whatsoever Claimeinge from by or Under me or any of / them: Shall and will warrant and defend by these presents, and I the Said THOMAS BEVAN / doe Covenant grant and agree to and With the Saide THOMAS WARD his heyres Executors and / and Every of them by these presents that all and Singular the fore / recited lands: with all and Singular the houseinge fences profits & appurtenancies there / unto belongeinge by these presents given and granted now be and for Ever hereafter shall / be Stand and Continue Unto the Said THOMAS WARD his heires Executors and assignes for Ever / from the Claime and Molestation of me my heires Executors or assignes for Ever, the Said / land to ly in Common for range of pasturadge betweene Us: without puttinge up of any fence / hedge ditch: or otherwise to be a hinderance of the Common range or any parcell thereof with / out the Consent of both parties dureinge our Naturall lives and further I doe bind myselfe / that if it should happen that I am minded to part with that part of land which I now hold / to lett THOMAS WARD have the refuseall of it uppon reasonable tearme: as Wittnesse my hand / and Seale this 18[th] day of September 1689 THO: BEVAN Seale
Signed Sealed and delivered
in the ꝑsence of Us
NICHOLAS FULLGHAM
RICH WILKISSON
JOHN PITT

Livery and Seizen was made and given / of all the before recited premisses in ꝑsence / of Us this 18[th] of Sept[r] 1689 NICHOLAS FFULGHAM
RICH WILKISSON
JOHN: PITT

Accknowledged in open Court / held for the Isle of Weight County / octob$^{r}$ the 9$^{th}$. 1689: by THOMAS BEVAN / to be his free act and deed and ordered to be recorded

Test JOHN PITT C$^{l}$ C$^{ur}$

**[21]**

Know all men by these presents that I WILLIAM BODDIE of the Isle of Weight County in Virginia / have bargained Sould and delivered Unto JOHN DUKE and to his heyres for Ever a plantation and / a parcell of Woodland ground there Unto adjoyneinge and the Said plantation is that plantation / which HENRY KINGE lately lived on: and the Sayd plantation and Woodland ground is bounded thus / it begineth at a little Shrubbie white oake which Standeth, by the Side of a little branch and from / thence alonge a parcell of Marked trees to a live Oake Standinge in a branch and from thence downe / the Said Branch to the Mouth thereof to a greater Branch and then downe the Said greater branch / soe far as a litle pokekerie tree marked with Sixe notches or marks in it three in the one Side and / three in the other, and it Standeth on a poynt on the other Side of a branch right over against / JOHN JACKSONs ould plantation, and it alsoe Standeth by the mouth of an other branch and then / up the Said other branch a litle Way and then over the branch to the mouth of another lesser bra / =nch and then up the Said lesser branch Soe far as to the first Station: or first mentioned litle shruby / white oake Now whether the plantation and woodland ground with in the bounds here above men / tioned, be one hundred acrers or two hundred acres or whether itt be moore or lesse wee doe not Certainely / know but bee it Moore or be it lesse the land with in the bounds here above mentioned and all the dues / & profits there Unto belongeinge I the foresaid WILLIAM BODDIE have Sould Unto him the foresaid / JOHN DUKE his heyres Executors administrators and assignes for Ever hee or they payinge Unto me or [ ] / soe much quitt rent or Kings rent as one hundred and fifety akers of land Cometh to yearely and every / yeare for Ever and further I the foresaid WILLIAM BODDIE doe hereby promise and ingadge my Selfe / that both I my Selfe and alsoe my wife Shall and Will in open Court accknowledge this deede of Sale / to be our free and Voluntary act and deed as Wittnesse my hand this 21$^{th}$ of august 1689

Wittnesse

ANTHONY **AD** DAVIS
his marke
WILLIAM **U** FOWLER
his marke
WALTER **H** HOWELL
his marke

WILLIAM BODDIE Seale
ELIZ: + BODDIE
her marke

Accknowledged in Court held / for the Isle of Weight County N$^{o}$ the 9$^{th}$ 1690 by WILLIAM BODDIE / and ELIZABETH his wife to be theire free act and deed

Test JOHN PITT C$^{l}$ C$^{ur}$

Seale

To all to whome these presents Shall Come I S^r^ W^M^ BERKELEY Kn^t^ Governo^r^ & Cap^t^ generall of / Virginia Send greetinge in our Lord God Everlastinge whereas by instructions from the Kings most Excellent Ma^tie^ / directed to mee and the Councell of State his Majestie was graciously pleased to authorize me the S^d^ Govern^r^ / and Councell to grant pattents and to assigne Such proportions of Land to all adventurers and planters as have bene Usuall heretofore in the like Cases Either for adventurers of Mony or transportation of people / into this Collony, accordinge to a Charter of orders from the late Tresurer and Company and that the Same / proportion of fifty acres of land be granted and assigned for Ever person transported hither Since Mid / =Somer 1624 and that the Same Course be Continued to all adventurers and planters Untill it Shalbe other / wise determined by his Ma^tie^ Now know yee that I the Said S^r^ W^M^ BERKELEY Kn^t^ & doe with the Consent of the / Councell of State accordingly give and grant Unto THOMAS POOLE one hundred Acres of land, lyeinge in the lower / parish of the Isle of Weight County begininge at a marked pokekory Joyneinge to the Said POOLEs land therein / runinge North 160 poles to a blacke Oake thence Northwest and by North 160 poles to the land of M^r^ ROBERT / BRACEWELL, thence by the marked trees of the Said BRACEWELLs Land South Southwest and South west and by / by [*sic*] South 320 poles to the Corner tree of the Said POOLEs Land thence retureinge by the marked trees of / the Said POOLEs land to the first Station the Said land beinge due unto the Said THOMAS POOLE by and for / the transportation of two persons into this Collony: whose names are on the records mentioned Under this / pattent to have and to hould the Said land, with his due Share of all Mines and mineralls therein Conteyned / with all rights and priveledges of huntinge Hawkinge, fishinge, & fowleinge with all woods waters and rivers / with all profits, Comodities and hereditaments whatsoever belonginge to the Sayd land to him the Said / THOMAS POOLE his heyres and assignes for Ever: In as large and ample Maner to all intents and purposes / as is Exprest in a Charter of orders from the late Treasurer & Company dated the 18^th^ of November 1618 / or by Consequence may be Justly Collected out of the Same or out of the letters pattents whereon they are / gounded to be held of our Sovereign Lord Kinge Charles his heyres & Successors for ever as of his Manor / of East Grenewich in fee and Common Sockage & not *in Capite* Nor by Knights Service yeldinge and / payinge to our Sovereigne Lord the Kinge his heyres and Successors for Every fifty acres of land here gran / =ted yearely at the feast of S^t^ Michaell the archangell the fee rent of one Shillinge which payment / is to be made yearely from the first grant hereof accordinge to his Ma^ties^ instructions the first Entry

**[22]**

Entry of the Survey and rights in the office beinge the 29^th^ of January last past provided that / if the Sayd THOMAS POOLE his heyres or assignes doe not Seate or plant or Cause to be planted or / Seated uppon the Sayd land with in three yeares next Ensueinge then it Shalbe lawfull for any / adventurer or planter to make Choyce & Seate thereon given Under my hand and Seale of the Collony / of James Citty this 16th. day of february 1662 and in the fiftenth yeare of the reigne of our / Sovereigne Lord Kinge Charles the Second &c WILLIAM BERKELEY

THOMAS POOLE his patt} FR^A: KIRKMAN TH^O LUDWELL Sen^r
for 100 acres of Land }

This pattent is rec^o by order of Court bearinge date July the 9th 1689
Test JOHN PITT C^l C^ur

Know all Men by these presents that I JOHN NEVILL and ELIZABETH NEVILL my Wife doe freely give / Unto BENJAMIN BEALE Jun^r and MARTHA his wife one hundred acres of Land beinge oute of a pattent / taken up by RICHARD STAPLES Containeinge Seven hundred and fivety Akers and bounding Joyneinge / uppon three hundred and fivety akers of land Sould from STAPLES unto WILLIAM THOMSON accord / inge to the Course of the pattent, to them or Either of them and theire heyres lawfully begotteng / theire boddies but in Case his Wife MARTHA Should dye with out heyres lawfully begotten of her / boddy as god forbid Shee Should and if the Said BENJAMIN BEALES Should Marry againe and have / heires Lawfully begotten of his owne boddy then the above Said Land to remaine to him and his / heires for Ever, butt in Case he the Said BEALE Should dye without heyres Lawfully begotten / of his owne Boddy, that then the Said land to return Unto BENJAMIN NEVILL my youngest / sonne this wee doe freely give with all previledges belongeinge thereto accordinge to pattent / Wittnesse our hands and Seales this 3d day of december 1689

Testes THO: GILES JOHN NEVILL Seale
JOHN NEVILL Jun^r ELIZABETH **E** NEVILL Seale
her marke

Acckknowledged in open Court held / For the Isle of Weight County dec^r: / y^e 9th 1689 by JOHN NEVILL & ELIZABETH / his wife to be theire free act and deed / and ordered to be recorded Test JOHN PITT C^l C^ur

Know all Men by these presents that wee JOHN SMITH and ANNE SMITH his wife of the Isle / of Weight County doe give and bequeath from us and form our heyres: Executors or assignes Unto / JOHN MICKMIHALL his heyres Executors or assignes for Ever a parcell of land beinge about twen / ty acres More or lesse, the Sayd parcell of Land: beinge part of the land which I Bought of Cap^t / WILLIAM OLDIS late of Nansamund & ROBERT RUFFIN of Surry which foresaid parcell of land lyeth / in the Westerne Corner of my land one Side there of Joyneinge uppon Cap^t GEORGE NORSWORTHY / late of the County of Nansamund and the other Side Joyneinge on MATHEW TOMLINs land & / the Inward Side bounded with a Branch and the other Side with a broad path: the aforesaid / JOHN MICKMIHALL his hayres Executors or assignes Shall not Sett out: or Sell any part or ꝑcell / of the aforeSaid land In wittnesse whereof wee have hererunto Sett our hands & Seale this 9th. day / of december in the yeare of our Lord God one thousand Sixe hundred Eighty nine

Signed sealed & delivered in the presence of Us
JOHN: BROWNE
ROBERT **RL** LAURENCE
his marke

JOHN SMITH Seale
ANNE + SMITH Seale
her marke & seale

Accknowledged in open Court held for / the Isle of Weight County decembr ye 9th. 1689 / by JOHN SMITH and ANNE his wife to be theire / free act and deed & ordered to be recorded

Test JOHN PITT Cl Cur

**[23]**

Know all Men by these presents that Wee JONATHAN SHIPLEY and ELLES his wife of the bridge Towne in / the Island of Barbados for divers good Causes and Considerations Us thereunto moveinge have made ordained / Constituted and appointed and by these presents doe make ordaine Constitute and appoint our trusty / good friends JACOB GREENE of Virginia otherwise called Capt JACOB GREENE, our true and lawfull atturny / for Us and in our names to aske demand recover and receive of all or any person or persons whatsoever all / debt or debts porke Tobacco and other Effects as shalbe found due to Us, Especially to demand recover or / receive of Coll ARTHUR SMITH JOSEPH WOORY and JAMES TULLAGH Executrs of the last Will and Testament of / JOHN BURNELL decd a Certaine Legacie or legacies bequeathed to the sd ELLES, by her late ffather the said / JOHN BURNELL: and uppon non payment of the Same legacie or legacies, the aforesaid Execrs of the Said / JOHN BURNELL for Us and in our Names to Sue implead prosecute for the Same, and uppon / Such Suite to procede to Judgment, decree Sentence and Execution and there uppon to leavy with Effect Un / till payment of Such Legacie or Legacies as aforesaid be made with all Costs and damages Susteyned and to / be Sustayned by occation of the deteyneinge the Said legacies or Legacies and uppon payment or payments thereof / from the Said Executrs accquittances Accquittances [*sic*] for the Same or any parte thereof for Us and in our name / to make Sale and deliver and alsoe to Compound doe performe and Execute all and Every other lawfull & reasonable / Acts and things whatsoever both for obtaineinge and dischargeinge of the Same as Shalbe nedefull to be done / in the premisses giveinge and by these presents grantinge Unto our Said Atturney our full and absolute power / in the premisses ratiffienge and houldinge firme all and whatsoever our Said Atturney shall Lawfully doe or / Cause to be done in or about the premisses by Vertue of these presents: And wee doe hereby further impower / the Said Capt JACOB GREENE if occassion be, to make and Constitute one or more Atturney or Atturneys under him / to aske demand recover and receive of all or any person or persons whatsoever all debt or debts pockes [*sic*] tobacco / and other Effects as Shalbe found due to us Especcially to demand recover or receive of the Execut[rs] of the Said / JOHN BURNELL dec[d]: as afores[d] the Legacie or legacies Soe bequeathed as aforesaid to the Said ELLES and finally / to doe act and performe all Such acts and things as wee our Selves might doe if wee were personally there / In Wittnesse whereof wee have hereunto Sett our hands and Seales this Seventeenth day of May in the first yeare / of the reigne of our Sovereigne Lord and Lady: William and Mary by the grace of God Kinge and Queene of / England & Anno[qu] Dom 1689

JONATHAN SHIPLEY Seale
ELLIS SHIPLEY Seale

Sealed and delivered in
the presence of Us
SAMUEL ASTENG
GEORGE BONFELL

Sworne to this 4th of July 1689 / before me

NATHANIELL BACON P[r] / Recorded the 1st of January 1689: by the request of Capt JACOB GREENE

To all Christian people to whome these ꝑsents Shall Come FFRANCIS BRIDLE and MARY his wife / of Nansamund parish in the Isle of Weight County Send greetinge in our Lord god Everlastinge / Know yee that wee the said FFRANCIS BRIDLE and MARY his Wife for divers good Causes and Conside / rations as hereunto moveinge butt nowe Espetially, for and in Consideration of the naturall affection / wee beare Unto THOMAS HAMPTON and ELIZABETH his wife have given and granted and by these ꝑsents / doe for Us our heires Executors and administrators give and grant Unto him the Said THOMAS HAMP / =TON and ELIZABETH his wife and after theire decease Unto MARY HAMPTON and the heires of her / body lawfully begotten the one halfe part or Moyetie of a parcell of Land to mee granted by patt / =ent dated the 21th day of January 1679: after THOMAS GALE is Satisfied his part by us heretofore / granted, Unto him the Said THOMAS HAMPTON as aforesaid his heires Executors administrators & / assignes for Ever, to gather with all howses Edeficies timber and timber trees: water and water / Courses profits previledges Comodities and advantages to the Same belonginge or in any maner of / waies appertaineinge boundinge Uppon JOHN THORNETON to have and to hould Unto him the Said / THOMAS HAMPTON and ELIZABETH his Wife as aforesaid free and Cleare and frely and Clearely / accquitted Exonerated and discharged of and of from all maner of former guifts grants bargaines / and Sales whatsoever in witnesse whereof wee the Said FFRANCIS BRIDLE and MARY my Wife have / hereunto Sett our hands and Seales this 8th day of feb[rij] 16$^{89}/_{90}$

Signed Sealed an ~~dd~~
on the ꝑsence of Us
JAMES DOUGHTIE
H

FFRANCIS **B** BRIDLE Seale
his marke
MARY **V** BRIDLE Seale

Accknowledged in Court held for the / Isle of Weight County feb$^{rij}$ the 10$^{th}$ 16$^{89}$/$_{90}$ / by FFRANCIS BRIDLE & MARY his wife to be theire / free act and deed and ordered to be recorded

Test JOHN PITT C$^{l}$ C$^{ur}$

**[24]**

To all Christian people to whome these presents shall Come THOMAS MAN of the Isle of Weight County / planter Sends greetinge in our Lord God Everlastinge Know yee that I the Said THOMAS MAN for divers / good Causes and Considerations mee hereunto moveinge but more Espetially: for and in Consideration of / a certaine Sume of tobacco to me in hand payd or Secured to be payd by HENRY HEARNE of Nansamund / County planter, the receipt whereof I doe hereby accknowledge and Confesse, have given granted bargai / ned Sold Aliened Conveyed Enfeofed and Confirmed, and doe by these presents for mee my heyres / Executors and administrators give grant bargaine Sell alliene Convey Enfeoffe and Confirme Unto him / the said HENRY HEARNE his heyres Executors administrators or assignes a Certaine parcell of land contey / =neinge one hundred acres Scituate lyeinge and beinge in the Isle of Weight County aforesaid and buting / and boundinge upon the north East Side of Corowake Swampe runninge up a branch North Eastward / ly to a red oake and Soe up the aforesaid MANs line to a Corner pine tree Joyneinge upon a parcell / of land by mee the Said THOMAS MAN letten unto JAMES JOHNSON unto him the Said HENRY HEARNE his / heires Executors and administrators or assignes to gather with all houses Edifices buildings timber and / timber trees Waters and water Courses profitts previledges Commodites and advantages to the Same / belongeinge or any maner of way appertaineinge To have and to hould Unto him the said HENRY / HEARNE his heires Executors administrators or assignes for Ever, free and Cleare & freely and Clearely / accquitted Exonerated and dischardges of and from all maner of former and other guifts grants / bargaines Sales or other incumbrances whatsoever and the Said THOMAS MAN doth further Cove / =nant, promise and grant to and with the Sayd HENRY HEARNE his heires Executors administrat$^{rs}$ / or assignes that he the Said THOMAS MAN, his heires Executors administrators or assignes Shall / and Will, at all times hereafter warrant Save defend and keepe harmelesse him the Said HENRY / HEARNE his heires Executors admis$^{rs}$ or assignes from all persons that Shall or may hereafter / Claime any right title or intrest to the Said land and ꝑmises or any part or parcell / thereof in Wittnesse wehereof I have hereunto Sett my hand and Seale this ninth day of february / in the yeare of our Lord God One thousand Sixe hundred Eighty and Nine

Signed Sealed and delivered<br>in the p$^{r}$sence of us<br>JAMES + BRYON<br>his marke<br>BRIDGMAN **B** JOYNER<br>his marke

THOMAS **M** MAN Seale<br>hir Marke

JAMES BENN

Accknowledged in open Court / held for the Isle of Weight County / feb$^{rij}$ the 10$^{th}$ 16$^{89}$/$_{90}$ by THOMAS MAN / to be his act and deed

Test JOHN PITT C$^{l}$ C$^{ur}$

this above bill of Sale returned in follio 32

Test JN$^{O}$. PITT C$^{l}$

Rec$^{d}$ of M$^{rs}$ SILVESTRA HILL the full and iust Sume of twenty two pound Sterlinge in plate / beinge for a negroe woman rec$^{d}$ ꝑ me THO: TABERER ꝑ Execution as atturny to JOSEPH SENIOR / beinge part of a debt from s$^{d}$ THOMAS to Said SENIOR I say rec$^{d}$ the aforesaid Sume quallified / as afores$^{d}$ ꝑ mee as the atturny of JOSEPH SENIOR

Test JA: POWELL THO: TABERER
ROB$^{T}$ PITT

Accknowledged in open Court held for / the Isle of Weight county aprill y$^{e}$ 9$^{th}$ 1690 / by Major THOMAS TABERER & ordered to be / recorded

Test JOHN PITT C$^{l}$ C$^{ur}$

**[25]**

Know all Man by these presents that I JOHN DUKE of the County of Isle of Weight planter haveinge / in hand already received Satisfaction to the Value of three thousand pounds of tobacco and Caske: doe hereby / these presents acknowledge, to have Sold and make Sale Unto JOHN BURNETT shoemaker of the Same County / a parcell of Land Conteineinge fifty Acres or there abouts, which land my ffather JOHN DUKE deceased, for / merly bought of JEREMIAH RUTTER of Chuckatucke then in Nansamund County beinge out a pattent of three / hundred acres lyinge and boundinge betwene the land of JOHN GOSELING and the house of my ffather JOHN / DUKE where he was then Scituated which Said land and I the Said JOHN DUKE doe accknowledge to have Sould / unto the abovesaid JOHN BURNETT for Ever with all right profitts Comodities and hereditaments whatsoever / thereunto belongeinge and that free and Cleare, and frely and Clearely defend keepe harmelesse the said / BURNETT from all or all maner of ꝑsons that Shall lay Claime or Claime any right title or intrest to the / above Mentioned fifty acres of land but the Same to hould and and injoy for Ever, with he the Said JOHN BUR / =NETT his heires Executors administrators or assignes accordinge to the tenor of my ffather DUKEs (deceased) / Conveyance Specifieith and to the true performance hereof I the Said JN$^{O}$. DUKE doe accknoweldge to have / sett my hand and Seale this 23$^{d}$ of Sept 1689

signu
JOHN I DUKE Seale
signu
ELIZABETH S MERCER Seale

Signes Sealed and delivered
in the presence of Us
WILL BRADSHAW

signu
RICH **R** BEALLE

BRIDGETT **O** DUKE
her marke

I ELIZABETH MERCER doe freely Consent with / my Sonne JOHN DUKE to this bill of Sale as Wittnesse / my hand and Seale the day and yeare above written

Accknowledged in open Court held for the Isle of Weight / County by JOHN DUKE ELIZ^A MERCER & BRIDGETT DUKE to be theire / act and deed and ordered to be recorded Test JOHN PITT C^l C^ur

Wee whose Names are Subscribed and Seales Sett beinge by order of the Worpp^ll Court of this County beareinge / date the 10^th of feb^rij Last Sumoned by the Sherrife of the Said County and Sworne togather with the S^d Sheriffe / and the Surveyor of the County aforesaid to lay out Seaven hundred and fifty acres of land In difference betwene / M^r RICHARD REYNOLDS plantiffe and M^r JOHN NEVILL and ELIZABETH his Wife defendants: accordinge to the ancient / Bounds of the pattent and alsoe to lay out Each parcell purchased out of the S^d pattent and then to make par / tition of the remainder ꝑsuant to the Said order Wee began at a marked white oake Standinge on the Northerly / Side of the Westerne branch of Nanzemond accknowledged all parties to be the ancient Corner tree in y^e / pattent mentioned thence N.E. by Severall antient marked trees 424 pole into a pecoson mentioned in the / pattent but not findinge the Corner tree wee markt a great pine in the sayd pecoson, thence by a line of / old markt trees: S. 47^d E as the Surveyor informed Us 400 pole to a markt white oake an ould reputed Corner / tree thence SW 502 pole to a red oake Stump by the Said Swampe where an ould Corner tree once Stood then up / the Swampe by Various Courses to the white oake first mentioned which Courses and distances the Survey^or / Sayeth includes 1085 acres out of which wee find 350 acres Sold by RICHARD STAPLES dec^d: unto M^r W^M THOMP / =SON dec^d and alsoe 200 acres Sold by Severall Conveyancies to M^r THOMAS BENBRIDGE and M^r W^M MURFREY w^ch / Severall parcells wee have likewise layd out accordinge to the directions of the Severall deeds of Sale the remain / inge 535 acres wee Equally devided thus, begininge at a light wood Stake Standinge in the 2^d Course of the / pattent 160 pole distance from the white oake the 3^d tree Expressed in the pattent thence S.W. downe / to the Swampe aforesaid dated Under our hands and Seales this 3^d day of aprill 1690

Test JOSEPH WOORY
SAMUELL SWANN Suv^ors

JAMES BENN : seale
W^M **W** WEST Seale
JACOB DURDEN Seale
WILL **I** GODWIN seale
JAMES TULLAGH: Seale
W^M BRADSHAW: Seale
W^M **W** POWELL Seale
DAN: **0** LONGE Seale
JOHN BOTTUST Seale

RICHARD **BH** HUTCHIN Seale
WALTER RUTTER Seale
JOHN **IM** MOORE Seale

The above Verdict of the Jury: is Confirmed and the land / beinge divided by the Jury M[r] JOHN NEVILLE is to have for his / Share that part which the houseinge is build on and / M[r] RICHARD REYNOLDS to have that part which have / not beene occupied, the above said divission is Consented / to: by Consent of both parties in open Court and soe doe / take the possesion of it with out any further delivery and Each / partie to pay his Share of the Chardge disburst about the / above Said land and M[r] RICHARD REYNOLDS to repay quitt rents / of that part of the land which he now have as M[r] NEVILLE Shall / make appeare due

at a Court held for the Isle of Weight County aprill the 9[th] 1690 then ordered to be recorded

Test JOHN PITT C[l] C[ur]

**[26]**

Seale:

To all to whome these presents Shall Come I FFRANCIS Lord Howard Baron Effingham his / Ma[ties] Governor generall of Virginia Send greetinge in our Lord god Everlasting whereas / his late Ma[tie] has benne gratiously pleased by his royall letters pattents Under the greate Seale of / England beareinge date at Westminster the 10[th]. day of october in the 28[th] yeare of his reigne / amongst other things in the Said letters pattents Conteined to Continue and Confirme the / ancient previledge and power of grantinge fifty acres of Land for Every person Imported / into this his Ma[ties] Collony of Virginia Now know yee that I the Said FFRANCIS Lord Howard / Gover[r]: &c doe with the advice and Consent of the Councell of State accordingly give and grant / unto FRANCIS DAVIS one hundred acres of Land Scituate and beinge in the Isle of Weight / County and begineth at a white oake Standinge in the line of ROBERT LAWRENCE Jun[r], and / and runeth alonge the said LAWRENCE his line northwest and by north Sixty nine poole [*sic, et passim*] / to a pine, then North tenn degrees East five and forty poole to a white oake then North / Sixty fower degrees west Sixteene poole to a white oake GILES LINSCOTTs Corner tree then / alonge the Sayd LINSCOTs line northwest and by north one hundred ninety and two poole / to JOHN SOMERLINs line, then by the Said SOMERLINs line South tenn degrees west one / hundred fifty and Six pole to a red oake RICHARD BOOTHs Corner tree thence alonge the / said BOOTHs line of marked trees to the first Station and is due by and for the transpor / tation of two persons into this Collony whose names are in the records mentioned Under / this pattent To have and to hould the said land with his due share of all mines and mine / rals, therein Conteyned, with all rights and previledges of huntinge Hawkeinge fishinge / and fowlinge with all woods, waters, and Rivers with all profitts, Comodities & heredita / ments, whatsoever belongeinge Unto the Said Land unto him the Said FRANCIS DAVIS his / heires and assignes for Ever in as large and ample maner to all intents and purposes / as hath bene Used and allowed Since the first plantation, to be held of our Sovereigne lord / the Kinge his heyres and Successors: as of his Manor of East Greenewich, in fee and Comon / Soccage, and not *in Capite*, nor by knights Service yeeldinge and payinge Unto our Said Sovereine / Lord the Kinge his heyres and Successors for Every fifty acres of land, hereby granted at the / feast of Saint Michaell the archangell, the fee rent of one Shillinge which payment is to / be made yearely from yeare to yeare accordinge to his Ma$^{ties}$ Instructions of the 12$^{th}$ of 7$^{b}$. 1662 / provided that if the Said FFRANCIS DAVIS heires & assignes doe not Seate or plant or Cause / to be Seated or planted Uppon the Said land within the Said three yeares now next Ensueing / the date hereof that then it shall and may be lawfull for any adventurer or planter to / make Choice thereof and Seate thereon Given under my hand and the Seale of the Collony / this 20$^{th}$ day of october Anno Dom 1688

Effingham

Indorssed on the backe of this pattent

Know all men by these ꝑsents that I FFRANCIS DAVIS of the Isle of Weight County planter and SARAH / my Wife, doe for a Valuable Consideration in hand already received for us our heires Executors / Admis$^{rs}$, assigne over Unto HODGES COUNCELL Jun$^{r}$ of the aforesaid County of the Isle of Weight / planter his heires Execu$^{rs}$ admis$^{rs}$ and assignes all our right title and Intrest in the with in / Pattent, in as large and ample Maner as Ever it was granted to us: In wittnesse whereof / wee have hereunto Sett our hands the thirtieth day of aprill Anno$^{qu}$ Dni one thousand & six / hundred and nynety

Signum
FRANCIS **X** DAVIS
Signum
SARAH **X** DAVIS

Testis
signum
HENRY + WEST
signum
BRIDGMAN **B** JOYNER

Accknowledged in Court held for / the Isle of Weight County May y$^{e}$ 1$^{st}$ / 1690 by FFRANCIS and SARAH DAVIS / to be theire free act and deed and / ordered to be recorded

Test JOHN PITT C$^{l}$ C$^{ur}$

**[27]**

To all people to whome these present deed or wrightinge Shall Come Know yee that I JOHN SHERER / Sen$^{r}$ of the Isle of Weight County in Virginia planter for a valuaeable Consideration already by me received in hand / before the assigneinge Sealeinge and deliveringe here of for which I doe acknowledge my Selfe fully Satisfied / JOHN BRITT of the County aforesaid blacke Smith, doe for me my heires Executors administrators and assignes / make over bargaine Sell alienate and Confirme to the Said JOHN BRITT and his heires Executors administrat$^{rs}$ / or assignes for Ever a Certaine parcell of Tract of land in the Upper parish of the Isle of Weight County / Called the blacke water, Containeinge by Estimation one hundred Acres more or lesse beinge part of a / Devidend and pattent of land granted to JOHN WAKEFIELD and I the Said JOHN SHEARER the Said parcell of / Land Soe Sould by me to the Said JOHN BRITT beigininge at the mouth of a Small Branch by my plantation / which I now lives [*sic*] on and Soe up the branch to a marked Gum and from thence South to a marked red / oake and Soe downe alonge by the Side of a Cart path Called ALLEXANDER WEBSTER path to a Swampe / and Soe round the Swampe to first station, To have and to hould to the Said JOHN BRITT his heyres Exect[rs] / administrators and assignes for ever the above Said Tract and parcell of land with all profits and heredi / taments and appurtenancies thereunto belongeinge, in as large and ample maner as I my Selfe my heires / Exequitors, Could have by vertue of a pattent granted for the Same, and further the Said JOHN SHERER doe / for my Selfe my heires Executors obleidge that the Said JOHN BRITT his heires Executors & assignes Shall / peaceable and quietly for Ever injoy the Same with out the lett hinderance or any Molestation of me / the Saide JOHN SHERER, my heires Executors or administrators with generall Warrantie aginst all / person or persons what Soever Which Shall disturbe Molest or disquiett the Said JOHN BRITT his heires / Executors administrators or assignes in the peaceable possesion of the above Said Land and doe obleidge / mySelfe and ELIZABETH my Wife to accknowledge this our deed at the next Court held for this County / in Wittnesse hereunto wee have Sett our hands and Seales the 29[th] day of Aprill Anno Domi 1690

Signed Seald and delivered
in the psence of
EDWARD CHITTY
JOHN **I** STEVENSON
his marke
MARGERY **U** CHITTY

his
JOHN **H** SHEARER Seale
marke
her
ELIZABETH **x** SHEARER Seale
marke

Accknowledged in open Court / held for the Isle of Weight County / May the first by JOHN SHEARER and / ELIZABETH his wife to bee theire free / act and deed
Test JOHN PITT C[l] C[ur]

Whereas Complaint is made to me NICHOLAS SMYTH Justices of the peace by JOHN PITT Sen[r] of the parish / of Newport of the Isle of Weight County that one RICHARD WILKISSON of the Same parish and County did one the / last day of June last: make aforcible Entry into a house and Tenement of land: wherein JOHN TURNER lived / and theire did by force Carry the goods and househould Stuffe out of the house whereby they may perish & / and [*sic*] doe still deteine the said hous and plantation or tenement by force Contrary to the peace of our / Soveraigne lord and Lady Kinge William and Queene Mary: The Said house and tenement belongeinge / to the foresaid JOHN PITT

These are therefore in theire Ma[ties] Names to Will and require you to Sumon an able Jury of ffreehoulders / to make theire repaire to the Said house and Tenement of JOHN PITT Sen[r] whereon JOHN TURNER lived / one friday next beinge the 4[th] of this instant there to make inquiry if the Entry of the Said RICHARD / WILKISSON Sen[r]. into the house and Tenement of the Said JOHN PITT was by forece or the deteiner be kept / by forces to meete at ten of the Clocke in the mourneinge given under my hand this 2[d] day of July 1690

NICHOLAS SMYTH

To M[r] JOSEPH WOORY high Sherrife of the Isle / of Weight County or his deputie / Executed ꝑ JOS WOORY high Sherrife / to Execute

The depotition of THO RICHARDS aged 28 or thereabouts Sayeth that he did see RICH[D]: WILKISSON turn / JOHN TURNERs goods out of doares and the Same declareth ROB[T] RICHARDS wittnesse our hands

ROBERT **R** RICHARDS
hir marke
THOMAS **T** RICHARDS

The Depatition of MARGARETT WHITLY aged 36 or thereabouts Sayeth / that RICHARD WILKISSON did Say if he had any thinge he would runn / JOHN TURNER through and further Sayeth not

MARGARETT **M** WHITLY
her marke

JOHN TURNER Sayd dame you y[e] have turned / all my things out of doares & keep s[ ] out of that which I have workt for this longe tyme

MARGARET WHITLY her m[r]k

Sworne the Same day and [ ] by both parties taken by me

JAMES BENNETT

**[28]**

In persuance to a writt granted L[t] Coll JOHN PITT by M[r] NICK SMITH dated July y[e] 2[d] 1690 / Wee the Jurors beinge Sumond and Sworne have made inquiry into the premisses and doe find as followeth / Wee doe find and it is our Judgments that M[r] RICHARD WILKISSON hath made aforeceable Entry uppon / the tenement of L[t] Coll JOHN PITT by a law in Dalton ~~fol~~[e] y[e] 194 and wee doe alsoe find that hee / hath made and kept aforeceable deteine unto which wee doe unto Sett our hands this 4[th] of July / 1690

JAMES BENN — JOHN CLARK
JAMES TULLAGH — THOMAS **T** WARD

| | |
|---|---|
| MICHAELL FFULGHAM | his marke |
| NICHOLAS FFULGHAM | JAMES **E** ENNIS |
| WALTER RUTTER | JOHN WHITLY |
| DANIELL LONGE | THOMAS **I** WHITLY |
| his marke | GEORGE **G** WRIGHT |

To the Worpp[ll] M[r] NICHOLAS SMYTH and Ma[jer] THOMAS TABERER Justices of the of the peace / for the Isle of Weight County JOHN PTIT humbly

Declareth: That RICHARD WILKISSON haveinge by force turned yo[r] Complainant out of the possession of / one house and tenement of land whereon JOHN TURNER lived beinge tenant to yo[r] Complainant / Contrary to the peace of theire Ma[ties] and doe stall detaine the possession of the Sayd house and / Tenement by force to the great losse and damage of yo[r] Complainant which damage will amount / to the quantity of thirty pounds Sterlinge Mony at least for which yo[r] Complainant humbly / Craves good Satisfaction accordinge to law in Such Cases provided and to be reposest againe / of the Said house and Tenement as formerly: and that he pay all Costs and Chardges of Suite / which Shalbe awarded accordinge to law

And yo[r] Complainant as in duty bound / shall every pray

Bee it knowne Unto all men by these ꝑsents that I ROBERT FULLERTON and ELLIONER my / Wife have for a valuable Consideration in hand already rec[d]. have bargained Sett to Sale / and delivered over Unto WILLIAM SCOT one parcell of land full out one hundred acres of / land lyinge and beinge in the lower parish of the Isle of Weight County uppon the head / of a Swampe Commonly Called Powells Swampe uppon the Westerne branch: bindeinge upon / the line of THOMAS GAILE, THOMAS POWELL and FFRANCIS HUTCHINS, and in Confirmation hereof / wee the Said ROBERT FULLERTON and ELLENER my wife doe bind our Selves our heires Execut[rs] / administrators to and with the Sayd WILLIAM SCOTT his heires Ex[rs]. administrators to warant / and mainetaine the Sale of the above Said parcell of land for Ever togather with all its previ / ledges thereunto belonginge in as stronge and firme a maner as may or Can be Expressed not / with Standinge anythinge to the Contrary in Confirmation hereof wee have hereunto: Sub / scribed our hands and Seales this first day of february in the yeare of oru lord 16$^{89}/_{90}$

| | |
|---|---|
| Signed sealed and delivered | ROBERT **x** FULLERTON Seale |
| in the ꝑsence of us | his marke and Seale |
| the marke of | ELINOR **T** FULLERTON |
| JOHN **I M** MORE | her marke and Seale |
| RICH[D] SCOT | |
| the marke of | |
| THOMAS **TH** HAMTON | |

Accknowledged in open Court held for the Isle of Weight / County July the 9th 1690: by ROBERT FULLERTON and ELLINER / his Wife, to be theire free act and deed and ordered to be / recorded

Test JOHN PITT Cl Cur

**[29]**

Know all Men by these presents that I JOHN POPE of the parish of Dawlish in England Mariner / have and hereby doe Constitute ordaine depute appoint and make my respected brother RICHARD / POPE of the County of Isle of Weight in Virginia my true and lawfull atturny for me and in / my name and Stead and for my Use to aske demand require receive and to use all lawfull me / anes to recover out of the hands of whome soever it may Concerne all Such Sume or Sumes of / mony debts goods lands or other Estate as now is or hereafter may become due owinge or pay / able to me the Constituant by bill bond book account or any other demand or by any other / waise or meanes whatsoever and in perticular to Use all lawfull meanses to recover out of the / hands of any that is due to mee giveinge and hereby grantinge to my Sayd Atturny full power / and authority to Sue arrest implead and prosecute to Effect in any Court and Courts and in any / behalfe appearance to make and any action or actions to defende and if nede be into prison to Cast / and there to deliver releases or other discharges uppon payment to give and Signe Compotition / if he See Cause to make atturnies one or more to Substitute and them at pleasure to revoke and / Every other way to act Execute and performe in my behalfe to all intents and purposes in as / full and ample maner measure and degree as I might or Could doe if I were personally present / to performe the Same alwaies and in all things ratifieinge allowinge and Confirmeinge what / my Said atturny Shall lawfully act or Cause to be done or acted in persuance of the premises / firmely by these presents in wittnesse whereof I the Sayd JOHN POPE have hereunto Sett my hand / and Seale this 22d day of July Anno Dom 1690

Signed Sealed and delivered JOHN POPE Seale
in the ꝑsence of us
JOHN PITT
JAMES BENNETT
JOHN FFRIZELL

Proved in open Court held for the / Isle of Weight County august the 9th. 1690 / by the oath of JOHN PITT and JAMES BENNETT

Test JOHN PITT Cl Cur

These are to Satisfie all parsons what Soever that I JOHN SOMMERVELL and I FFRANCIS SOMMERVELL / wife to JOHN SOMMERVELL doe freely and hartily accknowledge that wee have Unjustly and Unad / visedly and without Cause abused JOHN MACKLOUD in Sayinge of words to Severall persons / as if the aforeasaid JOHN MACKCLOUD had bewitched two of our Children to death and wee / doe freely and willingly aske him forgivenesse in open Court and doe owne that wee are Sory / for soe abuseinge the foresaid JOHN MACKCLOUD and doe desire it to be recorded as wittnesse our / hand this 9th day of July 1690

Owned in open Court by both parties
august the 9th. 1690 and forgivenesse Craved
Test JOHN PITT Cl Cur

the marke of
JOHN **I** SOMMERVELL
the marke of
FFRANCIS **2** SOMMERVELL

To the Sheriffe of Isle of Weight County / These
Virga: By the Rt: Honoble the Lt. Govr

For as much as Mr ROBERT THOMAS one in the Commission of the peace for yor County nomi / nated a Justice of the peace hath Carried and behaved himselfe very disorderly in this theire Maties / Government, and is Supposed not to be of Sound minde / I therefore FFRANCIS NICHOLSON Esqr their Maties Lt Govr: of this Collony doe in theire Maties / names order and Command that you Cause his name to putt out of the Said Commission of / of the peace and the record thereof given Under my hand this 2d day of august Ano. Dom / 1690

To theire Majesties Justices of
the pease for the Isle of Weight
County

FR NICHOLSON

**[30]**

Bee it knowen unto all men that I ROBERT LAURENCE the younger have Sould made / over & delivered unto GEORGE PEARCE Smith of the County of Nancemun all my right and / intrest of three hundred acres of Land Contayned in a pattent of Sixe hundred acres lyinge / in the County of Nancemun and granted Unto mee by Sr WM BERKELEY Knight Governor / and Capt Generall of Virginia the Eight and twentieth day of May in the yeare 1673 & / begininge at a marked oake Standinge by a Beaver dam Swampe Soe runinge North east / three hundred and twenty poles to a marked pine, Soe west Northwest 325 poles to a / marked Oake Soe South Southwest 320 poles to a marked pokekery Standinge by the beaver / dam: Swampe, Soe East South East 325 poles by the Branch side to the / first Station and the foresaid GEORGE PEERCE to take the land accordinge to the pattent / and to begin at the first marked tree therein mentioned runinge out the first mile for / length: and then the breadth of 300 acres accordinge to the Course of the pattent / To have and to hould the foresaid 300 Acres of land with all previledges and profits / theareunto belonginge by pattent for him the aforesaid GEORGE PIERCE his heyres Executrs / and assignes for Ever in as Stronge and firme a maner to all intents and purposes as / possibly may or might have bene Expressed and for the true performance hereof / accordinge to true intent and meaneinge the aforesaid ROBERT LAWRENCE the younger hath / here Unto Sett his hand and Seale bindinge not only himSelfe butt alsoe his heyres Executrs / and assignes for Ever to allow

the aforesaid Sale and doe accknowledge to have received / Sufficient Satisfaction for the Same ROBERT **R** LAURENCE
his marke Seale
Signed Sealed and delivered
in the presence of Us
WILL SCOTT Jun^r^
HENRY PLUMPTON

Accknowledged in Co^rt^ the 13^th^ apr^l^ 1674 / by ROBERT LAURENCE and order record: Test J PEASLEY dp^t^ C^lr^

Know all men by these presents that I GEORGE PIERCE in the Isle of Weight County / Smyth doe for a Valueable Consideration of tobacco received in hand before the assigne / inge and delivery heareof doe firmely by these presents assigne all my right title / Intrest of three hundred acres of Land which is here in Expressed in the bill of Sale which / is accordinge to pattent Unto HODGES COUNCELL in the Same County as aforesaid planter / the said parcell of Land, is to have & to hould unto the foresaid COUNCELL to him and his / heyres for Ever in as large and ample maner as Can be Expressed as Wittnesse hereof / I the above named GEORGE PIERCE have Sett my hand and Seale the 20^th^ day of this instant / November 1674
Testes: MARGARETT JONES GEORGE
**Eeee** y^e^ marke of **G** PIERCE Seale
her mark ANN + PIERCE
RALPH BOSEMAN her marke
NATH: TONAY

Accknowledged in Court held / for Nanzemund the 12^th^ of aug^st^ / 1675 by GEORGE PIERCE and *Uxor* / and is recorded Test JN^O^ BROMFIELD Depu^t^ C^lr^

The two above Conveyances at the request of HODGES COUNCELL in Court held for the / Isle of Weight County Sept^r^. the 10^th^. 1690 is orderd to be recorded in regard the records of / Nanzemund wherein they were recorded were Burnt
Test JOHN PITT C^l^ C^ur^

**[31]**

Know all Men by these presents that I Cap^t^ ROBERT THOMAS of the Isle of Weight Coun / ty in Virginia doe make Constitute ordaine and appoint M^r^ JOSEPH FORD of Virginia / my true and lawfull atturny for me and in my name and to my Use to demand Sue for / leave require recover and receive all Such Sumes of Mony or Tobacco or any other [ ] / whatsoever which is now due owinge or belongeinge to me or which hereafter shalbe / Come due unto me in the Collony of Virginia and uppon the receipt thereof accquittance / or any other lawfull discharge for me and in my Name to make Seale and deliver and I / doe hereby Ratiffie and Confirme all and Whatsoever my Said atturny Shall lawfully doe / as if I my Selfe were personably present as Wittnesse my hand and Seale this fowertenth / day of August one thousand Six hundred and Ninty

Signed Sealed & delivered ROBT THOMAS Seale
in the p$^{r}$sence of
THO: MOORE Sep$^{t}$. the 9$^{th}$ proved by M$^{r}$ THOMAS MOORE
JN$^{O}$ GAWEN

This Indenture made the 16$^{th}$ of august in thes yeare of our Lord God one thousand Six / hundred and Ninty and in the Second yeare of the reign of our Sovereigne Lord and lady / William and Mary of greate Brittaine ffrance and Ireland Kinge and Queene defenders of the / Faith Betwene GEORGE PIERCE of the lower parish of the Isle of Weight County of the one part / and WILLIAM JOHNSON of the Same one the other part Wittnesse, That the Said GEORGE PIERCE / for and in Consideration of a good Consideration to them already made and in hand paid / by the Said WILLIAM JOHNSON before the Ensealeinge and delivery of these presents where / with they accknowledge themselves fully Contented Satisfied and payd have granted demised / Bargained and Sould and by these presents doe fully Clearely and absolutely grant demise & / bargaine sell alienate Confirme and make over Unto the Sayd WILLIAM JOHNSON his heires / admis$^{rs}$ or assignes For Ever one hundred Acres of Land more or lesse lyinge and beinge in the aforesaid / parish and County beinge part of a pattent of two thousand one hundred acres of Land unto / the Said GEORGE PIERCE beareinge date y$^{e}$ 21 first of 7$^{ber}$ 1674 the Said hundred Acres of / Land more or lesse beinge bounded as followeth *Videlicet*, begininge at a white oak an ould / Corner tree thence northwest to a greate marked pine thence Southardly to a great pine in the / foote of a branch then up the Maine branch to the first Station, and the Said GEORGE PIERCE / doth for himselfe his heires Execut$^{rs}$ admis$^{rs}$ or assignes Covenant and agree to and with the S$^{d}$ / WILLIAM JOHNSON he his heyres Executo$^{rs}$ admis$^{rs}$ or assignes to and with Every of them that the / Said WILLIAM JOHNSON he his heyres Execut$^{rs}$ admis$^{rs}$ or assignes Shall from the day of this date / For Ever hereafter have hould occupy possese and quietly injoy the Sayd one hundred acres of / Land more or lesse before demised with all rights and profits Comodities and hereditaments / whatsoever there unto belonginge or in any wise thereunto belongeinge or in any wise there unto / appertaineinge with out the lett hinderance molestation incumbrance trouble or contra / diction of him the Said GEORGE PIERCE he his heyres Execut$^{rs}$ admis$^{rs}$ or assignes or by any other / person or persons whatsoever by theire knowledge Consent or procuration without any maner / of Condition or limitation of Use or uses Rent or rents the Kings only Excepted and for y$^{e}$ / better and more authenticke Confirmation of the before demist premisses the Said GEORGE / PIERCE doth hereby obleidge himselfe to accknowledge this deed of Sale in open Court when there / unto required to be his free and Voluntary act and deed and that his Wife shall doe the Same / alsoe in Wittnesse whereof the Sayd GEORGE PIERCE and ANNE his wife have hereunto Sett theire hands / and Seales the day and yeare first above written

*Sigilat et deliberat* The hand and Seale
*In presentia* JOHN BROWNE of GEORGE **D** PIERCE Seale
WILLIAM CRUMPLER The hand and Seale
of ANN **XX** PIERCE Seale

Accknowledge in open Court held / for the Isle of Weight County octob^r / the 9^th. 1690 by GEORGE PIERCE and ANNE / his Wife to be theire free act and deed
Test JOHN PITT C^l C^ur

**[32]**

I HENRY HEARNE and my Wife ELIZABETH HEARNE our heires and assignes doe assigne this bill / of Sale Unto THOMAS MAN and his heires for Ever as Wittnesse our hands this 9^th day of feb^rij 1690
Testes THOMAS LUCAS HENRY □ HEARNE
JOHN ROGERS his marke
ELIZABETH **E** HEARN
hir marke

Accknowledged in open Court held for the Isle of Weight County / ffeb^rij y^e 9^th 169^0/_1 by HENRY HEARNE and his wife to be theire free / act and deed
Test: JOHN PITT C^l C^ur

Seale

To all to whome these presents Shall Come I NATH BACON Esq^r president of his Ma^ties Councell of / State of Virginia Send gretinge in our lord God Everlastinge

Whereas his late Maj^tie hath bene gratiously pleased by his royall letters pattents under the greate Seale / of England beareinge date at Westminster the 10^th day of october in the Eight and twentieth / yeare of his reigne amongst other things in the s^d letters pattent Contained to Continue & Confirme / the ancient previledge and power of grantinge fifty acres of land for Every ꝑson imported / into this his Ma^ties Collony of Virginia Now know yee that I the Said NATHANIELL BACON Esq^r ꝑsident &c by / and with the advice and Consent of the Councell of State accordingly give and grante Unto JOHN / SOJOURNER one hundred Sixtie and two acres of land Scituate lyinge and beinge in the Isle of Weight / County begininge at three red oakes the said SOJOURNERs Corner trees of an other tract or devident / of land bought of M^r ROBERT WILLIAMSON and runinge thence East and by North Seventy fower pole / to a white oake by a branch JAMES ATKISSONs Corner tree then along the Sayd ATKISSONs line North / fiftie degrees westerlie Sixty two pole to a pine in the doctors branch, thence North Eighteene degres / west one hundred and Eightene pole to three Small Oake Saplins then west North west twenty / Eight pole to a blacke oake by a path thence South fortty Seven degrees West one hundred nintie / and five pole to a red oake in EDWARD BOYKINs line then alonge the Said BOYKINs line South / East and by East one hundred and Ninty pole to a red oake in the Said SOJOURNERs line, then / alonge the Said SOJOURNERs line to the place of begininge the Said land beinge due by and for the / Importation of fower persons into this Collony whose names are on the records mentioned under this / pattent. To have and to hould the Sayd land with his due Share of all Mines and Mineralls there in / Conteyned with all rights and previledges of huntinge hawekinge fishinge and fowlinge with all / woods waters and rivers with all profits Comodities and hereditaments whatsoever belongeinge to / the Said land to him the Said JOHN SOJOURNER his heires and assignes For Ever in as large and ample / maner to all intents and purposes as hath bene Used and allowed Since the first plantation to / be held of our Sovereigne Lord the Kinge his heires and successors as of his Mannor of East Greenwich in / fee and Common Sockage and not *in Capite* nor by Knights Service Yeldinge and payinge Unto our / Sovereigne Lord the Kinge his heyres and Successors for Every fifty acres of Land hereby granted at / the feast of S$^{t}$ Michaell The Archangell the fee rent of one Shillinge which payment is to be made / yearely from yeare to yeare accordinge to his Ma$^{ties}$ Instructions of the 12$^{th}$ of Sept$^{r}$. 1662 provided y$^{t}$ / if the Said JOHN SOJOURNER his heires or assignes doe not Seat or plant or Cause to be Seated and planted / uppon the Said land with in three yeares now next Ensueinge the date hereof that then it shall / and may be lawfull for any adventurer or planter to make Choice thereof and Setle there on / given Under my hand and the Seale of the collony this twentieth day of Aprill Anno: Dom 1689

This assignement written one the backe side of y$^{e}$ pattent

NATHANIELL BACON

Know all men by these presents that I JOHN SURIOURNOR of the Isle of Weight County with the / Consent of MARY my Wife doe assigne and make over from us our heyres for ever to JOHN DOLL his heires / Executors administrators or assignes for Ever all our right & Title of this within Mentioned pattent / as Wittnesse our hands with Seale this 23$^{d}$ day of January in the yeare of our lord 1690

| | |
|---|---|
| Signed Sealed and delivered | JOHN SURIOURNOR Seale |
| in the presence of Us | his + marke |
| JOHN DAVIS | MARY M SURJOURNOR |
| JOHN HARRIS | her marke Seale |

Accknowledged in open Court held for the / Isle of Weight County feb$^{rij}$ y$^{e}$ 9$^{th}$ 169$^{0}$/$_{1}$ by JOHN / SOJOURNOR and MARY his wife to be theire / free act and deed

Test JOHN PITT C$^{l}$ C$^{ur}$

**[33]**

Bee it kowne [*sic*] Unto all men by these presents that whereas I JOHN BROWNE of the Isle of White have / delivered a deed of Sale by Estimation two hundred acres of land Unto WILLIAM SCOTT his heires & assignes / bareinge date the ninth day of february one thousand Six hundred and ninety and alsoe the next Joyne / inge about one hundred acres Unto RICHARD SHOWELL beareinge date the tenth and the next Unto / THOMAS RIVES his heires and assignes about two hundred acres of land. It beinge a pattent granted / to me the twentieth day of octob[r] anno 1688

I doe hereby these presence declare to impower Constitute and ordaine my trusty welbeloved Wife to / act for me and in my name to make & acknowledgement in Courte to the aboveSaid WILLIAM SCOTT / his heires and assignes for Ever & RICHARD SHOWELL his heires and assignes for Ever and alsoe to THOMAS / REVES his heires and assignes for Ever and for what my Said loveinge wife and atturny Shall doe or act / in the perticular pattent to stand good firme Effectual in law as if I had bene there present / actinge in my owne person given Under my hand and Seal the ninth day of ffebruary 1690 and tenth / day of february 1690

Testis ROBERT SCOTT — JOHN ┬┬┬ BROWNE
RICHD SCOTT — his marke Seale

Proved in Court held for the Isle / of Weight County March y[e] 9[th] 169$^0/_1$
Test JOHN PITT C[l] C[ur]

Know all Men by these presents that I JOHN BROWNE of the Isle of Weight County with the / Consent of MARY my wife have for good Consideration Sould and made over Unto WILLIAM SCOTT / of the County aforesaid all my right title and intrest in a parcell of land granted to mee / by pattent in the yeare one thousand Sixe hundred Eighty Eight begininge at a live oake on / the South side of kingeSale Swampe and Soe runinge accordinge to pattent to a marked pine at y[e] / head of the aforesaid pattent then downe the Said Swampe to a branch Called the wolfe pitt / branch Joyneinge uppon RICHARD SHOWELLs line and Soe to the head of my land it beinge the / plantation I now live on it beinge for Estimation about two hundred acres of Land Wee say / to him and his heyres To have and to Hould for Ever to gather with all its previledges there / Unto belongeinge with all Tenements and other profits & Comodities there unto belongeinge / in as large and ample maner as is Expressed in the aforesaid pattent and I the Said BROWNE doe / bind my Selfe to mainetaine the Sale thereof against any that Shall lay Claime thereunto by / any pretence of right decedinge [*sic*] from me my heyres Execut[rs]. administrators & and [*sic*] assignes and for the preformance hereof accordinge to the true intent and meaneinge of the Said BROWNE and alsoe my / Wife in Confirmation of her Consent wee have hereunto Sett our hands and Seales this ninth day of feb[rij] / in the yeare of our lord one thousand Sixe hundred and ninety

Signed Sealed and delivered — JOHN ┬┬┬ BROWNE
in the psence of Us — his marke Seale
ROBERT SCOTT — MARY **R** BROWNE
RICHD: SCOT — her marke Seale
THOMAS **T** REEVES
his marke

Accknowledged by MARY BROWNE / atturny of JOHN BROWNE in open / Court held for the Isle of Weight / County March y[e] 9[th]. 169$^0/_1$ to be theire / free and Voluntary act and deed and / ordered to be recorded

Test JOHN: PITT C[l] C[ur]

This Indenture made the third day of June one thousand Six hundred and nintie Betwene JOHN BROWNE / the Elder of the one part and RICHARD SHEWELL one the other part Wittneseth that the Sayd JOHN BROWNE / for and in Consideration of one thousand pounds of tobacco and Caske to him before the Sealeinge and delivery / of these presents by the Said RICHARD SHEWELL well and truely payd the receipt whereof he the S[d] BROWNE / doe acknowledge & himselfe therewith fully Contented Sattisfied and paid & thereof doe clearely acquitt / and discharge the S[d] SHEWELL his heires Execut[rs] & administrators for Ever have bargained Sould and / Confirmed and by these presents doe allien bargaine Sell infeoffe & Confirme Unto the Sayd SHEWELL / his heires and assignes for Ever one hundred acres of land lyinge and beinge one kingsale Swampe / In the Countie of the Isle of Weight Called the Broadnecke begininge on the maine Swampe / and Soe runinge up the wolfe pit branch to a marked pine at the head of the s[d] branch & from / thence to the head of JN[O] BROWN's line Soe alonge the Said line to a marked Spanish Oake and / thence to a shruby white oake & soe downe the pipe Clay Branch to the Maine Swamp beinge part / of a pattent for five hundred acres of land bareinge date the twentieth day of october 1688 / with all its rights members Jurisdictions and appurtenancies and alsoe all the Estate Right title / Intrest use possesion propertie Claime & demand whatSoever of him the said BROWNE of in or to / the Same to have and to hould the said one hundred acres of land & all and Singular the ꝑmises

**[34]**

hereby bargained Sold or mentioned to be hereby bargained and Sould with theire and Every of theire / Rights members and appurtenancies whatSoever unto the said RICHARD SHEWELL his heires and assignes for / Ever. to the only proper use and behoofe of the Said SHEWELL his heires and assignes For Ever and the Said / JN[O] BROWNE for himselfe and his heires the Said one hundred acres of land and all and Singular the / ꝑmises before granted bargained and Sould with the appurtenancies Unto the Sayd RICHARD SHEWELL / his heires & assignes For Ever against him the Sayd JOHN BROWNE his heires and assignes and all and / Every other person or persons whatSoever lawfully claimeinge by from or Under him or any other / whatsoever Shall and Will warrant and for Ever defend by these presents and further the Said JOHN / BROWNE for himselfe his heires Executors & administrators doe promise Covenant and grant & agree / to and with the S[d] SHEWELL his heires and assignes and Every of them by these presents that hee the / S[d] JN[O] BROWNE shall and will From tyme to tyme and at all tymes hereafter at & Uppon the / reasonable request & at the cost and Charges in the law of the Said RICHARD SHEWELL his heires and / assignes Make or Cause to be made Such further assurance in the law for the better and more / perfect assurance Suertie

& Suere makeinge and Conveyinge all and Singular the before hereby granted / premises with theire & Every of theire rights members and appurtenancies Unto the Sayd SHEWELL his / heires and assignes as by the Sayd SHEWELL his heires & assignes or by his or theire Councell learned / in the laws shalbe reasonably devised advised or required In Wittnesse whereof the parties first / above named Unto these present indentures Interchangably have put theires hands and Seales / the day and yeare first above written Anno[qu] Nomini 1690

Signed Sealed & delivered before us
ED[W] **EF** FLOID
HEN BAKER
THOMAS + WICKINS

JOHN ┬┬┬ BROWN Seale
his marke

These ꝑsents wittneseth that I MARY BROWNE Wife of JOHN BROWNE doe hereby bind my Selfe / my heires Execut[rs] & admis[rs] with the Said JOHN BROWNE in the Sale of the within mentioned land / and Every part thereof fully absolutly to all intents and purposes as if I my Selfe my heires / &c had bene within named in Every of the Said premises Unto RICHARD SHEWELL his heires Execut[rs] / and admis[rs] firmely by these presents in wittnesse whereof I have hereunto put my hand and Seale / this 9[th] day of March $169^0/_1$

Sealed and delivered in the presence of
THOMAS **T** REVES
his marke
ROBERT SCOTT

MARY **R** BROWNE Seale

Accknowledged by MARY BROWNE atturny of JOHN BROWNE / in open Court held for the Isle of Weight County march y[e] 9[th] $169^0/_1$ to be hers and her husbands free act and deed

Test JOHN PITT C[l] C[ur]

To all to whome these ꝑsents shall Come I FFRANCIS Lord Howard Bacon of Effingham his Ma[ties] Lieu[t] / and Govr[r] of Virg[a] send greetinge in our lord God Everlastinge whereas his late Majestie has been gratiously / pleased by his royall letters pattents Under the greate Seale of England bareinge date at Westminster the / tenth day of octob[r] in the 28[th] yeare of his Reigne amongst other things in the Said letters pattents Conteined / to Continue and Confirme the ancient previledge and power of grantinge fifety acres of land for Every / person imported into this his Ma[ties] Collony of Virginia Now know yee that I the Said FFRANCIS Lord / Howard Gover[r]. &c doe with the advice and Consent of the Councell of State accordingly / give and grant Unto JOHN BROWNE five hundred acres of land lyinge in the Isle of Weight County / begininge at a live oake on the South side of KingSale Swamp and runinge thence South East Eighty / Chaines to a pine, then South west two hundred thirtie Seaven Chaines, then North West Sixtie / Sixe Chaines to a pine then north ten degres west twenty Eight Chaines to the Swamp aforesaid / then alonge the Said Swamp to the first Station and is due by and for the transportation of tenn / ꝑsons into this Collony whose Names are in the records mentioned Under this pattent. To: have and / to hould the Said land with his due Share of all mines and mineralls there in Conteined with all rights / and previldeges of huntinge hawkinge fishinge and fowleinge with all woods waters and rivers / with all profits Comodities and hereditaments whatSoever belonging as to the Said land to him

**[35]**
The Said JOHN BROWNE his heires and assignes for ever in as large and ample maner to all intents / and purposes as hath bene Used and allowed Since the first plantation to be held of our Sovereigne / Lord the Kinge his heires and Successors as of his manor of East Greenwich in free and comon Soccage and / not *in Capite* nor by knights Service yeldinge and payinge Unto our Said Sovereigne lord the kinge / his heires and Successors for Ever fivety acres of land hereby granted at the feast of S$^{t}$. Michaels the / Archangell the fee rent of one shillinge which payment is to be made yearely from yeare to yeare accor / dinge to his Ma$^{ties}$ Instructions of the 12$^{th}$ of Sept$^{r}$ 1662 ꝑvided that if the Said JOHN BROWNE his heires or / assignes Shall not seate or plant or Cause to be seated or planted uppon the Said land within these / three yeares now next Ensueinge the date hereof that then it shall and may be lawfull for any adven / turer or planter to make Choice thereof and Seate thereon: Given Under my hand and the seale / of the Collony this twentieth day of octob$^{r}$ Anno Dom 1688

Effingham

Know all men by these presents that I JOHN BROWNE and MARY my Wife have for a Valueable Consi / deration assigned over Unto THOMAS REVES this pattent it begininge at the pipe Clay branch and Soe down / the Swampe the lower Side of RICHARD SHEWELLs line to the Extent of the pattent warrantinge the Sale / to the Said REEVES his heires Ex$^{rs}$ & admis$^{rs}$ for Ever with all its previledges thereunto belongeinge as wittnes / our hands and Seales this tenth day of february in the yeare of our lord one thousand sixe hundred and / ninety before Signed I say from me the Sayd BROWNE my heires Ex$^{rs}$ & administrators

Signed Sealed and delivered
in y$^{e}$ ꝑsence of us
WILLIAM SCOTT
ROBERT SCOTT
RICHARD SCOTT

JOHN ┬┬┬ BROWNE Seale
his marke
MARY **R** BROWNE Seale
her marke

Accknowledged by MARY BROWNE / atturny of JOHN BROWNE in open Court / held for the Isle of Weight County / march the 9$^{th}$. 1690 to be hers and her / husbands ffree act and deed

Test JOHN PITT $C^l$ $C^{ur}$

In obedience to the within mentioned order wee the Subscribers have accordingly viewed the Sayd land of $M^r$ / NICHOLAS SMYTH and have Vallued it at two hundred and fifty pounds of Tobacco to be payd Conveniently Wittnesse / our hands this $18^{th}$ of March $169^0/_1$

THO GILES
JA BENN

The order of Court within mentioned bares date / March $y^e$ $9^{th}$. $169^0/_1$

Test JOHN PITT $C^l$ $C^{ur}$

Virginia

Know all Men by these $p^r$sents That I JOSEPH WOORY of Chuckatuck in the Isle of Weight County in / Virginia: doe for me my heyres Executors administrators and assignes freely accquit and dischardge $M^r$ / JOHN WYATT & $M^r$ JAMES FFOULES of London Executors of the last Will and Testament of my Brother / ROBERT WOORY late of London deceased of and from a Certaine legacy bequeathed unto me by the $s^d$ / Will therein mentioninge two hundred pounds of lawfull Mony of England hereby accknowledgeinge / to have received the foresaid Sume of two hundred pounds in full of the foresaid legacie Soe bequeathed / mee as by the Said Will appears In Wittnesse whereof I have hereunto sett my hand and Seale the / ninth day of Aprill 1691

Signed Sealed and delivered
in presence of us — JOSEPH WOORY Seales
HEN: BAKER
JOHN PITT

This accknowledged by $M^r$ JOSEPH WOORY / in open Court held for the Isle of Weight / County Aprill the $9^{th}$. 1691 to be his act / and deed and ordered to be recorded

Test: JOHN PITT $C^l$ $C^{ur}$

**[36]**

Know all men by these presents that I GEORGE WILLIAMSON of the upper parish of the Isle of Weight / County in Virginia for a Valueable Consideration to mee payd before the Sealeinge and deliveringe hereof / have bargained & Sould and doe hereby for mee my heires $Execut^{rs}$ $admis^{rs}$ for Ever bargaine Sell & deliver / infeoffe and Confirm unto JOHN SURJOURNOR of the County aforeSaid and to his heires and assignes for ever / aparcell of land Containeinge forty acres More or lesse beinge part of a pattent for five hundred acres / granted to my deceased brother ROBERT WILLIAMSON the $30^{th}$ of october 1686 the said land lyinge on the / west side of the third Swampe of the Maine blacke water in the parish and County $afores^d$. bounded begininge / at a white oake in the doctors Branch it beinge JOHN SURJOURNOR his Corner tree from thence to

JAMES / ADKINS his Corner tree from thence alonge a line of Marked trees to a white oake Standinge downe the / Doctors branch which is another of JOHN SURIOURNORs Corner trees: To have and to hould the Said / land with all appurtenancies thereto belongeinge to him the Said JOHN SOJOURNOR and his heires and / assignes for Ever in as full and ample manner as I might or Could have injoyed the Same by Vertue / of the aforesaid pattent & I doe hereby obleidge my Selfe my heyres Ex[rs] and admis[rs] to Warrant and / and [*sic*] defend this my Sale of all and Singular the premisses with theire appurtenancies to the S[d] / SURJOURNOR his heires and assignes for Ever against all maner of persons whatSoever pretendinge / any Claime or Intrest thereto. he the said SURJOURNOR his heires or assignes payinge the yearly / quitt rents of the Said land and therefrom wholly accquitt and discharge the Said WILLIAMSON / his heires Ex[rs] admis[rs] in wittnesse of all which I have hereuno put my hand and Seale the [--]

Signed Sealed and delivered in the<br>presence of Us the 9[th] of Aprill 1691<br>RICHARD STONE<br>WILLIAM EXUM Ju[r]<br>JO[N] DAVIS

GEO: WILLIAMSON Seale<br>Acknowledge in open Court<br>held for the Isle of Weight County<br>aprill the 9[th]. 1691 by GEORGE WILLIAMSON<br>to be his free act and deed<br>Test JOHN PITT C[l] C[ur]

Seale

To all to whome these p[r]sents Wrightinge shall Come I S[r]: HENRY CHICHLEY Kn[t] his Ma[ties] / deputy Governor of Virginia Send greetinge in our Lord god Everlastinge, whereas his Ma[tie] hath / bene greatiously pleased by his Royall Letters Pattents Under the greate Seale of England baring / date at Westminster the 10[th] of october in the Eight and twentieth yeare of his reigne amongst / other things in his letters pattents Contained, to continue and Confirme the antient previledges / and power of grantinge fifty acres of land for every person imported into this Collony of / Virginia Now know yee that I the said S[r] HENRY CHICHELEY Kn[t] deputie Governor doe with / the Consent of the Councell of State accordingly give and grant unto THOMAS MANDUE / three hundred and twenty Acres of land scituate on the blacke water branches in the Isle / of Weight County begininge at a red oake a Corner tree of GEORGE PIERCEs land now in the / posssesion of PHILLIP WRAFORD thence S. thirty nine degrees W. two hundred and Six poles to / a Small red oake, & then E.N.E. Eighty Six poles to the Coblers line, then by his lines N.W. one hun / dred Eighty two poles to a pine, & N. by E. one hundred and Eighty poles to a red oake in GEORGE / PIERCEs line and Soe by his line W.N.W. one hundred Eighty Six poles to the first station / the Said land beinge due by and for the transportation of Seaven persons into this collony whose / names are mentioned in the record Under this pattent To have and to hould the Said land / with his due Share of all Mines and mineralls there in Contained with the rights and previ / ledges of huntinge Hawkinge fishinge fowleinge with all Woods Waters & Rivers, with all / profits Comodities hereditaments what Soever belongeinge to the Said land to him the said / THOMAS MANDUE his heyres and assignes for Ever, in as large and ample Maner to all intents / and purposes as has bene used and allowed Since the first plantation, to be held of our Soverine / Lord the Kinge his heyres and Successors as of his mannor of East grenewich, in fee and Comon / sockage & not *in Capite* and by knights Service, yeeldinge and payinge to our sovereigne Lord / the Kinge his heyres and Successors for Every fifty acres of land hereby granted at the feast of / S[t] Michaell the archangell the fee rent of one shillinge which payment is to be made yearly

**[37]**
from yeare to yeare, accordinge to his Ma[ties] Instructions of the twelveth of September 1662 provided / that if I the Said THOMAS MANDUE his heires and assignes doe not Seate or plant or Cause to be Seated and / planted uppon the Said land with in these three yeares next Ensueinge the date hereof that then it shall / and may be lawfully for any adventurer or planter to mnake Choice & Seate thereof Given under my hand / and the Seale of this Collony this twentieth day of Aprill 1682

Recordatur HEN CHICHELEY
Teste
NICHO SPENCER Secrity

Endorsed on the pattent

Know all Men by these presents that I THOMAS MANDUE of the Isle of Weight County planter and SARAH / my wife for divers good Causes and Considerations us hereunto moveinge doe for us our heires Executors / and administrators assigne and Sett over Unto HENRY HEARNE of Nansamund County planter, his heyres / Executors administrators and assignes for Ever all our right title and intrest that wee have to the / within mentioned pattent, and all and Every part & parcell of land therein Contained and doe for us / our heyres Executors and administrators farther Covenant promise and grant to and with the Said / HENRY HEARNE his heyres or assignes to warrant Save defend and keepe harmelesse him the said HENRY / HEARNE his heyres or assignes against any person or persons that Shall or may lawfully Claime or / pretend to Claime any right tytle or Intrest to the land Mentioned in the pattent in the other side / In Wittnesse whereof I the said THOMAS MANDUE and SARAH my wife have hereunto sett our hands and / Seales this Sixtenth day of May in the yeare of our lord god one thousand Six hundred ninty and one

THOMAS **T** MANDUE Seale
his marke
SARAH **Z** MANDUE Seale
her marke

Signed Sealed and delivered
in the psence of Us
JAMES DOUGHTIE
THOMAS **T** KINDER
his marke

Accknowledged by THOMAS MANDUE / and SARAH his wife in open Court / held for the Isle of Weight County / to be theire act and deed June y[e] 9[th]. 1692

Test JOHN PITT C[l] C[ur]

Seale

To all to whome these presents shall Come I S^r^ HENRY CHICHELEY K^t^. deputie Gov^r^ & doe with the / Consent of the Councell of State accordingly give and grant Unto GILBERT ADAMS one hundred and fifty / acres of land Scituate on the branches of blacke Water in the lower parish of the Isle of Weight / County bounded (Viz^t^) begininge at a white oake neare a pocoson, beinge M^r^ NICHOLAS COBBs Corner / tree thence west thirteene poole to a red oake in M^r^ THOMAS TOOKEs Line and thence by the / said TOOKEs line North thirty five degrees Westerly thirty two pole North twenty five degres / westerly thirty two poles North forty degrees westerly Sixty pole North Eighty two pole South / Eighty degrees Easterlie Eighty Eight pole, North Eighty degrees Easterly twenty Sixe pole to / a Cart path and then alonge the said path, South Sixty Eight degrees Easterly one hundred / and forteene pole to a line betwixt the aforesaid TOOKE & M^r^ COBB and then by the Sayd line / South west one hundred Eighty Eighty pole to the first station. The said land beinge due &c / To have & to hould the S^d^ land &^c^ Given Under my hand and the Seale of the Collony the twenty sixth / day of September one thousand Sixe hundred and Eighty

HEN CHICHELEY

I GILBERT ADAMS doe with the Consent of my Wife ELIZABETH assigne over all my Right of this / Pattent accordinge as it is Survayed and Markt by Major ARTHUR ALLEN unto JOHN GOODRICH & his heires / for Ever with warranty that the bounds marked by Major ARTHUR ALLEN is the bounds of the Said / land accordinge to his draught given to mee as wittnesse our hands and Seales this 9^th^. day of June 1691 / haveinge already received a valueable Consideration for the Same

Signed Sealed & delivered — GILBERT **B** ADAMS Seale
In the presence of Us — his marke
JAMES BENN — ELIZABETH **2** ADAMS Seale
JAMES TULLAGH — her marke

Accknowledged in open Court held / for the Isle of Weight County July / the 9^th^ 1691 by GILBERT ADAMS and / ELIZABETH his wife to be theire free act and deed / and ordered to be recorded

Test JOHN PITT C^l^ C^ur^

**[38]**

The depotition of ROBERT FFLAKE aged 70 yeares or thereabout beinge Sworne / Sayeth

That WILLIAM EVANS did uppon his death Bed desire of mee beinge overSeer that M^r^ / JAMES BENN Should have a Conveyance for fower hundred Acres of Land out of his Conveya / nce of Eight hundred acres of Land lyinge at Kingsale for

M$^{r}$ BENN had paid for it and / it was his and that the Sayd WILLIAM EVANS had nothinge to doe with it ROBERT **R** FFLAKE
Sworne to in open Court held for the his marke
Isle of Weight County august the 10$^{th}$ 1691 Test JOHN PITT C$^{l}$ C$^{ur}$

The depotition of KATHERINE PIERCE Executrixe of WILLIAM EVANS dec$^{d}$ aged 25 yeares / or there about beinge Sworne Sayeth

That my former husband WILLIAM EVANS did uppon his death bed tell M$^{r}$ MOORE that the / halfe of his land which is fower hundred acres did belonge to M$^{r}$ JAMES BENN and did desire / that he may have it further Sayeth nott
Sowrne [*sic*] to in open Court august the 10$^{th}$. 1691 KATHERINE **K** PIERCE
Test JOHN PITT C$^{l}$ C$^{ur}$ her marke

The Depotition of THOMAS MOORE taken the 10$^{th}$ day of august 1691 beinge Sworne Saieth

That yo$^{r}$ deponent was requested by M$^{r}$ WILLIAM EVANS late of this County deceased to / wright his Will and at the bequeathinge of his land at Kingsale to his sonne THOMAS did informe yo$^{r}$ depo$^{t}$ that fower hundred acres of the Land bought of MATHEW STRICKLAND / Contained Eight hundred Acres did belonge to M$^{r}$ JAMES BENN as beinge purchaser within / for the Said land and that he had noe right for any then for fower hundred acres w$^{ch}$ / he then gave to his Sayd Sonne THOMAS by will and to the best of yo$^{r}$ depo$^{t}$ memory did / Say that M$^{r}$ JAMES BENN had honestly payd his part of the Sayd land and hed[2] hope that / he would Injoy it or words to that Effect
Sworne to in Court held of the Isle THO: MOORE
of Weight County august y$^{e}$ 10$^{th}$. 1691 Test JOHN PITT C$^{l}$ C$^{ur}$

This Indenture made the ninth day of June in the yeare of our lord God one thousand Sixe hun / dred nyntie one, and in the third yeare of the reigne of our Sovereigne lord and lady William / and Mary Kinge and Queene by the grace of god of England Scotland ffrance and Ireland &c / betwene THOMAS PIERCE and KATHERINE his wife Executrixe of WILLIAM EVANS dec$^{d}$ of the upper / parish of the Isle of Weight County of the one part and JAMES BENN of the lower parish / parish [*sic*] of the County aforesaid of the other part Wittnesseth that the said THOMAS PIERCE / and KATHERINE his wife in the quallity before Expressed for and in Consideration of the Sume / of two thousand pounds of tobacco and Caske paid by the Said JAMES BENN Unto the afores$^{d}$ / WILLIAM EVANS deceased: which tobacco was paid to the afforeSaid EVANS for the one halfe / of a parcell of Land which the Said WILLIAM EVANS did purchase of MATHEW STRICKLAND it / beinge Eight hundred acres more or lesse, as by the Said STRICKLANDs Conveyance to the said / EVANS may appeare which is part of a pattent granted to the Said MATHEW STRICKLAND /

[2] It is impossible to determine if "hed" is a misspelling of "had" or of "he'd."

Containeinge nine hundred and two acres and bareinge date the 26 day of September 1678 / the one halfe of which land the said WILLIAM EVANS did uppon his death bed Say he had / Sould Unto JAMES BENN and did desire that the said JAMES BENN Should have a Conveyance / for the Same and accordinge to the foresaid Consideration and the desire of the Said WILLIAM / EVANS deeceased Know yee therefore that wee the Said THOMAS PIERCE and KATHERINE my / wife in the quallity affore Said doe hereby accknowledge our Selves fully Satisfied / and payd and of Every part and parcell thereof doth Clearly accquit Exonerate and / discharge the Said JAMES BENN his heyres Executors and administrators for Ever by these

**[39]**
These presents have given granted aliened bargained Sould Enfeoffed and Confirmed and by / these presents doth fully clearely and absolutely give grant bargaine Sell alien Enfeoffe and / Confirme Unto the Said JAMES BENN his heyres and assignes for ever the one halfe of the aforeasaid / 800: acres of land more or lesse which is fower hundred more or lesse lyinge and beinge in the parish / and County aforesaid and Scituated uppon the Bever dam Swampe begininge at a marked dogwood / Standinge by the bever dam swampe Side from thence runinge South alonge an ould line of marked / trees 155 pole to a pine marked three wayes thence west South west halfe a point South (until / it doth meete with a parcell of land Leased by this Sayd MATHEW STRICKLAND for 99 yeares Unto THO / MAS JONES and Excepted out of the Sayd Conveyance of the Sayd EVANS, as by the Sayde Conveyance may / appeare) thence North and by west to the bever dam branch thence up the Sayd branch to the first / Station to have and to hould the aforesayd (400) Acres of land be it more or lesse with all woods / under woods previledges and appurtenancies what Soever Unto the Said JAMES BENN his heires and ass / ignes for Ever to the Sole and only Use and behoofe of the Said JAMES BENN and of this heyres and ass / -ignes for Ever against the Said THOMAS PIERCE and KATHERINE his wife theire heyres Executors ad / ministrators and assignes and all and Every other person or persons what Soever Claymeing by / from or Under them, and that they shall and Will warrant and for Ever defend by these presents / and that the Said THOMAS PIERCE and KATHERINE his wife doe Covenant and grant to and with y[e] / Sayd JAMES BENN his heyres executors administrators and Every of them by these presents that all / and Singular the Said (400) Acres of Land more or lesse by these presents Sould with all and Singular / theire appurtenancies now be and Ever here after Shalbe Stand and Continue to the Sayd JAMES / BENN and his heyres Clearely and freely dischardged and accquitted or other wayes from tyme to / tyme and at all tymes hereafter Shalbe well and Suffitiently Saved harmelesse by the Sayd THOMAS / PIERCE and KATHERINE his wife theire heyres Executors and adminsitrators of and from all and Sin / gular former bargaines and Sales Joyntures dowers guifts grants leases anuities charges Estates / titles and incumbrancies whatSoever in wittnesse whereof the said THOMAS PIERCE and KATHERINE / his wife have hereunto put theire hands and Seales the day yeare and reigne First above written

Signed Sealed and delivered as the act and deed of THOMAS PEIRCE and KATHERINE his wife in the presence of us whose names are under written
JOHN GILES
JAMES TULLAGH
HEN: APPLEWHAITE
JA DAY

THOMAS **T** PEERCE
hir marke Seale
KATHERINE **K** PEIRCE
her marke Seale

Accknowledged in open Court held / for the Isle of Weight County august the 10th. 1691 / by THOMAS PEIRCE & KATHERINE his Wife Executrixe / of WILLIAM EVANS decd to be theire free act and deed

Test: JOHN PITT Cl Cur

In the yeare and Reigne of Sovereigne Lord the Kinge ano: do: 1682/3 augst. ye ninth / Be it knowne to all persons to whome these may or Shall Concerne that I WILLIAM BUSH doe here / by firmely with the Consent of my Wife MARTHA BUSH Sell Unto GEORGE PERSIE a Sertain pcell / of land beinge and lyinge uppon the heads and branches of Currawaugh Swampe in the Isle of / Weight County in Verginia which parcell of land Containeinge two hundred Acres of which land / too to remaine to him the Said GEORGE PERSIE to him his heyres Executrs administrators and to / his assignes for Ever with all the profits previledges, thereunto belongeinge and further I the / said WILLIAM BUSH with my wife MARTHA BUSH doe warrant the Sale of the Sayd land unto / him the Said GEORGE PERSIE him his heires or assignes against any person or persons what Soever / that may or shall for the future lay and Claime Claimes or Intrest to or against the said land / but for the future to remaine his or theire true and proper right Unto which wee doe / here Unto Sett our hands this yeare and day above written. the above Said land beinge bounded / as followeth it lyinge on the South East side of the run the which the Said WILLIAM BUSH / liveth now on and Soe runinge up to the County line and than Endith wittnesse our hands & / Seales

Signed Sealed and delivered in ye psents of us
JOHN COGGAN
JOHN SELLAWAY

WILLIAM BUSH seale
MARTHA + BUSH seale
her marke

This Conveyance is recorded / augst the 9th 1683 / Turne over

**[40]**

Know all Men by these presents that I GEORGE PIERSIE doe for mee my heyres Executors and adminsitrators / assigne Sell and make over for Ever Unto JOHN SURBER of the Isle of Weight County and to his heyres / Executors administrators and assignes for Ever all my right title and Intrest of the within men / tioned two hundred acres of land Sould and made over to me by WILLIAM BUSH beareinge date / august the ninth $168^2/_3$ for which two hundred acres of land I doe acknowledge my Selfe fully / payd and Satisfied as wittnesse my hand and Seale this 27th of July 1692

Signed Sealed and delivered GEORGE **X** PIERSIE
In ꝑsence of Us his marke Seale
JOHN PITT
ADAM MURRAY

Accknowledged in open Court held / for the Isle of Weight County august / the 10th 1691 by GEORGE PIERSIE to be his / act and deed

Test JOHN PITT Cl Cur

Know all Men by these presents that I JOHN MORRIS Junr planter in the Isle of Weight / County doe for my Selfe my heyres Executors administrators or assignes for a valueable Con / Sideration by mee in hand already recived have bargained for & Sould Unto and by these ꝑsents / doe Sell allienate and make over Unto JOHN BARNES planter in the foresaid County his heyres / Executors administrators or assignes for Ever one hundred acres of land Scituated lyinge & / beinge in the Isle of Weight County and Joyneinge to the blacke water Swampe and beinge / one of the three hundred acres which my father WILLIAM MORRIS bought of CHRISTOPHER HOLLIMAN / beinge halfe of a pattent of Sixe hundred acres of the Said HOLLIMAN this hundred acres which / ꝑcell is my part of the three hundred which is one hundred acres and must be in the midle / betwene my brother MORGANs and my brother WILLIAM the Said JOHN BARNES his heyres Execrs / administrators or assignes for Ever to have and to hould the Said hundred acres of land with / all previledges Royalties and profits whatsoever there Unto belongeinge and further more / I the Said JOHN MORRIS Junior doth hereby bind my Selfe / my heyres Executors admisrs or assignes / to warrant and make good the Sale of the Said one hundred acres of land and to keepe harme / lesse and defend the foresSaid BARNES his heyres Executors administrators or assignes against / any person or persons whatsoever that Shall or may lay any Claime or pretend to have any / Intrest in or to any part or parcell of the foresaid hundred acres of land for Ever and further / more I the fore Said JOHN MORRIS Junr doth hereby obleidge my Selfe to accknowledge this my / Volluntary act and deed at the next Court to be held for the Isle of Weight County as / Wittnesse my hand and Seale this fifth day of august and in the yeare of our lord god 1691

his
Signed sealed and delivered JOHN: **IM**: MORRES seale
in the presence of Us marke
JNO JONES Senr
JOHN JONES Junr
his
JAMES **B** BARNES
marke

Accknowledged in open Court / held for the Isle of Weight County / august the 10th. 1691 by JOHN MORRES / to be his act and deed

Test JOHN PITT Cl Cur

To all to whome these ꝑsents shall Come I FFRANCIS NICHOLSON Esqr theire Maties Lt Governor / of Virignia Send Greetinge &c Now Know yee that I the Said FFRANCIS NICHOLSON Esqr Lt Goverr / doe with the advice and Consent of the Councell of State accordeingly give and grant Unto / HODGES COUNCELL the younger and THOMAS MAN: Two hundred acres of land lyeinge in Isle / of Weight County begininge at a markt Gumm JOHN BROWNEs Corner tree in Kingsale Swa / -mpe then alonge the Said BROWNs Line South tenn degrees East fivety Seven pole to a pine / then South East by another line of the Said BROWNE one hundred & fivetene pole to a pine / then South west one hundred forty Sixe pole and a halfe to a pine then South one hundred / forty two pole to a pine then South fivety Six degrees west forty Sixe pole to a Cypresse / in the Sayd Swampe thence up the maine Streame of the Said Swampe to the gumm / where it began The Sayd land being due to the Sayd HODGES COUNCELL the younger / and

**[41]**

and THOMAS MAN by and for the Importation of fower persons into this Collony whose names / are in the records mentioned Under this patent To have and to hould &c yeldinge and payinge unto / our Sovereigne Lord and Lady the Kinge and Queene theire heyres or Successors for Every fivety Acres / of land hereby granted at the feast of St Michaell the Archangell the fee rent of one Shillinge &c / Given Under my hand & the Seale of the Collony this 28d day of 8br 1690

Record WM COLE Secr FFR NICHOLSON

Know all Men by these presents that Wee HODGES COUNCELL Junr of the lower parish of the Isle / of Weight County and THOMAS MAN of the Same parish and County, doe both Joyntly and Severally / for Us our heyres Executors Admisrs assigne over Unto WILLIAM KEELL of the aforesaid lower / parish of the Isle of Weight County his heyres executors admisrs and assignes for Ever all our right / title and Intrest in this within pattent of land in wittnesse whereof wee have hereunto sett our / hands and Seales this 9th day of Septr Anno Dm 1691

Signed Sealed in
ꝑsence of
WM KERLE
Signu
BRIDGMAN **B** JOYNER

Signu
HODGES **HK** COUNCELL Seale
Signu
THOMAS **M** MAN Seale

Accknowledged in open Court held / for the Isle of Weight County Sept^r^ / the 9^th^ 1691 by HODGES COUNCELL and THOMAS MAN / to be theire act and deed and ordered to be rec^o^

Test JOHN PITT C^l^ C^ur^

To all people to whome this present deed or wrightinge Shall Come to be Seene Know yee, That I NICHOLAS / COBB of the Isle of Weight County the Sonne and Sole heyre of NICHOLAS COBB late of the County above / Said deceased & doe for a valueable Consideration, to me paid at and before the Sealeinge and delivery / hereof for which I accknowledge my Selfe to be fully Satisfied by EDWARD COBB my Brother of the Same Coun / tye doe for me and my heyres make over bargaine Sell alienate and Confirme to the Said EDWARD COBB & / his heyres Executors or assignes for Ever a Certaine parcell or Tract of land in the upper parish of the / Isle of Weight County Commonly Called JOHN JONES plantation, and now in the possesion of the said EDWARD / COBB Lyeinge and Boundeinge uppon a branch which runs up the ould fields Commonly called Major BONDs field / beginninge at the mouth of a Small branch ruuninge out of the maine branch and at the mouth of the s^d^ / stands a marked red oake runinge north alonge a line of marked trees to a red oake in M^r^ THOMAS / TOOKEs S.W. line and from thence to the horse Bridge includinge all the land to the Creeke which formerly / my deceased father held by what right or title what Soever with and Singular the houses orchards fences / Edifices profits previledges Royalties immunities and Commodities thereof and thereunto belongeinge to have / and to hould the premises to him the Sayd EDWARD COBB his heyres Executors administrators or assigns for / ever without the lett Molestation or disturbance of me the Said NICHOLAS COBB my heyres Executors / administrators or assignes in as large ample or Effectuall maner to all intents and purposes as I / the said NICHOLAS COBB my heyres Executors administrators or assignes might or Could injoy the Same / by force or Vertue of any pattent deed writinge what Soever and I the said NICHOLAS COBB doe bind / my Selfe heyres Executors administrators to Save and defend the Same EDWARD COBB his heyres Execut^rs^ / administrators or assignes harmelesse and Undamnified from all former bargaines Sales Joyntu^rs^ / dowers Morgages leases or incumbrances whatSoever may in any waise prove preiudiciall to the S^d^ / EDWARD COBB his heyres Executors administrators or assignes contrary to the true intent and meane / inge hereof with generall warrantie from all person or persons what Soever that Shall Molest dis / turbe the Sayd EDWARD COBB his heyres Execut^rs^ admist^rs^ or assignes from the peceable inioyment / of the premises and for the true Confirmation hereof I the Sayd NICHOLS COBB doe bind my Selfe / to make accknowledgement of the Sale hereof at our next Court held for the Isle of Weight County / in Wittnesse hereunto I have Sett my hand and Seale this 9^th^ day of August 1686

NICH N COBB
his Signall Seale

Signed Sealed and delivered in the ꝑsence of us
THO: MOORE

Vera Copia / Test JN^O^ PITT / C^l^ C^ur^

BENJA BEALE turne over

**[42]**

Know all Men by these presents that I EDWARD COBB of the upper parish of the Isle of / Weight County doe for my Selfe my heyres Executors administrators or assignes make over the / within deed of Sale with all the lands Edificies and buildings therein Contained with all the / appurtenancies thereunto belongeinge accordinge to the with in bounds as it is there described / Unto ANDREW WOODLEY of the parish and County aforeSaid and to the Said ANDREW WOODLEY / his heyres and assignes for Ever with generall warranty against all persons in wittnesse / whereof I have hereunto sett my hand and Seale this fourteenth day of September one thou / Sand Sixe hundred ninety one

EDWARD + COBB
his marke Seale

Test JOHN GILES
ROGER: STEVENS
JAMES TULLAGH

This Indenture made the 14th day of September in the yeare of our lord God one thousand and Six hun / dred nynety one and in the third yeare of the reigne of our Sovereigne lorde and Lady William / and Mary, by the Grace of God of England Scotland ffrance and Ireland Kinge and queene &c / Betwene EDWARD COBB and DOROTHY his wife for and in Consideration of the Sume / of Sixe thousand five hundred pounds of Tobacco, and Caske, to them in hand at and before / the Sealeinge and delivery of these presents, by the Said ANDREW WOODLEY well and truly paid / the receipt whereof he the Said EDWARD COBB and DOROTHY his wife doth hereby accknowledge / and them Selves there with fully Satisfied and paid, and thereof and of every part and parcel / thereof doth clearely accquit, Exonerate and discharge the Said ANDREW WOODLEY his heyres / Executors and administrators for Ever by these presents hath given granted aliened bargand / Sould Enffeofed and Confirmed and by these presents doth fully Clearely and absolutely / give grant bargaine Sell Alien Enfeoff and Confirme Unto the Said ANDREW WOODLEY his heires / and assignes for Ever a Certaine parcell or Tract of Land Scituate lyinge and beinge in ye / parish and County aforesaid Commonly called JONES his plantation and now in the possesion / of the Said EDWARD COBB (begininge and boundinge at the mouth of a branch which runs / up the ould feild Commonly Cald Major BONDs ould feild begininge at the mouth of a Smal / branch runinge out of the Maine branch and at the mouth of the Said Branch Stands a marked / red Oake runinge north alonge a line of marked trees to a red Oake in Mr TOOKEs South west / line and from thence to the horse Bridge includeinge all the land to the Creeke, which is / about 200 Acres more or lesse and it beinge part of a pattent of 900 Acres granted to / NICHOLAS COBB ffather to the Said EDWARD COBB) by pattent and beareinge date 17th day of / June 1664 To have and to hould the aforesaid 200 Acres of Land more or lesse accordinge to the / bounds before mentioned with all and Singular its Rights meembers [*sic*], Jurisdictions and appurtenancies / to gather with all howses

Edificies buildings orchards gardens Easements Lands tenements / pastures wayes woods underwoods water courses profits, Comodities hereditaments and appur / tenancies what Soever to the Said messuage or plantation and premises, or to any part or parcell / of them belongeinge or in any Wise appertaineinge thereunto, Unto the Said ANDREW WOODLEY his / heyres or assignes, to the only proper use and behoofe of the Said ANDREW WOODLEY his heyres and / assignes for Ever against him the Said EDWARD COBB his heyres and assignes and all and Every / other person and persons what Soever lawfully Claimeinge, by from or Under him them or any / of them, Shall and Will warrant and for Ever defend by these presents and that the Said EDWARD / COBB for himselfe his heyres Executors and administrators doe Covenant, promise grant and agree / to and with the Said ANDREW WOODLEY his heyres and assignes and Every of them by these presents / of all and Singular the foresaid premises with the apurtenancies thereunto belongeinge / now be and Ever hereafter Shalbe Stand and Continue to the Said ANDREW WOODLEY and his / heires and assignes for Ever. and that the Said ANDREW WOODLEY his heyres or assignes be frely

**[43]**

frely and Clearely acquited, Exonerated, and dischardged, and from tyme to tyme well and sufi / tiently, Saved and kept harmelesse by the said EDWARD COBB, his heyres Executors or administrators / of and from all and all maner of former and other guifts grants, bargaines, sales Leases Mortga / ges, Joyntures, dowers, of and from all and Singular other titles, troubles Charges, demands / and incombrances, whatsoever, had made, Committed Suffered, omitted or don by the Said EDWARD / COBB, his heyres or assignes, or by any other person or persons whatsoever, and that the Said / EDWARD COBB, his heyres or assignes, for and dureinge the space of Seaven yeares next Ensueinge / the date of these presents, Shall and Will at, and Uppon the reasonable request, and at the Cost / and Charges in the law of the Said ANDREW WOODLEY, his heyres or assignes, make Such further / lawfull and reasonable assurance, or assurances in the law, for the more better and perfict / assurance of the afforesaid premises as by the Said ANDREW WOODLEY his heyres or assignes or by / his or theire Councell learned in the law Shalbe reasoneable demised advised or required and / that the aforesaid premises with all the appurtenancies thereunto belongeinge, shalbe Estemed / and adiudged and taken to be and Ennure, to the only proper use and behoofe of the Said ANDREW / WOODLEY his heyres and assignes for ever, and to none other use intent or purpose whatsoever / In Wittnesse whereof wee have hereunto sett our hands and Seales the day yeares and Reigne / first above written

Signed Sealed and delivered in the presence of Us whose names are underwritten
JOHN GILES
JAMES TULLAGH
ROBERT STEVENS

EDWARD + COBB seale
his marke
DOROTHY + COBB seale
her marke

Accknowledged in open Court / held for the Isle of Weight County / Decemb^r^ the 15^th^. 1691 by EDWARD COBB / and DOROTHY his wife to be theire free / act and deed

Test JOHN PITT C^l^ C^ur^

Possesion Livery and Season of the lands within mentioned delivered unto the said / ANDREW WOODLEY his heyres and assignes for Ever this ninth day of october 1691

In the presence of us

his<br>
JOHN I SCRUES<br>
marke<br>
JOHN PORTIS<br>
ROGER STEVENS<br>
his<br>
PHILL **P** BRANTLY<br>
marke

his<br>
EDWARD + COBB<br>
marke<br>
DOROTHY + COBB<br>
marke

Know all men by these presents that I CORNELIUS CULLEY of the Isle of Weight County / planter have for a valueable Consideration beinge two thousand pounds of tobacco in hand / before the Sealeinge and delivery of this deed have bargained Sould and for ever quit cla / imed Unto JAMES TULLAGH of the Isle of Weight County his heyres and assignes for ever / a Certaine parcell or tract of land Contayneinge Sixty Acres more or lesse Scituate ly / inge and beinge in the lower parish of the Isle of Weight / County neare the Mill belonging / to THOMAS WEBB, and Commonly Called the Mill necke and bounded as followeth / begininge at a white oake Close uppon a run neare a springe formerly Called Webbs spring / and Soe runinge west uppon THOMAS WEBBs marked trees of this lands now in the posses / ion of the Said JAMES TULLAGH and soe to a bottome to a Corner tree beinge a red oake / betwene AMBROSSE BENNETT and this Devidend of land and from then said Bottome / runinge North to the Creeke to have and to hould the Said land with all houseinge / orchards fences previledges Royalties and Innuities what Soever, to him the Said JAMES / TULLAGH his heyres or assignes for Ever with generall Warrantie against all persons the / fore Said Tract of land beinge purchased by my father CORNELIUS SKULLY dec^d^ of AMBROSE / BENNETT as may appeare by deed beareinge date the 10^th^ day of July 1669 in Confirmation / hereof I have hereunto sett my hand and Seale this 15^th^ day of decemb^r^ 1691

CORNELIUS CULLEY Seale

Test THOS MOORE<br>
HEN APPLEWHAITE<br>
JA BENN<br>
JOHN GILES

Accknowledged in open Corut held for y^e^ Isle of Weight County dec^r^ y^e^ 15^th^ 1691 by CORNELIUS CULLEY to be his act and deed

Test JN^O^ PITT C^l^ C^ur^

**[44]**

This Indenture made the first of November in the yeare 1666 betwene NICHOLAS COBB of the / one partie of the Isle of Weight County of Virginia and JOHN JOANES of the other partie of the s[d] County / wittnesseth that the Said COBB the day of makeinge hereof hath granted demissed betaken and letten to / farme and by this indenture doth grant demise betake and to farme Lett Unto JOHN JONES his executers / administrators one parcell of moiety of land Scituatinge lyinge and beinge in the Isle of Weight County / afores Said and is bounded as followeth begininge at a red Oake which standeth by the horse path and Soe alonge / the horse path to a beech which is by the Swampe side a Joyneinge on M[r] NICHOLAS SMITH and soe alonge the / Swampe to a marked Beech by the Said Swamp side and from thence up the branch to a marked white oake / and from thence to the first Station, which the Said JONES is to have and to hould the said land for and / dureinge the tearme of twelfe yeares begininge the day of the date hereof fully to be Compleated and Ended yeldinge and payinge therefore yearly dureinge the said time to the said NICHOLAS COBB his heyres Executors / administrators or assignes at or uppon the tenth day of october the full and Just Sume of three hundred and / fifty pounds of good Sound well Conditioned tobacco and Caske Cleare of ground leaves or trash it is further / Covenanted and agreed Uppon that the Said JONES is to plant a Orchard Containeinge one hundred and fiftie / apple trees to be the one halfe Summer and the other halfe winter fruite to be planted the first or Second / yeare and to be fenced in with Sufficient fences and to be planted at Sixteene foote distance and kept tended / and to make Use of timber for his owne Use and buildinge Except Six Red Oakes the Said NICHOLAS COBB or his / assignes is to make Choice of and at his pleasure freely to Carry away and at the Expiration of the afore Said / tearme the said JONES is to leave a Sufficient dwellinge house of thirty foote longe tenentable with tobacco / house and other houses in repaire with Sufficient fences Standinge as they are in wittnesse hereof the parties / above mentioned have hereunto Sett theire hands and Seales the day and yeare above written

Signed Sealed and delivered p me NICHOLAS COBB seale
in the presence of us
WALTER JOHNSON
JOHN **P** PORTIS

This lease is proved by the oath of / JOHN JONES and JOHN PORTIS in Court / Held the 15[th] of decemb[r] 1691

Test JOHN PITT C[l] C[ur]

Know all Men by these presents that I ARTHUR ALLEN of Lawncs Creeke parish in the County of / Surry for a Valueable consideration to me in hand payd or secured to be payd by ROBERT FFLAKE of the / Upper parish of the Isle of Weight County have bargained and Sould and doe by these presents for mee / and my heyres for

Ever bargaine Sell and deliver Infeoffe and Confirme unto the Said ROBERT FFLAKE / and to his heyres and assignes for Ever a Certaine peece or parcell of land Containeinge one hundred / and Seventie acres, Scituate betwene the lands of THOMAS TOOKE Cap[t] ENGLAND THOMAS BLAKE and / EDWARD BRANTLY in the upper parish of the Isle of Weight County aforesaid the said one hundred / and Seventie acres of land being granted to mee by pattent dated the 20[th]. of octob[r] 1691 and this bounded / begininge at a Red Oake THOMAS BLAKEs Corner tree in M[r] TOOKEs line thence by BLAKE South Seventy thre / degrees west two hundred and Sixe poole to a small red oake, north Seventy fower degrees west Sixty pooles / to a pine and North thirty fower degrees west a hundred and two pole to a pine in M[r] NEWMANs line thence / by his line North north east twenty nine pole to a Stooping red oake in or neare Cap[t] ENGLANDs line then / by his Lines South: Sixty nine degrees east a hundred and Eight pole to a Small white oake markt by Con / Sent of GEORGE CRIPPS the present possesor of the Sayd land then North thirty one degrees East a hundred / and Seaven pole to two pines EDWARD BRANTLYs Corner trees neare the danceing place then by the said / BRANTLYs line South East fifty two pole to a pine & North East twenty pole to M[r] TOOKEs line and soe / by his line South east a hundred thirty Six pole to the first Station, To Have and To hould y[e] / Said 170 Acres of land with his due share of all mines and minerals therein Contained with free / priveledge of huntinge hawkinge fishing and fowlinge with allwoods wayes and Waters and all other / Royalties previledges Profits Comodities & hereditaments what Soever to the Sayd land belonging / or in any wise appertaineinge, to him the Sayd ROBERT FLAKE and to his heyres and assignes For Ever / in as full and Ample maner to all intents and purposes as I my Selfe might or Could have injoyed / the Same by Vertue of the before recited pattent, and I doe hereby Covenant provide declare & agree / to and with the Said ROBERT FLAKE his heyres and assignes that the Said land and Every part and parcell / thereof is Cleare and free from all and all maner of Incumbrances former bargaines & Sales Joyntures / mortgages Judgments and Executions and all other maner of Incumbrance what Soever & that / I have at the tyme of the EnSealinge and delivery hereof in and to all and Singular the premises

**[45]**

a good pure and Indefeazable Estate of inheritance in fee Simple w[ch]: I hereby transfer and doe obleidge / my Selfe my heires Execut[rs] admis[rs]: to warrant and defend this my Sale of all and Singular the ꝑmises w[th] / theire appurtenancies to the Said ROBERT FFLAKE to his heyres and assignes for Ever ag[t] all maner of persons w[t] / Soever by from or under me deriveinge any Claime title or Intrest thereto when thereto required will give to / him or any of them Such further lawfull assurance of all and Singular the premises as by his or theires learned / Councell Shalbe thoguht fitt and will alsoe acknowledge this Instrument of Conveyance to be my reall act & / deed in open Court next to be held for the Isle of Weight County aforesaid in testimony of all which I have here / unto putt my hand & Sale this [--] of [--] 1692

Signed and Sealed in AR[R] ALLEN Seale

Presence of
[--]

Accknowledged in open Court held for the / Isle of Weight County augs$^{t}$ the 9$^{th}$. 1692 / by Maj$^{r}$: ARTHUR ALLEN to be his act and deed

Test JOHN PITT C$^{l}$ C$^{ur}$

Know all Men by these presents that I ARTHUR ALLEN of Lawnes Creeke Parish in the County / of Surry for a Valueable consideration to me in hand paid & secured to be payd have bargained / Sould and delivered and doe by these presents for me and my heyres for Ever bargaine Sell and deliver / infeoffe and Confirme unto EDWARD BOYKIN, of the Upper parish of the Isle of Weight County a Certaine / parcell or devident of Land Conteyneinge five hundred twenty five acres Scituate on the North west side / of the third Swamp of the blacke water in the upper parish of the Isle of Weight County afores$^{d}$ the / said five hundred twenty five Acres of land being granted to me by pattent dated y$^{e}$ 20$^{th}$ day of octob$^{r}$ 1691 / and bounded (viz$^{t}$) Begining at a pine M$^{r}$ GEORGE WILLIAMSONs Corner tree there by his line north forty one / degrees East two hundred Sixe pole to a red oake in his Sayd line then, northwest by west three hundred & / twenty pole to a red oake by the Edge of a Pocoson, then South forty one degres west, two hundred & thirty two / pole to a Small pine & Small wite oake in M$^{r}$ THOMAS MOOREs line, then by his lines South forty Six pole to / a white oake his Corner tree, and South East by East two hundred & ninety fower pole to the first station / To: Have & to hold the said 355 acres of land with his due share of all mines and mineralls therein Conteyned / with free previledge of hunting hawking ffishing and fowling with all woods waies & Waters and all the / royalties previledges Profitts Comodities & hereditaments whatsoever to the Said land belonging or / in any wise appertaining to him the Said EDWARD BOYKIN and to his heyres and assignes for Ever in as / full and ample maner to all intents and purposes as I my selfe might or Could have injoyed the Same / by vertue of the before recited patt$^{t}$: and I doe hereby Covenant promise declare & agree that the / said land and Every part and parcell thereof is Cleare and free from all & all maner of former bargaines / and Sale Joyntures Judgments Mortgages & Executions and all other maner of incumbrances whatSoever / and that I have at the tyme of the Ensealeinge and delivery hereof in and to all the premises a good pure / and indefeazable Estate in fee Simple which I hereby transfer & doe obleidge my Selfe my heyres Executors and / adminsitrators to warrant and defend this my Sale of all and Singular the premises, with theire appurtenan / cies to the Said EDWARD BOYKIN his heyres and assignes for Ever ag$^{t}$. all maner of persons whatSoever by from / or under me laying any Claime Title or intrest thereto when thereto required will give to him or any of y$^{e}$ / Such further lawfull assurance of all and Singular the premises as by his or theire learned Councell shall / be thought fitt and will acknowledge this instrument: of Conveyance to be my reall act & deed in open / Court next to be held for the Isle of

Weight County aforesaid: in Testimony of all w$^{ch}$ I have hereunto / put my hand and Seale y$^{e}$ [--] of [--] 1692
Signed Sealed and delivered AR$^{R}$ ALLEN seale
In Presence of [--]

Accknowledged in oprn Court held / for the Isle of Weight County agu$^{st}$ y$^{e}$ 9$^{th}$ / 1692 by Majo$^{r}$ ARTHUR ALLEN to be / his act and deed
Test JOHN PITT C$^{l}$ C$^{ur}$

These presents wittneseth that whereas HODGES COUNCELL of the lower parish of the Isle of Weight / County and LUCY his wife by theire deed bareinge date the 20$^{th}$ day of december 1678 did give Unto / JOSEPH VICKE of the parish and County aforesaid his heyres and assignes a parcell of land Containeing / fifty acres more of lesse lying and being in the Said County with divers ande Sundry limitations pro / visors and agrements therein Expressed and declared as by the Said deed Under the hands and Seales / of the Said HODGES COUNCELL and LUCY his wife and by them accknowledged in the Isle of Weight / County Court the 9$^{th}$ day of march 168$^{1}/_{2}$ it may and doth more fully appeare, but for as much as / by the Said deed the land aforesaid is declared to lye uppon the heads of the branches of the beaver / dam Swampe the first branch runing north and by west unto ROBERT LAURENCE his ould line and y$^{e}$

**[46]**
the other Branch North and by East to the Said COUNCELLs head line with said courses of the for / Said branches not being then run or layd out by a Compase, but only guessed at and Since uppon tryall / made thereof by the Compass found Erronious and Untrue and run otherwise then in the said deed / is Expressed Now know all men by these presents that wee the Sayd HODGES COUNCELL and JOSEPH VICKE / doe for us our heyres Executors and administrators Covenant and agree Either with the other to stand / and abide the bounds hereafter mentioned and by us agreed one and that the Said VICKE shall from / this tyme and at all tymes hereafter peaceably and quietly Enjoy the Sayd land with in the Sayd / bounds now agreed on without the lett trouble or Molestation of him the Said COUNCELL his heyres / &c or any other person or persons whatSoever That is to Say from the foote of the branch on the / Southwest side of JOSEPH VICKs plantation to a Cypress marked with three Notches up the branch / and two up the Swamp Soe runing up the branch to a maple at the head marked with three not / ches in a side from thence to a red oake then Corner tree, from thence Eastwardly to a Stoopinge / Red oake marked with three Notches in a Side, soe downe uppon a Straite line to the head of a / branch on the north East side of the Said plantation and Soe downe to the foote of y$^{e}$ branch / to a Gum standing on the run side, marked with three notches up the branch and two downe / the Swamp and Soe downe the run side of the Swamp to the aforesaid Cypruss, which is the true / bounds by Us the aforesaid parties agreed upon, declareing all other bounds in the Sayd deed to be / Utterly Null Void and of None Effect as if they

had never bene anything in the Sayd deed to the / Contrary Notwithstanding In wittnesse whereof the parties above named have hereunto set their / hand and Seales this 6th day of october 1691

Signum

Signed Sealed and delivered in the presence of Us
WM KERLE
BRIDGMAN **B** JOYNER
his marke

HODGES **HK** COUNCELL Seale
Signum
JOSEPH **D** VICKE Seale

Ordered to be recorded augst / the 9th 1692
Test JOHN PITT Cl Cur

Know all men by these presents that I THOMAS HARRIS of the Lower parish of the Isle / of Wight County doe for me my heyres Executors administrators assigne over to WILLIAM CRUMP / LAR his heyres Executors administrators and assignes for Ever all my right title and Interest / in the above pattent, and doe acknowledge to have received full satisfaction for the same as / witnesse my hand and seal this 8th day of June 1692

Signum
THOMAS **T H** HARRIS (seales)

Signed Sealed and Delivered
in psence of us
WM KERLE
BRIDGMAN JOYNER
RICH REYNOLDS

Acknowledged in open Court held for the / Isle of Wight County August the 9th. 1692 / by THOMAS HARRIS to be his act and deed

Test JOHN PITT Cl Cur

The Above mentioned Convey / ance from PHILLIP RATFORD to / THOMAS HARREYS and from THO / HARIS TO WM CRUMPLAR is reco / in fol 546 in the last booke of / Conveyances

This Indenture beareinge date the Eight day of June in the yeare of our lord God one thousand / Sixe hundred ninty and two, wittnesseth that WILLIAM CARVER of the Lower parish of the Isle of / Weight County as intermarringe the daughter and heyres of JOHN MOORE late of this County / decd, to and with the Consent of of [*sic*] JANE his wife, and by these presents doth for them theire heires / Executrs administrators bargaine Sell allienate, transfer, give grant demise and fully and also / latly Lett and Sett over, Unto WILLIAM CRUMPLER of the aforesaid Lower parish of the Isle of / Weight County one part or parcell of land lyinge and being on the branches of the blackwater / in the Said County of the Isle of Weight by Estimation about one hundred Acres be it more or / lesse bounded as followeth, Vizt begining at the head of the branch on the north Side of the / ould plantation formerly JOHN MORREs Soe runing downe the Said Branch unto PHILLIP / RAFORDs line: soe runing along his line to THOMAS MANDEWs line Soe on the line to GEORGE / PIERCEs line of his great pattent and Soe along PIERCEss line to a direct line of marked trees

**[47]**

trees to the place where it began beinge a marked pine all which part or parcell of land lyinge and / beinge on the South side of the said branch and with in the forementioned bounds, with all the planta / tion: buildings woods wayes watters springs or water Courses or any other profits or appurtenancies / thereunto belonging or in any wise appertaineinge the Said WILLIAM CARVER doth by these presents for him / Selfe his heires Execut[rs] Adminis[rs] and Every of them, give grant demise Sell allienate transfer and fully & / absolutly lett and Sett over Unto WILLIAM CRUMPLER his heyres Execut[rs] admis[rs] assignes for Ever to / have and to hould without any lett hinderance molestation or Contradiction what Soever of him the / said WILLIAM CARVER his heyres Execut[rs] administrators or any of them or any other person or persons / what Soever, for by or Under them or any of them, claimeing without any maner of Condition or limitation / of Use of Use: Rent or rents, the Kings rent only Excepted which Said part or parcell of land afore demi / =sed in part of three hundred acres of land granted by pattent Unto JOHN MOORE deceased beareing date / the twenty third day of Aprill 1681 and for further Confirmation the Said WILLIAM CARVER and / JANE his wife doe obleidge themselves to accknowledge this deed of Sale in open Court held of the Isle / of Weight County when thereto required, and doe by these presents accknowledge before the Signeinge / and Sealinge of these presents to have received a full and Valueable Consideration for the Same in witt / nesse whercof wee have hereunto sett our hands and Sealcs the day and yeare above written

Signed Sealed and delivered<br>
in presents of<br>
W[M] KERLE<br>
BRIDGMAN **B** JOYNER<br>
his marke

Signum<br>
WILLIAM **WC** CARVER Seale<br>
Signum<br>
JEANE **I** CARVER Seale

Accknowledge in open Court held / for the Isle of Weight County august / the 11[th]. 1692 by W[M] CARVER and JANE / his wife to be theire free act and deed / and ordered to be recorded

Test JOHN PITT C[l] C[ur]

Know all men by these p[r]sents that I WILLIAM CARVER of the lower parish of the Isle of Weight / County for and in Consideration of divers and Sundry debts by WILLIAM CRUMPLER Engadged for and / paid on the account of JOHN MOORE late of this County deceased have and by these presents doe for / me Execut[rs] admis[rs] Bargaine Sell and for Ever lett and Sett over Unto WILLIAM CRUMPLER his heires / Execut[rs] admis[rs]: or assignes for Ever, three Cowes & two Steers about fower yeares ould and one / fower yeares ould bull beinge marked with a Crop and a Square on the upper Side of the right eare / and fower three yeare ould & heyfers marked with a Crop and a Square and halfe Moone / being marked by one LOVEDAY all Except one, which is marked with a Crop and hole in Each Eare and / halfe Moone on the left Eare, and one two yeare ould heyfer marked with a Crop on the right yeare / and Square on the left and two Calves marked a Crop halfe Moone & hole in Each Eare and all or / Singular what hoggs Soever any waies belonging to me, and all and Singular my Estate Reall and / personall goods Lands Chattels what Soever and doe accknowledge to have recived full satisfaction / for the Same wittnesse my hand and Seale this 9th day of June 169$^{2}/_{3}$

Test Sig

W[M] KERLE WILLIAM **WC** CARVER Seale

Signum

BIRDGMAN **B** JOYNER

Accknowledged by WILLIAM CARVER in open / Court held for the Isle of Weight County aug[st] / the 11[th]. 1692 to be his act and deed and ordered / to be recorded

Test JOHN PITT C[l] C[ur]

Know all men by these presents y[t] I ROBERT DRIVER hath bargained and Sould and doe by these / presents bargaine and Sell Unto CHARLES DRIVER that Tract or parsell of land that JOHN WILLIFORD had / on this last yeare, with all the appurtenancies thereunto belonging, which land was lately Escheated / by me the fore Said ROBERT DRIVER, and I the foresaid ROBERT DRIVER doe hereby by these presents obleidge my Selfe and / ELIZABETH my wife against us our heyres Execut[rs] and adms[rs] or assignes to Confirme and accknowledge / the fore said land with all the appurtenances thereunto belonging: to CHARLES DRIVER his heyres Ex[rs] / and adminstrators and assigns for Ever, with the assignement of the Escheate pattent belonging / to the foresaid land and Uppon the performance of all things and Every thing here above mentioned / I the foresaid CHARLES [*sic*] DRIVER doe hereby bind my Selfe my heyres Execut[rs] & admis[rs]. to pay ROBERT DRIVER / or his order the iust Sume of fower thousand pounds of good Merchantable tobacco and Caske Convenient / in the Isle of Weight County and further I the foresaid CHARLES DRIVER doe obleidge my Selfe as / above to take in and pay the bond for the Escheate of the above mentioned land of one thousand / pounds of porke to Coll JOHN LEAR or his order Note thus the forementioned thousand pounds of

**[48]**

is to be paid besides the with in mentioned fower thousand pounds of tobacco and Caske & / to the true performance of all things with in mentioned wee the within mentioned parties have / hereunto Sett outr hands this 2[d] day of decemb[r] 1691

Test RICH REYNOLDS ROBERT DRIVER

GILES DRIVER ELIZABETH **E** DRIVER

RICH$^{D}$ REYNOLDS Jun$^{r}$ her marke
CHARLES DRIVER

ordered to be recorded / Test JN$^{O}$ PITT C$^{l}$ C$^{ur}$

This Indenture made the Sixth day of august one thousand Six hundred ninty and two wittnesses / that ROBERT HOOKS of the Lower parish of the Isle of Weight County for a Valueable Considerati / =on, in hand allready recived have and by these presents doe for me my heyres Execut$^{rs}$ administ$^{rs}$ / give grant demise and fully, and absolutly Lett and sett over Unto JACOB DARDEN of the afore S$^{d}$ / lower parish of the Isle of Weight County his heyres Execut$^{rs}$ administrat$^{rs}$ or assignes for Ever / one part or parsell of Land and plantation now in the possesion of the Said JACOB DARDEN being / by Estimation about two hundred Acres of land, beinge part of fower hundred acres of Land gran / ted Unto ROBERT HOOKES deceased bareing date the 30$^{th}$ day of octob$^{r}$ 1662 as may more largely apeare / and a divission made by M$^{r}$ ARTHUR ALLEN, of the Said land formerly, which said part or parcel / of Land with all the buildings howses orchards buildings Edificies and all other Comodities profits / and appurtenancies thereto belonging I the Said ROBERT HOOKES doe for me my heyres Execut$^{rs}$ / administrators bargaine Sell allienate transfer unto the Said JACOB DARDEN his heyres Execut$^{rs}$ / adminsitrators the Same in the County Court when thereto required in wittnesse whereof I have / hereunto Sett my hand and Seale the day and yeare above Specified

Signed Sealed and delivered ROBERT **R** HOOKS Seale
In ꝑsents of Us his marke
THO: GILES
JAMES DOUGHTIE

Accknowledged in open Court held / for the Isle of Weight County aug$^{st}$ the 9$^{th}$ / 1692 by ROBERT HOOKES to be his act and deed

Test JOHN PITT C$^{l}$ C$^{ur}$

Know all Men by these presents that I ANNE MATHEWES of the Isle of Weight / County widdow doe Constitute ordaine and appoint my loveing Sonne JAMES BACON to be my true / and lawfull atturny to act and doe all my bussinesse Conserneing my debts to Sue implead Imprisson / acquit discharge or Sett at libertie if any Shall refuse him payment in as full and ample maner as / if I my Selfe were personally present to all intents and purposes what Soever in my stead and place / to aske demand recive and uppon refusall to act and doe as above Said with as full power / and Authoritie as I might or Could doe were I my Selfe personally present as wittnesse my hand / and Seale this Eight day of June in the yeare of our Lord 1692

Signed Sealed and Subscribed in the ANNE **X** MATHEWS
presence of us whose names are here her marke Seale
Under written

Testes ED PRIME
THEOPHILUS FFLEARE

Owned by ANNE MATHEWES in / open Court held for the Isle of Weight / County aug$^{st}$ y$^{e}$ 9$^{th}$ 1692 to be her act & deed

Test JOHN PITT C$^{l}$ C$^{ur}$

Know all Men by these presents that I ROBERT JOHNSON planter of the Isle of Weight / County & KATHERINE my wife have bargained Sould alineated and Confirmed Unto WILLIAM / BUSH of the Same parish and County a parcell of land Scituate lyinge and beinge uppon y$^{e}$ / Southwest side of Corawake Swamp begining at the mouth of a Swampe Caled the Locker / neare WILLIAM BUSH his howse and soe runing along WILLIAM JOHNSONs line Untill it Come / to RICHARD BOOTHs line and downe the said BOOTHs line to Corawacke Swamp and up the / run of the Said Swamp unto the first station whereof wee do hereby acknowledge and / and [*sic*] Confesse that we have given granted bargained Sould alienated and Confirmed / and doe by these presents for us our heyres Executors administrators for Ever given / granted bargained Sould alienated and Confirmed unto him the Said WILLIAM

**[49]**

WILLIAM BUSH and his heyres Executors administrators or assignes for Ever this land beinge part / of two thousand one hundred and fifty acres which I had by pattent of the right Hon$^{ble}$ HENRY / CHICHLEY in the yeare of our lord 1681 and wee doe by these presents further Covenant and agree / for us our heyres Executors administrators, warrant to Save defend and keepe harmelesse the / said WILLIAM BUSH, his heyres or assignes against any person or persons that Shall or may here / after lay any Claime Right title or intrest to any part of the Said land with all previledges / thereunto as firmely as I have it by pattent as wittnesse whereunto wee have Sett our hands and Seales / this 12$^{th}$ day of January in the yeare of our lord god one thousand Six hundred and ninety

Signed Sealed and delivered
in the presence of
WILLIAM DUCKE
marke
ELINER TTT JOHNSON
her

his marke
ROBERT **RI** JOHNSON Seale
her marke
KATTERIN **KI** JOHNSON Seale

Accknowledged in open Court / held for the Isle of Weight County / aug$^{st}$ the 9$^{th}$. 1692 by ROBERT JOHNSON / and CATHERINE his wife to be theire act / and deed

Test JOHN PITT C$^{l}$ C$^{ur}$

Know all men by these presents that I JOHN ROADS of the Isle of Weight County planter with my wife / ANNE ROADES doe for a Valueable Consideration already by us received and for divers and Sundry other Causes / to us reserved freely give and bequeath Unto RICHARD MATHEWES his heyres Executors or assignes my planta / tion whereon I doe now live togather with all the land that I doe now posses after the decease of me & / my wife ANNE togather with all moveable estate wee shall then be possest with both of us or one $w^{ch}$ / shalbe the longest Surveyvor only wee the above Said JOHN and ANNE ROADES doe reserve to our Selves two / Cowes one Iron pott two pewter dishes one bed to dispose of other waise according as wee shall then thinke / fit to dispose of them further the Said RICHARD MATHEWES is to have the liberty to build and Cleare upon / the Said Land forth with or when he Shall see fitt without any molestation or hinderance by me or my / wife and free from paying any rent or accknowlegement to us or Either of us as in wittnesse whereof wee / have hereunto Set our hands and Seales this $19^{th}$ day of November 1685

Signed Sealed & delivered
in presence of us
WILLIAM **M** MURPHRY
his mark
WILLIAM **M** HOOKS
his marke
THO: OGLETHORPE

JOHN **IR** ROADS Seale
his marke
ANN I\ ROADS Seale
her marke

This above wrighting was proved by the / oaths of $W^{M}$: MURPHRY and $W^{M}$ HOOKS to be / the act and deed of JOHN ROADS & ANNE his / wife this $10^{th}$ of august 1692 in Court and / ordered to be recorded

Test JOHN PITT $C^{l}$ $C^{ur}$

Know all Men by these presents that I ROBERT JOHNSON planter of the lower parish of / the Isle of Weight County doe freely give unto my daughter MARY JOHNSON a parcell of land to her / and her heyres lawfully begotten of her owne body for Ever, the aforesaid land lying and being up / on the north East side of Carrawake Swamp begining upon the Said Swamp at BOOTHs line at the run / of the Said Swamp and soe up the Said BOOTHs line North East to a pine, and Soe along THOMAS HOUL / DERs line the Same Course to a light wood Stump from thence downe a line of marked trees to the / head of a Small branch which runs out of the longe branch and Soe downe the long branch to Corra / wake Swampe soe downe the run of Corrawacke Swamp to BOOTHs line, which land I had by pattent / of $S^{r}$ HENRY CHICHELEY $K^{t}$. deputy Governor and $L^{t}$ Generall of Virginia in the Eight and twentieth / yeare of our Sovereigne lord King Charles the Second his reigne, and if the aforesaid MARY JOHNSON sho / uld depart this world before her husband that now is JAMES JOHNSON then he is not to be molested Soe / long as he lives but after his decease the Children is to have it as wittnesse my hand this fourth day of / august 1692

WILLIAM DUCK

marke
ROBERT **RI** JOHNSON

his

Accknowledged by ROBERT JOHNSON / and KATHERINE his wife in open Court / held for the Isle of Weight County aug^st^ / the 9^th^. 1692 to be theire act and deed
Test JOHN PITT C^l^ C^ur^

Know all men by these presents that I ANNE BREAD hath bargained Sould and delivered unto / ROGER RAWLINS two Cowes named Chera & browne with a Crop Under the right yeare the left / eare hole a blacke Sow & five Shoats & five piggs all of the Same marke. a feather bed a greene rug / and two blankets and a feather boulster & pillow & a flocke bed two Iron pots and pot hookes a tankard / and a pewter pint pot & Cullender a new bedsteed a fryinge pan & paire of pot links & a smothinge / Iron a darke bay horse and a Cartt & a hough harrow all these goods I doe warrant the Sale to be / good

**[50]**
good from any person or persons that may or shall lay any Claime or title to any of the / Same goods or Catles as wittnesse my hand this thirtenth of aprill 1692

Test JOHN THORNEHILL — ANN **n** BREAD
EDWARD **H** MATHEWES — her marke
his marke

To be Entred on the records / at the request of ROGER RAWLINS / aug^st^ the 11^th^ 1692

To all to whom &c. JEFFRA: NICHOLSON Esq: their Ma^ties^ L^t^. Governor &c. Whereas / y^e^ Now Know yee &c. give & grant unto JOHN JOHNSON two hundred & / fifty acres of Land lying in y^e^ Isle of Wight County beginning / at a Marked Pine, a Corner tree, between JAMES BRYAN, & BRIDGMAN / JOYNER, thence by y^e^ s^d^ BRYAN his Line of Markt Trees, North thir= / teen degrees East fifty foure poles to a Markt Pine, then by another / line of the s^d^ BRYANs, North, thirty degrees East, One hundred twenty / & seven poles to a red Oake, then by another line of y^e^ Said BRIANs / North by West, seventy one pole to a Markt Pine, JAMES ALLEN his / corner tree, then along y^e^ s^d^ ALLEN's Line, of Markt trees East / North East, two hundred & thirty poles, to a Markt Pine, then / along another line of y^e^ s^d^ ALLEN, N^o^: N^o^: West, One hundred / & Sixty poles to a White Oake, thence North nine degrees East / four pole & an halfe to a white Oake in WILLIAM MAYO his Line / then along y^e^ s^d^ MAYO his line, South fifty two degrees East / Sixty two pole to a live Oake near a Cypresse, the s^d^ MAYO's corner / tree in the Beaver=Dam=swamp, then downe the Beaver=dam= / swamp, to King Sale swamp, then downe KingSale Swamp, by / various courses to y^e^ Place of beginning. To have & to hold &c / Yeilding & paying &c *ut in alijs* Given under my hand & the / seal of y^e^ Colony the 29^th^ day of Aprill Anno Domi 1692

Exam: p WILLIAM COLE Sec^r^. FFR: NICHOLSON
Recorded p HUGH DAVIS C^l^ C^ur^

Know all Men by these p^r^sents y^t^ I JOHN JOHNSON & MARY my wife / of y^e^ lower pish of the Isle of Wight County, doe for us our heirs / Exec^rs^. & adm^rs^. assigne over into LUKE KENT of y^e^ afores^d^ lower / pish of y^e^ Isle of Wight County his heirs Exec^rs^ adm^rs^ & asignes for ever / all our right, title & interest in y^e^ within Patent, & doe acknowledge / to have reced y^e^ full & valuable consideracon of two thousand & five / hundred pounds of tob^o^: for y^e^ same, as Witnes our hands & seals / this twentieth day of October, Anno Domini 1692

Signed, sealed & ~~dd~~ in p^r^sence of W^M^ KERLE
HENRY **H** WEST

his
JOHN **I** JOHNSON seale
marke & seal
MARY **M** JOHNSON seale
her marke & seal

Accknowledged in Courte this 26^th^. day of X^ber^ 1692 by y^e^ s^d^ JOHN / JOHNSON & MARY his wife to be / their free & Voluntary act and / Deed
Test: HUGH DAVIS C^l^ C^ur^

**[51]**

To all to whom &c. I FFRA: Lord Howard Governor Gen^ll^ &c. Whereas &c / Now know yee &c. give & grant unto JAMES GARDNER two hundred / acres of land scituate on y^e^ heads of the branches of the Western / branch of Nantzemond in y^e^ lower pish of y^e^ Isle of Wight County / beginning at a Pine XTPHER WADEs corner tree, Thence North / sixty degrees east 34 poles to small pine, then N^o^:16 degrees / Westerly 116 poles to a small pine, then N^o^: 25 degrees East / 31 poles to two small saplyn pines, then N^o^: 88 p^o^: to a / small pine in a pocoson, then S^o^: 60 degrees N^o^: 60 p^o^: to / a white Oake by y^e^ edge of the Pocoson, then N^o^: 24 degrees / Westerly 52 p^o^: to a pine in y^e^ s^d^ GARDNER's owne Line / then by his owne Line S^o^: 39 degrees West 86 poles to a / dead Pine in M^r^ COLEMANs line, then by his Line S^o^: 40 p^o^: / to XTPHER WADEs Line, & soe by his Line East 240 p^o^: to y^e^ / first Station. To have & to hold &c yeilding & paying &c *ut / in alijs*, dated y^e^ 20^th^ day of Aprill 1684
Effingham

I JAMES GARDNER of y^e^ lower pish of the Isle of Wight doe assign / over unto WALTER WALTERS of the s^d^ county for myselfe my heirs &c / all my right title & interest to y^e^ within menconed Patent / Excepting a parcell of about 50 acres which I formerly sold / unto ALEXANDER CHESNUTT, as Wittnes my hand & Seal this 10^th^ / day of November 1692

Testes: THO^S^: HILL
GEO: ROCHFORD

y^e^ Marke of
JAMES **X** GARDNER Seale
ELIZ: TTT GARDNER Seale

X$^{ber}$ 26. 1692

This Patent & y$^{e}$ assignem$^{t}$ endorst hereon was this day acknow= / ledged in open Courte by y$^{e}$ subscribed JAMES GARDNER & ELIZ$^{A}$. his / wife to be their free & Voluntary act & Deed

Test: HUGH DAVIS C$^{l}$ C$^{ur}$

Isle of Wight County **December y$^{e}$ 20$^{th}$. 1692**

In p$^{r}$sence of M$^{r}$. JA: BENN one of their Ma$^{ties}$. Justices of / y$^{e}$ peace of this County. I have reced of Col$^{o}$. JN$^{O}$. PITT the / Records, both old, & now, belonging to his County, amounting to / twenty foure bookes in number, as alsoe y$^{e}$ last booke of Orders, / y$^{e}$ Acts of Assembly imprinted, & other bonds, docquets, peticons, / & old writings belonging to y$^{e}$ Clerkes Office in this County. I say / reced ꝑ me / X$^{ber}$ y$^{e}$ 26$^{th}$ 1692.

JAMES BENN ackn$^{o}$'. in Courte by y$^{e}$ s$^{d}$ HUGH DAVIS

HUGH DAVIS C$^{l}$ C$^{ur}$

**[52]**

Know all men by these presents, that I WILLIAM GODDIN of the Isle of / Wight County in Virg$^{a}$. planter, for a valuable consideration in hand reced / doe hereby bargaine, sell, alien & make over unto JOHN GRIFFINN of the / same County planter, two hundred acres of land, being ꝑte of foure hun= / ered acres of land purchased by me y$^{e}$ s$^{d}$ WILLIAM of ANTHONY FFULGHAM / & parte of a Patent for a divident of land granted to y$^{e}$ s$^{d}$ FFULGHAM & / M$^{r}$. W$^{M}$. BRESSIE dated y$^{e}$ 12$^{th}$ of July 1665, the s$^{d}$ two hundred acres / of Land lying between y$^{e}$ land, y$^{t}$ I now doe live on, & reserve for myselfe / & y$^{e}$ land belonging to JOHN WHEATLEY, bounded in more express termes / as followeth (viz$^{t}$) beginning at a red oake being THOMAS WHITLEY / corner tree, & running along y$^{e}$ head Line to a Pine, thence downe / to the swamp to a marked ash, & up y$^{e}$ s$^{d}$ Swamp to y$^{e}$ s$^{d}$ WHITLEY's / line, & then along y$^{e}$ s$^{d}$ Line to y$^{e}$ place where it first began. / To have & to hold y$^{e}$ s$^{d}$ two hundred acres of land (within y$^{e}$ / bounds afores$^{d}$) together with all p$^{r}$vildeges, hereditaments and / appurtences thereunto belonging, to him y$^{e}$ s$^{d}$ JOHN GRIFFIN & to / His heirs & assignes forever; And y$^{e}$ s$^{d}$ WILLIAM doth covenant and / agree to & with the s$^{d}$ JOHN GRIFFIN, that He y$^{e}$ s$^{d}$ JOHN GRIFFIN / & his heirs or assignes, shall for ever peaceably & quietyly hold & / enjoy y$^{e}$ s$^{d}$ Land & appurtenances, And y$^{t}$ He y$^{e}$ s$^{d}$ WILLIAM will / for ever warrant & defend y$^{e}$ same from y$^{e}$ lawfull claime of any / person or persons whatsoever, Wittnes his hand & seal this 26$^{th}$. day of / x$^{ber}$ Anno Domini 1692. the bounds herein menconed being according / to be pounds layd out by M$^{r}$. TH$^{O}$: GILES & M$^{r}$. JN$^{O}$. GILES.

Signed sealed & del: in p$^{r}$sence of all us y$^{e}$ marke ∤

THO: HILL. HEN: APPLEWHAITE of W$^{M}$. GODWIN

HEN: APPLEWHAITE jun$^{r}$.

x^ber^ y^e^ 26^th^ 1692 / Ackn°. in Courte by y^e^ s^d^ W^M^ GODWIN to be his act & Deed. Test HDAVIS CC

THO: HARRIS aged 25 years sworne sayth, That being at home Capt APPLEWHAITE comeing / there about busines unknown to me. I Coming in heard Cap^t^ APPLEWHAITE bed & / ROB^T^. STURDY hold his tongue for He would not concerne himselfe with Him, but / in words y^e^ Cap^t^. call'd ROB^T^ STURDY, foole, & STURDY made answear y^t^ He was / not such a foole but He made him a good plantacon, y^e^ Cap^t^ replyed y^t^ if He / did He payd him for it, & as y^e^ Cap^t^ was going ROB^T^ STURDY followed Him out & told / Him y^t^ He valued noe more then a farte of his arse, but GOODY STURDY sayd / somthing to y^e^ Cap^t^ but what I can't tell, & y^e^ Capt call'd Her black mouth'd Slutt / & GOODY STURDY told him, y^t^ she never hid y^e^ Key under y^e^ Dore. & furth^r^. sayth not THO: **T.H.** HARRIS
[ ] oct 20^th^ 1692 Test HD Cs

**[53]**

Whereas I RICHARD BOOTH of the Isle of Wight County upon the 20^th^ of / aprill 1680 obtained a Patent for five hundred & fifty acres of land / lying & being on y^e^ S°: side of the branch & near y^e^ head of Corawach / Swamp in lower ꝑish of Isle of Wight County, bounded as by the s^d^ Patent / doth more fully Appear, & upon y^e^ 8^th^ day of November 1681 I the said / RICHARD BOOTH having reced a Valuable consideration in hand pay & to me / by THOMAS MAN late of the s^d^ County of Isle of Wight did by deed under / my hand & seal make over all my right title & interest of the afores^d^ / Land to y^e^ afores^d^ THO: MAND [*sic, et passim*] & his wife ELIZABETH in ꝑsence of JOHN / ROGERS & CHARLES MAN evidenccs to y^e^ s^d^ Deed of Sale, as by y^e^ s^d^ Deed / will more fully appeare, & upon y^e^ 9^th^ of November 1681 I did acknow= / ledge y^e^ aforesaid Deed in Isle of Wight County Courte as by y^e^ records / of y^e^ s^d^ County will more fully appear, & whereas in y^e^ afores^d^ Deed / by y^e^ neglect or ignorance of y^e^ writer of thereof it was not inserted / in y^e^ following words (Viz^t^) y^t^ I y^e^ abovenamed RICHARD BOOTH did / from me & my heirs & all y^t^ did or hereafter might or Should ꝑtend / interest to me, make over all my right, title, & interest of y^e^ afores^d^ / five hundred & sixty acres of Land conteyned in y^e^ afores^d^ patent / with all rights & priviledges conteyned in the s^d^ Patent to the s^d^ / THO: MAND & ELIZABETH his wife & their heires for over, for y^e^ reason / aboves^d^ THOMAS MAND brought his action to Isle of Wight County / Courte ag^st^ me y^e^ s^d^ RICHARD BOOTH desiring y^t^ I y^e^ s^d^ BOOTH / might be ordered to make a good valuable & sufficient deed of Sale / of y^e^ afores^d^ Land to him y^e^ s^d^ THO: MAN & his heires for ever / according to y^e^ true intent & meaning of y^e^ agreem^t^ formerly made / as is above expressed betwixt me y^e^ s^d^ RICHARD BOOTH & THO: MAN / Sen^r^. deced, and it appearing by testimony of several evidences & the / Judgm^t^ of y^e^ Isle of Wight Courte, y^t^ it was the right of the said / THOMAS MAN Jun^r^ in right of his ffather THO: MAN Sen^r^ to have a good / & sufficient deed of Sale of the afores^d^ Land made & acknowledged / by me y^e^ s^d^ RICHARD BOOTH from me, & my heirs for ever, to the s^d^ THO: / MAN jun^r^ y^e^ son & heir of THO: MAN sen^r^ his heires & assignes for ever / as by order of y^e^ s^d^ Courte bearing date August y^e^ 10^th^ 1691 will more / fully appear, and I y^e^ s^d^ RICHARD BOOTH being well satisfyed in my / Mind & Conscience of y^e^ Justices of y^e^ Judgem^t^ of y^e^ Isle of Wight / Courte relating to y^e^ afores^d^ order, & y^t^ according to y^e^ afores^d^ Order / I ought to make an absolute deed in ffee simple of y^e^ afores^d^ Land / conteyned in y^e^ afores^d^ Patent to the afores^d^ THO: MAN his heires & / assignes for ever, Therefore, & for y^e^ reasons above expressed I the s^d^ / RICHARD BOOTH doe by these p^r^sents from me & my heirs, & all y^t^ can / or may pretend interest thereto in or from me transferr & make over / all my right title & interest of y^e^ 'fores^d^ Land conteyned in the fores^d^ / Patent

**[54]**

Patent to y^e^ afores^d^ THOMAS MAN son & Heir of THOMAS MAN sen^r^. / his heirs & assignes for ever, with all rights & privildges granted / to me by y^e^ fores^d^ Patent, alwaies excepting what right ELIZABETH / the wife of THOMAS MAN sen^r^. deced may pretend to by my former / Deed of Sale, and I y^e^ s^d^ RICHARD BOOTH doe further oblige myselfe / & my heirs at any tyme hereafter within the terme & tyme of seaven / yeares after y^e^ date hereof to signe, seale, & in Courte acknowledge / any other Deed of Sale y^e^ s^d^ THOMAS MAN shall produce to me, / which by his learned Councill in y^e^ Law he shall be advised to / draw for his, his heires or assignes, his, or their better security. And / I the said RICHARD BOOTH doe also oblige myselfe, y^t^ I & my / now wife [--] shall in open Courte in Isle of Wight at any tyme / wee shall be desired thereto to acknowledge y^e^ above written, & / on y^e^ other side to the before named THOMAS MAN y^e^ Son & heir / of THO: MAN deced, as Witnes our hands & seals this 9^th^ day of / ffeburary 169$^2/_3$

Signed sealed & delivered in prsence of us JOHN DAVIS
JOHN CAHAN

RICHARD **RB** BOOTH
his Marke ------- Seale

ffeb^r^: y^e^ 9^th^ 1692 / acknowledged in open Courte by y^e^ said RICHARD / BOOTH to be his act, & Deed.

Test HUGH DAVIS C^l^ C^ur^

To all Christian People to whom this present deed shall come, wee / Major THO: TABERER & Col: ARTHUR SMITH of y^e^ Isle of Wight Com: / send greeting,Whereas by order of Courte bearing date ffebruary / the 10^th^ 169$^1/_2$ Wee the said THOMAS TABERER & ARTHUR SMITH were / ordered & apppointed to be ffeoffees in trust for y^e^ disposing & passing / of Deeds for y^e^ Towne land according as is prescribed in y^e^ Act of / assembly begun at James City y^e^ 16^th^. day of Aprill anno Dom: / 1691 Now know yee, y^t^ wee y^e^ s^d^ aboves^d^ THO: TABERER & / ARTHUR SMITH for y^e^ Consideracon of One hundred sixty seven / pounds of tob^o^: & a halfe & Casq: by us already recited ffrate / for two lotts, doe for & in y^e^ behalfe of y^e^ courte & County give / grant, alien, sell, & confirme, & by these p^r^sents doe give, grant, / alien, sell & confirme unto JN$^{O}$. PITT sen$^{r}$. of y$^{e}$ s$^{d}$ County his / heirs Exec$^{rs}$. adm$^{rs}$. & assignes for ever, two halfe acres of Land / scituate, lying, & being in y$^{e}$ Towne of Newporte knowne / by

**[55]**

by y$^{e}$ Name of the twenty fifty & twenty sixth Lotts bounded as / followeth, beginning at a Stake in y$^{e}$ Out boundes y$^{t}$ divedes them / from N$^{o}$. 27 Thence East fowre degrees Northerly sixteen pole one / tenth to y$^{e}$ high Street, & then by y$^{e}$ street North, foure degrees / Easterly nine pole seven tenths to y$^{e}$ Corner by y$^{e}$ ffront=street / & soe by y$^{t}$ street Next foure degrees Southerly sixteen pole, & / very near five tenths to a stake in y$^{e}$ out bounds, & soe by the / Out bounds to y$^{e}$ place where it began, warranting y$^{e}$ sale of / y$^{e}$ s$^{d}$ two halfe acres of Land to be good lawfull & authentic / & firme in Law to the said JOHN PITT his heirs Exec$^{rs}$ adm$^{rs}$ or / assignes for ever, in as large & ample manner as it is made / unto us, the s$^{d}$ JN$^{O}$. PITT performing according to y$^{e}$ s$^{d}$ act of / asembly, otherwise it may & shall be lawfull for any other / person, to make choice of y$^{e}$ s$^{d}$ Lotts, or two halfe acres, and / build thereon, In Wittnesse hereof Wee have hereunto sett / our hands & seals this 31 day of December 1692

THO: TABERER seale
ARTH: SMITH seale

ffebruary y$^{e}$ 9$^{th}$. 1692 / Acknowledged in open Courte, by y$^{e}$ s$^{d}$ Coll ARTHUR SMITH / one of hte ffeoffees in trust, to be his act & Deed

Test: HUGH DAVIS C$^{l}$ C$^{ur}$

Virg$^{a}$: ffebruary y$^{e}$ 9$^{th}$ day 169$^{2}/_{3}$

ARTHUR SMITH Sen$^{r}$. aged fifty five, or thereabouts, of the Isle of / Wight County, living on Pagan Creeke, being examined & sworne / sayth as followeth. That One M$^{r}$. SAM$^{LL}$ BUCKNELL being parte owner / & supra Cargoe of y$^{e}$ Brigantine *Mary & Dorothy*, whereof is Master / EDMUND FFEBERYEAR as he told me being brought to my house the second / day this instant very ill, & after He had been there, two, or three / days, He desires me to send for M$^{r}$. FFEBERYEAR, Master of y$^{e}$ afores$^{d}$ / Brigantine, which I did, & when the afores$^{d}$ FFEBERYEAR came to / Him, & had a small discourse with him, & How He did, & seemingly / to me in perfect minde & memory. I heard him say, & understood / by his words, that it was his desire, y$^{t}$ every body should be satisfyed / y$^{t}$ He was obliged to, & that He gave to M$^{r}$. FFEBERYEAR his parte of y$^{e}$ / Venture y$^{t}$ was in y$^{e}$ Vessell, & One of his gunns, & y$^{e}$ other gun to / his son EDMUND FFEBERYEAR, & y$^{t}$ all y$^{e}$ Vessells company should have / something to remember Him, & y$^{t}$ He was willing that this should be / wrote

**[56]**

ffebruary y$^{e}$ 9$^{th}$. 1692

Wrote, but M$^{r}$. FFEBERYEAR asked him whether He would revoake his / Will in New England & He sayd, noe, for this was a Deed of gift, and He / desired FFEBERYEAR y$^{t}$

an Hundred pounds should be sent to His ffreinds / in England, & y$^{t}$ He should not see y$^{e}$ Woman Wrongd, this being the / fourth day of ffebruary, & He dyed y$^{e}$ sixth in y$^{e}$ night

*Juratur in Curiā nono die* & further sayth not
*ffebruarij* anno 1692 ARTH: SMITH sen$^{r}$.
Test HUGH DAVIS C$^{l}$C$^{ur}$

ARTHUR SMITH Jun$^{r}$. aged about 23 yeares old, or thereabouts being / examined & sworne sayth, as followeth / That y$^{e}$ same He heard as afores$^{d}$, Only y$^{t}$ He would have all y$^{e}$ Vessells / Comp$^{a}$. have something, & further I heard M$^{r}$. FFEBERYEAR aske him, what / He meant by his Venture, & He sayd, y$^{t}$ it was that which was be= / tween them. & further sayth not

*Juratur in Curiā, nono die* ARTHUR SMITH jun$^{r}$.
ffebruary anno 1692
Test HUGH DAVIS C$^{l}$C$^{ur}$

The Deposition of JACOB BARNES aged between forty three & foure / sayth That being at y$^{e}$ house of M$^{r}$. W$^{M}$. SMITH sen$^{r}$. upon y$^{e}$ 26$^{th}$. / day of December last, y$^{t}$ two of M$^{r}$. STYLES his men named SAM: LEYBURN / & CHA: EVANS did there say y$^{t}$ M$^{r}$. RICHD WILKINSON sen$^{r}$. was a going to / Courte, & y$^{t}$ y$^{e}$ s$^{d}$ WILKINSON had a bag of tob$^{o}$: stalke, did intend to / carey y$^{m}$. to Courte in order to prove y$^{t}$. Col. JN$^{O}$. PITT did make second Crops of / tob$^{o}$: & after y$^{e}$ above mentioned two men were gone, M$^{r}$. STYLES himselfe / did come to y$^{e}$ same house, & did there say to y$^{e}$ Depon$^{t}$ y$^{e}$ same words / & y$^{e}$ s$^{d}$ STYLES did further declare y$^{t}$ y$^{e}$ s$^{d}$ WILKINSON has carryed / y$^{e}$ s$^{d}$ Stalkes to Courte, if He had not disswaded him from soe doing / & further sayth no.

Jur: in Cur: nono die ffebruary JACOB BARNES
anno 1692 Test: HD C$^{l}$

The Deposicion of W$^{M}$. SMITH & MARY his wife He being aged 58 or thereabout / & she thereabout sayth, y$^{t}$ two of M$^{r}$. STYLES his men coming to yo$^{r}$. / depon$^{ts}$ house on y$^{e}$ 26$^{th}$. day of x$^{ber}$ these two men named SAM: / LEYBURNE & CHARLES EVANS, they did then & there declare in our hea= / ring y$^{t}$ M$^{r}$. RICHD WILKINSON sen$^{r}$. was going to Courte, & y$^{e}$ s$^{d}$ WILKINSON / had a bag of tob$^{o}$: stalkes & intended to carry y$^{m}$ to Courte in order / to

**[57]**

ffebruary y$^{e}$ 9$^{th}$. 1692

to prove y$^{t}$. L$^{t}$. Col. JN$^{O}$. PITT did make second Cropps of tob$^{o}$: / & further sayth not

Jur: in Cur: 9$^{o}$. die ffebruary WILL SMITH
1692 Test: HDAVIS C$^{l}$

The Deposition of M$^{rs}$ MARY SMITH aged 58 years or thereabouts / Sayth that RICHARD WILKINSON Coming to yo$^{r}$. Depon$^{ts}$ house / yo$^{r}$ Depon$^{t}$ did say to y$^{e}$ s$^{d}$.

WILKINSON y[t] she heard y[t] He had / inform'd ag[st] Col. PITT & y[t] yo[r] depon[t] did tell Him, y[t] she woud / not have done such a thing for never soe much, the s[d] WILL= / KINSON made answear y[t] all advantages were good against / an enemy, as Majo[r]. ALLEN says, & further sayth not

Jur in Cur nono die ffeb[r] 1692
Test HDC[l]

her
MARY M SMITH
signe

The Deposition of JN[O]. LUCKE aged about twenty two or there ab[ts] / doth declare y[t] He saw second upon Col JN[O]. PITT's plantation / & y[t] they had been turned out, & that they were Cutt downe.

Jan y[e] 2[d] 1692 sworne & examined before me, Col. JN[O]. PITT being p[r]sent
JN[O]. GOODRICH

JOHN LUCKE
Recorded p HD C[l]

The Deposition of RICHARD WILKINSON jun[r]. aged 28 yeares or / thereabouts says, y[t] He did see second Cropps of tob[o]: that they / were turned out, upon Col JN[O]. PITTs plantacon & were topt & / succored & Cutt downe & gon. I did see them in two several / peices, & three several tymes, & further says not.

Jan: y[e] 2[d] 1692 sworne & examined before, Col JN[O]. PITT being p[r]sent
JN[O]. GOODRICH

RICH WILKINSON jun[r].
Recorded p HD C[l]

The Deposition of RICHARD HAMPTON in y[e] difference betwixt HUGH CAMP= / BELL pl[t] & WILLIAM CARVER adm[r] of y[e] estate of JN[O]. MOORE deced def[t]. sheweth / That yo[r]. depon[t] was at y[e] house of JN[O]. CAMPBELL when y[e] s[d] JN[O]. MOORE / came there to speake with HUGH CAMPBELL who was there a lodger / it being soon in y[e] Morning, & with him there was one who called him= / selfe GEORGE LOVEDAY, & after the said CAMPBELL had veiwed several / papers, which y[e] s[d] CAMPBELL delivered to y[e] s[d] LOVEDAY, & y[e] s[d] LOVEDAY / & MOORE did then signe, seal, & deliver an obligation to y[e] s[d] CAMPBELL, to / which y[e] Depon[t] was an evidence, the s[d] MOORE was before to y[e] Depon[t]. / well knowne, & to what yo[r]. Depon[t] could observe y[e] s[d] MOORE was sober / and as much in his right minde as ever He knew Him before, neither did y[e] s[d] CAMPBELL give Him any drinke to y[e] best of his remembrance / till

**[58]**

ffebruary y[e] 9[th]. 1692

till they had ended their busines, & y[e] afores[d] bond was signed & sealed / & delivered after which y[e] s[d] CAMPBELL sent me for a single bottle of / drinke, y[e] s[d] CAMBELL having none in y[e] house, they asking if he y[e] s[d] / CAMPBELL would not make them drinke, then y[e] s[d] MOORE & LOVDAY / desires y[e] s[d] CAMPBELL to draw some paper betwixt them which the / s[d] CAMPBELL did when yo[r] Depon[t] went for y[e] bottle of

Drinke, yo[r]. / Depon[t] can farther declare y[t] he never knew y[e] s[d] CAMPBELL desire / either them or any else to take any drinke to doe them hurte. / This is what yo[r] Depon[t]. doth & will declare on his solemn oath. / & further sayth not.

Jur in Cur: RICHARD HAMPTON

Recorded p HDAVIS C[l]

JN[O]. PERMENTO one of y[e] grand jury informes ag[st] W[M]. JOLLEY for swearing / *Gods sounds*, JN[O]. LOWTER for swearing *Gods blood*, J[A]: JOLLEY for / bargaining & giving earnest on y[e] Saboth day, JN[O]. BUNKLEY for swearing / *Gods wounds*. JN[O]. SOJOURNER one of y[e] Grand Jury informs ag[st]. / JN[O]. COLLINS jun[r]. for fetching two bores from y[e] plantacon of W[M] / BALDWIN & carryed them to his ffathers plantacon & there did cutt / & marke the s[d] boars by his owne Confession.

Informacon ag[st] EDW[D] CHITTEE for Cropping y[e] left ear of a boar upon / his owne plantacon y[t] he doth owne to be none of his owne, & sayd / y[e] right owner may take him He sayd He cutt it off in roguery / RICH[D] WILKINSON sen[r]. p[r]sents Col JN[O]. PITT for making seconds

Recorded p HD C[l] p me JN[O]. SKELTON foreman

To all to whom &c. I FFRANCIS Lord Howard Baron of Effingham His Ma[ties] L[t]. / & Governor Gen[ll] &c. Whereas &c. now know yee &c give & grant unto / WILLIAM BALDWIN sixty seaven acres of land lying in y[e] upper parrish of y[e] / Isle of Wight County, beginning at a red Oake in JN[O]. HARRIS's line, and / running along y[e] s[d] HARRIS's Line South forty eight degrees & an halfe / West Sixty two pole, then South forty two degrees West, One hundred and / nine pole to a red Oake, thence North nineteen degrees east one hundred / thirty & three pole to a Dogwood, thence South east fifty two pole to y[e] place / of beginning To have & to hold &c. Yeilding & paying &c *ut in alijs* Given / under my hand & y[e] seale of y[e] Colony this 20[th] day of 8[ber]. Anno 1688

EFFINGHAM / turne

**[59]**

**Aprill y[e] 10[th] 1693**

I WILLIAM BALDWIN doe with y[e] Consent of my Wife ELIZABETH BALDWIN / assigne over all my right title & interest of this Patent, according as / it is surveyed, & markt by Capt SWAN unto JOHN CARROLL jun[r] and / his heirs for Ever, As Wittnesse our hands & seals this 9[th]. day of / Aprill 1693 having already received a valuable consideracon / for y[e] same.

Sealed signed & delivered in the p[r]sence of us
ROGER STEVENS
WILLIAM EXUM jun[r].

his
WILLIAM MB BALDWIN seal
Marke
ELIZABETH E BALDWIN seale
her marke

**Aprill y[e] 10[th] 1693**

Acknowledged in open Courte by y[e] s[d] WILLIAM / BALDWIN & ELIZABETH his wife to be their free & / voluntary act & Deed

Test HUGH DAVIS C[l]

I JOHN PORTIS doe give unto my Eldest son JOHN PORTIS a parcell / of Land lying & being in y[e] lower parrish of the Isle of Wight / County & bounded as followeth beginning at an Oake at y[e] head / of y[e] branch running westerly to a Line of Marked trees of THO: / TOOKES, & soe along THO: TOOKES Line Southerly, & soe to a marked / white Oake in ANTHONY MATHEWES's Line, which is my Corner tree & / then downe y[t] Line of now marked trees Northerly, & soe downe / the branch to y[e] maine swamp, & soe y[e] maine swamp to a / branch, & soe up y[t] branch to y[e] first station, this parcell of Land / I doe give unto my son JOHN PORTIS & to his heires for ever as my / free deed & gift, & I doe oblige myselfe to acknowledg this to be / my Voluntary free act & Deed at y[e] next Courte held for y[e] Isle of / Wight County, as Wittnesse my hand & seale this sixth day of aprill / 1693

Subnscribed in y[e] p[r]sence of us whose names are here under written

JN[O]. + BELL
his marke

JN[O]. **p** PRIME
his marke

EDM: PRIME

JOHN **P** PORTIS
his hand
and O seale

Aprill y[e] 10[th] 1693 / acknowledged in Courte by y[e] subscribed / JOHN PORTIS to be his act & deed

Test" HUGH DAVIS C[l]C[ur]

**[60]**

JN[O]. WILLIAMS Aged 18 yeares or thereabouts Sworne Sayth / That about the Last of August last, this depon[t] was at / worke on W[M]. WEST Mill dam, & then & there I did heare the / S[d] WEST Say, that he would Cutt his Mill dam, & Carry away / JAMES TULLAGHs mill dam in this County & further saith not

Sworne in Courte this 11 of Aprill 1693 HD C[l]

JN[O]. WILLIAMS

FFRANCIS CURTIS aged 30 yeares, or thereabouts, Sworne Saith / That about the beginning of X[ber] Last, this depon[t], was at worke / at, or near W[M]. WEST Mill, and divers tymes, whiles this depon[t] / was there at worke, to this depon[ts]. knowledge: the s[d]. W[M]. WEST & / his Son WILLIAM, have drawen up y[e] floodgates of y[e] s[d]. Mill dam / at very unreasonable tyme in y[e] Night & further Saith not

Recorded p HD C[l]

FFRA: **R** CURTIS

his marke

THO^S^. FFITZGERRARD aged twenty yeares or thereabouts Sworne / Saith. That this Last Winter, this Depon^t^. did live with M^r^: W^M^ / WEST, a Keeper of a Mill, in y^e^ Isle of Wight County, & y^e^ depon^t^ / hath Knowne that y^e^ s^d^. WEST, hath drawne up his Gates in divers / raines, and let y^e^ water run out of his Dam without giving notice / to M^r^ JAMES TULLAGH, and then he would shutt downe his gates / and keepe all y^e^ water up not Suffering the Naturall streame to / Run and further saith not
Swore in Court Aprill y^e^ 11^th^. 1693 THO: FFITZGERRARD
Test HD C^l^

Isle of Wight County CHARLES DIRHAM aged 38 yeares or thereabouts / Sworne Saith, That all this Last Summer WILL: WEST y^e^ Keeper / of a Mill in this County, hath continually kept y^e^ water in his Mill / Dam, to y^e^ height that his dam water hath drowned this depon^ts^ / Spring & other Springs in y^e^ adjacent Neighbourhood, which Springs / Lye a Sufficient distance from y^e^ customary verge of y^e^ Mill water / m^r^ke, but y^e^ s^d^ WEST hath this trespassed upon y^e^ Neighbourhood / by a continuall raising his Dam. and further Saith not

his
CHA: + DURHAM
m^r^ke

THO: BROWNE 34 yeares old deposeth / The very Same as above Express
Recorded HD C^l^ THO: **B** BROWNE

**[61]**

JN^O^. STREETE aged 41 yeares or there abouts Sworne Sayth that about / the 9^th^. of 7^ber^ Last being a dry Seasons this depon^t^ and ROBERT SCOTT / was a worke on M^r^ J^A^: TULLAGHs Mill wheele, and Just before / this depon^t^ and y^e^ s^d^. SCHOTT [*sic*], went to breake fast at y^e^ dwelling howse / being a Considerable distance from y^e^ s^d^ Mill, the water in y^e^ said / TULLAGHs Mill dam was very low, but when this depon^t^. and the s^d^. / SCOTT Returned to their S^d^. worke, the water in the S^d^. dam was / So high that this depon^t^. and the S^d^. SCOTT had much adoe to gett up / y^e^ gates of y^e^ S^d^. TULLAGHs Mill dame, to p^r^vent y^e^ dam from / being carryed away or broaken, which this depon^t^, does verily / believe was occasioned by W^M^. WEST y^e^ owner of a Grist Mill / above the s^d^. TULLAGHs Mill, who drew up his gates in y^t^ Juncture of / tyme without giving any notice thereof and further Saith not JN^O^: **J** STREET
Sworne in Court Aprill y^e^ 11^th^. 1693 his Signe

TRUSTRUM HILLMOTH aged 30 yeares or there abouts, Sworne Sayth / That this depon^t^. did keepe a Grist Mill belonging to M^r^. JAMES / TULLAGH of y^e^ Isle of Wight County from August Last till Xmas / last, within which tyme y^e^ depon^t^. was very Sensible that M^r^ / WILL: WEST the owner of a Mill Standing a little above the s^d^.

TULLAGHs / Mill did on a Sudden open his floodgates, or cause the Same to be / opened, without giving any Notice thereof, by which unexpected / Surprise, the s^d^. TULLAGH hath bine in greate dainger to Loose his / Mill dam, or receive very considerable damage thereby, Unlesse / the same had been after p^r^vented, by watching and vising [*sic*] in the night Season, and more pticularly one y^e^ 15^th^. of august Last in / The Night (without any notice given) the s^d^. WILL: WESTs dam / was cutt & the water poured downe Soe forcibly upon y^e^ s^d^. TULLAGHs / Dam, y^t^ y^e^ Strength thereof broake y^e^ s^d^ TULLAGHs Mill dam, spite / of all assistance to p^r^vent it (y^e^ cutting of which dam was done / by WILL WEST Jun^r^ as he confest to this depon^t^. and on the 14^th^. of ffb^r^y / Last (without notice given) the S^d^. WEST or his order, lett goe his / water out of his Mill dame, in Such a Measure, y^t^ it had Like to have / carryed away the s^d^. TULLAGHs mill dam and Mill house too, the / Cells being thereby removed out of place, and on the 14^th^. of M^r^ch / last y^e^ s^d^. WEST Did the same action as afore Exprest, by which he / blew up S^d^. WEST Comon Practice to Stop y^e^ Water in a dry Season / a weeke together & then let it goe againe and Stop it againe in / Like nature and further Saith not

Sworne in Court Aprill y^e^ 11^th^. 1693 TRUST: **C** HILLMOTH
Test HC C^l^ his M^r^ke

**[62]**

JOHN GRIFFIN aged 23 yeares or thereabouts Sworne Sayth / the very Same as is above declared & further Sayeth not

JOHN **I** GRIFFIN
Sworne in Court Aprill the 11^th^. 1693 his marke

DENNIS WILLIAMS aged 26 yeares or thereabouts Sworne Saith / about 5 or 6 weekes ago y^e^ deponent met THOMAS ALTMAN / looking of his Colt and Enquires of me If I saw any of them and y^e^ / deponent made him Answer in y^e^ Mash, and ALTMAN S^d^. If he met / that Rogue driving his Cattle he will Lick his back and further Saith not

Sworne in Court Aprill y^e^ 11^th^. 1693 DENNIS **DW** WILLIAMS
Test HD C^l^ his m^r^ke

JOHN ALTMAN Aged 30 yeares or there abouts Sworne Sayth / that I was one Sunday Morning at y^e^ howse of JAMES BAGNALL / & the s^d^: BAGNALL bid y^e^ depon^t^. take notice, he is driving his / cattle a crose my pastor, meaning THO: ALTMAN & further Saith not JOHN ALTMAN

Sworne in Court Aprill y^e^ 11^th^. 1693
Test HC C^l^

JOHN PARKER aged 27 yeares or thereabouts Sworne Saith / about a yeare ago did See THO: ALTMAN and his dog about 100 yards / from the S^d^. ALTMANs owne howse in y^e^ pastor did throw downe 2 or 3 / tymes a hog y^t^ I did Suppose to be JA:

BAGNALLs, and did with a Stick / pocke towards the Said hog and the hog did rise & further Saith not JN$^{O}$. **IP** PARKER
Sworne in Court aprill y$^{e}$ 11$^{th}$: 1693 his m$^{r}$ke
Terst HC C$^{l}$

MARY PARKER aged 21 yeares or thereabouts Sworne Saith / about 2 months ago I see THO: ALTMAN or his wife follow Cattel / up the Lane & JAMES BAGNALL Said Luck, Luck he drives his Cattel / through my pastor and further saith not
MARY PARKER

March y$^{e}$ 11$^{th}$. 169$^{2}/_{3}$
HUGH CAMPBELL y$^{e}$ action y$^{t}$ is now depending at Isle of Wight County / Court is against JOHN PORTEOUS, if he consent to pay four hundred / pownds of tobacho I desire y$^{e}$ may Except of y$^{e}$ Same and this for / advise from ye real freind
THO: TAYLER

Recorded ꝑ HD C$^{l}$

**[63]**

To all Christian People to whome this p$^{r}$sent writing of Award / Indented shall come, JAMES BENN and JOHN GILES both of y$^{e}$ Isle / of Wight County, Sendeth Greeting in o$^{r}$ Lord God Everlasting / whereas, Divers Questions, Controversies wranglings have / bene had, moved and debated, between GEORGE WRIGHT of th'one / ꝑty, and TH$^{O}$: WRIGHT of the other party bothe of y$^{e}$ afores$^{d}$. County / for and concerning their part and Share of their Land, whereon / they doe now dwell, for the appraseing whereof, Eighter of y$^{e}$ s$^{d}$. / ꝑtyes have Elected and Chusen us, the s$^{d}$. JA: BENN & JN$^{O}$: GILES / To be arbitrators indifferent Betweene them, and to that end / have bound them selves this day Either to other, by obligation / in the Sume of 100 pound Sterling to Stand to and abide the / award, arbitrem$^{t}$. and Judgem$^{t}$. of us, the s$^{d}$. JA: BENN & JN$^{O}$: GILES / touching y$^{e}$ ꝑmises, now know yee, that we JA: BENN / & JN$^{O}$: GILES, taking upon us the Charge of y$^{e}$ s$^{d}$. award and / minding y$^{t}$ a finall end, and agreem$^{t}$. Shall be had and continued / from thence forth, Betweene the s$^{d}$. ꝑtyes touching y$^{e}$ ꝑmises / doe make and declare this or award in manner and forme / following, That is to say, that wee the s$^{d}$. JA: BENN and JN$^{O}$: GILES doe / Award that y$^{e}$ valley y$^{t}$ Lyeth betweene the s$^{d}$. GEORGE WRIGHTs / and y$^{e}$ s$^{d}$. TH$^{O}$: WRIGHTs howses, beheld and reputed the bounds / between them y$^{e}$ s$^{d}$. GEORGE WRIGHT and y$^{e}$ s$^{d}$. TH$^{O}$: WRIGHT, and Soe / running up y$^{e}$ s$^{d}$. valley, unto a m$^{r}$ked pine by us m$^{r}$ked thence along / a line of m$^{r}$ked trees likewise m$^{r}$ked by us, y$^{e}$ s$^{d}$. / JA: BENN, and JN$^{O}$: GILES, which line Runneth East halfe a point to y$^{e}$ North / untill it doth meete with Mr. JN$^{O}$: CLARKEs line, and that y$^{e}$ s$^{d}$. JAMES / BENN and y$^{e}$ s$^{d}$. JN$^{O}$: GILES, doe Award y$^{t}$ y$^{e}$ s$^{d}$. line / of m$^{r}$ked trees, be ꝑpetua$^{ll}$ bounds betweene the s$^{d}$. GEORGE / WRIGHT, and the s$^{d}$. TH$^{O}$: WRIGHT and theire Heir$^{s}$: for Ever, in / Confirmation of y$^{e}$ s$^{d}$. Award, wee the said

JAMES BENN and the / s$^{d}$. JN$^{O}$: GILES have hereunto Sett o$^{r}$ hands and Seales this / 25$^{th}$: day of Jan$^{r}$y 169$^{2}$/$_{3}$

JA: BENN Seale
JN$^{O}$: GILES Seale

Aprill y$^{e}$ 10$^{th}$ 1693 / ackno' in Courte by y$^{e}$ subscribers, & ordered to be / recorded Test: HUGH DAVIS, C$^{l}$ C$^{ur}$

**[64]**

Know all men by theise p$^{r}$sents, that I WILLIAM BODDYE of the Isle / of Wight County in Virginia planter, for a Valuable Consideration / to me to be paid, by NICHO: CASEY of y$^{e}$ afores$^{d}$ County, have bargained / & Sold and Doe hereby for me my Heir$^{rs}$ Exec$^{rs}$ & Adm$^{rs}$: forever bargaine Sell / & deliver in fee of and confirm unto y$^{e}$ s$^{d}$. NICHO: CASEY and to his heir$^{rs}$: / and assignes for ever, A sertaine peace or ꝑcell of Land Conteining / one hundred eighty Acres More or lesse the s$^{d}$. ꝑcell of Land Lyeing ꝑ$^{t}$ of it / A plantation Scituate on the Northeast side of y$^{e}$ Sypress Swamp in / the fores$^{d}$. County, together with Some woodland ground Joyning there / unto, and alsoe all y$^{e}$ Groweing fencing Orchards old feild Joyning to y$^{e}$ / S$^{d}$. plantation, and this fores$^{d}$. plantation, old feild and Wood Land ground / is bounded thus. It begineth at a m$^{r}$ked whiteoak tree, which Standeth / by y$^{e}$ side of a path, which path lyeth betweene HEN: DAWSONs / plantation and y$^{e}$ s$^{d}$. plantation and from y$^{e}$ S$^{d}$. White oak along y$^{e}$ / Side of HENRY DAWSONs ground to a m$^{r}$ked pine tree, Standing by y$^{e}$ / Side of y$^{e}$ Syprus Swamp, and from there up the run of y$^{e}$ Syprus / Swamp to the to y$^{e}$ [*sic*] Mouth of another Swamp, and then up y$^{e}$ run / of that Other Swamp, So far as to another White oak, which oak is a / Corner tree, of JN$^{O}$. JONES his ꝑcell of Land, and from thence along by / the Side of JN$^{O}$. JONES his Land, to y$^{e}$ farther end thereof to a m$^{r}$ked / Spanish oak, and form thence Straight away to a black pine Stump / M$^{r}$ked and standing by y$^{e}$ Side of a branch and from thence to a marked white oak / and then over the S$^{d}$. branch to a m$^{r}$ked pokickrie tree standing neare / another branch, and from thence downe that other branch soe far as / as [*sic*] to a m$^{r}$ked White oak, which oak standeth on the other Side of a / branch, right over against JOHN DUKEs ꝑcell of Land, and from y$^{e}$ / m$^{r}$ked white oak, Straight away to a m$^{r}$ked Red oak, which red oak / Standeth near the head of a branch and also near a path which / path lyeth betweene this fores$^{d}$. plantation and a plantation / which y$^{e}$ s$^{d}$. JOHN JACKSON dwelt upon form$^{r}$ly and from y$^{e}$ afores$^{d}$. / a read oak downe into the head of y$^{e}$ s$^{d}$ branch, and then down y$^{e}$ run / of the S$^{d}$. branch Soe far as to HEN: DAWSONs grownd and then along / by y$^{e}$ side of HEN: DAWSONs ground to y$^{e}$ first Station or first / mention'd m$^{r}$ked white oak tree Standing by the side of a path / And I y$^{e}$ s$^{d}$. WILL: BODDIE doe heereby warrant y$^{e}$ Sale of this said / plantation and of all y$^{e}$ Land within y$^{e}$ bounds heerein mentioned / to have and to hold y$^{e}$ S$^{d}$. peace of Land with all woods wayes & waters / together with his due Share of all mines mineralls therein Cont= / ained, with free priviledge of hunting hawking fishing

**[65]**

Fishing and fouling and all other profitts Comodities and / Hereditam$^{ts}$. whatsoever to y$^{e}$ S$^{d}$. Land belonging or in any Wise / appertaining, to him y$^{e}$ S$^{d}$. NICHO: CASEY and to his Heir$^{rs}$: & assignes / for Ever, in as full and ample Manner as y$^{e}$ most learned in y$^{e}$ Law / can devise, And I doe heereby oblidge my Selfe my heir$^{rs}$: Exec$^{rs}$: and / adm$^{rs}$: to Warrant and defend this my sale of all and Singular the / p$^{r}$misees to y$^{e}$ S$^{d}$. NICHO: CASEY his heir$^{rs}$: & Assignes for Ever, against / all and and [*sic*] maner of ꝑsons whatsoever, and when thereunto Requi / =red to give y$^{e}$ S$^{d}$. CASEY such further Lawfull assurance of y$^{e}$ p$^{r}$misees / as his learned Counsell Shall think fitt, and acknowledge this / deed together with ELIZABETH my wife the Next Court to be held / I have heereunto put my hand Seale the [--] WILL: BODDIE Seale

Sign'd and Sealed and
delivered in p$^{r}$esence
of us

her
ELIZ$^{A}$: + BODDIE Seale
M$^{r}$ke

WILLIAM BODDIE & ELIZ$^{A}$ his wife / appear in Court this 1$^{st}$: May 1693 / & ackno' this to be their free & / voluntary act & Deed.

Test: HUGH DAVIS

I JOHN PORTIS doe give unto my Daughter SUSANNA THOMAS y$^{e}$ wife / of JN$^{O}$: THOMAS, which was form$^{r}$ly y$^{e}$ wife JN$^{O}$: FFRIZELL a ꝑcell of Land / Lyeing in y$^{e}$ upp$^{r}$ ꝑish of y$^{e}$ Isle of Wight County, & bounded as followeth / and to hold this Land dureing her Naturall Life; and in case she doth / dye before her son WILL FFRIZELL doth come to age of 18 yeares, then / my Grandson WILL: FFRIZELL to possese it, and doe give it to him, and / to his heir$^{rs}$ lawfully begotten of his body, & in case he shall dye without / Issue then to Returne to my Son JN$^{O}$ PORTIS and heir$^{rs}$. for Ever, As for y$^{e}$ / bounds I shall prescribe, *impri*: Beginning at a Syprus branch before / the house, which form$^{r}$ly JN$^{O}$: FFRIZELL did Live in, & soe up y$^{e}$ line y$^{e}$ / Jury made, betweene me and THO: MOORE, & soe to a gume which is / a corner tree which the two Surveyo$^{rs}$: made with the Jury, and frō / thence to a red oak y$^{t}$ is a Corner tree betweene my selfe & THO: / TOOKE and Soe along y$^{e}$ Line untill you come to a red oak standing / by y$^{e}$ blackwater Roade & Soe downe y$^{t}$ Road two hundred & twenty / pasees or there abouts and runing from thence along a line / of m$^{r}$ked trees to y$^{e}$ head of a branch of y$^{e}$ SouthSide of y$^{e}$ oyster / Shell necke, and soe downe aLong y$^{e}$ branch untill you come to / the maine Swamp and soe downe y$^{e}$ Maine Swamp untill / you come to the Spring and then up y$^{e}$ Spring branch untill

**[66]**

Untill you come to y$^{e}$ first Station, This being my Voluntary / free Gift, And I do oblidge my selfe to ackno: this my deed at y$^{e}$ / next Court held for Isle of Wight County at Wittnesse my hand / and Seale this Sixth day of Aprill 1693

Sign'd & Seal'd in p$^{r}$sence

of Us JN$^{O}$: + BELL JOHN **P** PORTIS
his m$^{r}$ke his m$^{r}$ke
JN$^{O}$ **P** PRIME & Seale
his m$^{r}$ke
EDM: PRIME

Apill y$^{e}$ 10$^{th}$ 1693 /. ackno. in Courte by y$^{e}$ s$^{d}$ JN$^{O}$. PORTIS / to be his act & Deed Test: HUGH DAVIS

In obedience to an ord$^{r}$ of Isle of Wight Court x$^{br}$: 26$^{th}$: 1692 / Wee the Subscribers have audited, the estate of RICH: BREAD dec$^{dd}$

| viz$^{t}$: | | li to |
|---|---|---|
| To ffunerall Expence ꝑ ord$^{r}$. | | 490 |
| To Clarkes acc$^{ts}$: | | 253 |
| To JN$^{O}$: THORNHILL ꝑ ord$^{r}$. | | 800 |
| To RICH: LEWISE ꝑ ditto | | 872 |
| To ROGER RAWLINS ꝑ ditto | | 2136 |
| To EDWARD COCKRELL ꝑ ditto | | 100 |
| To [ ]LL: BROWNE ꝑ RICH: BREAD bill | | 450 |
| May y$^{e}$ 12$^{th}$: 1692 | paide | 5101 |
| GEORGE MOORE | appraism$^{t}$ | 4720 |
| HEN: BAKER | overpaid | 381 |

Recorded ꝑ HUGH DAVIS Cl Cur

Know all men by theise p$^{r}$sents y$^{t}$ I WILLIAM BARNFIELD doe / Constitute and appoint HUGH CAMPBELL to be my Attorney at / Isle of Wight County Court in all actions, I am or shall be there / Concerned as Wittnesse my hand this 25$^{th}$: of Aprill 1693
Testis ISAACK MELYM WILL **&** BARNFIELD
EDW **2** RALLINGS his m$^{r}$ke
his m$^{r}$ke
Recorded ꝑ HD Cl

**[66a]**[3]

To all Xtian people to whom these p$^{r}$sents Shall come STEPHEN / POWELL & MARY his Wife of y$^{e}$ Isle of Wight County send greeting / in o$^{r}$ Lord God Everlasting. Know y$^{e}$ that y$^{e}$ s$^{d}$ STEPHEN POWELL and / MARY his Wife; for divers good Causes & Considerations us heere= / =unto Mooving, but more Especially for and in Consideration of a / Marriage lately Solemnized betweene HENRY ALLEN and MARY / Daughter of y$^{e}$ afores$^{d}$: MARY Wife of y$^{e}$ S$^{d}$. STEPHEN, hath given / & granted and by

[3] There is no page 67 in the book.

theise p$^{r}$sents doe for us o$^{r}$ heir$^{rs}$. Exec$^{rs}$: & adm$^{rs}$: / give and grant unto him y$^{e}$ S$^{d}$. HENRY ALLEN his heir$^{rs}$: and as= / Signes one hundred Acres of Land in the Isle of Wight County / afores$^{d}$. be it more or Lesse, within y$^{e}$ bounds heereafter meniton'd [*sic*] / Beginning at y$^{e}$ Corner tree by WILL: MURFREY, and from thence / to SIMON EVERETTs Line, and Soe a long y$^{e}$ s$^{d}$ EVERETTs Line to a white /oak by y$^{e}$ branch Side below HENRY ALLEN's Cornfield, & Soe along / y$^{e}$ S$^{d}$. branch to a white oake at y$^{e}$ head of y$^{e}$ branch and from thence / to a m$^{r}$ked Red oak, and Soe upon a Straight line to y$^{e}$ Side line and / Soe along y$^{e}$ Side line to y$^{e}$ first mention'd Corner tree by WILLIAM / MURFREY afores$^{d}$. being ꝑte of a ꝑcell of Land, Given unto y$^{e}$ s$^{d}$ / MARY, wife of y$^{e}$ aforeS$^{d}$. STPEHEN POWELL by ANTHONY BRANCH / late of this County dec$^{dd}$. together with all profitts priviledgees / Comodityes and advantages to y$^{e}$ Same belonging or any Manner of / way appertaining, to have and to hold unto him y$^{e}$ s$^{d}$. HENRY ALLEN / and his heir$^{rs}$. forever, ffree and Cleare, and freely and Clearly acquitted / & discharged off, and from all manner of former & other Gifts / Grants Bargaines & Sales by us done or offered to be done, or any / ꝑson from, by, or under us, In Wittnesse Whereof wee have heereunto / Sett o$^{r}$ hands and fixed o$^{r}$ Seales this third day of June in y$^{e}$ yeare / of o$^{r}$ Lord God
1693

Sign'd Seal'd & Delivered
in p$^{r}$sence of us
JAMES DOUGHTIE
FFRAN: **B** BRIDLE
his m$^{r}$ke

STEPH: **2** POWELL Seale
his m$^{r}$ke
MARY **4** POWELL Seale
her m$^{r}$ke

June y$^{e}$ 9$^{th}$ 1693 / ackno' in Courte by y$^{e}$ s$^{d}$ STEPHEN POWELL & / MARY his wife to be their free & voluntary / act & Deed

Test: HUGH DAVIS ClCur

**[68]**

What Coll$^{o}$: JOHN PITT has payd of y$^{e}$ charge of the Shute [*sic*] that was / betweene him and RICHARD WILKISON

| | li |
|---|---|
| # payd Major ALLIN | 1600 |
| # payd 4 Jurymen | 1200 |
| # payd 2 Chayn Carriers | 0400 |
| # Entry 4 Atturneys | 0080 |
| | 3280 |
| p$^{d}$ ROBT: BROCKE since audite p[ ]pt | 0440 |
| p$^{d}$ RICH: LOVEGROVE as above | 0300 |

| | |
|---|---|
| There being ꝑte of the Surplus left to pay / on M$^{r}$ WILKINSONs Side | |
| p$^{d}$. M$^{r}$ PENNY he being Contented with | 40 |
| 160 he gives which is deducted | 380 |

| What RICH: WILKINSON payd | li |
|---|---|
| payd Mr. ALLINGE | 1600 |
| payd 5 Jury men | 1500 |
| payd 4 Witnesse at 20li p day | 0280 |
| payd 2 Chayn Carrers | 0400 |
| # Entry ye Apeale Petiti filing Entry 2 Attorneys | 0077 |
| # Serch & coppi 3 Pattents Mones [*sic*] & Serch for 1 mor | 0130 |
| # bill of Cost PITT versus you | 0006 |
| # Cop of an ordr. | 0015 |
| # Pete Entri filing order MASON | 0042 |
| # Return of ye Order and Order Recording ye Jurys verdit | 0055 |
| # Order of Surveyers pay | 0015 |
| | 4120 |

In obedience to and ordr. of Court dated ye 9th. day of June 1693 have met / at ye Place appointed and has audit the acctt: Betweene RICHARD / WILKINSON & Collo: JNO: PITT as apeares above only ye charge of Enter= / =taining ye Jury and their Expences at James towne, wee leave it / to the Judgemt: of ye Court

ANTHO: HOLLIDAY
THO: GILES

Augst. ye 9th 1693

Recorded p HUGH DAVIS Cl Cur

**[69]**

Att a Court helden for ye Isle of White County **June ye 9th Anno Do: 1693**
By ye Majties Justicees &a:

Upon the Peticon of GEO: GREENE, Mr JAMES TULLAGH Mr: JNO: CLARKE / & Mr: DANNIELL LONG or any two of them, are requested & assigned (on / Thirsday next at ye house of NICHO: FFULGHAM) to apprize two Negroes / being pte of ye Estate of THO: GREENE decdd, In the hands of ye Said / GEORGE, One of ye Excrs. of the Sd. Decdd., and Mr. JAMES BEAMIS requested / to Swear the Sd. apprizers, and to returne this to ye next Court

Cop p HUGH DAVIS Cl Cur

We the Subscribers being Sworne Have in obedience to this within / mention'd order Apreized the Sd. Negroes att forty pounds Sterling / as Wittnesse or hands this 8th of June 1693

JOHN CLARKE
DAN **lo** LONG
his mrke

Aug[st]. y[e] 9[th] 1693 / Recorded ꝑ order of Courte ꝑ HUGH DAVIS Cl

M[r]: MARSHALL is D[r]: by porke

| M[r]: MARSHALL is D[r]: by porke | | ꝑ Contra is Cred[r] Porke | |
|---|---|---|---|
| To 11½[li] of Sugar | 52 | By severall paym[ts] | 1720 |
| To one Negro woman | 4500 | By 6 months Storidge & Comendacons | 1000 |
| To one barrell of Molassus | 400 | By one pound of yarne | 0038 |
| To one gall[o]: ditto W[M]. FRIZELL | 016 | By 7 gall[o]: & one q[t]. of drames | 0249 |
| | 5044 | By 6 Months dyet for y[e] Negro | 0260 |
| | 5013 | By 8 turnes with y[e] Carte | 0160 |
| Due to ballance | 13 | By makeing two Shirts fine | 0060 |
| | | By a looking glasse | 0050 |
| | | By one Month Storidg for porke | 0030 |
| | | By a Ba[ ]es | 0583 |
| | | By paid to M[r]. HOLLIDAY | 0868 |
| | | | 5013 |

In obedience to an ord[r]. of Court Wee the Subscribers have / ajusted the account in difference betweene M[r]: ANTHO: HOLLIDAY and / M[r] HUMPHEREY MARSHALL to y[e] best of o[r] knowledge and finde as above

Aug[st] y[e] 9[th] 1693
Recorded ꝑ HUGH DAVIS Cl

May y[e] 30[th] 1693
SAM: BRIDGER
HEN: BAKER

**[70]**

To all Christian people to whom this p[r]sent Deed shall come, Wee Major / THOMAS TABERER, & ARTHUR SMITH of y[e] Isle of Wight County, Send Greeting / Whereas by ord[r] of Court dated ffeb[r]ry y[e] 10[th] 1691. Wee the s[d]. THOMAS / TABERER and ARTH: SMITH were ordered and appointed to be ffeoffees in / trust for y[e] disposeing & passing of deeds for y[e] Towne Land, according as is / p[r]scribed in y[e] act of Assembly begun at James Cyty y[e] 16[th] day of Aprill / anno Domini 1691. Now know yee that wee the S[d]. THO: TABERER & ARTHUR / SMITH for the Consideration of one hundred Sixty & Seven pounds of tob[a]: / and an halfe 1 Caske by us already Rec[d]: ꝑ rate, for one Lot, doe for, & in behalfe / of the Court, and County Give, Grant, alien, Sell, and Confirme, and by theise p[r]sents / doe give, grant alien, Sell, & confirme, unto RICH: WILKINSON Jun[r]. of y[e] s[d] County / his heir[rs]. Exec[rs] adm[rs]: and Assignes for Ever, one halfe acre of Land, Scituate / Lying and being in the Towne of Newport, knowne by y[e] name of the / thirteenth Lot binded as followeth Beginning at a Stake in y[e] Streete / being one of y[e] Corners of the Lot No: 16, thence by the Streete North Sixty / one degrees Easterly seaven poles and one tenth, to a Stake y[t] divides this / from No: 12, Then South Eighty five degrees Easterly, twelve pole & eight / tenth to y[e] out bounds, and Soe by y[e] out boundes South, twenty two degrees / Westerly, five pole to a Stake y$^{t}$ divides this from No. 14 then North Eighty / five degrees westerly Seaventeene pole and five tenths, to y$^{e}$ Lot No. 16 / and Soe by y$^{t}$ North, five degrees easterly to y$^{e}$ place where it began. / Warranting y$^{e}$ Sale of y$^{e}$ S$^{d}$. Land to be good Lawfull & authentic, and firme / in Law, to be y$^{e}$ S$^{d}$. RICH: WILKINSON's Jun$^{r}$. his heir$^{rs}$. Exec$^{rs}$: adm$^{rs}$ or Assignes / for Ever, in as Large and ample manner as it is made unto Us, the S$^{d}$. RICH: / WILKINSON jun$^{r}$. ꝑforming according to y$^{e}$ S$^{d}$. Act of Assembly, Otherwise / it may or Shall be lawfull, for any other ꝑson to make Choysse of the S$^{d}$ / Lot or half Acres and build thereon, In Witnesse heereof, wee have / heereunto Set o$^{r}$ hands & Seales this 1$^{th}$ day of July 1693

THO: TABORER Seale
ARTH: SMITH Seale

Aug$^{st}$ y$^{e}$ 9$^{th}$ 1693 / Ackno. in Courte by y$^{e}$ subscriber ARTHUR SMITH
Test: HUGH DAVIS Cl

**[71]**

To all Christian people to whom this p$^{r}$sent Deed shall come, Wee Maj$^{er}$ / THOMAS TABERER, & Coll$^{o}$: ARTHUR SMITH of y$^{e}$ Isle of Wight County, Send / Greeting Whereas by ord$^{r}$ of Court dated ffeb$^{r}$ry y$^{e}$ 10$^{th}$ 1691 / Wee the s$^{d}$. THOMAS / TABERER and ARTH: SMITH were ordered and Appointed / to be ffeoffees in trust, for y$^{e}$ disposeing & passing of Deeds, for y$^{e}$ Towne / Land, according as is p$^{r}$scribed in y$^{e}$ act of Assembly begun at James / Cyty y$^{e}$ 16$^{th}$ day of Aprill anno Domini 1691. Now know yee, that / wee the S$^{d}$. THO: TABERER & ARTHUR SMITH, for the Consideration / of one hundred Sixty & Seven pounds of tobo: & an halfe 1 casq ue by us / already received ꝑ rate, for Onc Lot, doe for, & in behalfe of the Court & County / give, grant, alien, Sell, & Confirme, and by theise p$^{r}$sents doe give, grant alien / Sell, and confirme, unto HUMPHREY MARSHALL jun$^{r}$. of y$^{e}$ s$^{d}$ County his heir$^{rs}$ / Exec$^{rs}$ adm$^{rs}$: and Assignes for Ever, one half acre of Land, Scituate Lyeing and / being in the towne of Newporte, Knowne by y$^{e}$ Name of the thirtty second Lot / bounded as followeth, Beginning at a Stake in y$^{e}$ out bounds y$^{t}$ divides this / from N$^{o}$. thirty one, thence S$^{o}$: foure degreese Northerly five poles and four / tenths, to N$^{o}$: thirty four, thence East four degrees, Northerly fifteen poles / to y$^{e}$ Street, and Soe paralel to both y$^{e}$ aforeS$^{d}$. Lines, to y$^{e}$ place where / it began, Warranting y$^{e}$ Sale of y$^{e}$ S$^{d}$. halfe acre of Land, to be good Lawfull / and authentic, & firme in Law, to be y$^{e}$ S$^{d}$. HUMPHREY MARSHALL Jun$^{r}$. his heir$^{rs}$. / Exec$^{rs}$: adm$^{rs}$ or Assignes for Ever, in as Large and ample manner as it is made / unto Us, The S$^{d}$. HUMPHREY MARSHALL jun$^{r}$. ꝑforming according to y$^{e}$ S$^{d}$. act / of Assembly, Otherwise it may or shall be lawfull for any other ꝑson / to make Choice of the S$^{d}$ Lot or half Acre and build thereon, In Witt= / nesse heereof, wee have / heereunto Set o$^{r}$ hands & Seales this 9$^{th}$ day of July 1693

[--] Seale
ARTH: SMITH Seale

Aug$^{st}$ y$^{e}$ 9$^{th}$. 1693 / Ackno. in Courte by y$^{e}$ subscribed ARTHUR / SMITH
Test: HUGH DAVIS ClCur

**[72]**

Know all men by theise p$^{r}$sents that I LUKE KENT of y$^{e}$ Lower / ꝑish in the Isle of Wight County, doe heereby for me, my heir$^{rs}$ / & Assignes, Bargaine, Sell, Allien, enfeoffe, and Confirme, unto / JAMES TULLAGH of y$^{e}$ S$^{d}$. ꝑish & County & to his heir$^{rs}$ & assignes / forever, One tract of Dividend of Land Conteyning by Estimation / two hundred & fifty acres, more or lesse, Scituate, Lyeing & being / in y$^{e}$ ꝑish & County aforeS$^{d}$. and lately Granted, unto JN$^{O}$: JOHNSON / by pattent, and by him y$^{e}$ S$^{d}$. JOHNSON and MARY his Wife / assigned & Conveyed unto y$^{e}$ S$^{d}$. LUKE KENT, as by y$^{e}$ S$^{d}$. pattent / dated the 29$^{th}$. day of Aprill 1692 more at Large appeares / which S$^{d}$. Assignm$^{t}$. is also Endors'd, one y$^{e}$ Pattent aforeS$^{d}$. / To have and to hold y$^{e}$ S$^{d}$. tract of Dividend of Land together / with all howses, Edifices, orchards Gardens woods, Und$^{r}$woods / profitts, priviledges and appurtences thereunto belonging to him y$^{e}$ / S$^{d}$. JA: TULLAGH & to his heir$^{rs}$, & Assignes for Ever, and y$^{e}$ S$^{d}$. LUKE / KENT doth heereby Sell assigne & transferre unto y$^{e}$ S$^{d}$. JA: TULLAGH / and to his Exect$^{rs}$: & Adm$^{rs}$: or Assisgnes, theese goods & Cattell fol= / =lowing, foure Cowes & foure Calves, Withall their Increase, about / fifty heade of hogs, m$^{r}$ked with a Crop on y$^{e}$ right Ear & a Staple / in y$^{e}$ Crop & a Square under y$^{e}$ Left Ear, Eleven Sheepe and two / Iron potts, two feather beds & furniture, one horse named / archer branded **L K** two Chests, some earthen Ware, two / pewter dishes, one pewter tankard, one Iron pestle one gun, one table & forme, one frying pan, one Crosse cutt Saw, Which S$^{d}$ Land / goods and cattle, the said LUKE KENT do heereby Covenant and / promise to Warrant & defend, in y$^{e}$ quiet possession of him y$^{e}$ S$^{d}$ / JAMES TALLAGH & his heir$^{rs}$. Exec$^{rs}$: Adm$^{rs}$ & Assignes for Ever, Provided / Nevertheless, & it is y$^{e}$ true intent and Meaneing, of thees p$^{r}$sents / That if y$^{e}$ S$^{d}$. LUKE KENT, or his heir$^{rs}$, Exec$^{rs}$, or adm$^{rs}$. doe pay or / cause to be well and truly payd, unto y$^{e}$ s$^{d}$. JA: TULLAGH / or to his heir$^{rs}$, Exec$^{rs}$, adm$^{rs}$ or Assignes, the full Sume of Nine / Thousand, Seaventy Nine pownds of tobo & Cas$^{q}$. (the Cas$^{q}$. / already allowed for) at or upon or at any tyme before y$^{e}$ tenth / day of Octob$^{r}$. which Shall be in y$^{e}$ year of our Lord God, one / Thousand Six hundred Ninety & Seaven, which S$^{d}$. Sume / the S$^{d}$ LUKE doth promise to pay to y$^{e}$ S$^{d}$. JAMES TULLAGH

**[73]**

At five even & Equall paym$^{ts}$, y$^{t}$ is to Say, y$^{e}$ Sume of Eighteene / hundred and fifteene pownds Tobacho: & Cas$^{q}$. y$^{e}$ S$^{d}$. LUKE / KENT doth oblidge himselfe to pay, to y$^{e}$ S$^{d}$. JAMES or his assign's / convenient in this County, at or upon the tenth day of Octob$^{r}$. / next Ensueing y$^{e}$ date of theese p$^{r}$sents, and Soe the Like Sume / annually, y$^{e}$ S$^{d}$. LUKE doth promise to pay till y$^{e}$ full Summe / aforeS$^{d}$. be fully discharged & pay'd. If y$^{e}$ S$^{d}$. LUKE KENT Shall / a true ꝑformance make in y$^{e}$ p$^{r}$misees, then this deed to be / voyde and of none Effect, as if y$^{e}$ Sume had never bine / Otherwise to Stand & remaine in full force and Effect, in / y$^{e}$ Law any thing heerein Conteyned to y$^{e}$ Contrary, thereof in / any wise notwithstanding, In Wittnesse whereof y^e ꝑties / to theese p^r^sents have heereunto Sett their hand & Seales / July y^e 8^th anno 1693

his
LUKE V KENT Seale
m^r^ke
JAMES TULLAGH Seale

Sign'd, Seal'd & Delivr'd in the p^r^sence of us.
HUGH DAVIS
TRISTRAM **T** HILLMOTH
his Signe
ELIZA: **E** TULLAGH
her m^r^ke

Aug^st^. the 9^th 1693
Acknowleged in Courte by y^e / s^d JAMES TULLAGH & LUKE / KENT to be their mutual act & Deed
Test: H DAVIS Cl Cur

To all to whom I FFRANCIS NICHOLSON Esq^r^. lieutenant / Governo^r^ &c. Whereas &c: Now know yee, &c. Accordingly / give and grant, Unto JOHN JOHNSON Two hundred & fifty / Acres of Land Lyeing in Isle of Whight County begining / at a m^r^kt pine, a Corner tree, Betweene JAMES BRYAN and BRIDGEMAN JOYNER, thence by the S^d^. BRYAN his Line of m^r^kt / trees, North Thirteen degrees, East fifty four poles to a m^r^kt / pine, then by another Line of y^e Said BRYAN's North / thirty degrees East, one hundred twenty and seaven pole / to a red oake, then by another Line of y^e S^d^. BRIANs, North / by west, Seventy one pole to a m^r^ked pine JAMES ALLEN

**[74]**
ALLEN, his Corner tree, then along the s^d^. ALLEN's Line of markt trees / East north East, two hundred and thirty pole, to a markt pine, then / along another Line, of y^e S^d^. ALLEN, North, North, West, one hundred / and Sixty pole to a white oake, thence North nine degrees East / Sixty fowr pole and halfe to a white oake, in W^M^: MAYO, his Line / then along, the S^d^. MAYO his Line, South fifty two degrees East / Sixty two pole to a line oake near a Cyprus, the S^d^. MAYOs corner / tree in y^e Bever Dam, Swamp, then Down y^e beaver dam Swamp / to KingSale Swamp, then down KingSale Swamp, by various courses / to y^e place of Begining, the S^d^. Land being due unto y^e S^d^. JOHN / JOHNSON, by and for thImportacon of two ꝑsons into this Colony / whose names are in y^e Records, mention'd Und^r^. this Pattent / To have and to hold, &c: Yeeildeing and paying &c. provided / &c: as in others, given Und^r^. my hand and y^e Seale of y^e Colony / the 29^th^. day of Aprill 1692
Recorded / W^M^ COLE Sec^r^:

FFRANCIS NICHOLSON

Know all men by theise p^r^sents, y^t^ I [--] JOHNSON and MARY / my Wife of y^e Isle of Wight County, doe for us, or heirs, Exec^rs^ / and adm^rs^, Assigne over, unto LUKE KENT, of y^e aforeS^d^. Lower / ꝑish of y^e Isle of Wight County, his heirs Exec^rs^. Adm^rs^. & Assign's / for Ever, all our Right title and Intrest, in y^e within pattent / and doe acknowledge, to have rec^d^. the full and Valuable / Consideration of Two Thousand and five hundred pownds / of Tobaccho for y$^{e}$ Same as Wittnesse our hands & Seales / This Twentyeth day of octob$^{r}$ An$^{o}$. D$^{m}$. 1692

Signd Seal'd & ~~dd~~ in y$^{e}$ presence of
WILL: KERLE
HEN **H** WEST

JNO: **I** JOHNSON Seale
his m$^{r}$ke and
MARY **M** JOHNSON
her m$^{r}$ke and Seale

Isle of Wight County

Acknowledged in Court the 26$^{th}$. day of Decembr 1692 / by y$^{e}$ S$^{d}$. JN$^{O}$: JOHNSON & MARY his wife, to be their free / and Voluntary act & Deed

Test: HUGH DAVIS C$^{l}$. C$^{ur}$

Recorded ꝑ HD p$^{r}$dict

**[75]**

I doe Assigne, all my Right, title & Intrest, to this Pattent / & y$^{e}$ land & appurtenance therin Conteyned to M$^{r}$ JA: TULLAGH / and to his heirrs, and Assignes for Ever, having rec$^{d}$. a valuable / Consideration therefore, as Wittnesse my hand & Seale / this 8$^{th}$ day of July 1693

Testis
THOMAS HILL
MICHAELL WHARTON

his
LUKE **V** KENT, Seale
mke
HANNAH **H** KENT Seale

aug$^{st}$ y$^{e}$ 9$^{th}$ 1693 / ackn$^{o}$. in open Courte by y$^{e}$ s$^{d}$ LUKE / KENT & HANNAH his wife to be their / free & Voluntary act & Deed

Test: HUGH DAVIS C$^{l}$

At a Court holden for y$^{e}$ Isle of Wight County on y$^{e}$ **9$^{th}$ day / of June Anno Domini 1693**

By their Maj$^{ties}$ Justicees [*sic*] p$^{r}$st.

NICHOLAS WILLSON & MARGARET his Wife doe this day appeare / in the Courte & Set forth, that they are Willing to accept whatt / Legacies are given to them & their Children, by y$^{e}$ Last Will and testam$^{t}$: / of Coll$^{o}$: JAMES POWELL Dec$^{d}$:, and Capt$^{n}$: ROB$^{T}$: RANDOLPH (who / marryed the Exect$^{rx}$: of y$^{e}$ s$^{d}$: decd$^{t}$:) being in Courte, & willing to / Surrender the said Legacyes It is therefore Ordered that (on the / 19$^{th}$ day of this month, at y$^{e}$ howse of y$^{e}$ s$^{d}$: Capt$^{n}$: ROB$^{T}$: RANDOLPH's / in this County) the s$^{d}$: Capt$^{n}$: RANDOLPH Deliver, to y$^{e}$ s$^{d}$: WILLSON / the s$^{d}$: Legacys, to y$^{e}$ s$^{d}$: WILLSONs giving Sufficient Security to this / Courte, for delivery of What legacys, are due to y$^{e}$ Chilldren / of y$^{e}$ s$^{d}$: WILLSON, when they shall Lawfully claime the same / and alsoe, to signe, seale, and deliver Sufficient Receipts or / discharges to y$^{e}$ s$^{d}$: Capt$^{n}$: RANDOLPH & ANNE his Wife y$^{e}$ Exec$^{rs}$: / of y$^{e}$ s$^{d}$: Will, for y$^{e}$ s$^{d}$. Legacys, And Coll$^{o}$: ARTHE

SMITH and / Capt$^{n}$: JN$^{O}$: GOODRICH, are requested to be present at y$^{e}$ tyme and / place heeren mention'd

Copied p HUGH DAVIS Cl: Curiae / Recorded p H DAVIS Cl

**[76]**

Isle of Wight County

Know all men by theise p$^{r}$sents, y$^{t}$ I y$^{e}$ within Named NICH$^{O}$: / WILLSON (pursuivant to the within Mention'd ord$^{r}$.) doe heereby / acknowledge to have rec$^{d}$. of Capt$^{a}$: ROB$^{T}$: RANDOLPH & ANN his Wife / the Exec$^{rx}$: of y$^{e}$ Last will and Testam$^{t}$ of Coll$^{o}$: JA: POWELL Late of / this County Dec$^{d}$; the Sume of Twenty pounds Sterlg: and / fifteene Thousand pownds of Tobacho, togeather with a Cloth / Coate with Silver buttons, & britches of Plate buttons, which / are given to me the s$^{d}$. NICHOLAS & MARGARET my wife, by y$^{e}$ S$^{d}$ / Last Will & Testam$^{t}$. And also a Negroe Girle named ffrancke / given to ANN my Daughter & two young Negroes named Anne / & Doll & Nineteene barrells of Nailes, from N$^{o}$: 1 to 19, I have / also Received, which are given by y$^{e}$ S$^{d}$. Will to my Sonn / JAMES, and I y$^{e}$ S$^{d}$. NICHOLAS doe heereby, acquitt exonerate / and Discharge, y$^{e}$ S$^{d}$. Capt$^{a}$: ROB$^{T}$: RANDOLPH and ANN his wife / the Exec$^{rx}$: afores$^{d}$. from y$^{e}$ S$^{d}$. Legacys, & from all whatosever / That I y$^{e}$ S$^{d}$. NICHOLAS, my Wife or Children, can, or may heereafter / Clame from y$^{e}$ S$^{d}$. RANDOLPH and ANNE his Wife $^{ye}$ Exec$^{rx}$: afores$^{d}$: / By Vertue of y$^{e}$ S$^{d}$. Last Will: & Testam$^{t}$: of y$^{e}$ S$^{d}$. Dec$^{d}$. In Wittnesse / Whereof I have heereunto Sett my hand & Seale this / 19$^{th}$ day of June Anno Domini 1693

Sign'd Seal'd & Deliver'd in y$^{e}$ p$^{r}$sence of us

AR: ALLEN }
HUGH DAVIS } Sworne

his
NICHO: **WW** WILLSON Seale
M$^{r}$ke

august y$^{e}$ 9$^{th}$. 1693 / Proved in open Courte by y$^{e}$ Oaths of Majo$^{r}$. / ARTHUR ALLEN & HUGH DAVIS to be y$^{e}$ act & / Deed of NICH$^{O}$: WILSON

Test HUGH DAVIS C$^{l}$ C$^{ur}$

**[77]**

To all to whom &c: I FFRANCIS NICHOLSON Esq$^{r}$: Lieu$^{t}$ / Governour &c: Wheresas [*sic*] &c Now know yee &c: Accordingly / give and Grant Unto M$^{r}$ WILLIAM MAYO one hundred & Seventy / Acres of Land Lyeing in y$^{e}$ Isle of Wight County, begining / at a hickery, JOHN KINGs Corner tree, and running along / y$^{e}$ S$^{d}$. KING's Line of M$^{r}$ked trees, South twenty degrees / west two hundred pole to a pine, thence North, Seventy Six / degrees, west nineteene pole, to a dead pine, GYLES LYNSCOTEs / Corner tree in JOHN LAWRENCEs Lyne, thence North nine degrees / and a halfe West, one hundred Sixty & Six pole to a Small / white oake by a branch y$^{e}$ Said LAWRENCEs Corner tree / then Eleven Degrees East, one hundred ninety & Seven pole / to a white oake, upon y$^{e}$ banke of y$^{e}$ Maine black Water / being another Corner tree of y$^{e}$

S^d^. LAWRENCE, thence along the / S^d^. blackewater, North Seventy three degrees, East fifty four / pole, to a white oake Coll^o^: BRIDGER's Corner tree, thence South / Six degrees and a halfe East, one hundred Eighty & nine pole / to y^e^ place of begining, the S^d^. Land beind due unto y^e^ S^d^. M^r^: WILLIAM / MAYO, by for the Importation of four ꝑsons into this / Collony whose names are in Records, menconed und^r^. this ꝑ this / Pattent, To have & to hold &c: Yeilding and paying &c: / ꝓvided &c: as in others, given und^r^. my hand y^e^ Seale of y^e^ / Colony the 20^th^: day of octob^r^. anno Dom: 1691

FFR: NICHOLSON

Record^r^:
WILL: COLE Sec^r^.

Know all men by theise p^r^sents y^t^. I WILL: MAYO of the Isle / of Wight County in Virgin'a Planter, doe for mySelfe my Heirrs / Exec^rs^: Adm^rs^: or Assignes, Doe Assigne and make over all my right / title & Intrest, of this within mention'd Pattent unto THO: LEWIS / the Son of RICH: LEWIS of y^e^ afores^d^. County lately dec^d^, to him / the S^d^. THO: LEWIS his heir^rs^: Exec^rs^: Adm^rs^: or Assignes for Ever / In as free and ample manner, of the S^d^. pattent was granted / to me the S^d^. W^M^ MAYO, And I y^e^ S^d^. W^M^ MAYO, doe acknow= / ledge to have received, full Satisfaction, for y^e^ Land, men= / =tion'd within this Pattent, And I the S^d^. WILL: MAYO, doe / promise y^t^ upon reasonable Request,

**[78]**
Reqest [*sic*] to me made to acknowledge this Assigem^t^: with / my Wife ISABELL MAYO In y^e^ isle of Wight County Courte / In Wittnesse heereof I y^e^ S^d^. W^M^: MAYO & my Wife have / heereunto Sett our hands & Seales, y^e^ day asnd year above / Written

Sign'd Seal'd & De^dd^: In
y^e^ p^r^sence of us
his
HEN: **HB** BRADLEY
m^r^ke
HOGGES **HC** COUNCILL
M^r^ke
Jun^r^

WILL: MAYO Seale
her
ISABELL + MAYO Seale
M^r^ke

aug^st^ y^e^ 9^th^. 1693 / ackno^w^. in Courte by y^e^ S^d^ W^M^ MAYO / to be his act & Deed
Test: H DAVIS C^l^

Know all men by theise p^r^sents y^t^ I ISABELL MAYO, the wife of / WILL: MAYO doth make my Loveing Brother M^r^ HODGEES / COUNCELL my full & Lawfull Attorney to acknowledge with / my Husband W^M^. MAYO, all my Right title & Intrest of / a pattent for Land Conteining, one hundred & seventy acres / from me my heirs: Exec^rs^: adm^rs^ or Assignes, unto TH^O^: LEWIS / the sonn of RICH: LEWIS Lately Deced) to him his heirs, Exec$^{rs}$ / Adm$^{rs}$. and assigned for Ever, & further more, I give my Lawfull / Atturney as much power, as if I my selfe were p$^{r}$sent, to / Acknowledge the same in y$^{e}$ Isle of Wight Court, as wittnesse my hand / and Seale this 7$^{th}$ day of August 1693

Testis ISABELL ǀ MAYO Seale

HEN: **H B** BRADLEY his mke

HODGES **HC** COUNCELL Jun$^{r}$.

Recorded ꝑ HUGH DAVIS

**[79]**

I doe hereby Authorize and Impower M$^{r}$ W$^{M}$: EDWARDS Gent / to Sue and Implead, M$^{r}$ HUMPHREY MARSHALL of y$^{e}$ Isle of / Wight County, for what Sume or Sums of Money is due by / his bond past (to y$^{e}$ S$^{d}$. EDWARDS) in my Name as Security for and with: JOS: LEACH: M$^{r}$. of y$^{e}$ Shipp *Sarah* of Bristoll, for y$^{e}$ / well and good paym$^{t}$, of S$^{d}$. LEACH his bills of Exch$^{o}$: chargede / on M$^{r}$ GILES MERRICK of Bristoll for y$^{e}$ Virg$^{a}$ Dutyes and / Clearings of y$^{e}$ S$^{d}$. Ship *Sarah*, w$^{ch}$: w$^{th}$: the dammage of 15 ꝑ Cent / am$^{o}$ to £54.07.6 and by y$^{e}$ obligation & protests more / at large may appeare In Wittnesse Whereof I have / heareunto Sett my Hand and Seale this 9$^{th}$ of octob$^{r}$. 1693

Wittnesse JOHN LEAR Seale

CH: GORINGE

JOHN GEORGE

October y$^{e}$ 9$^{th}$. 1693 / Recorded ꝑ HUGH DAVIS C$^{l}$ C$^{ur}$

WILL: CARTER y$^{e}$ having deliver'd to M$^{r}$. W$^{M}$. EDWARDS Cattle to / The Valew of two thousand fife hundred & fifty pounds of / tobacho, which I doe Except of as paym$^{t}$. in part of an order / of Courte, I have against y$^{e}$ S$^{d}$. CARTER as heirs Administrator / of y$^{e}$ Estate of JOHN MORRE Dec$^{d}$, I have Sign'd theese p$^{r}$sents / this 9$^{th}$. of Octob$^{r}$. 1693 HUGH CAMPBELE

Testis W. EDWARDS

A[--]

October y$^{e}$ 9$^{th}$ 1693 / ackn$^{o}$. in Courte by y$^{e}$ s$^{d}$ HUGH / CAMPBELL to be his act & Deed Test: H DAVIS C$^{l}$

M$^{r}$: JOYLES [4]

S$^{r}$: I desre y$^{w}$ for to lett y$^{e}$ Shute[5] fall, y$^{t}$ is dependinge be= / =tweene, JOHN DAVIS & me for I am Soe Sike y$^{t}$ I cannot / come to y$^{e}$ Court, & Soe with my Love to y$^{w}$ I Rest y$^{e}$ Readdy friend / Decemb$^{r}$. y$^{e}$ [ ]$^{th}$ 1693

---

4 Mr. "Giles."

5 "Suit."

WILL LUCKE

Recorded ꝑ H DAVIS C$^{l}$

**[80]**

Know all men by theise p$^{r}$sents that wee JOHN LUTHER, and / MARY LUTHER of y$^{e}$ Isle of Wight County Send Greeteing / Know yee that wee the S$^{d}$. JN$^{O}$: LUTHER & MARY LUTHER, for / divers good causes & Considerations, to us in hand paid before / the Signing heereof, have given Granted alienated, effeoffed [*sic*] / bargained, Sold, and Confirmed, and by thesse p$^{r}$sents doe freely & / absolutely bargaine, Sell, and Confirme unto ROBERT MERCER / of y$^{e}$ Same County a ꝑcell of land being the plantacon, wee now live / on, according to y$^{e}$ bounds, wee now hold, which M$^{r}$. AMBROSSE BENNETT / form$^{r}$ly gave unto y$^{e}$ S$^{d}$. MARY LUTHER, (by Will) Scituate Lyeing / & being in y$^{e}$ County afores$^{d}$. to have and to hold, all y$^{e}$ S$^{d}$. ꝑcell of / Land, together with all howses & Edificees, buildings, with all bene= / fitts, priviledges thereunto belonging or appertaining to him / the s$^{d}$. ROBT: MERCER, his heir$^{rs}$, Exec$^{rs}$. Adm$^{rs}$. or Assignes for Ever / Without Lett, hinderance, Molestation or Eviction, Ejection of Wee / the S$^{d}$. JN$^{O}$: & MARY LUTHER or heir$^{s}$. Exs$^{rs}$: Adm$^{rs}$ or Assignes for Ever / free & freely acquitted, of and from all manner or former, Grants / leasees, deedes Incumbrancees Whatsoever, & of & from all manner / of ꝑsons, Clameing or p$^{r}$tending to Claime Any Rights title or Intrest / to y$^{e}$ demised p$^{r}$misees, or any ꝑt or ꝑcell Thereof, and Shall warrant / and defend for Ever, In Wittnesse heereof, Wee heereunto Sett o$^{r}$ hands / & Seales the first day of Decemb$^{r}$. in y$^{e}$ yeare One Thousand Six / hundred ninety & three

JOHN LUTHER Seale

her
MARY + LUTHER Seale
m$^{r}$ke

Sign'd Seal'd & Deliver'd
in y$^{e}$ p$^{r}$sence of us

his
JN$^{O}$. **T** BUTLER
m$^{r}$ke

RICHARD REYNOLDS

her
JOYCE **J** REYNOLDS
m$^{r}$ke

December y$^{e}$ 9$^{th}$. 1693 / Ackn$^{o}$. in Courte by y$^{e}$ S$^{d}$ JN$^{O}$. LUTHER / & MARY his wife to be their free & / voluntary act & Deed

Test HUGH DAVIS C$^{l}$ C$^{ur}$

**[81]**

Wee the Subscribers, being Sumoned by ord$^{r}$ of Court, bareing / Date y$^{e}$ ninth of Octob$^{r}$. 1693 to View a ꝑcell of Leather / Seized by JN$^{O}$: TYLERR, the Publick Sealer of this County / of ROBER [*sic*] KING, doe finde the S$^{d}$. Leather, to be well tann'd / and good Leather

JOHN TURNER

ARTHUR JONES
Decemb^r^. y^e^ 9^th^. 1693 THOMAS OWEN
Recorded p H DAVIS Cl JOHN SELLER
W^M^ **8** COOKE
WILLIAM GREENE

Know all men by theise p^r^sents, y^t^ I CHRISTOPHER HOLMES / of the Low^r^ pish of y^e^ Isle of Wight County in Virginia, / for a Valuable Consideration to me in hand paid, before / y^e^ Sealing and delivery of theise p^r^sents, by NICHOLAS SCASIE / of y^e^ piss and County aforeS^d^. have bargain'd & Sold, and doe / heereby, for me my heir^rs^. Exec^rs^ & adm^rs^. for Ever, bargaine, Sell / & deliver in feeoff & Confirme, Unto y^e^ S^d^. NICHO: SCASIE & to / his heir^rs^: & Assignes for Ever, a certayne peice or pcell of / Land Conteyning, Seventy acres. being pt of a pattent / of foure hundred & fifty acres, granted, to EPAPHRODITUS / LAWSON y^e^ 31^th^ of Jan^r^ry 1643, and by y^e^ S^d^ LAWSON assign'd to / CHESTER y^e^ 13^th^ of August 55 & from y^e^ S^d^. CHESTER desended to y^e^ / S^d^. HOLMES, y^e^ S^d^. 70 acres of Land, being Scituate about halfe / a mile to y^e^ Southwest ward, of Mout [*sic*] Lawsons bay Creeke in y^e^ / pish and County afores^d^. and thus Boarded, begining, at a m^r^ked / oake near a Cart path, being a Corner tree 'twixt this Land and / y^e^ Lande of JOHN MARSHALL, thence Southeast, a hundred Eighty / three pole, to a red oake, then Northeast, a hundred and Six pole / to a Small hickery by a branch Side , then North Seventy / degrees, Westerly a hundred and Eyhteene pole to a Small / hickory by y^e^ foremention'd Cart path, being a m^r^kt tree of JOHN / MARSHALLs Land, and soe by his m^r^kt tree South, Sixty two degrees / West, twenty four pole to the first Stat^o^. To have and / to Hold, y^e^ S^d^. Seventy Acres of Land, withall woods, waters, / together, W^th^ his due Share of all Mines & mineralls therein / conteyned, with full priviledge of hunting hawking, fishing

**[82]**

ffishing and ffowling, and all other profitts, Comodityes and / hereditam^ts^. w^t^Soever to y^e^ S^d^. Land belonging or any wise apptan= /=ing, to him y^e^ S^d^. NICHO: SCASIE, and to his heir^rs^. & assignes for Ever / in as full and ample manner, as y^e^ most lerned in y^e^ Law can / devise, And I doe heereby oblidge my Selfe my heir^rs^ Exec^rs^, adm^rs^ / to warrant and defend this my Sale of all Singular y^e^ p^r^mises / to y^e^ S^d^. NICHO: SCASIE his heir^rs^ & assignes for Ever, against all / and all manner of psons w^t^soever; and when thereto Required / to give y^e^ Said SCASIE Such farther Lawfull assurance of y^e^ p^r^mises / as his learned Counsill, Shall think fitt, and acknowledge this / deed with MARY my Wife y^e^ next Court to be held for the Isle / of Wight County aforeS^d^. Wittnesse whereof, I have heereunto / put my hand & Seale y^e^ 30^th^ of y^e^ 11^th^/mo: 1684

Sign'd, Seal'd and ~~dd~~ his
in presence of CHRISTO: ^ HOLMES Seale
DAN: SANBORNE mke
THO: CLARKE Recorded p HUGH DAVIS Cl Cur

SARAH SANBORNE

I MARY HOLMES doe heerby willingly Consent to y$^{e}$ Sale of y$^{e}$ within / mention'd Seventy acres of land Sold by my Husband XTOPHER / HOLMES, to NICHO: SCASIE, & doe freely and absolutely relinquish / my Right and Dower to all and Every ꝑt thereof as Wittnesse my / hand Seale y$^{e}$ 30$^{th}$ of y$^{e}$ 11$^{th}$/mo 1684

Sign'd & Seal'd MARY **M** HOLMES Seale
in p$^{r}$sence of DANIELL SANBOURNE
THO: CLARKE
SARAH SANBORNE

Acknowledged in open Court held / for y$^{e}$ Isle of Wight County feb$^{r}$ry / the 9$^{th}$ 1684 by CHRISTOPHER HOLMES / and MARY his Wife to be their free / and Voluntary act and deeds and ord$^{r}$ed / to be Recorded Test: JN$^{O}$: PITT ClCur

Know all men by theise p$^{r}$sents / that I NICHO: CASIE & ANNE my wife / doe, assigne, ov$^{r}$ all o$^{r}$ Right / title and Intrest of y$^{e}$ Within, mention'd bill of Sale unto EVE / BELLENGE to him his heir$^{rs}$: Exec$^{rs}$ & assignes for Ever as Wittnesse o$^{r}$ hands / ninth day of Septb$^{r}$. 1693

NICH: **N** CASIE
his m$^{r}$ke
ANN **K** CASIE
her m$^{r}$ke

Testis
THO: HAWKINS
ANN **A** AARON
her m$^{r}$ke

Decemb$^{r}$. y$^{e}$ 9$^{th}$ 1693 / ackno. in Courte by y$^{e}$ s$^{d}$ NICHO: / CASEY & ANNE his wife to be / ther Voluntary act & Deed. Test: H DAVIS Cl

**[83]**

Know all men by theise p$^{r}$sents that I DANIELL SANBORNE of / the Isle of Wight County doe & have for a Valuable Consideracon / already in hand Received, Bargain'd, Sell and make over a small ꝑcell / of Land, about Eight or ten Acres more or lesse, Unto NICHO: CASIE his / heir$^{rs}$: or Assianes [*sic*] for Ever, w$^{ch}$ ꝑcell of Land, was ꝑte of ꝑcell of Land / which Came out & granted Unto APAPHRADITUS LAWSON, in y$^{e}$ year one / thousand Six hundred & forty, w$^{ch}$ Land bought of him, by WATER BRUCE / & asended to ABRAHAM BRUCE, w$^{ch}$ Land lyeing betweene two / branches, w$^{ch}$ lyes upon a Small Creeke, w$^{ch}$ Cometh out of Lawson / bay, w$^{ch}$. Land lyeth, the greatest ꝑte in y$^{e}$ Isle of Wight County / formerly, planted and seated by one W$^{M}$. JONES, which Land / Joyneth upon A ꝑcell of Land, w$^{ch}$ y$^{e}$ S$^{d}$. CASIE bought of CHRISTO: / HOLMES of y$^{e}$ afores$^{d}$. County, which Land I y$^{e}$ S$^{d}$. SANBORNE doe / war$^{tt}$. to him & his heir$^{rs}$ for Ever from me or my heir$^{rs}$ Exec$^{rs}$ / or Assignes, or against any ꝑson or ꝑsons, in as full & ample / manner, as y$^{e}$ s$^{d}$. CASIE, and his Learned Counsill Shall thinke / fitt & further, I y$^{e}$ S$^{d}$. SANBORNE, doe bind my heir$^{rs}$ or Assigns / that if y$^{e}$ S$^{d}$. CASIE, his heir$^{rs}$ or Assignes, shall not thinke fitt / this Conveyance, that I y$^{e}$ S$^{d}$ SANBORNE, doe bynde my selfe / my heir$^{rs}$ or Assignes when y$^{e}$ S$^{d}$. CASIE his heir$^{rs}$ or Assignes shall / require it, to give him another, with all howses & priveledges / thereunto belonging, as wittnesse my hand & Seale the 6$^{th}$ day / of y$^{e}$ twelfth moth [*sic*] 1684

DAN SANBURN Seale

HUMPHREY MARSHALL
ROBT: KING
JAMES BENN

Acknowledged In open Court held for y$^{e}$ Isle / of Wight County Aprill y$^{e}$ 9$^{th}$ 1685 by DAN SANBORNE / to be his Act & deed, and ordred to be Recorded

Test JN$^{O}$: PITT Cl Cur

Know all men by theise p$^{r}$sents y$^{t}$ I NICHO: CASIE and ANN my wife / doe assigne over all o$^{r}$ Right title and Intrest of this within men / =con'd bill of Sale unto EVE BEHLONGE to him his Heir$^{rs}$, Exec$^{rs}$. and / assignes for Ever as wittnesse o$^{r}$ hands this 9$^{th}$ day of 7$^{ber}$ 1693

NICHO: **N** CASEY
his m$^{r}$ke

Testis THO: HAWKINS
ANN **A** ARON
her m$^{r}$ke

ANN **K** CASEY
her m$^{r}$ke

Decemb$^{r}$. y$^{e}$ 9$^{th}$ 1693 / ackno. in Courte by y$^{e}$ s$^{d}$ NICHO: / CASEY & ANNE his wife to be / their free & Voluntary act / & Deed

Test H DAVIS Cl Cur

**[84]**

Know all men by theise p$^{r}$sents that I JOHN PARKER of y$^{e}$ Isle of / Wight County planter doe by theise p$^{r}$esents, with y$^{e}$ Consent of my / Wife MARY give and Bequeath to my Brother FFRANCIS PARKER / and his heir$^{rs}$ for Ever, a ꝑcell of Land being scituate & lying uppon / the Western side, of y$^{e}$ Island comonly Called by y$^{e}$ name of Hughs / Iland, w$^{ch}$ Land my ffather THO: PARKER Deced: bought of W$^{M}$. ROGERS / it being ꝑte of a pattent for foure hundred and Seaventy acres or / there abouts, as by pattent will more plainely appeare / And further I y$^{e}$ s$^{d}$ JOHN PARKER, doe by theise p$^{r}$sents doe heereby / for Ever, unto my Brother FFRANCIS aboveS$^{d}$. all my Right title / and Intrest, that for any of my heir$^{rs}$. Exec$^{rs}$. adm$^{rs}$ at any tyme heere / after p$^{r}$tend to & further I the S$^{d}$. JN$^{O}$: PARKER, doe heereby binde / over the S$^{d}$. Land, I doe now Live on towards y$^{e}$ Confirmation of theis / p$^{r}$sents to him and his heir$^{rs}$, for Ever, but further it is considered / Betweene us That I y$^{e}$ aboveS$^{d}$. JN$^{O}$: PARKER, am to have free / outlett & inlett Convenient, through y$^{e}$ S$^{d}$. Land as alsoe timber / for my plantation's use, and this I y$^{e}$ aboveS$^{d}$. JN$^{O}$ PARKER doe / owne to be mine, & my wives fre deed of Gift to my Brother / FFRAN: PARKER & heir$^{rs}$ forEver, in wittnes of y$^{e}$ p$^{r}$mises, Wee / have heereunto sett o$^{r}$ hands & fix o$^{r}$ Seales this 9$^{th}$ day of Decemb$^{r}$. / 1693 and in y$^{e}$ 4 yeare of y$^{e}$ Reigne of o$^{r}$. Sovereigne King / William & Queene Mary

Testis JACOB BARNES — JOHN PARKER Seale

ELIZ$^{A}$: **O** ALTMAN — MARY PARKER Seale

DAN: MILES

Decemb$^{r}$. y$^{e}$ 9$^{th}$. 1693 / acknow: in open Courte by y$^{e}$ S$^{d}$ JN$^{O}$: PARKER / & MARY his wife to be their free & voluntary / act & Deed.

Test: ꝑ HUGH DAVIS Cl Cur

**[85]**

This Indenture made this ninth dgay [*sic*] of J$^{r}$ry An$^{o}$: Domy / 1693 and in y$^{e}$ fifth year of y$^{e}$ Reigne of o$^{r}$ Sovereigne / Lord & Lady William & Mary, over England Scotland / ffrance & Ireland King & Queene: Betweeen RICH: / HUTCHINS & ELIZ$^{A}$: his Wife of y$^{e}$ Western Branch ꝑish / in Nantzemond & Isle of Wight County of y$^{e}$ one part & / Coll$^{o}$. ARTHUR SMITH of y$^{e}$ Low$^{r}$ ꝑish in y$^{e}$ S$^{d}$. County of y$^{e}$ / other ꝑte, Wittnesseth, y$^{t}$ y$^{e}$ S$^{d}$. RICH: HUTCHINS & ELIZ$^{A}$: / his Wife, the Daughter and only Heiresse of JOSEPH / COBB y$^{e}$ Younger, who was y$^{e}$ Sonn and Heir$^{r}$. appa= / =rant of JOSEP COBB y$^{e}$ Elder now both decd. for & in / Consideration of two thowsand two hundred & fifty po$^{ds}$ / of Tobacho, to them, in hand pay'd or Secured to be pay'd / by y$^{e}$ S$^{d}$. Coll$^{o}$. ARTHUR SMITH have, given, granted, bar / =gained, Enfeeoffed, & Confirmed, & by theise p$^{r}$sents doe / for themselves, theire Heir$^{rs}$, Exec$^{rs}$ & Adm$^{rs}$, give, grant / bargaine, enfeoffe & Confirme unto him, the S$^{d}$. Coll$^{o}$. ARTH: / SMITH, & to his heir$^{rs}$ & Assignes for Ever, all their Right / title and Int'rest, which they now have, or heereafter / may or can claime, in & to a Certaine tract or divident / of Land Scituate, lying, and being, in y$^{e}$ S$^{d}$. Low$^{r}$ ꝑish / and County aforeS$^{d}$., & Conteining, about one hundred / & thirty acres, more or lesse, Beginning at a Small / Read oake Saplin, Standing in y$^{e}$ S$^{d}$. Coll$^{o}$. SMITHs line / of m$^{r}$ked trees, and from thence to a White oake Stand / ing close by a cart path & Soe North Something Easterly / to a Red Oake Saplyn Staning [*sic*] by a cart path Called M$^{r}$ Cobbs / cart path a corner tree, a straite line, & Soe downe the / S$^{d}$. Cart path, North East, or there about, to another red oake / Saplin, Standing by y$^{e}$ Side of y$^{e}$ S$^{d}$. Cart path, and soe / downe y$^{e}$ S$^{d}$. Cart path, North Easterly, or thereabout to ano= / =ther white oake Saplyn a m$^{r}$ked tree and Soe downe the / S$^{d}$. Cart path, north or there about to a pine Saplyn a m$^{r}$ked / tree, and Soe a Streight line to y$^{e}$ Westward of the north

**[86]**

North, to a white oake, a m$^{r}$ked tree, Standing on y$^{e}$ head of a branch / and soe downe the S$^{d}$. branch, to y$^{e}$ Creeke, and Soe up y$^{e}$ S$^{d}$. Creeke / to a branch W$^{ch}$ ꝑts M$^{r}$ HARDENs & y$^{e}$ S$^{d}$. COBBs Land, and soe up / the S$^{d}$. branch to a Spring Called M$^{rs}$: Hardens Spring, and Soe / up y$^{e}$ Valley to a red oake, a m$^{r}$ked tree Standing, on y$^{e}$ brow of a / hill by y$^{e}$ S$^{d}$. Valley, & Soe up y$^{e}$ Same Valley to a Hickory, a m$^{r}$ked / tree, and Soe up the Same

Valley to a White oake a m^r^ked tree / & thence to an Antient m^r^ked tree, Said to be M^r^ HARDENs m^r^ked / tree and soe running up South West, or thereabouts to a poplar / an old M^r^ked tree betweene M^rs^. HARDEN & PHAROAH COBB, & Soe / to a red oake M^rs^: HARDENs Corner tree, Soe South easterly / to a Corner tree being a Hickory of y^e^ S^d^. COBBs & y^e^ S^d^. Coll^o^. / ARTH: SMITHs to y^e^ first Stat. Wich S^d^. tract of Land is ꝑte / of greater divident of Land Conteyning about three hundred / Acres more or lesse & alsoe y^e^ S^d^. Land heereby bargained & / Sold was by Lease dated the one and twentieth day of ffeb^r^ry / One thousand Six hundred & Eighty Sixe Seaven Granted by / PHAROAH COBB to JN^O^. HOLE, as by y^e^ S^d^. Lease recorded in y^e^ Isle / of White County may fully appear, & whereof y^e^ S^d^. JOSEPH COBB / the Elder dyed Legally seized in fee, & y^e^ Same falls by Right / of Inheritance to ELIZABETH y^e^ wife of y^e^ S^d^. HUTCHINS and / Daughter of y^e^ S^d^. JOSPEH COBB, y^e^ younger, To have & to hold / y^e^ S^d^. tract or divident of Land together, with all howses / Edifices, orchards, Gardens, Woods, Und^r^woods, profitts / priviledges immunityes & appurtences whatsoever / thereunto belonging unto him y^e^ S^d^. Coll^o^: ARTH: SMITH / to his heir^rs^ & assign's for ever, and the s^d^. RICH: HUTCHINS / & ELIZ^A^: his Wife, doe heereby for themselfe or their heir^rs^ / Exec^rs^, and Adm^rs^, Covenant, Grant & agree to and w^th^ y^e^ S^d^ Coll / ARTHUR SMITH his heir^rs^ & asignes, that the S^d^. RICH HUTCHINS / and ELIZ^A^: his Wife & their Heir^rs^. shall and will for

**[87]**

for Ever heereafter, mainteyne, Warrant & defend the S^d^. / Coll^o^: ARTHUR SMITH & his heir^rs^ & Assignes in y^e^ quiet and / peaceable possession of y^e^ p^r^misees, with y^e^ appurtenances / free & cleare, from y^e^ let, hinderance, claime title Molest / =ation or disturbance of them y^e^ S^d^. RICH: HUTCHINS and his / Wife ELIZ^A^: or of their heir^rs^: or of or from any other ꝑson or / ꝑsons lawfully Claimeing, or to claime by from or und^r^ them / any or Either of them. In Wittnesse whereof the S^d^. RICH HUTCHINS and ELIZABETH his Wife have heereunto Sett / their Hands & Seales y^e^ day and year first above Written

his<br>RICH: **RH** HUTTCHINS<br>m^r^ke Seale

her<br>ELIZA: **EE** HUTCHINS<br>m^r^ke Seale

January y^e^ 9^th^. 1693<br>RICHD HUTCHINS & ELIZ^A^ his<br>wife ackno. the above instru=-<br>ment to be their free & volun=<br>tary Act & Deed

Test: HUGH DAVIS Cl Cur

This is to Certifie to all ꝑsons whome it may Concerne / that I whoose name is heereund^r^. written have / nothing to say, against WILL: BODDIEs Recording of the / Eare m^r^ke of his stock of Cattle and hoggs and other things / as wittnesse my hand this 3^d^. day of Jan^r^ry 1693 his

ROBT: **RC** COLLMAN
m$^{r}$ke

Recorded ꝑ HUGH DAVIS Cl Cur

**[88]**

Know all men by theise p$^{r}$sents y$^{t}$ ROB$^{T}$: MERSER of y$^{e}$ Isle of / Wight County Send Greeteing, Know yee y$^{t}$ I y$^{e}$ S$^{d}$ MERSER for / divers good Causes & Consideracon, to me in hand paid, before y$^{e}$ Signing / heerof which is twelve Thousand pounds of toacho [*sic*] & Caske, have / given, granted, alienated, enfeoffed, bargained Sold & confirm'd / and by theise p$^{r}$sents, doe freely and absoloutely bargaine & Sell and / Confirme, Unto JOHN LUTHER of y$^{e}$ Same county & ꝑcell of Land / Scituate lyeing & being in y$^{e}$ County aforesS$^{d}$., w$^{ch}$: y$^{e}$ S$^{d}$. JN$^{O}$ LUTHER / now liveth on form$^{r}$ly Sold unto y$^{e}$ S$^{d}$. ROB$^{T}$: MERSER, by y$^{e}$ S$^{d}$. JN$^{O}$: / LUTHER & his Wife MARY w$^{ch}$. will appeare by a deed past, from / Them to y$^{e}$ S$^{d}$. MERSER bearing date, the first day of Decb$^{r}$ last / past, in as large and ample Manner, as it was Conveyed to me / the S$^{d}$: MERCER, to have & to hold y$^{e}$ S$^{d}$. ꝑcell of Land, together w$^{th}$: / all howses & Edifices & buildings, w$^{th}$ all benefitts & priviledges / & hereditam$^{ts}$. thereunto belonging or appertaining to him the / S$^{d}$ JN$^{O}$: LUTHER his heir$^{rs}$: Exec$^{rs}$ Adm$^{rs}$ or assignes for Ever without / Lett hinderance, Molestation, or hinderance, Eviction Ejection / of me y$^{e}$ S$^{d}$. MERCER, my heir$^{rs}$: Exec$^{rs}$: adm$^{rs}$: or Assignes for Ever, / free, & freely acquitted, or & from all manner of former / grants, Leases deedes or Incumbrancees whatsoever, & of & from / all manner of ꝑsons, Claiming or p$^{r}$tending, to have any Right title / or Interest to y$^{e}$ demised p$^{r}$misees or any ꝑte or ꝑcell thereof / I shall Warrant & defend forEver, and doe oblidge my selfe & my / wife ELIZ$^{A}$. to acknowledge y$^{e}$ same at y$^{e}$ next Court holden for y$^{e}$ / Isle of Wight County, In Witnesse whereof Wee heereunto sett / our hands & Seales this 6$^{th}$ day of Jan$^{r}$ry in y$^{e}$ year of o$^{r}$ Lord God / 1693

Sign'd Seal'd & ~~dd~~ in y$^{e}$ p$^{r}$sence
of us

| | |
|---|---|
| her | ROB$^{T}$: **RM** MERCER |
| DOROTHY **W** BUTLER | his m$^{r}$ke Seale |
| m$^{r}$ke | ELIZ$^{A}$. **E** MERCER |
| JOYCE **J** REYNOLES | her m$^{r}$ke Seale |
| her m$^{r}$ke | |
| RICH: REYNOLDS | |

Jan$^{r}$ry. y$^{e}$ 9$^{th}$. 1693 / ackno$^{w}$. in Courte by y$^{e}$ / S$^{d}$. ROB$^{T}$: MERCER & ELIZ$^{A}$: / his wife to be their Voluntary act & Deed

Test H DAVIS Cl Cur

**[89]**

This Indenture, made y$^{e}$ Eight day of Jan$^{r}$ry in y$^{e}$ yeare of o$^{r}$ Lord / One Thousand Six hundred Ninty & three, and in y$^{e}$ fift year of / y$^{e}$ Reigne of o$^{r}$ Sovereignes

Lord King William & Queene / Mary of England Scotland ffrance & Ireland King &c: / Wittnesseth, that W$^{M}$: CARVER of y$^{e}$ upper pish of y$^{e}$ Isle of / Wight County to and with y$^{e}$ Consent of JANE his Wife, for / a full & Valuable Consideration, in hand already received, have / and by theise p$^{r}$sents, doe Grant demise Sell, alienate transfer / and for them their heir$^{rs}$: Exec$^{rs}$, Adm$^{rs}$. doe by theise p$^{r}$sents / Sell, grant, demise, and fully & absolutely Sett over unto / PHILLIP REYFORD pish of y$^{e}$ Isle of Wight County, his heir$^{rs}$ / Exec$^{rs}$. Adm$^{rs}$ & Assignes for Ever, one p$^{t}$ or pcell of land / lyeing and being in y$^{e}$ affores$^{d}$. pish & County Adjoyning to / Land of GEORGE PERCE, Conteyning one hundred Acres of / bounded as followeth Begining at a m$^{r}$ked pine and Soe / running along PEIRCE his Line of his Small Pattent, and form / the pine along y$^{e}$ line of y$^{e}$ great Pattent by Equally propor / tion, Untill y$^{e}$ afores$^{d}$. one hundred Acres, be fully accomp / =lished, to have and to hold, Unto y$^{e}$ S$^{d}$. PHILLIP REYFORD his / heir$^{rs}$: Exec$^{rs}$, adm$^{rs}$ & Assignes for Ever, Withall the pfitts / comodityes or appurtces theirto belonging only paying / the Kings Rents, Without any Lett troble or Molestation / of him y$^{e}$ S$^{d}$: W$^{M}$: CARVER of JANE his Wife their heir$^{rs}$. Exec$^{rs}$ / adm$^{rs}$ or any other pson by or Und$^{r}$. them Claming In / Wittnesse Whereof they have sett their hands & Seales / the day and year above Said

Signu

Testis W$^{M}$: KERLE — WILL: **WE** CARVER Seale

W$^{M}$. KINCHEN — JANE **I** CARVER Seale

THO HOWELL — her m$^{r}$ke

January y$^{e}$ 9$^{th}$ 1693. / Ackno. in Courte by y$^{e}$ S$^{d}$ WILLIAM CARVER & JANE / his Wife to be their free & Voluntary act & Deed / Test HUGH DAVIS Cl

**[90]**

Wee y$^{e}$ Grand Jurey Impan$^{ll}$. for y$^{e}$ Isle of Wight / County this p$^{r}$sent yeare 1693

Pres$^{ts}$: 1 ANDREW GRIFFIN for quarrelling, with Severall and / Beating of ROGER STEPHENS, at y$^{e}$ house of AND: WOODLEY the / 11$^{th}$ of Aprill last 1693 and Severall abuses given to y$^{e}$ Said / WOODLEY, by takeing y$^{e}$ priviledge of his howse from him / and disturbing y$^{e}$ whole Company, contrary to y$^{e}$ peace of o$^{r}$ / Sovereigne Lord & Lady William and Mary

2 Wee p$^{r}$sent CHARLES BAKER for Strikeing of GEORGE RIVERS / one of y$^{e}$ Grand jury, Seaven or Eight blowes with his fist, Soe / hard as he could Strike, Swearing many Oathes, he could Strike / a Jurey Man, Soe Well as another

3 Wee p$^{r}$sent JAMES JOLLEYs Howse keeper, who goes by y$^{e}$ name of / MARGARET GARDNER, that have lived theire this twelve monthe / for fornication haveing a bastard, and not Knowne to have a Husband / as by her owne Confession

Recorded p HUGH DAVIS Cl — AND: WOODLEY fooreman

Whereas PHAROAH COBB & ANN his wife by their deed Dated the / tenth day of Aprill anno: Domini 1671, did ratify & confirme / unto GEORGE WILLIAMS & to his heirs & Assignes for Ever a Certayne / Tract of Land Scituate lyeing & being in y[e] Lower pish in y[e] Isle of / Wight County which s[d]. Land was form[r]ly sold by y[e] s[d]. PHAROAH COBB / & ELIZ[A]: COBB his Mother, unto one SAM[LL]: HASEWELL, & is now in the / Lawfull possession of RICH: REYNOLDS Jun[r]: & ELIZI[A]: his wife y[e] / Daughter of y[e] s[d]. GEORGE WILLIAMS, & lawfull Inheretrix of y[e] s[d] / Land as by y[e] s[d]. deed more at Large may appeare Now Know / all men by these p[r]sents, that wee RICHARDE HUTCHINS and ELIZ[A]: my / wife, the daughter of y[e] Daughter of JOSEPH COBB j[nr]: decd. / the Eldest Sonn of JOSEPH COBB S[nor] Decd, who dyed Seized

**[91]**

Seized of the s[d]. Land in ffee, for yee consideracon of one thousand / pounds of tob[o]: & two Ewes in hand pay'd by y[e] s[d]. RICH: REYNOLDS / Jun[r]: as alsoe for a firme Establishm[t]: and Confirmation of him y[e] / said RICH: REYNOLDS Jun[r]: in y[e] quiet & peaceable possession of y[e] s[d]. / Land & appurtences, Wee the s[d]. RICH: HUTCHINS and ELIZ[A]:my wife / of y[e] Western branch pish in Nantzemond & in y[e] s[d]. Isle of Wight / County, doe by theise p[r]sents Assign assure grant Sell alien / transferr, & convey unto him, y[e] s[d]. RICH: REYNOLDS Jun[r]. & ELIZ[A]: / his wife and to their Heirs. & Assignes for Ever, all y[e] afores[d] / tract of Land Scituate in y[e] pish & County first above said / Conteyning by Estimation one hundred acres more or Lesse / and is bounded as followeth (Vizt) the first m[r]ked tree is a / Small white oak & Saplyn, by a branch Side running out of the / maine Creeke, from thence to a Cedar post Standing in y[e] roome / of a great poplar Stump (the former boundo) in y[e] s[d]. PHAROAH / COBB's Cornefeild, running from thence to another Cedar post / there fixed in y[e] roome of a Pokikory lately standing by a great / poplar, being a Corner tree, from thence runing to s small / Spannish oake, next to a Small Gume Standing by a pond side / from thence throw y[e] pond, to a Small Pokikory, & from / thence downe a Valley to y[e] s[d]. PHAROAH COBBs Line of m[r]ked / trees pting y[e] s[d]. PHAROAH COBBs land and M[r] ARTHUR SMITHs / to have & to hold thes[d]. tract of land together with all howses / Edifices, Orchards, Gardens, woods und[r]woods, Marishers, Marsh / grounds, pastures, feedings, pfitts, priviledges & appurtences / thereunto belonging, to them y[e] s[d]. RICH: REYNOLDS Jun[r] & ELIZ[A]: / his Wife their hei[rs]: & Assignes forever. And y[e] s[d]. RICH: HUTCHING / & ELIZ[A]: his Wife doe for themselves their hei[rs]: & Assignes / Covenant & agree to & with the s[d]. RICH: REYNOLDS & ELIZ[A]. his / wife and their hei[rs]: & assignes, y[t] they the s[d]. RICH: HUTCHINS / & ELIZ[A]: his wife will for Ever, heereafter Warrant & defend y[e] / the s[d]: RICH: REYNOLDS & his Wife ELIZ[A]: and their heirs & assigns / in y[e] peaceable possession of y[e] p[r]misees, w[th] y[e] appurtences / free

**[92]**

free & clear from any Lawfull claime Molestation or distur= / bance, frrom them y$^{e}$ s$^{d}$ RICH: HUTTCHINS and ELIZ$^{A}$. his Wife or / their hei$^{rs}$: or from any other ꝑson or ꝑsons Lawfully claiming / or to claime by, from, or und$^{r}$: him them , and or Either of them / Witness their Hands and Seales this 7$^{th}$ day of ffebrrij An$^{o}$: Dom / 1693

RICH: **R** HUTCHINS his m$^{r}$ke Seale
ELIZA **E** HUTCHINS her m$^{r}$ke Seale

ffebruary y$^{e}$ 9$^{th}$. 1693
Ackn$^{o}$. in Courte by y$^{e}$ s$^{d}$. RICH$^{D}$ HUTCHINS & ELIZ$^{A}$. / his wife to be their free & voluntary act & Deed / Test: HUGH DAVIS Cl Cur

I doe heereby Nominate Constitute and appoint BARTH: FOWLER / my true and Lawfull Atturney, to appear for me, and in my behalfe / in all Cawses & Actions now depending in y$^{e}$ County Court of y$^{e}$ Isle of / Wight, and in my Name to Implead, prosecute Sue, and defend / as if I my Selfe more ꝑsonally ꝑrsent, and heerby, Likewise / I Impower y$^{e}$ s$^{d}$. FOWLER, to Constitute another Attorney If sees / occasion in y$^{e}$ p$^{r}$misees, In Wittnesse whereof I have heereunto / Sett my hand this 8$^{th}$ day of ffeb$^{r}$y 169$^{3}/_{4}$ EDM: IRBY

Test W$^{M}$: HUNT
SARAH **x** HUNT
her m$^{r}$ke Recorded ꝑ HUGH DAVIS C$^{l}$ C$^{ur}$

Know all men by theise p$^{r}$sents, y$^{t}$ I WILL: CHAMBERS, of Lawnes Creek / in the County of Surry for a Valuable Consideration to me in hand payd / by THO: MOORE of y$^{e}$ upp$^{r}$ ꝑish of the Isle of Wight County / and w$^{th}$ w$^{ch}$ I acknowledge, my Selfe fully satisfyed, have bargai / =ned & Sold, & doe heereby for me and my heir$^{rs}$: for Ever bargaine / & Sell, & deliver, Enfeoffe, transferr & Confirme unto the S$^{d}$. THO: / MOORE, and to his heir$^{rs}$, & assignes for Ever, all y$^{e}$ my Estate / Right, title & Interest y$^{t}$ I have in & to a certain ꝑcell of Land / Scituate in y$^{e}$ maine Blacke water Swamp in y$^{e}$ uppr ꝑish of / y$^{e}$ Isle of Wight County aforeS$^{d}$. conteyning by Estimation

**[93]**
Estimation, Seaven hundred and fifty acres more or Lesse, being / ꝑte of a pattent for Eleven hundred and fifty acres to me Grant'd / the 20$^{th}$ of Octob$^{r}$. 1691 & thus bounded, beginning at a m$^{r}$ked Maple / in y$^{e}$ Maine black Water Swamp, aforeS$^{d}$. thence by a line of m$^{r}$ked / trees w$^{ch}$. divides y$^{e}$ S$^{d}$. ꝑcell of land from y$^{e}$ Residue of y$^{e}$ patent / to a red oake in y$^{e}$ head Line of y$^{e}$ S$^{d}$. Pattent, and then by y$^{e}$ Sever$^{ll}$: / head lines of y$^{e}$ S$^{d}$. Pattent, to a pine in a branch, w$^{ch}$: divides this / Land, from y$^{e}$ Land of M$^{r}$. GEORGE WILLIAMSON and soe downe / the S$^{d}$. branch to y$^{e}$ runn of y$^{e}$ Maine black Water Swamp / aforeS$^{d}$. & Soe up y$^{e}$ runn of y$^{e}$ S$^{d}$. Swamp to y$^{e}$ Maple first above / mentioned, To have and to hold y$^{e}$ S$^{d}$. 750 acres of Land more / or Lesse, together w$^{th}$ all howses ~~Edifices~~, Orchards, gardens / woods, wayes & waters, & all other Royalltyes priviledges

ꝑfits / Comedityes & hereditam$^{ts}$ w$^{t}$soever to y$^{e}$ S$^{d}$. Land, belonging or in / any wise appertaining to him y$^{e}$ S$^{d}$. THO: MOORE & to his heir$^{rs}$ / & assignes in as full and ample manner, to all intents and / purposees as I might my selfe ~~might~~ or could have enjoyed y$^{e}$ / Same, by virtue of y$^{e}$ before recited Patent, or as y$^{e}$ most Learn'd / in y$^{e}$ law, can devise, and I doe heereby declare affirme & agree / to and W$^{th}$ the S$^{d}$. MOORE his heir$^{rs}$ & assignes for ever, y$^{t}$ y$^{e}$ aforeS$^{d}$. Land / and Every ꝑte & ꝑcell thereof is clear & free from all & all / manner of former bargaines & Sales, Morgages, Joyntures / dowries Judgm$^{ts}$: Executions, and all manner of Imcumbrances / whatsoever, & that I have at y$^{e}$ tyme of y$^{e}$ Ensealing and delivery / heereof, to all and Singular, y$^{e}$ p$^{r}$misees, a good Sure and / Indefeazible Estate of Inheritance in fee, which I heereby / transfer & oblidge my Selfe my heir$^{rs}$, Exec$^{rs}$ & adm$^{rs}$. to warrat [*sic*] / & defend this my Sale of all & Singular y$^{e}$ p$^{r}$misees, with / their appurtencs, to him y$^{e}$ S$^{d}$ THO: MOORE & to his heir$^{rs}$ & assignes / for Ever, against all and all manner of ꝑsons, whatSoever by / from or under me deriving or p$^{r}$tending, any claime title or / Intrest thereto, when thereto Required, will give to him or any / of them all Such further & other confirmatiten [*sic*] of y$^{e}$ same / as

**[94]**

As his or their Counsill Learned in the Law shall thinke fitt / & will acknowledge this Instrum$^{t}$, or Conveyance together with / my Wives relinquishm$^{t}$. of her Right of Dower to y$^{e}$ Land / heerein above mention'd in open Court next to be held for y$^{e}$ Isle / of Wight County aforesS$^{d}$ in testimony of all which I have togeth$^{r}$ / with ROASEND: my wife heereunto put my hand & Seale the / 9$^{th}$ day of ffeb$^{r}$ry 1693

Sign'd Seal'd & ded, in p$^{r}$sence of us — WILL: CHAMBER Seale
ARTH: ALLEN THO: PITT — ROASA **9** CHAMBER Seale
Marke

ffebruary y$^{e}$ 9$^{th}$ 1693 / ackno. in Courte by ye S$^{d}$ W$^{M}$ CHAMBER & ROSAMOND his / wife to be their free & Voluntary Act & Deed

Test: HUGH DAVIS Cl

Know all men by theise p$^{r}$sents, y$^{t}$ I PHILLIP REYFORD of y$^{e}$ Isle / of Wight County, doe ordaine, & appoint for me and in my stead / JOHN GILES of y$^{e}$ aforeS$^{d}$. County my true and Lawfull attorney to / appear for me in y$^{e}$ Isle of Wight County Court, their to presecute / In my behalfe JOHN BROWN and JOHN WILLIAMS & his wife / untill both y$^{e}$ businesses are brought to Judgm$^{t}$. as Wittnesse / my hand this 9$^{th}$ day of Decemb$^{r}$. 1693

his
RICH: STONE — PHILL: **R** REYFORD
THO: MOORE — m$^{r}$ke

Recorded ꝑ HDCl

Know all men by theise p$^{r}$sents, y$^{t}$ I MARY WARD admr$^{x}$. / of THO: WARD decd: do Nominate & appoint for me and in / my Stead, JOHN GILES to be my true and

Lawfull attorney / to appear for me in y^e^ Isle of Wight County Court there to / ꝑsecute Capt^a^. HUGH CAMPBELL in an action of Debt / untill it be brought to Judgem^t^. give Und^r^ my hand this / day of March 169$^3/_4$

Testis GEORGE GREENE MARY ꟽ WARD
JN^O^: **IP** PILKINTON her m^r^ke
his m^r^ke

**[95]**

Aprill y^e^ 9^th^ 1694

This is to Certifye the Worp^ll^: Courte of y^e^ Isle of Wight / County y^t^ I NICHO: WILLSON of y^e^ Same County, doe Impow^r^ / my Wife MARGARET WILLSON to be my Lawfull attorney / in y^e^ difference now depending Betweene Cap^t^. ROBERT / RANDOLPH and M^rs^: ANN RANDOLPH Concerning a horse / as wittnesse my hand this 9^th^ of Aprill his

Tes. JN^O^: WHETSTONE } Sworne NICHO: **W** WILLSON
JN^O^: BROWNE } mark

Test: HD Cl

Know all men by theise p^r^sents MALLACK HAWLEY of y^e^ Isle / of Wight County doe Nominate, and appoint and make / my Lo: friend M^r^. JOHN GILES my Lawfull attorney for me / and in my Stead to act and doe in a Cause, as if I my Selfe / were p^r^sent, as wittnesse my hand this 7^th^: day of Aprill 1694

Testis GEO: GREENE MALLACKE **H** HAWLEY
WILL: + SMITH his m^r^ke
his m^r^ke

Recorded ꝑ HD Cl

An acc^tt^. of W^t^ I have recd: of y^e^ Debts due to y^e^ / Estate of my ffather Decd

| | |
|---|---|
| By Tobacho Rec^d^. of PETER FFRANKLIN | 144 [li] |
| of NICHO: BOONE | 406 |
| of M^rs^: WOORY for HINSON | 508 |
| of JN^O^: JOHNSON | 030 |
| of JN^O^: ROSSER | 106 |
| for a ꝑcell of Cattle as by receipt | 3500 |
| for a p^re^ of Iron dogs w^ch^. I gave a rec^t^. for & have y^me^ not | 0170 |
| | 4864 |

to Negroes praized at 40 ^li^ Sterl

GEO: GREENE

Recorded ꝑ HUGH DAVIS Cl Cur

**[96]**

This Indenture made the twenty Eight day of Aprill Anno / Domi: one thousand Six hundred ninety & foure, Wittnesseth / that WILLIAM WEST Sen$^{r}$: of the Low$^{r}$ ꝑish of y$^{e}$ Isle of Wight / County, to and with the free Consent of REBECCHA his Wife, for / the Valuable Consideracon of Two thousand & five hundred pownds / of Tobacho in hand already pay'd, have & by theise p$^{r}$sents doe / for me my heir$^{rs}$: Exec$^{rs}$ adm$^{rs}$, Give, grant, demise, alienate / Sell and for Ever, really & absolutely, Lett and sett over unto / ANTHONY ANTHONY [*sic*] HERRING, of y$^{e}$ afores$^{d}$. Low$^{r}$ ꝑish of y$^{e}$ Isle of / Wight County, his heir$^{rs}$, Exec$^{rs}$: adm$^{rs}$ & assignes for Ever, one ꝑte / or ꝑcell of Land, being by Estimation Two hundred Acres be it / more or lesse, and being one y$^{e}$ branches of y$^{e}$ Black water in / the aforeS$^{d}$. Low$^{r}$ ꝑish of y$^{e}$ Isle of Wight County, adjoyning to / JN$^{O}$. SMITH and WILL: WESTOWREY's Land, it being a ꝑte of a / ꝑcell of Land form$^{r}$ly purchased by y$^{e}$ S$^{d}$. W$^{M}$: WEST o [*sic*, of?] M$^{r}$ WILL / OLDIS, itt bering [*sic*] bounded as followeth, (Viz$^{t}$) Beginning at a / Red oake of NASWORTHY's, Standing in JOHN SMITH's Line / Soe running along SMITH's line to W$^{M}$. WESTOREYs Line / Soe along WESTOWRAY's Line to a branch Called y$^{e}$ Long / branch Soe up y$^{t}$ branch, to a m$^{r}$ked White oake, Standing in / the branch itt being a Corner tree, Soe along a line of m$^{r}$ked / trees to NASWORTHYs Line thence along that line to the first / Station, which Said ꝑte or ꝑcell of Land, with all the comodities / ꝑfitts & apꝑtences there to belonging viz. woods wayes / waters, Springs, buildings, or any other ꝑfitts or comodityes / theirto belonging, or in Any wise appertaining I the S$^{d}$. W$^{M}$ / WEST doe for me my hier$^{rs}$: Exec$^{rs}$ & adm$^{rs}$, give, grant demise / Sell, alienat transferr, and fully and absolutely Sett / over unto ANTHO: HERRING his heir$^{rs}$: Exec$^{rs}$: Adm$^{rs}$ & Assignes / to have & to hold for Ever, without any lett hinderance troble

**[97]**

Troble or Molestation of whatsoever of him y$^{e}$ afores$^{d}$ / W$^{M}$ WEST his heir$^{rs}$, Exec$^{rs}$: Adm$^{rs}$: or any other ꝑson or ꝑsons / from by or Under them claymeing and for further Confirmation / the S$^{d}$. W$^{M}$. WEST doth by theise p$^{r}$sents of [ ] himselfe / and REBECCHA his Wife to acknowledge the Same in y$^{e}$ County / Court of y$^{e}$ Isle of Wight when theirto Required in Wittnesse / whereof wee have heereunto, Sett o$^{r}$ hands & Seales the day / and yeare aforeS$^{d}$

Sign'd Seal'd & ~~dd~~
W$^{M}$: KERLE
ROBT. WEST
ELIZ$^{A}$: Λ BOAZMAN
signu

Signu
WILL: **W** WEST Sn$^{r}$. Seale
signu
REBEC: **R** WEST Seale

May y$^{e}$ 1$^{st}$ 1694 / Ackno. in open Courte by y$^{e}$ S$^{d}$ / W$^{M}$ WEST: & REBECCA his Wife / to be their free & Voluntatry act & Deed

Test: HUGH DAVIS Cl

This Indenture made y$^{e}$ fifth day of Aprill an$^{o}$: Domini / one thousand Six hundred ninety four, Betweene THOMAS / WICKINGS of y$^{e}$ one ꝑte and HENRY BAKER of y$^{e}$ Isle of Wight / County to y$^{e}$ other part, Wittnesseth, that y$^{e}$ S$^{d}$. WICKNIS [*sic*] for / and in Consideration of y$^{e}$ Sume of Eight thousand pn$^{ds}$ of tobacho / to him in hand pay'd before the Sealeing & delivery of theese / p$^{r}$sents by y$^{e}$ S$^{d}$. BAKER, The Receipt whereof [ ] y$^{e}$ Said / THO: WICKINS, doe Acknowledge & himselfe therewith fully / Contented, Sattisfyed & payd, & thereof doe Clearly, acquitt / & discharge The S$^{d}$. HENRY BAKER his heir$^{rs}$: Exec$^{rs}$: and adm$^{rs}$ / forEver, Have bargained Sold & Confirm'd, & by theise p$^{r}$sents / doe Allien, Bargaine Sell, Infeoff & Confirme unto y$^{e}$ S$^{d}$ / HEN: BAKER his heires & Assignes for Ever one hundred / acres of Land, bee it more or lesse, Lyeing and being in y$^{e}$ / Isle of Wight County, being ꝑte of a Conveyance Sold by / GEORGE ARCHER, unto M$^{r}$ ROBT: HILL and now in possession / of y$^{e}$ S$^{d}$. BAKER, w$^{th}$. all its Rights members, Juresdictions / and appurtenancees, together w$^{th}$ all woods, Und$^{r}$woods, feedings / wayes, waters, proffitts, Comodityes and appertenance, to

**[98]**

To the S$^{d}$. p$^{r}$misees or any ꝑt or ꝑcell thereof belonging or / in any wise appertaining, & alsoe all y$^{e}$ Estate Right title and / Interest, use, possession, prop$^{r}$ty Claime & demand whatsoever / of him y$^{e}$ S$^{d}$. THO: WICKINS of in, or to the Same, to Have & to / hold y$^{e}$ S$^{d}$. one hundred Acres of Land be it more or Lesse, and / all & Singuler other the p$^{r}$misees, heereby bargained & Sold or / mentioned, to be heereby Bargained and Sold, w$^{th}$ other, & every / of their Rights, & members & appurtenances, whatsoever, unto y$^{e}$ / S$^{d}$. HEN: BAKER his heir$^{rs}$ & asignes forever, to y$^{e}$ only proper use / & behoofe of y$^{e}$ S$^{d}$. BAKER his heir$^{rs}$ & assignes forEver, & the Said / THO: WICKINS, for himselfe & his heir$^{rs}$, the S$^{d}$. one hundrd acres / of Land be it more or lesse & all & all ye Singular y$^{e}$ p$^{r}$misees before: / ~~Mention'd~~ Granted, bargain'd & Sold with y$^{e}$ appurtenancies, unto / the S$^{d}$. BAKER his heir$^{rs}$ & assignes for Ever, against him y$^{e}$ S$^{d}$. THO / WICKINS his heir$^{rs}$ & assignes & all & Every other ꝑson or ꝑsons / w$^{t}$soever, Lawfull Claiming, by from or Und$^{r}$. him, them or / any of them, or any other Whatsoever, Shall and will warrant / and for ever defend, by theise p$^{r}$sents, And further the S$^{d}$. THO: / WICKINGS for himselfe his heir$^{rs}$, Exec$^{rs}$ & Adm$^{rs}$. doe covenant / promise grant and Agree to & with y$^{e}$ S$^{d}$. HEN: BAKER his heir$^{rs}$ / and Assignes & Every of them by theese p$^{r}$sents that he y$^{e}$ Said / THO: WICKINS Shall from time to time and at all tymes / heereafter, at & upon y$^{e}$ Resonable request & at y$^{e}$ Cost and / Charges in y$^{e}$ Law of y$^{e}$ S$^{d}$. BAKER his heir$^{rs}$ & assignes make / or cause to be made Such assurance & assurances in y$^{e}$ Lawe / for y$^{e}$ father & better & more ꝑfect assurances & Suretyes / and Sure makeing & Conveyinge all & Singular, the before heereby / granted, or mentioned, to be granted, p$^{r}$misees in all other and / Every of y$^{e}$ Rights, members and apurtenances, unto y$^{e}$ S$^{d}$. BAKER / his heir$^{rs}$, & assignes, by y$^{e}$ S$^{d}$. BAKER his heir$^{rs}$, assignes or by his / or their Counsell Learn'd in y$^{e}$ Law, Shall bee Resonably, devise / advise or Require, In Wittnesse whereof the ꝑty first / above named unto theise p$^{r}$sent Indenture have

**[99]**
Have putt his hand and Seale the day and year / first above Written
Sign'd, Seal'd & D[ed] THOMAS **T** WICKINS Seale
in y[e] p[r]sence of his m[r]ke
GEORGE MOORE
JOHN BROWNE

the first of May 1694 / Ackno[d]. in open Courte by the / within named THOMAS WICKINS / to be his free & Voluntary act / & Deed / Test HUGH DAVIS Cl

Know all Men by theise presents y[t] I MARY BAKER of y[e] Isle / of Wight County, doe heereby make ordaine constitue [*sic*] and / appointe, my Lo: friend, M[r] GEORGE MORE, my true & Lawfull / Attorney, for me & in my Name, & to my use to acknowledge unto / THO: WICKINS, in open Court, my Right of Dower in a Convey[a]. / for one hundred Acres of Land, Lyeing & being in y[e] County / of Nantzemond, Sign'd & Seal'd by HENRY BAKER & MARY his / Wife, bareing date Aprill y[e] Seventh An[o]: 1694, by theise / p[r]sents, Ratifying, Allowing & Confirming, that my S[d]. Attorny / may or Shall doe, Lawfully doe, in and about y[e] S[d]. p[r]misees as / fully & amply to all intents & purposes as if I my selfe / were then, & there p[r]sent, as wittnesse my hand & Seale y[e] / first day of May one Thousand Six hundred Ninety / and fower
Sign'd, Seal'd & delivered MARY BAKER Seale
in y[e] p[r]sence of
JN[O]: SKELTON
JAMES BRIGS

1[st] May 1694 / proved by y[e] Oathes of JN[O]. SKELTON / & JA: BRIGGS to be y[e] act & Deed / of M[rs]. MARY BAKER·
Test: HUGH DAVIS Cl

**[100]**
This Indenture made y[e] fifth day of Aprill An[o]: One Thou= / =Sand Six hundred ninety & foure. Betweene HEN: BAKER and / MARY his Wife of y[e] Isle of Wight County, of y[e] one part and / & [*sic*] THO: WICKINS of y[e] other part, Wittnesseth y[t] y[e] S[d]. BAKER / & MARY his Wife, for & in Consideration of y[e] Sume of three thousand / pownds of Tobacho to them in hand paid, before y[e] Sealing and / delivery of theise p[r]sents, by y[e] S[d]. BAKER, the Receipt whereof / they y[e] S[d]. BAKER and MARY his Wife doe acknowledge & themselves / therewith fully Contented Sattisfyed & payd, & thereof doe clearly / acquitt & discharge y[e] S[d]. WICKINS, his heir[rs]. Exec[rs] & adm[rs]. for ever / Have bargain'd Sold and Confirmed, and by theise p[r]sents doe Allien / bargaine Sell, Infeoff & Confirme unto y[e] S[d]. WICKINS his heir[rs] & / Assigns for Ever, one hundred Acres of Land, lyeing & being at / Buckland, in y[e] County of Nancemond, begining at a m[r]kt poplar / Standing by a fresh Rune side, & Soe up y[e] S[d]. Runn, to a Small / branch for y[e] breadth of y[e] S[d]. One hundred Acres of Land, and / aCrosse, againe for Length, & Soe downe againe to y[e] Corner Poplar / Withall its Rights, members Juresdictions Comodityes & appur= / tenances, together with all howseing, fenceing, woods &

Und$^{r}$woods / feedings, wayes, waters, profitts, & also all y$^{e}$ Estate Right title / Int'rest Use possess$^{o}$: ꝑperty's Claimes & demands w$^{t}$soever of / them y$^{e}$ S$^{d}$. BAKER, & MARY his Wife of in, or to, the same To / Have & to Hold, the S$^{d}$. One Hundred Acres of Land, and all & / Singular, other y$^{e}$ p$^{r}$misees heereby Bargain'd & Sold, w$^{th}$. theire / & every of their Rights, members, appurtenances whatsoever / unto y$^{e}$ S$^{d}$. WICKINS his heir$^{rs}$ & Assignes for Ever, to y$^{e}$ only / proper Use & behoofe of y$^{e}$ S$^{d}$. WICKINGS his heir$^{rs}$ & Assignes / for Ever, & the S$^{d}$. BAKER & MARY his Wife for themselves theire / Heir$^{rs}$, the S$^{d}$. One hundred Acres of L$^{a}$. & all & Singular the / before mention'd p$^{r}$mises, Bargained & Sold & with the

**[101]**
The appurtenances, unto y$^{e}$ S$^{d}$. WICKINS his heir$^{rs}$ & assignes for / Ever, against them the S$^{d}$. BAKER & MARY his Wife, theire heir$^{rs}$ / & assignes & all & Every, other ꝑson or ꝑsons whatsoever / Lawfully Claming from by or Und$^{r}$ them, or any of them, or / any other ꝑson W$^{t}$soever, Shall & will warrant, & forEver / defend by theise p$^{r}$sents, And further, the S$^{d}$. BAKER and / MARY his Wife for themselves their Heir$^{rs}$. Exec$^{rs}$ & Adm$^{rs}$. doe / covenant, Grant & Agree to & with y$^{e}$ S$^{d}$. WICKINS, his heir$^{rs}$ / and Assignes & Every of them by theise p$^{r}$sents, y$^{t}$ they y$^{e}$ S$^{d}$. / BAKER & MARY his Wife, Shall & will from time to time / & at all tymes heereafter, at & upon the Reasonable request / and at y$^{e}$ Cost and charges, in y$^{e}$ Law, of y$^{e}$ Said WICKINS his / heir$^{rs}$: & assignes, make or cause to be made Such further / assurance & Assurances in y$^{e}$ Law, for y$^{e}$ further better & / more ꝑfectt, assurance, Surety & Sure Makeing & Convey / =ing all and Singular the before & heereby granted p$^{r}$mises / with other, and Every of their Rights & appurtenances, unto / The S$^{d}$: WICKING, his heir$^{rs}$ & asisgnes, as by y$^{e}$ S$^{d}$. WICKINS his / heir$^{rs}$ & Assignes only his or their Counsell learned in y$^{e}$ lawe / Shall be reasonably devised, advised or required, In Wittnesse / The ꝑtyes above first Named, unto theise p$^{r}$sents Indentutre / Interchangeably have put their hands & Seales y$^{e}$ day and / year first above Written Anno: Dino 1694

Sign'd Seal'd & deliverd in y$^{e}$ p$^{r}$sence of
GEO: MOORE
JN$^{O}$: BROWNE

HEN: BAKER Seale
MARY: BAKER Seale

May y$^{e}$ 1$^{st}$: 1694 / Ackno' in open Courte by y$^{e}$ S$^{d}$. HENRY / BAKER & M$^{r}$. GEO: MOOR atturny of M$^{rs}$. / MARY BAKER

Test: HUGH DAVIS Cl Cur

**[102]**
Mem$^{d}$: That about y$^{e}$ 15$^{th}$ day of ff$^{r}$ry 1685 An agreem$^{t}$. was then / made betweene JACOB DARDAN, of y$^{e}$ one ꝑte and MARY WATTERS / and her Son JN$^{O}$. WATTERS To this Effect Viz$^{t}$.

That y$^{e}$ S$^{d}$. JN$^{O}$. WATTERS should Serve y$^{e}$ S$^{d}$. JACOB DARDAN twelve / yeares from y$^{e}$ date afores$^{d}$. and y$^{t}$ y$^{e}$ S$^{d}$. JAC: DARDAN, Should from / that tyme, take care and provide for y$^{e}$ S$^{d}$. JN$^{O}$ WATTERS, and finde / and provide him Sufficient accomodation, meate drinke & clothing / and alsoe use his uttermost Endeav$^{r}$. to teach & Instruct him in y$^{e}$ / trade of a Coop$^{r}$., and it was further agreed, that if y$^{e}$ S$^{d}$. DARDAN / Should happen to Marrye and afterwards, deceass, within y$^{e}$ afore / said terme, that they y$^{e}$ S$^{d}$. JN$^{O}$: WATTERS Should Serve the S$^{d}$ / DARDANs Wife dureing her Widdow hood and noe Longer, but / Should be free at her marrying, another man, and att y$^{e}$ Expiration / of y$^{e}$ S$^{d}$: tyme, y$^{e}$ S$^{d}$. WATTERS was to receive Two Shirts, a Searge / wasecoate and britchees, a Kersey Coate, a hatt & Shoes & Stockins / New, besides his Working clothes, a Cow & Calfe & three barr$^{lls}$ of / Indian Corne, W$^{ch}$ Said agreem$^{t}$. was Sign'd, Seal'd & delivered in y$^{e}$ / p$^{r}$sents of

JN$^{O}$. ROADES — JACOB DARDAN
ANN ROADES
& THO. OGLETORP — Recorded ꝑ H DAVIS Cl

The Subscriber, was Church Warden, in y$^{e}$ upp$^{r}$ ꝑish of Nansemund / in y$^{e}$ year of o$^{r}$ Lord Anno: Don: 1685

JAMES PETERS

The deference depending in ord$^{r}$ to y$^{e}$ within Mention'd, I have / forgotten, but yeare, as Church Warden, I bound W$^{th}$. Consent of / parents Severall Chilldren, whereof this might be one JA: PETERS

May y$^{e}$ 1$^{st}$ 1694 / The above agreem$^{t}$. was acknowledged in open Courte / by JACOB DURDEN

Test: HUGH DAVIS Cl

**[103]**

To all to whome &$^{c}$. I FFRANCIS NICHOLSON Esq$^{r}$: Lieut: / Govern$^{r}$ &$^{c}$: Whereas &$^{c}$: Now Know yea Accordingly give / & grant Unto JAMES CORLEY, one hundred Eighty seven acres of / Land, Lieing in y$^{e}$ Isle of Wight County, Beginning at a Stake / where a Red oake JAACK RIXEs Corner tree form$^{r}$ly Stood thence / by the S$^{d}$. RIXEs Line, West by South, thirty two pole, to a white / oake, thence North by east forty nine pole to a White oake / then North forty three degrees East one hundred thirty two / pole to a pine then Southeast, one hundred Eighty four pole / to a pine, then South West two hundred twenty & five pole / to a pine in S$^{d}$. RIXEs Line, then along the S$^{d}$. RIXEs line of M$^{r}$kt / trees to y$^{e}$ first Station, the S$^{d}$. Land being due, unto y$^{e}$ S$^{d}$. JA: / CORLEY, by and for y$^{e}$ Importation, of four ꝑsons into this / Collony whose Names are in y$^{e}$ Records mention'd Und$^{r}$. this Patt$^{t}$. / to Have, & to Hold &$^{c}$: Yeilding & paying &$^{c}$. ꝑvided &$^{c}$: / as in others Given Und$^{r}$. my hand, and the Seale of y$^{e}$ Colony / this 23$^{d}$: day of Octob$^{r}$. 1690 FFRA: NICHOLSON

Record: W[M]. COLE Secr

I underwritten JA: CORLEY, w[th] y[e] Consent of my Wife ELIZ[A]: doe / assigne & make over our whole Right title & Intr'est In the / within Pattent to THO: KERBEY his heir[rs]. & assignes Wittnesse / My hand this 9[th] day of fffebrry 169$^3/_4$

his m[r]ke<br>
Testis RICH: A BRACEWELL<br>
WILL W WEST<br>
his m[r]ke

his<br>
JAMES I CORLEY<br>
m[r]ke<br>
ELIZA: x t CORLEY<br>
/\/\/\/\/<br>
her m[r]ke

May y[e] 1[st] 1694 / Ackno.' in open Courte by y[e] s[d] JAMES / CORLEY & ELIZ[A]. his wife to be their free / & Voluntary Act & Deed.

Test: HUGH DAVIS Cl

**[104]**

This Indenture, made the ninth day of May Anno Dom: / 1694, & in y[e] Sixth year of the Rayne of o[r]: Soverayne Lord & / Lady William & Mary by y[e] Grace of God, of England Scottland / ffrance & Ireland, King & Queene Defendor of y[e] faith &[c]: / Betweene PETER BAYNTON, of y[e] Isle of Wight County in / the Colony of Virginia Gent of y[e] one ꝑte, And LUKE HAVEILD / of y[e] County of Nanzemond in y[e] Colony of Virginia Doctor in / physick of y[e] other part: Wittnesseth, that whereas one / WILLIAM PUDDINATT by Pattent und[r] y[e] Seale of y[e] S[d] Collony / & Under the hand of the Hon[ble] S[r]. W[M] BERKELEY K[t]: y[n] Govern[r] / bearing date the tenth day of Aprill Anno: Dom. 1642 was / Interested in & possessed of two hundred acres of Land, Scituate / being in y[e] Isle of Wight County afores[d]. Which lands after= / wards for want of hei[rs] did Excheat to y[e] Crown, and whereas y[e] / Same soe Escheated was by pattent dated the twenty fourth of / July anno Dom. 1669 by y[e] s[d]. S[r]. W[M]: BERKELEY granted, unto / ELIZ[A]: BOURCHER, who afterwards, Inter Marrying w[th] y[e] s[d]. PETER / BAYNTON, y[e] s[d]. Lands Came to y[e] possession of y[e] s[d]: BAYNTON / and y[e] s[d]. ELIZ[A]: & her Issue dyeing, the s[d]. Land was by Escheat / Pattent beareing date the Sixteenth day of Aprill anno dom: / 1683, und[r]. y[e]. Seale of y[e] Colony, an und[r]. y[e] hand of y[e] Right Hon[ble] / THOMAS Lord CULPEPPER granted, unto y[e] s[d]. PETER BAYNTON / as by y[e] s[d]. Severall recited Pattents relacon being thereunto / had may more fully & at Large appeare, Now this Indenture / Wittnesseth that y[e] s[d]. PETER BAYNTON for an in Considera= / =tion, of y[e] Sume of Ninety Eight pownds of lawfull money / of England, to him in hand paid & secured, before y[e] Ensealeing / and delivery of theese p[r]sents, the receipt whereof y[e] s[d]. PETER / BAYNTON doth hereby Acknowledge Every ꝑt thereof to be / fully Satisfyed by y[e] s[d]. LUKE HAVEILD, hath bargained, Sold / aliend Enfeoffed & Confirmed, and by theise p[r]sents doth for / himselfe his hei[rs]: Exec[rs]: adm[rs] & assignes, Bargaine, sell alien / Enfeoffe & confirme unto y[e] s[d]. LUKE HAVEILD his heires, and

**[105]**
And Assignes, the s$^{d}$. two hundred Acres of land, together with all / Edifices, Structures buildings Emoluments and appurtences, what= / =soever, to y$^{e}$ Same belonging or in any wise apperteyning, To have & / to hold, to y$^{e}$ s$^{d}$. LUKE HAVELD his heirs & assignes for Ever, And y$^{e}$ s$^{d}$ / PETER BAYNTON for himselfe his heir$^{es}$: Exec$^{rs}$: adm$^{rs}$ & assignes, doth Coven$^{t}$: / promise & grant to, & w$^{th}$: y$^{e}$ s$^{d}$. LUKE HAVEILD y$^{t}$ y$^{e}$ s$^{d}$. bargained p$^{r}$m: / =isees, are at y$^{e}$ time of y$^{e}$ Ensealeing & delivery of theise p$^{r}$sents, free / & clear from all manner of incumbrances whatsoever, And y$^{e}$ s$^{d}$. PETER / BAYNTON for himselfe his hei$^{rs}$: & adm$^{rs}$, doth Coven$^{t}$: promise & grant / to and w$^{th}$: y$^{e}$ s$^{d}$. LUKE HAVEILD his heirs: & assignes, y$^{t}$ he y$^{e}$ s$^{d}$. PETER / BAYNTON his hei$^{rs}$: Exec$^{rs}$ & adm$^{rs}$, the s$^{d}$. bargained p$^{r}$misees & every / ꝑte and ꝑcell thereof, against all & all manner of ꝑsons & ꝑsons [*sic*] / whatsoever, claimeing or to claim the same, shall will warrant / and forever defend In Wittnesse whereof the s$^{d}$. PETER BAYNTON / hath to theise p$^{r}$sents, Sett his hand & Seale the day & year first above / written

Sealed & Deliver'd
in y$^{e}$ p$^{r}$sence of — PETER BAYNTON Seale
GEORGE MOORE
THO TABERER
ROBT: KAE
CHAR: CHAPMAN

May y$^{e}$ 4$^{st}$ 1694 / Acn$^{o}$ in open Courte by M$^{r}$. / P$^{R}$. BAYNTON y$^{e}$ subscriber to be / his act & Deed

Test HUGH DAVIS C$^{l}$

Know all men by these p$^{r}$sents, y$^{t}$ I ANN WILLIAMS of y$^{e}$ Isle of / wight County, the Widdow of JN$^{O}$: WILLIAMS Dec$^{d}$. of y$^{e}$ fores$^{d}$. County / for divers good causes & consideracons me hereunto Expecially / moveing, have given, and by this my prsent deed of gift, doe give / and bequeath, unto my L$^{o}$: Children in manner & forme follow / =ing: I doe give unto my Son JN$^{O}$: WILLIAMS, my great Cheste he for / to have it at my Death if he is y$^{e}$ Longest Liver, If not to my next / Eldest Son y$^{t}$ is a live, and further I give unto my son s$^{d}$. son And / his heirs, one Ewe & lamb, & y$^{e}$ Increase, to have it delivered next spring / I doe give unto my Son W$^{M}$ WILLIAMS And His Heir$^{S}$: two Cowes / and their Increase, one Steer above five years old & a pewter dish

**[106]**
Dish to have y$^{t}$ delivered next spring, I doe give to my son TH$^{O}$: / WILLIAMS, and his heir$^{S}$: one feather bed & boulster one blanket / one sheate, one stear one pewter dish two cowes a Ewe and a Lamb / and y$^{e}$ Increase to be delivered next Spring, I doe give unto my daughter / MARY WILLIAMS and her heires, one Cow and Calfe or with Calfes & / y$^{e}$ Increase, a Ewe & Lamb, a pewter dish, my Great table & forme & one / Iron pott, to

be deliver'd unto her, when she comes to y$^{e}$ age of Eighteen / yeares or marryed, I doe give unto my Son NICHO$^{S}$: WILLIAMS & his heire$^{S}$: / two Cowes & Calves, or with Calfes one Ewe & lamb; & y$^{e}$ Increase one / Steare about five yeares old, one feather bed and boulster one blankett one / Sheat one pewter dish, and his ffathers Muskett NICH$^{O}$: cannot be / above seaven years old, to be deliver'd unto him, when he is eighteene / yeares old, I doe give unto my Son RIC$^{H}$: WILLIAMS & his heires, two Cowes / & calves or with Calve about Seven yeares old one Ewe & lamb and y$^{e}$ Increase / one Stear about five years old, one feather bed & boulster, one blanket / one Sheate one pewter dish & his ffather's Sword to be deliver'd unto him / when he is Eighteene yeares old. I doe give unto my Daughter JANE / WILLIAMS / & her heir$^{S}$: two Cowes about Seven years old with Calfe or calves / one Ewe & lamb and y$^{e}$ Increase one feather bed & boalster that her father / gave her, to be her ticken, a pewter dish a Iron pott a steare about / six yeares old, to be delivered unto her, when she comes to y$^{e}$ age Eigh / =teene yeares old, and for the true and faithfull Delivery of y$^{e}$ fores$^{d}$ / thing to my fores$^{d}$. Children or their heir$^{S}$: I doe by these p$^{r}$sents / deed, oblidge my Selfe my hei$^{rs}$: Ex$^{rs}$: & adm$^{rs}$: to y$^{e}$ fores$^{d}$ delivery / of the things at y$^{e}$ tymes appointed, in testimony of all which / I have hereunto sett my hand & Seale y$^{e}$ 9$^{th}$ day of Aprill 1694 and / farther I give to my Daughts ELIZ$^{A}$: RIGHT MARY WILLIAMS, and JANE / WILLIAMS all my wearing clothes, both linen & woollen that I / shall have att my Death, to be Equally divided amonst them or any / of them y$^{t}$ shall be Liveing

her<br>
ANN ∤ WILLIAMS Seale<br>
mark

Sign'd & Seal'd in<br>
p$^{r}$sence of<br>
ARTH SMITH Jun$^{r}$.<br>
JN$^{O}$: **X** CRAINE<br>
ARTHUR SMITH

May y$^{e}$ 21$^{st}$ 1694 / Acko. in Courte by y$^{e}$ s$^{d}$ ANNE / WILLIAMS to be her ack & Deed

Test HUGH DAVIS C$^{l}$

**[107]**

I doe give my five Children voluntary Consent to the w$^{th}$in / Deed made by now Wife, when She was in her widdowhood / witnesse my hand and Seal May 21$^{st}$: 1694 / May y$^{e}$ 21$^{st}$. 1694 ARNOLD **S** SHEWMACKE Seale

ackn$^{o}$. in Courte by y$^{e}$ his m$^{r}$ke / to ARNOLD SHUMACKE to be / his act & deed / Test: HUGH DAVIS C$^{l}$C$^{ur}$

Know all men by theise p$^{r}$sents, That I WALTER RUTTER of / y$^{e}$ Low$^{r}$ ꝑish of y$^{e}$ Isle of Wight County for y$^{e}$ love and affection I beare Unto my L$^{o}$: Daughter MARTHA RUTTER, and for divers / other Causes me theirunto Moving have, and by theise p$^{r}$sents doth / for me my heir$^{rs}$: Exec$^{rs}$: adm$^{rs}$., give grant demise and for Ever lett /

and Sett over Unto my aforeS$^{d}$. Daughter MARTHA RUTTER, all that / ꝑt or ꝑcell of Land & plantation, on w$^{ch}$: DAVID PRICE now lives on / it being bounded as followeth, vizt: Beginning at a red oake on y$^{e}$ / mill path thence along a line of m$^{r}$ked trees to a white oake near / GREENs lyne thence on y$^{t}$ lyne to y$^{e}$ Milldam, downe y$^{e}$ dam to / a stoney Valley and from thence to y$^{e}$ first Station, all w$^{ch}$. S$^{d}$. Land / & plantation, w$^{th}$ all y$^{e}$ profitts and appurtenances theirto belonging / or in iny wyse appertaneing. I the S$^{d}$. WALTER RUTTER doth for me / my heir$^{rs}$: Exec$^{rs}$. Adm$^{rs}$. give grant demise to my aforeS$^{d}$. L$^{o}$. Daughter / MARTHA RUTTER, and to y$^{e}$ heir$^{rs}$. of her body lawfully begotten to have / and to hold for Ever, only Excepting what timber or fensinge I / my Selfe may have occasion to make use of on my plantacon / during my Naturall Life, And for further Confirmation, I doe / oblidge my Selfe, y$^{t}$ I and my Wife MARTHA, shall acknowledge / this S$^{d}$. deed of gift in y$^{e}$ County Court, when their to Required / Wittnesse o$^{r}$ hands & Seales this 31$^{th}$. day of M$^{r}$ch 1694

Sign'd Seal'd & ~~dd~~
in p$^{r}$sence of
W$^{M}$. GREENE
sig ud [*sic*]
MARY **M** GREENE
W$^{M}$. KERLE
ARTH: PURSELL

WALTER RUTTER Seal
Signu
MARTHA **M** RUTT$^{R}$ Seale

May y$^{e}$ 21 1694 / ackno. in Courte by y$^{e}$ s$^{d}$ WALTER RUTTER & MARTHA his Wife to be their free & Voluntary Act & Deed
Test H DAVIS Cl

**[108]**

This Indenture made y$^{e}$ twenty Second day of ffebru$^{r}$ry in y$^{e}$ yeare of / o$^{r}$ Lord God one Thousand Six hundred ninety and three and in y$^{e}$ fifth / year of y$^{e}$ Reigne of o$^{r}$ Sovereigne Lord & Lady, William & Mary, by y$^{e}$ / grace of God King & Queene of England, Scotland, ffrance & Ireland / &c: Betweene JAMES BARON of y$^{e}$ Upp$^{r}$ ꝑish of y$^{e}$ Isle of Wight / County of y$^{e}$ one ꝑt, and ANDREW WOODLEY of y$^{e}$ ꝑish & County afores$^{d}$. / of y$^{e}$ other ꝑt Wittnesseth the y$^{e}$ S$^{d}$. JAMES BARON, for & in Consi= / =deration of y$^{e}$ Sume of seven thousand pownds of Tobacho to him / in hand, at and before y$^{e}$ Sealing & Delivery of these p$^{r}$sents, by y$^{e}$ S$^{d}$. ANDREW / WOODLEY well & truly paid, y$^{e}$ Receipt whereof, he the S$^{d}$. JAMES / BARON doth heerby Acknowledge, and himselfe therew$^{th}$: fully Satis= / =fyed & paid & thereof & of Every ꝑt & ꝑcell thereof, doth clearly acquitt / Exonerate & discharge the S$^{d}$. ANDREW WOODLEY his heir$^{rs}$ Exec$^{rs}$ & adm$^{rs}$ / for Ever By theise p$^{r}$sents hath given granted aliened bargained / Sold, Enfeoffed & Confirmed, And by theise p$^{r}$sents doth fully / clearly & absolutely give, grant Bargaine, Sell, alien, Enfeoff and / Confirme unto y$^{e}$ S$^{d}$. ANDREW WOODLEY his heir$^{rs}$ & assignes for / Ever, one ꝑcell of tract of Land, Scituate Lyeing & being in y$^{e}$ ꝑish / & County aforeS$^{d}$. Containing Six hundred & forty acres (form$^{r}$ly / Granted unto ANTHO: MATHEWS by pattent bearing date y$^{e}$ first / day of ffeb$^{r}$ruary 1664 and by y$^{e}$ S$^{d}$. ANTHO: MATTHEWS Conveyed unto / y$^{e}$ S$^{d}$. JAMES BARON, by his last Will & Testam$^{t}$. in Writing bareing / date y$^{e}$ 6$^{th}$ day of May 1681) Begining at a m$^{r}$ked old oake neare y$^{e}$ / head of CRANAGEs Swamp on y$^{e}$ West Side of EDMUND / PALMERs land, thence West by north 320 pole thence South by West / 320 pole thence East by South 320 pole thence North by East / along PALMERs Line of m$^{r}$ked trees to y$^{e}$ first Station to Have / & to hold y$^{e}$ fores$^{d}$ 640 acres of Land according the foreS$^{d}$. bounds / withall and Signular its Rights, members, Jurisdictions & appur / =tenances, to gather withall howses, Edifices buildings, barns, Stables / orchards, gardens yards, backsides, Easem$^{ts}$, Lands, tenem$^{ts}$: meddowes / feedings pastures, Woods Und$^{r}$woods, Wayes profitts Comodityes / Comon of pasture, hereditaments and appurtenances w$^{t}$soever / to y$^{e}$ Said Messuages or tenem$^{ts}$. and p$^{r}$misees or to any part or / parcell

**[109]**

parcell of them belonging or in any Wise appertaining thereunto / unto y$^{e}$ S$^{d}$. ANDREW WOODLEY his heir$^{rs}$ & assignes for the only proper / use and behoofe of y$^{e}$ S$^{d}$. ANDREW WOODLEY his heir$^{rs}$ & assignes for / Ever, against him y$^{e}$ S$^{d}$. JAMES BARON, his heir$^{rs}$: or Assignes, & all, & / Every other ꝑson & ꝑsons W$^{t}$soever, Lawfully Claiming by from / or Und$^{r}$ him, them or any of them, Shall and Will warrant & / forEver defend by theise p$^{r}$sents, and y$^{t}$ the S$^{d}$. JAMES BARON for / himselfe his heir$^{rs}$, Exec$^{rs}$ & adm$^{rs}$, doth Covenant promise, grant & / agree to, and with y$^{e}$ S$^{d}$. ANDREW WOODLEY his heir$^{rs}$ & assignes and / Every of them, by theise p$^{r}$sents, that all & Singular y$^{e}$ foreS$^{d}$. 640 / acres of Land, according to y$^{e}$ fore Recived bounds, with all the / appurtenances thereunto belonging, Now be and Ever here af= / =ter Shall be, Stand and Continue, to y$^{e}$ S$^{d}$. ANDREW WOODLEY & / his heir$^{rs}$, & assignes for Ever, And y$^{t}$ y$^{e}$ S$^{d}$. ANDREW WOODLEY his heir$^{rs}$ or / Assignes, be freely and clearly acquitted, Exonerated & discharged, / & from time to time, well & Sufficiently Saved as Kept harmlesse by / the S$^{d}$. JA: BARON his heir$^{rs}$, Exec$^{rs}$ or adm$^{rs}$ of and from all manner of / former & other gifts grants, bargaines, Sales, Leases, Morgagees, / Joyntures Dowres, of & from all & Singular other titles, troubles / Charges, demands and Incumberances whatsoever, had, made, Com= / mitted, Suffered, omited or done by y$^{e}$ S$^{d}$. JA: BARON his heir$^{rs}$ or assigns / or by any other ꝑson or ꝑsons what / soever, And that y$^{e}$ S$^{d}$. JAMES BARON his heir$^{rs}$, or assignes for and / dureing the Space of Seven yeares next Ensueing the date of / theise p$^{r}$sents, Shall & will at & uppon y$^{e}$ reasonable request & / at y$^{e}$ Cost & Charges in y$^{e}$ Law of y$^{e}$ S$^{d}$. ANDREW WOODLEY, his heir$^{rs}$ / or assignes, make Such further Lawfull and Reasonable assurance / or assurances or conveyances in y$^{e}$ Law, for y$^{e}$ more & better / and ꝑfect Assurance of y$^{e}$ foreS$^{d}$. p$^{r}$mises as by y$^{e}$ S$^{d}$. ANDREW / WOODLEY his heir$^{rs}$ or assignes or by his or their Counsill learn'd / in y$^{e}$ Lawes, Shall be reasonably devised, advised or Required / and that y$^{e}$ aforeS$^{d}$. p$^{r}$misees with all y$^{e}$ appurtenances thereunto

**[110]**

Thereunto belonging, Shall be Esteemed, adjudged & taken / to be enure [*sic*] to y$^{e}$ to y$^{e}$ only proper use & behoofe, of y$^{e}$ S$^{d}$. ANDREW / WOODLEY his heir$^{rs}$ & Assignes for

Ever, & to name other Use, intent / or purpose Whatsoever, In Wittnesse heereof I have heere unto / Set my hand & Seale y[e] day and year first above Witten [*sic*]
Sign'd Seal'd & d[d]. in y[e] p[r]sence
of whose name are Und[r] written JAMES BARON Seale
JOHN GILES
JOHN TURNER
JOHN **P°** PORTIS Jnor
his m[r]ke

Poss[o]: Livery Seazin of the / within mention'd p[r]misees, given & / granted, unto the w[th]in mention'd AND: / WOODLEY his heir[rs] & assignes for Ever / in y[e] p[r]sence of
his
JN[O]: P PORTIS Snor
m[r]ke
JANE **I** PORTIS
her m[r]ke
THO: **D** DAVIS
his m[r]ke

June y[e] 9[th]: 1694 / ackno.' in Courte by the s[d] / JA: BARON to be his act / & Deed Test: HUGH DAVIS Cl Cur

M[r] JAMES BENN

pay y[t] four hundred & fifty pownds of Tobacho & Caske / which I had Judgm[t]: against yow, to CUTHBERT HYINGTON / or his ord[r]. & this Shall be y[e] discharge from it, the feese pmised / to pay, I know not of any ord[r], that M[r] CAMPBELL had from me / to demand it of you JAMES
March y[e] 21[th]: 169$^0/_1$
y[r] ffriend
HEN: GAWLER

Aprill y[e] 9[th]. 1691

Rec[d] of JAMES BENN y[e] full contents of this Note p me
CUTHBERT **H** HYINGTON
his m[r]ke

June y[e] 9[th] 1694 / Recorded at y[e] request of HUGH / CAMPBELL
Test: HUGH DAVIS Cl

**[111]**

I doe Impow[r]. M[r] JN[O]: GILES to be my Attorney against MALAK / HALEY Wittness my hand this 8[th] of June 64
Wittnesse JAMES TULLAGH ROB[T]. COLLMAN
Recorded p HD Cl

Know all men by theise p$^{r}$sents, y$^{t}$ I W$^{M}$. WHITTFIELD of Isle of / Wight County planter doe Constitute & appoynt HUGH CAMPBELL to / be my Attorney at y$^{e}$ next Generall Court held for this Colony in / two action in w$^{ch}$ I have appealed from y$^{e}$ orders of Isle of Wight / County Court, & this my Lett$^{r}$: of Attorney doth also Impow$^{r}$ y$^{e}$ S$^{d}$. / HUGH CAMPBELL, to take to his Assistance, Some other able Attorney / and theese p$^{r}$sents Shall oblidge me to pay to y$^{e}$ S$^{d}$. to y$^{e}$ S$^{d}$. CAMPBELL, / his Attorny's fees according to Law, or Custome, also Such other / atturny As he Shall Imploy, given Und$^{r}$ my hand this 20$^{th}$ of / august 1692

Testis JN$^{O}$: PITT:

his<br>
W$^{M}$: **W** WHITFEILD<br>
m$^{r}$ke

Recorded ꝑ HD Cl

Know all men by theise p$^{r}$sents, y$^{t}$ I W$^{M}$: BODDIE of y$^{e}$ Isle of / Wight County in Virginia, have with y$^{e}$ free Consent of ELIZAB: / BODDIE my Wife, bargain'd, Sold, & deliver'd, unto NICHO: CASEY of y$^{e}$ foreS$^{d}$. / County, a Certaine ꝑcell of Land, lyeing and being in y$^{e}$ foreS$^{d}$. County / near y$^{e}$ Syprus Swamp, it lyeth by y$^{e}$ Side of a branch w$^{ch}$ commeth / out of y$^{e}$ Siprus Swamp, And y$^{e}$ S$^{d}$. ꝑcell of Land Sume of it is / wood Land ground, Some old feild, Some orchard, and Some howseing / there is thereon, and y$^{e}$ bounds of it, is thus, It begineth at a m$^{r}$ked white / oake which Standeth by y$^{e}$ Side of y$^{e}$ aforeS$^{d}$: branch, that ꝑcell / of Land which I form$^{r}$ly Sold to JN$^{O}$: DUKE, lyeth on y$^{e}$ other Side / of this foreS$^{d}$. branch, and from y$^{e}$ foreS$^{d}$. White oake along by y$^{e}$ / Side of ꝑt of y$^{t}$ Land w$^{ch}$ I form$^{r}$ly sold to the fores$^{d}$. NICH: CASEY / soe far as to a m$^{r}$ked Red oake which Standeth by a path and near a / pond and also near a Valle and then down y$^{e}$ S$^{d}$. Valle to the head

**[112]**

head of a little branch and then down y$^{e}$ S$^{d}$ Little branch to y$^{e}$ mouth / thereof into y$^{e}$ first mention'd branch and then up y$^{e}$ first mention'd / branch Soe far as y$^{e}$ first station or m$^{r}$ked white oake this foreS$^{d}$. / ꝑcell of Land is thought to be fifty acres of Land or there abouts / now whether this fores$^{d}$. ꝑcell of Land be more then fifty acres of L$^{d}$. afs$^{d}$. / then fifty acres, all y$^{e}$ Land, either y$^{e}$ bounds heere before mention$^{d}$: / I the fores$^{d}$. W$^{M}$. BODDIE have bargained Sould & deliver'd unto him / y$^{e}$ fores$^{d}$. NICHO: CASEY, And I doe heerby in y$^{e}$ behalfe of my Selfe / my heir$^{rs}$ Exec$^{rs}$: and adm$^{rs}$: warrant y$^{e}$ Sale of this fores$^{d}$. ꝑcell of / Land, withall y$^{e}$ Just and Lawfull ꝑfitts, thereunto belonging / to be good & Lawfull unto him y$^{e}$ foreS$^{d}$. NICHO: CASEY his heir$^{rs}$ / Exec$^{rs}$: and Adm$^{rs}$ for Ever, this foreS$^{d}$ ꝑcell of Land was form$^{r}$ly called / by y$^{e}$ name of JN$^{O}$: JACKSONs plantation, And further I y$^{e}$ foreS$^{d}$: / W$^{M}$ BODDIE, doe heereby promise and Ingage my Selfe / that all any Convenient tyme, whensoever NICHO: CASEY shall / require me or desire mee, that then both I my selfe and also my / wife W$^{th}$ me shall and will acknowledge in open Court in y$^{e}$ Isle / of Whigt County this to be o$^{r}$ act & deed, as wittnesse o$^{r}$ hands / and Seales this 9$^{th}$ of June 1694 xxx

Sign'd Seal'd & ~~dd~~ in y$^{e}$
p$^{r}$sence of us
W$^{M}$: WILLIAMS
GEORGE GREENE
W$^{M}$: GREENE

W$^{M}$: BODDIE Seale
ELIZ$^{A}$: **X** BODDIE Seale

June y$^{e}$ 9$^{th}$ 1694 / Ackno. in Courte by y$^{e}$ s$^{d}$ W$^{M}$. BODDIE / & ELIZ$^{A}$: his wife to be their free & / Voluntary Act & Deed / Test H DAVIS CL

I doe heereby Impower M$^{r}$ JN$^{O}$: GILES, to be my Attorny, for me / and in my name, to appear in any action y$^{t}$ Shall be brought / against me in y$^{e}$ isle of Wight Courte. Witnesse my hand / this 8$^{th}$ day of June 1694 SAM: COHOONE
Test: HUGH DAVIS Recorded ꝑ HDCl

**[113]**

I und$^{r}$.written doe heerby Constitute and appoynt WILL / ARCHER to be my Attorny to Answer all Sutes or matt$^{rs}$ / now depending in y$^{e}$ Isle of Wight County for or ag$^{nst}$ mee & w$^{t}$ my S$^{d}$ / Attorny shall do in y$^{e}$ p$^{r}$misees I do & will ratify allow and / Confirme, Wittnesse my hand this 9$^{th}$ day of June 1694

Sign'd Deliver'd in
p$^{r}$sence of
JN$^{O}$. WHETSTONE
JN$^{O}$: BELL

NICHO: **NW** WILLSON
marke

Recorded ꝑ HD C$^{l}$

Know all men by theise p$^{r}$sents that wee JN$^{O}$: PITT & NICHOLAS / FFULGHAM, adm$^{rs}$. of y$^{e}$ Estate of PHILLIP MACODINE doe / authorize Constitute and ordaine M$^{r}$: JN$^{O}$: GILES our Lawfull / attorney to act in o$^{r}$ behalfe in any matter Cases or actions / in y$^{e}$ Isle of Wight County Court or Elsewhere concerning / y$^{e}$ s$^{d}$. Estate, and w$^{t}$ he Shall doe therein, wee Confirme as if / wee were ꝑsonally p$^{r}$sent as Wittnesse our hands this 9$^{th}$. of / Aprill 1694

Test Recorded ꝑ HD C$^{l}$

JN$^{O}$: PITT
NICHO: FFULGHAM

RICHARD JONES aged about 22 yeares or there abouts / doth declare, that THOMAS WILLIAMSON told him that Coll$^{o}$: / POWELL hired to breake this horse, and when he had broke / this, hee sayd, hee was to deliver, him y$^{e}$ sayd horse to / M$^{rs}$: WILLSON, and further THOMAS WILLIAMSON told / me, that hee might have bestowed a better horse to / her then that Was or ever woold be, and did tell me / hee was to give him tenn shillings and further / Saith not

it was about 9$^{ber}$ Last
was twelve month
RICH: **R** JONES
hir m$^{r}$ke

RICH: **R** JONES
his m$^{r}$ke

Recorded ꝑ HD C$^{l}$

**[114]**

THOMAS WILLSON aged 28 yeares or thereabouts doth decla$^{r}$ / Last Generall training, in y$^{e}$ Upp$^{r}$ pish I see THO: WILLIAM= /=SON there, and he Knowing that I was goeing to JOHN BRANT= / LEYs, hee desired me to call at M$^{r}$ NICHO: WILLSONs, and desire / him to fetch hime the horse, for hee could not learn him / to pace, nor hee beleiv'd noe other man, & further Saith not

Ju$^{r}$: in Cur nono die Junij — THO: **T** WILLSON
anno 1694 Test HD C$^{l}$ — his m$^{r}$ke

JOHN BROWNE aged 25 years or thereabouts doth declare / that my Uncle WILLSON brought me a horse to break and / told me that my Aunt would pay me for it, and they did / finde him provender, and after I had Kept him three Months / they sent me word, to deliver him to THO: WILLIAMSON / who came for him in Coll$^{o}$: POWELLs Name, and I questioned him / whether Coll$^{o}$: POWELL sent for him, And he made Answer / & said the black horse y$^{t}$ is y$^{r}$ Ant WILLSON's, and I riding from / Church in Company, Coll$^{o}$: POWELL being there, Asked me / whether, I could bring y$^{e}$ horse Gentle or noe, I Made answer / & say'd yes S$^{re}$ I believe I can, and Coll$^{o}$: POWELL replyed pray / doe, y$^{r}$ Ant shall pay y$^{w}$ honestly for itt. for it is her / horse and further Sayth not — JNO: BROWNE

Ju$^{r}$ in Cur. nono die Junij
anno 1694 Test HD C$^{l}$

Memorand$^{m}$:

A deede made by W$^{M}$. CHAMBERS & ROZAMOND his / wife to THO: MOORE bearing date y$^{e}$ 9$^{th}$ day of ffebr$^{r}$y 1693 / for seven hundred & fifty acres of Land, and by y$^{e}$ s$^{d}$. CHAMBERS / & his Wife acknowledged in this County Court, and Recorded on / y$^{e}$ 9$^{th}$. day of ffeb$^{r}$y 1693 is Assign'd by y$^{e}$ s$^{d}$. MOORE to JN$^{O}$: JONES / of this County in theese words (viz$^{t}$)

**[115]**

Know all men by theese p$^{r}$sents y$^{t}$ I WILLIAM CHAMBERS of Lawns / Creeke Parrish of y$^{e}$ County of Surry for a Valuable Consideration / to me in hand pay'd by THO: MOORE of y$^{e}$ Upp$^{r}$ pish of y$^{e}$ Isle of / Wight County, and w$^{th}$ which I acknowledge my Selfe fully Satisfy'd / Have bargained & Sold, And doe heereby for me and my heir$^{rs}$ for Ever / Bargaine sell & deliver, Infeoff, Transferr, & confirme, unto / y$^{e}$ S$^{d}$. THO: MOORE & to his heires Assignes for Ever, all y$^{t}$ my Estate / right, title & Interest y$^{t}$ I have in and to a Certaine pcell of Land / Scituate on y$^{e}$ Maine black water Swamp, in y$^{e}$ upp$^{r}$ pish of y$^{e}$ / Isle of Wight County afores$^{d}$. Conteyning by Estimation Seven / hundred & fifty acres, be the Same more or Less, y$^{e}$ said Seven / hundred & fifty acres more or Less, being pt. of a pattent, for / Eleven hundred & fifty acres to me granted y$^{e}$ 20$^{th}$ of October / 1691 and thus bounded, beginning at a m$^{r}$ked Maple in the /

Maine black water Swamp aforeS$^{d}$. thence by a line of m$^{r}$ked / trees, w$^{ch}$ devides y$^{e}$ S$^{d}$. ꝑcell of Land from y$^{e}$ residue of y$^{e}$ pattent / to a Red oake in y$^{e}$ head line of y$^{e}$ s$^{d}$. pattent, and then by y$^{e}$ Severall / headlines of y$^{e}$ S$^{d}$. Pattent, to a pine in a branch w$^{ch}$ devides this L$^{d}$ / from y$^{e}$ land of M$^{r}$. GEORGE WILLIAMSONs and soe downe y$^{e}$ S$^{d}$. brāch / to y$^{e}$ Runn of y$^{e}$ main black water Swamp aforeS$^{d}$. and Soe up y$^{e}$ / Runn of y$^{e}$ S$^{d}$. Swamp to y$^{e}$ Maple first above menttioned

To have & to Hold y$^{e}$ said 750 acres of Land more or lesse / together with all y$^{e}$ howses, orchards, gardens Woods, waies / & Waters, and all other Royalltyes, Priviledges, profitts Comodity's / & hereditam$^{ts}$: whatsoever to y$^{e}$ Sd. Land belonging or in any wise / apperteyning, to him y$^{e}$ S$^{d}$. THO: MOORE and to his hier$^{rs}$ and / assignes for Ever, in as full and ample Manner to all in= / =tents & purposes, as I my Selfe might or could have Enjoyed / the Same by vertue of y$^{e}$ before Recited pattent, or as the / most Learned in y$^{e}$ Law can devise, And I doe heereby declare / & affirme, Covenant & agree to & w$^{th}$ y$^{e}$ S$^{d}$. MOORE his heir$^{rs}$ & / assignes for Ever, y$^{t}$ y$^{e}$ aforeS$^{d}$. Land and Every ꝑt and

**[116]**

And ꝑcell thereof is clear & free from all & all manner of former / bargaines, & Sales, Morgages, Joyntures, Dowries, Judgm$^{ts}$. Execut$^{ns}$ / and all other manner of Imcumbrances w$^{t}$Soever, And y$^{t}$ I have at y$^{e}$ tyme / of Ensealing & delivery heerof to all & Singular y$^{e}$ p$^{r}$imises a good / Sure & Indefezable Estate of Inheritance in fee w$^{ch}$ I heereby trans= / =ferr & oblidge my Selfe my heir$^{rs}$ Exec$^{rs}$ & Adm$^{rs}$, to warrant & defend / this my Sale of all and singular y$^{e}$ p$^{r}$mises w$^{th}$ their appurtenances / to him y$^{e}$ S$^{d}$. THO: MOORE unto his heir$^{rs}$ & assignes for Ever, against / all & all maner of ꝑsons w$^{t}$soever by from or under me deriving / or p$^{r}$tending any Claime title or Interest thererto, When thereto / required will give to him or any of them, all Such further and other / Confirmat$^{o}$: of y$^{e}$ Same of his or their Cousell [*sic*] learned in y$^{e}$ Law / Shall think fitt, And will acknowledge this Instrum$^{t}$: of Conveyance / together w$^{th}$ my wives Relinquishm$^{t}$: of her Right of Dowre / to y$^{e}$ land heerein above mention'd in open Court next to be held / for y$^{e}$ Isle of Wight County aforeS$^{d}$. in testimony of all w$^{ch}$. I have / together w$^{th}$ ROAS$^{D}$. my wife heereunto put my hand & Seale the / 9$^{th}$ of ffeb$^{r}$ry 1693

Sign'd Seal'd in y$^{e}$ p$^{r}$sence
of ARTH : ALLEN
THO: PITT

W$^{M}$: CHAMBERS Seale
ROSA$^{D}$: **R** CHAMBER Seale
her m$^{r}$ke

Isle of Wight County the 9$^{th}$ of ffeb$^{r}$ry 1693 / The Within Subscribed W$^{M}$ CHAMBERS / and ROZAMOND his Wife, acknowledged this / to be their free & Volantary act & deed / in open Court

Test HUGH DAVIS Clr Cur
Recorded ꝑ HUGH DAVIS ꝑdict

**[117]**

Know all men by theise p$^{r}$sents, that I THOMAS MOORE of y$^{e}$ / upp$^{r}$ ꝑish of y$^{e}$ Isle of Wight County, for a Valuable Considert$^{o}$ / by me already Rec$^{d}$. of JN$^{O}$. JONES of y$^{e}$ Lower ꝑish of y$^{e}$ afores$^{d}$. / County, doth Assigne over & deliver into y$^{e}$ S$^{d}$. JN$^{O}$: JONES and / to his heir$^{rs}$ or Assignes for Ever all my Right title and Intrest / y$^{t}$ I have in or to this Seven hundred & fifty acres of Land as / within is Specifyed, in as full and Ample maner, & to all / intents & purposes, as with all other priviledges w$^{t}$soever / to me Confirmed and will acknowledge this my Assignm$^{t}$: / unto y$^{e}$ S$^{d}$: JN$^{O}$: JONES or his heir$^{rs}$ or assignes for Ever. to ge= / ther with my Wifes Reinquishm$^{t}$. of her Right & Dowre / to this S$^{d}$. Land, or any ꝑt thereof w$^{th}$in Mention'd in open / Court next to be held of [ ] the Isle of Wight County. In / testimony of all w$^{ch}$. I have together with ELIZ$^{A}$: my Wife / heereunto put my hand Seal August y$^{e}$ 9$^{th}$ 1694

Sign'd Seal'd & Deliver'd — THO MOORE Seale

in y$^{e}$ p$^{r}$sence of

GEORGE WILLIAMSON

RICH: ROYALL

Aug$^{st}$. y$^{e}$ 9$^{th}$ 1694 / Ackno. in open Courte by the S$^{d}$ / THO: MOOR, & ELIZ$^{A}$. y$^{e}$ wife of y$^{e}$ S$^{d}$ THOMAS relinquisheth her / dower by her subscribed attorny

Test: H DAVIS Cl

Know all men by theise p$^{r}$sents y$^{t}$ I ELIZ$^{A}$: MOORE y$^{e}$ Wife of THO: MOORE / doe Constitute & appoynt my L$^{o}$: Brother M$^{r}$: GEO: MOORE, of y$^{e}$ County / of Isle of Wight my true & Lawfull Attorny for & to acknowledge / unto JN$^{O}$: JONES Sn$^{r}$: of y$^{e}$ aboveS$^{d}$. County all my Right title & Intrest, w$^{ch}$ / I have, by Right of Dowry in and to a Certayne track of Land, Contein / =ing Seven hundred & fifty acres bought by my Husband of M$^{r}$ WILL / CHAMBERS of Surry County, Granting to my Attorney full power / & Lawfull Authority to acknowledge y$^{e}$ aboveS$^{d}$. Land, as if I my Selfe / where [*sic*] ꝑsonally p$^{r}$sent, In wittnesse heereunto I have sett my hand & / Seale this 6$^{th}$ day of August 1694

ELIZ$^{A}$: **E** MOORE Seale

Sign'd Seal'd in y$^{e}$ p$^{r}$sence of

AND: GRIFFIN

JN$^{O}$: GOODRICH

TH$^{O}$: THROPP

Aug$^{st}$ y$^{e}$ 9$^{th}$ 1694
proved by y$^{e}$ Oaths of JN$^{O}$: GOODRICH & TH$^{O}$: THROPP
Test: H DAVIS Cl Cur

**[118]**

In obedience to an ord$^{r}$. of Court Dated y$^{e}$ 9$^{th}$ of June Instant / Wee the Subscribers have apaised y$^{e}$ Estate of CHRISTOPHER / BATEMAN

| | |
|---|---|
| (viz) To 15 peeces of Earthen Ware | 100 [lb] |
| to 1 Chaffe bed boalster bedstead & hide | 130 |
| to 1 Couch & bed & 3 pillows & two bobbin Coushings | 150 |
| to two Chests at | 120 |

| | |
|---|---|
| to Tw [*sic*] tables and 1 forme at | 250 |
| Three Chaires att | 060 |
| 4 trayes | 020 |
| 1 Iron pott at | 100 |
| 1 ffrying pan and hamer at | 051 |
| 5 pailes and a baskett with a ꝑcell of Wooll in it at | 075 |
| 1 Lennen wheele | 070 |
| 2 old barrells a baskett of feathers & a Pametahood | 020 |
| a ꝑcell of Stinking beefe | 080 |
| 1 tinn pot & a tinn pann att | 025 |
| Sworne to this appraism[t] | 1171 |

this 14[th] of June 1694 befor me

JA: BENN

THO: NORSWORTHY
JNO: ꟼ WHETLEY
his m[r]ke

Recorded ꝑ HUGH DAVIS Cl

This is to Impower M[r] JN[O]: GILES to be my Attorny to plead or / doe any businesse in o[r] Court, & Especially against MALACK HAULEY / for me and in my Stead wittnesse my hand this 8[th] of August 1694

his
ROB: **R** COLLMAN
m[r]ke

Wittnesse
JA: TULLAGH
W[M]: JOLLEY

Recorded ꝑ H DAVIS Cl

**[119]**

Know all men by these p[r]sents that I ELIZABETH EDWARDS of / y[e] Isle of Wight County in y[e] Colony of Virginia widdow / for and in Consideration that THOMAS THROP of y[e] County / afores[d]. Carpenter, has beene (& Still is) at charge troble of / providing convenient house roome & much provision for my / Support & Maintenance, without which care & kindnesse, my / Small matt[r] w[ch] I had left me by my husband, could nor would not / Support me in my now infirme & old age, in so much y[t], I must / of Necessity proove a burthen to y[e] ꝑish, where I now live, & for / divers other good & Reasonable Considerations me thereunto movu= / ing [*sic*]. Have given & granted, & by these p[r]sents doe fully & absolute / =ly give grant Assigne transferr, & Sett over unto y[e] S[d]. THO: THROPP / all and Singular, my moneys, goods, Debts, household Stuffe and / Whatsoever Estate I have now in my posession or due & of / Law belonging to me, Immediately to be by him Enjoyed & to / his assignes for Ever, not doubting his care of me Soe long as / it shall please God to Continue my life in this World, In / Wittnesse whereof, I have heereunto Sett my hand & Seale / this Twenty Third day of ffeb[r]ry Anno Dom: one Thousand / Six hundred Ninety & Three

her
ELIZ[A]: W EDWARDS

Sealed & Deliverd

in y$^{e}$ p$^{r}$sence of her m$^{r}$ke
JN$^{O}$: GOODRICH
ROB$^{T}$: KAR
WILL FFISHER

**[120]**

**August y$^{e}$ 21$^{th}$ day 1694**

An acc$^{tt}$: of what was p$^{r}$sented to us of JN$^{O}$: ALTMANs Estate whose / are [*sic*] heereund$^{r}$. Written

| | |
|---|---|
| Imprimis, three pewter dishes 2 plates one porringer 16 Spoones one beaker at | 0170 |
| Item one Chest one table one Couch all old at | 0060 |
| Item 6 flecees of wooll | 0090 |
| Item one gunn | 0140 |
| Item 4 pailes & 2 bowls | 0030 |
| Item 2 iron potts & pothookes & one Skimer | 0160 |
| Item one pestle & one Cutting Knife | 0070 |
| Item one horse with Saddle & bridle at | 1100 |
| Item 4 hogs at 100 a peece 17 shotes at 50 & 5 pigs at 25 | 1375 |
| Item 6 Cowes at 380 peece | 2280 |
| Item 2 heifers & one young bull | 0750 |
| Item 3 Calves | 0300 |
| Item 5 Sheepe | 0500 |
| Item 7 Sider barrels at 20 ꝑ peece | 0140 |
| | 7215 |

Testis o$^{r}$ hands y$^{e}$ day & year above written
W$^{M}$. SMITH
ROB$^{T}$: KING

8$^{ber}$ y$^{e}$ 9$^{th}$ 1694 / p$^{r}$sented to y$^{e}$ Courte on Oath of y$^{e}$ / widdow of y$^{e}$ s$^{d}$ JN$^{O}$. ALTMAN deced:

Test: HUGH DAVIS Cl

Know all men by theise p$^{r}$sents that I THO:MAN of y$^{e}$ Isle of Wight / County, planter, doe, firmely give & bequeath from me my heir$^{rs}$ Exec$^{rs}$. / Adm$^{rs}$: or Assignes, unto SARAH MAN the wife of FFRANCIS DAVIS [*sic*] of / the Same County a ꝑcell of land Containeing one hundred acres / more or Lesse, Scituate lyeing and being in y$^{e}$ Isle of Wight county / aforeS$^{d}$. and butting & bounding one y$^{e}$ North east side of Curawaok / Swamp, Beginning at a pine Standing in y$^{e}$ aforeS$^{d}$. MAN's line / m$^{r}$ked with three Noches in one Side, and Soe runing along y$^{e}$ Line / North West to a pine a Corner tree, thence runing along y$^{e}$ line y$^{t}$ / was CHARLES MAN's north twenty Six pole to a Small white oake / in Coll$^{o}$: BRIDGERs Line then by y$^{e}$ line west to Curawaok Swamp / then up y$^{e}$ Swamp to a gume m$^{r}$ked, Standing in or near y$^{e}$ Runn / of the S$^{d}$. Swamp, thence North east or near y$^{e}$ Matter along a line / of m$^{r}$ked trees, m$^{r}$ked with three m$^{r}$ks in East Side, by y$^{e}$ Side of a / little branch near CHARLES MANs old feild Running up to the

**[121]**

the foreS$^{d}$. pine m$^{r}$ked in y$^{e}$ aforeS$^{d}$. MANs Line, which Land being / bounded as above namely, I the S$^{d}$. THO: MAN do make firmly unto the S$^{d}$ / SARAH MAN & her heir$^{rs}$. Lawfully begotten of her own body for Ever / withall Commodityes apurtenances & hereditam$^{ts}$. thereunto belonging / further it is agreed upon that if y$^{e}$ aforeS$^{d}$. SARAH MAN dieth before / her husband FFRANCIS DAVIS, he is not to be molested Soe long as he liveth / and after his decease, her heir$^{rs}$, is to have it for Ever, and for y$^{e}$ more / Confirmation of y$^{e}$ S$^{d}$. THO: MAN doe binde me my heir$^{rs}$, or assign's / to make firme unto SARAH DAVIS & her heir$^{rs}$, the aforeS$^{d}$. Land / Voluntary and to acknowledge it in open Court, the Said deed / to be free & Voluntary, as Wittnesse my hand & Seale this / thirteenth day of Septemb$^{r}$. In y$^{e}$ year of o$^{r}$ Lord God one thous= / =and Six hundred ninety three

Sign'd Seal'd & Del$^{dd}$.
in y$^{e}$ p$^{r}$sence of Us
W$^{M}$: DUCK
her
MARG: ∞ DUCKE
m$^{r}$ke

It is further agreed upon that if y$^{e}$ / aforeS$^{d}$. SARAH MAN dieth and her heir$^{rs}$ w$^{th}$out / Issue after y$^{e}$ death of FFRANCIS DAVIS, the / Said Land Shall returne to y$^{e}$ Said MAN or / his heir$^{rs}$. againe

his
THO: **M** MAN Seale
m$^{r}$ke

Ackno.' In Courte by the S$^{d}$ THO: MAN this 9$^{th}$ / day of October 1694
Test: HUGH DAVIS Cl

Know all men by theise p$^{r}$sents that I THOMAS MAN of y$^{e}$ Isle of / Wight County planter for divers good Causes & Considerations / but more Especially for and In Consideration of a certaine sume / of Tobacho to me in hand paid or Sured to be paid, by JAMES / CURLEY of y$^{e}$ Same County planter, the Receipt whereof I doe / heereby acknowledge and Confesse, Have given, Granted, bargain'd / Sould aliened and Confirmed, and doe by theise p$^{r}$sents for me my heir$^{rs}$. / Exec$^{rs}$. & Adm$^{rs}$. Give Grant bargaine Sell alien and Confirme unto him / the S$^{d}$. JAMES CURLEY his heir$^{rs}$. Exec$^{rs}$. Adm$^{rs}$: or Assignes, a Certaine / pcell of Land Conteining one hundred & fifty acres more or lesse / Scituate lyeing and being in y$^{e}$ Isle of Wight County aforeS$^{d}$ / and butting & bounding upon y$^{e}$ Northeast Side of Currewaoke / Swamp. Beginning at y$^{e}$ foreS$^{d}$. MANs line in the runn of Carawaok / Swamp, and running up y$^{e}$ S$^{d}$. line Northeast to a pine a Corner tree / near JAMES JOHNSON thence North west along the S$^{d}$. MANs line / to a pine m$^{r}$ked with three Noches in a Side, thence running down / a Line of m$^{r}$ked trees South m$^{r}$ked with three Noches in a Side to a

**[122]**

A gume Standing in or near y$^{e}$ run of Curawoak Swamp near y$^{e}$ mouth of / a Little branch Issuing out of y$^{e}$ S$^{d}$ Swamp and running up by y$^{e}$ Side of CHARLES / MANs old feild, thence Runing up y$^{e}$ run of Curewaok Swamp to y$^{e}$ aforeS$^{d}$. / MANs line unto him the S$^{d}$. JAMES CURLEY his heir$^{rs}$. Exec$^{rs}$: Adm$^{rs}$: and assignes / for Ever, free and clear and freely & Clearly acquitted exonorated & dischar / =ged of & from all manner of former and other titles, grants bargaines / Sales or other Incumbrances whatsoever with all priviledges thereunto / belonging, houses buildings fencees woods timber & timber trees waters & / water Cources, profitts priviledges, commodityes and advantages to have / and to hold to him the S$^{d}$. JA: CURLEY his heir$^{rs}$ Ex$^{rs}$ Adm$^{rs}$ a$^{ss}$s: for Ever And y$^{e}$ S$^{d}$. THO: / MAN doth further Covenāt ℘mise and grant to and w$^{th}$ y$^{e}$ S$^{d}$ JAMES CURLEY / his heir$^{rs}$. Exec$^{rs}$. adm$^{rs}$ or assignes, that he y$^{e}$ S$^{d}$. THO: MAN his heir$^{rs}$: Exec$^{rs}$. / adm$^{rs}$ or assignes Shall and Will at all tymes heereafter, warrant Save / defend and Keepe harmlesse y$^{e}$ S$^{d}$. JA: CURLEY his heir$^{rs}$: Exec$^{rs}$: adm$^{rs}$: or / Assignes from all ℘sons that Shall or may heereafter claime any / Right title or Intrest in y$^{e}$ S$^{d}$. Land or any ℘t or ℘cell thereof further / I the S$^{d}$. THO: MAN doe oblidge my Selfe my heir$^{rs}$ & assignes to give / unto him the S$^{d}$. JA: CURLEY his heir$^{rs}$: or assignes any further assu= / =rance as his learned Councill Shall advise, In Wittnesse whereof / I have heereunto Sett my hand and Seale this thirteenth day of / Septb$^{r}$. in y$^{e}$ year of o$^{r}$ Lord one Thousand Six hundred ninty foure

Sign'd Seal'd & deli$^{d}$. in y$^{e}$ p$^{r}$sence of us
W$^{M}$ DUCK
W$^{M}$ BUSH
EDM$^{D}$. BRIAN

his
THO: **M** MAN Seale
m$^{r}$ke

ackno.' Courte by the S$^{d}$ THO: MAN this / 9$^{th}$ of October 1694

Test: HUGH DAVIS Cl

Know all men by theise p$^{r}$sents y$^{t}$ I THOMAS MAN of y$^{e}$ Isle of Wight / County planter for divers good Causes & Considerations, but more / Especially for and in Consideration of a Certaine Sume of Tobaccho / to me in hand paid or Sured to be paid by WILL DUCKE of y$^{e}$ Same / County planter, the receipt whereof I doe heereby acknowledge and / Confesse, have given granted bargained Sould aliened and Confirmed / and doe by theise p$^{r}$sents for me my heir$^{rs}$: Exec$^{rs}$: & adm$^{rs}$: Give Grant bargaine / Sell Alien & Confirme Unto him y$^{e}$ S$^{d}$. W$^{M}$: DUCKE his heir$^{rs}$. Exec$^{rs}$. adm$^{rs}$ and / assignes a Certayne ℘cell of Land Conteyning one hundred and Eighty acres / more or lesse, Scituate Lyeing and being in y$^{e}$ Isle of Wight County aforeS$^{d}$.

**[123]**

AfordS$^{d}$. and butting and bounding upon y$^{e}$ South west Side of Curowaok / Swamp, Begining at a Gum m$^{r}$ked with three Noches In each Side Stand= / ing in or near y$^{e}$ Run of Currawaok Swamp in y$^{e}$ mouth of a great / branch Issueing out of y$^{e}$ South west Side of y$^{e}$ fores$^{d}$. Swamp, thence / to a white oake thence up y$^{e}$ run of y$^{e}$ s$^{d}$. branch to a gum

Standing / in y$^{e}$ mouth of a Little branch Issuing out of the aforeS$^{d}$. great branch / and running up South West or near the master marked to a gum / Standing in y$^{e}$ head of y$^{e}$ little branch near unto THO: MANs old plan / =tation thence running along the S$^{d}$. MANs line Southerly to a pine / thence runing along y$^{e}$ S$^{d}$. MANs Line Easterly or Northeast to / Curawaok Swamp, thence downe the run of y$^{e}$ S$^{d}$. Swamp to the / afores$^{d}$. Gume, unto him y$^{e}$ S$^{d}$. W$^{M}$. DUCK to his heir$^{rs}$. Exec$^{rs}$. adm$^{rs}$. / and assignes for Ever. free & Clear & freely & Clearly acquitted / Exonorated and discharged of and from all manner of former / and other gifts grants bargaines Sales or other Incumbrances / whatsoever with all priviledges thereunto belonging howses / buildings fences woods timber & timber trees, waters & water / Courses profitts priviledges Comodityes and advantages. To / have and to hold to him y$^{e}$ S$^{d}$. W$^{M}$. DUCKE his heir$^{rs}$. Exec$^{rs}$. adm$^{rs}$. / & assignes for Ever, And y$^{e}$ S$^{d}$. THO: MAN doth further Covent / ꝑmise & grant to and with y$^{e}$ S$^{d}$. W$^{M}$. DUCK his heir$^{rs}$. Exec$^{rs}$. / adm$^{rs}$. & assignes that he y$^{e}$ S$^{d}$ THO: MAN his heir$^{rs}$ Exec$^{rs}$. adm$^{rs}$. / & assignes, Shall and will at all tymes hearafter warrant / Save defend and Keepe harmelesse y$^{e}$ S$^{d}$. W$^{M}$. DUCK his heir$^{rs}$. Exc$^{rs}$. / adm$^{rs}$ & Assignes from all ꝑsons that Shall or may hearafter claime / any Right title or Interest to y$^{e}$ S$^{d}$. Land or any ꝑt or ꝑcell / thereof further I y$^{e}$ S$^{d}$. THO: MAN doe oblidge myselfe my heir$^{rs}$ / Exec$^{rs}$. adm$^{rs}$. & assignes, to give unto him y$^{e}$ S$^{d}$. W$^{M}$. DUCKE his / heir$^{rs}$. Exec$^{rs}$. adm$^{rs}$ & assignes any further Assurance as his / learn'd Coucell shall advise, In Wittnesse whereof I have / heereunto Set my Hand and Seale this thirteenth day of 7$^{ber}$ / In y$^{e}$ year of o$^{r}$ Lord one Thousand Six hundred ninety fower Sign'd Seal'd & Deliv$^{rd}$: in y$^{e}$ p$^{r}$sence of us

his<br>
THO: **M** MAN & Seale<br>
m$^{r}$ke

W$^{M}$. BUSH<br>
EDW: BRIAN<br>
JA: I CURLEY<br>
his m$^{r}$ke

Ackno.' in Courte by the S$^{d}$ THO: MAN / this 9$^{th}$ day of October 1694<br>
Test HUGH DAVIS Cl

**[124]**

To the Wors$^{ll}$ their Majt$^{s}$ Justices these are to Sertrtifie [*sic*] / that I CATHREN PERCE doe empower THOMAS MOORE to= / be my Attorney at this Court held the 9$^{th}$ day of this / Instant to answer to an accion entred ag$^{t}$ me by MATHEW / STRICKLAND in wittnes here unto I have sett my this [*sic*] 6$^{th}$ day / of October 1694

ROBERT KAE<br>
WINN, THOMAS

CATH: **K** PEERCE<br>
her marke

Recorded ꝑ HD Cl

To the Worshippfull their maiesties Justices / for the Isle of Wight County THOMAS GROSS humbley / Sheweth that M$^{r}$. THOMAS PITT in his life time & / this pett$^{r}$: had som difference a bout this pett$^{er}$: Land / which Difrence was fully endede & Concluded before Coll= / ARTHUR SMITH & Capt HENRY APPLEWAITE which the

/ said M^r^. PITT did reduce into writing under his own / hand which was left in the hands of y^e^ said Coll.= / SMITH to which y^e^ said Coll: SMITH & Capt. APPLEWITE / and witnesses: and this pett^r^ Considering that all / men are mortall & that that writing being all / that this pett^r^: hath to show for his said Land y^t^ if / Coll: SMITH sholde die would be loste, this pett^r^:= / doth desier therfor that Coll SMITH might produce y^e^ / same to the Court y^t^ this pett^r^ may have it recorded & / this pett^r^. shall pray and &c
8^ber^. y^e^ 9^th^
1694

Upon this pet^n^ y^e^ following deed was de^l^: into y^e^ / Office by Col. SMITH by order of Courte Test H DAVIS Cl

Thes Presents witnesseth that THOMAS GROSE & / THOMAS PITT bothe of the Isle of Wight County / have mutually a Gread betweene them for & / Conserning the Land in diference betwene them / *videliset* that THOMAS PITT is to let THO: GROSE his / heyres exeq^r^ or assines all his wright title & Intrust / of the land the saide GROSE now houlds up as far as / Coll BRIDGERS new line to his heyres and Assines for / Ever [ ] [*escheat*] / the s^d^ THOMAS GROSE paying / unto THO: PITT his heyres exeq^rs^ administre^rs^ or

**[125]**
Assines six thousand pounds of to bacco and Caske at two / payments that is thre thousand redy downe & three / thousand y^e^ next yeare if M^r^ NICHOLUS SMITH wants / in his breadth of two hunderd acers runing his mile / according to patting and Comes soe much as thare wa / nting in y^e^ breadth THO: PITT is to make Good proporsina / ble out of y^e^ six thouand [*sic*] pounds of tobacco accounting / the land to be 200 Acres that THO: GROSE now / houlds witnes our handes the 9^th^ of october 1686
ARTH: SMITH y^e^ m^r^ke of **T** THO: GROSE
HEN: APPLEWHAITE 8^ber^ 9^th^ 94 THO: PITT

ARTHUR SMITH & HEN: APPLEWHATE / sworne as evidence to this deed / & upon GROSSE pet^n^: y^e^ same lyes / in y^e^ office Test: H DAVIS Cl

Know all men by these presence that I EDMUND / IRBY of Charles sitty County do here by authorise / and impower W^M^: ARCHER or Such other persons as / he shall appoint to be my atturny to prosecute / all actions as are now depending betwene me and / person or persons in the Isle of wite County and what / my sade atturny shall do or Caus to be done in the / premisses I will allow & Conferm In witnes where of / I have here to set my hnad this 2^th^ day of october / In the yeare of ower Lord 1694
Seald & Delivered in the presence of
JOHN DELK EDMUND IRBY
JAMES DINFORD Recorded ꝑ HD Cl

These are to sertifie that I W$^{M}$ ARCHER doe authorizes / and impower THOMAS MOORE to execute the with in / power in witnes here unto I have set my hand this 9th / day of x$^{ber}$ 1694 WA.

test JOHN DELK
M$^{r}$ JOHN GILES JN$^{O}$. DELKE sworne as an / evidence hereof 8$^{ber}$. 9$^{th}$ / 1694
Test: HUGH DAVIS Cl

I dow Constitute yow my lawfull atturny / to implead M$^{rs}$ MARY WORD and to obtaine an order of / Court ag$^{t}$ her for my debt according to the bill of five pounds / assigned by me by M$^{r}$ EDWORD C[ ]LTON: for w$^{ch}$ I will pay you / or ffes as wittnesse my hand this 28$^{th}$ of Sep$^{r}$ 1694

Test JOHN PITT ELIZEBETH **E** GREANE
OLIVE PITT hur marke

**[126]**

At a Courte holden for the Isle of Wight County on the / **9$^{th}$: day of August Anno Domini 1694**

By their Ma$^{ties}$ Justices

On the 25$^{th}$ day of this month Coll ARTHER SMITH Cap$^{t}$. / HENRY APPLEWHAITE M$^{r}$: THO: GILES & Cap$^{t}$ JA: BENNE / or any three of them are requested & impowered / to meet at the hous of M$^{r}$ HUMPHREY MARSHALL / in the County & audite acc$^{ott}$ betwene JN$^{O}$: MAR / SHALL Pl$^{t}$ & y$^{e}$ s$^{d}$ HUMPHRY MARSHALL def$^{t}$ & to reporte / the same to the next Courte

In obedience to the with in order of this / Court we subscribed have met at the hous of M$^{r}$. / HUMPHRY MARSHALL and have proused theyr / Accounts and finde M$^{r}$: JN$^{O}$: MARSHALL to except / aganst sume artickes in the first ꝑte of his sonns / account which he have prodused a receipt for some and sat= / tice=facktory reasons to us for the nexte which / he proffers to sware to when required the ballance / of which acc$^{ott}$. we finde to be 100$^{li}$ of tobacco due / to M$^{r}$ HUMPHRY MARSHALL within our hands this / 11 day of Sept 1694

ARTH: SMITH
HEN: APPLEWHAIT
THO: GILES
JAS: BENN

October y$^{e}$ 9$^{th}$. 1694 / Recorded ꝑ HUGH DAVIS C$^{l}$ C$^{ur}$

**[127]**

In a be deants to a order of Court of the Isle of Wight / County baring date August the 9: 1694

We of the Jury hath not upon the plantashun / of M^r ROBART COLEMANs that is menshed in the order / of Co^rt and we find by evidenc that M^r COLEMAN / hath ousted the s^d mallit holle and we find no dam / ing against the defendent and we of the Jure hath / set our hands this: 11: day of september in the / year: 1694

| | |
|---|---|
| NICHOLASS FULLGHAM | JOHN **IP** PENNE |
| RICH: WILKINSON: Jun | his mark |
| CHARLS **&** DURRIM | WILLIAM **W** PENNE |
| his marck | THO **T** GROSE |
| WALTER RUTTER | his mark |
| JOHN LUTHER | JOHN **I** WATS |
| THO: **I** WHITLE | his mark |
| his mark | ROBARD **R** RICHARDS |
| | mark |
| | EDWARD **N** BROUN |
| | mark |

Decemb^r. y^e 10^th 1694 / Compared, & it agrees with y^e Original both in / tense & pseudography Test: HDAVIS C^l

An acco^t: of debts paid by y^e widow SUSANA WADE / Since her husbands death w^ch he owed before he / died

| | ^lb tobacco |
|---|---|
| To THO: GILES | 0269 |
| To M^r: JOSEPH WOORY | 0240 |
| To M^r: W^M WEST | 0150 |
| To W^M JOHNSON | 0040 |
| To Coll JN^O. PITT | 0300 |
| To Madan [*sic*] HESTER BRIDGER | 0400 |
| To Cap^t: THO GODWIN | 1190 |
| To Mair: ARTHER ALLIN | 0300 |
| To docter JOHNSON | 0400 |
| To TIMOTHY WALKER | 0400 |
| To Coll JAMES POWELL at severall payments | 2573 |
| To Coll JAMES POWELL 534^lb porke at 1½ | 0301 |
| To M^r JAMES BENN | 0090 |
| turne in all | 7091 |

**[128]**
Wee finde by y^e Acct^tt prsented to us by SUSAN: WAIDE / Execu^t. of CHRISTOPHER WAIDEs by severall receipt / past to her which her decd^d. husband was In debted / amounting to the sume of 7091

Octob^r^: y^e^ 9^th^ 1691 — THO: MOORE, WILL BRADSHAW

Octob$^{r}$: y$^{e}$ 9$^{th}$
1691

THO: MOORE
WILL BRADSHAW

Recorded HDAVIS C$^{l}$

| | |
|---|---|
| on white faced hefer ab$^{t}$: | 4 yeares old |
| on pyd Cow | 6 ditto |
| on brown Cow | 7 ditto |
| on Ditto heifer | 3 Do |
| on Ditto seare | 3 Do |
| on hifer at FRA: W$^{M}$.SONS | 3 Do |

1 head of hoggs yonge & old
on small
Chest & Iron pott
on fether bed & bolster
on Iron pot
on powdring tubb
pon friing pan
on postell
on pare tongs
August 13$^{th}$: 1694 then delevered into the Custody / of JN$^{O}$. SHERRER & RID LOYDE the above pticulirs

p HEN BAKER sheriffe

This is y$^{e}$ acc$^{ott}$. of y$^{e}$ estate of JN$^{O}$. RICHARDSON deb: JN$^{O}$ / SHERRER which is recorded this 9$^{th}$. 8$^{ber}$ 1694

p HUGH DAVIS C$^{l}$

JEMIMA DRAKE[6] aged 43 yeares on or thare about / being examined & sworne: Saith that some / time in July Last I hearde SAMMUELL COHOON / say that THOMAS NORSWORTHY fuckt FRANCES / MEACOM, & yo$^{r}$ deponant told y$^{e}$ said COHOON Shee / did not beleive it the said COHOON replyed it was / as sure as ever his father fuckt his mother & as

**[129]**

As sure as ever my husband fuckt me, & that he / wolde take his oath of it and the said COHOON went / over to WILLIAM JOHNSON's and when he Came back / again he asked this deponant if THOMAS NORSWORTHY / was rid out to Coll himselfe now he had put him / selfe in a heate with fucking the Girl, [ ]d / Saith the said COHOON, I thought to have had / the first bout with her my selfe but now / he may keep her & further this deponant / Saith not

JEMIMA | DRAKE

6 Herewith commences a bitter parable about the ruin of a young maiden's reputation. *Incipit nunc fabula miserrima dē ruinā famae virginis.*

Sworn in Courte y$^{e}$ 11$^{th}$ of her marke
x$^{ber}$ 1694 Test HD C$^{l}$

The deposition of WILLIAM JOHNSON aged 44 yeares / or thare a bout being examined & sworn: / saith that sometime in July last, SAMMUELL= / COHOON Came to this deponants house, puffing & / blowing this deponant asked the said COHOON what / was the matter, God saith he yonder is my / Land lord A swineing the garl this deponant / asked him what Girl, the said COHOON answered / FRANSES MECOM, this deponant answered I Could / not beleive it the saide COHOON replied it is / sure WILLIAM as ever you swined your wife, / and as sure as ever my father begot me, this dep= / onant bid him have a cear for it was a hard thing / to sware, he answered he wold take his oath / of it, & further this deponant saith not:
Sworne in Courte y$^{e}$ 11$^{th}$. x$^{ber}$ 94 WILLIAM JOHNSON
Test HDAVIS C$^{l}$C$^{ur}$

**[130]**

The Deposition of MARABLE FRANKLIN aged 44 / yeares of thare aboute being exa[m]ened & sworn / saith that som time in July last SAMUELL= / COHOON & THOMAS NORSWORTHY Came to this deponants / hous whare the said COHOON told this deponant / that THOMAS NORSWORTHY Commited Carnall Coper= / lation with FRANS MECOM as sure as ever my ~~father~~ / husband did with me, & as sure as his father be / God him, THOMAS NORSWORTHY bed him have / A care for he wold sue him, the said COHOON replyd / he did not Care he would sware it before any mag= / estrate or Court in Virginia and further this deponant / saith not
MARABLE **P** FRANKLING Recorded HDAVIS C$^{l}$
her mark

JOHN GARLLAND aged 23 years or thare abouts being / examined & sworn saith that some time in July / Last: this deponant Came to the house of THO: NORSWORTHY / About his action: & thare this deponant heard / SAMUELL COHOON say that THO: NORSWORTHY had / swift FRANCES MEACOM: & God saith the said COHOON / If he had not A swifed her I would but now he hath / Done it the said: COHOON said he wold have nothing / to do with her & further this deponant saith not JOHN **H** GARLLAND
Sworne in Courte y$^{e}$ 11$^{th}$ x$^{ber}$ 94 his mark
Test Test: HD C$^{l}$

I Doe heirby Impower JOHN WATTES for to Administer / upon my Dest husbands Estat for me in my place / Giving from under my hand the 7$^{th}$ day des 1694
Test Recorded HD C$^{l}$
JAMES BROWN proved by y$^{e}$ Oaths of both / wittnesses Test HD C$^{l}$
JOHN WATTS Juiner

**[131]**

ROBERT EDWARDs Estate Debt$^{r}$

| | |
|---|---|
| Im$^{ps}$: paid to WILL: WILLIAMS by bill | 400 |
| paid to Coll: PITT for the / lett$^{r}$: of Administraton | 192 |
| to Coll ARTHUR SMITH for levie | 200 |
| to ROB$^{T}$: LITTLEBOY | 075 |
| to JN$^{O}$: SUMMERELL | 060 |
| to Widdow MATHEWS | 050 |
| to my Selfe for 2 ells of / Canvas 6 Shaines of Silk and 3 doz: buttons | 045 |
| to funerall Charge | 140 |
| December y$^{e}$ 10$^{th}$ 1694 | 1162 |

OWEN GRIFFIN p$^{r}$sents this acco$^{tt}$ on oath & y$^{e}$ / same is admitted to Record

Test HDAVIS C$^{l}$

This bill bindeth me NICHOLAS ASKEW my hei$^{rs}$ / Exec$^{rs}$: adm$^{rs}$: to pay or Cause to be paid Unto JOHN: / ASKEW his hei$^{rs}$: Exec$^{rs}$: & Admin$^{rs}$ the full and Gest [*sic*] / Sume of ninety and nine thousand pounds of good / marchantable tobacco & Caske to be paid Convenient in y$^{e}$ / Low$^{r}$ ꝑish of y$^{e}$ Isle of Wight County upon demand In wit= / nesse here of I have sett my hand & seale this 24$^{th}$ of 9$^{br}$: 1694

The Condition of this obligation before mentioned / is Such that Whereas the aboves$^{d}$ NICHO: ASKEW & JN$^{O}$: / ASKEW being posest w$^{th}$: y$^{e}$ plantation which was formerely / THO: OGLETHORPE Contaning one hundred and seventy / acres of Land and y$^{e}$ s$^{d}$ NICHO ASKEW hath with the Consent / of his Wife for a Valuable Consideration to him in hand / paid before the Signing and Seleing of theis p$^{r}$sents, and / doth heereby owene him selfe fully Satisfyed that the / fore s$^{d}$: JN$^{O}$: ASKEW Shall have y$^{e}$ plantation where he / now liveth that is alredy Cleard: with all y$^{e}$ housees / garding occherds and fencees with all other y$^{e}$ a purtenancies / thereunto belonging with as much Wood land ground / Joyn:

**[132]**

Joyning to y$^{e}$ s$^{d}$ plantation as, as shall Compleate the one / halfe of y$^{e}$ afore one hundred and and [*sic*] seventy acers / of land to him the s$^{d}$. JN$^{O}$: ASKEW & his hei$^{rs}$: for their / Sheares for ever; Without lett hinderance molestation / or troubl by me the s$^{d}$ NICHO ASKEW on my heir$^{es}$ or any / other ꝑson or ꝑsons by or procuration and if y$^{e}$ s$^{d}$ NICHO: / ASKEW is heir$^{es}$ doe att all tymes for ever heere after / Let y$^{e}$ s$^{d}$ JN$^{O}$: ASKEW & his heir$^{es}$ Inioy the fores$^{d}$ plantation / with y$^{e}$ p$^{c}$ of y$^{e}$ wood land Ground peaceably and quietly / and acknowledge this as their Act & Deede in open Court / When so required then this p$^{r}$sent obligation to be / Voyde & of no affect or else to Stand in full force and / Virtu

NICHOLAS N ASKEW

WILL BRADSHAW
JOHN LUTEN
Sign' Seald & Deliverd December y[e] 10[th]. 1694
In y[e] p[r]sence of us
FFRAN **FS** SEGRAVE
signd

SARAH **X** ASKEW
Their m[r]ks

Acn[o]. in Courte by y[e] s[d] NICHO: ASKEW / & SARAH his Wife Test H DAVIS C[l] C[ur]

M[r]: SKELTON in forme me that JOHN WILLIAMS the precher / Keepe people from Coming to Church & I doe present him / And I doe present MARY JACKSON the Dafter of RICHARD / JACKSON for the ofence for bring of a base borne Child

JOHN BRANTLY
fore man

The Gran iury prese[t]. JEAMES JOLLY for Ceeping a woman / In his hous y[e] which he has to Childrion by her fur= / ther wee doe present ROBBART DRIVER for stoping up y[e] / high way & one of y[e] Grand Jury did tell him to Clean it / again & his anser was M[r] JOLLE mite Cleanit him selfe

Recorded H DAVIS C[l]

**[133]**

†In the name of God Amen I JOHN GRIFIN being sick / and weke of Body but in perfit mind and / memorey / After my body being intered at the desction of my / Executor hear after mentioned as for my Land, I give and / bequeath unto my sister ANNE TALLOCH to her and her / heirs for ever and my bead and furniture I Give all soe / to my said sister.

Item I Give and bequeth unto my sister SARAH TALLOCH / what tobacco my Father THOMAS GRIFING gave my brother / THO: GRIFIN being five thousand my funirell Charges paid / out of it, and all soe my puter I give to my sister / SARAH, and as for my Executor my Loving father JAMES TALLOCH / I doe appoint and ordaine my hole and sole Executor of this my / Last will and testiment As Witness my hand and Seall / December: 4[th]: 1694

Signde and Seald in
The Presents of
JAS: BEEN
ARTH: SMITH: Jun[r]
EDWARD **N**[7] GOODSON
his Marke

JOHN **I** GRIFFEN
agrees with y[e] Original
in Pseudography Test: HD

---

[7] More like an upside "U".

December $10^{th}$.1694 / proved in open Courte to be / $y^e$ last Will & Testament of / $JN^O$. GRIFFIN deced by $y^e$ oaths / of all $y^e$ witnesses hereto & / a probate granted $y^e$ $Exo^{rs}$ / Test: HUGH DAVIS

Isle of Wight County

In obedence to an $ord^r$ of Court baring date the $10^{th}$ day / of $ffeb^ry$ $169^2/_3$ we the Subscribers being sworne by $Cap^t$: / $JO^N$: GOODRICH to Appraze the estate of RICHARD TOWLE deseased / Doe appraze the said Estate viz

| lb s d | |
|---|---|
| 3 Cows at 03 05 00 | 05 05 00 |
| 1 Steare 4 yeare ould and one yearelen | 02 10 00 |
| one hors and ould Saddell | 03 00 00 |
| 9 Shoots and piggs | 01 00 00 |
| one ould bead and blanket | 01 10 00 |
| a parsell of ould Iron as ould pott frie pan | 01 00 00 |
| a Small parsell ould Puter | 00 00 00 |
| a parsell of ould wooding Lumber | 00 12 00 |
| To the above $s^d$ in all | 13 05 00 |

$Apprazem^t$ we have sett our hands this $20^{th}$. day of $ffeb^ry$ $169^2/_3$

THO: MOORE
THO: THROPP

Recorded Test: H DAVIS $C^l$

**[134]**

Know all men by these Presents that I JOHN PORTIS $Sen^r$. / of the Isle of Wight County planter & JANE my wife / Doe for us our heirs Executors or adminsitrators for / A valyable Consideration by us in hand alredy receved have / bargained for & sould unto and by these presents doe / Sell allinate and make over unto JOHN JONES $Sen^r$ in $y^e$ / ffore said County Cooper his heires or assigns for Ever / one hundred acers of Land situated liing & being / in the Lower parish of $y^e$ fore $s^d$ County begining at / a Red oake a Corner tree Joying to $y^e$ Land of $y^e$ $s^d$. / JOHN JONES so along by $y^e$ $s^d$. JONES is land to a pine mentioned / in $y^e$ Drught but that being down thare is marked / in its Steed a Red oake sapling from thence Long a / Line which by $y^e$ Draught Run is w: by:s: so far as / Shall make up $y^e$ hundred acers of Land with a / Line Runing from thence to $y^e$ first mentioned Red oake / this hundred a Ceres of Land is part of a patent of nine / hundred a Ceres of Land Granted to $y^e$ $s^d$. JOHN PO[ ] / and HENRY WEST, $y^e$ $s^d$. Land to have & to hold with all / prevelidges profits Regallityes what so Ever thare / unto belonging to him $y^e$ $s^d$. JOHN JONES his heires or / assigns for Ever with: Genarall waranty against any / person or persons that Shall or may Lay any Clames or / pretend to have any intrest to $y^e$ $s^d$. hundred acres of / Land or to any part or parsell thare of & farther more / I y$^{e}$ s$^{d}$. JOHN PORTIS Sen$^{r}$. Dooth obledge my self my heires / or assignes to Give unto y$^{e}$ s$^{d}$. JOHN JONES or to his hires / or assignes what further assureans that he

**[135]**

He the s$^{d}$. JONES his heires or assigns or his on / Ether off heyrs Councell in law Shall at any / time Requier & doe obledge our Selfes to acknowledg / this our Vallantary act & Deed at y$^{e}$ next Court / to be held for y$^{e}$ Isle of Wight County as witness / our hands & Seales this 10$^{th}$ Day of December 1694

his<br>
Test ROBERT SCOTT — JOHN **Y** PORTIS Sen$^{r}$.<br>
JOHN JORDAN — mark<br>
JANE **Z** PORTIS seale<br>
mark

Know all men by thees Presents y$^{t}$ I WILLIAM COOKE of y$^{e}$ / Upper Parish of y$^{e}$ Isle of Wight County for a Valluable / Consideration to me in hand paid by JOHN PROCTER of y$^{e}$ / Same Parish & County & w$^{th}$: which I acknowledge my Selfe / ffully satisfied have Bargained & Sold and doe here by / for me & my heires for ever Bargaine Sell & Deliver / Infeeoff Transfer & Confirme unto y$^{e}$ s$^{d}$. JOHN PROCKTER / and to his heires and Assignes for Ever one hundred / twenty five aceres of Land Scittuated near y$^{e}$ maine / blackwater in y$^{e}$ Parish & Cot$^{y}$. afores$^{d}$. being y$^{e}$ westward / halfe of a Patt$^{t}$: for two hundred & fifty acers to me granted / y$^{e}$ 9$^{th}$: day of aprill last past To have & to Hold y$^{e}$ s$^{d}$. one hundred / twenty and five aceres together w$^{th}$ all y$^{e}$ howses ortchards / Gardens woods ways & waters and all other Roytallties / Priveledges Proffits Comodities & hereditam$^{ts}$. whatsoever / to y$^{e}$ s$^{d}$. Land belonging or in any wise apperteining to / him y$^{e}$ s$^{d}$. JHON PROCTER & to his heires & assignes for Ever in / as full & ample maner to all intents & purposes as I my / Selfe might or Could have Enjoyed y$^{e}$ Same by vertue / of y$^{e}$ before recited Patt$^{t}$: and I doe hereby Declare / and affirme Covenant / And

**[136]**

And Agree to & with y$^{e}$ S$^{d}$. JOHN PROCTER his Heires & Assignes y$^{t}$ the / afore S$^{d}$. Land and Every Part & Parsell theireof is Clear / and free from all & all maner of former & other Bargaines / And Sales mortgages Joyntures Dowries Judgm$^{ts}$: & Executions / And all other maner of Incomberance what so Ever & y$^{t}$ I have / at the time of y$^{e}$ Sealing & Delivery here of to all and / Singular y$^{e}$ Premises A Good Pure & Indefeazable Estate of / Inheritance in fee simpell w$^{ch}$: I hereby Transfeir and / oblige my self my Ex$^{rs}$: & Ad$^{rs}$: to warrant & Defend this / my Sale of all & Singular y$^{e}$ Premises w$^{th}$: theire / Apurtenanses to him y$^{e}$ S$^{d}$. JOHN PROCKTER & to his Heires / and Assignes for ever a Gainst all & all maner of Persons what / Soever by from or Under me Deriveing or pretending any / Claime title or Interest theireto, When theire to required / Will Give to him or any of them all Such farther and / other Lawfull Assureence and Confirmat: of y$^{e}$ Same as his / or their Learned Councill Shall think fitt and will allso / acknowledge this

Instrum$^{t}$: of Conveyance to be my Reall Act: / and Deed in open Court next to be held for y$^{e}$ Isle of Wight / County above S$^{d}$: together w$^{ch}$: JONE my wife Relinquishm$^{t}$: of / her Right of Dower to y$^{e}$ Land herein a bove mentioned In / Testimony of all w$^{ch}$ I have together w$^{th}$: JONE my wife here / unto Put my hand and Seall this 9$^{th}$ day of ffebry 1694

signed Seald & Deliverd
In presence of
THO: MOORE

W$^{M}$: **A** COOCK Seal
his mark
JONE **I** COOCK
her mark

**[137]**

ffebruary the 5$^{th}$, 169$^{3}/_{4}$

An Inventory of M$^{r}$: WILLIAM DENSONs Estate / Deced

one Dowlis Sheet & bed ticking
A Rudg [*sic*] and blankit & five Elles of Canvis
one quier of paper & a box of pouder some nailes
one pound of thred one beed Corde
one pane of Stirrup lethers
one bridel Raines five baeles of Cotton yarnes
Some buttones & Case of knives
Eight pinte pott & a bibell a brasink dish
one pare of Scaled & wights Eight Dear Skins
two porringers one Cameblet Cotte
two pare of stillards, neare one barrell of Salt
two hors a sett of Irons for Carte wheles
nine Gimblets six plaining Irons & a round Shave
one adz & hand Saw & lathing hamer
three pare of Sisors twenty two Glas bottles
halfe a Case of bottells a Colde Chissell & a punch
Some Drapshott one wrighting
one quart pott, & pinte pott, one Glass Cup
one mug and Jally pott Som alloways
fore iron potts & three pare of pott hoks
Seaven augers & seaven Chisels two gouges
thre whole Gouges two hand Saws
two broade hoes fore broade axes
one tomahake one frieing pan one Ladel
and fork & steel fox trape one file
and fros two brase paness
one gun & one pare of fleams [flearns?] & one Crascut Saw
two Drawing knives one wedge
one hamer & Cuting Knife three bill hooks
one pare of balers Sheres & one horse

and one collen & sadell & hackny sadell
and two negro boys p me JER[E]. EXUM

**[138]**

Know all men by these Presents that I HENRY HARTWELL / of James Citty Doe Constitute and appoint and in my Stead / and place putt my welbeloved ffriend JN[O]: GILES my Law / full attorny for mee & in my name and on my behalf / to presecute all Such actions as I Shall have Depending / in the Isle of Wight County Court hereby ratifying and / Confirming whaty [*sic*] Said attorney Shall act or doe on my / behalfe as wittness my hand this 5[th] Day of Jan[r]y. 169$^4/_5$

Test CHA: CHAPMAN HEN: HARTWELL
HUGH DAVIS

The Deposicon of GILES DRIVER aged thirty four yeares / or their abouts Doth Declare to y[e] best of my Knowledge / that WILL JOLLEY Did removed of, of [*sic*] Brothers RICH: / RENYNOLDS [*sic*] his plantation abouty y[e] middle of Jan[rr]y / Last was a twelve m[o] and JAMES JOLLEY Remaynd their / and worked att his trade Some Consederable tyme / after and further Saith not GILES DRIVER

JOHN LUTER aged thirty nine yeares or there abouts / Doth declare that betwen y[e] tenth & y[e] fiftenth of Jan[rr]y / Last was a twelve m[o]: hapening to be at WILL JOLLEYs / hous, and he was a removing some of his Goods & his / Landlord made seison of Some of his Goods for his rent / and further Saith not.

JOHO LUTHER

**[139]**

The Deposion [*sic*] of JAMES TULLAGH aged forty six yeare / or there abouts y[t] by the Request of M[r]: RICH. RANALDS / and WILL JOLLEY I Did make up y[e] acc[o]. betwene them / the Plantation of that M[r]: RENALDS for worned / him to Draw aney nailes or to tak away any / Locks or born aney fencin stuff, and forther / Saith not

JAMES TULLAGH

Know all men by these Presents that I ISABELL / MAYO y[e] wife to WILL: MAYO Advs [*sic*] make my Loving brother M[r] HOGES COWNCELL my ffull & Lawfull / attorny to acknowlege with my hus band WILL: MAYO / all my rite title & intrust of a paten Lands / Containing one hundred & Seaventy A cers / ffrom me my hares executors administrators / or asigns Unto THO: LEWES y[e] sone of RICH / LEWES Lately deced: to him his ares exetors / adme[tor]: or asigns for Ever and forthermore / I Give my Lawfull attorny with as much / power as if I my self ware present and to / acknoleg y[e] same in y[e] Isle of Wight Court / as witness my hand and Seale this 7 day / of August 1693

her
Test his ISABELL **X** MAYO Seal

HENRY **HB** BRADLY mark
his
HOGES **HC** COWNCELL Junr$^{r}$.
mark

**[140]**

The Enventory of the Estate of WILL JONES / apprayz this 19$^{th}$. Day of Desem$^{r}$: 1694

| | |
|---|---|
| It 1 ould Cowe | 0300 |
| It 2 steares of 4 yeare old: | 0700 |
| It 2 hefers of 3 year old: | 0500 |
| It 1 bulle of 4 year old | 0250 |
| It 2 yearling Calves | 0120 |
| It 5 barrous of a bought 2 years old | 0325 |
| It 4 Sowes | 0240 |
| It 15 Shots at 35 ꝑ peace | 0525 |
| It 3 yewes 2 wethers 1 ram | 0600 |
| It 1 old Cart & wheles yoke ring and stap[ ] and pin 1 sider hogghed 2 Sider barrels old | 0180 |
| It 1 Spinning whele & bed stead | 0180 |
| It 1 Cheste | 0050 |
| It 1 Table | 0150 |
| It 1 Cubberd and Couch | 0150 |
| It 3 old Cheares | 0040 |
| It 1 bedsted & Cord firme and stool | 0060 |
| It 1 young horse of 2 years old | 0600 |
| It 1 musket and Sword | 0300 |
| It 2 payls 2 pigins 1 Chern | 0100 |
| It 2 friing pans 1 potrack | 0800 |
| It 1 parsell of Erthen ware | 0050 |
| 1 Spit 1 pare of fire tongs | 0080 |
| It 1 flesh forks 1 Ladell | 0040 |
| It 2 hamers 1 Auger 1 hand Saw Draw knife and Raspe | 0060 |
| It 2 wedges 2 Smothin Eyrins a pare or Sheap Shears 1 Iron Candelstick 1 Cokin Iron 1 old reaphoock 1 ege 1 hatchet 1 old bill hoock | 0100 |

**[141]**

| | |
|---|---|
| It a parsell of ou[l]d axeses and hows and som old Iron | 0030 |

| | |
|---|---|
| It 1 Gimblet 2 paire of Sisors 1 paSp[ ] | 0010 |
| It 3 Glas bottls 3 trays, bole | 0046 |
| 1 pane of wool Cards | 0015 |
| It 2 Runlets 1 Gun | 0060 |
| It 2 Iron potts & pot hooks 1 skilit | 0160 |
| It 2 Doz ½ of wood trensers | 0015 |
| It 2 tinn pans 1 funnill | 0020 |
| It 17 of Peweter at 8$^{li}$ ꝑ li | 0136 |
| It 21 Spoones | 0045 |
| It 2 Chests | 0150 |
| It 1 fether bed 2 Rugs 1 pillo | |
| 1 Sheat 3 old blankits 1 bed Cord | 1300 |
| It 15$^{li}$ of wool at 8$^{li}$ ꝑ li | 0220 |
| It a parsell of flaxe | 0050 |
| It 11 turckes | 0100 |

HUM MARSHALL
WILL WILLIAMS
his
NICHO \/\ CASEY
mark
THO **T** SAYOR
his mark

June the 5$^{th}$ 1694

Reccd of Cap$^{t}$ JN$^{O}$ GOODRICH A bill of Exchang / Drawn by M$^{r}$ DANUEL PEUGH upon M$^{r}$ JONATHAN / WILLS for Seventy four pounds five Shillings / If that mony Is paid I am to Lay it out in / Such Goods as the aboveS$^{d}$. JOHN GOODRICH / Shall order and to Doe with it as he Shall / order witnes my hand

ROB$^{T}$: KAE W$^{M}$ FFISHER
W$^{M}$: THOMAS

**[142]**

To all Christian people To whom these presents / Shall Come I WILLIAM ARCHER Late of Charles Citty County for Divers Good Causes & Considerations / me there unto moving, one whereof being y$^{e}$ / exceeding & xtian Cause & Deligent paynes taken / and Done for me by MARGETT WILLSON now wife / of NICHO WILSON I doe hereby Give & Grant unto / HENRY CROAKER of Surey County in trust to and / for y$^{e}$ Sole use in trust and benefit of SAMPSON / WILSON Son of y$^{e}$ S$^{d}$. MARGARETT when he shall Come / to y$^{e}$ age of one & twenty yeares, that is to say / the severall Goods marchant Dizes and Chattells / here under mentioned Viz$^{t}$: one ~~hh~~d of Rumm / Containing ab$^{t}$. Sixty Gallons, two barrels of / Molasses Each Containeing ab$^{t}$. thirty Gallons / one cask of Salt Containeing ab$^{t}$: Eight bushells / one white Gelding

Branded **T K** Called Turk ab$^{t}$: / tenn yeares old also one Sorrell horse w$^{th}$: a blaze / Doune his face w$^{th}$: flaxen mane and tale Called / blaze ab$^{t}$. ten yeares old, also two barrells of Salt / both ab$^{t}$: seaven bushells in y$^{e}$ storehous of / M$^{r}$: BUSH in Elezebeth River also an unsertaine / quantity of Salt now being at y$^{e}$ house of M$^{r}$ J$^{A}$: / PETERS Little Creek in norfuck County all w$^{ch}$: / is to be Sold & Disposed of for Ready mony by y$^{e}$ s$^{d}$: / HENRY TOCKER & after all Reasonable trouble / Charge & Expences is taken out of it & allowed / the S$^{d}$. TOCKER then y$^{e}$ neat proced thereof to be / paid at y$^{e}$ tyme and in y$^{e}$ maner as afore sayd / to y$^{e}$ s$^{d}$: SAMPSON proved never y$^{e}$ lesse / and

**[143]**
And it is that true intente and meaning of y$^{e}$ S$^{d}$. WILL / ARCHER, that if y$^{e}$ S$^{d}$: NICHO WILSON & MARGARETT his / wife, Shall happen to Seperate & Live A parte / That in Such Case upon Security Given to y$^{e}$ S$^{d}$: TOCKER / by MARGARETT WILSON y$^{e}$ mother of y$^{e}$ S$^{d}$: SAMPSON she / may and Shall have y$^{e}$ use and occupaton thereof / the s$^{d}$: ARCHER Doth further think fitt to Declare / his meaning (that is to say) that if it Shall pleas / God to take y$^{e}$ s$^{d}$: SAMPSON out of this world before / before [*sic*], he Coms to y$^{e}$ age of one and twenty yeares / then I Give y$^{e}$ s$^{d}$: money in trust unto y$^{e}$: s$^{d}$ HENERY / TOOKER for y$^{e}$ Sole use benifit & behoufe of / MARGRET WILSON to have & in Joy after y$^{e}$ / Death of NICHOH WILSON & in Case She Shall / Give Security to y$^{e}$ S$^{d}$: TOOKER that y$^{e}$ s$^{d}$. mony / after her Decease & y$^{e}$ Deceas of y$^{e}$ s$^{d}$ SAMPSON / Shall be well & truely payd unto JAMES WILSON / son of y$^{e}$ s$^{d}$. MARGRET then She y$^{e}$ S$^{d}$. MARGRETT / Shall have y$^{e}$ use & occupacon thereof & / in Case y$^{e}$ s$^{d}$ SAMPSON & JAMES shall happen to Dye before thay Come to y$^{e}$ age of one / and twenty yeares that y$^{e}$ s$^{d}$ TOOKER shall & / may Dispose of y$^{e}$ s$^{d}$: money as y$^{e}$ s$^{d}$. MARGRET / Shall Direct Delivery of all y$^{e}$ s$^{d}$ Goods being / made herewith by y$^{e}$ actuall Delivery of an / hand full of y$^{e}$ s$^{d}$: Salt in y$^{e}$ maine [?] of y$^{e}$ whole / by WILL ARCHER to y$^{e}$ s$^{d}$: TOOKER in witness where / of y$^{e}$ s$^{d}$. WILL ARCHER hath hereunto assined / his hand and Seal this fifteenth day of november
Anno Domi 1694

the mark of
WILL **A** ARCHER

Signed Seald & Delivered in y$^{e}$ presents of
THOMAS THROPP
the mark of
WILL **W** SMITH

**[144]**
A Envatory of the widdoo PEARSE$^{es}$

To one hefer fore yeares old
To one Gunn and ould small Chest
To one Pigen

her
KATH **K** PEIRCE
mark

In p^r suante to an ord^r: of the Isle of Wight County / Court Dated y^e 10^th Day of December 1694 / Wee whose names are heere Subscribed / being Inpanneled on a Jury in a Difference / betwixt M^r: ROBT COLMAN Plan^tt. & MALUCK / HAWLEY Defn^tt. and being Sworne Doe Give / o^r: Verdict

Wee Doe finde by oath that y^e Def^tt. was / ousted by M^r. COLLMANs ord^r. Wee find y^e Def^t. / hath not performed his ꝑte. of y^e Lease in / planting of one hundred and fifty Apple trees / therefore we aword him four hundred / pounds of tobacho Dammage to y^e Pl^t f

RICH: REYNOLDS Juni^or
WILL BRADSHAW
GEORGE **X** WRIGHT
THOMAS **R** WRIGHT
JOHN CLARKE
RICH: WILKISON

W^M: GREEN
BEN **BB** BEALE Jury
THO: NORWARTHY
JOHN NEVILL
HEN **9** TURNER
his mark
TH^O BEVAN

January y^e 31^th 1694

Wee the Jury by y^e assistance of M^r GEORGE / WILLIAMSON survayer of y^e County in obedienc / to y^e order of Court Dated y^e 11^th of Decm^r. / 1694 / have mett and Devided y^e Land / be

**[145]**

Between JN^O. BRANTLY and GEORGE BARLLOW / an Equall Devision according to y^e best of our / Knowledg, as Wittness our hands

ROBT: KAE
THO: CARTER
JN^O: DAVIS
JAMS BRIGGES
HENRY **G** OLEHAM
his
JN^O **V** COLLLINGS
mark
his
ROBT **RH** HOGGES
mark
his
JN^O: **I** BRANSH
mark
his
JA: **I** ADCHISON
mark
his

JA: Ɨ LOPER
mark
his
FFRANS **F** RAYNARD
mark
PETER VASSER

**[146]** blank

**[147]**

†In the Name of God Amen / I PETER BEST of the Isle Wight County being Sick and / weake in body yet blessed be almighty God in perfect / Sences and memory, doe ordaine this my Last will & / testament first I bequeath my Soule / to allmighty God who Gave it to me Secondly I be / queath my body to y$^e$ Earth from whence it Came in / hopes of a Joyfull Resurrection, and for my woroldly / goods I Give in manner & forme following

ffirst I give to my oldest Sonn WILLIAM BEST all / this plantation that I now Live upon to him and / his haires Lawfully begotten of his body for ever / and if it Should pleas God that my sonn WILL: Should / die with out heires then my Will is that this my / Land shall Return to my Sonn PETER BEST in y$^e$ / Same maner and forme as afore said

Next I Give to my Sonn CHRISTOPHER BEST all my / Land that I am now possest with all at king Saile / to him and his heires for Ever & if it Should / please god that my Son CHRISTOPHER Should die / with out hair Lawfully begotten of his body then / my will is that y$^t$ my Land Shall Return to my / youngest son THOMAS BEST & his heires for Ever

And for all the Rest of my personall Estate I doe / give to my Loving wife MARY BEST as wholy Executrix / after my depts are paid

and for the true performance there of I have here / Unto set my hand and Seales this twentieth day of / october 1693

Signd & Seald in y$^e$ presents of us
THO: HAWKINS
his
JAMES Ɨ MACFADDEN
mark
CHRISTOPHER BEST

his
PETER **PB** BEST seal
mark

**[148]**

SILVESTRA HILL widdow maketh oath y$^t$ being / with her daughter MARTHA BEST (wife / of JN$^O$. BEST then deced) she then lying on / her death bed & discowrsing about y$^e$ disposal / of y$^e$ Land then in her possession, she the s$^d$. MARTHA / did then declare she did give y$^e$ same to M$^r$ LUKE / HAVILD & his heires and she was then in her / right mind & Lived till y$^e$ day following

SILL HILL

Know ye by these p$^{r}$sents that I JOHN JENNINGS / of the upper parish of y$^{e}$ Isle of Wight County in y$^{e}$ / Colony of Virg$^{a}$: & MARY my wife for & in Consideration / of Phisicke administered and labour & pains under / Gone by LUKE HAVILD of Chuckatucke Gent: as / likewise in consideration of y$^{e}$ sume of five shillings / by y$^{e}$ s$^{d}$. LUKE HAVILD to us in hand payed as allsoe / in consideration of y$^{e}$ intent of our late loveing sister / MARTHA BEST who upon her death bed did volintarily / and of her owne free will by words by her then spoken / gave unto ye s$^{d}$. LUKE HAVILD & his heires forever all / y$^{t}$ parsell of Land scituated lying & being in y$^{e}$ / western branch of Nanzemond where of the s$^{d}$. / MARTHA dyed seized Have bargained sold assigned / and set over and doe by / these p$^{r}$sents for our selves our heirs Exer$^{s}$. & adm$^{rs}$ / bargain sell assigne & sett over unto y$^{e}$ s$^{d}$. LUKE / HAVILD his heires and assigns for ever all our right / title & interest to y$^{e}$ s$^{d}$: Land & p$^{r}$misses & every

**[149]**

pte and parsell thereof as being heir at law / unto y$^{e}$ s$^{d}$: MARTHA BEST, to have and to hold / to y$^{e}$ s$^{d}$. LUKE HAVILD his heires and assignes / for ever free and clear of all manner of incomb / rances by us heretofore made in any manner whatsoever in wittnes where of wee have / hereunto sett our hands & seals this 20$^{th}$ day / of October Anno Dom$^{i}$ [--]

Seald and deleverd in p$^{r}$sents of
JN$^{O}$. GOODRICH
CHA: CHAPMAN

JOHN JENNINGS seale
MARY JENNINGS seale

JOHN JENNINGS by his attorny M$^{r}$ CHA: CHAPMAN / and MARY y$^{e}$ wife of y$^{e}$ s$^{d}$ JN$^{O}$: acknowledge this / Conveyance to be their free volintary act & deed.

Where as I have signed & seald together with my wife / One deed or Conveyance bearing date y$^{e}$ 20$^{th}$ of 8$^{ber}$: / last of certain lands scituate on y$^{e}$ westerne branch / of nanzemond to LUKE HAVILD & his heires for ever / Now these p$^{r}$sents wittness that I have made or / dained and constitute CHA: CHAPMAN my true and / lawfull attorney to acknowledge y$^{e}$ same in Courte / and confirming his acknowledgment / firm & good in law as if I were personally / p$^{r}$sent in Court & wittnes my hand this the 9$^{th}$ day / of aprill 1695

Test JN$^{O}$. GOODRICH

JOHN JENNINGS

**[150]**

Cap$^{t}$ EVANS

S$^{r}$ I desiere yo$^{w}$ will lay out the Sixteene / pownd five Shillings A[ ] in halfe a peace / of good frensh dowlas & y$^{e}$ remaind$^{r}$ / in blew linin brown white brin [sic] bridges

/ and one peace of stuf for my best advantage / and make return to me in Virginia & yo$^{w}$
/ will Olidge S$^{r}$ yo$^{r}$: hub$^{l}$ Sar$^{t}$
Varinia the 9$^{th}$ of AW
July 1692

Rec$^{d}$ this 9$^{th}$ day of July 1692 of ANDREW WOODLY / the Sume of Sixteene pownds five shilings & / the Return to be made in goods Bristoll as / ꝑ advise
Test LUKE HAVILD ꝑ me JN$^{O}$. EVANS
JO$^{S}$: ASHELLEY

To all Christians people in whome these p$^{r}$ests / writing Shall Com wee THOMAS THROPP & MARTHA / his wife of y$^{e}$ Isle of Wight County in Virginia / Send Greeting know yee that wee s$^{d}$: THO: THROPP / and MATHA his wife witneseth that for & in Con / Sideration of y$^{e}$ Just full Sume of four thousand / and two hundred pounds of Virginia leave toboccos / and Casque in hand payd & secured to be payd / by PETER BAYNTON before sealling & delivery / heare of the recept where of the s$^{d}$: THO: THROPP / and MATHA his wife doe hereby ackolege & Confess / them selfs full payd and Satisfied by y$^{e}$ s$^{d}$: PETER / and

**[151]**

And there of & of Every part & parsell there / of doe fully Clearely & absolutely acquite / Exonerate and Discharg y$^{e}$. s$^{d}$: PETER BAYNTON / his heires Execu$^{rs}$: and admin$^{rs}$. and Every of them by / these presents have Given Granted aleened / bargained Sould Enfeoffed and Confirmed and / by these p$^{r}$sents doe firmely & Absolutely / give grant aleene bargan sell Enfoeff & Confirme / unto y$^{e}$ s$^{d}$. PETER BAYNTON his heires Exec$^{rs}$ / admin$^{rs}$ assigns or order one hundred acres of land / Scituated lying and being on James river in the / Isle of Wight County being apart of y$^{e}$ tract of / land of three hundred and fifty acres of land / formerly granted by S$^{r}$: WILLIAM BARKLEY Kn$^{tt}$. / and Govene$^{r}$: unto WILLIAM LEWERD deced / which may at Larage Appeare by patent bare / ring dat y$^{e}$ 14$^{th}$: day of october 1665 since which / time is found to Excheat to there magesties & / Confirmd by an Escheat patten Granted unto / y$^{e}$ above s$^{d}$: THO: THROPP and MARTHA his wife / as may more at large appear by said pattent / Granted by Sir: EDMOND ANDROS kn$^{tt}$. & Governor / of Virginia baring date y$^{e}$ year 1694 beginning / the bounds of y$^{e}$ s$^{d}$. one hundred ackers of land / beginning at or neare a holly tree near y$^{e}$ river / side and soe runing back in y$^{e}$ woods to y$^{e}$ end of / y$^{e}$ line that devides betwene Cap$^{t}$. JN$^{O}$ GOODRICH / and y$^{e}$ s$^{d}$: THROPP & MATHA his wife and from / y$^{e}$ s$^{d}$. holly tree one y$^{e}$ river Side a dew Corse / towards y$^{e}$ dweling hows of y$^{e}$ s$^{d}$. THO: & MARTHA y$^{e}$ / bredth of one hundred acers land as it hath / bene survayed and Lade by Mag$^{r}$. ARTHER ALLEN / and M$^{r}$ GEORGE WILLIAMSON survayer and

**[152]**

and soe keeping its bredth of a hundred acers back / into y^e woods to y^e ende of the line as it hath / been out by y^e s^d. Maj^r: ALLEN & M^r WILLIAMSON / for the accon^t. of Cap^t JOHN GOODRICH and y^e s^d. / line & bounds which hat benn don by y^e s^d survay / also with y^e Consent of y^e s^d. THOMAS & MARTHA / his wife shall be & Remaine as y^e lawfull / bounds to be for Ever y^e lines of Devision / betwene y^e s^d. THOMAS & MARTHA his wife & / the s^d. PETER & theire heires & assigns for Ever / with all y^e housing fenceing orchards woods / under wood marshe & marsh land ways / privliges profits Comodities hereditments & / Appurtenances what soever belonging & appretaining / to the mentioned one hundred acers land unto / the fores^d. PETER BAYNTON his assigns for ever all / the above bownded premises of y^e s^d one hundred / acres Land wtih all & every of y^e appertenances / theire to belonging unto y^e s^d. PETER BAYNTON & to / his heires assigns or order & y^e s^d. THO: THROPP and / MARTHA his wife both for their selves there / heires Exec^rs. & admin^rs and for Every of us or eyther / of them to Keep save & Defend from all maner / of harme damage or molistation whatsoe ever / the s^d. PETER BAYNTON & his heires or assigns for / Ever there on eyther of them there peasable / in Joyment in y^e s^d. Premises for Ever with warrinty / against all maner of Clames right title or / demand of and from all maner of person or / Persones what so ever y^e s^d. PETER BAYNTON his / heires or assigns yealding & paying yearely & / Every year at y^e useall time of payment of / the

**[153]**
the quitt rents y^e s^d. Sume of twenty foure / pownds of tob^o: a yeare where unto wee the / above named THO: THROPP & MARTHA his / wife hath to y^e Confermation here of have / here unto sett theire hands and Seales the / ninth day of Aprill 1695

Signd Seald & deliverd
in y^e presents of us — THO: THROPP seal
JA: DAY — MARTHA THROPP seall
HEN BAKER

Acknoledged in Open Court held for y^e / Isle Wight County y^e 9^th. Aprill 1695 / & by vertue of an Order of y^e 9^th of June / 1698 Recorded ꝑ CHA CHAPMAN Cl Cur

Know all men by these presents that I the / within named PETER BAYNTON that for & in / Consideration of y^e Just & full Sume of / ffoure thowsand & two hundred pownds of / tob^o. & Casque in hand payd & secured to be / payd by Cap^t JN^O: GOODRICH before sealing & / delivery here of y^e Recept heare of y^e s^d: / PETER doe hereby acknowledge hiumselfe / fully payd & satisfied by y^e s^d: JN^O: GOODRICH / and y^e within named PETER BAYTON doe warrant / the sale of y^e within mentioned deed of Effeoffment / and premises with all its profits & appurtenances / whatsoever theire to belonging or any ways apper / taining against himself y^e s^d: PETER BAYTON his / heires Exec^rs: & admin^rs or any eyther of them & from / all maner of any Clames of any person or persons what / soever Claminmg by y^e s^d: PETER PAYNTON [*sic*] his heires /

Exec$^r$ & admin$^{rs}$. or any or eyter of them: but to bee / and remaine unto y$^e$ above nmed [*sic*] JN$^O$: GOODRICH his heires / Executors adm$^{rs}$ & assignes for ever as witnes my hand & / Seale this ninth day of Aprill 1695 PETER BAYNTON
signd Seald & deliverd in y$^e$ presents of us Seal
JA: DAY
HEN : BAKER

Recorded as above CHA CHAPMAN Cl

**[154]**

This Indenture made the fourth day of march, in y$^e$ yeare / of our Lord God one thousand six hundred ninty foure / and in y$^e$ Seaventh yeare of the Reign of our Soveraign / Lord and Lady William & Mary: by y$^e$ Grace of God / King and Queen of England, Scotland, france & / Ireland, Betwen GEORGE GREEN of y$^e$ lower parish / of the Isle of Wight County of the one part and / RICHARD WILKISON Junior of y$^e$ parrish & County / afforesaid of y$^e$ other part witnesseth that the / s$^d$. GEORGE GREEN for and in Consideration of y$^e$ sum / of five thousand pounds of tob$^o$. in Cask to him in / hand at and before y$^e$ sealing & delivery of these / presents by y$^e$ s$^d$. RICHARD WILLKISON well and truly / paid y$^e$ receipt whereof he the s$^d$. GEORGE GREEN / doth hereby acknowledge and himselfe theirwith / fully sattisfied & paid and thereof & of every parte / and parcell therof doth clearly acquit, exonerate & / discharge y$^e$ s$^d$. RICHARD WILLKISON his heires, Executrs / and administrators for ever, by these presents have / given granted alined, barganed, solde enfeoffed and / Confirmed, & by these presents doth fully, clearly and / absolutly give, grant, bargaine, sell alien enfeoff / and Conferm unto the s$^d$. RICH: WILLKISON Juner his / heires and assignes for ever one parcell of land / Containing by estimation one hundred & fifty acers / setiated Lying and being in y$^e$ parrish and County / affore s$^d$: now in y$^e$ tener and occupation of y$^e$ s$^d$. / GEORGE GREEN it being part of a pattent Containing / two hundred acres, granted to Cap$^t$ JOHN MOON the 20$^{th}$ / of november 1642, and by the s$^d$. MOON give by his will / to his daughter MARY MOON after words by marriag / MARY

**[155]**

MARY GREEN from whom it did desend to her sonn / THOMAS GREEN and from the s$^d$. THOMAS it did decend / unto the s$^d$. GEORGE GREEN, Called by the name of / the poplar neck, y$^e$ land hereby Convayed is / all that part of y$^e$ s$^d$. pattent which lyeth on y$^e$ / west side of a rode Commanly Called namzemond / path it being bounded on y$^e$ west side by a branch / of pagan Creek Called y$^e$ back bay Creek, & to the / South & north by lines of marked trees belonging / to y$^e$ s$^d$. pattent, and to the east by y$^e$ fores$^d$. road / or path to have and to holde y$^e$ fores$^d$. parcell / or tract of land according to the afforcs$^d$. / bounds with all Singular its rights members / Jurisdictions and appurtenances to gather with / all houses edifices, buildings, barns, & stables, orchards / gaardens, yards backsides easments Comon of pasture / hereditaments and appurtinances what soever to y$^e$ / s$^d$.

messuages or tenements & premisses or to any / part or parcell of them belonging or in anywise / appertaining theireunto unto [*sic*] the s$^{d}$ RICHARD / WILLKISON his heires or assignes to y$^{e}$ only proper / use and behoofe of the s$^{d}$. RICH: WILLKISON his heires / and assignes for ever, against him y$^{e}$ s$^{d}$. GEORGE / GREEN his heires and assigns and all and every / other person and persons whatsoever lawfully / claming by from or under him them or any of them / Shall and will warrnt and for ever defend by thes / presents: and that the s$^{d}$. GEORGE GREEN from himselfe / his heires Executors and administrators doe Covenant / promise grant and agree to & with y$^{e}$ s$^{d}$ RICH: WILLKISON / his heires and assigns & Every of them by these / pressents that all and Singalar the fores$^{d}$. 15 acres / of

**[156]**

of land more or less according to the before recited bounds / with all y$^{e}$ appurtinances theire unto belonging now / be and ever here after Shall be Stand & continue / for ever & that y$^{e}$ s$^{d}$: RICH: WILLKISON his heires or / assignes, be freely and clearly acquited exonerated / and discharged and from time to time well and suffitently / keept harm lesse by the s$^{d}$: GEORGE GREEN his heires / Executors or administrators of & from all & all / manner or former and other gifts grants bargans / Sailes Leasses Mortgages Joynters dowers of and from / all & singular other titles troubles charges damages / and incumberances what soever had made commit / =ed Suffered omited or don by y$^{e}$ s$^{d}$. GEORGE GREEN his / heires or assignes or by any other person or persons / whatsoever and that y$^{e}$ s$^{d}$. GEORGE GREEN his heires / on and dureing the Space of seaven yeares next / inSueing y$^{e}$ date of these presents Shall and will at / and upon y$^{e}$ reasonable request and at the costs & charges / in the law of y$^{e}$ s$^{d}$. RICH: WILLKISON his heires or assigns / make Such further lawfull and reasonable assurance / or assurances or convayances in y$^{e}$ law for y$^{e}$ more / better and perfect assurance of y$^{e}$ afores$^{d}$. premisses / as by y$^{e}$ s$^{d}$. RICH: WILLKISON his heires or assignes or by his or / their Councill lerned in y$^{e}$ law Shall be reasonably / devised advised or required & y$^{t}$ y$^{e}$ affores$^{d}$. premisses / with all y$^{e}$ appurtinences thereunto belonging shall be / be [*sic*] esteemed & Judged & taken to be & ever to y$^{e}$ onely / proper use & behoofe of y$^{e}$ s$^{d}$. RICH: WILLKISON his heires & / asignes for ever and to none other use intent or purpose / what soever witnesse in witnesse here of I have hereunto / sett my hand

Signed sealled & deliverd in y$^{e}$ presents of us GEORGE GREEN seale

GEO: MOORE
JOHN GILES
PHILARETE GILES

**[157]**

Know all men by these presents that I GEORGE GREEN of y$^{e}$ lower / parrish of y$^{e}$ Isle of Wight County doe Stand & am firmly bounden / and obliged to RICH WILLKISON Jun$^{r}$: of y$^{e}$ parish & County affores$^{d}$: / in y$^{e}$ Sum of two hundred pownds of good & lawfull money of / England to be paid to y$^{e}$ s$^{d}$: RICH: WILLKISON or his true &

lawfull / atturney executors or administrators to y$^{e}$ which payment well / and truly to be paid I doe bind me my heires executors & admin= / istrators firmly by these pressents Sealed with my Seale / dated y$^{e}$ fourth day of march, in y$^{e}$ yeare of our Lord God / one thousand Six hundred ninty foure.

The Condition of this obligation is Such that if y$^{e}$ within / named RICH WILLKISON his heires & assignes and every of / them shall & may every from hence forth peacebly & / quietly have holde use occupy possess and injoy all that / messuage or tenements & land Situated lying & being / in y$^{e}$ parrish and County within named & every part / and parcell thereof mentioned to be bargained and / solde by y$^{e}$ within bounded GEORGE GREEN, to y$^{e}$ s$^{d}$: / RICH: WILLKISON in and by a Certaine Indenture of / bargaine & sale bearing date y$^{e}$ day of y$^{e}$ date / within written made betwene y$^{e}$ within bounded / GEORGE GREEN on y$^{e}$ one part and y$^{e}$ above named / RICH: WILLKISON of y$^{e}$ other part clearly discharged / or otherwise Suffitiently Saved & keept harmlesse / of and from all & all maner of estates titles troubles / charges & incumberances whatsoever or any time / heretofore had made commited permited sufered or / don by the s$^{d}$: GEORGE GREEN or by his meanes or pro= / curement that then this present obligation to be / void & of none effect or else Shall Stand remain and be / in fullo force power effect and Virtue GEORGE GREEN seal

Signd Seald & deliverd in y$^{e}$ pressence of us
GEO: MOORE
JOHN GILES
PHILARETE GILES

**[158]**

March y$^{e}$ 9$^{th}$ 169$^{4}/_{3}$

Then deliverd by GEORGE GREEN to possession of y$^{e}$ house / and plantion: Called y$^{e}$ poplar neck by tworf [*sic*] and twigs / according to y$^{e}$ bunds mentioned in this Indenture In y$^{e}$ / presence of us

W$^{M}$ SAYWELL GEORGE GREEN
THO: BIVEN
mark of
GEORGE **W** WILLIAMS

This bill byndeth us EDWARD COBB & WILLIAM BALDING / Joyntly & Severally our heires Executors to pay unto the / justices of y$^{e}$ Isle of Wight County or theires Successors for / the use of y$^{e}$ orphants of RICHARD BLUNT deced y$^{e}$ / full & Just sum of foure hundred & twenty pownds / of good tob$^{o}$: in Cask to be paid Conven$^{t}$: in y$^{e}$ aboves$^{d}$. / County one demand in witness here unto we have / sett our hands this 29$^{th}$ of June 1688

EDW$^{D}$. **x** COBB
his mark

Test THO: MOORE
GEORGE GRENE

W$^{M}$ **WB** BALDWIN
his mark

I JOHNS SKRUSE doe asin my Rite of this / bill to my Cyscon SUAN BLUNT
JOHN **I C** SCRUSE
his mark

Isle of Wight County y$^{e}$ 10$^{th}$ June 1695

I subscribed doe hereby certified (& to w$^{ch}$: I will be ready / at any time to make outh) y$^{t}$ in my voyage before this to / Virginia I brought severall tabells for M$^{rs}$: ELEZEBETH / CAUFIELD & M$^{r}$ JAMES DAY by the matting of som of them / whare on they were marked falleing of I could not / distinguis but Sent to each their numb$^{r}$: of tabells but / Some Small time after I understood by y$^{e}$ s$^{d}$: DAY that hee / had a large table of M$^{rs}$. CAUFIELDs, Sente him in y$^{e}$ / Room of a small one of his that hee understood was

**[159]**
at the s$^{d}$: CAUFIELDs and Desired y$^{t}$ as I sent to both places for / [ ] I would contrive to have them rechanged in order to / which my sloope bro$^{t}$: y$^{e}$ s$^{d}$: lit[ ] table from y$^{e}$ s$^{d}$: M$^{rs}$. CAUFIELDs / and Imediately Sent it to y$^{e}$ s$^{d}$: DAYs but hee never yet / that I know of returnd y$^{e}$ other. RICH$^{D}$. TIBBOTT
Sworne be fore me
this 10$^{th}$: of June 1695
GEO: MOORE

Know all men by these precents that that I FFRA: DENSON / widdoe do authorize Constitute & apoynt my Sonne / JAMES DENSON to be my true & Lawfull attorny / in a sutte depending between BRIAN MACKCLAM & my / self: to actt & do for me & in my Sted in as full a maner / as: as [*sic*] if I my selfe were theare present witnes my hand / this 9$^{th}$ day of Aprill 1695 FRANSIS DENSON: seal
Test JERI: EXUM

Know all men by these presents thay JAMES DAY of y$^{e}$ / Isle of Wight County march$^{t}$: doe constitute & appoint / my Loving frend JOHN GILES my true & Lawfull / attorny for me and in my Stead to defend Suite / brought against me in the Isle of Wight County Courte / by M$^{rs}$. ELAZABETH CAUFEILD giving unto my s$^{d}$: attorney / full power & lawfull authority to act & doe on my / behalfe as if I were actually present my self in / witnes here of I have hereunto sett my hand this / third day of June 1695
JA: DAY
95

**[160]**
M$^{r}$: GILES

I desire if yo$^{w}$: heare me Called at our Court in / an action of ROB$^{T}$: LITTLEBOY for a ~~hhd~~. of tob$^{o}$. give him / Judmg$^{t}$. for it & if any thing Els: Should happen in any / absence I desire yo$^{w}$: will appeare for me & sattisfation / Shall be made by my Sarvis to yo$^{w}$ & wife AW: June the 9$^{th}$ 1694

Yo$^{r}$: ffriend to Com$^{rs}$:
AND$^{W}$: WOODLEY:

Know all men by these presents y$^{t}$ I SAMWELL COHOON do / Constitute & appoynt HUGH CAMPBELL to be my / attorney at Isle of Wight County Court in all actions / brought against me to y$^{t}$ Courte as witnes my hand / this 10$^{th}$ of June 1695

SAMWELL COHOONE

M$^{r}$: GILES

S$^{r}$: on fryday Last M$^{r}$: BAKER arrested me in the / Suite of RICHARD REYNOLDS Sen$^{r}$: S$^{r}$: Thest are thare fore / to Request you to appeare in my Steed to answer y$^{t}$ matter / Layd to my Charge at our nexte Courte by y$^{t}$ fores$^{d}$: REYNOLDS / and this my note Shall oblidge paym$^{t}$: for the same / from Yo$^{r}$: servant to Comand June the 10$^{th}$ 1695

JN$^{O}$: **ID** DAVIS

The Depossition of ANN KEEBELL aged aboute 50 yeares Sayth / That about y$^{e}$ 23$^{th}$: or 24$^{th}$: day of 8$^{br}$: 1692 I did bring a sarvant / wench by name MARTHA TALL to bed of a basterd Childe / belonging to Mad$^{m}$: HESTER BRIDGER & y$^{e}$ s$^{d}$: MARTHA did Lay / her basterd to M$^{r}$ WILLIAMSON mate of Cap$^{t}$ TIBBOTTs Ship / and the s$^{d}$: MARTHA & Child were bad after She was / brought

**[161]**

Brought to bed & I was Imployed by Mad$^{m}$. BRIDGER to / dress & cure y$^{e}$ Childe & look after y$^{e}$ woman a Considerable / while to y$^{e}$ greate trouble & Charge of Mad$^{m}$. BRIDGER / for she Provided every thing for her as was Convenient / ither for y$^{e}$ woman & childe in y$^{e}$ Condition thay were / and want$^{d}$ for notnhing & Likewise Mad$^{m}$. BRIDGER payed / mee fowr hundred pownds of tob$^{o}$: for my peculiar troble / and if any occassion Shoulde bee I am willing & free to / Sware to y$^{e}$ same on my coporall oath & further / Sayth not

ANN KEEBELL **Δ** med wife
her marke

The deposition of HENRY TOOKER aged forty yeares or / Thare a bout Sheweth y$^{t}$ ab$^{t}$ two days before y$^{e}$ death / of Cap$^{t}$. WILL$^{M}$ ARCHER late of Charles Citty County y$^{e}$ / ARCHER did tell y$^{e}$ depon$^{t}$: y$^{t}$ MARGARETT y$^{e}$ wife of NICHOLAS / WILSON had lent him thirty po$^{ds}$: for w$^{ch}$ he had given her / his recep$^{t}$: & y$^{t}$ he cold noe otherwise make her satis / faciton for y$^{e}$ same then by making deed of Gift to the / depon$^{t}$ in trust for y$^{e}$ s$^{d}$. WILSONs Children & further / Saith not

June y^e^ 10^th^ 1695 HENRY TOOKER
Sworne in Courte
Test HC

†In the name of God amen I RICHARD PYLAND being sick of / body but of Sound and perfect memory thanks be to almighty / God doe make & ordaine this my last will and testament / in manner and forme Viz first I Give my Sole to God / my Creator in Sure & Sartane hopes through the / merritts of my Saviour Christe y^e^ forgiveness of all / my Sinnes and my body to y^e^ Earth from whence it / Came as two my worldly Estate as followeth [*stained*]

Viz first I Doe give unto my loving wife one horse & two young / Mares to Runn for a stock for my wife and my five / Children

**[162]**
Children and for y^e^ Remanens of all my Estate I give to my / Loveing wife ELINOR PYLAND dureing her widowhood / and wheresoe Ever She Marries y^e^ Estate then left to be / equally devided betweene my said wife and my five children / my debts being first paide and I doe appoynt my Loveing / wife my full & hole Executrix of this my last will / and testament in Witnes hereunto I have set my hand / and put my Seale this Second day of ffebry: Anno / Domini 169^2^/~3~
Sind Seald y^e^ p^r^senc: RICHARD **R S** PYLAND
of THO: MOORE his Marke seal
HENRY WHITE

Thesc are to In power M^r^: JOHN GILES to Presecute any / action or actions y^t^ I y^e^ Suscriber have or Shall have / in y^e^ Isle of Wight County witness my hand this / 5^th^ day march 169^4^/~5~ Sign
Test ROBERT BALLARD ELIZ **E** GREEN
HUGH DAVIS

June the 10^th^: 1695

These are to impower you Cap^t^: HUGH CAMBELL to answer / in my buisness y^t^ depends att this Courte Given under / my hand this tenth day of June
ꝑ me SAM^LL^: BRIDGER

May the 27 1695

An Inventory of the Estate of JOHN WHITLY deced:

Item a Cowes one steare & a booll & heffer of 3 yeare old / 3 heffs of 2 years ould one yeare old heffers 6 Calves

Item 4 yews 5 wathers & a Ram & a lambs & a parsell of woll

Item one Riding Horse one Breeding Mare & a horse / Coulte of a yeare old one bridle & Sadle & a pare of / pistil & houlsters and a Carbine & one Sword

Item 12 hogges of 3 yeares old & 17 Shotes Item 3 feathers / beds & boulsters & flock bed & boulster and / 4 Ruggs

Item

**[163]**

Item 4 pare of Blankets 3 pare of sheets 6 Napkins & 10 / Small Table Clous: & 2 towel 3 Looking glases

Item one dozen of glass bottels & a warmeing pann

Item 4 besteads 3 tables & 3 formes 4 Chests 1 trunks

Item 2 Box's & 2 Couches A Small passell of feathers

Item one dozen of puter Dishes & a puter bason 7 puter plates / 4 puter tanker 5 puter poringers 3 dozen of puter spones

Item one puter Candel stick 2 wyer Candel Stikse tinn panns / 3 tinn Cups a tinn Cullinder & a tinn Scimmer

Item 4 Iton potts & pott hooks 2 frying pans 2 pitts a gridiron / one possell Iron & a Chafing dish one Small brass Skilit

Item 14 trays & 3 boles 4 pales & pigans 2 dozen of round / trenchers 2 dozen of Earthen Cups & gugs 2 dozen of earthen / of pans & potts togather

Item 4 old Sider Barells 2 Meall trays & 3 meall sifters

Item one old: Cort Cubbard one Sickell & pare of bellose

Item one Cuting knife & old handsaw

Item one box Iron 2 spinning wheeles 1 Carte & wheeles

Item one Sett of Iron wedgges & one Grindstone

her
Sworne MARY **m** WHITLY
mark

This is to impower yo[w] JOHN GILES to be my attorney in / all Causes y[t] I have in Courte to pled for me witnice my / hand this 8th day of June 1695 in y[e] Isle of Wigh County

ROBART **S** COLMAN
his mark

witnes
JAMES TULLAGH

**[164]**

The Deposition of ANN LANE aged fifty yeares or / thare abouts hath often tymes heard THO: JOYNER / Sener: say that in his health & in his Sickness / what Little he had left was his son JOHN JOYNERs / after his Deceds for all y[e] Rest have had / thare Shaeares & further Saith not

her
**X** ANN LANE
mark

ELIZABETH COOKES aged fourty seven years or thereabout hath often / times heard THOMAS JOYNER Sen^r say That in his health, & / sickness w^t little he had left was his son JN^O: JOYNERs after his / deseas & farther saith not

ELIZABETH COOKES
her **3** marke

The deposicon of THOMAS LUCAS aged about thirty four years old / I THO^S: LUCAS did hear THOMAS JOYNER Sen^r say a little before his / deseas, y^t his son JN^O: JOYNER should injoy all the Estate y^t She s^d / THO^S: JOYNER was possessed withall for all y^e rest of y^e bretheren / have had their Share before

THOMAS LUCAS

The deposicon of THEOPHILUS JOYNER aged thirty & five or thereabout / has oftimes heard his Father say in his health & his Sickness / that w^t little he had was his son JN^O: JOYNERs after his deseas

THEOPHILUS + JOYNER
his marke

**[165]**

In Obedience to an order of y^e Isle of Wight / County Courte bareing Date y^e 19^th of June / 1694 Wee whose names are Underwritten / have Inventoried & appraised y^e Estate / of JOHN WHITLY deced which was Showen unto / us by his Rellike, which we Vallued in tob^o

| | lb |
|---|---|
| 3: tables and 3 formes at | 900 |
| 2: Couches at | 180 |
| 3: old Chests & two old boxes | 350 |
| 2: old trunks & a Little round box | 130 |
| 3: Lookeing glasses at | 070 |
| The best bead rug blankets & beadst^d | 1050 |
| One old feather bed bedsted rug & blak^ts: | 0700 |
| one Canvis feath^r bead & Stead rug & blank^ts | 0540 |
| one old flock bead rug & blankets | 0250 |
| 3: p^r of Canvis Sheets at | 0240 |
| 2 Table Cloths 6 napkins, 2 towells | 0100 |
| 1 Courte Cubearde at | 0750 |
| 62 pounds of peuter at | 0720 |
| A parsell of Iron ware wate 30^li at | 0120 |
| A parsell of wooden weare | 0155 |
| A parsell of old Iron at | 0050 |
| A warming pann & littell old kittell | 0070 |
| A mare and Colte at | 1100 |
| A horse at | 0800 |

| | |
|---|---|
| 6 Cowes & 6 calves & a bool at | 3000 |
| A Steare of 3 yeares old at | 0250 |
| 4 hefers of 2 yeares old at | 0700 |
| one hefer yearling at | 0090 |
| 5 weathers at | 0400 |
| JOHN GILES | 13465 |

JAMES TULLAGH
JOHN CLARKE

**[166]**

Deposicon of JOSEPH JORDAN aged twenty three / or thare abouts saith y$^t$ I did see WILL NEAVELL / Very much burnte upon his arme & thye and / sweld very much & I asked him who did it & / he Replyed CHA: DERROM and WILL GREEN / and said w$^t$ he was a going to Coll LEARES / and farther saith not
the 8$^{th}$ of august 1695 JOSEPH JORDAN

An Inventory of y$^e$ Estate of HENRY ALLEN / deced taken this 8$^{th}$ of aug$^t$ 1695 VIZ 1 horse about 16 yeares
1 Cow at home & what more is to be found / Shall be Redey to Give acco$^t$: of
A Small parsell of hodgs y$^e$ Cwantity not / Knowne but will Give acco$^t$ when found a nursey / of apple treas planted & tended by HENRY / ALLEN at FRANSES BRIDLEs, hone for a rasor / at FRANSES BRIDLEs a linnin Spining wheale

2 Small Chests
1 trunk
2 framed Cheares
2 matted Ceares [*sic*]
1 Couch
3 or 4 milk trase & bols
1 sider h~~hd~~ 3 smal sider Cask
1 feather bed & bolster
1 p$^r$ of Blankets
1 p$^r$ of Sheats
a parsell of his wareing cloths
1 Gunn
2 tinn panns
1 frying pann 1 Iron pott

2 puter tankerds
2 porringers ditto
1 Dozen of spoones
6 puter plates
1 Candell stickes
3 dishes
5 Earthen Cuppes
1 tinn Saus pann
pre of Small Stillards
4 weaven Slays
1 Saddel w$^{th}$out stirrops
4 Course towels
12 p$^r$ of mens fall shoes

**[167]**

2 Small Rundlets Dets Due from M$^r$ THO: GILES & / THO: POWELL bill 49

his
THO: |- BULLOCK
marke

MARY BULLOCK
her marke

The Deposion [*sic*] of ANN WILKISON aged 23 yeares / or thare abouts Saith when SAM^LL^. COHOONE / Came for his things my father Demanded / five hundred pounds of tob° & SAM^LL^ / COHOONE Sed no he wodd Give him 400 / hundred of tob° to & my father Said / he woldd take it & he wolde take it / in shoes & for his one ware & his wives / and Daughters he wolde Give him / 60 p^r^ pare & COHONE Swore Dam / him he woldd not Lett him have / Shoes if he wolde Give him a hundred / p^r^ pare & farther saith not

and father sed he wolde not take his bill

her
ANN **A** WILKISON
mark

I MALLUCK HALLEY of y^e^ Isle of Wight County / Doe heare by impower M^r^ CHA CHAPMAN / to be my attorney for me & in my name / to appeare in y^e^ s^d^ County Courte & answer / a Sute brought aganste me by M^r^. ROB^T^ / COLEMAN & what my s^d^: attorney Shall / Lawfully doe tharein I doe heare by Ratify / and Conform witnes my hand this 2^th^ day of augus^t^ / 1695

his
NATH^LL^. **P** PERMETER
JOHN WILLIAMS
RICH REYNOLDS

MALL^K^. **x x** HAWLY
his marke

**[168]**

I The Subscriber do testifie to y^e^ Courte that I Saw W^M^ NEVEL / walking from CHARLES DURRUM's with his arm [ ] burnt / and his cloths not so much as [ ], but how it came fur. / saith not

y^e^ 6^th^: Aug^t^. 1695 ꝑ me JAMES JORDAN

Know all m en by these p^r^sents that I SARAH GREEN of y^e^ / lower parish of y^e^ Isle of Wight, have made, ordained, and con / =stituted, and by these p^r^sents do for me, my heirs, Exect^rs^, and Adm^rs^ / make, ordain, and constitute, and in my Stead and Place put / JOHN DAVIS, of y^e^ upper Parish of y^e^ said County, my true and / lawfull Attorney, for me and in my name, and to my use, to / ask and demand, Sue for, levy, recover and receive of , and from / all and every p^r^son and p^r^sons whatsoever, all debts due and / demands, due, and payable to me in this Colony of Virginia, from / any p^r^son or p^r^sons, in any manner, accruing to me by Acco^ts^ / specialty debt, or in any manner to me belonging, or to belong / and for all, or any Such debt or debts, to give such release, or releases / as may or Shall be necessary, or convenient in law to be given / and upon refusall of payment, to Sue for y^e^ Same, and to impow^r^. / such other Attorney, or Attorneys, as to my Said Attorney shall seem / meet, and convenient, and to prison to commit, or out of Prison to / deliver, or to give any release or Releases, discharge, or discharges as may / be requisite, in and about any business, whatsoever to me belonging / as if I were p[r]sonally p[r]sent ratifiing, and confirming, and I do / hereby ratify and confirm whatsoever my Attorney shall legally do / in for touching any and every of my concerns, whatsoever in any / manner hearsoever. In Witnes whereof, I have hereunto sett my hand / and Seal, this ninth day of July Anno Dom. one Thousand / Six hundred, and ninety & five

Sealed and delivred
in y[e] p[r]sence of
JN[O]. SKELTON
HUM: MARSHALL

SARAH **G**: GREEN
her marke Seal

**[169]** [*right side of page torn off*]

Bee Itt Knowne unto all Men by these ꝑsons / that I ELISABETH BOOTH y[e] wife of RICH: / BOOTH of y[e] blackwater doe Constitute Im / =power & ordaine my Loving frends M[r] JEREMIAH / EXUM to be my true Lawfull attorney to actt / for me & in my name & Place & Steade & / in my Behalfe to Acknowledg before y[e] Courte / of y[e] Isle of Wight a deed of Sale made to / ISACK REAKES to be my Reall actt and deed & y[e] / assignem[t] upon y[e] backsid of y[e] Pattent to be / my Reall actt & deed also & doe give unto / my afores[d]: attorney my Good Right & full / power to perform full fill & finish all / things bee fore mentioned Rattifying & Conferm= / =ing & allowing all & whatsoever Shall be done / aboute y[e] same & to be as Goode and Effecttuall / in Lawe If I had performed y[e] same in my owne / person as wittines my hand & seale this 23 / of July in y[e] yeare 1695

wittines
WILL BROWN
JOHN ROGARES

her
ELIZABETH **O** BOOTH
mark [Seal]

Be itt Knowne unto all men by these presen[ts] / that I RICH. BOOTH & ELIZEBETH his wife for / Good Consideration in hand allready Recd ha[ve] / bargained Solde & deliverd over unt [*sic*] IAAC / REAKES all my Right titell and Intrest of [a] / Pattent of Land y[t] I now live upon that [is] / to say two hundred & Sixty five acers be [--] / onerly oun dew & full Interest in y[e] s[d]. patt[ent] / lying and being as is Exprest in y[e] abo[ve] / s[d]: pattent bareing date y[e] 23[th] of Aprill / And / turne over

**[170]**

And for farther Confermation heare of wee y[e] s[d] / RICH. BOOTH & ELEZEBETH his wife doe binde / our selves our hares Executors Administrators / and assignes to warrent and maynetaine / the a bove s[d]: deed of Land unto y[e] s[d]: ISAAC REAKES / his hares Executors administrators & assigns / for Ever in as strong & firme a maner Can / bee Expreste by woords or writing not with= / =standing any thing above mentioned to y[e] / Contrary & further wee doe binde our selves / In y[e] Penalty of twenty Thousand Pounds /

of tob$^{o}$: in cask forfeiture to make and / Acknowledg$^{t}$ at our nex$^{t}$ w$^{ch}$: is to be held / the Ninth of y$^{e}$ nex$^{t}$ M$^{o}$: Called July 1695 / In wittenes heare of wee have heareto / sett our hands and Seales this 29$^{th}$ of / June 1695

Wtnes
JOSEPH MEREDETH
HENRY POPE

Signum
RICH **RB** BOOTH seal
signum
ELIZABETH **E** BOOTH & Seal

The Deposion of THO: NORSWORTHY aged 30 / Yeares or thare abouts being Sworne and / Examened Saith

That som time in or a bought y$^{e}$ Latter end / end [*sic*] of January 169$^{3}$/$_{4}$ this Deponant wente / along with SAM$^{LL}$: COHOON to M$^{r}$: RICH WILKISON senr / hous to remove y$^{e}$ s$^{d}$ COHOONs things from thence / at which time y$^{e}$ s$^{d}$: WILKISON did demand of y$^{e}$ s$^{d}$: / COHOON sattisfaction for y$^{e}$ s$^{d}$: COHOONs accomadation / at his hous, upon which y$^{e}$ s$^{d}$: COHOON & y$^{e}$ s$^{d}$: / WILKISON did settelle thare accompts Conserning / Shoes which y$^{e}$ s$^{d}$: WILKISON had had of y$^{e}$ s$^{d}$: COHOON

**[171]**

COHOON which did amounte to about 300$^{lbs}$ of tobo / which y$^{e}$ s$^{d}$: COHOON did a gree Should goe on part / of Satis faction for his s$^{d}$: diet, y$^{e}$ s$^{d}$: WILKISON did / then demand of y$^{e}$ s$^{d}$: COHOON five hundred pounds / of tobo on ore about w$^{ch}$: thare arrose a grate / Difference be twene y$^{e}$ s$^{d}$: COHOON & y$^{e}$ s$^{d}$: WILKISON / but at length y$^{e}$ matter being Som what palle= / =ated [*sic*] y$^{e}$ s$^{d}$: COHOON did say y$^{t}$ in consideration of his s$^{d}$: / diett & to have a small end of all Controverses / betwen them he would pay unto y$^{e}$ s$^{d}$: WILKISON / 400$^{lb}$ pounds of tobo more Then these Shoes before / accompted for to w$^{ch}$: y$^{e}$ s$^{d}$: WILKISON did agree upon / which y$^{e}$ s$^{d}$: COHOON did offer to pas his bill to / y$^{e}$ s$^{d}$: WILKISON for y$^{e}$ s$^{d}$: 400$^{lb}$ of tobo & y$^{e}$ s$^{d}$: / WILKISON Replyed that he would take it out / in shooes but y$^{e}$ s$^{d}$: COHOON Swore *God dam him / he Should never have a Shooe more of him* / and y$^{e}$ s$^{d}$ WILKISON replyed he would not then / take his bil, and farther this deponant saith not

THO: NORSWORTHY

I the within mentioned THO: NORSWORTHY do say / farther y$^{t}$ y$^{e}$ s$^{d}$: COHOON did say that if y$^{e}$ s$^{d}$: / WILKISON did not take y$^{r}$ 400 pounds of tobo then / he Should have no more then his dew or then / the Law would a low him & farther saith not

THO: NORSWORTHY

**[172]**

This Indenter made this sixth day of august in / the yeare of o$^{r}$: Lord God one thousand six / hundred ninety & five Betweene JOHN LUTHER / of y$^{e}$ Isle of Wight County planter (with y$^{e}$ / Consent of his wife MARY) of y$^{e}$ pt: and / RICH: BEALE planter of y$^{e}$ other p$^{r}$t of y$^{e}$ / a fore s$^{d}$: County Wittnesseth that y$^{e}$ s$^{d}$: / JOHN LUTHER for a Valuable Sume of tobo & / caske to him in hand pade & deliverd before / the Ensealing & delivery of these p$^{r}$sents / whare with y$^{e}$ s$^{d}$: JOHN LUTHER doth acknoledg / him selfe fully satisfyed Contented & paide / Hath granted bargained & sold & these / p$^{r}$sents doth fully clearly & absolutely / grante bargaine & sell Unto y$^{e}$ fores$^{d}$: RICH / BEALE his hares Exec$^{rs}$: adm$^{rs}$: & assignes for / Ever a ꝑcell of Land Contaning Twenty acers / more or lesse which ꝑcell is parte of the / plantatyon that AMBROS BENNET by will gave / to y$^{e}$ s$^{d}$: JOHN LUTHERs wife MARY & is bounded / as followeth, all y$^{e}$ Land that is Upon y$^{e}$ south / side of a littelle branch at y$^{e}$ head of y$^{e}$ s$^{d}$: / LUTHERs plantation & y$^{e}$ line of GILES DRIVER / to y$^{e}$ path that form$^{r}$ly wente from AMBROS / BENNITT to RICH: REYNOLDS his old plantation / whare on ROB$^{T}$: DRIVER now liveth to have / holde occupy & quietly Injoy y$^{e}$ s$^{d}$: Land / with all rights profitts & priveledgs in / free or ample maner in all & Every / respect as y$^{e}$ s$^{d}$: JN$^{O}$: LUTHER him selfe hath or / can have uppon y$^{e}$ s$^{d}$: Land, by these p$^{r}$sents / bargained & sold to him y$^{e}$ s$^{d}$: RICH: BEALE / his hares Exec$^{rs}$: adm$^{rs}$: & assignes for Ever / and y$^{e}$ s$^{d}$: JN$^{O}$: LUTHER for him selfe his heir$^{rs}$: / Exec$^{rs}$: adm$^{rs}$: doth Covenant and Grante to / and

**[173]**

And with y$^{e}$ s$^{d}$: RICH: BEEALE his har$^{rs}$: Exec$^{rs}$: / adm$^{rs}$: and assigns y$^{t}$ y$^{e}$ ꝑcell of Land before / demised & sold & Every ꝑt & ꝑcell thare= / =of at y$^{e}$ tyme of y$^{e}$ Ensealing and delevery / of these p$^{r}$sents in and soe all tymes heare= / =after for Ever, & from tyme to tyme shall= / =be remaine & Continue unto y$^{e}$ s$^{d}$ RICH: / BEALLE his her$^{rs}$: Exec$^{rs}$: adm$^{rs}$: or assigns / Clearely acquitted & discharged or otherwise / Sufficiently Saved & kept harmelesse / of & from all, and all manner of former / or other bargans, Sales gifts, Grants leases / Joynturs wills Doweres, Executions Seizures / Intrusons & Extents & off and from all and / Singular other charges titles trobles Incum= / brances & demands, what so ever had made / Comited consented unto procured or done by y$^{e}$ / s$^{d}$: JN$^{O}$: LUTHER or by any other ꝑson or ꝑsons / by his Consent knowledge or p$^{r}$curem$^{t}$ the / rents and service due to the kings mai$^{tis}$: for / y$^{e}$ demised p$^{r}$mises & every parte or ꝑcelle / thare of unto y$^{e}$ s$^{d}$: RICH: BEALL and his / har$^{rs}$: Exec$^{rs}$: adm$^{rs}$: & assigns for Ever y$^{e}$ s$^{d}$: / JOHN LUTHER doth heereby Coven$^{t}$ & promis / to & with y$^{e}$ s$^{d}$: RICH: BEALLE y$^{t}$ upon reasnable / request to him made he and his wife will / acknoledg this p$^{r}$sent deed & Convayance / y$^{e}$ nexte Courte in y$^{e}$ Isle of Wight County in / wittnes whare of y$^{e}$ s$^{d}$ JN$^{O}$: LUTHER & his wife hath / heare unto sett thare hands & seales y$^{e}$ day & / yeare first a bove written

| Signed seald & deliverd in | | JOHN LUTHER seall |
|---|---|---|
| y$^{e}$ ꝑnes of us | WILL BRADSHAW | her |
| | signed | MARY + LUTHER seale |
| | ELIZ: **7** BRADSHAW | marke |
| | signed | |
| | THEOPH. + JOYNER | |

**[174]**

The Deposion of BENIA: BEALLE sen$^{r}$ being sixty too / yeares of age or thare abouts & his wife being / about sixty yeares of age or thare abouts / sworne & Examined Saith y$^{t}$ y$^{e}$ Land that / Leieth one y$^{e}$ other side of y$^{e}$ Branch betwen / JN$^{O}$: LUTHER and GILES DRIVER along as y$^{e}$ markt / treas gooeth up to y$^{e}$ path that goeth to RICH / REYNOLDS plantation we Can both Sware y$^{t}$ / wee Ever held & payed Rent for & was possesed / of y$^{e}$ Same by AMBROS BENNET & farther / Saith not June 7$^{th}$ 1690

Sworne before me — BENIA: BEALL se$^{r}$
THO: GILES — her
MARY **MB** BEALL

†In the name of God amen y$^{e}$ 23$^{th}$ day of may anno / Domini 1695

I WILLIAM PENNY of y$^{e}$ Isle of Wight County of / Virginia being sick & weake of boddy but / of sound & perfect memory blessed be / Allmight [*sic*] God doe make & ordaine this / my laste will & testam$^{t}$ in manner & / forme following

viz I give and bequeath my sole to allmight / God my maker & hopeing with a surenc that / by merrets of Jesus christe my saviour to / Receve Everlasting life with y$^{e}$ sayme in / heaven & I bequeath my body to y$^{e}$ Earth / with Christian beuraill & as for my woorldly / goods I bequeath in manner & forme as / followeth

Itom I give & bequeath unto my daughter ELESABETH / one feather bed bolster & pillows with / farniture & she to take her Choyes / Itom

**[175]**

Itom I Give and bequeath unto my Daughter MARY / one fether bed with the furniture / belonging to it

Itom I Give unto JN$^{O}$: VOLINGTINE one breading sowe / and three barrowes & he to take his Choys / of all my hogges & I give unto JN$^{O}$: VALLINGTINE / and to JAMES VALLINTINE to flock beds and / firniture be Longing to them & JOHN VALLINTIN / to take his furstoe [*sic*] Choys

Itom I Give unto my sister FRANCES one bussell / of Corne

Itom I Give unto my sister ELESABETH one / busshell of Corne

Itom I Give unto JAMES VOLLINTINE one hogg / of two yeares ould and as for y[ ] of my / personall Estate after my Debts / being paide and my funerall Expence / to be Equall devided amongst my two / Daughters Except y$^{e}$ Provision in y$^{e}$ / hows of Corne & one ate which I Leave / for JN$^{O}$: VOLLINTINE & JAMES VOLLINTINE & / my two Daughters while thay stay / and I make and appoynte Daughter / ELESABETH my whole & Sole Exec$^{rx}$ of t[his] / my Laste will & testam$^{t}$ as wittness / my hand & Seale this Day & yeare / above written

Signed Seald & deleverd — WILL **3** PENNE[Y]
in y$^{e}$ p$^{r}$sents of Us — his mark
ANTHO: HOLLADAY
his
ROB$^{T}$: **RM** MARSHALL

mark

[176]

*Inter* RICH REYNOLDS *quer* & JOHN DAVIS Deft / NATHANIELL PERMENTO & CHARLES DURROM / both of this County make oath y$^{t}$ thay / were p$^{r}$sent att y$^{e}$ hous of y$^{e}$ Deft about / the beginning of June Laste when y$^{e}$ pl$^{t}$: / Demanded y$^{e}$ Deft to give him posestion / of y$^{e}$ hous and plantation y$^{e}$ s$^{d}$: DAVIS now / Lives on & deft gave y$^{e}$ s$^{d}$: REYNOLDS for Answer / that he Colde not would not deliver / possestion for that he had order to y$^{e}$ Contrary / wittnes our hands this day of augst / 1694

his
CHA: + DURHAM
mark
NATH: **X** PERMENTO
his marke

**R**

Receved this 11$^{th}$ day of June 1694 of MARGRET / WILLSON y$^{e}$ som of thirty pounds star$^{ll}$ w$^{ch}$: / I have borrowed of her for one yeare / and do oblige my self my Exec$^{rs}$: adm$^{rs}$: / to pay y$^{e}$ same to her or accordingly / with ten pounds advance for y$^{e}$ yeares use / thare of witnes my hand this day above s$^{d}$:

W$^{M}$: ARCHER

Octob$^{r}$ y$^{e}$ 6$^{th}$ 1695

In obedience to an ord$^{r}$ of Courte Dated y$^{e}$ 9$^{th}$ / day Sept$^{br}$ 1695 we y$^{e}$ Subscribers have / Inventories & appraized y$^{e}$ Estate of / THOMAS JOYNER deced as followeth

| | |
|---|---|
| 39$^{lb}$ of pewter att 12$^{li}$ ꝑ pound | 0468 |
| 5 of old broken peweter | 0030 |
| 1 brass pann weight 3$^{lb}$ att 16 ꝑ pd | 0048 |
| 1 Iron pott & pott hookes | 0160 |
| 1 frying pann & 1 spitt | 0171 |
| 1 gonn and 1 sworde | 0230 |

[177]

| | |
|---|---|
| a ꝑcell of old Carpenters tooles | 0200 |
| 1 old Croscut saw & a ꝑcell of old Iron | 0204 |
| 2 pre of hooks & hinges & 1 Iron bullet | 0050 |
| 1 Ring staple & hooks | 0050 |
| 2 pre of potracks & 2 hookes | 0120 |
| 1 old gridiron | 0025 |
| 1 pre of old brasse Scales & wates / and box | 0140 |
| one Table & 3 old barrells | 0190 |

| | |
|---|---|
| 4 deale planks & 2 old boles | 0060 |
| 1 Grinstone | 0040 |
| 1 Cheste 1 box 2 trunks & a small Cabenett | 0280 |
| 1 feather bed & bolester 2 pillows / 2 pillow beare 1 shagg Rugg one / hamacker 2 sheats 1 Chafe bed / 3 Curtaines & Vallins and one / bedstead | 2800 |
| 1 old flock bed in a Canvis tick and 1 old rudg & old hamacker | 0300 |
| 1 Campaign Coverlid | 0450 |
| 1 Kersey Cote and briches 1 penistone / waste Cote & 2 pre of Virginia / Stokings, 2 new corce dowlas shert | 0460 |
| 1 blew sherte & 2 old neckcloths | 0140 |
| a ꝑcell of old Clothes & 2 old hatts | 0250 |
| 2 plow Chanes | 0300 |
| one Looking glasse | 0100 |
| 1 stuffe petticote & wesecoate one / striped petticote a pre of parragan / boddice & 2 sleave & one pre of / worsted stockins | 1000 |
| 1 red cloth suite & 1 old flowerd / demity peticote | 0400 |
| 1 sheate 2 shiffs 2 aprons a ꝑcell / of head linnen & an old black / scarfe | 0500 |
| 10 y$^{ds}$ of low linen | 0120 |
| 6 Ells of sheating holland | 0240 |

**[178]**

| | |
|---|---|
| 3 Ells of holland & ¾ of dowlas | 0180 |
| 15 2/5 Ells of Canvis | 0231 |
| 2½ y$^{ds}$ searge | 0100 |
| 1¼ of Cotton | 0030 |
| 1¼ of brown thred | 0050 |
| a pre of spectacles & 2¼ y$^{rd}$ of narro lace | 0026 |
| 1 steare 2 Cous & a yerling hefer | 1550 |
| by a bill of THO: SMITH | 0500 |
| BRIDGMAN JOYNER by acc$^{tt}$ | 0400 |
| NICKLAS CASEY | 0050 |
| | 5477 |
| one Small Silver bodkin | 7165 |
| one old gold rindg & 6$^{s}$ 6$^{d}$ in mony the totall | 12642 |

one Womans Caster hat
one bible
one Iron pott

one bras pann
one hamer
one Swash
one Ivory hafted knife
one Chafing dish

ARTH: PURSSELL
WILL I GODWIN
ALEK * MATHEWS
WILL BRADSHAW

An accont of MARY WHITLY widdoe adminitiks [*sic*] of / her husband JN[O]: WHITLY deced aganst her deced / husbands Estate

| | |
|---|---|
| To a Letter of administration & other Clarks fees | lb |
| To y[e] Sheriffs fees | |
| To a Coffin for my hisband | 150 |
| To 2 gall of brandey for y[e] funerall | 100 |
| To 4 Shillings pade M[r] COPELLAND | 150 |

**[179]**

| | |
|---|---|
| paide to JAMES JOLLEY for a kee | 050 |
| paid to M[r]. NICHOLAS FULGHAM in tobo | 469 |
| paid to M[r]: GEORGE MOORE for Leavies [ ] | 306 |
| for my troble & panes in y[e] admininstration what yo[w] worship think fitt | |
| dew to Cap[t] APPLEWHAIT | 190 |
| shues | 542 |
| dew to Coll SMITH for y[e] beleyake | 500 |
| dew to RICH: TUNNER | |
| dew to NICHOLAS FULGHAM | |
| dew to ROB[T] MARSHALL | 400 |
| dew out of my husbands WHITTLYs / Estate 1000 pounds of tob[o]. for a Steare & a Cow which my s[d]: husband solde which was given my Daughter OLIVE MACKDOWELL / by her father JAMES MACKDOWELL | 1000 lb |
| Dew to my husband in tob[o] / by THO: OWEN | 500 |
| by the widdow PITT | 100 |
| by RALFE FRISSELL | 090 |
| by WILL SMITH 2½ barrells of Corne | |

**[180]**

Know all men by these p$^{r}$sents that I SYLVESTRA / HILL Widdow Relique of L$^{t}$ Coll NICH$^{O}$ HILL Latte / of y$^{e}$ County of y$^{e}$ Isle of Wight for & in Consid / = Eracon of y$^{e}$ Sume of twenty Pounds of Good / and Lawfull money of England to me by / LEWES BURWELL of y$^{e}$ County of Yorke before / the Sealing and Delivery of these p$^{r}$sents / in hand p$^{d}$: y$^{e}$ Receipt whare of and that I / am thare w$^{th}$: fully Satisfyed Contented & p$^{d}$: / I do heare by acqnowledge and y$^{e}$ s$^{d}$: LEWIS BURWELL / his heires of & from y$^{e}$ Same & Every p$^{t}$: thare of / I do fully freely & absolutely acquit & Discharg / have given granted bargained, Sold & Con / =firmed and by these p$^{r}$sents do for my selfe / my Exec$^{rs}$: & adm$^{rs}$: give grante bargane sell & / Conferme unto y$^{e}$ s$^{d}$: LEWIS BURWELL his heires & / my Righte title Claime Intrest & Estate / which I have or ought to have of in and / to one Seat tract of Plantacon of Land scituate / lying and being in y$^{e}$ s$^{d}$: County of y$^{e}$ Isle of / Wight a little a bove y$^{e}$ head of Laien Creek / where y$^{e}$ s$^{d}$: L$^{t}$ Coll$^{o}$: NICH$^{O}$ HILL formerly lived / and by y$^{e}$ last will and Testament of the s$^{d}$: / NICH$^{O}$: HILL gave unto me y$^{e}$ s$^{d}$: SYLVESTRA HILL / for and Dureing y$^{e}$ terme of my Natrall / Life with all Priveladges Rites profets Com / =odeties & advantages, to the Same belonging / or in any wise appertaining to have and to / hold y$^{e}$ s$^{d}$: Tract: or Plantacon & other the / Prebargained primises w$^{th}$: the appaurtenances / to y$^{e}$ s$^{d}$: LEWIS BURWELL his hares & assignes / for Ever and further for me my hares Exec$^{rs}$: / adm$^{rs}$: I do Covenante Promise grante & / agree to and with the s$^{d}$: LEWIS BURWELL

**[181]**

His hares & that I will Upon y$^{e}$ Reasonable Costes / and Charges in the Law of y$^{e}$ s$^{d}$: LEWIS BURWELL his [ ] / Do make Suffer acqnowledge Performe & Deliver / and Execute all & Every such further & other / Deeds grants Confermances and assurances in y$^{e}$ / Law ꝑsuant to the true Intent & meaning of theise / ꝑsents as by y$^{e}$ s$^{d}$: LEWIS BURWELL & or his or thare / Councell lerned in the law shall be Reasonable / Devised advised or Required in witness whare / of I have heare unto set my hand and fixed / my Seael this Twelfth Day of Sep$^{r}$ annoq$^{u}$ / Dom one thousand Six hundred ninety / five

Signed seald & livery &
Seizin of y$^{e}$ Land above mencond — SIL: HILL Seale
given to y$^{e}$ above named maj$^{r}$
LEWIS BURWELL by y$^{e}$ above named
M$^{rs}$: SILVESTRA HILL by Delivery of
a twig & turfe ꝑt of y$^{e}$ Premises in
Presents of

J[ ]
JS ALLEN
THO: MOORE
JOHN JENINGS
JN$^{O}$: SKELTON

The account & Invitary of JN$^{O}$: THORNETONs Estate deced

To one Cow and Calfe & two too yeare old hefers
To one two yeare old steere
To one old decriped Stoone horse
To one Rugg & one blankitt
To 2 old Chests
To 2 rush bottomed Cheares
To 3 old pales
To 12 old puter spoones
To 4 old trays
To one forty galland Caske
To some od Shomakers tooles
To one old falling ax & spade
To 18 Shoots a boute between 9 & 12 months old

**[182]**

JOHN JOLIFE aged 39 yeares or there abouts sath y$^{t}$ he / was at y$^{e}$ hous of Coll SMITH y$^{e}$ 4$^{th}$ of august I did / heare WILL: GREEN & his wife MARY GREEN say / that JOHN BUNCLY his wife or his Daughter / did milke JOHN JOLIFEs Cattell & said y$^{t}$ will / prove it & after y$^{e}$ cattle was drove over / to y$^{e}$ sd GREENes penn and farther saith not

JOHN JOLLIFF

The Deposion of SUSANAH GARNER & ELEZABETH / ROYALL being Sworne saith

That yo$^{r}$ Deponant did hare JAMES PARTRIDGE / say that after his Debts payd y$^{e}$ remainer of / of [*sic*] his Estate to be Equally to be Devided betwene / his wife & Daughter & that his Daughter / Law had three head of cattell all Ready of / her owne & farther saith not

her
SUS **Z** GARNER
marke
her
ELIZ **E** NEYALL
marke

The Deposion of ELEZIBELL BROWN aged about 56 / yeares or thare abouts saith y$^{t}$ about June last / past being at y$^{e}$ hous of THO BOONEs did there / thare [*sic*] to W$^{M}$: JOLLY up two halfe Crowns to M$^{r}$: / ROB$^{T}$: COLEMANs negro siscoe & toald him he would / not have to doe with him upon no score it being / money y$^{r}$ M$^{r}$: COLEMANs negro Tom had left with / y$^{e}$ s$^{d}$: JOLLEY to by a hatt but he not finding it / safe would not be Conserned with one no Eiter / of y$^{e}$ s$^{d}$: negroes but bad y$^{e}$ negroe Returne y$^{e}$ / money whare he had itt and farther saith / not

This Deponant being sworne to / be for me Octob y^e^ 7^th^ 1695

JERI: EXUM

**[183]**

M^r^: CHAPMAN October y^e^ ferst 1695

Pray appear and prosecute an Accon for me ag^t^. / the Adm^rs^: of PHILLIP MACKCODDING and for yo^r^: Soe / doeing this Shall be yo^r^: ware^r^: witnes my hand

MICHALL WHARTON

Virgenia

To the wor^ll^: y^e^ Isle of Wighte Courte the / humbell petion of JOHN WOKINS / Sheweth / That yo^r^: Pet^r^: father JOHN WATKINS did in / his life make the Nuncupative will annexed to / Pet^n^: in y^e^ p^r^sents of W^M^: CRUMPLOE & W^M^ / DAVIS w^ch^: yo^r^: Pet^nr^: prays may be admitted / to Record & administracion of y^e^ estate of yo^r^: / s^d^: Pet^nr^: fathers estate may be granted to / yo^r^: Petn^r^: w^ch^: y^e^ will annexed in his mothers / behalfe yo^r^: Petn^r^: Shall

Pray &^c^

Jeneway y^e^ 7^th^ 1695

†JOHN WATKINS sin^r^: Laste will by words be fore / the s^d^: WILL: CRUMPLEE [*sic*] & WILL DAVIS [ ] y^e^ plantation that I / now live one y^e^ one halfe I give unto my wife / MARY and falfe [*sic*] y^e^ orcherds & the other falfe / to my son JOHN WOCKINS y^e^ s^d^ JOHN WOCKINS Jun^r^ / to have y^e^ hole plantation to plante one & to / give his mother a sheare of Corne yearley if / he makes good youes of it to her Living and after / her deceas to returne to his sonn JOHN WATCKINS & / from hare to hare for Ever y^e^ parsell of Land y^t^ / THOMAS ENGLISH lives one he is to have one / hundred

**[184]**

Hundred acers one y^e^ South Side of y^e^ Swamp and what / is a bove a hundred acers I doe Give to my Grandson / JAMES WATKINS and if he dies with out Ishew / then to Returne to my Grandson GEORGE ENGLISH / and his hei^rs^: for Ever and my hole movable / Estate I give unto my wife MARY WATKINS and / if my wife MARY dies to Give my Riding horse / to my sonn JOHN WACKINS

WILL: DAVIS his
WILL CRUMPLER JOHN ł WATKINS
mark Seal

In Obedience to an order Courte helde y^e^ 9^th^ day / of Septembr 1695 the Estate of WILL = / DENSON Apprased

| | |
|---|---|
| 2 Negro Men at | 11000 |
| 8 augers at | 00100 |

| | |
|---|---|
| 6 Chisels 4 Gouges 2 hamers | 00140 |
| 4 Broadaxes 1 froe 1 drawing / Knife 1 tomahak 1 adze & Gouge | 00245 |
| 3 hand Saws & Croscut Saw & Sledge | 00220 |
| 1 Sett of Carte wheales Rings & boxes / and Drawing Knife | 00150 |
| 2 hoes flesh forke & Ladle / and Rounde Share | 00011 |
| 2 pare of Stillerds & horse / Cambe Geare | 00450 |
| 4 & 1/8 Ells of brown Linnin | 00706 |
| 4 & ½ Ells of Linnin | 00072 |
| 1 Ells of Kenting | 00040 |
| 1 Quire of paper | 00004 |
| 3 Dows Skins | 009[ ] |
| 1 bridle & Cruper Lether | 0030 |
| bed | |

**[185]**

| | |
|---|---|
| Bed ticking | 00070 |
| 1 Sheete | 00065 |
| 1¼ [ ] of Cotton Yarne & ½ [ ] of thred | 00040 |
| 1 coate | 00250 |
| 3 Iron Potts at 3[li] pd | 00279 |
| 3 Pare of Pothwoks | 00060 |
| 2 Brass Panns | 00110 |
| 1 fring Pann | 00025 |
| 2 Porringers & ½ gills 2 pare of / Sixsurs 1 Pare Sheares | 00056 |
| 1 Bible 1 paro of Goulde Scales / and Glass buttons | 00200 |
| 1 ffox trap | 00750 |
| 1 Rugg and blankett | 00250 |
| 2 Gunns | 00550 |
| 1 Compas Dyall & pre of fleems | 00040 |
| 2½ Bushells of Sault | 00225 |
| 1 Parsell of nayles | 00030 |
| 1 Saddle | 00035 |
| 1 writeing Slate | 00030 |
| 2 Mesen Potts | 00080 |
| 1 horse | 07000 |

JOHN COGAN sen[r]

his
JN[O] IM MOORE
marke

**[186]**

At a Courte holden for y[e] Isle of Wight County on / y[e] 9[th] of 9[ber]. 1695

Then order was Granted for y^e Devision of y^e Land / of RICH^D BRIGGS deced Left to his two Sonn

3^d December 1695

In obedience to y^e order w^th:in mentoned wee whose / Names are heare to Subscribed have veiwed y^e / Land in y^e s^d: order menconed and Devided & marked / out a Deviding Lyne to y^e best of our Judgm^t / betwen JAMES and EDWARD BRIGGS According / to will of RICH^D BRIGGS thare father

HEN BAKER
ROBERT KAE
THO: MOORE
JN^O: SKELTON

November y^e 26^th: 1695 Receved then of MARY WHITLEY / widdow for y^e use of THO: WHITLEY orphant of JOHN / WHITLEY deced y^e Sum of One Thousand Eight hundred / fifty one pounds of tob^o: being his Share of his fathers / Estate I Say Received by me

Test — EDWARD **N** BROWN
his marke

JOHN GILES
JAMES TULLAGH
NICHOLAS FULLGHAM
JOHN CLARKE

November y^e 26^th: 1695 Received then of MARY WHITLEY widdow / for y^e use of JN^O: WHITLEY & WILL WHITLEY orphans three / Thousand Seaven hundred & two pounds of tob^o: it being / in full for theire Share of thare fathers Estate / I Say Received by me

Test JN^O: GILES — CHARLES **X** DURHAM
his marke

JAMES TULLAGH
NICHOLAS FALLGHAM
JN^O: CLARKE

**[187]**

Know all men by theste [*sic*] presents that I JN^O: BROWNE Sen^r of the / Isle of Wight County doe authorize and impower JOHN / BROWNE to be my Lawfull attorney to answer at Courte / in y^e difirence between me & Cap^t HUGH CAMBELL & / what Soever my s^d: attorney Shall act or doe in my / name I doe heareby Rrattifie [*sic*] allow and Conferme / as Given Under my hand this 2^th day of Desemb^r 1695

Test DAN^LL LEIGH — signum
signum — JN^O: Ш BROWNE
MARY **M** BROWNE

Isle of Wight County

To y^e^ wor^ll^. his ma^tes^ Justices for the s^d^ County / GEORGE HARDY Humbly Sheweth

Whare as y^e^ Petn^r^ being very week and not / able to Come to Courte desieres y^t^ yo^r^ worships / will be pleased to lett y^e^ bearer heare of / CALEB TAYLER stand tryall for [ ] / attorney in any Suite y^t^ Shall be [ ] / this or any other [ ] held for y^e^ s^d^ County

Jann^r^y y^e^ 3^d^ 1695 And yo^r^ Petn^r^ shall

GEORGE HARDY

M^r^: CHAPMAN [ ] 12^th^ Octob^r^ 1695

Please to pete^n^ y^e^ Isle of Wight County [ ] / order for devision of Land in y^e^ s^d^: County Given / by my ffather Will between my Brother JAMES / BRIGGS & my self doe further thare in as [ ] / Land may be requisite in y^e^ Judgm^t^ seem meet / for my interest & for y^e^ soe doeing this shall / be y^e^ warn^r^ witnis my hand

Test HEN: BAKER EDM^D^ BRIGGS

**[188]**

A true Inventory of y^e^ Estate of GEORGE HARDY Jun^r^ / deced taken y^e^ 6^th^ of Jan^r^y 1695

Imp^rs^ 1 old fether bed & pillow

1 Iron pott with pot hooks & potracks 1 frying pan

3 old puter dishes 1 olde Small puter flaggon

1 Long seader table 2 old Chests 1 old broad axe

1 old adz 1 hetchet 2 hand saws 1 old whip saw 2 small / augers 1 Gouges 5 Chisels 23 Joyners 7 planes

2 Small hamers 1 pump bore 2 old Iron wedges

[ ] 2 pr compases a Small p^r^sel of Coopers / tooles 1 tile & a p^r^sell of small tools for stocking of / [ ] 1 pr fire tongs & some debts but / [ ] Know not

RICHARD HARDY

To all to whom these p^r^sents Shall Come I FRANCIS / Lord Howard Baron of Effingham his Mai^ties^ Leiu^t^ & / Goven^r^ Gen^ll^. of Virginia Send Greeting in o^r^ Lord / God Everlasting Whereas his Mai^ties^ hath been graci= / ously pleased by his Royall Letters pattants under y^e^ / [ ] seale of England bearing date att westminster / the tenth day of October in y^e^ Eight & twentieth yeare / of his Reigne amongst other things in y^e^ s^d^: Letters pat= / =tents Conteined to Continue and Confirme y^e^ Auncient / priveledge and power of granting fifty acers of Land / for Every p^r^son Imported into this his Ma^ties^: Collony of / Virginia now Know y^e^ that I y^e^ s^d^: FRANCIS Lord Howard / Goven^r^ &c^r^ doe with y^e^ advice & Consent of y^e^ Councell of / State accordingly give and grante unto CHRISTOPHER / WADE Ninety two acers of land lying betweene the / Lands of M^r^: COLEMAN & M^r^: JN^O^: NEVELL in y^e^ Lower p^r^ish / of Isle of Wight County Begining att a Small Live / oake

**[189]**

Oake Sapling by a branch, thence up y^e s^d: branche / East North East nine by fore po: to a small sapling / Gum then north forty Eight deg^r: west ninety four / po: to a white oake M^r: COLEMANs Corner tree by a / meadow, then by M^r: COLEMANs north west one hundred / twenty two po: to a small white oake. then by M^r: / NEAVILL South weste seventy six po: & South Easte / one hundred and Eighty po: to y^e firste station / of two p^r sons into this Collony whose names are / in the Record mentoned under this pattent to / have and to hold the s^d: Land with his due sheare / of all Mines & minerells therein Contained [ ] / Rights & priviledges of Hunting Hauking fishing and / fencing with all woods watters & Rivers with all / profitts Comodits & Hareditaments what soever be= / =longing to y^e s^d: Land to him y^e s^d:CHRISTOPHER WADE / his heires and assines for Ever in as Large & am / =ple manner to all intents & purposes as have / been used and all [ ] / to be held of [ ] / and senesis as of [ ] / free & Comon senses [ ] / Knight Service yeilding & [ ] / Lord the King his heires & successors for [ ] / aiers of Land heare by Granted by ye [ ] / michall the arch angel y^e ffee Rent of [ ] / w^ch: payment [ ] made yearely from yeare to yeare / according to his Ma^ties: Instructions or [ ] / provided that if y^e s^d CHRISTOPHER WADE his heires or / assigns doe not seate or plant or Caus to be seated / or planted upon y^e s^d: Land within these three yeares / next Ensuing the date heare of that then itt shall and / may be law full for any adventurer or planter to [ ] / Choys thare of & seate thare on Given under my hand & y^e / seale of y^e Collony 20^th day of Aprill 1684 Effingham

**[190]**

Know all men by these presences that I SAMWELL WAIDE of y^e / County of the Isle of Wight planter doe assigne over / all my write & titell of this within mentioned pattent / of Land from me my heires Exec^rs: Admini^rs: or assignes unto / JOHN NEVILL Jun^r: his heir^rs: Exec^rs: Admin^rs or assignes of y^e / Same County for Ever as witnes my hand January y^e 23^th / day 169$^5/_6$ and doe acknoldeg to be fully Sattisfied and Contented / for the Same

Test JOHN NEVILL Sen^r

WILIAM **Y** NEVILL
his marke

I the above named SAMUELL WADE doe heare by desire a / pointe and Constitute my well beloved brother JN^O: BARDING / for me and in my name to acknowledg this Signmen^t / [ ] written in Courte to bee my free and Volluntary / act and deed and his acknowledgm^t I doe heare by hold / and Esteem as good as if my self were personally present to all / intents and purposes witnes my hand and Seales y^e first / day of febro^ary anno dom 169$^5/_6$

Signed Seald and Deliverd in y^e presents of us
THO: GILES

I SUSANNAH give my free Con= sente to y^e above mentioned assignm^t: witnis my hand y^e

his
JN$^{O}$: **I** BARDEN
mark
[ ] **IS** SEAMER
`his mark

day & yeare above writine

his
SAM$^{LL}$: **S** WADE Seale
marke
her
SUSANA **D** WADE Seale
marke

Know all men by these presents that I HEN$^{R}$: MARTIN of the Isle / of Wight County Planter & MARY my wife doe for us our hares / Exec$^{rs}$: make over bargan Sell and alineat unto HEN$^{R}$: APPLEWHAIT / of y$^{e}$ s$^{d}$: County his hares Exec$^{rs}$: or assigns a parsell of Land Con= / taining forty acers more or less Setuatin and Setinated [*sic*!] Liing= / and binding in y$^{e}$ fore s$^{d}$: County begining at a Line tree which / Devids the Land of y$^{e}$ s$^{d}$: APPLEWHAITE which formerly bought of / EDMUND PALLMER and y$^{e}$ Land of WILL: BODDY neare y$^{e}$ old feald / whare JAMES RIDIN Lived and bind in and runing westerly / the s$^{d}$: BODDYs Line to y$^{e}$ Land that now AMBRUS HADLY now Lives / uppon and Easterly one the Land of HEN$^{R}$: APPLEWHAITE being / formerly purchased by him from EDMUND PALLMER and / so

**[191]**
So doune to the furst Station with all priveledgs & Royaltys / what Soever is or Shall be Long thare unto to have / and to holde the premises him y$^{e}$ s$^{d}$: HEN$^{R}$: APPLEWHAITE / his heires Exec$^{rs}$: or assigns for Ever with Generall war= / renty against any purson or pusons that Shall Lay any / Clame or Clames to any part or parsell thare of for all / which wee y$^{e}$ s$^{d}$: HEN$^{R}$: MARTIN & MARY my wife doe / acknowledge our sevels [*sic*] fully Satisfied be fore y$^{e}$ Sealing / and delivery heare of and for a full and Abcollute / Confermation heare of doe ohblige our Selfes to acknow= / ledge this our Valantary act and deed at y$^{e}$ next Court / to be heild [*sic*] in y$^{e}$ Isle of Wight County as wittnes owr / hands and Seales
Test: RICH: REYNOLDS
THO: **O2g** JOYNER

his
HENRY **H** MARTIN
mark
MARY **x** MARTIN
hur: marke

This Indenter bearing date the Seventh day day [*sic*] of / October in y$^{e}$ yeare of our Lord God one thousand / Six hundred Ninty & five wittnesseth that / MATHEW TOMBLING of y$^{e}$ lower pish of y$^{e}$ Isle of / Wight County to and with y$^{e}$ free & Volantary Con / =sent of MARY his wife for a full and Valuable Con / =sidcration in hand allredy Reseved have barganed / solde and by these presents doe for us our heirs Exec$^{rs}$: / Admin$^{rs}$ bargain sell allienate transfer & for Ever / Lett & sett over unto WILLIAM BRIDGERS of y$^{e}$ afores$^{d}$: / Isle of Wight his heires Exec$^{rs}$: Adm$^{rs}$: and assigns

/ for Ever one part or ꝑsell of Land being by Estemation / one hundred acers be it more or Les lying and being / on y$^{e}$ branches of the black Watter in y$^{e}$ Upper ꝑshe / of y$^{e}$ s$^{d}$ Isle of Wight County being p$^{t}$: of a pattent / of twelve hundred twenty acers of land granted / to y$^{e}$ s$^{d}$: MATTHEW TOMBLING baring date the twentyth / seaventh day of Aprill anno Dom: one thousand six / hundred Eighty & six being bounded on y$^{e}$ North / with y$^{e}$ run and JN$^{O}$: SMITHs line & westerly on JN$^{O}$: FULGAMs / Line to a Corner white oake y$^{t}$ being allready Leased / to JN$^{O}$: MAINNALL to have and to hold y$^{e}$ s$^{d}$: Land unto / him

**[192]**

with all y$^{e}$ buildings housses woods wayes / watters Springs or watter Courses or any other profits / priveledgs Comoditis or apurtanances whatsoever in as Large / and ampell maner as ever first Granted by pattent / with out any Lett hinderance Controdicon or molestation / of him y$^{e}$ s$^{d}$: MATTHEW TOMBLING his heires Exec$^{rs}$ adm$^{rs}$ / or any other p$^{r}$son or p$^{r}$sons whatsoever from / by or under them Claiminge & for further Confermation / y$^{e}$ s$^{d}$: MATTHEW TOMBLING & MARY his wife doth by / these ꝑsents obleige them selves to acknowledge y$^{e}$ / same in y$^{e}$ County Courte held for y$^{e}$ Isle of Wight / when thare to bequested in wittness whare of / thay have heare unto sett their and seale y$^{e}$ day and / yeare above Specified

Signed Sealed & deliverd in
p$^{r}$sents

MATHEW TOMLIN seal
signi
MARY **III** TOMLIN seal

W$^{M}$ KERLOR
RICHARD **R** WORRELL
signi
W$^{M}$ **W** WORRELL
signi

Jan$^{r}$y y$^{e}$ 6$^{th}$ day 169$^{5}/_{6}$

A trew and p$^{r}$fect inventory of y$^{e}$ Estate of THO: ELMES deced / as followeth

2 Cowes & one Calfe one Steare 1 mare & 1 sowe and
2 Shotes 1 fether beed bolster & p$^{re}$ of blankets / and one beedsted 2 tables 1 Couch & 4 Cheares
1 Chest 1 Coberd & Loocking glas 1 p$^{re}$ of andirons 1 p$^{re}$ / of tongs 2 Iron pots 1 fring pan 1 warming pan
1 Spitt 1 driping pan 2 p$^{re}$ of potracks 8 puter dishes
8 plates 10 spoones 1 flagan 1 Candellstick 1 beaker
1 Chambert pott 1 silver Cupe 1 Gun 1 Sorde 2 Coates
2 p$^{r}$. of briches & 1 perigwig dew to him for wages from / Cap$^{t}$. BOSSE £2=3=0
dew in Surry by RICH$^{D}$ JONES 400 tobo
by NOAH BAREFOOT 450: dew by M$^{r}$: CHAPMAN 450
1 poudring tub & half dozen of trenchers wooden bool 1 p$^{r}$: bools
1 Sadell a p$^{r}$cl of Carpenders twoles W$^{M}$ BROWNE

**[193]**

†Know all men by these present y[t] I WILL POWILL of the / Isle of Wight County being at present very sick & weake / in body but yet in psent senns & memory doe if it / shall please god to take me out of this present Life / make this my last will & testament as followeth

first I doe give unto my Loving wife ELEZ[H] POWELL y[e] plantation / I now Live upon dureing her Life w[th]: all y[e] stock thare unto / belonging dureing her a fore s[d]: Life and then y[e] s[d]: Land / I doe give unto my sonn JN[O]: POWELL y[e] broad neck at y[e] / uper end of my line likewise I doe give my sonn NATHANELL / from that neck down y[e] Swamp to my orch[a]erd side and y[e] Rema / ining part of this Land unto my sonn JACOB to them / and theire heires Lawfully be gotten of theire own / bodyes for Ever

second I doe give unto my sonn WILL: POWELL my sonn THOMAS / POWELL all my Land upon y[e] hed of bowanarrows Swamp / to be Equally devided betwixt them my sonn WILL: to have / his first Choys to them and theire heire Lawfully begotten / of theire own bodies for ever

third I doe give unto my daughter ELEZEB[T]: wife of JN[O]: COOPES / that plantation thay now live upon to them & theire / heires for Ever this being my laste will & testam[t] / Revoking all other will & testam[ts]: what soever in / witnes heare of I have heare unto set my hand & seale / this Eleaventh day of Decemb[r]: in y[e] yeare of our Lord / God Sixteen hundred ninety & five

Signed sealed & deliverd in y[e] presents of us

WILL **M** POWELL sell
his marke

THO: **TP** POWELL
his mark
THO: **TE** GALE
his marke
RICH[D]: **P** HUCHINS
his marke

The prais ment of HEN[R]: ALLINs Cattell and hodggs

| | |
|---|---|
| 2 Cows 1 steare & 1 hefer at | 1100 |
| to 11 hoggs at | 0720 |
| to 4 thrays at | 0032 |
| | 1852 |

Test y[e] s[d]: apprasers this 9[th]: of June 1695
JACOB DURDEN
SIMON EVERITT
WILL **W** MURFRE
his mark

**[194]**

By Verty of an order of Isle of Wight County baring date / august y[e] 9[th]. 1695

Wee whose names are under written have apprased y$^{e}$ / Estate that THOMAS BULLOCK have presented [ ] of HEN$^{R}$: ALLINs deced this 26$^{th}$: day of august 1695

| | tobo |
|---|---|
| viz to a bed and furnture | 800 |
| to a Barrell stock & lock plate for a Gun | 220 |
| to 3 dishes 6 plates at 11 ꝑ $^{li}$ | 154 |
| to a Candlestick 2 tankerds 2 porringers 2 tin pans / 1 doz of spoons | 212 |
| to 1p$^{r}$ of stilerds | 050 |
| to 1 old hors ould saddel &c: | 800 |
| to a q$^{t}$ bottel & 4 earthen Cups | 010 |
| to a Couch 4 Cheares 2 Chests & a trunk | 350 |
| to a p$^{r}$sell of old Cask old wheels | 050 |
| to 3 littell ould towells | 008 |
| to an old Rundlit at | 010 |
| we finde a p$^{r}$sell of old cloths of little worth | |
| to a ꝑsell of appel treas in y$^{e}$ possetion of / FFRANSES BRIDDLE of noe vallu whare they stand | |
| to a ~~hhd~~ of tobo dew by bill from THO POWELL | 490 |
| to M$^{r}$ THO: GILE also | 030 |
| to 4 weavers slays we not staning Knowing / the value but as we Can apprehend at | 010 |
| | 3269 |

Test JACOB DURDING
WILL **W** MURFREA
SIMON EVERIT

as to y$^{e}$ Cattell & hoggs none and as yet to be found but when p$^{r}$ddused wee will be Ready to set a Vallu upon them in obedience to y$^{e}$ order of Court

**[195]**

†I NICHOLAS SMITH of y$^{e}$ Isle of Wight County in Virginia / being weake in body but of Reasonable Understanding & / Disposeing minde and Calling to minde y$^{e}$ certainty of my death / but y$^{e}$ uncertainty of y$^{e}$ time when, doe make & ordeyn my / Last will & Testam$^{t}$ in maner foll: that is to say

ffirst & Principally I comitt my Sowle to God y$^{e}$ father of / Spirits trusting & firmely believing thro y$^{e}$ merritts & bitter / passion of my alone Saviour & Redeemer Jesus Christ to reseve / full Pardon & Remission of all my Sins when Ever this mortall / life Shall Cease: & my body to be decently intered at y$^{e}$ discretion / of my Ex$^{rs}$: heare after named & for w$^{t}$ wordly Estate it hath / pleased y$^{e}$ lord to possess me with all I Give Bequeath and / Dispose as foll:

Itt I Give & Bequeath to my Lo: wife ANN y$^{e}$ one halfe of my / whole personall Estate & y$^{e}$ other remaining half to my Grand / Daughter y$^{e}$ Daughter of THOMAS POWELL now Living in y$^{e}$ province of Mary$^{ld}$: & her two Children but if my s$^{d}$: Grand Daughter / or Either of her Childeren Should hapen to dye before me / 'tis then my will &

desier y$^{t}$ his heirs or theire parts shall / Remaine to & be possest by y$^{e}$ Surviver: or Survivo$^{rs}$: of them / Excepting only out of y$^{e}$ whole one good feather bed & bolster / by me bought in Hol$^{ld}$: & now standing in my Dineing Roome / which I Give to NICHOLAS MILLER

Itt I Give & Bequeath to my Grand Daughter aforenamed / all my lands y$^{t}$ I now posses in Virginia or Else wheire for / and Deuring her naterall life and at her decease to y$^{e}$ Heires / of her body lawfully begotten for Ever, Excepting only / the trackt or Devidend of Land whare on I now live w$^{ch}$: / I Give to my Loving wife a fore s$^{d}$: for and dureing her naturell / Life and at her decease to my afore s$^{d}$: Grand Daughter for & during her naturall life & y$^{t}$ to y$^{e}$ Heires of her / body lawfully begotten for Ever

I doe heare by make ordayne & Constitute my a fore S$^{d}$: Lo: / wife ANN & my afores s$^{d}$: Grand Daughter Ex$^{rs}$ of this my / Last will & Testam$^{t}$: & declareing all former wills heare to / fore by me made to be null & voyd I have heareunto sett / my hand & Seal this 19$^{th}$ day of November 1695

Signed & Sealed publisht & declared
by y$^{e}$ Subscriber NICHOLAS SMITH to be his
Last will & Testam$^{t}$: in presence of us

NICHOLAS Seale
SMITH

AR$^{R}$ ALLEN
JOHN DAVIS
WILL **W** WEBES
marke
EDWARD MILLER

**[196]**

This Indentur Made y$^{e}$ Eight day of ffebruary in y$^{e}$ Second yeare of / the Reigne of our Sovereigne Lord James y$^{e}$ second of England Scotland / ffrans Ireland and Virginia King defender of y$^{e}$ ffaith &c$^{r}$ / and in y$^{e}$ yeare of our Lord God one thousand Six hundred Eighty / and ffive Betwene ISACK GEORGE of y$^{e}$ Uper parish of y$^{e}$ Isle of / Wight County & HESTER his wife on y$^{e}$ one party & L$^{t}$ Coll JAMES / POWELL of y$^{e}$ afores$^{d}$: p$^{r}$st: & County gen$^{t}$ on y$^{e}$ other parte witnesseth / that y$^{e}$ s$^{d}$: ISACK GEORGE & HESTER his wife for & in Consideration / of a Valuable Some of tob$^{o}$: to theme in hand payed before / y$^{e}$ Ensealing & delivery of thease presents by y$^{e}$ s$^{d}$: L$^{t}$ Coll JAMES / POWELL whare of & whare with thay y$^{e}$ s$^{d}$: ISACK GEORGE and / HESTER his wife acknowledg them Selves to be fully Satisfied / Contented & payed have by thease presents demised granted / Sett & to ffarme Lett unto y$^{e}$ L$^{t}$ Coll: JAMES POWELL his heires / Exec$^{rs}$: adm$^{rs}$: and assigns all that plantation whare on y$^{e}$ s$^{d}$: ISACK / GEORGE & HESTER his wife formerly lived uppon y$^{e}$ which plant$^{on}$: / was given unto him y$^{e}$ s$^{d}$: ISACK GEORGE by y$^{e}$ last will & testam$^{t}$. / of his late father JN$^{O}$: GEORGE Scituated lying and being / on the noarth Side of a Creeke Comonly Caled or knowne / by y$^{e}$ name of Castell Creeke in y$^{e}$ Uper parish of y$^{e}$ Isle of Wight / County bounded as is Exprest and laide downe in y$^{e}$ s$^{d}$: JN$^{O}$: GEORGE's / last will togeather with all houeses Edefises buildings gardens / orcherds fences & pastueres thare unto belonging with all / woods

Underwoods Comons feedings wast grounds moors marshes / profitts Comodities & heriditam^ts: what soever of them y^e s^d: / ISACK GEORGE & HESTER his wife or Either of them to have & / to houlde y^e s^d: plantation togeather with all y^e houses Edefices / buildings, gardings orcherds fences pastures with all woods under / woods Comons feedings waste grounds moors marshes & all & sing= / ulere other y^e pemices with thare & every of theire appertanance / be fore by thees presents demised & Every parte & parsell thare / of unto y^e S^d: L^t: Coll: JAMES POWELL his heirs Exe^rs: adm^rs: & assig^ns: / from y^e day of y^e date heare of unto y^e full end & terme of ninety / and nyne years from thence next insuing & fully to be compleated / and Ended yealding & paying thare fore yearly during y^e s^d: / terme unto y^e S^d: ISACK GEORGE and HESTER his wife theire / Her^rs: exe^rs: adm^rs: or asigns one Eare of Indian Corne at y^e / feast of y^e nativity of Jeasus Christe if y^e Same be Law fully / demanded & y^e S^d: ISACK GEORGE for him Selfe & HESTER his wife / theire Heires Exe^rs: & adm^rs: & Every of them doth Covenant / promise and grante to and with L^t: Coll: JAMES POWELL / his heires Exe^rs: adm^rs: and assigns that thy [*sic*] the s^d / ISACK

**[197]**

ISACK GEORGE & HESTER his wife or one of them now have / or hath full power and othority to Demise and grant to / and with L^t Coll: JAMES POWELL his hei^rs: Exe^rs: adm^rs: / and assignes y^t thay y^e s^d: ISACK: [--] / y^e s^d: plantation with other y^e premices which thare and / every of theire appurtanances and Every parte & parcell / thare of unto y^e s^d: L^t Coll: JAMES POWELL his hei^rs: Exe^rs: adm^rs: / and assignes in maner & forme a fore s^d: & y^e s^d: L^t Coll JA: / POWELL doth by thees presents for him selfe his hares / Exe^rs: adm^rs: & assignes Covenant & promis to & with y^e s^d: / ISACK GEORGE & HESTER his wife theire hei^rs: Exe^rs: adm^rs: and / Every of them at y^e end & expiration of y^e s^d ninty nyne / yeares to deliver up y^e plantation with Good housing / and fencing thare on in good order & tenant able in witnes / whare of all y^e partys to these presents have in terchan^bly / put theire hands & seales y^e day & yeare & Reigne above / written

| | |
|---|---|
| Sealed and delivered by all y^e partyes | his |
| on this indenter named in pesents of | ISAAC I GEORGE seall |
| SAM^L LUCK | mark |
| MILIHESEDER DUCKE | HESTER **H** GEORGE |
| MARY BRASHUR | her mark seall |
| | JAS POWELL seall |

acknoledged in open Courte / held for y^e Isle of Wight County octob^r y^e 9^th 1696 / by ISACK GEORGE & HESTER his wife to be / theire free & volintary act & deed & ordered / to be recorded

We the Subscribers doe assigne over y^e within Spesifide / Lease unto WILL SMITH or his assignes with warinty for us our / hei^rs: Exe^rs: & adm^rs: or from any person or persons as Shall / Claime from by or under us, as wittnes our hands this 9$^{th}$ day / of Aprill 1696 ROB$^{T}$: RANDALL

Test RICHARD STONE ANN: RANDALL

JOSEPH COREN

Aprill y$^{e}$ 9$^{th}$. 1696

Acknowledged in Courte by y$^{e}$ subscribers / ROB$^{T}$ RANDALL & ANNE his wife, the s$^{d}$ / ANNE relinquiching all her right of / Dower by her attorny JN$^{O}$: SKELTON

Test HUGH DAVIS C$^{l}$ C$^{ur}$

**[198]**

To all People whome this p$^{r}$sent Wrighting Shall Com to be / Seen Knowe y$^{e}$ y$^{t}$ I JN$^{O}$: PORTIS sen$^{r}$: of y$^{e}$ Isle of Wight County & / JANE my wife doe for a Valuable Consideration to us in hand paide / five Thousand two hundred & fifty pou$^{ds}$: of tob$^{o}$: before / the Sineing & delivery heare of for which Sum we doe acknoledg / to be fully Sattisfied by JOHN BRITT of y$^{e}$ County a fore s$^{d}$: doe / for our Selves our hei$^{rs}$: make over bargane sell a linate & / Conferme to y$^{e}$ s$^{d}$: JN$^{O}$: BRITT his hei$^{rs}$: Exe$^{rs}$: or assignes for Ever a / Sertaine Tract or Percell of Land in y$^{e}$ Isle of Wight County / Containing three hundred & Fifty acures byeing one Sum of y$^{e}$ / blackwater branches being parte of a patant of nine hundred / and fifty acers Granted to JN$^{O}$: PORTIS & HENRY WEST baring date / y$^{e}$ twentieth five day Septemb$^{r}$: 1673

The s$^{d}$: Land being Devided by JN$^{O}$: PORTIS & HENRY WEST / as by a devision under theire hands and Seales Recorded in y$^{e}$ / Isle of Wight County Records baring date 10$^{th}$ day of July 1675, / all w$^{ch}$: parte of y$^{e}$ Land & patant as by y$^{e}$ Devision made by me y$^{e}$ s$^{d}$: / JN$^{O}$: PORTIS & HENRY WEST Excepting one hundred acers of / Land Sould to JN$^{O}$ JONES w$^{ch}$: he y$^{e}$ s$^{d}$: JN$^{O}$: JONES is to Survaye the / Remaine parte being three hundred & fifty acers of Land / wee doe by these p$^{r}$sents Sill unto y$^{e}$ s$^{d}$: JN$^{O}$: BRITT his hei$^{rs}$: / Exe$^{rs}$: adm$^{rs}$: & assig$^{ns}$: for ever all y$^{e}$ above s$^{d}$: Land mentioned / in the above s$^{d}$: Pattant and Devision Excepting one one / hundred acers of Land a bove Mentioned with all profits / theire unto belonging to have and to holde y$^{e}$ s$^{d}$ Land w$^{th}$: / all Privelages profitts Royalties Inmunities & Commodityes / thare of & thare unto belonging to have & to hold the premices / to him y$^{e}$ s$^{d}$: JN$^{O}$: BRITT his hei$^{rs}$: Exe$^{rs}$: adm$^{rs}$: or assignes for Ever / with out y$^{e}$ Lett Mollestation or Disturbance or procurem$^{t}$: / of me y$^{e}$ s$^{d}$: JN$^{O}$: PORTIS my hei$^{rs}$: Exe$^{rs}$: adm$^{rs}$: with all Right that / I had of Could have by y$^{e}$ s$^{d}$ pattant and furder I doe obliege / my Selfe my hei$^{rs}$: Exe$^{rs}$: & adm$^{rs}$: to defend Save & keep Undamnified / the s$^{d}$ JN$^{O}$: BRITT his hei$^{rs}$: Exe$^{rs}$: & adm$^{rs}$: for Ever all person or / ꝑsons that Shall Disturbe or laye Clayme to y$^{e}$ Land & furder I doe / obleige my self with my wife JANE to acknoledg this deed of Sale / at our next Courte held for y$^{e}$ Isle of Wight County in wittnes / heare unto we have sett our hands & Seales this 8$^{th}$ day of / Aprill 1696

his mark

Sind Seal'd and ~~dld~~ in y$^{e}$ inter lined before sined JN$^{O}$: **P** PORTIS seale

Acknowledged in open Cu$^{rr}$ JANE **I** PORTIS

p$^{r}$sents: JN$^{O}$: x SERER held for y$^{e}$ Isle of Wight her marke seale
WILL EXUM Ju County y$^{e}$ 9$^{th}$ of Aprell
ALECK SERER 1696 by JN$^{O}$ PORTIS & JANE his wife
to be their acte & Deed & Ordered to be Recorded

**[199]**

Know all men by these p$^{r}$sents that I ROB$^{T}$ LACY of Lawne Creeke / parish in Surrey County & MARY my wife have barganed sold & delivred / and doe by these p$^{r}$sents for a Valuable Consideration to us in hand / pade by GEORGE TEATHER of y$^{e}$ Uper parish in y$^{e}$ Isle of Wight County / for us o$^{r}$: hei$^{rs}$ Exe$^{rs}$ & adm$^{rs}$: for Ever bargain Sell & Deliver / Enfeoff: & Confirme un to y$^{e}$ s$^{d}$: GEORGE TEATHER his heirs & assigns / for ever a sertane p$^{r}$sell of Land Containing ninty acers situated / in y$^{e}$ Uper parish of y$^{e}$ Isle of Wight County afore s$^{d}$: being parte / of a Eleven hundred acers formerly granted to W$^{M}$: MILES & W$^{M}$: / COOKE late of Surrey County deced dated y$^{e}$ 29$^{th}$ of Septemb$^{r}$ / 1664 y$^{e}$ s$^{d}$: ninty acers being bounded as followeth beginning at / a Sickemore in ~~or neare y$^{e}$ head of y$^{e}$~~ Beaver Dammitt [*sic*] Branch / near JN$^{O}$: PARSONSes bridg thence south 81$^{o}$E220 pole to a / Small live Oake Saplin thence north 80: pole to a Sickemore / in or neare y$^{e}$ head of y$^{e}$ Beaver Damms Branch thence downe / y$^{e}$ s$^{d}$: branch to y$^{e}$ furst Station to have & to holde y$^{e}$ s$^{d}$: ninty / acers of Land togeather with all y$^{e}$ houses orcherds / tenem$^{ts}$: & oth$^{r}$: hereditm$^{ts}$ whatsoever to him y$^{e}$ s$^{d}$: / GEORGE TEATH$^{R}$: his hei$^{rs}$ & assignes for Ever in as full / and ampell maner to all in tentes & purposes as y$^{e}$ most / learned in the Law can devise & I doe heareby oblige / my selfe my hei$^{rs}$: Exe$^{rs}$: & adm$^{rs}$: to warrant & defend / this my sale of y$^{e}$ afores$^{d}$: ninty acers of land ag$^{st}$: all / maner of p$^{r}$sons: whatsoever to y$^{e}$ s$^{d}$: GEO: TEATHER his heirs / and assignes for Ever & when thare two required to Give / y$^{e}$ s$^{d}$: GEO: TEATHER his hei$^{rs}$: & assignes such further lawfull / assueranc of y$^{e}$ p$^{r}$mises w$^{th}$: th:appurtanances as by his learned / Counsell shall be thot fitt at y$^{e}$ propp$^{r}$ Cost & chearges one / of y$^{e}$ s$^{d}$: GEO: TEATHER his hei$^{rs}$: or assignes in witnes whareof / we have heare unto putt our hands & seales y$^{e}$ / [--] day of [--] Anno Car scd xxxj$^{o}$ Annoqu / dom 1680[8]

the marke of
ROB$^{T}$ **R** LACY Seale
the marke of
MARY **8** LACY: Seale

Signed Sealed & deliverd
In y$^{e}$ p$^{r}$sents: of Us:
WILL BRESSE
the marke of
HEN: **IK** KING

Acknowledg in open Court by ROB$^{T}$: LACY and / MARY his wife held for y$^{e}$ Isle of Wight / County y$^{e}$ 9$^{th}$ of Feb$^{r}$ 1680 to be thare free / act & deed & ordered to be recorded

Test JOHN PTIT Cl

[8] Abbreviated form of "Anno Caroli secundi xxxj$^{o}$ Annoque domini 1680."

To all to whom these pesents [*sic*] shall Come / Know y$^{e}$ that I GEORGE TEATHER of Isle of / Wight for divers good Causes & Considerations / moveing me theire unto do Leet and Lease grant and asigne / unto GEO MORELL of y$^{e}$ County of Surres [*sic*] all my Right & title / preroguietive & prilivig [*sic*!] of y$^{e}$ with in mentioned peace or p$^{r}$sell / of land to him and his hei$^{rs}$: ore assignes for y$^{e}$ full terme or time / of ninty one yeares paying one eare of Indian Corne yearely to y$^{e}$ s$^{d}$: / TEATHER his heirs or assignes upon demand in witnis whare of I have set my / hand & Seall this 4 of April 1695

his
Signed Sealed & deliverd in p$^{r}$sents of THO: LANE GEORGE I TEATHER
[ ] **M** GORDIN GEORGE **M** MORELL Sen$^{r}$ mark Seall

**[200]**

I GEORGE MARRELL of Lawnes Creek Parish in y$^{e}$ County of Surrey doe heare by assigne / and Sett over unto JN$^{O}$ MANGUM of y$^{e}$ Same Parish & County his Ex$^{rs}$ and h$^{rs}$ adm$^{rs}$: / y$^{e}$ above mentioned p$^{r}$cell of Land by me Purchesed of GEO: TEATHER for y$^{e}$ / full terme above mentioned and will warrant and Defend him & them / in y$^{e}$ peasable possession of y$^{e}$ Same he & thay paying y$^{e}$ yearly acknoledgm$^{t}$ / above mentioned in testimony of which I have heare unto put my / hand & Seale y$^{e}$ 23$^{d}$ day of March 169$^{5}$/$_{6}$

Signd & Sealed in Presents of
RICH$^{D}$: HALLOMAN
his
JNO: I ATKISON
mark

It is agreed upon before y$^{e}$ signing & inSealing heare of y$^{t}$ y$^{e}$ s$^{d}$: GEO: MORRELL doth warrant but fifty acres of / Land
GEO: MEARILL
J M marke

In obedience to an order of Courte Dated y$^{e}$ 10$^{th}$ of febwary 1695 / wee y$^{e}$ Subscribers have been at y$^{e}$ hous of JN$^{O}$: COLLINS sen$^{r}$ to apras / the Estate of JN$^{O}$: COLLINS [ ] what was p$^{r}$sented to our vew have / Effected y$^{e}$ s$^{d}$: according to y$^{e}$ best of our Judgm$^{t}$ as ffolloweth

| | |
|---|---|
| To: 20 pounds of pheathers y$^{e}$ thicking belongs to y$^{e}$ old man | 160 |
| To: [ ] gunes | 400 |
| To: ones Little Iron pott & pott hooks | 100 |
| To: one virginia bed stead | 080 |
| To: one Chest & lockw$^{th}$: out Key | 100 |
| To: thirten pounds pewter | 130 |
| To: two new England old Barrells & fifteen for meale | 030 |
| To: tobo: in Leafe | 124 |
| To: one bill dew 186 | 186 |
| To: PITT | 050 |
| App$^{rll}$ y$^{e}$ 4$^{th}$ 1696 Sum: in all | 1360 |

JN^O^: CARRELL | Errors Excepted
THO: THROPP | Sworne by me GEO: MOORE

In obedience to an order of Courte dated y^e^ [--] of ffebwary 1695 / wee y^e^ subscribers have been uppon y^e^ Plantation of THO: ELEMES / to apraise what was sett to our vew s^d^: to be y^e^ s^d^ ELEMES Estate / and have Effected y^e^ same according to y^e^ best of our Judgm^t^ / as followes

| | |
|---|---|
| To: one Cubbord two tables foure Cheares one Couche | 400 |
| To: two Iron potts to paire pott racks to paire pot hoks | 250 |
| To: to pare of old Stilerds one warming pan one looking glas | 200 |
| to: one pare of and Irons one sitt: one frying pan | 200 |
| to: one fouling peece one old bras Cittle | 250 |

turne turne over

**[201]**

| | |
|---|---|
| To: one Chest a parsell of Carpenders tooles | 200 |
| To: one Pheather bed & bolster one halfe flocke one p^re^ of blankets one bed steade | 400 |
| To: to: old: Cotes to pare of briches & a serge | 290 |
| To: a p^r^sell of pewter & a parsell of wooden ware and old bible | 420 |
| To: one p^r^: of fire tongs & a driping pan 1 gridiron | 060 |
| to: two Cous one mare | 1300 |
| to: a Small sack Cup | 0120 |
| App^rll^ y^e^ 4^th^: 1696 Su: | 4070 |

JN^O^: CARRELL | Errors excepted
THO: THROPP | Sworne by me / GEO: MOORE

†In y^e^ name of god amen I JN^O^: JEININGS being sick & weak / of body by [*sic*] of perfect sences & memory praised be to all / all [*sic*] Mighty god for it doe make & ordaine this my last / will & testam^t^ in manner & forme following

Imp: I Bequieth my soule to god that gave it & my body to y^e^ Earth / to be buried in Christian buriall at y^e^ decreson of my Ex^rs^: as / shall be heare after named trusting through y^e^ merits of my / blesed saviour and Redeemer Jesus Christ to have a Shure / & Certaine Resurrition [*sic*] at y^e^ Last day as for my worldly / Estate as followes

Itt: I Give unto my sister SARAH LUCKES one gould Ring

Itt I Give unto my Brother WI^LL^ THOMAS one new Castor[9] / hatt & three y^rds^ of broad Cloth

Itt I Give unto my son GEORGE JEINNINGS all my Land y^t^ Lyes in worrisq^k^ / Bay & at Loyons Crick & one Cow three heaveres [heifers] of / three yeares old three

---

[9] A hat made of beaver or rabbit fur.

hefers of two yeares old Eleven / yeoues & Ram & all y$^e$ Rest of my p$^r$sonall Estate both / goods & Chattles after my Legices & debts being payed when / y$^t$ he comes to y$^e$ Eage of twenty one

**[202]**

Itt I give unto my mother SILVESTER HILL forty shillings Hard / money for to buye her two morning Ringes & doe make her my / Exectricks of this my Last will & testam$^t$: & I doe Reaceve / my Brother WI$^{LL}$ THOMAS Likewise to be an assistance as / Executor with M$^{rs}$: HILL as witness my hand and seale this 31$^{th}$ Day of Decemb$^r$ 1695

sealed signed in y$^e$ presents of us — JN$^O$ JENNINGS seall

FFR$^A$: JOYN$^R$
MARTHA THROPP
TH$^O$: HEATHFIELD
WI$^{LL}$ THOMAS

It has pleased god to visit me with Sickinis which is y$^e$ meanes of / my abcence to day thare for I Confes a Judgm$^t$: to Doctor / HAVIELD for four hundred and thirty pounds of tob$^o$ / aprill y$^e$ ninth 1696

THOMAS WILLIAMSON

Theese p$^r$sents wittnis y$^t$ I ROBT: BRACWELL of y$^e$ Isle of Wight / County in Virginia doe Constitute & appointe my Loving / wife SUSANA BRASWELL to be my Law full atturney for me / and in my name to procecute and Sue all Such persons as are / in debt to me and to answer to all Suites which I have / Depending in y$^e$ Isle of Wight Courte in wittnis heare / unto I sett my hand this 27 day of march 1696

Wittnes THO: MOORE — ROBERT BRCELL
EDW$^D$: **EC** CHAMPION
his mark

Ap$^{ll}$: y$^e$ 6$^{th}$: 169$^5/_6$ [10]

Wee y$^e$ Subscribers have aprased y$^e$ s$^d$: Cattel attached by / M$^r$: THO: GILES accordin to y$^e$ best of our iudgm$^t$ in obidience / to y$^e$ Order of Court see for y$^e$ order dated y$^e$ 9$^{th}$ of ffeb$^r$ 1695 / at three hundred & fifty poundes / of tob$^o$, wee have Appraised them

THO: APPLEWHAITE
WILL **W**: FFILLEPS
his marke

**[203]**

**Apr$^{ll}$ y$^e$ 6$^{th}$: 1696**

---

[10] This is clearly inaccurate. The date is 1696.

Wee y^e^ Subscribers being sworne Returneth our Valluation / of y^e^ Corne with in mentioned in a p^r^sell of [ ]b[ ]gs

the which Comes to ba: 1875
and allsoe in tob^o^ 0588
in all is 2463

ARTH: PURSLEY} see for y^e^ order dated
THO: JOYNER } y^e^ 9^th^ day of January 1695

Apr^ll^ y^e^ 6^th^ day 1696

Wee y^e^ Subscribers being sworne Returnes this our Valuation / of y^e^ Goods within mentioned y^e^ w^ch^: Comes to in tob^o^: 473^lbs^

See for y^e^ order dated y^e^ 9^th^ day of Jan^ry^ 1695

Sherr fees to serve attachm^ts^ / at four sverall places 60

455^lb^ [11]

RICHO: REYNOLDS: sub Sherr

a true and perfect inventory given by MARY WATTKINS / adm^rs^. of y^e^ Estate of WATTKINS Deced. as forloweth [*sic*] / one Bed & bolester one rugg three blanketts three / pilloes i bedstead 3: pillocases i sheate i: table Cloth / 3: napkins i: peuter Dish 2: plates i: Small peut^r^. Dram Cup / ii peuter Spoones 9: woodin traies 2: pales 2: Small pigans / i Couch: i Chest i: tables i: fforme 2: cheares i Iron Cettle / i Craws: cut Saw two Iron wedges 3: Sider cas^q^ a ꝑsell / of old: Lumder [*sic*] i ꝑ pott hokes ii: ꝑ pott racks one ꝑ bellos / 7: head Cattle, 5: barroues; 6 Sowes; 5 Sheep; one horse

ꝑ me MARY WATTKINS
her 8 mark

**[204]**

This indenture made this Thirtheth day of March in y^e^ yeare / of our Lord God one thoushon six hunred nienty & six Betwene / JAMES BAGNALL of y^e^ Isle of Wight County of y^e^ one ꝑrty: / and WILL: WEST: sen^r^ of y^e^ other ꝑt of y^e^ afores^d^: County witniseth / that y^e^ s^d^. JAMES BAGNALL for a Valuable Sum of tobo to him / in hand paid & Deliverd before y^e^ Ensealeing & delivery / of these p^r^sents whare w^th^: y^e^ s^d^: JA: BAGNALL doth acknoledge him / Selfe fully satisfied contented & paied Hath Granted / bargained & Solde & by these p^r^sents doth fully clearely & / absolutely grant bargan & sell unto y^e^ s^d^: WILL: WEST sen^r^: / and his he^rs^: Exe^rs^ adm^rs^ & assign^s^ for Ever a ꝑcell of Land / containing by estimation therty acers with y^e^ hous & / Orchard, which was form^r^ly M^r^: ROBT BRASWELLs more or les & / bounded as followes begining at a gutt Runing out of y^e^ fores^d^: / WILL: WESTs sen^r^ Mill Dam westward to JAMES TULLAGHs Line / and soe doun y^e^ s^d^. line to y^e^ s^d^: JA: TULLAGHs Dam from thence / up y^e^ Dams to y^e^

[11] The math, if that is what it is, eludes me.

first station to have hold occupy and quietly / Enioy y$^{e}$ s$^{d}$ Land with all fences houses orchardes & buildings / priviledges in as free and ample manner in all & Every Respect as y$^{e}$ / s$^{d}$: JA: BAGNALL hath or can have to y$^{e}$ fores$^{d}$: land by these p$^{r}$sents / bargained Sold to him y$^{e}$ s$^{d}$: WILL: WEST sen$^{r}$ & to y$^{e}$ onely prop$^{r}$ / Use of him his hei$^{rs}$ Ex$^{rs}$: adm$^{rs}$ & assig$^{ns}$: for Ever & y$^{e}$ s$^{d}$: JA: / BAGNALL for him selfe his hei$^{rs}$: Exec$^{rs}$: adm$^{rs}$: doth Coven$^{t}$ and Grant / that he the s$^{d}$: JA: BAGNALL for and not with standing any other / act by him done to y$^{e}$ Contrary at y$^{e}$ tyme of y$^{e}$ Ensealing and / delivery of these p$^{r}$sents is and Standeth law fully sezed of an / Undefeable [*sic*] Estate in y$^{e}$ simple of all singular y$^{e}$ before demised / ꝑmises with y$^{e}$ apurtanances with out any maner of Condition / or limitation of use or Uses to altere hange [*sic*!] or determine y$^{e}$ / Same and that y$^{e}$ s$^{d}$: JA: BAGNALL now hath full power / true title & absolute authority to demise grant bargan / Sell and assigne y$^{e}$ s$^{d}$: ꝑcell of Land with y$^{e}$ apurtenances / and Every ꝑt & ꝑcell: thare of unto y$^{e}$ s$^{d}$: WILL WEST sen$^{r}$. his / his [*sic*] hei$^{rs}$: Exec$^{rs}$: adm$^{rs}$ & assign$^{s}$: for Ever and alsoe y$^{e}$ s$^{d}$: JA: / BAGNALL for himselfe his hei$^{rs}$: Exe$^{rs}$: & adm$^{rs}$ Doth furthe / coven$^{t}$ & grant to and with y$^{e}$ s$^{d}$: WILL WEST sen$^{r}$: his hei$^{rs}$: / Exe$^{rs}$: adm$^{rs}$: & assign$^{s}$: that y$^{e}$ s$^{d}$: ꝑcell of Land before demised / & Solde, and y$^{t}$ Every ꝑt or ꝑcell: thare of at y$^{e}$ tyme of y$^{e}$ / Ensealing and delivery of these p$^{r}$sents is and soe all tymes / heeafter for Ever and from time to time hallbe [*sic*] remaine / and continue unto y$^{e}$ s$^{d}$: WILL WEST sen$^{r}$ his hei$^{rs}$: &c clearely / requested & discharged or other wise sufficiently Save / and

**[205]**

and Kept harmeles of and from all & all manner of form$^{r}$: or other / bargaines sales giftes Grants Leases Joyntu$^{rs}$: Judgm$^{t}$ & Executions / intrutions & Extentes and of and from all Singular other charges / titles & damages what soever had made consented unto ꝑcured / or done by y$^{e}$ s$^{d}$. JA: BAGNALL or by any other ꝑson or p$^{r}$sones by / his consent Knoledg or prucurtion[12] y$^{e}$ Rentes & service deu to y$^{e}$ / Kings Ma$^{tis}$ for y$^{e}$ demised p$^{r}$misees only Excepted Lastly for y$^{e}$ / further better absolute & more ꝑfect assurance and Convaying / of all & Singular y$^{e}$ before Demised ꝑmices and Every ꝑt & ꝑell: / thare of unto y$^{e}$ s$^{d}$: WILL WEST sen$^{r}$ & his hei$^{rs}$ Exec$^{rs}$ adm$^{rs}$: / and assign$^{s}$: for Ever y$^{e}$ s$^{d}$: JA: BAGNALL doth heare by covn$^{t}$ / and promise to & w$^{th}$: y$^{e}$ s$^{d}$: WILL WEST that upon reasonable / Request to him made he will acknoledg this p$^{r}$sent deed and / Convayance in y$^{e}$ Isle of wight County Courte in wittnis / whare of y$^{e}$ s$^{d}$ JA: BAGNALL hath heere unto sett his hand / and Seall y$^{e}$ day and yeare first before written

| | |
|---|---|
| Signd Seald & Deliverd | JAMES BAGNALL seale |
| in prsents of us: | her |
| BENIA: BEALLE sen$^{r}$ | MARY M BAGNALL seale |
| TRUSTRUM NORSWOTHY | mark |
| WILL: BRADSHAW | |

**[206]**

[12] Almost certainly "procuration."

Know all men by theise presents that I THOMAS REEVES and ELIZ[A]: my Wife have / for a Valuable Consideration Assigned over all o[r]: Right & title of this within written / patten, it begining at y[e] pipe Clay branch and Soe downe the Swamp the lower Side of / RICH: SHEWELLs line, to y[e] Extent of y[e] Patten, warranting y[e] same to y[e] S[d]: THOMAS / HAMTON his heir[rs]: Exec[rs]: adm[rs]: or Assignes for Ever withall priviledges there unto / belonging as wittnesse o[r] hands and Seales this 30[th] day of Jan[r]ry: $169^5/_6$

Signed

Testis JN[O]: RICKES — THO: **T** REEVES Seale
JAS: DENSON — ELIZA: **E** REEVES Seale
Signd
FFRAN: **B** BRIDLE

Know all men by theise prsents, that I JOHN CREWES of y[e] upp[r] pish of y[e] Isle of / wight County in Virg[a]: planter for a Valuable consideration to me in hand paid Att / & before y[e] Sealing and delivering heere of, and for which I doe acknowledge my Selfe / Satisfied by THOMAS NEWMAN of y[e] Same pish & County doe from me & my heir[rs] / Exec[rs]: adm[rs]: & assignes, Convey Make over Bargaine Sell Alinate & Confirme to y[e] / s[d]: THO: NEWMAN & his heir[rs]: exec[rs]: adm[rs]: & Assignes for & dureing the full terme / and time of Ninety & Nine years, begining from y[e] time of [ ] Conveyance Lease / deed or Writings, which he firmly holds his land by Dureing the time theron Pos[ ] / untill it be fully compleated & ended It being about one hundred and thirty acres of / land more or les, lying and Joyning to y[e] land he now Liveth upon Butted & bounded / as followeth That is to Say, Begining at a live Oake standing in y[e] mouth of a Smal branch / to y[e] first Station, withall y[e] Singular howses orchards ffences, Edifices profitts / Priviledges & Commodities theirof & thereunto belonging To have & to hold y[e] p[r]misees / without Lett or Molestation or Disturbance of me the s[d]: JOHN CREWES or my heir[rs] / Exec[rs]: Adm[rs]: or Assignes In as Large ample and Effectuall Manner to [ ] / and purposes whatsoever as I y[e] s[d]: JOHN CREWES or my heir[rs]: Exec[rs]: adm[rs]: or assignes might or / could Injoy y[e] same by force and Virtue of my Conveyance Leased, deed or Writing which I / firmly hold my land by, And I y[e] s[d]: JOHN CREWES doe binde my Selfe my heir[rs]: Exec[rs]: adm[rs]: / or Assignes, to Save and defend y[e] s[d]: THO: NUMAN & his heir[rs]: Exec[rs]: adm[rs]: or Assignes from / all form[r]: Bargaines Sales, Joyntures, Dowries Morgages, Leases or Incumbrances whatsoever / may in any wise prove prejudiciall Hinderance lett or Incumbrance to y[e] s[d]: THO: NUMAN / and his heir[rs]: Exec[rs]: adm[rs]: or Assignes, and for y[e] Confirmation heereof I sett my hand & Seale / this first day of May In y[e] 3 year of o[r] Lord, one Thousand Six hundred Ninety & Six

Sign'd Seal'd & Deliver'd — Signd
in y[e] p[r]sence of us — JOHN |-|-| CREWES Seales
THO: MOORE
RICH: STONE

I find upon searching the ould Ruffs that thes Deed was acknowledged in Open Co[rt] held For y[e] Isle of Wight County y[e] 1[st] of May 1696 by JOHN SCREWES

To THOMAS MEWMAN & were Recorded by mee
Witnesse my hand y[e] 10 1703
CHAP CHAPMAN C C[ur]

**[208]**

Know all men by theise p[r]sents that I FFRAN: DENSON Widdow of y[e] Isle of Wight / County doe Authorise Constitute and apoint my Son JAMES DENSON to be my / true and Lawfull Attorney to Answer y[e] Suite depending betwixt ROB[T]: SCOTT & / my Selfe and all other Suites as Shall be heereafter depending or to Answer in / my behalfe as if I my Selfe were there p[r]sent, or to prosecute any Suet in my / behalf or forme at any time Soever wittnesse my hand this 8[th]: day Aprill 1696
Testis JERI: EXUM FRANCIS DENSON

Acc[tt]. whatt things the widdow hide left
one Bedd 2 Rugs and one blankett & boalster one pillowe
5 pewter dishes one bason one Salt Seler one quart pott one CandleStick / and grater 2 earthen dishes two Iron potts two Ladles three p[re] of / pothookes one pot rack one p[re] of tonges one Spitt one Tinny Kettle
2 bottles one Looking glasse one old table one chest one Chamber pott
one Iron pestle one petticoate & wasecoat 6 Quives & one Shift
two [ ]head clothes one handker cheif one pameto baskett 2 trinchers
one p[re] of Small Stillards one handSaw 2 augurs one Apron
JACOB BARNES D[r]: 76[lb] Tobacho
Signed
EDWARD N BROWN

This Indenture made y[e] twelft day of May 1696 Between MATH: STRICKLAND / Jun[r]: of y[e] Isle of Wight County of y[e] one p[t] & HENRY BAKER m[r]chant of y[e] Same County / of y[e] other p[t] Wittnesseth that y[e] s[d]: STRICKLAND for & in Consideration of three / Thousand pounds of Tobacho to him before the Sealing and delivery of theese / p[r]sented by y[e] s[d]: BAKER; well and truely paid the Receipt whereof he y[e] S[d]. / STRICKLAND doe acknowledge & himselfe therewith fully Satisfiyed and paid, and / thereof doe clearly acquit & discharge the s[d]: BAKER his heir[rs]: Exec[rs]: adm[rs]: for Ever / Have bargained Sole & Confirmed and by theise p[r]sents doe Alline, Bargaine / Sell, Inffeoff & Confirme unto y[e] S[d] BAKER his heir[rs]: & Assignes for Ever, one / Hundred Acers of Land, Scituate Lying and being on y[e] Southside, of y[e] Bever dam / Swamp and bounded by KingSale Swamps on y[e] East Side, being p[t]. of a patten granted / to MATHEW STRICKLAND for Nine hundred and two acres of Land, & in y[e] Same land / that form[r]ly THOMAS JONES Lived on, with all its Rights members Jurisdictions & / appurtenances, as Howses orchards gardens ways waters &c: to y[e] S[d]: p[r]mises or any / p[t]: or pcell thereof belonging or anywaise appertaining & also all y[e] estate, Right / tytls Intrests, use, possession, property, Claime & Demand whatsoever of him y[e] s[d] STRICK= / LAND, of , in or to the Same To Have and to Hold the s[d] one hundred acres of Land / &

all and Singular the prmisees heerby bargained & Sold, with their and Every / of their Rights members and appurtenances Whatsoever unto y[e] s[d] BAKER

**[209]**

BAKER his heir[rs] and Assignes fror Ever, and to y[e] onely proper use and Behoofe of / the s[d]. BAKER his heir[rs] & assignes for Ever, and y[e] S[d]: STRICKLAND for himselfe / his heir[rs]: Exec[rs]: adm[rs]: for Ever, against him y[e] S[d]: STRICKLAND his heir[rs]: Exec[rs]: Adm[rs]: / & assignes, & all, & every other pson & psons whatsoever Lawfully claiming / by, from, or und[r]: him them, or any of them, or any other pson Whatsoever, / Shall and will warrant, and for Ever defend By theise p[r]sents, In Wittensse / whereof the pty first above Names unto this p[r]sent Indenture have put / their hand and Seale y[e] day and year first above written – Anoq[u] Dom 1696 Signed

Sign'd Seal'd & Deliver'd in p[r]sence of MATH: **E** STRICKLAND Seale

ANTHO: HOLLADAY

CHA[R] CHAPMAN

Acknowledged in / y[e] Isle Wight Co[rt]
By vertue of an Order of y[e] 9[th] of June 1698
Recorded by CHA[R] CHAPMAN C Cur

M[r]: CHAPMAN 8[th] August 1696

Pray appear for me in Whatsoever business relates to me as [ ] defd[t]: / In y[e] Isle of Wight Court and for yo[r] soe doing this shall be yo[r] warrant

THO: MOORE

This is to Satisfie that I THOMAS MOMFORD planter in y[e] Low[r] pish of y[e] Isle / of Wight County have for a valuable Consideration already in hand Received / have bargained and Sole & Made over Convey'd unto DANIELL SANBORNE of y[e] afores[d] / County one pcell of Land, being pt of y[e] Land wherein I now Live upon [ ] / creeke formrly in y[e] possession of one ROB[T] STEVENS and now Assended to me / by an Escheate granted to me In y[e] yeare one Thousand Six hundred & Ninety and / Six, which land lying and bouding upon a branch that comes forth of timber / neck Creek & Adjoining upon y[e] Land of y[e] afores[d]. SANBORNs, which he bought / of GILES LAWRENCE, which land RICH: RATLIFFE joyned upon, all the land on / the North Side of y[e] afores[d]. branches belonging to my Devident whereon I now / live, which land is Judged to be about thirty or forty Acres more or Lesse / which land I doe warrant the Sale unto the S[d]. DAN: SANBORNE his heir[rs] / Exec[rs]: adm[rs]: or Assignes for Ever with all benefitte thereunto belonging / from me my heir[rs]: Exec[rs]: adm[rs]: or Assignes in as full as the lawe can devise / without fraud, And further I y[e] S[d]. MOMFORD doe binde my heir[rs]: Exec[rs]: adm[rs]: / or assignes unto y[e] S[d]. SANBORNE his Heir[rs]: Exec[rs]: adm[rs]: or Assignes that if / him or them or his learned Councell in y[e] Law Should not thinke this con= / veyance Sufficient that then I y[e] S[d]. THO: MOMFORD my heir[rs]: Exec[rs]: adm[rs]: / or Assignes is to give him better Assurance when Ever he or they shall / demand it upon y^e^ penalty of twenty Thousand pounds of good m^r^chantable / Tobacho to be Rcov^r^able by the S^d^. SANBORN or his heir^rs^: Exec^rs^: adm^rs^: or Assignes

**[210]**

Assignes of me my heir^rs^ Exec^rs^ adm^rs^: or Assignes as Wittnesse my hand and Seale / 23^d^: day of y^e^ third month 1696

Signed
DOROTHY **O** GIBS
Signed
THO: **T** SAWER
ELIZ^A^: SANBORNE

Signd
THO: **TW** MOMFORD Seale

The Deposition of ROB^T^: STURDY aged fifty Six or thereabouts Sheweth to y^e^ / Wor^pps^. that y^e^ depon^t^: was comeing through MATH: STRICKLANDs Cornfeild / about an hour by Sun in y^e^ Evennig [*sic*] homewards bound, he see PHILIP REYFORDs / bull in y^e^ feild eating of corne y^e^ Depon^t^ calls to MATH: STRICKLAND, and told / him y^e^ PHILIP REYFORDs bull was in y^e^ field, and before he came y^e^ depon^t^ / turn'd y^e^ bull out of y^e^ field and after y^e^ boy was in y^e^ Cunstables hand I saw / MATH STRICKLAND and W^M^. GANY profer to be y^e^ boys Security and they would / not be Excepted and further y^e^ depon^t^. Saith not.

Know all men by these p^r^sents y^t^ I FFRANCIS DENSON of y^e^ Isle of Wight County / widdow doe heereby authorize constitute and appoint JOSEPH MEREDITH to be / my true and lawfull attorney to answer y^e^ Suite depending betweene me & ROBERT / SCOTT in y^e^ Isle of White County as wittnesse my hand this 3^d^. day of August 1696
Test GEO: SMITH

FFRANSIS DENSON

Sept^r^: y^e^ 24^th^ 1696

In obedience to an Order of y^e^ Isle of Wight Court dated the / 9^th^ day of M^r^ch 1695 and renewed by a latter ord^r^. of y^e^ 10^th^ of August 1696 / Wee y^e^ Jury & Survey^r^: have met w^th^: y^e^ Intent to lay out y^e^ land betweene / W^M^. GREEN & GEO: GREEN, W^M^ WEST & JA: BAGNALL, but by no Meanes can / proceede by reason no patten is produced to us to goe by

RICH: REYNOLDS
W^M^ **S** BRADSHAW
THO **X** JOYNER
THO: **TP** POPE
JN^O^: **I** PARNELL
BENJ^A^: **BB** BEALLE Jun^r^:

RICH **RB** BEALLE
GEO: **J** WRIGHT
THO: **R** WRIGHT
RICH: WILKISON Ju.
JN^O^: CLARKE
WALTER + WATERS

GEORGE WILLIAMSON
Surveyor

**[211]**

Know all men by Theise p$^{r}$sents that I XTOPHER HOLMES of y$^{e}$ Low$^{r}$ ꝑish of y$^{e}$ / Isle of Wight County in Virg$^{a}$: for a Valuable Consideration to me in hand paid / before y$^{e}$ Sealeing and delivery of these p$^{r}$sents, by NICHO: CASEY of y$^{e}$ ꝑish / and County afores$^{d}$. have bargained & Sold and doe heereby frome my heir$^{rs}$: Exec$^{rs}$: / & adm$^{rs}$: for Ever bargaine sell and Deliver in ffe off & Confirme unto y$^{e}$ s$^{d}$. / NICHO: SCASIE & to his heir$^{rs}$. & Assignes for Ever a Certaine paire or ꝑcell / of Land Conteining Seventy Accers, being p$^{t}$ of a pattent of four hundred & / fifty Acres granted to EPAPHRODITUS LAWSON y$^{e}$ 31 of Jan$^{r}$ry 1643 and / by y$^{e}$ S$^{d}$. LAWSON assigned to CHESTER y$^{e}$ 13 of August 58 and from y$^{e}$ S$^{d}$ / CHESTER desended to y$^{e}$ S$^{d}$. HOLMES y$^{e}$ S$^{d}$. 70 acres of Land being Scituate / about halfe a mile to y$^{e}$ South westward of Mount Lawsons Bay Creeke / in y$^{e}$ ꝑish and County afores$^{d}$. & thus bounded, Beginning at a m$^{r}$ked red / oake near a cart path being a Corner tree betwixt this land and the / Land of JN$^{O}$: MARSHALL thense Southeast a hundred Eighty three pole / to a red oake then Northeast a hundred & Six pole to a Small hickery by / a branch Side then North Seventy degrees Westerly a hundred and / Eighteene pole to a Small hickery by y$^{e}$ aforemention'd cart path / being a markt tree of JN$^{O}$: MARSHALLs Land & Soe by his m$^{r}$kt trees / South Sixty two degrees west 24 pole to y$^{e}$ first Station To Have / and to Hold y$^{e}$ s$^{d}$. Seventy acres of land withall woods waies waters / together w$^{th}$: his due Share of all Mines and Mineralls therein Conteined w$^{th}$ / free priviledge of hunting Hawking fishing and fowling, and all other / profitts and Comodityes & hereditam$^{t}$: Whatsoever to y$^{e}$ s$^{d}$ land belonging / or in any wise appurtaning to him y$^{e}$ S$^{d}$. NICHO SCASIE and to his heir$^{rs}$: / and assignes for Ever in as full and ample Manner as y$^{e}$ most learned / in y$^{e}$ Law can devise, And I doe heerby oblidge my Selfe my heir$^{rs}$. / Exec$^{rs}$. & Adm$^{rs}$. to warrant and defend this my Sale of all and Singular / y$^{e}$ pomise to y$^{e}$ S$^{d}$. NICHO: SCASIE his heir$^{rs}$. & Assignes for ever / against all & all manner of ꝑsons whatsoever and when there to / required to give the s$^{d}$. SCASIE Such farther lawfull assurance / of y$^{e}$ p$^{r}$misees as his learn'd Cousill Shall thinke fitt and acknowledge / this deed together with MARY my Wife y$^{e}$ next Court to be held for y$^{e}$ / Isle of Wight County afores$^{d}$. In Wittnesse whereof I have heereunto / put my hand & Seal y$^{e}$ 30$^{th}$ of y$^{e}$ 11 M$^{o}$: 1684

Signd

Sign'd Seal'd and deliver'd in p$^{r}$sense of
DAN: SANBORNE
THO: CHARKE [*sic*]
SARAH SANBORNE

CHRIST: **Ω** HOLMES Sealle

Recorded in y$^{e}$ Isle of Wight Records
ꝑ HUGH DAVIS C$^{r}$ C$^{ur}$

I MARY HOLMES doe heereby Willingly Consent to y$^{e}$ Sale of y$^{e}$ w$^{th}$in. / mention'd Seventy acres of land Sold by my Husband XTOPHER HOLMES to / NICHO: SCASIE & doe freely and absolutely Relinquish my Right of Dow$^{r}$. / to all & Every p$^{t}$: thereof as wittnesse my hand & Seal y$^{e}$ 30$^{th}$ of y$^{e}$ 11$^{th}$ M$^{o}$: 1684

Sign'd Seal'd in p$^{r}$sence of us
DAN: SANBORNE

MARY **M** HOLMES Seale

THO: CLARKE　　　　Recorded ꝑ HUGH DAVIS Cl$^{r}$ C$^{ur}$
SARAH: SANBORNE

**[212]**

Acknowledged in open Court held for y$^{e}$ Isle of Wight County ffeb$^{r}$ry / the 9$^{th}$. 1684 by CHRISTOPHER HOLMES and MARY his wife to be their free and / Voluntary Act and deede and ordered to be Recorded
Test JOHN PITT Cl Cur　　　　Recorded ꝑ HUGH DAVIS Cl Cur

Know all men by theise p$^{r}$sents that I NICHO CASEY and ANN my Wife / doe Assigne over all our right title in [*sic*] Intrest of this within Mentioned / bill of Sale unto EVE BELLONGE to him his heir$^{rs}$: Exec$^{rs}$: & assignes / for Ever as wittnesse o$^{r}$ hands this 9$^{th}$: day of Sept$^{br}$: 1693　　　　Signed
Testis THO: HAWKINS　　　　NICHO **N** CASKEY
ANN **A** ARON　　　　ANN **K** CASEY

Isle of Wight Dec$^{br}$: y$^{e}$ 9$^{th}$ 1693 / Acknowledged in Court by y$^{e}$ s$^{d}$. NICHO CASEY / and ANN his Wife to be their voluntary / Act & deed / Test HUGH DAVIS C$^{l}$ C$^{ur}$ / Recorded by HD C$^{l}$

Know all mne by theise p$^{r}$sents y$^{t}$ I EVE BELLONGE of y$^{e}$ Isle of Wight County / Weaver for y$^{e}$ Valuable Consideration of thirty five pownd Sterling Money / to me in hand paid by GEORGE NORSWORTHY of Nansemand County Gent doe / transferr Assigne and make over all my right title and Interest to a tract / of Land, Conteining about Seventy acres mentioned in a Conveyance on this / Sheete of paper made from XTOPHER HOMES to NICHO: CASEY and by y$^{e}$ s$^{d}$ / CASEY assigned to me together w$^{th}$ all y$^{e}$ tenem$^{ts}$: priviledges & appurtenances / thereunto belonging unto him y$^{e}$ s$^{d}$ GEO: NORSWORTHY and to his heir$^{rs}$: & assignes / for Ever and I doe heereby ꝑmise to warr$^{tt}$: & defend y$^{e}$ Same ag$^{st}$: all ꝑsons / whatsoever wittnesse my hand and Seale this 9$^{th}$. day of 9$^{br}$ 1696
Sign'd Seald & Deliver'd in the p$^{r}$sence of Us whose name are und$^{r}$ Written　　　　EVE BELLONGE Seale
JOHN GILES
GEO: SMITH
RICH$^{D}$: REYNOLDS

Acknowledged in open Co$^{rt}$ held for y$^{e}$ Isle of Wight County y$^{e}$ 9$^{th}$ of 9$^{br}$ 1696 & by vertue of an Order of June Co$^{rt}$ 98 Recorded ꝑ me
CHA CHAPMAN C$^{l}$C$^{ur}$

**[213]**

Know all men by theise p$^{r}$sents that I DAN$^{L}$ SANBORNE of y$^{e}$ County of Isle of / Wight doe & have for a Valuable Consideration already in hand Rec$^{d}$: Bargain / Sell and Confirme and make over a small ꝑcell of Land about Eight or tenn acres / more or less unto NICHO: CASEY his heir$^{rs}$ or Assignes for Ever which ꝑcell of Land / was p$^{t}$. of a ꝑcell of Land which came out and granted unto APAPHRODITUS / LAWSON in y$^{e}$ year one Thousand Six hundred & forty, which land bought of / him by by [*sic*] WALTER BRUCE & Assended to ABRAHAM BRUCE which land / lying betweene two branches which lyes upon a Small Creeke which / cometh out of Lawsons bay which land lyeth the greatest p$^{t}$: in y$^{e}$ Isle / of Wight County form$^{r}$ly planted & Seated by one W$^{M}$. JONES, which land / Giveth upon a ꝑcell of land which y$^{e}$ S$^{d}$. CASEY bought of XTOPHER HOLMES / of y$^{e}$ afores$^{d}$. County, Which land I y$^{e}$ s$^{d}$. SANBORNE doe warrant to him / and his heir$^{rs}$: for Ever from me or my heir$^{rs}$. Exec$^{rs}$. of Assignes, or / against any ꝑson or ꝑsons in as full as ample manner as y$^{e}$ s$^{d}$. CASEY and his Learned Counsill shall think fitt & further I the S$^{d}$. SANBORNE / doe binde my heir$^{rs}$: or Assignes that if y$^{e}$ s$^{d}$. CASEY his heir$^{rs}$: or assignes / Shall not think fitt this Conveyance, that I y$^{e}$ s$^{d}$. SANBORNE doe / binde my Selfe my heir$^{rs}$. or Assigne when y$^{e}$ S$^{d}$. CASEY hsi heir$^{rs}$ / or Assignes Shall require itt, to give him Anuther, all howses and / priviledges thereunto belonging as Wittnesse my hand & Seale / the 6$^{th}$ day of y$^{e}$ twelvth Month 1684

HUM: MARSHALL — DAN SANBORNE Seale
ROB$^{T}$: KING
JA: BENN — Recorded ꝑ HUGH DAVIS C$^{l}$ C$^{ur}$

Acknowledged in open Court held for y$^{e}$ Isle of Wight County / Aprill y$^{e}$ 9$^{th}$: 1685 by DAN: SANBORNE to be his act & deed / and ordered to be recorded
Test JOHN PITT C$^{l}$ C$^{ur}$

Know all men by theise p$^{r}$sents y$^{t}$ I NICHO: CASEY and ANN my Wife / doe Assigne over all our Right title & Intrest of this within men / ton'd bill of Sale to EVE BELLONGE to him his heir$^{rs}$: Exec$^{rs}$: & assignes / for Ever as Wittnesse o$^{r}$ hands this ninth day of [ ] 1693

Testis THO: HAWKINS — signd NICHO: **N** CASEY
signd ANN **A** ARONN — Signd ANN **K** CASEY

Isle of Wight / County Decem$^{br}$: y$^{e}$ 9$^{th}$. 1693 / Ackn$^{o}$. in Court by y$^{e}$ S$^{d}$. NICHO: CASEY & ANN his Wife / to be their free and Voluntary Act & deed test / HUGH DAVIS C$^{l}$ C$^{ur}$ / Recorded ꝑ HD C$^{l}$

**[214]**

Isle of Wight County Know all men by theise p$^{r}$sents that / I EVE BELLONGE of this County, Weever, for y$^{e}$ Valuable Consideration of / thirty five pound Sterling money to me in hand paid by GEO: NORSWORTHY / of Nandsemond County Gent, doe transferr Assigne & make over all my / Right title & Intrest to y$^{e}$ ꝑcell of Land tenem$^{ts}$: & appurtenances within / Mention'd unto him the S$^{d}$. GEO: NORSWORTHY, &

to his heir^rs^: & assignes for / Ever And doe heereby ꝑmise to warr^tt^: & defend y^e^ same / ag^st^ all / ꝑsons Whatsoever, Wittnesse my hand and Seale this 9^th^: day of 9^br^: 1696
Sign'd Seal'd & deliver'd in y^e^ p^r^sence of us whose
Names are und^r^. Written                EVE BELLONGE Sealle
JOHN GILES
GEO: SMITH                Acknowledged in open Co^rt^ held for
RICH^D^: REYNOLDS                the Isle Wight County y^e^ 9^th^ of Novem^br^
1696 and by vertue of an Order of y^e^ 9^th^.
June 1698 recorded
ꝑ CHA CHAPMAN C^l^ C^ur^

MaryLand Ss Memorandum that upon y^e^ 28^th^ day of Sept^br^ in the / eight yeare of the Reigne of o^r^ Soveraigne Lord William the third by / the Grace of God of England Scotland ffrance & Ireland King defender of / the faith &^ca^: Annoq^u^ Domini 1696. Before me ROBERT GOULDSBOROUGH / of Talbot County Gen[ ] of his Maj^ties^ Justicees of y^e^ Peace for y^e^ s^d^. County, and / Notary and Tabellion Publick Legally thereunto admitted, Personally appear'd / NICHOLAS GOULDSBOROUGH of Talbot County afores^d^. and ANN his Wife one of the / Executrix of y^e^ Last Will and Testam^t^: of NICHO: SMITH late of Isle of / Wight County in y^e^ Coll^o^: of Virg^a^: Geaid [*sic*] deceased, And y^e^ S^d^. Notary acknowledge / as Likewise by these p^r^sents they doe acknowledge to have Rece^d^. of / HUMPHREY MARSHALL and ANN his Wife the Relict and Other Execut^x^: / of y^e^ s^d^ NICHO: SMITH deceased, the one full Moyety of y^e^ ꝑsonall Estate / of y^e^ S^d^. NICHO: SMITH to her y^e^ s^d^. ANN Wife of y^e^ S^d^. NICHO: GOULDSBOROUGH / by y^e^ S^d^. Last Will and Testam^t^: Bequeathed Amounting to y^e^ Sume of one hundred / Sixty and three pownds Eleven Shillings & four pence, And therefore they / the S^d^. NICHOLAS and ANN his Wife doe by theise p^r^sents for themselves / their heir^rs^: Exec^rs^: and Adm^rs^: Release and for Ever acquit to them y^e^ Said / HUMPHREY and ANN his Wife, all manner of Claime w^ch^. they at any time / heereafter may have to y^e^ S^d^. ꝑsonall Estate or any p^t^ thereof.

**[215]**
In Wittnesse whereof the said NICHO: and ANN have heereunt [*sic*] Sett their / hands & Seales in y^e^ p^r^sence of me the s^d^. Notary and JAMES BENSON, ad [*sic*] JAMES / SANFORD Wittnesses Subscribed
JA: BENSON        *Quod in Testim Veritatis*        NICHO: GOLDSBOROUGH Seale
JA: SANFORD        *Sigillum meum Efficu*        signd
*Apposua die et Anno Sup^r^*        ANN **A** GOULDSBOROUGH Seale

ROB^T^: GOULDSBOROUGH Seale
Acknowledged by y^e^ S^d^. NICHO GOULDSBOROUGH before us
HUGH DAVIS
JN^O^: DUNN

Know all men by theise p$^{r}$sents that I NICHO: GOLDSBOROUGH of Talbot / County in y$^{e}$ province of Mary Land have ordained Constituted authorized / and Impowered & by theise p$^{r}$sents doe ordaine constitute Authorize and Impower / my Trusty fried [*sic*] WILL: SMITH of y$^{e}$ Isle of Wight County in Virginia my true / and Lawfull attorney for me and in my Name; and to my ꝑticular use and / behoofe, to ask demand Sue for recover & receive; all Such Debts goods cattels / wares Merchaneizes. or other Effect Whatsoever as are or may be any waies / oweing or belonging to me in Virg$^{a}$: as also to take care of & [ ] / Such goods Chattels or Effects Whatsoever as y$^{e}$ S$^{d}$. W$^{M}$: SMITH [ ] / Shall be by me instructed with & them to Impower or [ ] / and benefitt as occasion Shall Require In Wittnesse whereof I / have heereunto Sett my hand Seal this thirty first day of Octo$^{br}$ 1696

Testis JOHN DUNN: Sworne      NICHO: GOULDSBOROUGH Seale
Signed
HANNAH + SMITH
signed
WILL **W** SMITH Sworne

Proved in open Co$^{rt}$ held for y$^{e}$ Isle of Wight County y$^{e}$ 9$^{th}$ of / November 1696 & by Veitue [*sic*] of an Order of y$^{e}$ 9$^{th}$ of June 1698

Recorded ꝑ me CHA CHAPMAN C$^{l}$ C$^{ur}$

**[216]**

Know all men by theise p$^{r}$sents that I RICH: REYNOLDS of y$^{e}$ Isle of Wight County / Sen$^{r}$. doe for my Selfe my heir$^{rs}$: Exec$^{rs}$ adm$^{rs}$: & Assignes, Assigne and make / over all y$^{e}$ Right title and Intrest of one hundred Acres of Land, Scituate Lying / and being in y$^{e}$ Low$^{r}$ ꝑish of y$^{e}$ fores$^{d}$: County, unto WILL: MURFREY his heir$^{rs}$ Exec$^{rs}$: / adm$^{rs}$. and Assignes for Ever, Which S$^{d}$. hundred acres of Land was form$^{r}$ly con= / =veyed from RICH: WEBB to RICH: GADSBEY, and is now in y$^{e}$ tenor and / occupation of y$^{e}$ above S$^{d}$. W$^{M}$. MURFREY, further I doe oblige my Selfe to / Acknowledge this to be my reall act and deed in open Court, whensoever / required thereunto as alsoe ELIZ$^{A}$: my Wife as wittnesse o$^{r}$ hands / the 9$^{th}$ day of feb$^{r}$ry 168$^{5}$/$_{6}$

Sign'd in y$^{e}$ p$^{r}$sence of us
JOHN NEVILL      RICH: REYNOLDS
ROBT. [ ]      Signed
ELIZ$^{A}$: **X** REYNOLDS

Acknowledged in open Court held for y$^{e}$ Isle of / Wight County febr$^{r}$y y$^{e}$ 9$^{th}$ 1685 by M$^{r}$ RICH / REYNOLDS & ELIZ$^{A}$: his Wife to be their Act & dede / and ordered to be Recorded

Test JOHN PITT C$^{l}$ C$^{ur}$

I WILL: MURFREY and my Wife FFRANCIS doe Assigne this within / mention'd Assignem$^{t}$: of RICH: REYNOLDS withall o$^{r}$ Rites and titles / and Intrest unto DANIELL NOLOBOY Jun$^{r}$: his heir$^{rs}$: Exec$^{rs}$: & Assignes / for Ever Wittnesse o$^{r}$ hands and Seales this 7$^{th}$ of Octob$^{r}$. 1696 Signd

MICHAEL **M** MURFREY WILL: **M** MURFREY Seale
JN$^{O}$. **Q** WATTERS Signed
FRANCIS **E** MURFREY Seale

Acknowledged in Open Co$^{rt}$ held For y$^{e}$ Isle of Wight / County y$^{e}$ 9$^{th}$ day of October 1696 by W$^{M}$ MURFRY / & FRANCIS his Wife & Ordered to be recorded
Test CHAP CHAPMAN C$^{l}$C$^{ur}$

**[217]**

To all X$^{an}$ people to whom these p$^{r}$sent writing of award Inden / =ted shall come wee M$^{r}$ ANTHONY HOLLIDAY M$^{r}$ JAMES BENN M$^{r}$ / HUMPHREY MARSHALL Sendeth Greeting in o$^{r}$ Lord God Everlasting / Whereas divers Questions Controversies and Sutes have [ ]ed had moved & / depending Betweene JAMES BAGNALL of y$^{e}$ Isle of Wight County of y$^{e}$ one / ꝑty and FFRANCIS PARKER of y$^{e}$ s$^{d}$ County of th'other ꝑty as well for and / Concerning y$^{e}$ bounds of their Lands as alsoe for other Cause & actions for / appeasing Whereof Either of y$^{e}$ s$^{d}$ ꝑtyes have Elected and Chosen us / the S$^{d}$: ANTHO: HOLLYDAY JA: BENN & HUMPHREY MARSHALL to be Arbi / trators Indifferently Betweene them, and to that End have bound / themselves to ANTHO: HOLLIDAY by obligation, in y$^{e}$ Sume of one hundred / pounds of good and Lawfull money of England to stand and abide in y$^{e}$ / a ward of abitriment and judgm$^{t}$ of us the s$^{d}$. ANTHO: HOLLIDAY / JA: BENN & HUMPHREY MARSHALL, touching the p$^{r}$misees Now Know / y$^{e}$ that wee the s$^{d}$: ANTHO: HOLLIDAY, JA: BENN & HUMP: MARSHALL / taiking [*sic*] upon us the Charge of y$^{e}$ s$^{d}$ award and mindeing that a finalle / end and Agreem$^{t}$. Shall be had and Continued from hence forth behind / the s$^{d}$ ꝑtyes touching y$^{e}$ prmisees doe make and declare this o$^{r}$ award / in manner and forme following that is to say first we award JAMES / BAGNALL shall hold y$^{t}$ ꝑt of y$^{e}$ land he now liveth on, beginning att the / Mouth of a branch, and Soe runing up the branch to a m$^{r}$ked white oake / Standing on y$^{e}$ North side of y$^{e}$ old dwelling house and Soe runing S: 45½° / W a long a line of m$^{r}$ked trees to a white oake in y$^{e}$ head line which is y$^{e}$ / deviding line, Betwee [*sic*] the s$^{d}$. PARKER and BAGNALL layd out by M$^{r}$ / GEORGE WILLIAMSONS in o$^{r}$ p$^{r}$sence, and FFRANCIS PARKER to hold that p$^{t}$ / Joyning upon ROB$^{T}$: KINGs land and y$^{e}$ S$^{d}$. PARKER pay to y$^{e}$ S$^{d}$: BAGNALL / four hundred & five pounds of tab$^{o}$: in Caske it being his p$^{t}$ of the / Charge for y$^{e}$ Surveying & devision of y$^{e}$ S$^{d}$. Land and y$^{e}$ S$^{d}$: land being / devided b [*sic*] y$^{e}$ 7 day of August 1674
as Wittnesse o$^{r}$ hands

ANTHO: HOLLIDAY
JAMES BENN
HUM: MARSHALL

**[218]**

To all Christian People to whom these p[r]sents Shall come THOMAS MAN S[n] / and heire of THO: MAN late of y[e] Isle of Wight County Deceased Sends Greeting / in o[r] Lord God Everlasting. Know yee that I y[e] S[d]. THO: MAN for divers good / Causes and Considerations wee heerunto Moveing, but more Especially for and / in Consideration of y[e] Sume of two thousand pounds of Tobacho to me in hand / paid by NICHOLAS TYNER of y[e] Same County, the Receipt whereof I doe heerby / acknowledge & Confess have given granted bargained Sold Aliened Conveyed Enfeofed / and Confirmed and doe by theese p[r]sents for me my heirr[s:] Exec[rs]: & adm[rs]. give / grant, bargaine Sell Alien Convey Enfeof and Confirme, unto him y[e] S[d] / NICHO: TYNER his heir[rs]: Exec[rs]: & Adm[rs]: A Certaine ꝑcell of land, Scituate / Lyeing and being in y[e] Isle of Wight County and butting & bounding on the / Southside of Corowake Swamp, and y[e] Southwest Side of y[e] great branch / and hear the land of HODGES COUNSILL and W[M]. FFOWLER Conteining by Estimation / Two hundred Acres be itt more or less within y[e] bounds aforemention'd / being ꝑ[t]: of a ꝑcell of Land Conteining five hundred & Sixty acres made over / unto the S[d]: THOMAS MAN by RICH: BOOTH as by a deed of Sale or writing under / the hand and Seale of y[e] S[d]. BOOTH bearing date y[e] 9[th] day of ff[e]bry 169$^2/_3$ / may appeare To have and to hold unto him y[e] S[d] NICHO: TYNER his heir[rs] / Exec[rs]: adm[rs]: & Assignes for Ever, Together w[th] all howses Edifices build / ings timber & timber trees waters & waters Courses wayes Easem[ts]: profitts / priviledges Comodityes and advantages to y[e] same belonging or in any / manner of way appertaining unto him y[e] S[d]: NICHO: TYNER his heir[rs] / Exec[rs]: Adm[rs] or assignes for Ever free and Clear, freely and Clearly / acquitted Exhonerated and discharged of and from all manner of other / & former gifts grants bargains Sayles Joyntures Dowers Executions / or other Incumbrances Whatsoever, And y[e] S[d]. THO: MAN doth by theese / p[r]sents for himselfe his heir[rs] Exec[rs] & adm[rs]. Coven[t]: ꝑmise grant and / agree to and w[th] the S[d] NICHO: TYNER his heir[rs] Exec[rs]: & adm[rs]: to Warr[tt]. Save / defend & keepe harmlesse the S[d]. NICHO: TYNER and his heir[rs]: from & against / any ꝑson or ꝑsons that Shall or may heerafter Lawfully Claime or p[r]tend / to claime any right title or Intrest to y[e] s[d] Land & p[r]misees or any ꝑ[t] / or ꝑcell thereof. In Wittnesse whereof I the S[d]: THO: MAN have / hearunto Sett my hand and Seale this Eight day of Novemb[r]. in y[e] year / of o[r] Lord God one thousand Six hundred Nynety and Six

Sign'd Seald and ~~Ddd~~: — Signed
in y[e] p[r]sence of Us — THO **M** MAN Seale
BOAZ GWIN
Signu
PHILIP **R** REYFORD

Acknowledged in open Co[rt] held For the Isle Wight County y[e] 9[th] day of November 1696 & Recorded
ꝑ HUGH DAVIS C[l] C[ur] then
Teste CHA CHAPMAN C[l] C[ur]

**[219]**

Know all men by theise p$^{r}$sents that wee JAMES BAGNALL, & FFRANCIS PARKER / both of y$^{e}$ County of y$^{e}$ Isle of Wight doe Stand and are firmely bounden and / obliged unto M$^{r}$ ANTHO: HOLLIDAY of y$^{e}$ fores$^{d}$. County in y$^{e}$ Sume of one hundred / pounds of good and lawfull Money of England to be payd to y$^{e}$ S$^{d}$. M$^{r}$. ANTHO / HOLLIDAY or his true and lawfull attorney Exec$^{rs}$. & adm$^{rs}$. to the which paym$^{t}$ / well and truely to be made, Wee binde o$^{r}$selves, and Either of us by him / Selfe Joyntly & Severally for y$^{e}$ whole our and Either of o$^{r}$ heir$^{rs}$. Exec$^{rs}$. / and Adm$^{rs}$. and Every of them firmely by theise p$^{r}$sents Sealed with / o$^{r}$ Seale dated y$^{e}$ 10$^{th}$: day of July 1694

The Condition of this obligation is Such that if y$^{e}$ within bounden / JAMES BAGNALL & FFRANCIS PARKER their heir$^{rs}$. Exec$^{rs}$: & adm$^{rs}$: & Every / of them for his and their ꝑ$^{ts}$. and behalfe in all things doe well, and / truly Stand to, and abide, and observe ꝑforme obey fullfil & keep / all and every y$^{e}$ award, arbitrem$^{t}$: doom determination finall end / and judgm$^{t}$: of Capt$^{a}$: JA: BENN M$^{r}$ ANTHNO: HOLLIDAY, M$^{r}$ HUMPHREY / MARSHALL Arbitrators, Indifferently Nominated Elected & chosen / as well on y$^{e}$ ꝑ$^{t}$ and behalfe of y$^{e}$ Within Named JA: BAGNALL, as / on y$^{e}$ ꝑ$^{t}$ and behalfe of y$^{e}$ Within Named FFRANCIS PARKER to award / arbitrate determine & judg of for, upon or Concerning y$^{e}$ bounds / of o$^{r}$ Lands, as also Judmg$^{ts}$: Executions, actions Suites Cause & Causees [*sic*] / of action & Suit, Trespasses, strifes variances quarrells controversies / and demands, whatsoever, had, made, moveing or depending or having / being & begining betweene the s$^{d}$. ꝑties, as any time or tymes / before y$^{e}$ day of y$^{e}$ date of theese p$^{r}$sents, soe Alwayes y$^{t}$ y$^{e}$ S$^{d}$: / award, arbitrem$^{t}$, doom, determination, & judgm$^{t}$: of y$^{e}$ S$^{d}$ Arby / trators of, for, or upon y$^{e}$ p$^{r}$misees be made or putt in writing / indented und$^{r}$. their hands and Seales and ready to be delivered / to y$^{e}$ s$^{d}$. ꝑtyes or to such of them as Shall come & require y$^{e}$ same / of y$^{e}$ S$^{d}$. Arbytrators on this side or before octob$^{r}$. next and if y$^{e}$ s$^{d}$ / arbitrators Shall make and put in writeing no Such award or / arbitrem$^{t}$. as afores$^{d}$. ffor & upon y$^{e}$ p$^{r}$misees at or before y$^{e}$ S$^{d}$. Octob$^{r}$ / next that then this obligation to be Void and of non Effect / or otherwise to Stand in full force & Vertur [*sic*]

Sign'd Sealed & Deliver'd — JA: BAGNALL Seale
in y$^{e}$ p$^{r}$sence of Us — FFRAN: PARKER Seale
GEO: WILLIAMSON
NICHO: **N** CASEY
DAN: **DB** BETTEN S$^{r}$

**[220]**
M$^{r}$ JOHN GILES S$^{r}$. I am Arested to the Court by M$^{r}$ BULLMANT for what / I knowe not. there is no petition Entred pray Crave a non suite soe rest yo$^{r}$ friend

JOHN PITT

To all to whomee theese p$^{r}$sents Shall Come I WILL: MURFREY Send Greiting / Know y$^{e}$ that I y$^{e}$ afores$^{d}$: MURFREY have for a Valuable Consideration / already Rec$^{d}$. have bargained Alienated and Changed with DANNIELL / NOLIBOY Jun$^{r}$ of y$^{e}$ Isle of Wight County a ꝑcell of Land Containing one / hundred Acres for two hundred more or less, his hundred Acres Begining / at a m$^{r}$ked pine Standing att y$^{e}$ mouth of a Small branch, which runneth / out of the meddow Swamp runing up the S$^{d}$. Line to a m$^{r}$ked pine / runing South east, crossing y$^{e}$ Land of M$^{r}$ THO: BEMBRIDGE dec~~dd~~. to a m$^{r}$ked / pine a Corner tree joyning upon JOHN ASKEW Soe runing north a / Crossing y$^{e}$ Meddow Swamp to a m$^{r}$ked pine a Corner tree soe runing / halfe a Mile S. West to the first Station, which Said Land w$^{ch}$ is ꝑ$^{t}$ of / a ꝑcell of Land which I bought of RICH: REYNOLDS, & Confirmed by him / and his Wife in Court the which S$^{d}$. Land I y$^{e}$ s$^{d}$. W$^{M}$: MURFREY together / with my Wife FFRANCIS doe warr$^{tt}$: the S$^{d}$. Land unto y$^{e}$ above S$^{d}$. DAN: NOLIBOY / Jun$^{r}$. his heir$^{rs}$: Exec$^{rs}$: adm$^{rs}$: and Assignes for Ever to have & to hold with / all rights & priviledges houses orchards and apurtenances thereunto / belonging or apertaining, And further I y$^{e}$ S$^{d}$. MURFREY my heir$^{rs}$: Exec$^{rs}$: / or Asignes doe warr$^{tt}$: to keepe and defend the S$^{d}$ NOLIBOY Jun$^{r}$ harmless / from any ꝑson or ꝑsons whatsoever that Shall lay Claime title or Intrest / to this said land or any ꝑcell or ꝑ$^{t}$ thereof, and for y$^{e}$ true ꝑformance / I y$^{e}$ S$^{d}$. MURFREY with FFRANCIS my Wife doe sett o$^{r}$ hands & Seales / This 7$^{th}$ of Octob$^{r}$. 1696

Sign'd Seal'd in y$^{e}$ p$^{r}$sence of Us

Signed
MICHAEL **M** MURFREY

Signd
JOHN **O** WATTERS

Signd
WILL **W** MURFREY Seale
FFRAN: **E** MURFREY Seale

Acknowledged in open Co$^{rt}$ houlden For y$^{e}$ Isle of Wight / County y$^{e}$ 9$^{th}$ day of Octob$^{r}$ 1696 & Recorded ꝑ / CHA CHAPMAN C$^{l}$ C$^{ur}$

**[221]**

Know all men by theise p$^{r}$sents that I SAM: SWANN of pequimns p$^{r}$cinct / in Albemarle county in North Carolina Gen$^{t}$: have Constituted appointed ordained / & made in my place & Stead putt and in and [*sic*] by theise p$^{r}$sents, doe Constitute appoint / ordayne and make and in my place & Stead putt and place my trusty & well / beloved friend HEN: BAKER of y$^{e}$ Isle of Wight County in y$^{e}$ Dominion of / Virginia gen$^{t}$: my true and Lawfull Attorney, for me and in my name & to / my use to Aske demand & Receive and take of any ꝑson or ꝑsons within y$^{e}$ / Dominion of Virg$^{a}$: and Sume or Sums of Money tobacho Corne porke / or any other goods or M$^{r}$chandize due to me in y$^{e}$ Dominion of Virginia / afores$^{d}$. and upon refusall or nonpaym$^{t}$: of y$^{e}$ Same or any ꝑ$^{t}$ or ꝑcell / thereof the ꝑson or ꝑsons Soe neglecting or refuseing to arrest Sue / in prison Implead and proceede to judgm$^{t}$, & Execution, And in prison / to Deteine and keepe untill Satisfaction had and made, and upon Such / satisfaction had & made out of prison againe to deliver & one or / more receipts or Receipts discharge or discharges acquictance or / acquittances of me and in my Name to make Signe Seale deliver / for the Same or any ꝑ$^{t}$ or ꝑcell thereof And one or more Attorney or / Atturneys und$^{r}$ him to make ordayne Constitute and appoint & againe / to revoke, Heereby ratifyeing Confirming Allowing & holdeing firme / and Stable all and Whatsoever Lawfull act or acts Thing or Things my

S[d]. / Attornyes for y[e] better Recovery of y[e] Same or any p[t] thereof In wittnesse / whereof I have heereunto Sett my hand & Seale y[e] 21[th]: day of May

SAM SWANN Seale

Sign'd Seal'd & Deliver'd
in y[e] p[r]sence of
THO: MOORE
JN[O]: GILES
HUM: MARSHALL

| 1693 | |
|---|---|
| 9[br] the 22[d]: THO: PEARCE D[r] | Contra Cred[tr]: |
| To Severall goods 532 | By M[r] FFLAKEs acc[tt]: 532 |
| | HEN: TOOKER |

Xber y[e] 9[th] 1696 / Cap[t]: Sworne by this / Test HD C[l] C[ur]

**[222]**

Know all men by theise p[r]sents y[t] I ROB[T]: HOOKER of Isle of Wight / County for divers good Considerations me thereunto Mooveing, but more / Especially for and in Consideration of y[e] love and Affection y[t] I have to / RALPH BOOZMAN Sonn of my Wife doth give grant inffeoff & alienate / unto y[e] S[d]. RALPH BOOZMAN and his heir[rs]. a Certayne tract of Land Scituated / in y[e] North west Branch of Nazemond river, being formrly granted to ANTHO: / BRANCH by a patten bearing date August y[e] 16[th] 1664 and by y[e] S[d]. branch / bequeathed by Will to my Wife Mother to y[e] aboveS[d]. RALPH BOOZMAN / to him y[e] S[d]. RALPH BOOZMAN and to his heir[rs] for Ever, to have & to hold with / all priviledges and profitts of y[e] S[d] land onely Excepting and / and alsoe Whatt tymber I shall have occation for not to sell but for my / plantacons use all other proffits priviledges &c[a]: of y[e] afores[d]. tract of / Land I doth heereby give grant and Assigne unto y[e] aboveS[d]. RALPH BOOZMAN / and his heir[rs] for Ever Wittnesse my hand & Seale this 7[th] day Dec[br]: 1696

Signed
ROB[T]: **R** HOOKER Seale
Signed
MARY + HOOKER Seale

Recorded by vertue of an order of
y[e] 9[th] 10[br] 1696 & by vertue of an ord[r]
of June 98 Finding y[e] same acknowledged
in y[e] s[d] Co[rt] I attest it
CHAP CHAPMAN C[l] C[ur]

Att a Courte holden for y[e] Isle of Wight County on y[e] 9[th] day of ffeb[r]ry anno / 1694 / By their Maj[ties] Justices

This day y[e] Last will and Test[a].m[t]: off Maj[r]. THO: TABBERER dec[dd]. & / was proved in open Court by y[e] oathes of JN[O]: DAVIS NICHO MILLER & M[r] CHARLES / CHAPMAN y[e] Wittnesses thererto, The S[d]: CHAPMAN Makes oath alsoe to the /

Codicill to y$^{e}$ S$^{d}$. Will annexed, and order for Commission of adm$^{tion}$ *cum / testamento Annexo* is granted to M$^{r}$ JOHN NEWMAN on y$^{e}$ Estate of y$^{e}$ S$^{d}$ / Dec$^{dd}$: dureing the Minority of JOSEPH COPLAND now in Wardship of y$^{e}$ / S$^{d}$. NEWMAN who p$^{r}$sents an Inventory of y$^{e}$ S$^{d}$. Estate on his oath & M$^{r}$. GEO: / MORE M$^{r}$ JA: DAY Capt$^{a}$. JN$^{O}$: GOODRICH and M$^{r}$. THO: MOORE or any three of / them are Requisted & assigned by this Courte to make a division of y$^{e}$ S$^{d}$ / Estate according to y$^{e}$ Intent and meaning of y$^{e}$ S$^{d}$. Will, & of Such convenient / time as y$^{e}$ S$^{d}$ Gent: Shall appoint betwixt this and y$^{e}$ next Courte, for / their proceeding therein they are desired to give Notice to y$^{e}$ S$^{d}$. M$^{r}$ / JOHN NEWMAN.

True Coppy Test GEO: SMITH ꝑ H DAVIS C$^{l}$ C$^{ur}$

**[223]**

Sept$^{br}$: y$^{e}$ 16$^{th}$ 1695

In Obedience to the Within Ord$^{r}$: Wee the Subscribers have made / an Equal Division to y$^{e}$ best of o$^{r}$ judgm$^{ts}$: according to the Will / of Major THOMAS TABERER

GEO: MOORE
JN$^{O}$: GOODRICH
THO: MOORE

Whereas I y$^{e}$ Subscriber having rec$^{d}$: the full fift p$^{t}$. of y$^{e}$ Estate of / Major THO: TABERER given to my Wife ELIZABETH WILLIAMS and her / Children by Will I do therefore oblidge my Selfe my heir$^{rs}$. Exec$^{rs}$ / to pay unto JOHN NEWMAN his heir$^{rs}$: Exec$^{rs}$: the full fift p$^{t}$ of all / Just Debts due from y$^{e}$ estate of y$^{e}$ s$^{d}$ THO: TABERER Wittnesse my / hand the Second day of octob$^{r}$.

NICHO: OGBORNE — JN$^{O}$: WILLIAMS
Signd
THO: **TH** HOBBY

Whereas the Subscriber heareof have Rec$^{d}$: a third of the fift p$^{te}$. / of y$^{e}$ Estate of Major THO: TABERER given to my Wife CHRISTIAN / JORDAN and her Daughter CHRISTIAN given by Will doe therefore oblidge / my Selfe my heir$^{rs}$. Exec$^{rs}$: to pay Unto RICH NEWMAN her heir$^{rs}$. Exec$^{rs}$: / the full third of y$^{e}$ fifth p$^{te}$. of all just Debts due from y$^{e}$ Estate of / y$^{e}$ S$^{d}$. THO: TABERER as Wittnesse my hand this twelveth of Sept$^{br}$: / 1696 — ROB JORDAN

AND$^{W}$: GRIFFIN
JA: JORDAN

Rec$^{d}$. of JN$^{O}$. NEWMAN a feather bed & furniture and a Rideing / horse being a legacy left to my Wife MARY WEBB by y$^{e}$ Will of / her ffather THO: TABERERER [*sic*] as Wittnesse my hand this 17 ff$^{br}$ 1695

GEO: MOORE — WILL: **3L** WEB was
MECHEZIDEC DUCHER — M$^{r}$ke

Whereas I y[e] Subscriber have rec[d]: the fifth p[t]: of y[e] Estate of / Maj[r]: THO: TABERER Given to my Wife MARY WEB and her Children / by Will, I doe therefore oblidge my Selfe my heir[rs] Exec[rs]: to pay / unto JOHN NEWMAN his heir[rs]: Exec[rs]: the full fifth p[t]: of all / Just Debts due from y[e] Estate of THO: TABERER according to y[e] Will / as wittnesse my hand this 19[th]: day of 7[br] 1695 Signd
GEO: MOORE WILL: **W** WABB
MELCHESIDEC DUCHE

**[224]**

Isle of Wight. JAMES SAMPSON and JAMES HORSENELL being Sworne / doe upon their Severall oathes Corporall oathes, Say that they being in y[e] / Store of y[e] P[tr] JOHN WILSON in Sept[br]. Last the defd[t]. and one HUGH / CRAWFORD came to y[e] S[d]. Store to buy goods this S[d]. WILLSON refused to Creditt / the S[d]: CRAWFORD Whereupon y[e] S[d]. defd[t]: did Say M[r] WILLSON y[w] need not / fear him for he has tobacho at my house and is an honest man and there / y[e] tobacho Shall be paid
Sworne in Courte 10 X[br]: 96 JA: SAMPSON
HD C[l] C[ur] JA: HORSNELL

Rec[d]: of JN[O]: NEWMAN one ffeather bed and furniture being a Legacy / Given to my wife CHRISTIAN and her Daughter by y[e] Will of her ffather / THO: TABERER as wittnesse my hand y[e] 12[th]: of Sept[br]: 1696
AND[W] GRIFFIN ROB: JORDAN
JAMES JORDAN

Bee it Known unto all men that I doe Constitute and apoint JOHN / GILES my Atturney in my Stead to defend a Suite att y[e] Isle of Wight / County Court brought against me ꝑ Capt[a]: ROB[T]: THOMAS wittnesse / my hand this 7[th] day of Dec[br]. 1696
Signd
JOHN **T** THOMAS

M[r] CHARLES CHAPMAN Jan[r]y y[e] 27[th] 1696

Theese are to Impower to act as my lawfull atturny on y[e] Cause / [ ] depending att y[e] Next Court betwixt Major SAMM[LL]: / SWANN and mee the Subscrib[r] & to act in y[e] S[d]. Cause as farr forth as if I / Ware thare Personally my Selfe as Wittnesse my hand the day and date / above Mention'd GILES DRIVER
Testis RICH: REYNOLDS
To M[r] CHARLES CHAPMAN p[r]sent

**[225]**

Pray Appear for me In any Suite I have depending in y^e^ Isle / of Wight County Court and prosecute the Same and this Shall be your / Sufficient Warr^tt^: as Wittnesse my hand this 3^d^. day of X^br^: 1696
To JN^O^: GILES Attorney at law JA DAY

To all to whome theese p^r^sents Shall Come, I S^r^. WILL BERKLEY K^nt^ / Gov^r^: and Cap^ta^: Gen^r^all of Virginia, Send Greeting in o^r^ Lord God / Everlasting Whereas by Instructions from y^e^ King's most Ex / cellent Maj^tie^ directed to me and the Counsell of State his Maj^tie^ / was gratiously pleased to Authorize me y^e^ S^d^ Gov^r^: and Counsell to grant / pattens and to Assigne Such proportions of Land to all advent^rs^ & plant^rs^: / as have bine heeretofore, Usuall in y^e^ Like Cases, Either for Advent^rs^: or / Money or tran^s^ of people into this Colony according to a Charter of / of [*sic*] Ord^r^. from y^e^ Late treasurer: & Company & that y^e^ Same propor / tion of fifty Acres of land be granted or Assigned for Every ꝑson / tra^s^: hither Since midd^s^ 1625. And that y^e^ Same Course be Continued / to all adventurers and planters untill it Shall otherwise be deter / =mined by his Maj^tie^ Now know y^e^ y^t^ I y^e^ S^d^. Sir WILL BERKLEY K^nt^ / Govern^r^: &^ca^: doe with y^e^ Consent of y^e^ Counsill of State accordingly give / and grant unto RICH: GROSSE, two hundred Acres of land according / to y^e^ Antient bounds thereof lyeing and being in y^e^ Isle of Wight / County, y^e^ S^d^: land being lately found to Escheated to his Majestie / as by an Inquisition Recorded in y^e^ Secretaryes office Under / the hands & Seales of M^r^: JOHN JENNINGS Deputy Escheat^r^: for y^e^ S^d^ / County, and a Jury Sworne before him for y^t^ purpose bearing date the / 17^th^: of 7^br^: 1670 may appear and is now granted to the S^d^: / RICH: GROSSE, who hath made his Composition according to Act. To / have & to hold y^e^ S^d^. land with his due Share of all mines & Miner^ls^: / therein Conteined, with all rites and priviledges of hunting / hauking fishing and fowleing withall woods waters & Rivers / withall proffits Comodityes and hereditam^ts^: to y^e^ S^d^: land be / longing to y^e^ S^d^. RICH: GROSS his heir^rs^: and Assignes for Ever / in as ample Manner, to all intents and purposes as is Expressed / in a Charter of ord^rs^: from y^e^ Late Treasurer & Company dated y^e^ / 18^th^: of 9^br^: 1618 or by Consequence may be Collected out of the / Same or out of the Letters pattens where on they are

**[226]**
Grounded to be held of o^r^ Soveraigne Lord y^e^ King his heir^rs^ & Success^rs^: / for Ever, as of his manno^r^. of East Grenwich in ffee & Comon Soccage / and not *in Capite* nor by Kn^tt^: Service yeilding and paying to o^r^ Soveraine / Lord y^e^ King his heir^rs^: & Successo^rs^ for Every fifty Acres of land heerby / granted, yearly at y^e^ feast of S^t^. Michaell y^e^ Archangell the fee rent / of one Shilling, which paym^t^: is to be Made yearly from year to year / according to his Maj^ties^ Instructions of y^e^ 12^th^ of Sept^br^. 1662 provided / that if y^e^ s^d^. RICH: GROSSE his heir^rs^: or assignes doe not seate plant or / Cause to be Seated or planted upon y^e^ S^d^. land within three yeares next / Insuing then it Shall be lawfull for any Advent^er^. or planter to make / Choice and Seate thereupon Given und^r^. my hand and y^e^

Seate of y^e^ / Colony this Sixt day of Aprill One Thousand Six hundred / Seventy one Anno R^g^ 8 Car. 2^d^ xxiij
RICH: GROSS his patten for 200 acres of Land WILL: BERKLEY
in y^e^ Isle of Wight County
Recordat^r^. Test / PHILL: LUDWELL C^l^ offc

Know all men by theise p^r^sents that I JANE RIGANE *als* JANE GROSS / Widdow y^e^ Daughter & Sole heiresse of y^e^ Within Named RICH: GROSSE / Dec^dd^. doe heereby for y^e^ Consideration of five Thousand pownds of tobo / in hand paid as p^rt^: of the Satisfaction of this Land as also for divers / other Considerations me thereunto Mooveing bargaine Sell assigne / and make over all my right title & Interest to y^e^ land & appurtences / in this pattent conteyned to NICHOLAS CASEY & his heir^rs^: & Assignes for / ever as wittnesse my hand and Seale this 9^th^ of ffeb^r^y 1696
Testis: GEO: NORSWORTHY Signed
RICH: WILKINSON Jun^r^ JANE I RIGANE Seale
JAME [*sic*] TULLAGH
RICH: REYNOLDS

Acknowledged in Open Co^rt^ For y^e^ Isle / Wight County y^e^ 9^th^ ffebr 1696 & by vertue / of an Order of y^e^ 9^th^ June 1698

Recorded p CHA CHAPMAN C^l^ C^ur^

**[227]**

Know all men by these p^r^sents that I ROBERT FFLAKE Sen^r^ of y^e^ Upper Parish of y^e^ Isle of Wight / County for A valluable Consideracon to me in hand p^d^ or secured or secured to be p^d^ by THOMAS / SMYTH lately of y^e^ County of Surry, have bargained & Sould & doe by these p^r^sents For me & / my Heires For ever bargaine Sell & deliver Infeoffe & Confirme unto the said THOMAS / SMYTH and to his Heir^es^ & Assignes For ever Two hundred & ffifty Acres of Land being / part of A Patten of Six hundred Acres, the said Parcell of Land lyeing in the upper Parish / of y^e^ Isle of Wight County and bounded as Followeth, The said parcell of Land includeing the / Mill Comonly knowne by y^e^ name of flakes Mill y^e^ said land beginning att A Branch / between y^e^ Mill & the plantacon Eastward & soe up the Mill swamp to A Branch / Comonly called Porters Branch running Eastward & up Porters branch to the Cart Path & / soe Cross streight to y^e^ first named branch To have & to hould the said two hundred & fifty / Acres of Land w^th^ the Mill and Such Utensills belonging to y^e^ Mill as are agreed upon between / the said FFLAKE & SMYTH, & alsoe his due Share of all Mynes & Mineralls therein / Conteyned w^th^ free priviledge of Hunting hawking fishing & Fowleing w^th^ all woods Ways / & Waters w^th^ all other Regallityes priviledges proffitts & Comodities & all Hereditamen^ts^ / whatsoever to y^e^ said Land belonging or in any wise apperteyning as Mill houses and / whatsoever is upon the said Land to him the said THOMAS SMYTH and to his Heir^rs^ / & Assignes that y^e^ s^d^ Land & Mill & every part & pcell thereof is Clear &

Free From all and / all manner of Former bargaines & Sales Joyntures & Mortgage Judgm^ts Execucon and / all other manner of Incumbrances Whatsoever and that I have at y^e tyme of Insealing / & delivery hereof in and to all & singuler y^e p^rmises A good true & Indefeizable Estate / of Inheritance in ffee simple which I hereby doe transfer & oblidge my selfe my heires / Ex^rs & Adm^rs to warrant & defend this my Sale of all & Singuler the p^rmises w^th their / apperences to y^e said THOMAS SMYTH to his Heires & Assignes for ever ag^st all manner / of persons whatsoever by From or under me deriveing any Clayme tytle or Interest / thereunto when required thereto will give him or any of them such further Lawfull / assurance at all & singuler y^e p^rmises as by his or their Learned councell shall be thought / Fitt and Will acknowledge this my reall Act & Deed in Open Court next to be houlden at / y^e Isle of Wight County in Testimony of all I have sett my hand & Seal the 2^d day of / Aprill 1697 ROBERT FFLAKE Sen R his mark
Sealed & Delivered in y^e p^rsence of
THOMAS WALLER
CHARLES BASS **B** his marke

Acknowledged in Open Courte held For the Isle of Wight County / y^e 9^th day of Aprill 1697 by ROBERT FFLAKE Sen^r and / Recorded ꝑ / CHA CHAPMAN C^l C^ur

**[228]**

This Indenture made y^e second day of September in the year of o^r Lord God 1697 Between / HENRY MARTYN & MARY his Wife of y^e upper parish in y^e Isle of Wight County of y^e one part / planter, & JN^O THOMAS of y^e Lower Parish in y^e Same County Planter Witnesseth y^t y^e s^d HENRY / MARTYN & MARY his wife hath demised granted & to Farme letten & by these p^rsents dowe demise / & to Farme lett one hundred Acres of Land situated lyeing & being in the Lower parish of y^e / Foresd County bounding att y^e upper end on y^e Land of Coll SMYTH & soe downe on one side / by Coll SMYTH & on y^e other side by THOMAS PARNELL soe betweene these two till y^e Hundred / Acres be Compleated & ended the said JN^O THOMAS to have & to hould he his Heires Ex^rs Adm^rs / or Assignes y^e said Hundred Acres of Land From y^e day of y^e date hereof to y^e Full end & Terme / of Ninety Nine Yeares Fully to be Compleated & ended Yeilding & payeing yearly For yearly / Rent & duty to y^e said HENRY MARTYN & MARY his Wife their Heires Ex^rs Adm^rs or Assignes / if Lawfully demanded by y^e said MARTYN & MARY his Wife their Heires Ex^rs Adm^rs or Assignes / of y^e said JN^O THOMAS or his Heires Exc^rs Adm^rs or Assignes upon the sd Land one year [*sic*] of Indian / Corne in att or upon y^e First day of January dureing y^e said Terme of Ninety Nine yeares / The Said HENRY MARTYN & MARY his Wife doe For themselves their Heires Ex^rs Adm^rs or / Assignes For y^e Consideracon & made according to y^e Rent aforesd Covent & warrant / unto y^e said JN^O THOMAS his Heires Ex^rs Adm^rs or Assignes quietly & peaceably to enjoy / the said Land without any lett or molestacon togeather w^th all y^e Woods underwoods / Mines Mineralls Waters, Hunting Hawking made by y^e said HENRY MARTYN & MARY his / Wife their Heires Ex^rs Adm^rs or Assignes or any person or persons whatsoever, / Att y[e] expiracon of y[e] said tyme of Ninety Nine yeares, to deliver up quiett possession of y[e] said / Land to y[e] said HENRY MARTYN & MARY his Wife their Heires Ex[rs] Adm[rs] or Assignes / In Witness whereof y[e] said partyes have severally sett to their hands & Seales y[e] day / & year above written

his
HENRY **H** MARTEN O
mark

Sined Sealed & delivered in
y[e] p[r]sence of us
JN[O] JONES Sen[r]
FFRAN: LEE
RICH: LEWIS

her
MARY + MARTEN O
mark

his
JOHN I THOMAS O
marke

Acknowledged in Open Court held For / y[e] Isle of Wight County y[e] 9[th] day / of October 1697 by HENRY MARTYN / & his Wife & Recorded by / CHA CHAPMAN C[l] C[ur]

**[229]**

Know all men by these p[r]sents y[t] I RICHARD BEAL & MARY my Wife doe acknowledge to Assigne / over all o[r] right Title & Interest of this within menconed sayl of Land From us o[r] / Heires &[c] For ever unto TRUSTRAM NORSWORTHY his heires &c For ever & doe Acknowledge / to have reced Satisfaccon For y[e] same as witnesse o[r] hands & seales this 9[th] day / of Aprill 1697

Signed Sealed & delivered
in y[e] p[r]sence of
JOS: BRIDGER
JACOB HARDY

of Land first Interlined

his marke
RICHARD **R:B:** BEAL
MARY **2** BEAL
her marke

Acknowledged in open Co[rt] / held For y[e] Isle of Wight County / the 9[th] day of Aprill 1695 / Vera: Copia: Entred in Record / p CHA CHAPMAN C[l]C[ur]

Barbados:

Know all men by these p[r]sents that I JOHN POLGREEN of the Island / afforesaid For diverse good causes & Consideracons me hereunto moveing / have made ordeyned deputed & appointed and in my stead & place putt / And by these presents doe make ordeyn depute and appoint and in my / stead & place putt my trusty & welbeloved ffreind M[r] ANDREW WOODLY / of Virginia a Merchant to be my true & lawfull Attrorney For me and in my name and to & / For my use to ask demand & suc For Levy require recover & receive & / every Such sume or sumes of money or other Comodityes whatsoever / which now are or hereafter Shall bee due & oweing unto me From any / person or persons whatsoever in Virginia affores[d] by any manner or wayes / or meanes whatsoever especially of & From M$^{rs}$ FRANCES POLGREEN of / Virginia widdow late wife of GEORGE POLGREEN deced For one negro Man / named Willy And upon my Said Attorneys recovery & receipt of any sume / or sumes whatsoever From any ꝑson or ꝑsons one or more discharge / or discharges or sattisfaccon Release or Releases For me & in my Name / to signe Seal & deliver and alsoe to acco$^{t}$ Compound refer & agree / to & w$^{th}$ the said FFRANCES POLGREEN her heires Ex$^{rs}$ & Adm$^{rs}$ and all other / person or persons whatsoever indebted to me otherwise to prosecute them to / y$^{e}$ utmost Extent of y$^{e}$ Law For y$^{e}$ speedy recovery of my Just right Giveing / & by these p$^{r}$sents granting to Act & doe all Such Act & Acts thing & / things devise & Devises in the Law as to my said Attorney shall seem / necessary & Convenient satisfieing and by these p$^{r}$sents alloweing & Confirmeing / For good and sufficient in Law all and whatsoever my said Attorney shall / Lawfully doe or Cause to be done in the p$^{r}$mises and punctually rely

**[230]**
And absolutely to all intents Construccons & purposes whatsoever as if I my selfe / were there personally p$^{r}$sent In witness whereof I have hereunto putt my hand / & seal the Eight day of January 1695 Seal

Signed sealed & delivered in presence of JOHN POLGREEN O

CHARELS DRYVER}
JOHN BURNELL }
ABRAHAM TOOKE }
THOMAS HARDY }
ANDW WOODLY }

Proved in open Court held For y$^{e}$ Isle of Wight County the 9$^{th}$ day of ffebr 169$^{7}/_{8}$ to be the Act & Deed of JOHN POLGREEN by the Oathes of M$^{r}$ ANDREW WOODLY & THOMAS HARDY and / Recorded

by CHA CHAPMAN C$^{l}$ C$^{ur}$

To all to whome these p$^{r}$sents shall come, I S$^{r}$ W$^{M}$ BERKLEY K$^{t}$ Governo$^{r}$ & / Cap$^{t}$ Generall of Virginia send greeting in o$^{r}$ L$^{d}$ God Everlasting, whereas / by intruccons from y$^{e}$ Kings most Excellent Ma$^{tie}$ to me and y$^{e}$ Councill / of State his Ma$^{tie}$ was gratiously pleased to authorize me y$^{e}$ S$^{d}$ Govern$^{r}$ / & Councell to grant pattents & to Assigne such proporcons of Land to / all Adventurers or Planters as have been heretofore usuall in y$^{e}$ like / Cases either for Adventurers of mony or transportacon of people into / this Colony accordeing to A Charter of Orders From y$^{e}$ late Treasurer / & Company & that y$^{e}$ same proporcon of ffifty Acres of Land be granted / or Assigned For every person transported hither since Midsumer 1625 / And that y$^{e}$ same Course be Continued to all adventurers & Planters / untill it shall otherwise be determined by his Ma$^{tie}$, Now know yee / that I y$^{e}$ said S$^{r}$ W$^{M}$ BERKELY K$^{t}$ Govern$^{r}$ &c doe w$^{th}$ y$^{e}$ Consent of y$^{e}$ / Councill of State accordeingly give & grant unto RICHARD GROSS / Two hundred Acres of Land accordeing to y$^{e}$ antient bound thereof / lyeing & being in y$^{e}$ Isle of Wight County, y$^{e}$ said Land being lately / Found to Escheat to his Ma$^{tie}$ on an Inquisicon Recorded in the / Secretaries Office under y$^{e}$ hand & Seal of M$^{r}$ JN$^{O}$ JENNINGS Deputy / Escheator For y$^{e}$ said county and A Jury sworne before him

**[231]**

For that purpose bearing date y$^{e}$ 14$^{eenth}$ day of September 1690 may appear and is now / granted to y$^{e}$ said RICHARD GROSS whose hath made his Composicon accordeing to Act / and to hould the said Land w$^{th}$ his due share of all Mines & mineralls there[ ] / Conteyned w$^{th}$ all rights & priviledges of Hunting Hawking Fishing & Fowleing w$^{th}$ / all Woods waters & Rivers w$^{th}$ all profitts Comodities & Hereditam$^{ts}$ to y$^{e}$ said Land / belonging to y$^{e}$ said RICHARD GROSS his Heires & Assignes For ever, in an ample manner / to all intents & purposes as is Expressed in A Charter of Orders From the late / Treasurer out of y$^{e}$ same, or out of y$^{e}$ Letters Pattents whereon they are grounded / to be held of o$^{r}$ Soveraigne Lord y$^{e}$ King his Heires & Successo$^{rs}$ For ever as of his / Manner of East Greenwich in ffee & Comon Soccage & not *in Capite* nor by K$^{ts}$ service / Yeilding & payeing to o$^{r}$ Soveraigne Lord y$^{e}$ King his Heires & Successo$^{rs}$ for every fifty / Acres of Land hereby granted yearly att y$^{e}$ Feast of S$^{t}$ Michaell y$^{e}$ Archangell y$^{e}$ fee / Rent of one Shilling, w$^{ch}$ paym$^{t}$ is to be made yearely From year to year accordeing / to his Ma$^{ties}$ instruccons of y$^{e}$ 12$^{th}$ of Sept$^{br}$ 1662 Provided that if y$^{e}$ said RICHARD / GROSS his Heires or Assignes doe not seat & plant or Cause to be planted upon y$^{e}$ / s$^{d}$ Land w$^{th}$in three yeares next ensueing then it shall be lawfull For any / Adventurer or planter to make choice & seat thereupon Given under my hand / & the Seal of y$^{e}$ Colony this Sixth day of Aprill One Thousand Six hundred and / seaventy one *Anno RgGs Caroli secundi* 23°

WILLIAM BERKELY

Recordatur Test PHILL LUDWELL C$^{l}$ Off

Know all men by these p$^{r}$sents that I JANE REGAN *als* JANE GROSS widdow y$^{e}$ / Daughter & sole Heiress of y$^{e}$ w$^{th}$in named RICHARD GROSS doe hereby (For the / Consideracon of ffive Thousand pounds of Tobaccoe in hand p$^{d}$ as part of y$^{e}$ / sattisfaccon For this Land, as alsoe For diverse other Consideracons me / thereunto moveing) Assigne & make over all my right Tytle & intrerest / in y$^{e}$ Land & apptences in this pattent Conteyned to NICHOLAS CASEY and / to his Heires and Assignes For ever, as witness my hand & seal this / 9$^{th}$ day of ffebr 1696 Seal

Test GEORGE NOSWORTHY — JANE ł REGING O<br>
JAMES TULLAGH — Signum<br>
RICH$^{D}$ WILKINSON Jun$^{r}$<br>
RICH$^{D}$. REYNOLDS

Acknowledged in Open Court held For y$^{e}$ Isle of / Wight County y$^{e}$ 9$^{th}$ day of ffeb$^{r}$: 1696 by JANE / REGING as her Act & Deed & Recorded by order of y$^{e}$ 9$^{th}$ / of June 98

p CHA CHAPMAN C$^{l}$ C$^{ur}$

**[232]**

This Indenture made y^e^ 2^d^ day of September 1694 Between HENRY MARTYN & MARY his / Wife of y^e^ Upper parish in the Isle of Wight County planter of y^e^ one part & JOHN / JONES sen^r^ of y^e^ Lower Parish in the Same County Cooper of y^e^ other part Witnesseth / that the said HENRY MARTYN & MARY his wife, hath demised granted & to farme / letten, & by these p^r^sents doe demise & to Farme lett, one hundred Acres of / Land situated lyeing & being in y^e^ Lower parish of y^e^ County, Joyneing to / one end on y^e^ s^d^ JONES's Land, purchased of EDMOND PALMER, & one side to y^e^ / Land of y^e^ said JONES, purchased of JOHN PORTIS sen^r^, and on the other side / to y^e^ Land of M^r^ WILLIAM BODY & soe by those two Lynes, till the hundred / Acres be Compleated, y^e^ said JONES to have & to hould, he his / Heires Ex^rs^ Adm^rs^ or Assignes, y^e^ said Hundred Acres of Land From y^e^ day of / the date hereof to y^e^ Full end & Terme of Ninety Nine Yeares Fully to be / Compleated & ended, Yeilding & payeing Yearly For Yearly rent & duty / to y^e^ said HENRY MARTYN & MARY his Wife their Heires Ex^rs^ Adm^rs^ or Assignes / if Lawfully demanded by y^e^ said MARTYN & MARY his Wife their Heires / Ex^rs^ Adm^rs^ or Assignes, of y^e^ said JONES his Heires Exc^rs^ Adm^rs^ or Assignes / upon y^e^ said Land One Ear of Indian Corne in at or upon the First day / of January dureing the Tearme of Ninety Nine Yeares, / And The said / HENRY MARTYN & MARY his Wife doe For themselves their Heires Ex^rs^ / Adm^rs^ or Assignes For y^e^ Consideracon & made according to y^e^ rent / aforesaid Covent & warr^t^ unto y^e^ said JOHN JONES sen^r^ his Heires Ex^rs^ / Adm^rs^ or Assignes quietly & peaceably to enjoy y^e^ said Land w^th^out any Lett / or molestacon, togeather w^th^ all y^e^ Woods underwoods Mines / Mineralls, Waters, Hunting Hawking made by y^e^ said HENRY MARTYN & / MARY his Wife their Heires Ex^rs^ Adm^rs^ or Assignes or any ꝑson whatsoever / and att y^e^ Expiracon of y^e^ said tyme of Ninety Nine yeares to deliver up / quiett possession of y^e^ said Land to y^e^ said HENRY MARTYN & MARY his / Wife their heires Ex^rs^ Adm^rs^ or Assignes, In Witness whereof the / said ꝑties have severally sett to their hands & seales y^e^ day & year / above written

Signed Sealed & delivered in y^e^
p^r^sence of us
FFRANC LEE
RICHARD LEWIS
JN^O^ THOMAS --- Mark

HENRY MARTYN
his **H** m^r^ke
her
MARY + MARTYN
m^r^ke
JOHN JONES Sen^r^

Acknowledged in Open Co^rt^ held / For y^e^ Isle of Wight County y^e^ 9^th^ / day of October 1697 by y^e^ s^d^ / MARTYN & his Wife & Ordered / to be Recorded / [ ] CHA CHAPMAN C^l^ C^ur^

**[233]**

Know all men by these p^r^sents, that I JAMES LONG of North Carolina Eldest / sonne & Heir to JAMES LONG, Formerly & Inhabitant in the Westerne Branch / of Nanzimond River, For good Consideracon in hand already reced, have bargained / sould

& delivered over unto ROB$^{T}$. SCOTT his Heires & Assignes For ever, Two hundred / Acres of Land, scituate lyeing & being on y$^{e}$ South side of y$^{e}$ Maine Swamp / begining att a marked Cyprus, & soe to hould all y$^{e}$ Land on y$^{e}$ aforesaid Swamp / that belongs to y$^{e}$ afforesaid JAMES LONG as Sonne & Heir afforesaid w$^{ch}$ said / Two hundred Acres of Land my ffather JAMES LONG did Convey A Deed of Sale / out of his owne proper pattent of Three hundred Acres unto ROB$^{T}$ STOCKES / dureing his life, which said Two hundred Acres of Land I the abovesaid / JAMES LONG, doe bind my selfe my Heires Ex$^{rs}$ & Adm$^{rs}$, that the abovesaid / ROB$^{T}$ SCOTT his Heires & Assignes, shall quietly & peaceably enjoy, togeather w$^{th}$ all / the appertences thereunto belonging For ever, For Further Confirmacon hereof / I hereunto sett my hand & seall this second day of August 1697

his Seal
JAMES **S** LONG O
Mark

Signed Sealed & delivered in
y$^{e}$ p$^{r}$sence of us
CHARLES ROADS
JACOB DARDEN
WILLIAM PARKER

Acknowledged in Open Court held For y$^{e}$ / Isle of Wight County by y$^{e}$ said JAMES / LONG y$^{e}$ 9$^{th}$ day of Aug$^{st}$ 1697 & / Recorded ꝑ CHA CHAPMAN C$^{l}$C$^{ur}$

I doe hereby Assigne my Full Tytle & interest of one Servant Boy / Called JOHN CAVENOE unto JOHN NEVILL Jun$^{r}$ For y$^{e}$ Tearme and / tyme accordeing to y$^{e}$ Judgem$^{t}$ of Co$^{rt}$ as witness my hand the / 16$^{th}$ day of December 1697

H$^{N}$ HAWKINS

Recordedꝑ CHA CHAPMAN C$^{l}$ C$^{ur}$

[234]

To all to whome these p$^{r}$sents shall Come I S$^{r}$ HENRY CHICHLEY K$^{t}$ his / Ma$^{ties}$ deputy Govern$^{r}$ of Virginia send greeting in o$^{r}$ Lord God Everlasting / Whereas his Ma$^{tie}$ hath been gratiously pleased by his Royall Letters Pattents / under y$^{e}$ great seal of England, beareing date att Westm$^{er}$ y$^{e}$ tennth day of / October in y$^{e}$ & Twentieth Year of his raigne amongst other things / in y$^{e}$ said Letters Pattents Conteyned, Continue & Confirme y$^{e}$ antient / priveledge & power, of granting Fifty acres of Land For every ꝑson / imported into his Ma$^{ties}$ Collony of Virginia, Now know yee that I / the said S$^{r}$ HENRY CHICHLEY K$^{t}$ Dep$^{ty}$ Governor &c doe w$^{th}$ y$^{e}$ Consent / of y$^{e}$ Councell of State accordeingly give & grant unto THOMAS MANN / three hundred acres of Land in y$^{e}$ Isle of Wight County begining att at / marked Cyprus in a Cove by Chowan River side thence East One / hundred & Sixty pole to a Small Hickory thence South one hundred / & Fifty pole to two White Oakes thence West one hundred & Sixty / pole to A Cyprus in y$^{e}$ mouth of a Branch by y$^{e}$ River side & soe up / the River to y$^{e}$ First station the said Land being due to y$^{e}$ said THOMAS / MANN by & For y$^{e}$ transportacon of Six persons into this Colony whose / names are menconed in y$^{e}$ Records under this pattent To have & to hould / the said Land w$^{th}$ his due share of all Mines & Mineralls therein / conteyned, w$^{th}$ all rights & priveledges of hunting Hawking Fishing & / fowling, w$^{th}$ all Woods Waters

& Rivers w$^{th}$ all profitts Comodities and / hereditam$^{ts}$ whatsoever belonging to y$^{e}$ said Land to him y$^{e}$ s$^{d}$ THOMAS / MANN his Heires & Assignes For ever, in as large & ample manner, to / all intents & purposes as has been used & allowed since y$^{e}$ First / plantacon, to be held of o$^{r}$ Sov$^{r}$aigne Lord the King his Heires and / Successors of as of his manner of East Greenwich in Free & comon / Soccage & not *in Capite* or by K$^{t}$ service Yeilding & payeing to our / said Soveraigne Lord y$^{e}$ King his Heires & Successors For every fifty / Acres of Land hereby granted att y$^{e}$ Feast of S$^{t}$ Michaell y$^{e}$ Archangell / the ffee rent of one Shilling w$^{ch}$ paym$^{t}$ is to be made yearly From

**[235]**
Year to year accordeing to his Ma$^{ties}$ instruccons of y$^{e}$ Twelfth of September / 1662 provided that if y$^{e}$ s$^{d}$ THOMAS MANN his Heires or assignes doe not / seat or plant or Cause to seated [*sic*] or planted upoon y$^{e}$ said Land w$^{th}$ these / Three yeares next ensueing the date hereof, That then it shall & may be / lawfull For any adventurer or planter to make choice & seat thereon / Given under my hand & seal of y$^{e}$ Colony this 22$^{d}$ day of September 1682 HEN: CHICHLY
Recorded
Teste PHILL LUDWELL ꝑ M$^{r}$ Sec$^{r}$

Know all men by these p$^{r}$sents that I THOMAS MANN doe Assigne & / make over all my right, Tytle & interest of y$^{e}$ w$^{th}$in menconed Pattent / to WILLIAM BUTLER & his Heires & Assignes For ever, witnesse my hand / & seal this 9$^{th}$ Day of ffebruary 169$^{7}/_{8}$

his seal
Sealed & delivered in y$^{e}$ p$^{r}$sence of us — THOMAS **M** MANN O
m$^{r}$ke

RICHARD REYNOLDS
JOYCE **J** REYNOLDS
her m$^{r}$ke

Acknowledged in open Co$^{rt}$ held For y$^{e}$ Isle of Wight County y$^{e}$ 9$^{th}$ day of ffebruary 169$^{7}/_{8}$ by y$^{e}$ said THOMAS MANN to be his Act and Deed and ordered to be Recorded
Test CHA CHAPMAAN C$^{l}$ C$^{ur}$

Be it knowne unto all men by whome these p$^{r}$sents shall Come I MARTHA DAWSON of y$^{e}$ parish of Lower in / the County of y$^{e}$ Isle of Wight in the Colony of Virginia Widdow send greeting / that whereas my Aunt MARGARY SHEPPARD, of Warwick County in Virginia / hath lately departed this Lyfe, seized of a Tract of Land & plantacon Whereon / shee lately lived & dyed, and alsoe a Small ꝑsonall Estate, within the said / County, the which said Land does descend unto me the said MARTHA as Heir / att Law, & the ꝑsonall Estate as next of Kin, And For as much as the said MARTHA / DAWSON, being Sickly & weak, & no table [*sic*] to look after y$^{e}$ same, have authorized / Confirmed & appointed, and by these p$^{r}$sents doe authorize & appoint, my derely / &

well beloved Sonne, HENRY DAWSON whoe is now in possession, of the said / Estate, to be my true & Lawfull Attorney, For me & in my name & to my / use, to Enter & take & keep possession, of what Land & ꝑsonall Estate / my said Aunt MARGARY dyed possessed of, and alsoe For me & in my / names to peticon & obteyn From Warwick County Co$^{rt}$ a Letter of Adstracon / of all y$^{e}$ goods & Chattells w$^{ch}$ my said Aunt MARGARY dyed possessed of as / alsoe all things actions rights & Credits which of right did belong to my / said Aunt MARGARY SHEPPARD, and I the said MARTHA DAWSON doe / Further authorize & impower, my said Attorney to make one or more / attorney or attorneys as he shall soe occasion and alsoe to doe all other / other

**[236]**

Lawfull thing & things For me & in my name & to my use, as I my selfe might / lawfully doe, in as Full & ample manner as I my selfe might dooe and w$^{t}$ / my said attorney or attorneys, Shall doe herein I doe hereby ratifie & / Confirme to all intents & purposes, as witness my hand & Seal (these / words interlined before signed) by these p$^{r}$sents doe authorize & appoint

Mark O
MARTHA **M** DAWSON
her

Test JN$^{O}$ PORTIS Jun$^{r}$
marke
JAMES **I M** MERCER
his

Acknowledged by MARTHAH DAWSON to be her / Act & Deed in Open Court houlden For the Isle / of Wight County the 2$^{d}$ day of May 1698 and / Recorded by Order of s$^{d}$ Court

ꝑ CHA CHAPMAN C$^{l}$ C$^{ur}$

This Indenture made y$^{e}$ Second day of may in y$^{e}$ yeare of our lord god / on thousand six hundred ninty Eight & in y$^{e}$ tenth yeare of the Reign / of our Soveraigne Lord William by y$^{e}$ grace of god King of England / Scotland france and Ireland &$^{c}$: Between JOHN SMITH of y$^{e}$ Isle weight / County of y$^{e}$ on part and GEORGE NOSWORTHY of Nanzemond County / Gentleman of y$^{e}$ other part wittnesseth y$^{t}$ said JOHN SMITH for & in / Consideration of y$^{e}$ sume of thirty pounds of good and Currant mony of / Virginia to him in hand, at and before the sealing and delivery of / these presents by y$^{e}$ said GEORGE NORSWORTHY Gent, well and truly paid y$^{e}$ zec$^{t}$ [*sic*] / whereof he y$^{e}$ said JOHN SMITH doth hereby acknowledge and him self / therewith fully satisfied and paid, and thereof and of every part & parcell / thereof doth Clearly acquite, exonerate, and discharge, the said GEORGE / NORSWORTHY, his heires executors and administrators for ever, by these / Presents, hath given and granted Alliened bargained sold Enfeoffed and Confer / by these presents doth fully Clearly and absolutely give grant bergaine / Sell Allein enfeoff and confirm unto y$^{e}$ said GEORGE NORSWORTHY / Gent his heires and Assigns for ever one percell or trace of land lying y$^{e}$ Isle of / Wight County being part of a pattent of two thousand and fiftie Acers / granted unto WILLIAM

OLDIS and ROBERT RUFFIN / dated y^e^ of September 1694 Containing one hundered Acres wich I y^e^ said / JOHN SMITH did purchase of y^e^ said WILLIAM OLDIS and ROBER RUFFIN / by deed bearing date y^e^ Eight day of June 1677 it being now in y^e^ tenure and / occupation of the said JOHN SMITH, y^e^ said one hundered Acers of land being / being bounded as followeth (Viz) beginning at a marked poplar being

**[237]**

M^r^ LASWELLs NW corner tree and runing thence west about 126 / pole along M^r^ MATHEW TOMLINs line to A read oake marked for / A corner tree and from thence south about 126 pole by A line of / marked trees to A Small white oake marked for a corner tree and / from thence Est about 126 pole by a line of marked trees to the / said M^r^ LYSEWELLs line of marked trees and down the said line North / to the first station or marked popler to have and to hold the said one / hunered acures of Land according to the said recited bounds (Excepting / out of the said one hundered and twenty Aceres of y^e^ said land / wich is by deed of gift Conveyed unto JOHN MACKMIALL with / all and Singuler its rights members Juridictions & appurtenances to authenc all houses / Edifices buildings & barnes stables orchards gardings / yards backsides Easments common of pasture heridataments & appurtenances / whatsoever to the said Lands or tenements and premeses or to any part on / parcell of them belonging or in any wise appertaining thereunto / unto the said GEORGE NORSWORTHY Gent his heirs or assignes to the only / proper use and behoofe of the said GEORGE NORSWORTHY Gent his heirs / or assignes for ever against him the said JOHN SMITH his heirs and / asigns and all and every other person and persons whatsoever / Lawfully Claming by from or under them or any of them Shall / and will warrant and for ever defend by these presents and that the / said JOHN SMITH for himself his heirs Executors and administrators / doe covenant promise grant and agree to and with the GEORGE / NORSWORTHY Gent his heirs and assigns and every of them by these / presents that all and Singuler the afforesaid on hundered acres of Land / (except before Excepted) according to the forerecited bounds with all the / apurptenances [*sic*] thereunto belonging now be and ever hereafter / shall be stand and continue to the said GEORGE NORSWORTHY Gent / and his heires and assignes for ever and that y^e^ said GEORGE / NORSWORTHY Gent his heirs or assigns be freely and Clearly acquited / exonerated and discharged and form time to time well and sufficient / kept harmless by the said JOHN SMITH his heirs Executors or / administrators of and from all maner of former and other gifts / grants bagains [*sic*] sailes Leases mortgages Joynters dowers and from all / and singler other titles troubles Charges demands and incumbrances / whatsoever had made committed suffered omitted or done by the said JOHN / SMITH his hers or assignes or by any other person or persons whatsoever and that / the said JOHN SMITH his heirs or assignes for and dureing the space of / sevn yeare Next ensueing the date thereof presents shall and / will at and upon the reasonable request and at the Cost and Charges / in the law of the said GEORGE NORSWORTHY Gent his heirs or / assigns make such further Lawfull and Reasonable assuranc / or assurances or conveyances in the law for the more better and perfect

**[238]**

of the afforesaid premises as by the said GEORGE NORSWORTHY his heirs / his Assignes of by his or there Councell Learned in the law shall / be reasonable devised or advised or requierd and that the afforesaid / premises with all the appurtenances thereunto belonging shall be / Esteemed and Judged and taken to be and annewe to the only proper / use and behoof of the said GEORGE NORSWORTHY Gent his heirs and / assignes for ever and to none other use intent or purpose whatsoever In witnesse / hereof I have hereunto sett my hand and seal the day yeare and / Reign of the first above written

Signed sealed & delivered in y^e^ seal
p^r^sence of us JN^O^ SMYTH O
JOHN GYLES
RICH^D^ REYNOLDS
THO: BO[*blotted*]N

Acknowledged in open Co^rt^ held For y^e^ Isle of Wight County y^e^ 2^d^ day of May 1698 by the said JOHN SMYTH and ordered to be Recorded Test CHA CHAPMAN C^l^ C^ur^

To all to whome these presents shall come I FRANCIS MORYSON / Es^qr^ Govern^r^ and Cap^t^ Gen^ll^ of Virg^a^ Send Greeting in our Lord / God Everlasting Whereas by instruccons from the Kings most / Excellent Ma^ty^ Directed to me & the councell of State his Mai^ty^ / was gratiously pleased to authorise me the said Gove^r^ & Councell to grant / pattents as have bene Usuall heretofore in the like Cases either for / adventuo^rs^ of mony or transportaton of people into this Collony accord [*sic*] / to A Charter of orders form the late Tresurer and compony and y^t^ / there be the same p^r^portion of ffiftie Acers of Land granted and / assigned for every ꝑson transported hirthere [*sic*] Since Midsum^r^ 1625 & / that the Same Course be continued to all adventuro^rs^ and planters / untill it shall be otherwise determined by his Ma^ty^ Now Knowe / yea that I the said FRANCIS MORYSON Esq^r^ &^c^: Doe with the Consent of / of [*sic*] the Councell of State accordingly Give and grant unto M^r^ RICHARD / ISERD three hundered and ffiftie Acers of Land Scituat lieng or being / in the County of y^e^ Isle of Wight begining att A Marked oake and soe / runing West South west 200 poles Joyning to the Land of M^r^ ROBERT / PITT and to A marked tree butting on the Land of THOMAS POOLE / and soe Northerly 320 poles Joyning to the Land of the said POOLE and / butting on the Land of Cap^t^ UPTON now in the occupation / of M^r^ JOSEPH BRIDGER and M^r^ ROBERT BRACEWELL and now East north East / 200 poles Joyning to Cap^t^ UPTONs Land and so againe Southerly / 320 poles to the first mentioned marked tree and Joyning to the / Land of W^M^ LEWIS including or bounding the said Quantity

**[239]**

the said Land being Due unto the said JOHN ISEARD by and for transpor / tation of one person into this Collony whose Names are in the Records / mentioned under the pattent To have and to hold the said Land with / his due share of all Mynes & minerells therein

Conteyned whith all / Rights and prviledges of hunting hawking ffishing and fowleing with all / woods waters and rivers with all profites Comodities and heridataments / whatsoever belonging to the said Land, to him the said M^r^ RICHERD / ISEARD his heires and assignes for ever in as Large and ampell manner / to all intents and purposes as is expressed in a Charter of orders from the / late Tresuerer and company Dated 18^th^ Nove^r^ 1618 or by Consequnce / may be jusly Collected out of the same or out of the Letters pattents / whereon they are grounded To be held of our sovereigne Lord the King / his heires and Successo^rs^ for ever as of his Mano^r^ of East Greenwich / in free and Comon Sonotige [*sic*] and not *in Capite* not by Kn^ts^ service / Yeilding and paying unto our s^d^ Sovereigne Lord the King his heires & / Successo^rs^ for every ffiftie Acers of Land hereby Granted yearly att the / feast of S^t^ Michall the Arkaingell the fee rent of one Shilling [*sic*][13] which / payment is to be made seaven yeares after the Date hereof and not / before according to the said Charter of orders and since confirmed by his / Ma^tys^ instructions, As olsoe by Act of assembly of the Second of March / 1642 Provided that if the said ISARD his hires or assignes Doe not plant or seat / or Cause to be planted or Seated upon the said Land within three yeares / next ensuing, that then it shall be Lawfull: for any adventuro^rs^ or / planter to make Choice & Seat thereupon Given att James Citty / under my hand and the seat of this [--] of the Collony this 20^th^ of / Jenuary: 1661: and in the thirteenth yeare of the Reigne of our / soevereigne Lord the King Charles the second: &c

FRANCIS MORISON
THOMAS LUDWELL

Know all men by these presents y^t^ I WALLTER RUTTER of y^e^ Isle of weight county / w^th^ y^e^ ffree Consent of MARTHA my Wife have bargained & Sold all my right / Tittlle & interest of this within mentioned pattent from me my hieres / Execut^rs^ adm^rs^ and assigns for ever unto JOSEPH BRIDGER his heirs Ex^qrs^ / adm^rs^ & assignes for ever as Wittness our hand seales this Eight of ffebuary / 1697

Signed sealed & delivered — seals
in y^e^ p^r^sent of us — WALTER RUTTER O
TRUSTRAM NOSWORTHY — Her
THOMAS OWEN — MARTHA **M** RUTTER O
marke

Acknowledged in open Court / held For y^e^ Isle of Wight County y^e^ 9^th^ of Aprill 1697 And by vertue of An order of y^e^ 9^th^ / of June 1698 Recorded p me

CHA CHAPMAN C^l^C^ur^

**[240]**

[13] Some later scribal swell cleverly crossed the "ll"s in the word "shilling" to make the obvious obscene, and therefore, meaningful transformation.

To all to whom these presents shall come I FFRANCIS Lord Howard / of Effingham his Mai$^{ties}$ L$^{d}$ & Govener Gen$^{ll}$ of Virg$^{ae}$ send Greeting in / our Lord god Everlasting Whereas his late Maj$^{ty}$ hath been graciously / pleased by his Royall Pattents under y$^{e}$ great seat of England / bearing Date att Wesminster y$^{e}$ tenth Day of October in 28$^{th}$ of this / Reigne amongst other things in y$^{e}$ said Letters Pattents Conteined to / Continue and Confirme y$^{e}$ ancient priviledges & power of / granting ffiftie Acres of Land for every person Imported into his Maj$^{ties}$ / Collony of Virg$^{a}$ Now Know yee y$^{t}$ I the said FFRANCIS Lord Howerd / Govn$^{r}$: &$^{c}$: doe w$^{th}$ y$^{e}$ advise and Cosent [*sic*] of y$^{e}$ Councell state accordingly / give & grant unto WALTER RUTTER one hundered & ffiftie Acers of / Land Between the Land of Coll BRIDGER Coll PITT & THOMAS POOLE / in y$^{e}$ Lower perish of y$^{e}$ Isle Wight County itt being all that / Could be found within a pattent of three hundered & ffiftie Acers / granted to M$^{r}$ RICHARD ISERD y$^{e}$ 20$^{th}$ of of [*sic*] January 1661: y$^{e}$ remainder / being within Elder grants and by y$^{e}$ s$^{d}$ IZARDs last will & testament / dated y$^{e}$ 2$^{nd}$ of May 1669 Given to his two Daughters MARY & MARTHA / MARY Dying both without Issue, & allso before any Division was / made thereof y$^{e}$ whole fell to MARTHA the Now Wife of y$^{e}$ said RUTTER / the said 150 Acers being thus bounded Beginning at A pine Coll / BRIDGERs Corner tree of SEWERDs land in or nere Coll PITTs line / very neere y$^{e}$ fish pond thence by Coll PITTs South ffiftie five deg$^{r}$: West / two hundered & four pole to A white oake Very Neere THOMAS STANTONs / (*als* POOLEs) Corner red oake y$^{n}$ by POOLEs line North North East one / hundered & Eighty pole to A small red Oak [*erased*] / North North West one hundred sixty six pole to A hickery on Turky / hill &$^{c}$ North one hundred twenty six pole to A red oke Saplinn / y$^{e}$ said RUTTERs one corner tree and soe by his one line North East / thirty pole to A red oak Coll BRIDGERs corner tree in s$^{d}$ line and / so by his line south south East three hundred Ninty six pole to y$^{e}$ first / station: To have and to hold y$^{e}$ said Land with his Dew share of all / mines & Mineralls therein Contained with all Rights & priviledges / of hunting Hauking ffishing & ffowlling with all & woods Watters / & Rivers with all profitts Comodities & Heridatatments [*sic*] / whatsoever belonging to y$^{e}$ said Land to him y$^{e}$ Said WALLTTER RUTTER his heirs & / assigns for ever in as large and ample maner to all intents & / purposes as hath been used & allowed sence y$^{e}$ first plantation to be / held of our sovereign lord y$^{e}$ King his heirs & successers [*erased*] / as of his mann$^{r}$ of East Greenwich in free & common soccage and / not *in Capite* nor by Kn$^{ts}$ Service Yeilding and paying unto our / said Soveraigne Lord y$^{e}$ King his heirs & successors for Every ffiftie / Acers of Land hereby Granted att y$^{e}$ feast of S$^{t}$ Michaell y$^{e}$

**[241]**

Arch Angell y$^{e}$ fee reent of one shilling wich payment is to be made / yearly from yeare to yeare according to his Maj$^{ties}$ Instructions of / y$^{e}$ 12$^{th}$ of September 1662 Dated this thirtieth [*erased*] day of october / Anno Dom 1686

Effingham

Know all men by presents y$^{t}$ I WALTER RUTTER with y$^{e}$ free / Consent of MARTHA my wife have sould all my Right Tittle / & interest of this within mentioned pattent from me my heirs / Execut$^{rs}$ adm$^{rs}$ & asignes for Ever unto JOSEPH BRIDGER his heirs / Ex$^{rs}$ adm$^{rs}$ & assignes for ever as wittness our hand & sealles this Eight / day of febuary 1696

Seal

Signed Sealed & Delivered
in y$^{e}$ presents of us
TRUSTRUM NORSWERTHY
THOMAS OWEN

WALTER RUTTER O
her
MARTHA **M** RUTTER O
[--]

Acknowledged in open Co$^{rt}$ houlden For y$^{e}$ / Isle of Wight County y$^{e}$ 9$^{th}$ of Aprill 1697 / and By vertue of an Order of y$^{e}$ 9$^{th}$ of / June 1698

Recorded ꝑ me CHA CHAPMAN C$^{l}$C$^{ur}$

To all to whome these presents may or shall come Know yee that / I WALTER RUTTER and MARTHA my Wife of y$^{e}$ Isle of wight county for / divers good Causes & considerations, Us theire unto moveing more espetially / for & in consideration of twelve thousand pounds of tobacco to us in / hands payd y$^{e}$ Receipt whereof wee acknowledge, have bergained sold / Enfeofe from us our heirs Ex$^{rs}$ adm$^{rs}$: or assignes Unto JOSEPH BRIDGER his / heirs Ex$^{rs}$ adm$^{rs}$, for ever A certaine percell of Land lyeing and / being in y$^{e}$ lower parrish of y$^{e}$ Isle of wight couty [*sic*] called by y$^{e}$ Name / of Herrings plantation wich is Now in y$^{e}$ tenner & occupation of / EDWARD BROWNE & y$^{e}$ said Land is bounded as followeth Viz$^{t}$: / beginning att y$^{e}$ mouth of A Branch w$^{ch}$ is called Herrings / branch wich Runeth into y$^{e}$ mille rune A little above y$^{e}$ cart way / over y$^{e}$ rune & soe up along y$^{e}$ s$^{d}$ branch w$^{ch}$ branch Eastern to y$^{e}$ head of it / Butting one C[ ] JAMES BENNs line wich is y$^{e}$ bounds betwen y$^{e}$ said land / & y$^{e}$ s$^{d}$ RUTTERs dwelling platation [*sic*] & from thence along Cap$^{t}$ BENNs line to a / marked Red oake standeing neare y$^{e}$ Road side butting one y$^{e}$ head of a / ready Branch over y$^{e}$ road w$^{ch}$ runeth Northerly into y$^{e}$ Creeke & soe down / along y$^{e}$ said Branch into y$^{e}$ Creeke & from y$^{e}$ mouth of said Branch / up y$^{e}$ Creek & rune to y$^{e}$ mouth of Herrings Branch over y$^{e}$ Cart path / to y$^{e}$ first Station, wich said plantation & percell of land being by / Estemation about sixty Acers more or less according to y$^{e}$ aforementioned / bounds I y$^{e}$ said WALTER RUTTER & MARTHA my wife doe acknowledge / to have sold unto JOSEPH BRIDGER his heirs Ex$^{rs}$ adm$^{rs}$ & assignes for ever

**[242]**
with all maner of privelidges & apurtenances thereunto belonging of Hawking / hunting fishing & fowling Mines Watters Mineralls woods under woods / as was granted to MARTHA my Wife & MARY her sister by as Escheate / pattent bearing date: 1670: To have & to hold y$^{e}$ said Land w$^{th}$ / all appurtenances thereunto belonging for ever from Us our heirs / Ex$^{rs}$ adm$^{rs}$ or assignes Laying any Clame or interest thereunto or / any person

or persons whatsoever from by or und$^{r}$ us or them / Laying any Clame thereunto as Wittness our hands & Seals this 8$^{th}$ day / of ffebruary: 169$^{6}$/$_{7}$ Seal

Signed Sealed & delivered in WALTER RUTTER O
y$^{e}$ p$^{r}$sence of us by M$^{r}$ RUTTER her
THO: GODWYN MARTHA **M** RUTTER O
EDWARD STREETER Marke
TRUSTRAM NOSWORTHY

Acknowledged by WALTER RUTTER / & MARTHA his Wife in Open Co$^{rt}$ held / For y$^{e}$ Isle of Wight County y$^{e}$ 9$^{th}$ of / Aprill 1697, And by order of y$^{e}$ 9$^{th}$ / of June 1698 Recorded ꝑ me / CHA CHAPMAN C$^{l}$C$^{ur}$

Know all men by presents y$^{t}$ I WALTER RUTTER of y$^{e}$ Isle of wight / county doe acknowledge to owe & am Justly indebted to JOSEPH / BRIDGER his heirs Ex$^{rs}$ adm$^{rs}$ or assignes y$^{e}$ full & Just sum of / Twenty four Thousand pounds of good sound Merchantable tobacco / & Cask to be paid Convenient in y$^{e}$ Isle of wight county upon / demand to y$^{e}$ true performance of y$^{e}$ Same I bind my self my heirs / Ex$^{rs}$ adm$^{rs}$ & assignes feirmely by these presents as Wittness my / hands & seal this Eight day of ffebruary 169$^{6}$/$_{7}$

The Condition of this obligation is such y$^{t}$ For as much as y$^{e}$ above / bound WALTER RUTTER & MARTHA his Wife hath made / saile of two parcells of land Unto JOSEPH BRIDGER his heir$^{rs}$: &$^{c}$: / for ever, one y$^{e}$ s$^{d}$ percells of Land being Three hundered & / fiftie Acers granted of M$^{r}$ RICHARD IZERD by pattent bareing date / Jenuary y$^{e}$ 20$^{th}$ 1661 y$^{e}$ other being parte of an Excheate patttent / Granted to MARTHA y$^{e}$ said WALTERs RUTTERs Wife & MARY hir Sister as by / a coveyance [*sic*] or saile of sixty Acers more or less acording to y$^{e}$ bounds / out of y$^{e}$ Excheate pattent bareing date w$^{th}$ these prescents from under y$^{e}$ hands / & Seales of y$^{e}$ s$^{d}$ WALTER RUTTER & MARTHA his Wife may appeare / Now if y$^{e}$ s$^{d}$ JOSEPH BRIDGER his heirs Ex$^{rs}$ adm$^{rs}$ or assignes doe from / time to time & all times peaceably hold & Quietly Injoy & possess y$^{e}$ / above s$^{d}$ two percells of Land [ ] w$^{ch}$ for every parte & percell theirto belong / ing and all y$^{e}$ appurtenances there w$^{th}$: out any Lett Molestation trrable / or any damages what soever by y$^{e}$ s$^{d}$ WALTER RUTTER his / heirs Ex$^{rs}$ adm$^{rs}$ or assignes or any person or persons whatsoever / from by or uunder [*sic*] us or them or any person otherwise then this

**[243]**

obligation to [be] Voide & of none Effect Ece to remaine in full force / Strength & vertue

Signed Sealed & deliverd Sea[--]
in y$^{e}$ p$^{r}$esents of us WALTER RUTTER O
THO: GODWYN
EDW$^{D}$ STREETER

Acknowledged in open Co$^{rt}$ held For y$^{e}$ isle of / Wight County y$^{e}$ 9$^{th}$ of Aprill 1697: and by / an Order of y$^{e}$ 9$^{th}$ of June 1698 Recorded p me / CHA CHAPMAN C$^{l}$C$^{ur}$

Whereas there is A Marridgee [*sic*] intended between Cap$^{t}$. ROBERT KAE / and M$^{rs}$ ANNE GOODRICH y$^{e}$ Relict of Cap$^{t}$ JOHN GODORICH deced Now / Know all men by these presents that y$^{e}$ said Capt KAE for & in Consider / ation of y$^{e}$ Said Marridge does here by Obledge himself his Heirs / Ex$^{rs}$ & adm$^{rs}$ lands & tenem$^{ts}$ unto FFRANCIS WREN of y$^{e}$ Isle of Wight / County Planter in y$^{e}$ penaltey of fortie thousand pounds of to~~bb~~$^{o}$ / upon Conditon that said ROBERT KAE (If it shall please God he shall / depart this Life before y$^{e}$ said ANNE) Shall make good out of his / said Estate unto y$^{e}$ said ANNE GOODRICH or her Assignes y$^{e}$ sume of twenty / thousand pounds of good To~~bb~~ & Cask to be paid Convenient in y$^{e}$ Isle Wight / County immeadiatly after y$^{e}$ decease of y$^{e}$ said Cap$^{t}$ KAE in Consideracon / of y$^{e}$ said sume of to~~bb~~$^{o}$ All Claime of Dower or of any part of ye / Estate of y$^{e}$ s$^{d}$ Cap$^{t}$ KAE are hereby Release, that being in full of all / Claimes whatsoever that may be demanded by any Law whatsoever / in witnesse whereof y$^{e}$ said ROBERT KAE hath hereunot sett his hand / & Seal this first Day of March 169$^{7}/_{8}$ seal

Sealed in presents of (before y$^{e}$ Said ANNE being first interlined  ROBERT KAE O

his
JOHN **IW** WREN
marke
CARLES [*sic*] CHAPMAN

Acknowledge in Open Co$^{rt}$ houlden For y$^{e}$ Isle of Wight County y$^{e}$ 9$^{th}$ of ffebr 169$^{7}/_{8}$ by y$^{e}$ s$^{d}$ Capt KAE & Recorded p CHA CHAPMAN C$^{l}$C$^{ur}$

Know all men by these prsents that I W$^{M}$ RANDOLPH of Henrico / County in Collony of Virginia Esq$^{r}$ Ex$^{r}$ of M$^{r}$ HUGH DAVIS late of y$^{e}$ / Isle of Wight County in Collony affores$^{d}$ Gen$^{t}$ dated have made ordeyned / & Constituted & by these p$^{r}$sents doe for me my heires Ex$^{rs}$ adm$^{rs}$ / make ordeyne & Constitute RICHERD REYNOLDS of y$^{e}$ Isle of Wight / County afforesaid my true & Lawfull Attorney for me in Name & / to my use to aske demand sue for Levy recover & receive all / & all manner of Debts dues & demands Whatsoever that are due / to me in y$^{e}$ quallity afforesaid from all & every pson or p$^{r}$sons / whatsoever in any manner howsoever & upon Receipt thereof / to give any Release or Releases Discharge or discharges Necessary / and Convenient in y$^{e}$ Law to be given And in Case of Non paym$^{t}$ / to sue for y$^{e}$ Same and into prison to Comitt & from thence to discharge

**[244]**
& Release and in every thing to Act & doe as if I were personally / p$^{r}$sent: And as occasion requires to imploy & impower such other / Attorney or Attorneys under him as he she [*sic*] shall think most & / Convenient Ratifieing & by these presents Conferming whatsoever / my said Attorney shall lawfully doe or Cause to be done in & / about y$^{e}$

premises In witness whereof I hereunto sett my hand & seal this / first day of march Anno Dom 169$^{7}/_{8}$
Seal
Seald & Deliverd
W^M RANDOLPH O
in y^e p^r sents of
HEN BAKER
CHA CHAPMAN

Proved in open Co^rt held For y^e Isle of Wight County y^e 9^th day of Aprill 1698 by both y^e Witnesses & recorded

p CHA CHAPMAN C^l C^ur

Knowne unto all men by these p^r sents y^t JOHN DAY of y^e / Citty of Bristoll Merchant have made assigned ordeyned & Deputes / & in my stead & place by presents put & Constitute my well - / beloved freind HUMPHRY MERSHALL my true & Lawfull Atturny / for me and in my [*sic*] & to my Use to all Leavy recovery & receive / all & Singuler Such Debts Duteys Sums & Sume of tobacco as / are or Shall be Due or owing unto me the said JOHN DAY / by any p^r son or p^r sons whatsoever in Virgi^a: Giveing & / by these p^r sents granting Unto my said Atturny full power / and Authority for me & in my Name & to my use to sue and / implead Condem & Imprison Every of my Debters aforesaid and / att his Liberty and pleasure Such p^r sent & p^s ons out of / Prison to delever or Cause to be delevered & Upon y^e Rec^t of any / Sume or Sumes of to~~bb~~ to my use to be Rece^d of any psons / aforesaid acquittance or other Lawfull discharge for the same / for me & in my stead and Name to Marke seal & delever as my / deed or deeds & one Attorny or more Under him to Make / substitute & Att his free will againe to Revocke & all ev^r y / other thing & things wich Shall be neadfull as nessesary to be done / in or about y^e premeses y^e Same to doe as fully & wholly as I my / self might doe if I were there personally p^r sent holding ferm & / stable all & whatsoever my said Atturny Shall doe or Cause to / be done in or abought y^e premeses in Wittness heareof I have / heareunto sett my hand & seal this: 28^th Day of Aprill 1697
Signed Sealed & Delevered
Seal
in p^r sents of Us
JN^O DAY O
ANTHONY HOLLIDY
ROB^T: BROCK

Proved in open Co^rt held For y^e Isle of Wight County y^e 9^th day of June 1697 & by vertue of an Order of y^e 9^th of June 1698 Recorded by me

CHA CHAPMAN C^l C^ur

**[245]**

By this publick Instrm^t of Procuracon or L^re of Attorney Be it knowne and / manifest unto all people, That on y^e last day of Sept^br 1697 Before me W^M / SCOREY Notary puiblick, admitted & Sworne dwelling in London & in y^e p^r sence / of y^e Witnesses affernamed, personally appeared Cap^t JOHN PURVIS of London / aforesaid Marrin^r, & hath made ordeyned & Constituted & by these p^r sents / doth make ordeyn & Constitute RICHARD WYNN of Nanziman River in Virginia / M^r ch^t his true & Lawfull attorney, Giveing & to him granting Full power / & authority in y$^{e}$ name of y$^{e}$ said Constituant but to & For y$^{e}$ sole use & attorn / of ELIZABETH CARTER of London Widdow, to ask demand sue For recover and / receive of & From THOMAS MOUNTFORT & HENRY JENKINS of Virginia or either / of y$^{m}$ or of their or either Heires Ex$^{rs}$ Adm$^{rs}$ or Estates y$^{e}$ Impost & Contents / of a Certeyn Bill of Exchange dated in Virginia y$^{e}$ Tenth of Janry 1693 / For Seaventeen pounds Eleaven Shillings Sterling payable att twenty / dayes after sight to y$^{e}$ said HENRY JENKINS on Order w$^{ch}$ said THOMAS MOUNTFORT / on M$^{r}$ GEORGE RICHARDES M$^{r}$chant in London, w$^{ch}$ Bill was protested For Non- / paymt by M$^{r}$ NIC$^{O}$ HAYWOOD Notary publick in London y$^{e}$ Nineteenth day of / October 1694 as by y$^{e}$ Protest in that behalfe made may appeare Alsoe / to demand sue For recover & receive of and From HENRY ROYALL of Virginia / aforesaid, and y$^{e}$ said HENRY JENKINS or either of them, or of their or either / of their Heires Ex$^{rs}$ Adm$^{rs}$ [ ]ds or Estate, y$^{e}$ Impost & Contents of a / Certyn Bill of Exch$^{a}$ dated in Virginia the Eighth of Aug$^{t}$ 1693 For / seaven pounds two shillings sterleing payable att Twenty dayes after / sight to y$^{e}$ said HENRY JENKINS or Order, w$^{ch}$ said HENRY JENKINS Endorsed / & sent y$^{e}$ same to y$^{e}$ said Constituant drawne by y$^{e}$ said HENRY ROYALL / on M$^{r}$ JOHN HANFORD M$^{r}$ch$^{t}$ in London, w$^{ch}$ Bill was protested For non / paym$^{t}$ by y$^{e}$ s$^{d}$ M$^{r}$ NICHOLAS HAYWOOD, y$^{e}$ 15$^{eeth}$ day of y$^{e}$ said month of Octob$^{r}$ / 1694 as by y$^{e}$ protest in y$^{t}$ behalfe made may alsoe appear, upon the / recoveryes & receits, to make & give due & sufficient acquittance and / discharge, And if needFull toucheing all other y$^{e}$ p$^{r}$mises to appeare and / y$^{e}$ person of y$^{e}$ said Constituant to represent, in All Co$^{rts}$ & before all / Lords Govn$^{rs}$ Judges & Justices and to ꝑsue implead, Seize, Sequester / attach, arrest imprison & to Condemne, and out of prison againe where / need shall be, to deliver, *Cum Faculte substituendi* And gen$^{r}$all in and / Conceiveing y$^{e}$ p$^{r}$mises & y$^{e}$ dependcs to doe say transact & accomplish / in Judgem$^{t}$ Count as w$^{th}$out, w$^{t}$soever y$^{e}$ s$^{d}$ Constituant himselfe / might or Could doe ꝑsonally, He hereby promiseing to hould and / ratifie For good & Vallid whatsoever his said Attorney or his substitutes / shall lawfully doe or Cause to be done in y$^{e}$ p$^{r}$mises by vertue hereof / In witness whereof the said Constituant hath hereunto put his / hand

**[246]**
The day & year First abovewritten in y$^{e}$ p$^{r}$sence of JOSEPH RUCK / & W$^{M}$ BROOKEHOUSE
Seal
JOHN RUCK JN$^{O}$ PURVIS O
W$^{M}$ BROOKHOUSE

*In Testimonium Veritatis* / GUILL SCOREY Not$^{r}$ pub$^{c}$ / Alsoe sealed & delivered by y$^{e}$ s$^{d}$ Cap$^{t}$ / JN$^{O}$ PURVIS in y$^{e}$ p$^{r}$sence of us

JAMES MORGAN
RICHARD TIBBOTT

Proved in open Co$^{rt}$ held For y$^{e}$ Isle of Wight County / y$^{e}$ 9$^{th}$ day of Aug$^{t}$ 1698 by y$^{e}$ s$^{d}$ TIBBOTT to be y$^{e}$ Act & Deed / of y$^{e}$ said Cap$^{t}$ JN$^{O}$ PURVIS & Ordered to be / Recorded Test CHA CHAPMAN C$^{l}$C$^{ur}$

Know all men by these p$^{r}$sents That I / ROB$^{T}$ RANDALL of Surry County in Virginia doe make / have made ordeyned Constituted & appointed and by these p$^{r}$sents / ordeyn Constitute & appoint HENERY TOOKER of the Same / County in Virginia aforesaid my true & Lawfull Attorney for / me & in my name & for my use to ask demand sue for / recover & receive all Such sume or sumes of Tobacco & mony / as are or shall be due to me in Virginia of & from any ꝑson or / p:$^{r}$sons whatsoever & upon satisfaction & payment of any y$^{e}$ s$^{d}$ / sume or sumes of Tobacco or mony y$^{e}$ said p$^{r}$son or ꝑsons to / acquitt & discharge And allso to bergaine sell or dispose of all & / Singuler my Lands tenem$^{ts}$ & Hereditaments att y$^{e}$ blackwater / in y$^{e}$ County of Surry aforesaid & to convey & assure the Same / in fee Simple to any ꝑson or p:$^{r}$sons willing to make purchase / thereof & Likweise under him to make Constitute & appoynt one / or more Attorny or Attorneyes & att his pleasure againe to / Revoke and make voyd & finally, to Act performe & doe all / & every things & thing Act & Acts that I my self might or Could / doe yf I were personally p$^{r}$sent Rattyfieing Confirming & holding / for firme & effectuall what soever my said Attorney Shall / Lawfully doe or Cause to be done In all & Singuler y$^{e}$ premises In / Testimony wherof I Have hereunto sett my hand & Seal

**[246]**

this thirteenth day of August Anno Doni: 1698 Seal
Signed Sealed and delivered ROBERT RANDALL O
I [*sic*] p$^{r}$sence of Us
A$^{R}$ ALLEN
HENERY BAKER
THO HOLT
JOHN LEES

Proved in Open Co$^{rt}$ held For y$^{e}$ Isle of Wight County the 9$^{th}$ day of Sept$^{r}$ 1698 to be y$^{e}$ Act & Deed of y$^{e}$ said ROBERT RANDALL by HENRY BAKER & JN$^{O}$ LEES and Ordered / to be Recorded / Test CHA CHAPMAN C$^{l}$C$^{ur}$

Whereas WILLIAM SMELLY late of the Isle of Wight County / deceased by his last will and Testament bearing date the / 5$^{th}$: day of August 1689 gave unto his three Sonns, ROB$^{T}$: / LEWIS and JOHN, his land, and y$^{e}$ said JOHN being deceased

Now know all men by these pressents that I LEWIS / SMELLY of the County aforesaid doe for me, my heirs, / Execut$^{rs}$: and administrators make & assinge [*sic*] over unto ROB$^{T}$: / SMELLY all my right title Claime and Interest of, in and / unto, the plantation and houses given unto the said JOHN / SMELLY deceased by my aforesaid father WILLIAM SMELLY in / [ ] & Exchange of land made over this day unto mee by / the said ROBERT SMELLY To have and to hold unto him / the said ROBERT SMELLY his heires Executors and administrat$^{rs}$ / for ever, Together all proffitts, privilidges, Comodities, & Advantages / to same belonging or any manner of way appertaineing, In wittness / whereof I the Said LEWIS SMELLY have hereunto Sett my hand / & Seal this Twenty fifth day of August in the year of o^r Lord God / one thousand Six hundred ninety and Eight Seal

Signed Sealed and delivered LEWIS SMELLY O
in y^e p^rsence of
THO: GILES
JAMES DOUGHTIE
EDWARD BRIAN
ROBERT **RT** HORNEING
his marke
WILLIAM **M** MURFREY
his marke

Acknowledged in open Co^rt held for y^e Isle of Wight Counthy y^e 9^th day of Sept^br 1698 to be his Act & Deed and Ordered to be Recorded
Test CHA CHAPMAN C^lC^ur

**[247] missing**

**[248]**

Whereas WILLIAM SMELLY late of the Isle of Wight County deceased / by his last will and Testament bearing date y^e 5^th: day of August / 16[--] gave unto his three sonns ROBERT, LEWIS, and JOHN his land / and y^e said JOHN being deceased

Now know all men by these p^rsents that I the said ROBERT / SMELLY of y^e County aforesaid Do for mee, my heires, Executors / and Administrators make and assigne over unto LEWIS SMELLY / all my right title Claime and Intrest of in and unto one plantation / houses and parcell of land given unto mee by my father / WILLIAM SMELLY in Exchaing of a parcell of land given by my / ffather unto JOHN SMELLY deceased, begining upon the / Swampe, called the dirty swamp, up as high as the first / long branch, called the Wight March branch to a marked / trees to the head line and soe along the line to the corner / tree of WILLIAM MURFREY and ROGER TARLTON, and from thence / along ROGER TARLTONs line to M^r HENERY PLUMPTONs line to / the Swampe, Together with a small parcell of land Lying / betweene the land given JOHN SMELLY given him by his ffather / and y^e plantation where LEWIS SMELLY now lives, and formerly / purchased by the said W^M SMELLY his heires Males, To have / and to hold unto him the said LEWIS SMELLY his heires, Execu^rs: and / Administrators for ever, Together with all proffitts, priviledges, / Comodities, and Advantages to the same belonging, or any manner / of way appertaineing; In wittness whereof I the said ROBERT / SMELLY have hereunto Sett my hand and Seal this Twenty / fifth day of August in the year of our Lord God One / Thousand Six hundred Ninety and Eight seal

Signed Sealed and delivered ROB^T SMELLY O
in the p^rsence of
The word (given) interlined before
the Sealing and delivery hereof

THO: GILES
JAMES DOUGHTIE
EDWARD BRYAN
ROBERT **RH** HORNEING
his mark
WILLIAM **W** MURFREY
his mark

Acknowledged in Open Co^rt^ held For y^e^ Isle of Wight County y^e^ 9^th^ day of Sept^br^ 1698 & Ordered to be Recorded
Test CHA CHAPMAN C^l^C^ur^

**[249]**

Know all men by these presents that I THOMAS SMITH of y^e^ County / of Surry for & in Consideration of seventeen thous^d^ five hundred / pounds of marchantable tobaccos in caske to me in hand paid & well / and sufficiently secured to be p^d^: by WILL: GOODMAN of y^e^ s^d^: County & w^th^: / w^ch^: I acknowledge my self to be wholly satisfied Have Bargained and / sold and do hereby for me & my Heires for ever Bargained sell and deli / =ver In feeoffeffe [*sic*] Transferr & Confirme unto y^e^ s^d^. WILL: GOODMAN & to his / Heires, & Assignes with all & singular y^e^ Geere, & utensils y^e^ property belong / unto her. All w^ch^: was lately by me purchased of M^r^ ROBERT FFLAKE / late of y^e^ Isle of Weight County deceased and is Scittuate p^t^ in y^e^ upper / parrish of y^e^ s^d^. County & p^t^: in y^e^ County of Surry aboves^d^: & thus / bounded begining at y^e^ mouth of a small branch Issueing into y^e^ mill / Swamp a little below y^e^ s^d^: mill, thence up y^e^ s^d^ mill swamp to y^e^ mouth of a / branch known by y^e^ name of Porters branch, then up that branch to a Cart / path w^ch^: crossing y^e^ s^d^: branch leads to y^e^ s^d^: mill & from thence such a course / to y^e^ head of y^e^ first mentioned branch as will w^th^: y^e^ said branch include / the s^d^: mill and quantity of land. To Have & To Hold the s^d^: two hun= / =dred & fifty acres of land w^th^: y^e^ s^d^ mill thereon standing together with / his due share of all mines & mineralls, therein conteyned and all other Royalties / Privelidges Proffitts, Comodities, & Advantages w^t^soever to y^e^ s^d^: land belonging / or in any wise Appertaineing to him the s^d^: WILL GOODMAN, & to his heires, / Assignes, for ever in as full & Ample manner to all intents & purposes / as I my selfe or y^e^ aboves^d^: M^r^ ROBERT FFLAKE could have enjoyed y^e^ same: / And I doe by these Presents Covenant, promise, declare, and Agree to & w^th^: y^e^ s^d^: / GOODMAN his heires, & Assignes that all & every p^t^ of y^e^ s^d^ land & mill is clear / & free from all & all manner of former & other Bargaines, & sales, Joynture / Mortgages, Judg^ts^: & Executions, and all other manner of Incumbrance w^t^soever / & y^t^ I have at y^e^ time of th'insealing & delivery hereof in & to all & Singular the / p^r^mises a good, pure, and indefeazable estate of inheritance in fee simple / which I hereby transferr & oblige my selfe, Ex^rs^ & Ad^rs^ in y^e^ penall Sume of Thirty / Thousand pounds of good marcht^ble^: tobaccoe in caske payable to y^e^ s^d^ GOODMAN his / Heires & asignes on demand to warrant & defend this my sale of all & singul^r^ / the premises w^th^: their Appurttenances to him y^e^ s^d^. WILL: GOODMAN his Heires / and Assignes for ever against all & all manner of persons w^t^soever when / thereto required will give to him or to any of them such farther & other lawfull / Assurance & assurances, Conveyance & Conveyances of all & singular y^e^ premises as by / his or their learned Councell shall thincke fitt: and in open Court will acknowledge / this deed or instrument of Conveyance together w$^{th}$: ELIZABETH my wifes Relin / quishm$^{t}$ of her right of Dower to y$^{e}$ land herein abovementioned In testimony / of all w$^{ch}$: I have together with ELIZABETH my s$^{d}$ wife hereunto put o$^{r}$ hands & / seals y$^{e}$ first day of August 1698

Testis CHARLES SAVIDGE THO: SMITH
NICHOLAS **N** SESUM ELIZABETH SMITH
Signa

Acknowledged in Open Co$^{rt}$ held For y$^{e}$ Isle of Wight County y$^{e}$ 9$^{th}$ of Aug$^{t}$ 1698 by / THOMAS, SMYTH, & by vertue of y$^{e}$ Power of Attorney Following by ELIZABETH / his Wife & Ordered to be Recorded

Test CHA CHAPMAN C$^{l}$C$^{ur}$

**[250]**

Know all men by These present y$^{t}$: I ELIZABETH SMITH y$^{e}$ wife of / THO: SMITH of Surry County doe by These presents make Appoint & / ordain WILLIAM WILLIAMS of y$^{e}$ affores$^{d}$: County of Surrey my true and / Lawfull Atturney for me and in my stead & place to acknowledge all my Right title / and Intrest of a parcell of Land with a mill and w$^{t}$: other Conveniences / thereto doth Belong. y$^{e}$ s$^{d}$ Land and mill being in y$^{e}$ Isle of Wight County / (Viz$^{t}$:) y$^{e}$ major p$^{t}$ of y$^{e}$ Land, and p$^{t}$ in Surrey County and lately sold by y$^{e}$ s$^{d}$ / THO: SMITH my husband to WILL GOODMAN of y$^{e}$ County of Surrey and / I y$^{e}$ s$^{d}$ ELIZABETH SMITH y$^{e}$ wife of y$^{e}$ s$^{d}$ THO SMITH doe appoint W$^{M}$: WILLIAMS / of y$^{e}$ County of Surry my Lawfull Atturney to Aknowledge all y$^{e}$ abovenamed / Conveniences w$^{th}$: y$^{e}$ Land & Mill to WILL: GOODMAN In y$^{e}$ next Co$^{rt}$: as shall be / held in Isle of Wight County & doe confirm y$^{e}$ same by setting my hand / and Seal to this Letter of Atturney This first day of August 1698

Testis: CHARLES SAVIDGE ELIZABETH **E** SMITH
her mark
NICHLAS **N** SESUM
his mark

Proved in Open Co$^{rt}$ held For y$^{e}$ Isle of Wight County / y$^{e}$ 9$^{th}$ of Aug$^{t}$ 1698 to b$^{e}$ y$^{e}$ Act & deed of y$^{e}$ said / ELIZABETH by both y$^{e}$ witnesses & Ordered to be / Recorded

Test CHA CHAPMAN C$^{l}$C$^{ur}$

Att a Co$^{rt}$ houlden for y$^{e}$ Isle of Wight County y$^{e}$ 9$^{th}$ day of August 1698

p$^{r}$sent

Cap$^{t}$ HENRY APPLEWHAIT } M$^{r}$ GEORGE MOOR} M$^{r}$ ANTHONY HOLLYDAY}
L$^{t}$ Co$^{ll}$: SAMUELL BRIDGER} M$^{r}$ THOMAS GILES} M$^{r}$ HUMPHRY MARSHALL}

Justices

This Co$^{rt}$: (upon y$^{e}$ petition of GEORGE WILLIAMS & JAMES BRAGG paying Lycence / to sell Liquors att Co$^{rts}$: & trayneings) haveing duely Considered y$^{e}$

same, and y$^{t}$ by reason / of y$^{e}$ great distance of some of his Ma$^{ties}$ Justices, & divers other of y$^{e}$ Inhatibants, some / reasonable refreshm$^{t}$: is very needfull, & to avoid y$^{e}$ many disorders y$^{t}$ have been, & may be / comitted, by Multiplicity of subtellors & others bringing too much Liquors to such / publick places, doe thinck fitt to Order & it is hereby Ordered, y$^{t}$ y$^{e}$ Clerk doe forthw$^{th}$: / make out a Lycence to be signed by y$^{e}$ Judge of this Co$^{rt}$. to y$^{e}$ s$^{d}$ pet$^{rs}$: to sell / Liquors att y$^{e}$ places aboves$^{d}$:, & Cakes, & other reasonable accomodations, they / payeing his Ex$^{ncys}$ dues: & not permitting any Enormityes to be Comitted by selling / in tyme of y$^{e}$ Co$^{rt}$: sitting or otherwise to any person, or persons, beyond w$^{t}$. may be / for reasonable refreshm$^{t}$, under payn of forfeiting y$^{e}$ liberty hereby granted, and / incurring such further penaltyes as by Law are to be inflicted, And it is Ordered / y$^{t}$ noe other persons p$^{r}$sume to sell drink att any of y$^{e}$ said places, under / penalty of being proceeded ag$^{st}$: according to Law

Test CHA CHAPMAN C$^{l}$C$^{ur}$

**[251]**

By vertue of y$^{e}$ order above mentioned & under y$^{e}$ restrictions therein conteyned y$^{e}$ s$^{d}$ / GEORGE WILLIAMS & JAMES BRAGG are Lycenced hereby & impowered to being & sell / any liquors all y$^{e}$ places above specified, given under my hand this 9$^{th}$ day of 7$^{ber}$ 1698

HEN: APPLEWHAITE

This Indenture made y$^{e}$ one and Twentieth day of March in y$^{e}$ year of our Lord one / thous$^{d}$ six hundred Ninety Eight between JOHN HALL of y$^{e}$ one party & WILL: GREEN of / y$^{e}$ other partie Witnesseth, y$^{t}$ I y$^{e}$ afores$^{d}$ JOHN HALL w$^{th}$: y$^{e}$ consent of my father in Law / & Mother doo hereby Coven$^{t}$. to & w$^{th}$: y$^{e}$ afores$^{d}$ WILL GREENE or his heires to serve him or / them y$^{e}$ full terme of fower yeares from y$^{e}$ date of this present Indenture, full to be / compleated & ended; in y$^{e}$ trade or trades of a Cordwinder, *als* Shooemaker & tanner, faithfully / & truely to y$^{e}$ utmost of my endeavour & ability not purloining or Imbexeling [*sic*] any of my / afores$^{d}$: Masters or his heirs goods by rioting or keeping companie w$^{th}$ lewd or vile persons or / Unlawfull gameing nor making y$^{e}$ secrets of my occupation known to any w$^{th}$: y$^{e}$ consent of my / afores$^{d}$ Master or his heirs during y$^{e}$ afores$^{d}$ terme of servitude neither to enter into y$^{e}$ state of / Matrimony or Commit carnall coppulation nor to absent my self from my afores$^{d}$. Masters / house or his heirs house with either of their consents during y$^{e}$ s$^{d}$ terme

And I y$^{e}$ afores$^{d}$ W$^{M}$. GREENE doe for me & my heirs coven$^{t}$ to & w$^{th}$: y$^{e}$ afores$^{d}$. JN$^{O}$: HALL, to teach in / y$^{e}$ afores$^{d}$: trade of a Cordwinder, *als* Shooemaker, & tanner either by my self or my procurement, / to y$^{e}$ utmost of my endeavour, & ability & to imploy him wholly & soley in y$^{e}$ afores$^{d}$: trade / of a Cordwinder *als* Shooemaker, & tanner, excepting to make provision or any other imploy / =ment usuall, & customary for a prentice to doe & I y$^{e}$ afores$^{d}$ term of servitude to / finde for in sickness & in health during y$^{e}$ afores$^{d}$. terme of servitude & all y$^{e}$ expiration of y$^{e}$ afores$^{d}$ terme of servitude,

& to give a new suit of apparell, to white shirts, & a paire of shooes / & stockings, a new hatt, a Seat of working Gear as Journymen shooemakers use to have / to w^ch^: y^e^ s^d^ Indenture wee y^e^ aforesaid parties have hereunto set our hands & seale y^e^ day and / year abovewritten

Signed sealed & delivered
in y^e^ p^r^sence of
W^M^: SAYWELL
GEORGE GREEN

y^e^ mark of
JOHN I HALL
WILLIAM GREEN

Att A Co^rt^ here under For y^e^ Isle of Wight County y^e^ 9^th^ / day of Aprill 1698 the said ꝑties attended in Court & y^e^ / Indenture being read, ordered y^e^ s^d^ HALL doe serve y^e^ / tearme in y^e^ indenture menconed and that y^e^ same be / Recorded

Test CHA CHAPMAN C^l^C^ur^

**[252]**

Be it knowne unto all men by these presents y^t^ I JOHN GOODRICH sen^r^: w^th^ y^e^ / consent of my wife REBECAH for divers good causes & considerations me hereunto / moveing doe make over unto my son CHARLES GOODRICH & y^e^ male heirs of his body / a firme deed of gift of one hundred acres of land lying & being in y^e^ County of y^e^ / Isle of Wight & upon y^e^ first branch of blackwater & bbging [*sic*] on y^e^ west side of / y^e^ s^d^ branch along FFRANCIS ENGLANDs line into y^e^ woods to y^e^ utmost bounds of y^e^ / s^d^ land & up y^e^ s^d^ branch towards y^e^ Chinkapin neck, w^ch^: s^d^ land I JOHN GOODRICH / sen^r^: w^th^ y^e^ consent of my wife REBECKAH. doe freely & volantary make over y^e^ / s^d^. land w^th^ all priviledges & profitts as is granted by pattent unto my s^d^ son CHARLES & his / male heirs afores^d^: peaceably & quiettly for ever to enjoy ffurther we y^e^ s^d^. JOHN & / REBECKAH Doe obleige o^r^selves freely & vollantary to aknowledge y^e^ same in / open Co^rt^. either o^r^selves or by an Attorney to y^e^ true performance hereof we / have hereunto sett o^r^. hands & seals this thirteenth of 7^ber^. one thous^d^ six hundred / ninety three

Signed, sealed, & delivered
in y^e^ p^r^sence of us
NICHOLAS PASFEILD
y^e^ mark
**FR**
FFRAN: of RAYNER
JOSEPH FFORD

signum
JOHN I GOODRICH
senior
Signum
REBECKAH **R** GOODRICH

Acknowledged in open Co^rt^ / held For y^e^ Isle of Wight County y^e^ 9^th^ / day of June 1698, by y^e^ said REBECKAH the s^d^ JN^O^ / being dead & ordered to be Recorded

T: CHA CHAPMAN C^l^C^ur^

Isle of Wight County

I y$^{e}$ subscriber doe hereby Testifie & declare upon oath to y$^{e}$ best of my remem= / brance five or six & twenty years agoe I was summoned by y$^{e}$ Sheriff / of this County on a Jury of escheat to meet att y$^{e}$ house of Coll: JOSEPH BRIDGER / lately deced w$^{ch}$ was to finde whither a parcell of land belonging to Cap$^{t}$: JOHN UPTON / lately deced did Escheat to his Majesty or not [--] / w$^{ch}$ was to y$^{e}$ best of my remembrance Eight hundred & fifty acres [--] / lying & being in a place Called y$^{e}$ white march in the County y$^{e}$ Jurors being sworne / & in those times y$^{e}$ custom was to goe on y$^{e}$ very land then to be tryed y$^{e}$ s$^{d}$ Coll / JOSEPH BRIDGER did request y$^{e}$ Jurors to walk out w$^{th}$ him saying y$^{u}$ are not upon / y$^{e}$ land & if you will walke along w$^{th}$ me, or to y$^{e}$ purpose I will shew you y$^{e}$ land, / w$^{ch}$: accordingly we y$^{e}$ Jurors did proseed and when wee came to a parcell of pare / trees, standing between y$^{e}$ s$^{d}$: house, & a branch between y$^{e}$ s$^{d}$ house & where JOHN / GOODWIN formerly lived. y$^{e}$ s$^{d}$ Coll JOSEPH BRIDGER tolde y$^{e}$ Jury y$^{t}$ & y$^{t}$ was y$^{e}$ / land, which upon y$^{t}$: y$^{e}$: Jury proceeded, & found it to Escheat to his Majesty / and further sayeth not.

RICH$^{D}$ REYNOLDS

Sworne in open Co$^{rt}$ y$^{e}$ 9$^{th}$ Aprill 1698 / Test CHA CHAPMAN C$^{l}$C$^{ur}$

**[253]**

Know all men by these presents that I JOHN NEVILL of Nanzemond / County for & in Consideration of Eight thous$^{d}$ P$^{ds}$ of Tobaccoe paid down / in hand the receipt whereof I doe aknowledge to have received, have Bar= / gained, sold, sold [*sic*], allienated, made over, & doth hereby Grant, sell Allien, & / deliver unto M$^{r}$ JN$^{O}$: JOHNSON of y$^{e}$ County afores$^{d}$ to him, his heires, Ex$^{rs}$, & / Adm$^{rs}$: or Assignes one hundred Acres of land scituated, Lying, & being in the / Isle of Wight County upon the westerne Branch of Nanzemond River & opposit / to an old Indian towne Bounded as may appeare more att Large by Pattent for y$^{e}$ / s$^{d}$ land Granted by y$^{e}$ hon$^{ble}$: y$^{e}$ Gov$^{r}$ to HENERY BRADLEY datted y$^{e}$ sixth of March / 1664 & by y$^{e}$ s$^{d}$ HENERY BRADLEY sold, & assigned to me y$^{e}$ second of feb$^{r}$. 1663 & / acknowledged in Nanzemond County Court y$^{e}$ 12$^{th}$ of y$^{e}$ aboves$^{d}$ feb$^{r}$. as may appear by / a testimony Given by y$^{e}$ Clerke of y$^{e}$ Court on y$^{e}$ pattent afores$^{d}$. To have, & To / hold y$^{e}$ aboves$^{d}$ hundred acres of land w$^{th}$: all y$^{e}$ appertinances thereto belonging / both housen [*sic*], orchards, woods, pasture & all Priveledges, Rights, Profitts & / hereditam$^{ts}$ thereto Belonging to y$^{e}$ aboves$^{d}$ M$^{r}$. JOHN JOHNSON & his heires Ex$^{rs}$ / & Adm$^{rs}$, or Assignes for ever. From me, my Heires, Ex$^{rs}$, & Adm$^{rs}$ in as full & / ample manner as I my selfe Ever Possest, or Enjoyd y$^{e}$ same & I doth hereby / oblige my selfe my heires, Ext$^{rs}$. & Adm$^{rs}$, in y$^{e}$ Penall forfeiture of sixteen / thous$^{d}$ p$^{ds}$ of Good Tobaccoe Payable convenient in Nanzemond County / upon demand to M$^{r}$. JOHN JOHNSON his heires, Ext$^{rs}$ &$^{c}$: to save, & defend y$^{e}$ aboves$^{d}$ / M$^{r}$. JOHN JOHNSON his heires, Ext$^{rs}$ & Adm$^{rs}$, or Assignes harmeless from any / Claims, title, or Intrest, y$^{t}$ may, or shall be made, or Pretented to be made to y$^{e}$ / aboves$^{d}$ land, By any Person or Persons w$^{t}$soever, & also to Confirme this / above sale of land By makeing acknowledgement both my self & ELIZABETH my / wife in open Co$^{rt}$: in y$^{e}$ Isle of

Wight County y^e^ next Co^rt^: after y^e^ date hereof wittness / my hand, seale this 9^th^: day of August 1698

Signed, sealed, & delivered in y^e^ p^r^sence of Us
JOHN GILES
HENEREY **H** BULLARD
his mark
HUGH CAMBELL

JOHN NEVILL
ELIZABETH **EN** NEVILL
her mark

Acknowledged in open Co^rt^ held For y^e^ Isle of Wight County / y^e^ 9^th^ day of Aug^t^ 1698, by the said JOHN NEVILL / & ELIZABETH his Wife & Ordered to be Recorded
Test CHA CHAPMAN C^l^C^ur^

**[254]**

This Indenture made y^e^ eighth day of June in y^e^ year of o^r^: Lord God one Thous^d^ six / hundred ninety eight; & in y^e^ tenth year of y^e^ Reign of o^r^ Soveraigne Lord William by y^e^ / Grace of God King of England, Scotland, France, & Ireland, &^c^: Between RICH^D^ / REYNOLDS senior of y^e^ lower ꝑish of y^e^ Isle of Wight County of ^y^e one part; & RICH^D^ / REYNOLDS Junior of y^e^ s^d^ ꝑish, & County of y^e^ other part: Wittnesseth y^t^ y^e^ s^d^ RICH^D^ / REYNOLDS Sen^r^: for and in Consideration of y^e^ sume of thirteen thous^d^ p^ds^ of Tob^o^ to him / in hand, at, & before y^e^ Sealing, & delivery of these p^r^sents by y^e^ s^d^ RICH^D^ REYNOLDS jun^r^: / well, & truely p^d^ y^e^ Receipt whereof he y^e^ s^d^ RICH^D^ REYNOLDS Sen^r^: doth hereby acknow= / ledge & himselfe therew^th^ fully sattisfied, & p^d^, & thereof & of every part, & parcell thereof doth / clearly acquit, exonerate, and discharge y^e^ s^d^ RICH^D^ REYNOLDS junior his heirs, Ex^rs^: & / Adm^rs^: for ev^r^: by these presents: hath given, granted, Alien'd, bargained, sold, effeoffed & / Confirmed: And by these p^r^sents; doth fully, clearely, & absolutely, give, grant, bargaine, / sell, & feoffe & Confirm unto y^e^ s^d^ RICH^D^ REYNOLDS Junior his heirs, & assignes for ev^r^: / one parcell, or tract of Land Contained in a patten for three hundred & eighty acres granted / by y^e^ Honourable S^r^ HENERY CHICHLEY Governour & bearing date y^e^ twenty third of / Aprill 1681 Scituate, lyeing & being in y^e^ parrish & County afores^d^ now in y^e^ tennure, occupation of / EDWARD GOODSON WILLIAM WEST, & JOHN TYLER & y^e^ afores^d^ RICH^D^ REYNOLDS, Senior / bounded as followeth begining att a marked Hickery on y^e^ lower bay creeke side / being Coll ARTHUR SMITHs uppermost corner tree thence North fifty nine degrees / West 320 pole to a Hickery; thence South West by South 100 pole to an ash Standing / on y^e^ North West side of WESTs freshett thence down y^e^ run of y^e^ s^d^ freshett to y^e^ / lower bay Creeke & soe down y^e^ s^d^ Creeke to y^e^ first station; To have & to hold y^e^ s^d^ / parcell, or tract of Land according to y^e^ fores^d^ bounds w^th^ all & singular its rights, / members, Jurisdictions, and Appurtenances together w^th^ all houses, edifices, buildings, / barnes stables, orchards, gardens, yards; backesides, easmen^ts^ Common of pasture, / heridatem^ts^, Appurtinances w^t^soever to y^e^ s^d^ Messuages, or tenements, & premises / or to any part, or parcell of them belonging or in anywayes appertaining thereunto / unto y^e^ s^d^ RICH^D^ REYNOLDS Junior his heires, or assignes to y^e^ onely proper use & / behoof of y$^{e}$ s$^{d}$ RICH$^{D}$ REYNOLDS Junior his heires & assignes for ever, against / him y$^{e}$ s$^{d}$ RICH$^{D}$ REYNOLDS Senior his heires, & assignes & all & every other / person & persons whatsoever lawfully claiming by, from, or under him, them, / or any of them shall & will warrant, & for ever defend by these presents; And y$^{t}$ / y$^{e}$ s$^{d}$ RICH$^{D}$ REYNOLDS Senior for himselfe, his heires, Ex$^{rs}$; & Adm$^{rs}$ doe Covenant / promise, grant, & agree to, & w$^{th}$ y$^{e}$ s$^{d}$ RICH$^{D}$ REYNODLS Junior his heirs, & assignes / & every of them by these presents y$^{t}$ all & singuler the fores$^{d}$ three hundred & / eighty acres of land according to y$^{e}$ before recited bounds w$^{th}$ all y$^{e}$ Appurtinances / thereunto belonging Now by & ever hereafter shall be stand & continue to y$^{e}$ s$^{d}$ / RICH$^{D}$ REYNOLDS Junior and his heirs, & Assignes for ever; & y$^{t}$ y$^{e}$ s$^{d}$ RICH$^{D}$ / REYNOLDS Junior his heirs, or Assignes be freely & clearely acquited, exsonerated / & discharged, & from time to time well & sufficiently kept harmless by y$^{e}$ s$^{d}$

**[255]**

RICH$^{D}$ REYNOLDS senior his heires, Ex$^{rs}$ or Adm$^{rs}$ of & from all & all manner / of former & other gifts, grants, bargaines, sailes, leases, mortgages, Joyntures, / dowers of & from all & singular other titles, troubles, charges, demands, & incumberances / whatsoever had made, Committed, suffered, omitted, or done by y$^{e}$ s$^{d}$ RICH$^{D}$ REYNOLDS / senior his heires, or Assignes or by any other person or persons w$^{t}$soever And y$^{t}$ y$^{e}$ s$^{d}$: / RICH$^{D}$ REYNOLDS senior his heires or assignes for & during y$^{e}$ space of seven years / next ensueing y$^{e}$ date of these presents shall & will at & upon y$^{e}$ reasonable request / & att y$^{e}$ Cost & Charges in y$^{e}$ law of y$^{e}$ s$^{d}$ RICH$^{D}$ REYNOLDS Junior his heires, or / Assignes made such further lawfull & reasonable assurance, or assurances, or Convey= / =ances in y$^{e}$ law for y$^{e}$ more better, & perfect assurance of y$^{e}$ affores$^{d}$ premisses / w$^{th}$ all y$^{e}$ appurtinances as by y$^{e}$ s$^{d}$ RICH$^{D}$ REYNOLDS his heirs, or assignes or by his / or their Councell learned in y$^{e}$ laws shall be reasonably devised, advised, or required, / & y$^{t}$ y$^{e}$ afores$^{d}$ premisses w$^{th}$ all y$^{e}$ appurtinances thereunto belonging shall be / esteemed & Judged & taken to be & ennure to y$^{e}$ only proper use & behoofe of y$^{e}$ / s$^{d}$ RICH$^{D}$ REYNOLDS Junior his heirs & assignes for ever & to another use / intent or purposes w$^{t}$soev$^{r}$: in wittness hereof I have hereunto sett my hand & / Seale y$^{e}$ day, years, & Reign, [ ] abovewritten

Signed, sealed, & delivered in the p$^{r}$sence of us whose names are under Written — RICH$^{D}$ REYNOLDS

FFRANCIS + FFLOYD his mark
JOHN **X** BUTLER his mark
RICH$^{D}$ **R** WOOTTON his mark

Acknowledged in open Court held For y$^{e}$ Isle / of Wight County y$^{e}$ 9$^{th}$ day of Aug$^{t}$ 1698 / by M$^{r}$ RICH$^{D}$ REYNOLDS his Wife Consenting in Co$^{rt}$ & Recorded
p CHA CHAPMAN C$^{l}$C$^{ur}$

Know all men by these prsents that I ARTHUR SMITH of y$^{e}$ Isle of Wight / County Doe give, grant, make over, & confirm unto ROB$^{T}$ BROCK fifty acres / of Land lying & being in y^e Isle of Wight County being part of five hundred / acres of Land formerly taken up by EDMUN BARR [--] and Called by y^e name / of y^e timber purcotion the s^d fifty acres of Land is on y^e Norrwest End of y^e / s^d five hundred acres of Land to have & to hold y^e afores^d fifty acres of Land / unto ROB^T BROCK for ever with all profitt thereunto belonging as / wittness my hand & seale this 9^th of September 1698

seale

HEN: APPLEWHAITE J^r AR: SMITH O

RICH^D REYNOLDS

Acknowledged in Open Co^rt held For y^e Isle of Wight / County y^e 9^th of Sep^tr 1698

Recorded ꝑ CHA CHAPMAN C^lC^ur

**[256]**

This Indenture made y^e ninth day of June in y^e yeare of o^r: Lord God / one Thous^d six hundred ninty eight And in y^e tenth yeare of y^e Reign of / o^r: Soveraign Lord William by y^e grace of God of England, Scotland, france / & Ireland King &c: between RICH^D REYNOLDS Junior of y^e lower parrish / of y^e Isle of Wight County of y^e one part; And RICH^D REYNOLDS Sen^r. of / y^e s^d parish & County of y^e other part; Wittnesseth y^t y^e s^d RICH^D REYNOLDS / Jun^r for & in Consideration of the sum of Three thous^d p^ds of tob^o to him / in hand at & before y^e sealing, & delivery of these pressents by y^e s^d RICH^D / REYNOLDS sen^r well, & truly p^d y^e receipt whereof he y^e s^d RICH^D REYNOLDS / Jun^r: doth hereby aknowledge & himselfe therewith fully sattisfied & p^d & / thereof. & of every part & parcell thereof doth clearly acquit exonerate & / discharge y^e s^d RICH^D REYNOLDS Senior his heirs, Ex^rs. & Adm^rs. for ev^r by these prsents / hath given, granted, Alien'd, sold, enfeofed, & Confirmed, And by these p^rsents doth / fully, Clearly, & absolutely give, grant, bargain, sell, enfeoff, & Confirm unto y^e s^d / RICH^D REYNOLDS Sen^r. his heirs, & Assignes for ever one parcell or tract of l^d Containing / by estimation 100 acres more or less scituate, lying, & being in y^e ꝑish & County afores^d / Contained in A patten of three hundred & eighty acres of Land beareing date y^e twenty / third day of Aprill 1681 w^ch patten was granted to y^e s^d RICH^D REYNOLDS sen^r & lately / purchased by me. The land herein Convayed is bounded as foloweth, begining att / A marked Pine standing upon y^e side of a hill at y^e head of A branch w^ch. comes / out of y^e freshett Swamp called Wests freshett thence along a line of marked / trees by us marked runing near North East unto a stooping Read Oak a line / tree in Coll ARTHUR SMITHs line; Thene North 59 degrees West along y^e s^d / line of Coll SMITHs unto Hickery being a corner tree of y^e s^d patten, thence / South West & by South Along a line of Marked trees it being y^e head line of / y^e s^d patten w^ch parts this land from y^e land of CHARLES DRIVER unto a / marked Ash by y^e freshett Swamp side; thence down y^e s^d Swamp unto / the mouth of y^e first mentioned Branch; thence up the s^d branch unto y^e / fores^d Pine it being y^e first station. To Have & to hold y^e fores^d parcell or / or tract of l^d according to y^e fores^d bounds w^th. all & singular its rights /

members, Jurisdictions, & appurtainances, together w$^{th}$ all houses, edifices / buildings, barnes, stables, orchards, gardens, yards, backsides, easments, / Common of pasture, hereditaments, & appurtinances w$^{t}$soever to y$^{e}$ s$^{d}$ / messuag, or tenem$^{t}$, premisses or to any part or parcell of them belonging / or in any wise appertaining thereunto unto y$^{e}$ s$^{d}$ RICH$^{D}$ REYNOLDS Sen$^{r}$.

**[257]**
His heirs, and assignes for ever; against him y$^{e}$ s$^{d}$ RICH$^{D}$ REYNOLDS Jun$^{r}$ his / heirs, & assignes & all & every other person & persons w$^{t}$soever lawfull / Claiming from, by, or under them, them, or any of them shall & will warr$^{t}$: / & for ever defend by these presents: And that y$^{e}$ s$^{d}$ RICH$^{D}$ REYNOLDS Jun$^{r}$ for / himselfe his heirs, Ex$^{rs}$. & Adm$^{rs}$. doe Coven$^{t}$. promise, grant, & agree to & with y$^{e}$ s$^{d}$ / RICH$^{D}$ REYNOLDS Sen$^{r}$. his Heirs, & assignes & every of them by these presents / that all & singular y$^{e}$ fores$^{d}$ one hundred acres of land more or less according / to y$^{e}$ before recited bounds with all y$^{e}$ appurtinances thereunto belonging now be [*sic*] / & ever hereafter shall be stand, & continue to y$^{e}$ s$^{d}$ RICH$^{D}$ REYNOLDS sen$^{r}$ & his / heires & assignes for ever & y$^{t}$ y$^{e}$ s$^{d}$ RICH$^{D}$ REYNOLDS Sen$^{r}$ his heires or assignes / be freely & clearly acquited, exonerated, & discharged & from time to time well & / suficiently saved harmless by y$^{e}$ s$^{d}$ RICH$^{D}$ REYNOLDS Junior his heirs, Ex$^{rs}$, & / or Adm$^{rs}$: of & from all & all manner of former and other gifts grants, bargains, / sailes, Leasess, demands, & incumbrances whatsoever had made Committed, suffered / omited or done by y$^{e}$ s$^{d}$ RICH$^{D}$ REYNOLDS Junior his Heires, or Assignes or by any / other person or persons whatsoever. And that y$^{e}$ s$^{d}$ RICH$^{D}$ REYNOLDS Junior his / Heirs or assignes for & during y$^{e}$ space of seven yeares next ensueing y$^{e}$ date of / these presents shall, & will att & upon y$^{e}$ reasonable request, & at y$^{e}$ Cost, & charges / in y$^{e}$ Lane of y$^{e}$ s$^{d}$ RICH$^{D}$ REYNOLDS Senior his heires or assignes make such furth$^{r}$ / lawfull & reasonable assurance or assurances or Conveyances in y$^{e}$ law for y$^{e}$ more / better & perfect assurance of y$^{e}$ afores$^{d}$ premises as by y$^{e}$ s$^{d}$ RICH$^{D}$ REYNOLDS his / hiers or assignes or by his or their Councell learned in y$^{e}$ laws shall be reasonably / devised, advised or required & that y$^{e}$ afores$^{d}$ premises w$^{th}$ all y$^{e}$ appurtainances / thereunto belonging shall be esteemed, & Judged & taken to be & ennure to y$^{e}$ / only proper use & behoof of y$^{e}$ s$^{d}$ RICH$^{D}$ REYNOLDS senior his heires & assigsnes / for ever And to noe other use intent or purpose w$^{t}$soever: In wittness hereof I / have hereunto sett my hand & seal the day yeare & Reign first above written. Seal
Signed, sealed & delivered in y$^{e}$ presence of us RICH$^{D}$ REYNOLDS jun$^{r}$ O
whose names are underwritten
FFRANCIS + FFLOYD his mark
JOHN **x** BUTLER his mark
RICH$^{D}$ **R** WOOTTEN his mark

Acknowedged in open Co$^{rt}$ held For y$^{e}$ Isle of Wight / County y$^{e}$ 9$^{th}$ day of Aug$^{t}$ 1698 by M$^{r}$ RICHARD / REYNOLDS; his wife Consenting in Co$^{rt}$ & Recorded
p CHA CHAPMAN C$^{l}$C$^{ur}$

**[258]**

To all to Whom these p^r^sents shall Come I S^r^ EDMOND / ANDROS Kn^t^ his Ma^ties^: Lieu^t^. & Govern^r^: Gen^r^all of Virginia send Greeting / Whereas his late Ma^ties^. King Charles y^e^ 2^d^. hath been Graciously pleased / by his Royall letters Pattents Under y^e^ great Seale of England beareing / date at Westminster y^e^ 10^th^ day of Octob^r^ in y^e^ Eight & twentieth year of his / Reign. Amongst other things in y^e^ s^d^ Letters Pattents Contained to Continue & / Confirme y^e^ Antient priveldge & power of granting fifty Acres of l^d^ for every / person Imported into this Colony of Virginia Now Know yee / that I y^e^ s^d^ S^r^ EDMOND ANDROS Kn^t^ Govern^r^: &c: doe with y^e^ / Consent & advice of y^e^ Councell of State Accordingly give & grant / unto Cap^t^ HUGH CAMPBELL three hundred & eighty Acres of l^d^ Scituate / lying & being in y^e^ Isle of Wight County begining at a marked Spanish / Oake at y^e^ head of a parcell of Land formerly taken up by GYLES DRIVER / Soe runing SE by S two hundred & forty poles unto a marked white oake / nigh unto Parson BROICESWELLs Land from thence SW by West three / hundred & sixty poles to a Marked red oake from thence parallel from y^e^ / first line Ninety Eight poles upon y^e^ head of AMBROSS BENNETTs Divid^t^ / of land for Eleven hundred & fifty acres from thence along y^e^ head or / Miles End of y^e^ s^d^ BENNETTs Divident of land and along y^e^ s^d^ DRIVERs / parcell of Land formerly taken three hundred & ninety poles to y^e^ / first station or Marked Spanish Oake. The s^d^ three hundred & Eighty / Acres of L^d^ being y^e^ part Added in a patent for Nine hundred & thirty / Acres granted to GILES DRIVER by Patent Dated the 29^th^ of Septemb^r^ / 1674 & by him deserted, & since granted Unto y^e^ s^d^ Cap^t^ HUGH / CAMPBELL by Ord^r^ of y^e^ Gen^r^all Co^rt^. bearing date y^e^ 24^th^ day of octob^r^ / 1695, & if further due by & for y^e^ Importation of Eight persons into / this Collony all whose Names are to be in y^e^ Records Mentioned und^r^. this / Patent. To have and to hold y^e^ s^d^ Land with his due / share of all Mines and Mineralls therein Contained with all / rights & priveledges of Hunting, Hawking, fishing, & fowling w^th^ all woods wat^rs^ & / rivers withall

**[259]**

proffits, Comodities & Heridetam^ts^ W^t^soever belonging to y^e^ said Land / to him y^e^ s^d^ Capt HUGH CAMPBELL his heires & assignes for Ev^r^, / in as large & Ample Manner to all intents & purposes as hath been / used & allowed Since y^e^ first plantation. To Bee held / of o^r^ Soveraign Lord the King his heires & success^rs^ as of his man= / ner of East Greenwich in free & comon Soccage & not *in capite* / not by Kn^ts^ Service Yeilding and paying unto o^r^ / s^d^ Soveraign Lord the King his heires & success^rs^ for / every fifty Acres of Land hereby granted at y^e^ feast of Saint Michael / y^e^ Archangell y^e^ fee rent of one shilling which paym^t^ is to be made / yearly from yeare to yeare provided that if y^e^ s^d^ Cap^t^ HUGH / CAMPBELL his heires or assignes doe not Seat or plant Nor cause to be / Seated or planted thereon within three yeares next ensueing y^e^ date / hereof that then it shall & may be Lawfull for any Adventurer / or planter to maker choice thereof & seat

This Indenture made this 19$^{th}$ day of Sept$^{br}$ 1698 betwixt HUGH CAMPBELL of Norfolk / County of y$^{e}$ one part & OWEN BURNE of Isle of Wight County on y$^{e}$ other part / wittnesseth y$^{e}$ s$^{d}$ HUGH CAMPBELL for & in Consideration of four thous$^{d}$ p$^{ds}$ / of Tob$^{o}$ to him in hand paid before y$^{e}$ signing & sealing hereof by y$^{e}$ s$^{d}$ OWEN / BURNE y$^{e}$ receit whereof y$^{e}$ s$^{d}$ HUGH CAMPBELL doth hereby acknowledge / & therefore doth acquit & discharge y$^{e}$ s$^{d}$ OWEN BURN his heirs Ex$^{rs}$ & Adm$^{rs}$ / for ever & by these presents have given, granted, Alinated, sold, & confirmed / & by these presents doth fully, clearly, & absolutely, give, grant, bargain, sell, / & for ever confirm unto y$^{e}$ s$^{d}$ OWEN BURN his heires & assignes for ever one / parcell of Land containing two hundred Acres of Land scituate, lying, & being / on y$^{e}$ main Blackwater in Isle of Wight County being part of an Escheat / Patten for thirteen hundred & eleven Acres of land granted to y$^{e}$ s$^{d}$ HUGH / CAMPBELL beareing date y$^{e}$ 21$^{st}$ of Aprill 1695 begining upon blakwater / runing up into y$^{e}$ woods a mile upon RICH$^{D}$ BRASELLS branch or on y$^{e}$ / branch betwixt y$^{e}$ s$^{d}$ HUGH CAMPBELL & y$^{e}$ s$^{d}$ RICH$^{D}$ BRASSELL & so running / such a breadth as will make two hundred Acres so running a mile back again / to y$^{e}$ main swamp, & then to y$^{e}$ first station [--] ~~the foresd land~~ / to contain two hundred Acres & no more to have & to hold y$^{e}$ s$^{d}$ two hundred / acres of land w$^{th}$ all & singular its rights & priveledges Jurisdictions, & / appertinances w$^{t}$soever to y$^{e}$ same belonging or anyway appertaining unto / y$^{e}$ s$^{d}$ OWNE BURNE his heires & assignes & to his & their only proper use / for ever from y$^{e}$ s$^{d}$ HUGH CAMPBELL his heirs & asignes & all & every / person or persons w$^{t}$soever lawfully Claimaing by from or under him or / them or any of them & shall & will warrant & for ever defend by these / presents & y$^{t}$ y$^{e}$ s$^{d}$ HUGH CAMPBELL for himself his heirs Ex$^{rs}$. & Adm$^{rs}$ / do covenant, promise, & grant w$^{th}$ y$^{e}$ s$^{d}$ OWEN BURNE his heirs & assignes / & every of them by these presents y$^{t}$ all & singular y$^{e}$ fores$^{d}$ two hundred / Acres of Land with all y$^{e}$ Appertinances thereto belonging now be & ever / hereafter be stand & continue to y$^{e}$ s$^{d}$ OWEN BURNE, his heires & assignes for / ever, & y$^{t}$ y$^{e}$ s$^{d}$ OWEN BURNE his heires & assignes be freely & Clearly acquited / exonered [*sic*] & discharged from time to time well, & sufficiently kept harmless / by y$^{e}$ s$^{d}$ HUGH CAMPBELL his heires, Ex$^{rs}$ & Adm$^{rs}$ of & from all manner of

**[263]**

Former & other gifts, grants, bargains, sailes, leases Morgadges, Joynters / dowers of & from all & Singular other titles, troubles, omitted, or done by y$^{e}$ s$^{d}$ / HUGH CAMPBELL his heires or Assignes; or by any other p$^{r}$son or persons w$^{t}$soever / & y$^{t}$ y$^{e}$ s$^{d}$ HUGH CAMPBELL his heirs or assignes for & during y$^{e}$ space of seven / yeares next ensueing y$^{e}$ datte of these p$^{r}$sents shall & will & upon y$^{e}$ reasonable / request & att y$^{e}$ Cost, & Charges of y$^{e}$ s$^{d}$ OWEN BURN his heires & assignes make / such other lawfull & reasonable asewrance & asewrances in y$^{e}$ law for y$^{e}$ more / & better asewrance of y$^{e}$ afores$^{d}$ premises as by y$^{e}$ s$^{d}$ OWEN BURNE his heires / or assignes or his or their learned Councell in y$^{e}$ law swhall be reasonably de= / =vised, advised, or required & y$^{e}$ fores$^{d}$ two hundred Acres of land being as / afores$^{d}$ two hundred Acres & no more: shall be marked & laid out by y$^{e}$ s$^{d}$ / HUGH CAMPBELL his heires & Ex$^{rs}$ upon y$^{e}$ equall Charge of y^e^ s^d^ HUGH / CAMPBELL his heirs, Ex^rs^, & Adm^rs^ & y^e^ s^d^ OWEN BURN his heirs, Ex^rs^ & assignes / & if it shall happen y^t^ any more then two hundred Acres shall be in y^e^ bounds / beforenamed or laid as afores^d^ then y^e^ s^d^ OWEN BURN his heirs or assignes / shall pay to y^e^ s^d^ HUGH CAMPBELL his heirs, Ex^rs^ for what shall be more / then two hundred Acres proportionably as he y^e^ s^d^ OWEN BURN hath p^d^ for / y^e^ fores^d^ two hundred Acres of land (Viz^t^) at y^e^ rate of two thous^d^ p^ds^ of / Tob^o^ for each hundred Acres & y^t^ y^e^ fores^d^ premises with all y^e^ apperti= / nances thereto belonging shall be esteemed & judged, & taken to be to y^e^ only / proper use & behoofe of y^e^ s^d^ OWEN BURN his heirs, & Assignes for ev^r^. as it is / before inserted & to no other use, intent, and purpose w^t^soev^r^. in witnesse wereof / I have hereunto set my hand & seale y^e^ day & year first above written Seal

Signed, sealed, & delivered in y^e^ p^r^sence of us HUGH CAMPBELL O
Whose names are und^r^ written
JER: ELLIS
THO: **T** GROSE
his marke

Acknowledged in open Co^rt^ held For y^e^ Isle of Wight County y^e^ 10^th^ day of Octobt^r^ 1698 & Recorded
p CHA CHAPMAN C^l^C^ur^

**[264]**

Whereas M^r^ HENRY BAKER & M^r^ JOHN CREWES are att my request bound to / Cap^t^ HENRY APPLEWHAITE prsident of y^e^ Isle of Wight County & his seccoss^rs^: [*sic*] / by bond beareing datte w^th^. these presents in penalty of one Hundred p^ds^ & / twenty p^ds^ sterling for y^e^ paym^t^ of Sixty two p^ds^ Eight shillings to / JAMES WILSON son of NICH^O^ WILSON w^n^ he shall attain y^e^ age of one & twenty / yeares, & for y^e^ maintenance of y^e^ s^d^ JAMES dureing y^e^ s^d^ terme as by y^e^ s^d^ / Bond may appeare Now for y^e^ secureing of y^e^ s^d^ HENRY BAKER & JN^O^ / CREWES their heires Ex^rs^ & Adm^rs^ from all damages y^t^ may acrew to them / for & by reason of their Bond as above, I THOMAS CLERKE doe by these / p^r^sents bind my selfe my heires Ex^rs^ & Adm^rs^ in y^e^ penalty of one hundred / & Twenty p^ds^ to y^e^ s^d^ HENRY BAKER & JN^O^ CREWES their Ex^rs^ Adm^rs^ & / hereby make ov^r^ by these presents to y^m^ their Ex^rs^. & Adm^rs^. as a further / security ag^t^ y^e^ s^d^ Bond these things following (Viz^t^) Tenne pewt^r^ dishes / three pewter Basons, Tenne Pewt^r^ plates, three ffeather bedds, & / furniture, one Silver Tankard, six small silver Cupps, four silv^r^ spoons / In wittnesse whereof I have hereunto sett my hand & seal this twentieth / day of July Annoq Dom 1698 Seale

Sealed & delivered in y^e^ p^r^sence of THO: CLERKE O
GEORGE MOORE
CHA CHAPMAN

Acknoled [*sic*] in open Co^rt^ held For y^e^ Isle of Wight / County y^e^ 10^th^ day of October 1698 & / Recorded p CHA CHAPMAN C^l^C^ur^

I acknowledge to have reced of THOMAS CLERKE the sume of Twenty p$^{ds}$ / Eight p$^{ds}$ sterling mony & doe hereby obledge my selfe my heires Ex$^{rs}$ Adm$^{rs}$ in y$^{e}$ / penalty of Sixty p$^{ds}$ for y$^{e}$ paym$^{t}$ of y$^{e}$ money to JAMES WILSON his heires / or Assignes y$^{e}$ s$^{d}$ Twenty Eight p$^{ds}$ w$^{n}$ he shall attain y$^{e}$ age of one & twenty / yeares y$^{e}$ sume being part of y$^{e}$ s$^{d}$ WILSONs Estate & pay for y$^{e}$ schooling of y$^{e}$ s$^{d}$ / JAMES att my owne Charges. Witness my hand & seale y$^{e}$ twentieth day of July 1698 Seale

Sealed & delivered in y$^{e}$ presence of HEN BAKER O

GEORGE MOORE

CHA CHAPMAN

Acknowledged in Open Co$^{rt}$. held for HEN BAKER y$^{e}$ Isle Wight County y$^{e}$ 10$^{th}$ day of / October & Recorded p CHA CHAPMAN

**[265]**

Be it knowne who all men by these p$^{r}$sents y$^{t}$ whereas I y$^{e}$ subscriber hereof / JACOB DURDEN of y$^{e}$ County of y$^{e}$ Isle of Weight Planter having a Pattent given & / Granted unto Mee by S$^{r}$ EDMOND ANDROS his Ma$^{ties}$. Leu$^{t}$ Gen$^{r}$all & govern$^{r}$ of Virginia / for 330 Acres of Land Bearing Date y$^{e}$ 28$^{th}$ day of Octob$^{r}$. In y$^{e}$ year 1697 scituated / lying & being In y$^{e}$ aboves$^{d}$ County of y$^{e}$ Isle of Wight now know yee whom Itt may or / Shall, Concern y$^{t}$ I y$^{e}$ aboves$^{d}$ JACOB DARDEN doe & with y$^{e}$ consent of ANN his wife or heirs / Ex$^{rs}$. Adm$^{rs}$, or Assignes for good Consideration in hand already Reced have / bargained, sold, & delivered over unto HENRY POPE y$^{e}$ aboves$^{d}$ County of y$^{e}$ Isle / of Wight or unto his heires, Ex$^{rs}$, Adm$^{rs}$, & Assignes to say by Estimation one hundred / sixty five Acres of y$^{e}$ aboves$^{d}$ Pattent of land for To have & to hold for ev$^{r}$. being / & equall share to witt y$^{e}$ one half of y$^{e}$ abovs$^{d}$ Pattent with all priveledges of / hunting, hawking, fishing, & fowling & w$^{t}$soever Priveledge belonging within y$^{e}$ / Precincts of y$^{e}$ abvoves$^{d}$ 165 Acres & for further Confirming hereof wee y$^{e}$ aboves$^{d}$ / JACOB DURDEN & ANN his wife o$^{r}$. heires, Ex$^{rs}$. Adm$^{rs}$, & Assignes y$^{t}$ they shall Quietly / Peaceably Injoy for Ever together with all y$^{e}$ Appertinances thereunto belonging / In as full & firm a manner as may or can be Expressed to All True Intents / Meanings & Proposes Afores$^{d}$ In Confirmation hereof to y$^{e}$ premises aboves$^{d}$ wee / have hereunto sett o$^{r}$. hands & seales this seventeenth day of Sep$^{t}$. I [*sic*] y$^{e}$ year 1698

The abovementioned land is to be at y$^{e}$ West end of the Tract Land seal

JACOB DURDEN O

Witness JN$^{O}$ RICKES

THO: PITT

her seal

ANN A DURDEN O

mark

Acknowled [*sic*] y$^{e}$ 19$^{th}$ of 8$^{br}$ / Recorded p CHA CHAPMAN C$^{l}$C$^{ur}$

The deposition of BEJAMIN BALDWIN Aged twenty seven years / or thereabouts being Examined & sworne saith that when JOHN / CHRISTOPHER FIRABANT was at my house a Giving directions about the / Iron work of THOMAS

NORSWORTHYs saw Mill y$^{e}$ deponant Askt him / that he was to have for building of the Mill, he told y$^{e}$ deponant / that he durst venter to charge Tob$^{o}$ with y$^{r}$ deponant & y$^{r}$ depon$^{t}$ / as not willing to that, & then y$^{r}$ deponant, askt him what he / was to have & he told me Nine hundred & furthur y$^{r}$ deponant saith / that all the Iron work for the said mill was done according to his / directions & he said it would doe well enough.

BEN: BALDWIN

Sworne in open Co$^{rt}$ held for the Isle of / Wight County y$^{e}$ 9$^{th}$ day of 10$^{br}$ 1698 / Recorded ꝑ CHA CHAPMAN C$^{l}$ C$^{ur}$

**[266]**

The deposition of WILLIAM JOHNSON aged 50 years or thereabouts / being examined & sworne saith that y$^{e}$ deponant heard JOHN / CHRISTOPHER FIREABANT say that THOMAS NORSWORTHY did offer / him nine hundred pounds of Tob$^{o}$ to build him a saw Mill & / he told him it was well enough we should not fall out & fuither / y$^{e}$ deponant saith not.

his
WILLIAM **WI** JOHNSON
mark

Sworne in open Co$^{rt}$ held for the Isle / of Wight County y$^{e}$ 9$^{th}$ day of Decem$^{br}$: / 1698 Recorded ꝑ CHA CHAPMAN C$^{l}$ C$^{ur}$

The Deposition of THOMAS WHITLEY aged 40 years or thereabouts / being examined & sworne saith y$^{t}$ I heard JOHN CHRISTOPHER / FIRABANT say that he would make y$^{e}$ Mill saw 500 foot of / plank ꝑ day & that he would make y$^{e}$ Mill works with 5 / saws & further your deponant saith not

his
THO: **T** WHITLEY
mark

Sworne in Open Co$^{rt}$ held for the Isle / of Wight County y$^{e}$ 9$^{th}$ day of Decemb$^{r}$ 1698 / Recorded ꝑ CHA CHAPMAN C$^{l}$ C$^{ur}$

Whereas there is a marriage intended between me BLACKABY / TYRRELL of the Isle of Wight County and SARAH JONES of the same / County spinster, whereas it is agreed that my so intended / wife shall have free liberty to give, devise bequeath, & dispose of all that part of the Estate she now possesses w$^{ch}$ / is underneath written to such uses as to her shall seem / meet Now know yee that I the said BLACKABY TYRRELL / doe in full & open Court (in consideration of the said / intended marriage) freely, voluntary, & irrevocably / release all the right & Interest that by Vertue of the / said marriage, I may att any time Claime, in that part / of her said Estate or any part thereof, Giving & by these / presents granting to my said intended wife full power / & free liberty, by any Act, or Acts, deed, or deeds, or by / her last Will & Testament in writing to give, devise, or / dispose, y^e^ same or any thereof, to such person, or persons, / use or uses, as she shall thinck fitt, In wittness whereof / I have hereunto sett my hand, and Seal this Eighth day

**[267]**

of Decemb[r] Anno Domini 1698
The ꝑticulars above reserved are as followeth (Viz[t])
The Plantation & Land she lived on in Blackwater
Two Negroes Called Franck & Rachell
Two feather beds & all furniture
Four pewter dishes
A Large Bible
Two Cedar Boxes
Two Breeding Cowes & two breeding Ewes

Sealed delivered in the p[r]sence of us
CHA CHAPMAN
JN[O] CHAPMAN y[e] marke of BLACKABY **B** TYRRELL (Seal)
Recorded ꝑ CHA CHAPMAN ClC[ur]

Know all men by these presents that I JOHN CREWES of y[e] upper / parrish of y[e] Isle of Wight County planter Doe with my free and / voluntary will give & grant unto my Cousin RICHARD BLUNT & / to the Heires lawfully begotten of his body all my Right & title of / the house & land which RICHARD BLUNT Senior died posest with for / the whole time that y[e] said RICHARD BLUNT Senior had writ By Vertue / of a leas for 99 years granted by M[r] JN[O]. GILES to mee & if the said / RICHARD BLUNT Junior die without Issue then the said land to re= / =turn to the next & nearest of his kindred, & I the said CREWES / doe Obleidge my self to Acknowledge y[e] same in open Co[rt] next / held for y[e] Isle of Wight County. as wittness my hand w[th] seal / this 26[th] day of November Anno Domini 1698

Signed & sealed in y[e] presence of Us
JN[O] DAVIS
THO: **T:** FLOYD (his mark)

JOHN **I** CREWES (his mark) O (seale)

Recorded ꝑ CHA CHAPMAN C[l]C[ur]

**[268]**

A List of debts due to me the subscriber in my own Right in / the R[t] of ANNE my wife, & in her Right as Ex[tx]. of Coll: JA: POWELL deced

| | [lb] Tob[o] |
|---|---|
| RICH[D] HANSCOMES bill & Account | |
| JOHN CHAMPIONs bill | 0727 |
| THOMAS CLERKs bill & Account | 1038 |

| | |
|---|---|
| GEORGE BARLOWs bill | 0741 |
| W$^{M}$ BALDWINs bill | 0460 |
| RICH$^{D}$ BENNETT Senior 4 bills & Account | 4000 |
| RICHARD BENNETT Juniors bill | 2193 |
| JAMES BRIGGS Bill | 0421 |
| JOHN GREENs Bill | 0425 |
| THOMAS THROPs Bill | 0463 |
| RICHARD PYLANDs Bill | 0450 |
| M$^{r}$ ROBT PARKs not [*sic*, note] on Cap$^{t}$ HENRY APPLEWHITE | 0931 |
| Sum Tot: | 12149 |

These presents witness y$^{t}$ I y$^{e}$ abovenamed ROB$^{T}$ RANDALL / doe assigne all my Right, title, & Interest of y$^{e}$ above specified / debts amounting to Twelve Thous$^{d}$ one hundred & forty nin= / pounds of Tob$^{o}$ (due to me in y$^{e}$ quallityes abovesaid) to NICH$^{O}$ / WILSON or his assignes with warranty that they are justly / due, Witness my hand this 19$^{th}$ day of June 1693 ROB$^{T}$ RANDALL

Test JN$^{O}$ GOODRICH
RALPH SHIRLEY Recorded ꝑ / CHA CHAPMAN C$^{l}$C$^{ur}$

Cap$^{t}$ HENRY APPLEWHAITE

Pray be pleased to pay M$^{rs}$ ANNE POWELL Two Thousand three / hundred p$^{ds}$ of Tob$^{o}$ Convenient & this note shall be y$^{e}$ discharge. / for soe much
Who am y$^{r}$ ffr$^{d}$ & S$^{r}$vant ROB$^{T}$ PARKE
march y$^{e}$ 27$^{th}$ 1693

**[269]**

The Deposition of JN$^{O}$ GOODRICH of the Isle of Wight County aged / Eighty years or thereabouts sworne, & examined saith, y$^{t}$ INDIAN / COOPER,[14] about sixty years agoe gave a parcell of Land for a / Gleab, in Orisqueake Bay, where MARY DICKSON non [*sic*, now] liveth / & her father WILLIAM PHILLIPS lived, on this Land sev$^{r}$all / years by lease from the Vestery, Before which time M$^{r}$ OISER, / & M$^{r}$ DUNSTAN Ministers, lived on the said Land, as belonging / to the Church (or as Gleabe Land that INDIAN COOPER Gave) / & further saith not.

Dated March y$^{e}$ 5$^{th}$ 1697/8 signum
Sworne by us ꝑ Ord$^{r}$ of Co$^{rt}$ JOHN I GOODRICH
GEO: MOORE CHA CHAPMAN C$^{l}$C$^{ur}$
HEN: BAKER

[14] This is almost certainly "Julian" Cooper.

The Deposition of WILLIAM MILES of y$^{e}$ Isle of Wight County, / Aged seventy five years or thereabouts, sworne & examined & / Saith that about sixty years agoe, the plantation wheron / WILLIAM PHILLIPS, severall years since lived On, went by the / name of the Gleab, (& was then Owned by all) & y$^{t}$ One M$^{r}$ OISER a Minister lived on this / Gleab, and One M$^{r}$ FFAUKNER Minister Lived there alsoe.

Dated March 5$^{th}$, 169$^{7}/_{8}$ his
before Us W$^{M}$ **M M** MILES
GEORGE MOORE mark
HEN: BAKER

Recorded ꝑ CHA CHAPMAN C$^{l}$C$^{ur}$

**[270]**

Know all men by these ꝑsents y$^{t}$ I JAMES JOLLY of y$^{e}$ / Isle of Wight County in Virg$^{a}$ Smith, doth depute, Impow$^{r}$ / Authorize WILLIAM JOLLY Smith of y$^{e}$ same County my / true, Lawfull Attorney, to Act & doe in my absence as / my self in all causes: to sue & Recover for me the afores$^{d}$ / JAMES JOLLY. in wittness whereunto I have sett to my / my [*sic*] hand this 18$^{th}$ day of June 1698

his JAMES JOLLY
Test JAMES Ɨ RIGHT
mark Acknowledged in Open Co$^{rt}$ y$^{e}$ / 9$^{th}$ day of August
OLIVER SLAUGHTER 1698 / & Recorded ꝑ me / CHA CHAPMAN C$^{l}$C$^{ur}$

This Indenture made y$^{e}$ 9$^{th}$ day of 10$^{br}$. in y$^{e}$ year of o$^{r}$ Lord / God 1698 & in the 10$^{th}$ yeare of the Reign of o$^{r}$ Soveraigne / Lord William the third by the Grace of God of England, Scotland / France, & Ireland King &c: betweene JN$^{O}$ GILES of y$^{e}$ County of y$^{e}$ / Isle of Wight of y$^{e}$ one part & GILES DRIVER of y$^{e}$ s$^{d}$ County of the / other part Wittnesseth; That y$^{e}$ s$^{d}$ JN$^{O}$ GILES for, & in Consideration / of y$^{e}$ sum of one Thous$^{d}$ p$^{ds}$ of Tob$^{o}$ in Cask, to him in hand / paid at, & before y$^{e}$ sealing, & delivery of these presents by y$^{e}$ / said GILES DRIVER well & truly paid y$^{e}$ receipt whereof y$^{e}$ s$^{d}$ / JN$^{O}$ GILES doth hereby acknowledge; & himself therewith / fully satisfied & paid; hath given, granted, Allien'd, bargained / sold, enfeoffed & Confirmed, unto y$^{e}$ s$^{d}$ GILES DRIVER his heires / & assignes for ever; all his Right, title, & interest in & to / a parcell of land lying in y$^{e}$ lower parrish of y$^{e}$ s$^{d}$ County / Contained in a patten granted unto y$^{e}$ s$^{d}$ JN$^{O}$ GILES by S$^{r}$ / EDMOND ANDROSS Knight for six hundred eighty seven / Acres dated y$^{e}$ 26 day of Aprill 1698, as deserted from / GILES DRIVER it being y$^{e}$ added part of A patten granted

**[271]**

To y$^{e}$ said DRIVER bearing date y$^{e}$ 21 day of Septemb$^{r}$ 1674 / To have & to hold y$^{e}$ foresaid tract of land according to the / meets, & bounds laid down & sett forth in y$^{e}$ s$^{d}$ patten: unto y$^{e}$ said / GILES DRIVER ~~beareing date~~ his heires & Assignes for ever; / against y$^{e}$ s$^{d}$ JN$^{O}$ GILES & his heires with all & singular its rights, members,

Jurisdictions and / Appurtinances whatsoever to y$^{e}$ s$^{d}$ Land belonging or to any / part or parcell thereof to y$^{e}$ only proper use of y$^{e}$ s$^{d}$ GILES / DRIVER, his heires, & assignes, & to noe other use, intent or / purpose w$^{t}$soev$^{r}$. In Wittness hereof I have hereunto sett my / hand & Seale the day & yeare first abovewritten:

Signed, sealed, & delivered in y$^{e}$ p$^{r}$senc of us whose names are underwritten.
ARTHUR SMITH
JO$^{S}$ BRIDGER
THO: PITT

JN$^{O}$ GILES Sigellum

The words (against the said JN$^{O}$ GILES & / his heires) interlined before y$^{e}$ signeing and / sealing

Acknowledged in open Co$^{rt}$ held For y$^{e}$ Isle of / Wight County y$^{e}$ 11$^{enth}$ day of ffeb$^{r}$ 169$^{8}$/$_{9}$ by M$^{r}$ / JOHN GYLES & Recorded ꝑ / CHA CHAPMAN C$^{l}$C$^{ur}$

This Indenture made y$^{e}$ Thirtieth day of y$^{e}$ tenth month / Called Decemb$^{r}$ one Thous$^{d}$ six hundred ninety Eight between / EDWARD GRIFFEN of y$^{e}$ Isle of of Wight County Planter / of y$^{e}$ one party, & DANIELL SANBORNE of y$^{e}$ fores$^{d}$ Coupnty on y$^{e}$ / other party. Agreed upon as followeth. I EDWARD GRIFFEN / with y$^{e}$ free Consent of MARY GRIFFEN my wife; formerly / known by y$^{e}$ name of MARY MUMFORD, Kinswoman of / THOMAS MUMFORD deced. have Bargained, & sold, & Made ov$^{r}$ / unto y$^{e}$ afores$^{d}$ DANIELL SANBORNE y$^{e}$ remaineing p$^{t}$ of a / ꝑcell of land lying, & being in y$^{e}$ Afores$^{d}$ County in y$^{e}$ Corasid / Necks w$^{ch}$ y$^{e}$ afores$^{d}$ SANBORNE had a parcell of before / belonging to y$^{e}$ Afores$^{d}$ Escheat patten of my Uncle THOMAS / MUMFORD granted to him in y$^{e}$ year one thous$^{d}$ six hundred / Ninety seven which land as sending to my wife MARY / GRIFFEN by the death of her uncle THOMAS MUMFORD.

**[272]**
Which according to y$^{e}$ Antient bounds w$^{ch}$ is mentioned in / y$^{e}$ escheat Patten to be two hundred acres beginning upon a / Creek Called Beverly creeke, & Joyning upon y$^{e}$ land / of RICHARD RATTLIFs formerly one VANCLORIEs running / by North East three hundred twenty five poles to a marked / Oake, & to a branch side which devides betwen GEO: NORSWORTHYes / land & soe running East due East to a line of marked trees / to timber Neck Creeke, soe running South three hundred / twenty five pole Joyning upon y$^{e}$ land of one CHRISTOHPER / BEST to befferly Creeke, from thence to y$^{e}$ first station w$^{ch}$ / land I y$^{e}$ said EDWARD GRIFFING, & MARY GRIFFING my wife / doe warrant y$^{e}$ saile of y$^{e}$ afores$^{d}$ land unto DANIELL / SANBORNE his heires, Ex$^{rs}$, Adm$^{rs}$, & Assignes for ever. / from us o$^{r}$ heires, Ex$^{rs}$, Adm$^{rs}$, & Assignes for ev$^{r}$. from any / other person or persons w$^{t}$soev$^{r}$ in as full & as ample manner / as y$^{e}$ Law can devise without fraud, or quivocation, or taking / any advantage if any word within this deed should allow / of it: being fully & clearly satisfied; by a Valueable Consideration / alread [*sic*] in hand received. & further I y$^{e}$ s$^{d}$ EDWARD GRIFFING w$^{th}$ / MARY GRIFFING my wife doe

bind o$^{r}$selves, or heires, Ex$^{rs}$, or Assignes / that if this deed within mentioned should not be sufficient / w$^{n}$ y$^{e}$ s$^{d}$ SANBORNE, or his Learnd Councell in y$^{e}$ Law has advised / or his heires, or Ex$^{rs}$ ~~Adm$^{rs}$~~ they being not satisfied with this / Asseurance within mentioned; y$^{t}$ wee doe ingage o$^{r}$selves, our / heires, Ex$^{rs}$, or Assignes better aseurance whenever he or they / shall require it, we refuseing soe to doe, doe bind o$^{r}$selves, our / heires, Ex$^{rs}$, or Assignes to pay unto y$^{e}$ s$^{d}$ SANBORNE his heires, / Ex$^{rs}$, or Assignes y$^{e}$ full Sum unto y$^{e}$ s$^{d}$ SANBORNE his heires, / Ex$^{rs}$, or Assignes y$^{e}$ full Sum of thirty thous$^{d}$ p$^{ds}$ of good sound / Marchantable Tob$^{o}$ in Caske to y$^{e}$ true ꝑformance of These / Articles and agreements within mentioned we have

**[273]**

Sett o$^{r}$ hands & seales y$^{e}$ day & year first / abovementioned his Seal
RICHARD REYNOLDS EDWARD **E** GRIFFING O
JN$^{O}$ LUTHER mark Seal
ROB$^{T}$ THOMAS MARY **M** GRIFFING O
GEO: NORSWORTHY mark

Acknowledged in open Co$^{rt}$ held For y$^{e}$ Isle of Wight / County y$^{e}$ 11$^{enth}$ day of ffeb$^{r}$ 169$^{8}$/$_{9}$ by EDWARD GRIFFIN & MARY his Wife to be their act & Deed

Recorded ꝑ CHA CHAPMAN C$^{l}$C$^{ur}$

To all people to whom this p$^{r}$sent deed, or wrighting shall come, know / y$^{e}$ y$^{t}$ I HENERY MARTYN, & MARY my wife, of y$^{e}$ upper parrish of y$^{e}$ Isle of / Wight County in Virginia planter for a Valueable Conseration already / by me Received in hand before y$^{e}$ Assigning, sealing, & deliveryng hereof / for which I doe Acknowledge my self fully satsified by ANN JONES exex / widdow in y$^{e}$ lower parrish of y$^{e}$ same County, doe for me, my heires, Ex$^{rs}$ / Adm$^{rs}$, & Assignes, make over, bargaine, sell, Alienate, & confirme to y$^{e}$ said / to y$^{e}$ s$^{d}$ [*sic*] ANN JONES, & her heires, Ex$^{rs}$, Adm$^{rs}$, & Assignes for ever a / certaine parcell, or tract of land; in y$^{e}$ Lower parrish of y$^{e}$ aforesaid / County Containeing by Estimation one hundred acres of land, being / part of a dividant of land Granted EDMOND PALMER, & I y$^{e}$ s$^{d}$ HENERY / MARTIN y$^{e}$ said parcell of Land soe sold by me, to the said ANN JONES begining / & Joyning to one End of JN$^{O}$ JONES his land, purchased of EDMOND / PALMER, & one side WILL BODY line, & soe by these two lines till the / hundred acres of land be compleated. To have, & to hold to y$^{e}$ said ANN / JONES her heires, Ex$^{rs}$, Adm$^{rs}$, & Assignes for Ever, y$^{e}$ abovesaid tract and / parcell of land w$^{th}$ all profitts & herediments [*sic*] & appurtinances thereunto / belonging in as large, & Ample manner as I my self my heires, Ex$^{rs}$, Adm$^{rs}$, / could have by vertue of a Pattent Granted for y$^{e}$ same, & further the / said MARTIN doe for my self, my heires, Ex$^{rs}$, Adm$^{rs}$, Oblidge y$^{t}$ y$^{e}$ said / ANN JONES her heires, Ex$^{rs}$, & Adm$^{rs}$ shall peaceably, & quietly for ever / enjoy y$^{e}$ same without y$^{e}$ lest hinderance, or any Molestation of me / y$^{e}$ said HENERY MARTIN, my heires, Ex$^{rs}$, Adm$^{rs}$, with Genarall warranty / against all person or persons whatsoever which shall disturb, molest, or disquiet / y$^{e}$ said ANN JONES her heires, Ex$^{rs}$, Adm$^{rs}$, or Assignes in y$^{e}$ peaceable / possession of y$^{e}$ abovesaid land, & doe Oblige my self, & MARY my wife / to acknowledge this our free Act, & Deed at y$^{e}$ next Co$^{rt}$ held for this / County the fores$^{d}$ land, Delivered to ANN JONES by HENERY MARTIN / by turff & twigg in y$^{e}$ presence of us. / In Wittness our hands & seale this / 28$^{th}$ day of March in y$^{e}$ year of lour Lord / God 1699

his Seal
HENERY **H** MARTIN O
mark Seale
MARY + MARTIN O
her mark

his
JN$^{O}$. **I** THOMAS
mark his
ALEXANDER + MATHEWS
mark
JN$^{O}$ **P** PORTIS
Signum

Acknowledged in open Co$^{rt}$ / held for y$^{e}$ Isle of Wight County / the 10$^{th}$ day of Aprill by y$^{e}$ said / HENERY MARTIN & MARY his wife / 1699 & Recorded ꝑ / CHA CHAPMAN C$^{l}$C$^{ur}$

**[274]**

This Indenture made y$^{e}$ 6$^{th}$. day of Aprill 1699 in y$^{e}$ 11$^{enth}$ year of / y$^{e}$ Reigne of our Lord King William y$^{e}$ 3$^{d}$ over England &c between MARGARETT EDWARDS of y$^{e}$ Isle of Wight County in y$^{e}$ Collony of Virg$^{a}$ / Spinster of y$^{e}$ one ꝑte (she being one of y$^{e}$ Daughters, & Coheires of / ROB$^{T}$ EDWARDS deced) & JAMES BRAGG of y$^{e}$ same County planter / of y$^{e}$ other ꝑte Witnesseth that y$^{e}$ said MARGARETT EDWARDS for & / in Consideration of y$^{e}$ sum of one Thousand p$^{ds}$ of Tob$^{o}$ to her in hand / paid by y$^{e}$ said JAMES BRAGG, y$^{e}$ receipt whereof she doth hereby / acknowledge, & for divers other Causes, & Considerations her thereunto / moveing Hath bargained, sold, aliened, Enfeofed, & Confirmed, & by these / p$^{r}$sents doth for her self, her Heires, Ex$^{rs}$, Adm$^{rs}$, & Assignes, ~~all that her~~ / ~~third part, & propotion~~ bargaine, sell, alien, Enfeoff, & Confirme unto / y$^{e}$ said JAMES BRAGG his Heires & Assignes, all that her third part / & proportion, (the whole in three equall parts to be devided) of a / certain tract of [*sic*] parcell of land Containing by Estimation One / hundred acres or thereabouts purchased by her father ROB$^{T}$ EDWARDS / of EDMOND PALMER, & lyeing in y$^{e}$ County afores$^{d}$ bounding upon / y$^{e}$ Lands of Cap$^{t}$ HENERY APPLEWHAIT & W$^{M}$ FFRIZELL together with all / Mines, & Mineralls, Waters, & Water Courses, to y$^{e}$ same belonging, / With liberty of fishing, Hunting, & fowling & all priviledges / Accustomed, To have & to hold y$^{e}$ s$^{d}$ Land above conveyed & every / ꝑte thereof, to y$^{e}$ said JAMES BRAGG his Heires, & Assignes forever, / with warranty y$^{t}$ y$^{e}$ same is free from all Incumbrances w$^{t}$soever, / with Warranty y$^{t}$ y$^{e}$ same is free from all incumbrances w$^{t}$soever, / And y$^{e}$ said MARGARETT EDWARDS for herself, her heires, Ex$^{rs}$, & Adm$^{rs}$ / doth Covent, & promise to, & with y$^{e}$ said JAMES BRAGG, his Heires, / & Assignes, that y$^{e}$ said JAMES BRAGG his Heires, & assignes Shall, & may / peaceably Enjoy y$^{e}$ said Land, from all ꝑsons Claiming, or to Claime / by, from, or under her in any manner howsoever. In Witness / whereof y^e^ said MARGARETT EDWARDS hath hereunto set her hand / and Seal y^e^ day & year first Above written

Signed, Sealed, & delivered in the presence of us
JOHN JONES
his
W^M^ **W** WEST
mark

her seal
MARGARET **M** EDWARDS O

Acknowledged in open Co^rt^ held for y^e^ Isle of / Wight County y^e^ 10^th^ day of Aprill 1699 by MARGARETT EDWARDS & Ordered to be Recorded
ꝑ CHA CHAPMAN C^l^C^ur^

**[275]**

This Indenture bearing Date y^e^ 5^th^ day of Aprill, in y^e^ year of / our Lord 1699 Witnesseth: y^t^ JN^O^ MOORE of y^e^ Lower ꝑish of y^e^ Isle / of Wight County to & with y^e^ free & voluntatry Consent of MARGARETT his Wife / for y^e^ full, & Valueable Consideration of Six Thous^d^ p^ds^ of Tobaccoe / In hand already paid; & secured to be paid, have & by these p^r^sents / doth for us, or heirs, Ex^rs^, & Adm^rs^ Give, grant, sell, alienate, transfer / & fully, & Absoloutely Lett, & sett over for ever unto JACOB REEKS of / y^e^ aforesd Lower ꝑish of y^e^ Isle of Wight County To him, his heirs, and / Assignes for ever one part, or parcell of Land being by Estimation about / One hundred & twenty Acres be itt more or less, being part of A Patent / of four hundred and Ninety Acres of Land granted unto y^e^ s^d^ JN^O^ MOORE / of four hundred and Ninety Acres of Land granted unto y^e^ s^d^ JN^O^ MOORE / bearing date y^e^ twentieth day of Aprill in y^e^ year of o^r^ Lord God 1682, / being in y^e^ branches of y^e^ Indian creek begining at a Wight Oake / being a Corner tree adjoyning to y^e^ land of HENERY BOAZMAN by / a percousand, Thence West by South the pattent Line fifty Eight / poles, Thence West South West on y^e^ Pattent Line one Hundred twenty / eight poles to a dead Pine in M^r^ LOVEGRAVEs Line, Thence by M^r^ / LOVEGRAVEs Line South by East to y^e^ head of a deep Branch to a marked / Wight Oake, Thence down y^e^ branch to the main Run being a Branch / of y^e^ Indian Creek, Thence up y^e^ said Run to y^e^ foot of a Branch on y^e^ / East side of y^e^ plantation y^t^ JN^O^ COGAN formerly lived on, Thence / up y^e^ s^d^ Branch as y^e^ Run goes twenty five poles, Thence on a strait / Line South East to a line deviding y^e^ land of M^r^ THOMAS PITTS, & y^e^ / said JN^O^ MOOREs Land & plantaiton withall y^e^ buildings houses / of edifices, Orchards, Woods, wayes, & Waters, Mines & Mineralls w^th^ / all appurtinances thereunto belonging, in as large, & ample a / manner as ever it was granted at first by Pattent unto the / afores^d^ JN^O^ MOORE his heires, or Assignes for ever, without any Lett / hinderance, Contradiction, or Molestation of him y^e^ s^d^ JN^O^ MOOREs or / MARGARETT his Wife, Doth by these p^r^sents bind ourselves, or Heires / Ex^rs^, Adm^rs^. To acknowledge y^e^ s^d^ saile, In y^e^ County Co^rt^ held for y^e^ / Isle of Wight County in wittnesse whereof They have hereunto / sett their hands, & fixed Seales y^e^ day & year abovewritten

Signed, Sealed, & delivered his

in p^r^sence of us JOHN IM MOORE Seal
JN^O^ SIKES mark Seal
RICH^D^ ✠ BRADLY her
his mark MARGARET MM MOORE O
ROB^T^ REEKES mark

Acknowledged in open Co^rt^ / held for y^e^ Isle of Wight County / y^e^ 10^th^ day of Aprill 1699 by / JN^O^ MOORE & MARGARETT his Wife / & Ordered to be Recorded
p CHA CHAPMAN C^l^C^ur^

**[276]**

To all to whome these p^r^sents shall or may Come know yee / y^t^ I HESTER BRIDGER of y^e^ Isle of Wight County doe nominate & / appoint my well beloved son JOSEPH BRIDGER to be my true & / Lawfull Attorney in any, & all manner of Cases whatsoever either / either [*sic*] for me, or ag^t^ me, to demand, or Receive any Tobaccoes or / Money w^ch^ is owing either in Virginia, or elsewhere &c to me, & upon y^e^ / non payment of any debts due to me I doe hereby Impower my s^d^ / son JOSEPH BRIDGER to be true, & Lawfull Attorny as afores^d^ / to arrest, Imprison, Release out of prison as he my s^d^ Attorney / think fitt to doe, or to apply any Attorney or Attorneys in any / suit w^t^soever either depending for me, or ag^t^ me: more especially / in any suit, or suites y^t^ my sonns SAM^LL^. BRIDGER, or W^M^. BRIDGER / shall have ag^t^ me in y^e^ Isle of Wight Court, or elsewhere or y^t^ y^e^ s^d^ / HESTER BRIDGER shall have ag^t^ them (& w^t^soever my loving son / JO^S^: BRIDGER shall have as aforesaid nominated to be attorny / shall doe) I doe hereby & allow to be as good & Authentick in Law as / although I had bin [*sic*] present, & Consented to y^e^ same as Wittness / my hand this 9^th^: 10^br^: 1698
Testes
KINGSMAN MINERD HESTER BRIDGER
RICH^D^ GLOVER
his + Mark Recorded p CHA CHAPMAN C^l^C^ur^

Know all men by these p^r^sents, That I W^M^. MACKY of y^e^ Isle of Wight / County M^r^chant, Have by these p^r^sents made, Ordained, Constituted, & in / my place, & stead put & Deputed my trusty, & Loving friend ROB^T^ TUCKER / my true & Lawfull Attorney, for me, & in my name, & for my use, to ask / Demand, Sue, for, Levy, recover, & receive all such Sum & Sums of mony / Debts, goods, Wares, Dues, Accounts, & other Demands w^t^soever, w^ch^ are, or shall / be due, owing, payable, & belonging to me, or detained from me, any manner / of wayes, or means w^t^soever, by any Person, or Persons w^t^soever, giving, and / granting unto my Said Attorney, by these p^r^sents, my full & whole power, & / strength, & Authority, in & about y^e^ p^r^emises, to have, use, & take all Lawfull / wayes, & meanes, in my Name for y^e^ Recovery thereof, & uppon y^e^ Receipt of / any such debts, Dues, or Sums of Mony afores^d^ Acquittances, or other / sufficient discharges, for me, & on my Name, to make Seal, & Delivery / & generally, all & every other Act, &

Acts, thing, & things, Device & / & Devices in y$^{e}$ Law w$^{t}$soever Needfull, & necessary to be done in & / about y$^{e}$ P$^{r}$mises, for y$^{e}$ Recovery of all or any such Debts, or sums / of Money afores$^{d}$ for me, & in my Name to doe, Execute, & perform, / as fully, Largly, & amply, to all intents, & purposes, as I my self / might, or could doe, if I was Personally P$^{r}$sent or as if y$^{e}$ matter / required more Speciall Authority then is herein Contained, & Attorney / one or more und$^{r}$ him, for y$^{e}$ purpose afores$^{d}$, to make, & Constitue, & again

**[277]**

All Pleasures to Revoke, Ratifying, Allowing & holding for firm / & effectuall all, & whatsoever my Said Attorny shall Lawfully doe / in & about y$^{e}$ P$^{r}$mises, by Vertue hereof In Witness whereof I / have hereunto Sett my hand, & Seal y$^{e}$ 7$^{th}$ day of March 169$^{8}/_{9}$

his<br>
Witt: NATH: **N** SMITH<br>
mark

WILLIAM MACKIE

his<br>
NICHOLAS **N** SMITH<br>
mark

Proved in open Court held For y$^{e}$ Isle of Wight County / y$^{e}$ 10$^{th}$ Aprill 1699 by y$^{e}$ oathes of both witnesses & / Recorded ꝑ CHA CHAPMAN C$^{l}$C$^{ur}$

To all people to whom this p$^{r}$sent Deed or writing shall / come, Know yee y$^{t}$ I JN$^{O}$ BRETT, & SUSANA my Wife of y$^{e}$ uper ꝑish / of y$^{e}$ Isle of Wight County in Virg$^{a}$ Black Smith for a Valueable / Consideration all Already by me reced in hand before y$^{e}$ Assigning / sealing, & delivering hereof for w$^{ch}$ I doe acknowledge my self / full satisfied by JN$^{O}$ PORTIS Jun$^{r}$ of y$^{e}$ County aforesd in Butt [*sic*] in / y$^{e}$ Lower ꝑish doe for me, my heires, Ex$^{rs}$, Adm$^{rs}$, & Assignes / make over, bargaine, sell, Alienate, & Confirme to y$^{e}$ s$^{d}$ JOHN / PORTIS Jun$^{r}$ & his heires, Ex$^{rs}$, Adm$^{rs}$ or Assignes for ever a / certaine ꝑcell or tract of Land in y$^{e}$ Lower ꝑish of y$^{e}$ Isle of / Wight County Containing by Estimation one hundred Acres more / or less being part of a devidant of Land, Patten Granted to JN$^{O}$ / PORTIS Sen$^{r}$ & HENERY WEST dated y$^{e}$ Septemb$^{r}$ 25 1673 & I y$^{e}$ s$^{d}$ / JN$^{O}$ BRETT y$^{e}$ s$^{d}$ ꝑcell of land soe dold by me to y$^{e}$ s$^{d}$ JN$^{O}$ PORTIS / begining att White Oake Corner tree of JN$^{O}$ SHERRERs, stand / =ing in Low Meadow ground; & soe along a line of New marked / Trees. S:S:W: half a point Westerly through a Pocoson to a / Swamp, to a marked Gumm Comonly Called y$^{e}$ fish pond, & soe / up y$^{e}$ Swamp to a marked Pine att y$^{e}$ head by a Pocoson, & from / y$^{t}$ Pine Easterly to JN$^{O}$ JONES line of Marked trees, & soe along / that Line to a Red Oak a Corner tree, & from thence 200 pole / N:NW, to y$^{e}$ first station. To have, & to hold to y$^{e}$ s$^{d}$ JN$^{O}$ PORTIS / his heires, Ex$^{rs}$, Adm$^{rs}$, & Assignes for Ever, the aboves$^{d}$ tract, of / & parcell of Land with all profitts, & heridiments [*sic*], purtinances / thereunto belonging in as Large, & ample manner, as I my / self, my heires, Ex$^{rs}$, Adm$^{rs}$ could have by Vertue of a Patten / granted for y$^{e}$ same. & further y$^{e}$ s$^{d}$ JN$^{O}$ BRETT doe for my self, / my heires, Ex$^{rs}$ oblidge y$^{t}$ y$^{e}$ s$^{d}$ JN$^{O}$ PORTIS, his heires, Ex$^{rs}$, & Assignes / shall peaceably and quietly enjoy for ever the same / without y$^{e}$ Lest hinderance or any Molestation of me y$^{e}$ s$^{d}$ JN$^{O}$ / BRETT, my heires, Ex$^{rs}$, or Adm$^{rs}$ with generall waranty agan$^{st}$ / all ꝑson or Persons w$^{t}$soever w$^{ch}$ shall disturb molest, or /

disquiett y$^{e}$ s$^{d}$ JN$^{O}$ PORTIS, his heires, Ex$^{rs}$, Adm$^{rs}$ or Assignes in the / peaceable possession of y$^{e}$ aboves$^{d}$ Land. & we doe give to each / other y$^{e}$ priviledge of a Cart path between y$^{e}$ Meadow, & y$^{e}$ swamp / for our own Occations & our heires & asignes for ever & doe oblidge my self & SUSANNA my wife

**[278]**
To Acknowledge this our free Act, & deed att y$^{e}$ next Co$^{rt}$ held / for this County y$^{e}$ afores$^{d}$ Land delivered to JN$^{O}$ PORTIS by turff / & twigg by JN$^{O}$ BRETT in y$^{e}$ p$^{r}$sence of us JN$^{O}$ SHERRER, and / THOMAS SHERRER. Interlined with Oake, & Our Heires for ever / berfore assigned, In Witness our hands, & Seales y$^{e}$ 14$^{th}$ day of March / in y$^{e}$ year of our Lord God 169$^{8}/_{9}$

JN$^{O}$ BRETT Seal

Signed, sealed, & delivered<br>
in y$^{e}$ psence of us<br>
JN$^{O}$ SHERRER

her<br>
SUSANNA **H** BRETT Seale<br>
mark

his<br>
THO: **T:** SHERRER<br>
mark

Acknowledged in open Co$^{rt}$ / held for y$^{e}$ Isle of Wight County / the 10$^{enth}$ of Aprill 1699 by y$^{e}$ s$^{d}$ JN$^{O}$ BRETT, & SUSANNA his / Wife to be their Act, & Deed, & / Ordered to be Recorded

Test CHA CHAPMAN C$^{l}$C$^{ur}$

To all to whome these p$^{r}$sents shall come know yee y$^{t}$ I S$^{r}$ / EDWARD ANDROSS K$^{nt}$ his Ma$^{ties}$ L$^{t}$. Gov$^{r}$. Gen$^{ll}$ of Virg$^{a}$ send / Greeting. Whereas his late Ma$^{tie}$; King Charles y$^{e}$ 2$^{d}$ hath been / graciously pleased by his Royall Letters under y$^{e}$ great Seal of / England bearing date att Wesminster y$^{e}$ tenth Day of Octob$^{r}$ in y$^{e}$ / Eight & twentieth year of his Reign Amongst other things in y$^{e}$ / s$^{d}$ Letters patents Contained, to Continue, & Confirm y$^{e}$ Ancient / power & priviledge of granting fifty Acres of Land for every p$^{r}$son / Imported into this Collony of Virg$^{a}$. Now know yee y$^{t}$ I y$^{e}$ s$^{d}$ S$^{r}$ / EDMOND ANDROSS K$^{nt}$ Gov$^{r}$ &c: doe w$^{th}$ y$^{e}$ advice & Consent of y$^{e}$ Councell / of State Accordingly give & grant unto JAMES DOUGHTYs one / hundred ninety eight acres of Land in y$^{e}$ Lower pish of Isle Wight / County near King Saile begining at a red Oake a marked tree in / JAMES COLLINS his Line, thence North Seventy seven degrees, & a half / West thirty poles to a pine, thence North one hundred seventy / six pole to a White Oake, thence North thirty seven degrees, East one / hundred & Eleven poles to a Pine, thence East five degrees, South / one hundred forty six pole to a White Oake to a Corner tree of JAMES / COLLINS, thence along y$^{e}$ s$^{d}$ COLLINS line South thirty three degrees & / three quart$^{rs}$: West three hundred twenty eight poles to an Oake, / thence North Six degrees, West Eight poles to y$^{e}$ begining. The s$^{d}$ Land / being due unto y$^{e}$ s$^{d}$ JAMES DOUGHTY by & for y$^{e}$ transportation of / four persons into this Collony. whose names are to be in the Records / mentioned under this patent. To have & To hold y$^{e}$ s$^{d}$ Land w$^{th}$ due / share of all mines & mineralls therein Contained w$^{th}$ all rights,

**[279]**

of privildeges of hunting, hawking, fishing, & fowling with all / Woods, waters, & Rivers with all profitts, Comodities, & heraditaments / w$^{t}$soever belonging to y$^{e}$ said Land, to him y$^{e}$ s$^{d}$ JAMES DOUGHTY his / heires & Assignes for ever in as Large & ample manner to all / intents & purposes as hath been used & allowed since y$^{e}$ first / Plantation. To be held of o$^{r}$ Sovoraign Lord y$^{e}$ King his heires and / Successors as of his manner of East Greenwich in free & common / Soccage, & not *in capite*, nor by Knights Service / Yeilding & paying unto our said Sovoraign Lord y$^{e}$ King his heires, & / Success$^{rs}$ for every fifty Acres of Land hereby granted at y$^{e}$ feast of / S$^{t}$ Michaell y$^{e}$ Arch Angell y$^{e}$ fee rent of one Sh~~ill~~ w$^{ch}$ payment is to / be made yearly from year to year Provided y$^{t}$ if y$^{e}$ s$^{d}$ JAMES DOUGHTY / his heires or Assignes doe not seat, or plant, nor Cause to be seated, / or planted thereon within three yeares next ensueing y$^{e}$ date hereof / y$^{t}$ that it shall & may be Lawfull for any adventurer, or planter / to make choice thereof & seat thereof Given under my hand & y$^{e}$ / Seale to y$^{e}$ Colony this 26$^{th}$ day of Aprill in y$^{e}$ tenth year of his / Ma$^{ties}$ reign Anno$^{q}$ Dom 1698

JAMES DOUGHTYes patent for } EANDROSS
198 Acres of Land in Isle Wight }
County E JENINGS Dep$^{ty}$ Sec$^{rie}$

Know all men by these p$^{r}$sents y$^{t}$ I JAMES DOUGHTY & ELIZABETH my wife / of Nansimond County for divers good Causes & Considerations whereunto / moveing but more especially for; & in Consideration of y$^{e}$ sume of one / Thous$^{d}$ p$^{ds}$ of Tob$^{o}$ to us in hand paid before y$^{e}$ sealing & delivery hereof / wee doe hereby Acknowledge & Confess to bee paid, by ROB$^{T}$ ELLY of y$^{e}$ / Isle of Wight County; & are fully Contented, satisfied, & paid, doe fore us / o$^{r}$ heires, Ex$^{rs}$, & Adm$^{rs}$ Assigne, & set over unto him y$^{e}$ s$^{d}$ ROB$^{T}$ ELEY / his heires, Ex$^{rs}$, Adm$^{rs}$, & Assignes all our right, title, & Interest of, in & unto / y$^{e}$ within mentioned Patent, & every part, & pcell of land therein / mentioend to him his heires for ever in Wittness whererof I y$^{e}$ said / JAMES DOUGHTY & ELIZABETH my wife have hereunto to sett o$^{r}$ hands / & Seales this 8$^{th}$ day of June in y$^{e}$ year of o$^{r}$ Lord God 1699

Signed, sealed, & delivered JAMES DOUGHTIE sigellum
in y$^{e}$ p$^{r}$sence of ELIZABETH **E:** DOUGHTY seal
HUGH GOUGH her mark
THOMAS GILES

Acknowledged in open Court / held for y$^{e}$ Isle of Wight County / y$^{e}$ 9$^{th}$ of June 1699 by y$^{e}$ said / JAMES DOUGHTY & ELIZABETH his / wife & ordered to be Recorded

Test CHA CHAPMAN C$^{l}$C$^{ur}$

**[280]**

Know all men by these p^r^sents y^t^ I EDMOND PALMER of y^e^ Isle of / Wight County. house Carpenter, & ALICE my Wife doe for us o^r^ heires, Ex^rs^, / Make over, bargaine, Sell & Alienate unto HENERY MARTIN of y^e^ s^d^ / County, his heires, Ex^rs^, or Assignes Seven hundred Acres of land scituated / lying, & being In y^e^ fores^d^ County begining at a pine upon ARTHUR / SMITHs line Seventeen Outs [*sic*], and half, & some odd Chaines running West / North West, & from y^e^ Pine to M^r^ BRESSIEs line seventeen Outs & / half, & some odd Chaines running North East by East y^e^ same to have / & to hold to him y^e^ said HENERY MARTIN, his heires, Ex^rs^, or Assignes with / all housing, ffences, Orchards, priviledges, & Royalty for ever / w^th^ generall warrant against all persons to Every part, or ꝑcell / thereof for all w^ch^ wee y^e^ s^d^ EDMOND & ALICE doe Acknowledge o^r^selves / fully satisfied before y^e^ Sealing & delivery hereof, & for a full, & / Absolute Confirmation hereof doe Obleidge o^r^selves / to Acknowledge this o^r^ voluntary Act & Deed all y^e^ next Court / to be held in y^e^ Isle of Wight County as Wittness o^r^ hands & / Seales this 5^th^ day of September 1677

Sealed, Signed, & delivered in y^e^ p^r^sence of
his
MATHEW: **MW:** WAKLY
mark
JOSHUA TURNER

EDMOND PLAMER Seal
her
ALICE **A** PALMER Seal
mark

By vertue of an Order of y^e^ Isle Wight / County y^e^ 10^th^ Aprill 1699
Recorded ꝑ CHA CHAPMAN C^l^C^ur^

Know all men by these p^r^sence y^t^ I JN^O^ JOHNSON doe appoint HUGH / CAMPBELL to me my Attorney at Isle of Wight County Court in / an action depending JAMES DAY pla^t^: & in all other action y^e^ s^d^ / DAY shall bring against me to Isle of Wight County Court as / Wittness my hand this 9^th^ June 1699 y^e^ word Isle of Wight int^r^lin'd / before Signing

Test his
JN^O^ G COOKES
mark

his
JN^O^ **I** JOHNSON
mark

Recorded ꝑ me / CHA CHAPMAN C^l^C^ur^

**[281]**

To all people to whome this p^r^sent writing shall Come / I HENERY MARTIN in y^e^ Isle of Wight County planter; & MARY / his Wife for a very Valueable Consideration them thereto moveing w^th^: w^ch^: / they Acknowledge themselves fully satisfied, Contented, & paid by ROB^T^ / BROCK of y^e^ said County of y^e^ Isle of Wight County Brick=layer & thereof / doe acquit, & Discharge him for ever. By these p^r^sents have granted / assigned, sold, Covayed [*sic*], Confirmed, & sett over. & by these p^r^sents, doe fully / freely & absolutely grant, assigne, sell, Convey, Confirme & sett over / unto y^e^ said ROB^T^ BROCK his heires, Assignes for ever three hundred Acres / of Land lying, & being in y^e^

fores$^{d}$ County of y$^{e}$ Isle of Wight the foresaid / three hundred acres of Land being p$^{t}$ of a patent two thousand one hundred / acres of Land Granted EDMOND PALMER & by y$^{e}$ said PALMER seven hundred of y$^{e}$ said patten / granted, & Conveyed to my ffather HENERY MARTIN being y$^{e}$ outermost end / of y$^{e}$ patten as more at large is sett forth y$^{e}$ said PALMER Conveyance to / my father y$^{e}$ w$^{ch}$ three hundred acres of Land is to be bounded as / followeth (Viz$^{t}$) begining upon y$^{e}$ Lore Line of JOHN THOMAS hundred / Acres it is Least by y$^{e}$ said MARTIN, to y$^{e}$ said THOMAS. & upermost / hundred Acres of of [*sic*] y$^{e}$ seven hundred Acres sold by y$^{e}$ fores$^{d}$ PALIN or / to y$^{e}$ foresaid MARTIN & Comonly Called by y$^{e}$ name of Martin / folley, & soe extending downwards towards & upon y$^{e}$ Line of / HUGH BRACY, & W$^{M}$ BODY soe including three hundred Acres of / Land as aforesaid y$^{e}$ abovesaid tract or parcell of Land with all / there priviledges, proffitts, & Comodities w$^{t}$soever to the same / granted, Together with all right, title, interest, use, / pertestions, Revacation, propertyes, claimes, & Demand w$^{t}$soever / of them y$^{e}$ said HENERY MARTIN & MARY his wife their heires, or / assignes of in or to y$^{e}$ same, or w$^{ch}$ they now have, or Claime, or / hereafter shall, or may have or claime to y$^{e}$ said Land, w$^{th}$ y$^{e}$ / appurtinances by force, vertue, or meanes of y$^{e}$ said Conveyance / of EDMOND PALMER, or by any other right, or title, wayes, or meanes / w$^{t}$soever, or howsoever. To Have, & to hold y$^{e}$ s$^{d}$ Land, woods, waters / priviledges, or royalties & Appurtinances to y$^{e}$ said ROB$^{T}$ BROCK his / heires & assignes for ever more, & y$^{e}$ said HENERY MARTIN & y$^{e}$ / said MARY his Wife from henceforth for ever to y$^{e}$ only use of y$^{e}$ s$^{d}$ ROB$^{T}$ BROCK his heires or assignes theires [*sic*] heires, & assignes doth hereby Covenant / promise, & agree with y$^{e}$ said ROB$^{T}$ BROCK his heires, & assignes that / they y$^{e}$ said HENERY MARTIN & MARY his Wife theires, or his heires y$^{e}$ / said Land, or tract of Land before mentioned w$^{th}$ y$^{e}$ appurtinances to / y$^{e}$ said ROB$^{T}$ BROCK his heires, & assignes ag$^{st}$ all person or persons / whatsoever claiming under them shall & will warrant, & for / ever defend by these p$^{r}$sents, & that y$^{e}$ s$^{d}$ ROB$^{T}$ BROCK his heires and / Assignes shall & may from henceforth for ever Lawfully peaceably / & quietly have, hold, possess, & enjoy y$^{e}$ said tract of Land with the / appurtinances without y$^{e}$ Lett, suites, trouble, molestation or inter / =ceptions of any person or persons w$^{t}$soever. And lastly y$^{t}$ y$^{e}$ said / HENERY MARTIN & MARY his Wife theires, & his heires or any / Claiming, or to Claiming under him, or them shall and Will att / any time hereafter upon y$^{e}$ Reasonable request of y$^{e}$ s$^{d}$ ROBERT

**[282]**
BROCK his heires or assignes make such farther assurance & / Confirmation of y$^{e}$ said land to y$^{e}$ said ROBERT BROCK & his heires / as by y$^{e}$ said ROB$^{T}$ BROCK his heires or assignes, or his or theires / Counsell Learned in y$^{e}$ Law shall be Reasonable devise, advise / or required. In Wittness hereof they the said HENERY MARTIN & MARY / his wife have to this their deed of bargain & saile put theire hands / & Seales y$^{e}$ 9$^{th}$ day of June 1699

his Seal
HENRY **H** MARTIN O
mark

Signed, sealed, & Delivered
in y$^{e}$ P$^{r}$sence of

ARTHUR SMITH                                                                 her      Seal
KINGMIN MINARD                                                  MARY + MARTIN O
                                                                                  mark

Acknowledged in open / Co[rt] held for y[e] Isle of / Wight County y[e] 9[th] of June / 1699 by HENERY MARTIN & / MARY his Wife to be their Act / & Deed & Orered [*sic*] to be Recorded

Test CHA CHAPMAN C[l]C[ur]

Virginia

To all to whome these p[r]sents shall come. That I THOMAS / JOYNER Senior of y[e] Isle of Wight County send greeting know / yee that I y[e] said THOMAS JOYNER of y[e] County aforesaid for / divers good Causes, & Considerations hereunto moving, but more / especially, for a valueable Consideration have given, granted, / bargained, sold, Aliened, enfeoffed, assigned, & made over, & by / these p[r]sents doe give, grant, bargaine, sell, allienate, enfeoffe, / acquit, & made over unto ARTHUR PURSILL of y[e] foresaid Isle of / Wight County Joyner a ꝑcell of Land Containing four hundred / Acres scituate; & being in y[e] Isle of Wight County bounding / Cap[t] JN[O] FFULGHAMs Land begining on y[e] Maine blackwater / Swamp, & Running from y[e] edge of y[e] Swamp North 37 degrees, / East 458 pole, thence South, & by West ¼ poynt Westerly 72 pole, / Thence East 240 pole, thene South & by East 180 poles to y[e] / Swamp, & soe along y[e] Swamp to y[e] first station. being p[t] / of devident of Land granted to y[e] foresaid, THOMAS JOYNER Sen[r] / by Patten beareing date y[e] 15[th] day of octob[r] Anno Domini 1698 / To have, & to hold, the afores[d] four hundred Acres of Land

**[283]**

Withall y[e] proffitts, commodities, priviledges, Immolliments, herediments [*sic*], & appurtinances thereto belonging, or in any wise / Appertaining, to him y[e] said ARTHUR PURSELL, his heires, Ex[rs], Adm[rs], & / Assignes forever Without Lett, hinderance, or Molestation of him y[e] / said THOMAS JOYNER, or ELIZABETH his Wife, their heires, Ex[rs], Adm[rs], / & Assignes for ever. In & fully accquitted from all manner of / Legacies, Deeds, Dowers, or Conveyances w[t]soever, &, of, & from / all manner of ꝑson or ꝑsons Claiming, or p[r]tending to Claime / any right, Title, & Intrest to y[e] said ꝑcell of Land or any p[t] or / parcell thereof, warranting to make good & defend y[e] same & / for further Confirmation I y[e] said THOMAS JOYNER & ELIZABETH my / Wife doe for us, our heires, Ex[rs], Adm[rs] for ever quitt claime to the / same, & doe obleidge o[r]selves to acknowledge this said deed in y[e] / County Court held for y[e] Isle of Wight County when thereto / required in Wittness whereof we have hereunto sett o[r] hands & / fixed o[r] Seales y[e] [--] day of Aprill one thousand six hundred / Ninety & Nine

Signed, Sealed & ~~dd~~
in p[r]sence of us                                                              THOMAS JOYNER seal
his                                                                                    her

BRIGEMAN B JOYNER mark
THOMAS MANDEW

ELIZABETH E JOYNER Seal mark

Acknowledged in open Co[rt] held for y[e] Isle / of Wight County y[e] 9[th] of June / 1699 by the said THOMAS / JOYNER & his Wife to be / their Act & Deed & / Recorded ꝑ CHA CHAPMAN C[l]C[ur] / By his Excellency / a Proclamation

Virginia Sc[t]

SEAL Whereas his sacred Ma[tie] hath by his Royall Comission / bearing date att Wesminster y[e] twentieth day of July / in y[e] tenth year of his Ma[ties] Reigne Constituted, & appointed / me FFRANCIS NICHOLSON Esq[r] L[t] & Govern[r] Gen[ll] of this his / Ma[ties] Collony & Dominion of Virginia thereby giveing and / granting unto me full power to Exercise & all manner of / Jurisdictions, powers, & Authorities to the same belonging

**[284]**
Now to the end that y[e] Peace of this his Ma[ties] Dominion / may be y[e] better secured, & all proceedings at Law continued, / & that y[e] Ordinary Course of Justice may not be Int[r]rupted / I have thought fitt by & with y[e] advice of his Ma[ties] / Councell of this Collony in his Ma[ties] name to publish & Declare / y[t] All Majestrates & Officers both Civill, & military doe continue / & remaine in all & singular their powers, Authorities, and / Jurisdictions untill further Order be taken therein hereby / requireing them to proceed in y[e] Execution of their sev[r]all / Duties, and all his Majesties Subjects within this Collony / are to be Aiding & Assisting to them therein & to Yeild all / due Obedience to this Proclamation Given under my hand and / & Seale of y[e] Collony the ninth day of December in y[e] tenth year / of y[e] Reign of Our Soveraign Lord William y[e] third by y[e] / Grace of God of England, Scotland, ffrance, & Ireland / King, Deffend[r] of y[e] faith Anno[q] Dom 1698

FFR: NICHOLSON

A Ploclamation [*sic*] for
Continueing Officers

God Save y[e] King / A true Copy Test CC THACKER C[l]Gen[ll]C[ur]

To y[e] Sherriff of Isle / of Wight County / CC THACKER C[l]GenC[ur]

**[285]**
To all to whome this p[r]esent writing shall come / that I POOLE HALL of the Isle of Wight Countyy in Vig[a] / Planter being heir unto THOMAS POOLE my Grandfather Deced / as by his Will appear being prov'd in Co[rt]: for y[e] Isle of Wight / County June y[e] 9[th] Day 1682 wi[ch]: by that Will was given / me & my heires all y[e] Land that my s[d] Grandfather Died possest / withall, being part of a patten of five hundred acres, Granted / to my Grandfather THO: POOLE by S[r]: WILL BERKELEY. & I y[e] s[d] /

POOLE HALL have bargained, & sold unto JN$^{O}$: WATTS one hundred / acres of y$^{e}$ s$^{d}$ Land bounded as follows; begining att a White / Oake in y$^{e}$ thickett y$^{e}$ parts DANIELL LONG land & my Grandfath'r / soe running South from thence seventy five Degrees, West one / hundred & thirty two poles throw COKERs thickett to a corner / tree that p$^{ts}$: JAMES TULLAGH, & THOMAS POOLE, & from thence / North one hundred & twenty six poles to a White Oake, & from / thence North Seventy five Degrees, East one hundred / ten poles, & then East ten Degrees, South to y$^{e}$ Swamp, & / soe up y$^{e}$ Said Swamp to y$^{e}$ first station. including y$^{e}$ hundred / acres y$^{e}$ w$^{ch}$: Land I POOLE HALL have sold unto JN$^{O}$ WATTS, & his / heir for ever. for y$^{e}$ Consideration of six Thous$^{d}$ p$^{ds}$ of Tob / & y$^{e}$ said Tob$^{o}$ I acknowledge fully satisfied & paid by y$^{e}$ said / WATTS. & I y$^{e}$ said POOLE HALL doe by these p$^{r}$sents acquitt, Discharge, / & Release y$^{e}$ s$^{d}$ JOHN WATTS, his heires, Ex$^{rs}$, Adm$^{rs}$, for ever of y$^{e}$ afores$^{d}$: / Tob$^{o}$. And I doe by these P$^{r}$sent fully & absolutely Discharge y$^{e}$ / s$^{d}$ JN$^{O}$ WATTS for ever; by this P$^{r}$sent deed of Saile I POOLE HALL / for me my heires, Ex$^{rs}$, Adm$^{rs}$, & Every of them for ever, Give, / Granted, Alliened, bargained, sold, enfeoffed, & confirmed, And by / These p$^{r}$sents Doth fully, clearly & absolutely Give, grant, / Bargain, sell, alien, enfeoff & Confirme unto y$^{e}$ s$^{d}$ JN$^{O}$: WATTS, his / heires for ever y$^{e}$ fores$^{d}$ hundred acres of Land with all, & / singular its rights, members, Jurisdictions, and appurtanances, / together with all Woods, underwoods, springs, wayes, water, / Proffitts, Comodities w$^{t}$soever appertaining or belonging / y$^{e}$ s$^{d}$ hundred acres of Land; unto y$^{e}$ said JN$^{O}$ WATTS, his heires, for / ever. To have, & to hold from hence forth for ever the s$^{d}$ track / of Land, & y$^{e}$ s$^{d}$ POOLE HALL, for himself, his heires, Ex$^{rs}$, Adm$^{rs}$, / y$^{e}$ said hundred Acres of Land, & all, & singular other y$^{e}$ ꝑmises / before Granted, Bargain'd & sold with y$^{e}$ appurtinances, unto y$^{e}$ y$^{e}$

**[286]**
The s$^{d}$ JOHN WATTS his heires for ever, to y$^{e}$ only use & behoof / of y$^{e}$ s$^{d}$ JOHN WATTS his heires, or assignes for ever against him / y$^{e}$ said POOLE HALL his heires, Ex$^{rs}$. or assignes, and all or every / Person or Persons w$^{t}$soever Lawfull claiming, by, from, or / under him, them or any of them; shall & will warrant; & / for ever Defend y$^{e}$ s$^{d}$ JN$^{O}$ WATTS, his heires or Assignes for ever / By these p$^{r}$sents: & y$^{e}$ said POOLE HALL for himself, his heirs, Ex$^{rs}$, / & Adm$^{rs}$: Doth Covenant, promise, grant, & agreant [*sic*], & agree / to & with y$^{e}$ s$^{d}$ JOHN WATTS, his heires, & assignes, & every of / them, By these presents in manner & forme following y$^{t}$ / Is to say y$^{t}$ y$^{e}$ s$^{d}$ POOLE HALL att y$^{e}$ time of Sealing, & Delivery / of these p$^{r}$sents, has a pure, ꝑfect, & absolute Estate of / Inheritance of all & singular y$^{e}$ fores$^{d}$ p$^{r}$mises, & every part / thereof shall be fully vested, setled, & Executed in & upon y$^{e}$ / said JN$^{O}$: WATTS, his heires for ever. According to y$^{e}$ true meaning / of these p$^{r}$sents, shall Continue, & be seized of & in y$^{e}$ said / hundred acres of Land, & that y$^{e}$ s$^{d}$ POOLE HALL att y$^{e}$ time of the / Sealing & Delivery of these p$^{r}$sent hath full power & Authority / to grant, bargain & sell, & convay all & singular mentioned / ꝑmises with their and every of their appurtinances unto / y$^{e}$ said JN$^{O}$ WATTS, his heires, & Assignes, & every of them shall / & may by Vertue of these

p$^{r}$sents from time to time, & att / all times for ever hereaft$^{r}$: Lawfull, peaceable & quiettly / have, hold, use, possess y$^{e}$ s$^{d}$ hundred are [*sic*] of land, & all and / singular y$^{e}$ before Granted ꝑmises, to take all y$^{e}$ proffitts for / ever; without lett, suit or trouble, Deniall or Disturbance / of y$^{e}$ s$^{d}$ POOLE HALL, his heir, or assignes, or any person or p$^{r}$sons / w$^{t}$soever Lawfull claiming by, from or under him, or by his or / their meanes act, consent, title, intrest, privity or procurem$^{t}$ / & fatther I y$^{e}$ s$^{d}$ POOLE HALL for me, my heires, Ex$^{rs}$, & / Adm$^{rs}$, covenant & agree to & with y$^{e}$ s$^{d}$ JOHN WATTS his / heires, or assignes to make any farther Right y$^{t}$ or either / of them shall Desire or their, or his learned Councell in y$^{e}$ / Law shall Deny & y$^{t}$ this p$^{r}$sent Deed of bargain & saile I & / my wife will each acknowledge att y$^{e}$ next Court held for y$^{e}$ / Isle of Wight County to be our free & Voluntary Act / & Deed where my s$^{d}$ Wife Shall relinquish her

**[287]**
Dower hereby Wittness our hand & Seal this 9$^{th}$ / 1699

POOLE HALL (Seal)
her
ANNE **B** HALL (Seal)
mark

These presents wittness y$^{t}$ I CHRISTIAN STANTON / doe hereby relinquish & Discharge all my right / to the abovesaid hundred Acres of Land

Signed, Seale & Delivered
in y$^{e}$ presence of
ARTHUR SMITH

her Seal
CHRISTIAN **N** STANTON O
mark

Acknowledged in open Co$^{rt}$ held For y$^{e}$ Isle of Wight County the / 9$^{th}$ day of Aug$^{t}$ 1699 by y$^{e}$ said POOL HALL & ANNE his / Wife to be their acts & Deeds, and Relinquishm$^{t}$ of Dower / Confessed & declaired by y$^{e}$ said ANNE, And Ordered to be / Recorded

Test CHA CHAPMAN C$^{l}$C$^{ur}$

To all to whome these p$^{r}$sents shall come I S$^{r}$: EDMOND ANDROSS / K$^{nt}$: his Ma$^{ties}$ L$^{t}$: & Gov$^{r}$: Gen$^{l}$: of Virg$^{a}$ send Greeting. Whereas / his late Maj$^{ti}$ King Charles y$^{e}$ 2$^{d}$ hath been graciously pleased / by his Royall Letters patents Und$^{r}$. y$^{e}$ Great Seal of England, / bearing date at Westminster y$^{e}$ 10$^{enth}$. day of October, in y$^{e}$ Eighth / & twentieth year of his Reign, amonst [*sic*] other things in y$^{e}$ said / Letters Patents Contained to Continue & Confirme y$^{e}$ antient pow$^{r}$: / & priviledge of granting fifty Acres of Land for Every p$^{r}$son / Imported into this Collony of Virginia. Now know yee y$^{t}$ I the / said EDMOND ANDROSS K$^{nt}$: Gov$^{r}$: &c doe with y$^{e}$ advice & Consent / of y$^{e}$ Councell of State acocrdingly give & grant unto HENERY / SANDERS one hundred & eighteen Acres of Land In y$^{e}$ Lower / Parrish of y$^{e}$ Isle of Wight County near Kingsaile begining at / a Pine a Corner tree to THO: PARKERs, thence along y$^{e}$ said / PARKERs Line South

Eleven & a Quarter degree, West forty / Poles to a Pine,thence South thirty four degrees, West / Eighty four poles to a White Oake, thence South fifteen / degrees, West twenty six poles to a White Oake, thence South / forty six poles, thence South twenty Nine Degrees,

**[288]**
West fourteen pole to a Pine standing in EDW$^{D}$: TELWELLs / Line, North thirty five degrees, West fifty five pole to a / Pine, thence North thirty three deg$^{s}$, West Sixteen poles / to a Pine a Corner tree of JN$^{O}$ BRIANTs, thence North / fourteen deg$^{s}$, West one hundred twenty six poles to an / Old Pine, thence North Eight deg$^{s}$, East Ninety four poles / to a Pine standing in JN$^{O}$ ROBERTs Line, thence along y$^{e}$ said / ROBERTs Line South seventy degrees, East one hundred fifty / five poles to a Gum, standing in a Branch, thence South / thirty nine degrees, West sixteen poles to y$^{e}$ begining, y$^{e}$ / said land being due unto y$^{e}$ said HENRY SANDERS by & for y$^{e}$ / Transportation of three p$^{r}$sons into this Colony whose / names are to be in y$^{e}$ Records mentioned under this patent. / To have & To hold y$^{e}$ s$^{d}$ land with due share of all mines / & Mineralls therein Contained, with all Rights & priviledges / of hunting, hawking, fishing & fowling; with all Woods / Waters & Rivers, with all profitts, Comodities & heradem$^{ts}$: / w$^{t}$soever belonging to y$^{e}$ s$^{d}$ land to him y$^{e}$ s$^{d}$ HENERY SANDERS / his Heires & Assignes for ever, in as Large & ample manner / of ~~East Greenwich~~ to all intents & purposes as hath been used / & allowed since y$^{e}$ first Plantation to be held of o$^{r}$ Soveraign / Lord y$^{e}$ King his heires & Successors as of his Mannor of / East Greenwich in free & common Soccage, & not *In capite* / nor by K$^{nts}$: service, Yeilding & paying unto our s$^{d}$ Soveraign / Lord y$^{e}$ King his heires, & Successors, for every fifty Acres of / Land hereby granted, att y$^{e}$ feast of S$^{t}$ Michaell y$^{e}$ Arch Angell / y$^{e}$ fee rent of one S~~hill~~ which paym$^{t}$ is to made [*sic*] Yearely, / from year to year, Provided y$^{t}$ y$^{e}$ said HENERY SANDERS his / heires or Assignes doe not seat or plant, nor Cause to be / Seated or planted thereon within three years next / ensueing y$^{e}$ date hereof y$^{t}$ then it shall and may be Lawfull / for

**[289]**
For any adventurrer to make Choyce thereof, & seat thereon / Given under my hand, & y$^{e}$ Seale of y$^{e}$ collony this 26$^{th}$ day of / Aprill in y$^{e}$ tenth year of his Maj$^{s}$ Reign Anno~~q~~ Dom 1698

HENRY SANDERS his patent for 118 } ANDROS
Acres, of Land in y$^{e}$ Isle of Wight County}

E JENINGS Dep$^{ty}$ Sec$^{ry}$

Know all men by these p$^{r}$sents y$^{t}$ I HENERY SANDERS of y$^{e}$ Isle of / Wight County planter & MARGERETT my Wife for divers good Causes & / Considerations us hereunto moveing. but more especially for & in / Consideration of a certain sume of Tob$^{o}$ to us in hand paid, or secured / to be paid by THOMAS COOPER of y$^{e}$ afores$^{d}$ County of y$^{e}$ Isle of Wight y$^{e}$ / receipt whereof wee doe hereby Acknowledge & Concess, doe for us our / heires, Ex$^{rs}$ & Adm$^{rs}$ Assign & sett over unto y$^{e}$ said THOMAS COOPER all / our Right, title & Interest of in & unto y$^{e}$ within mentioned Patten / unto him y$^{e}$ said THOMAS COOPER, his heires, & Assignes for ever, free & / Clear & freely & Clearely Acquitted & Discharged from all manner of / former gifts & grants W$^{t}$soever In Wittness whereof wee have / hereunto sett our hands, Seales this 9$^{th}$ Day of Aug$^{st}$ 1699

HENERY SANDERS<br>
MARGARETT **M** SANDERS<br>
her mark

Signed Sealed & Delivered<br>
in y$^{e}$ p$^{r}$sence of us<br>
Signum<br>
THOMAS Ŧ DAILE<br>
JN$^{O}$ Ɨ [ ]LINT

Acknowledged in open Co$^{rt}$ / held for y$^{e}$ Isle of Wight County / y$^{e}$ 9$^{th}$ of Aug$^{st}$ 99 by y$^{e}$ s$^{d}$ HENERY SANDERS / & MARGARETT his Wife to be their / Act & Deed & Ordered to be / Recorded 1699

Terst CHA CHAPMAN C$^{l}$C$^{ur}$

**[290]**

This Indenture made y$^{e}$ 6$^{th}$ day of June Anno 1667 betweene / JN$^{O}$ MARSHALL of y$^{e}$ one party, & W$^{M}$ WEST of y$^{e}$ Isle of Wight / County of y$^{e}$ other party, Wittnesseth y$^{t}$ y$^{e}$ s$^{d}$ MARSHALL for / & in Consideration of fifteen hundred p$^{ds}$ of Tob$^{o}$ & Cask to / paid [*sic*] before y$^{e}$ Sealing, & delivering of these p$^{r}$sents, by y$^{e}$ s$^{d}$ / W$^{M}$ WEST. y$^{e}$ receipt whereof y$^{e}$ s$^{d}$ JN$^{O}$ MARSHALL doe hereby / Acknowledege himself fully satisfied thereof, & of every ꝑt & / ꝑsell thereof doe hereby acquit, & discharge y$^{e}$ s$^{d}$ W$^{M}$ WEST / his heires, & Assignes for ever. By these p$^{r}$sents have granted / Alienated, bargained, sold & Confirmed unto y$^{e}$ s$^{d}$ W$^{M}$ WEST his / heires & Assignes for ever, a Certain ꝑcell of Land Lying & / being In the Isle of Wight County Containing one hundred / & sixty Acres more or Less, being on y$^{e}$ Western side / of a divident of Land granted unto JN$^{O}$ MARSHALL by / Patent beareing date y$^{e}$ 5$^{th}$ day of Aprill Anno Dm / 1667 And bounded about with marked trees, w$^{th}$ all it's / Rights, prviledges, & profitts, & heredim$^{ts}$ to y$^{e}$ s$^{d}$ divident / of Land belonging, or any ꝑt or ꝑcell thereof, or in any / wise appertaining, & all y$^{t}$ Estate, right, title, Interest / or Claime of him y$^{e}$ s$^{d}$ JN$^{O}$ MARSHALL, of, in or to y$^{e}$ / p$^{r}$mises or any ꝑt or ꝑcell thereof. To have & to / hold y$^{e}$ s$^{d}$ divident of Land, & all & singular y$^{e}$ p$^{r}$mises / with y$^{e}$ appurtinances before bargained & sold unto y$^{e}$ s$^{d}$ / W$^{M}$ WEST to y$^{e}$ onely proper use & behoofe / of y$^{e}$ s$^{d}$ W$^{M}$ WEST his heires & Assignes for ever. & y$^{e}$ s$^{d}$ / JN$^{O}$ MARSHALL for him, his heires & Assignes doe Covenant / & grant y$^{t}$ Notwithstandinge any Act of him att time of / Sealeing & delivering these p$^{r}$sents, done to y$^{e}$ Contrary / is & standeth Lawfully seized of an Infiazable Inheritance / of all & singular, of all & singular & before demised / p$^{r}$mises and of every ꝑt & ꝑcell thereof unto y$^{e}$ s$^{d}$ W$^{M}$ / WEST, his heires, Ex$^{rs}$, & Assignes for ever, & y$^{e}$ s$^{d}$ MARSHALL

**[291]**

MARSHALL doe further Covenant & assure y^e^ s^d^ W^M^ WEST his / heires & Assignes y^t^ y^e^ s^d^ divident of Land, & all other y^e^ / p^r^mises with y^e^ appurtinances, att y^e^ time of ensealing and / delivering of these p^r^sents shall remaine & Continue unto y^e^ s^d^ / W^M^ WEST, his heires & Assignes Clearely acquited & discharged / of & from all manner of former bargaines, Sales, Gifts, / grantes, Legacyes, doweryes, Judgm^ts^, of & from all manner / of other Charges, troubles, Incumbrances w^t^soever, had / made, acknowledged, Consented unto, done, suffered by y^e^ s^d^ / JN^O^ MARSHALL his heires or assignes or by any other ꝑson or / ꝑsons w^t^soever Lawfully Claimeing under him, or by / his Act, meanes or procurem^t^ y^e^ rents & services from / henceforth due, to his Ma^tie^ only excepted. In Witness / Whereof I have hereunto sett my hand & Seale y^e^ day & / year abovewritten

The above being a Coppy of a grant from / my father JOHN MARSHALL, I doe by these / p^r^sents for me, my heires, Ex^rs^ & Assignes / ratifie & Confirme to y^e^ s^d^ W^M^ WEST his / heires & Assignes for ever Wittness my / hand & seal this 16^th^ day of October 1699

Seal

Signed, Sealed & delivered HUM: MARSHALL O

in y^e^ p^r^sence of

AR: SMITH

CHAP CHAPMAN

Acknowledged open Co^rt^ held For y^e^ Isle of Wight County / y^e^ 16^th^ day of October 1699 & Recorded

ꝑ CHA CHAPMAN C^l^C^ur^

**[292]**

This Indentutre made y^e^ 5^th^ day of July Anno Dom 1699 Between RICH^D^ / BENNETT in y^e^ Upper Parish of y^e^ Isle of Wight County and RICH^D^ BENNETT / Jun^r^ of y^e^ other Party of y^e^ same parish, Witness y^t^ I the said RICH^D^ / RICHARD [*sic*] BENNETT Sen^r^ for a valluable consideracon reced of y^e^ said / RICHARD BENNETT Jun^r^ doe For my selfe my Heires Ex^rs^ Adm^rs^ or A^ss^ / Rattifie Confirme avouch, and by these p^r^sents For ever putt over unto / him y^e^ said RICHARD BENNETT Jun^r^ his Heires Ex^rs^ adm^rs^ or assignes / all my right & Tytle of a certeyn quantity of Land be it more or / begining att y^e^ mouth of y^e^ Branch, that is Called Hickory Vally / and From thence a streight Lyne to a Corner tree w^ch^ stands in a / Hedge Row, that belongs to EDWARD JONES, Then takeing in the / plantacon where RICHARD BENNETT Jun^r^ now dwells, The said / Land being part of y^e^ Land, that was bought of W^M^ MYLES in / y^e^ year 1656 Know this that I RICHARD BENNETT Sen^r^ doe / Confirme & putt over to RICHARD BENNETT my Sonne his Heires / Ex^rs^ Adm^rs^ & Assignes, that parcell of Land, to be & to hould / possess & Enjoy w^th^out any molestacon or trouble, w^th^ all share / of Mynes

Mineralls therein Conteyned, w$^{th}$ all rights profitts and / Comodities thereunto belonging, the said RICHARD BENNETT Jun$^{r}$ / to pay y$^{e}$ Quitrents For y$^{e}$ same accordeing to y$^{e}$ Tean$^{r}$ of y$^{e}$ pattent / In witness I y$^{e}$ aforesaid RICHARD BENNETsen$^{r}$ have hereunto sett / my hand y$^{e}$ day & Year above written

Signed sealed delivered in p$^{r}$sence of
RICHARD HOLLYMAN
PETER VASSER
W$^{M}$ HOLLYMAN

RICH$^{D}$ **R:B:** BENNETT Sen O
Signum

Acknowledged in open Co$^{rt}$ held For y$^{e}$ Isle Wight Count y$^{e}$ 9$^{th}$ day of Octob$^{r}$ 1699 & Recorded
p CHA CHAPMAN C$^{l}$C$^{ur}$

This Bill binds us ROB$^{T}$ KAE & GEORGE MOORE, us or either / of us Joyntly & severally o$^{r}$ heires Ex$^{rs}$ & Adm$^{rs}$, to pay or cause / to be paid to Cap$^{t}$ HEN: APPLEWHAITE p$^{r}$sident of y$^{e}$ Isle of Wight / County Co$^{rt}$. to him, or his Success$^{rs}$. y$^{e}$ sum of six Thous$^{d}$ three / hundred & fifty p$^{ds}$ of good sound M$^{r}$chantable Tob$^{o}$ in cask / convenient in y$^{e}$ Isle of Wight County payable in year of o$^{r}$ Lord / 1701 upon y$^{e}$ 10$^{enth}$ Day of Octob$^{r}$ it being Due for goods bought

**[293]**

bought an Outcry, out of y$^{e}$ Estate of Cap$^{t}$ JN$^{O}$ GOODRICH deced / Wittness o$^{r}$ hands this 17$^{th}$ Day of July 1699

Testes
CHA CHAPMAN
RICH$^{D}$ REYNOLDS

ROBERT KAE
GEORGE MOORE

Recorded p CHA CHAPMAN C$^{l}$C$^{ur}$

This bill Bindeth us JAMES MICE & RICH$^{D}$ HOLLIMAN or either / of us Joyntly & severally o$^{r}$ heires, Ex$^{rs}$. & Adm$^{rs}$ to pay or cause / to be paid to Cap$^{t}$ HEN: APPLEWHAIT P$^{r}$sident of y$^{e}$ Isle of Wight Co$^{rt}$. / to him, or his Successors, y$^{e}$ full sum of four hundred & ten pounds / of good sound M$^{r}$chantable Tob$^{o}$ & Cask Convenient in y$^{e}$ Isle of / Wight County payable upon y$^{e}$ tenth day of Octob$^{r}$ in y$^{e}$ year 1701 / it being for goods bought at an Outcry out of y$^{e}$ Estate of Cap$^{t}$ / JN$^{O}$ GOODRICH deced Wittness o$^{r}$ hands y$^{e}$ 17$^{th}$ of July

Testes
CHA CHAPMAN
RICH$^{D}$ REYNOLDS

JACOBUS MICE
RICH$^{D}$ HOLLYMAN

Recorded p CHA CHAPMAN C$^{l}$C$^{ur}$

This Bill binds us GEORGE WRIGHT & JN$^{O}$ TURNER or either of / us, Joyntly & severally O$^{r}$: heires, Ex$^{rs}$, Adm$^{rs}$, to pay or cause / to be paid to Cap$^{t}$ APPLEWHAIT p$^{r}$sident of y$^{e}$ Isle of Wight County / Co$^{rt}$. to him, or his Success$^{rs}$. y$^{e}$ full sum of four hundred and / thirty pounds of good sound M$^{r}$chantable Tob$^{o}$ in Cask conveni / ent in y$^{e}$ Isle of Wight County; payable upon y$^{e}$ 10$^{th}$ day of Octob$^{r}$. / in y$^{e}$ year 1701 It being for goods bought at an Outcry out / of y$^{e}$ Estate of Cap$^{t}$ JN$^{O}$ GOODRICH deced Wittness o$^{r}$ hands y$^{e}$ 17$^{th}$ / day of July 1699

Testes his mark
CHA CHAPMAN GEORGE & WRIGHT
RICH$^{D}$ REYNOLDS JNO + TURNER
signum

Recorded p CHA CHAPMAN C$^{l}$C$^{ur}$

This Bill bindeth us JN$^{O}$ TURNER & GEO: WRIGHT or either of us / Joyntly & severally, O$^{r}$ heires, Ex$^{rs}$ & Adm$^{rs}$, to pay or cause to / be paid to Cap$^{t}$ HEN: APPLEWAHIT P$^{r}$sident of y$^{e}$ Isle of Wight / County Co$^{rt}$, to him, or his Success$^{rs}$, y$^{e}$ full sum of Eleven / hundred & Eighty pounds of good, sound M$^{r}$chantable Tob$^{o}$ in Caske convenient in y$^{e}$ Isle of Wight County payable upon y$^{e}$

**[294]**

Tenth day of Octob$^{r}$ in y$^{e}$ year of o$^{r}$ Lord 1701 It being due for goods / bought out of y$^{e}$ Estate of Cap$^{t}$ JN$^{O}$ GOODRICH deced att an / Outcry Witnesse o$^{r}$ hands this 17$^{th}$ day of July 1699

Testes his mark
CHA CHAPMAN JN$^{O}$ + TURNER
RICHD REYNOLDS his mark
GEO: **J:** WRIGHT

Recorded p CHA CHAPMAN CC$^{ur}$

This bill bindeth us JN$^{O}$ WHETSTONE & GEO: BARLOW or eitther / of us Joyntly & severally o$^{r}$ heires Ex$^{rs}$, & Adm$^{rs}$. to pay or cause / to be paid, to Cap$^{t}$ HEN: APPLEWHAIT P$^{r}$sident of y$^{e}$ Isle of Wight / County Co$^{rt}$. to him, or his Success$^{rs}$ y$^{e}$ full sum of five & / & twenty hundred & fifty pounds of good, sound M$^{r}$chantable / Tob$^{o}$ in Caske Convenient in y$^{e}$ Isle of Wight County payable upon / y$^{e}$ 10$^{th}$ of Octob$^{r}$ in y$^{e}$ year of o$^{r}$ Lord 1701 It being due for / goods bought at an Outcry out of y$^{e}$ Estate of Cap$^{t}$ JOHN / GOODRICH deced Wittnesse o$^{r}$ hands this 17$^{th}$ day of July 1699

Testes JN$^{O}$ WHETSTONE
CHA CHAPMAN GEO: BARLOW
RICH$^{D}$ REYNOLDS

Recorded p CHA CHAPMAN C$^{l}$C$^{ur}$

This Bill bindeth us PETER DEBERRY & FRA: RENN or either / of us, Joyntly & severally o$^{r}$ heires Ex$^{rs}$ & Adm$^{rs}$. to pay or / cause to be paid to Cap$^{t}$ HEN: APPLEWHAIT P$^{r}$sident of y$^{e}$ Isle of / Wight County Co$^{rt}$. to him, or his Success$^{rs}$. y$^{e}$ full Sum of Nine / hundred pounds of good, sound M$^{r}$chantable Tob$^{o}$. in Cask convenient / in y^e^ Isle of Wight County payable upon y^e^ 10^th^ day of 8^br^ in y^e^ year / 1701 It being for goods bought at an outcry out of y^e^ Estate / of Cap^t^ JN^O^ GOODRICH deced Wittness o^r^ hands this 17^th^ Day of / July 1699

Testes
CHA CHAPMAN
RICH^D^ REYNOLDS:

PETER DEBERRY
his
FFRA: **FW** WRENN
mark

Recorded ꝑ CHA CHAPMAN C^l^C^ur^

This Bill bindeth us EDW^D^ CHITTY & JN^O^ DAVIS or either of us, / Joyntly & severally o^r^ heires Ex^rs^, & Adm^rs^ to pay to Cap^t^ HEN: / APPLEWHAIT p^r^sident of y^e^ Isle of Wight County Co^rt^. to him or his / Success^rs^, y^e^ full sum of fourteen hundred & forty pounds of good / Sound

**[295]**

Sound M^r^chantable Tob^o^ in Cask Convenient in y^e^ Isle of / Wight County payable upon y^e^ 10^th^ day of Octob^r^. in y^e^ year of o^r^ / Lord 1701 it being due for goods bought at an Outcry of y^e^ Estate / of Cap^t^ JN^O^ GOODRICH deced, Wittnesse O^r^ hands this 17^th^ day of July 1699

Testes
CHA CHAPMAN
RICH^D^ REYNOLDS

EDW^RD^ CHITTY
JN^O^ DAVIS

Recorded ꝑ CHA CHAPMAN C^l^C^ur^

This Bill bindeth me GEO: BARLOW, & PETER DEBERRY or either of / us Joyntly & severally o^r^ heires, Ex^rs^. & Adm^rs^ to pay or cause to / be paid to Cap^t^ HEN: APPLEWHAIT P^r^sident of y^e^ Isle of Wight County / Co^rt^. to him or his Success^rs^. y^e^ full sum of two thous^d^ three / hundred & twenty p^ds^ of good sound M^r^chantable Tob^o^ in Cask / Convenient In y^e^ Isle of Wight County payable upon y^e^ 10^th^ day of / Octob^r^. in y^e^ year of o^r^ Lord 1701 it being due for goods bought att / an Outcry out of y^e^ Estate of Cap^t^ JN^O^. GOODRICH deced / Wittnesse o^r^ hands this 17^th^ Day of July 1699

Testes
CHA CHAPMAN
RICH^D^ REYNOLDS

GEO BARLOW
PETER DEBERRY

Recorded ꝑ CHA CHAPMAN C^l^C^ur^

This Bill bindeth us JA^S^ CAUFIELD, & RICH^D^ BENNETT, or either of us / Joyntly, & severally O^r^ heires, Ex^rs^, & Adm^rs^ to pay, or Cause to be p^d^ / to Cap^t^ HEN: APPLEWHAIT p^r^sident of y^e^ Isle of Wight County Co^rt^. to / him or his Success^rs^. y^e^ sum of sixteen hundred & fifty pounds of / good, sound, merchantable Tob^o^ in Caske Convenient in y^e^ Isle of Wight / payable y^e^ year of o^r^ Lord 1701 it being due for goods bought / att an Outcry out of y^e^ Estate of Cap^t^ JN^O^ GOODRICH Deced Wittness our / hands this 17^th^ of July 1699

The aboves^d^ Tob^o^ to be p^d^ upon y^e^ 10^th^ day of 8^br^ / in y^e^ year above written

Testes<br>CHA CHAPMAN<br>RICH^D^ REYNOLDS

his mark<br>JAMES **IC** CAUFIELD<br>Signum<br>RICH^D^ **RB** BENNETT

Recorded ꝑ CHA CHAPMAN C^l^C^ur^

**[296]**

This Indenture made y^e^ 9^th^ of 10^br^ in year of our Lord God 1699 & / in y^e^ 11^th^ year of y^e^ Reign of o^r^ Sov^r^aign Lord Will y^e^ 3^d^ by y^e^ grace / of God of England, Scotland, France & Ireland King &c: between / EDWARD COBB of y^e^ Lower ꝑish of y^e^ Isle of Wight County of y^e^ one ꝑt & ANDREW / WOODLY of y^e^ upper ꝑish & County fores^d^ of y^e^ other ꝑt Wittnesseth y^t^ y^e^ s^d^ / EDW^D^ COBB for & in Consideration of six thous^d^ five hundred p^ds^ of Tob^o^ / & Cask to him in hand at & before y^e^ sealing & Delivery of these / P^r^sents by y^e^ s^d^ ANDREW WOODLY well & truely & p^d^ y^e^ receipt whereof he / y^e^ s^d^ EDW^D^ COBB doth hereby acknowledge, & himselfe therew^th^ fully / satisfied & p^d^; & thereof & of every ꝑt & ꝑcell thereof doth clearly / acquit, exonerate & discharge y^e^ s^d^ ANDREW WOODLY his heires, Ex^rs^ & Adm^rs^ / for Ever by these p^r^sents hath given, granted, Aliened bargained, sold, / enfeoffed & Confirmed, & by these p^r^sents doth fully clearly & Absolutely Give, grant, bargain, / sell, alien, Enfeoffe & Confirme unto y^e^ s^d^ ANDREW WOODLY his heires / and Assignes for ever. a certain ꝑcell or tract of land Scituate, lyeing / & being in upper ꝑish & County afores^d^ called y^e^ little Neck, & now in y^e^ possession / of y^e^ s^d^ ANDREW WOODLY. Beginning at a marked Oake standing upon a / Point on y^e^ Southward side of a creek Called Ffloyds Creek Issueing / out of Pagan Creek, & running up a long y^e^ side of y^e^ s^d^ Creek three / hundred fifty two poles, Westerly unto a Swamp Called Gualkine Swamp / from thence along a Swamp called JN^O^ CROWEs Swamp south Eighty / six poles to a marked Oake to y^e^ head of y^e^ s^d^ Swamp, from thence / South East & by South, Southerly Joyning upon M^r^ NICH^O^ SMITH a / hundred Sixty four poles to a swamp, from thence a long Down y^e^ / s^d^ Swamp forty six poles to a marked Spanish Oake joyning upon / Major JN^O^ BOND. from thence Northwest to a marked White Oake / Sixty four poles to a Swamp, from thence along Downe y^e^ said / Swamp w^ch^ runneth into Ffloyds Creek, Northerly two hundred / & two Acres of land being granted by patent to NICHOLAS COBB, / father to y^e^ s^d^ EDW^D^ COBB Dated y^e^ 21^st^ Day of ffeb 1663 To have & / & to hold y^e^ afores^d^ two hundred & two Acres of Land according / to y^e^ bounds aforementioned & exprest. With all & singular its / Rights, members, & Jurisdictions & appurtinances, together withall / houses, Edifices, Buildings, Orchards. Gardens, hereditam^ts^ & appurtinances

**[297]**

Whatsoever, to y$^{e}$ s$^{d}$ Messuage, plantation or plantations & p$^{r}$mises / or to any ꝑt, or ꝑcell of them belonging on in any wise apprtaining / thereunto; unto y$^{e}$ s$^{d}$ ANDREW WOODLY, his heires, Assignes to y$^{e}$ onely / proper use & behoofe of him y$^{e}$ s$^{d}$ ANDREW WOODLY, his heires or assignes / for ever, against him y$^{e}$ s$^{d}$ EDW$^{D}$ COBB his heires and assignes, and all / & every other ꝑson and ꝑsons whatsoever Lawfully claimeing by / form or under him, them or any of them shall & will warrant, & for / ever Defend by theser p$^{r}$sents: And that y$^{e}$ s$^{d}$ EDW$^{D}$ COBB for himselfe, his / Heires, Ex$^{rs}$, & Adm$^{rs}$ Doe Covenant, promise, grant & agree to & with y$^{e}$ s$^{d}$ / ANDREW WOODLY, his heires & Assignes, & every of them by these p$^{r}$sents, that / all & singular y$^{e}$ afores$^{d}$ p$^{r}$mises, with all y$^{e}$ appurtinances thereunto / belonging; Now be & Ever hereafter shall be, stand, & continue to y$^{e}$ said / ANDREW WOODLY & his heires and assignes for ever: that y$^{e}$ s$^{d}$ ANDREW / WOODLY, his heires or Assignes be freely & clearly acquited, Exonerated / & discharg'd; & from time to time well & sufficiently saved & kept / harmless by y$^{e}$ s$^{d}$ EDW$^{D}$ COBB, his heires, Ex$^{rs}$ & Adm$^{rs}$ of & from all manner / of former & other gifts, grants, bargains, sails, mortgages, Joynters, Dono$^{rs}$. / by y$^{e}$ s$^{d}$ EDW$^{D}$ COBB, his heires or assignes, or by any ꝑson or ꝑsons w$^{t}$soevr, / & y$^{t}$ y$^{e}$ s$^{d}$ p$^{r}$mises w$^{th}$ all y$^{e}$ appurtinances thereunto / belonging shall be esteemed & adjudged & taken to be & Ennure to / y$^{e}$ onely proper use & behoofe of him y$^{e}$ s$^{d}$ ANDREW WOODLY, his heires / & assignes for Ever. & to no other use, Intent or purpose w$^{t}$soever / In Wittness whereof I have hereunto sett my hand y$^{e}$ day, yeare, & reigne / first abovewritten

his
Signed Sealed & Delivered in y$^{e}$ prsence} EDWARD + COBB (seal)
of us whose names are underwritten } mark
RICH$^{D}$ REYNOLDS
W$^{M}$ MAYO Acknowledged in open Co$^{rt}$ held for y$^{e}$
HEN: WOODLY Isle of Wight County y$^{e}$ 9$^{th}$. of 10$^{br}$. 1699
by y$^{e}$ s$^{d}$ EDW$^{D}$ COBB

Recorded ꝑ CHA CHAPMAN C$^{l}$C$^{ur}$

**[298]**

Know all men by these p$^{r}$sents, y$^{t}$ I DORITHY COBB doe hereby appoint / Constitute & ordain my Loveing husband EDW$^{D}$ COBB my Lawfull / Attorny to acknowledge & relinquish all my right of Dower to M$^{r}$ / to [*sic*] M$^{r}$. ANDREW WOODLY, his heires & assignes y$^{t}$ I have to y$^{t}$ track / of Land Calld y$^{e}$ little Neck as Wittness my hand this 14$^{th}$ of Novemb$^{r}$ / 1699 / y$^{e}$ words EDWD COBB interlined afores signeing Acknowledged & Recorded her
Signed & delivered & before DORITHY + COBB
AR. SMITH mark
W$^{M}$: MAYO

Recorded ꝑ CHA CHAPMAN C$^{l}$C$^{ur}$

To all to whome these p$^{r}$sents shall come, I FFRANCIS NICHOLSON / Esq$^{r}$. their Ma$^{ties}$ L$^{t}$ Gove$^{r}$n$^{r}$. of Virg$^{a}$ Send greeting. Whereas his late / Ma$^{tie}$. King Charles y$^{e}$ 2$^{d}$. hath been graciously pleased by his Royall / l$^{rs}$ patents under y$^{e}$ great Seal of England beareing date at Westminst$^{r}$. / y$^{e}$ 10$^{th}$ day of Octob$^{r}$ in y$^{e}$ 28$^{th}$ year of his Reign amongst other thing, / in y$^{e}$ s$^{d}$ L$^{rs}$ patents Contained to continue & Confirme y$^{e}$ Ancient pow$^{r}$. / & priviledge of granting fifty Acers of Land for every ꝑson Imported / into this Collony of Virginia. Now Knowe yee y$^{t}$ I y$^{e}$ s$^{d}$ FFRANCIS NICHOLSON / Esq$^{r}$. their Mat$^{es}$. L$^{t}$ & Gov$^{r}$: &c: doe w$^{th}$ y$^{e}$ Advice & Consent of y$^{e}$ Councell / of State accordingly give & grant unto Maj$^{r}$. ARTH$^{R}$: ALLEN one hundred / & seventy acres of Land scituate betweene y$^{e}$ lands of M$^{r}$ TOOKE Captain / ENGLAND, THOMAS BLAKE, & EDW$^{D}$ BRANTLY in y$^{e}$ upper ꝑish of y$^{e}$ Isle of / Whight County begining at a Red Oake THO: BLAKEs Corner tree in M$^{r}$. / TOOKEs Line thence by y$^{e}$ s$^{d}$ BLAKEs Line South Seventy three degrees / West two hundred & six poles to a small Red Oake, North Seventy / four degrees, West sixty poles to a Pine, & North thirty four degrees, / West a hundred & two pole to a ~~stooping Red Oake in or near Cap$^{t}$ / ENGLAND's Line then by~~ Pine in M$^{r}$ NEWMANs Line & soe by his Line / North North East twenty nine pole to a stooping Red Oake in or / near Cap$^{t}$. ENGLANDs Line, then by y$^{e}$ s$^{d}$ ENGLANDs Line South / sixty nine degrees, East a hund an [*sic*] eight pole to a small White Oak, / and

**[299]**
And North thirty one degrees; East a hundred & seven pole to two markt / Pines EDW$^{D}$ BRANTLY's Corner tree, near y$^{e}$ dancing place, & then by y$^{e}$ s$^{d}$ / BRANTLY's Line South East fifty two pole to a pine, & North East twenty / pole to M$^{r}$. TOOKEs Line, & soe by his Line South East a hundred thirty / six pole, to y$^{e}$ first Station. The s$^{d}$ Land being formerly granted to / M$^{r}$ ROB$^{T}$ FLAKE by patent dated y$^{e}$ 20$^{th}$ day of Aprill 1685 & by him / deserted, & is since granted to y$^{e}$ s$^{d}$ Maj$^{r}$. ARTHUR ALLEN by Order of y$^{e}$ / Genall Co$^{rt}$. dated at James Citty y$^{e}$ 17$^{th}$ day of Aprill 1691. & is due by & / for y$^{e}$ Importation of four ꝑsons into this Collony; whose names are / in y$^{e}$ Records menconed under this patent. To have & to hold y$^{e}$ said / land w$^{th}$ his due share of all Mines & Mineralls therein Contained: with / Right & priviledges of hunting, hawking, fishing & fowling: with / all Woods, Waters & Rivers: w$^{th}$ all profitts, Commodityes & hereditam$^{ts}$ / w$^{t}$soever belonging to y$^{e}$ s$^{d}$ Land to him y$^{e}$ s$^{d}$ Maj$^{r}$. ARTHUR ALLEN his / heires & Assignes for ev$^{r}$. in as large & ample manner to all / intents & purposes as hath been used and allowed since y$^{e}$ first / Plantation. To be held of O$^{r}$. Sov$^{r}$aigne Lord & Lady y$^{e}$ King and / Queen their heires & Success$^{rs}$; as of their mannor of East Greenw$^{ch}$. / in free & common Soccage & not *in Capite*, nor by Knights / S$^{r}$vice Yeilding & paying unto o$^{r}$ s$^{d}$ Sov$^{r}$aigne Lord & Lady the / King & Queen, their heires & Successo$^{rs}$ for every fifty acres of / Land hereby granted at y$^{e}$ feast of S$^{t}$. Michael y$^{e}$ Arch Angell / y$^{e}$ fee rent of one shilling w$^{ch}$: paym$^{t}$ is to be made yearely / from year to year according to his Ma$^{es}$: Instructions of y$^{e}$ 12$^{th}$ / of Septemb$^{r}$. <u>1662</u> Provided y$^{t}$ if y$^{e}$ s$^{d}$ Maj$^{r}$: ARTHUR ALLEN, his / heires, or Assignes doe not seat or plant, nor cause to be / seated or planted thereon, w$^{th}$in three yeares next ensueing / y$^{e}$ date hereof y$^{t}$ then it shall & may be Lawfull for any

/ Adventurer or planter to make choice thereof & seat / thereon. Given under my hand, & year Seal of y$^{e}$ Collony y$^{e}$ / 20$^{th}$ day of Octob$^{r}$. Anno Dom 1691
Record WILLIAM COLE Sec$^{ry}$: FFR: NICHOLSON

**[300]**

Know all men by these p$^{r}$sents y$^{t}$ ARTHUR. ALLEN of Laiones Creek Parrish / in y$^{e}$ County of Surry for a valuable Consideration to me in hand p$^{d}$ [ ] / Secured to be p$^{d}$. by ROB$^{T}$. FFLAKE of y$^{e}$ upper ꝑish of y$^{e}$ Isle of Wight County / have Bargain'd & sold & doe by these p$^{r}$sents for me and my Heires bargaine & sell & deliver, enfeoff & / Conferme unto y$^{e}$ s$^{d}$ ROB$^{T}$ FFLAKE, his heires or assignes for ever, a certain / peice or ꝑcell of land containing a hundred & seventy acres / scituate between y$^{e}$ lands of THO: TOOKE, Cap$^{t}$. ENGLAND, THO: BLAKE & EDW$^{D}$ / BRANTLY in y$^{e}$ upper ꝑish of y$^{e}$ Isle of Wight County afores$^{d}$ y$^{e}$ s$^{d}$ 170 acres of land / being granted to me by patten dated y$^{e}$ 20$^{th}$ of Octob$^{r}$. 1691 & thus bounded / Begining at a red Oake THO: BLAKE's Corner trees in M$^{r}$. TOOKEs line, / Thence by BLAKE: Seventy three degrees, W two hundred & six / pole to a small red Oake, North seventy foure degrees, W: Sixty pole / to a pine, & :N: thirty four degrees, W: a hundred & two pole to a / Pine in M$^{r}$. NEWMANs line, thence by his line :N:N:E: twenty nine / pole to a stooping red Oake in or near Cap$^{t}$ ENGLANDs Line then by his line :S: sixty nine degrees, :E: a hundred thirty six & seven / Pole to two Pins EDW$^{D}$ BRANTLY's Corner trees near y$^{e}$ danceing place y$^{n}$ / by y$^{e}$ s$^{d}$ BRANTLY's lines :S:E: fifty two pole to a pine, NE twenty pole / to M$^{r}$. TOOKEs line, & soe by his line :SE: a hundred thirty six pole / To y$^{e}$ first station; To Have & to hold y$^{e}$ s$^{d}$ 170 acres of land w$^{th}$ his / due share of all mines & mineralls, thereon Contained w$^{th}$ free / priviledge of Hunting, Hawking, fishing & fowling, w$^{th}$ all woods / waye & waters, And all other Royaltyes, Priveledges, profitts, / Comodotyes & Heridatam$^{ts}$: w$^{t}$soever to y$^{e}$ s$^{d}$ land belonging, or in any wise / Appertaining to him y$^{e}$ s$^{d}$ ROB$^{T}$ FFLAKE & to his heires & Assignes for ever / in as full & Ample manner to all intents, & purposes as I my selfe / might or could have enjoyed y$^{e}$ same by vetue [*sic*] of y$^{e}$ before recited patten

**[301]**

And I doe Hereby Convent, promise, declare & agree to & w$^{th}$ y$^{e}$ s$^{d}$ ROB$^{T}$ / FFLAKE his heires & assignes, y$^{t}$ y$^{e}$ s$^{d}$ land, & every p$^{t}$ & ꝑcell thereof is / clear & free from all, & all manner of former ~~Leases~~ bargains & Sales / Joyntures, Mortgages, Judgm$^{ts}$: & Excecutions, and all other manner of / Incumbrances, w$^{t}$soever, & y$^{t}$ I have att y$^{e}$ time of y$^{e}$ ensealing, & delivery / hereof in & to all & Singular y$^{e}$ Premises a good pure & indefeazable / Estate of inheritance in fee simple w$^{ch}$ I hereby transfer & doe oblidge my / selfe, my heires, Ex$^{rs}$ & Adm$^{rs}$ to warrant & defend this my sale, of all & / Singular y$^{e}$ P$^{r}$mises w$^{th}$ their appurtinances to y$^{e}$ s$^{d}$ ROB$^{T}$ FFLAKE, & to y$^{e}$ [*sic*] / his heires & assignes for ever ag$^{st}$: all maner of p$^{r}$sons w$^{t}$soever, by, from / or under me deriveing any claims, title or Interest thereto: When / thereto required, will give to him or any of them such farther Lawfull assurance / of all & singular y$^{e}$ p$^{r}$mises as by his or their learned Councell / Shall be thoguht fitt; & will also acknowledge this instrum$^{t}$ / of Conveyance to be my Reall act & Deed in open Co$^{rt}$ next to be / held for y$^{e}$ Isle of Wight County afores$^{d}$ in Testimony of all w$^{ch}$: / I have hereunto putt my hand & Seal this [--] of [--] 1699

A$^{R}$R. ALLEN

Signed & Sealed
in p$^{r}$sence of
[--]

Acknowledged in open Co$^{rt}$ held for y$^{e}$ / Isle of Wight County Aug$^{st}$. 9$^{th}$ 1692 by Maj$^{r}$: / A$^{R}$R: ALLEN to be his Act & deed / Test JOHN PITT C$^{l}$ C$^{ur}$

Know all men by these p$^{r}$sents y$^{t}$ I ROB$^{T}$ FFLAKE & MARGARET my wife / doe assigne all o$^{r}$. Right, Title, & Interest of y$^{e}$ w$^{th}$in specified land / from us o$^{r}$. heires, Ex$^{rs}$, Adm$^{rs}$, or Assignes, unto JN$^{O}$ WALLIS his heires & / for ever all y$^{e}$ land w$^{th}$in menconed in this Bill of sale, as Wittnesse / o$^{r}$ hands this 9$^{th}$ of x$^{br}$. 1699

Testes PHILLIP SHELLY — ROB$^{T}$ FFLAKE
JO$^{S}$ BRIDGER — signum
MARG$^{T}$. **CM** FFLAK

Acknowledged in open Co$^{rt}$. held / for y$^{e}$ Isle of Wight County y$^{e}$ 9$^{th}$ X$^{br}$ / by y$^{e}$ s$^{d}$ FFLAKE & his Wife MARG$^{T}$. / to be their deed / & Recorded ꝑ me CHA CHAPMAN C$^{l}$ C$^{ur}$

**[302]**

To all Xpian ꝑsons where these p$^{r}$sents shall come MAT: STRICKLAND / & W$^{M}$ STRICKLAND sons of MATHEW STRICKLAND late Deceas, have made, / concluded, & agreed for Division betweene y$^{m}$ & either of them, & their / heires for ever Devided & bounded as followeth, I y$^{e}$ s$^{d}$ MATH: STTRICKLAND / doe give & make over my whole Right & title for me, & my heires unto / him & his heires for ever, a ꝑcell of land wehreon my father lived / on begining att y$^{e}$ mouth of y$^{e}$ horse swamp, soe running up y$^{e}$ horse / Swamp to y$^{e}$ Gum Branch, & soe running up y$^{e}$ s$^{d}$ Branch to Coll$^{o}$ PITTS / Line soe Running y$^{e}$ Course of y$^{e}$ s$^{d}$ Line unto y$^{e}$ Plantation whereon / y$^{e}$ s$^{d}$ MAT$^{W}$: STRICKLAND Deced dwelt now all that Land above y$^{e}$ fore= / menconed Branch joyning unto afores$^{d}$ Plantation, & alsoe all y$^{e}$ Land y$^{t}$ / lieth on y$^{e}$ South side of y$^{e}$ horse Swamp; now I y$^{e}$ s$^{d}$ MATHEW / STRICKLAND doe give one hundred and fifty acres of Land att y$^{e}$ / old Plantation unto my Brother JN$^{O}$ STRICKLAND & his heires / for Ever never to goe out of y$^{e}$ name of y$^{e}$ STRICKLANDs. alsoe I / y$^{e}$ s$^{d}$ MAT$^{W}$. STRICKLAND Doe give one hundred & fifty Acres of land / unto my Brother SAM$^{LL}$. STRICKLAND, & his heires for ever nev$^{r}$. / to goe out of y$^{e}$ name. Lying att y$^{e}$ hand of y$^{e}$ Watery Branch / Joyning upon ARTHUR WHITEHEAD, now all y$^{e}$ rest of y$^{e}$ Land above / y$^{e}$ for menconed Branch & on y$^{e}$ South side of y$^{e}$ horse Swamp / I y$^{e}$ s$^{d}$ MAT$^{W}$: STRICKLAND doe give unto my brother W$^{M}$. STRICKLAND / & his heires, & alsoe I y$^{e}$ s$^{d}$ MATHEW STRICKLAND doe give unto / my brother JOSEPH STRICKLAND one hundred & fifty acres / of Land Joyning upon Blackwater Branch between my /

Plantation, & y$^{e}$ Line of M$^{r}$. WOODWARDs being w$^{th}$in my own / p$^{t}$ according to y$^{e}$ Devision Bounds after menconed between me / & my brother W$^{M}$ STRICKLAND, Every one to have his p$^{t}$ according / to his Articles att age to Receive. further more if I or either of us

**[303]**

Should defraud them or either of them he y$^{e}$ defrauder shall / forfeit his own p$^{t}$ according unto these Articles to him or them y$^{t}$ / Shall be defrauded. Well Remembred y$^{t}$ y$^{e}$ afores$^{d}$ 150 acres of / land y$^{t}$ is given unto JN$^{O}$ STRICKLAND & his heires Shall not encroach / or defraud a late saile of a ꝑcell of Land Joyning upon y$^{e}$ Black / =pond; att y$^{e}$ head of y$^{e}$ horse Swamp bargained, & sold from me WILL / STRICKLAND unto ARTHUR WHITEHEAD. As Wittnesse o$^{r}$ hands & Seal this / 14$^{td}$ day Aug$^{st}$. In y$^{e}$ year of o$^{r}$. Lord God 1699

signum
MAT: **E** STRICKLAND sigillum
WILL: **W**: STRICKLAND sigillum

The contents within menconed
Signed, Sealed & delivered
in y$^{e}$ p$^{r}$sence of us
BARNABY MACKINNEY
THOMAS MARKS

Acknowledged att a Levy / Co$^{rt}$. held for y$^{e}$ Isle of Wight County / y$^{e}$ 16$^{th}$ 8$^{br}$. 99 by y$^{e}$ MATHEW STRICKLAND / & W$^{M}$. & Ordered to be recorded
Recorded ꝑ CHA CHAPMAN C$^{l}$C$^{ur}$

Know all men by these ꝑsents y$^{t}$ I THO MAN of y$^{e}$ Isle of Wight / County & ELIZABETH my wife for & in Consideration of 2050$^{li}$ of good marcht$^{bl}$: / Tob$^{o}$: & Caske to us in hand p$^{d}$ (before y$^{e}$ sealing hereof) by THEOPHILUS JOYNER of y$^{e}$ / County aforesd, have bargained & sold, & doe by these p$^{r}$sents for us & o$^{r}$ heires for ever bargain & sell & / deliver enfeoff & Confirme unto y$^{e}$ s$^{d}$ JOYNER & his heires & assignes forever, a / certain peice or ꝑcell of land con$^{T}$:g one hundred & fifty acres scituate on y$^{e}$ maine / Blackwater acres to me granted y$^{e}$ 22$^{d}$ of Septemb$^{r}$. 1682 bounded (viz$^{t}$) W upon y$^{e}$ / River, N upon y$^{e}$ land of W$^{M}$. MAYO, E$^{t}$ upon BRIDGEMAN JOYNER, & S: upon y$^{e}$ land of / HODGES COUNCELL. To have & to hold y$^{e}$ s$^{d}$ land w$^{th}$ his due share of all mines & min$^{r}$als / therein con$^{T}$d: w$^{th}$ all Rights & Priviledeges of hunting, hawking fishing & fowling, / w$^{th}$ all woods, waters & Rivers, & all other profitts, comodities & heriditam$^{ts}$: w$^{t}$soever / to y$^{e}$ s$^{d}$ land belonging or in any wise appertaining, to him y$^{e}$ s$^{d}$ THEOPHILUS JOYNER / his heires & assignes for ever in as full & ample manner to all intents & purposes as / I my selfe might or could enjoy y$^{e}$ same by vertue of y$^{e}$ before recited, patt$^{s}$: & I / doe hereby oblidge my selfe my Ex$^{rs}$ & Adm$^{rs}$ to warr$^{t}$ & defend this my sale of all & / singular y$^{e}$ p$^{r}$mises against all, & all manner of p$^{r}$sons w$^{t}$soever; to acknoledge this deed (together / w$^{th}$ my Wife) to ackno in open Co$^{rt}$. held for y$^{e}$ Isle of Wight County: & if thereto required to / give y$^{e}$ s$^{d}$ JOYNER, his heires, & assignes Such father lawfull assurance of y$^{e}$ Premises:

**[304]**

As by his Councell learn'd in Lawe shall be thought fitt In Wittness whereof we / have hereunto put o$^{r}$. hands & seals y$^{e}$ 9$^{th}$ of June 1683

Signed sealed & delivered — THOMAS MAN O seal
in p$^{r}$sence of — her
WILL. MAYO — ELIZA: **E** MAN O seal
RICH$^{D}$ BOOTH — mark

Acknowledged by THO: MAN & ELIZ / his wife in open Co$^{rt}$. held for y$^{e}$ Isle of / Wight County y$^{e}$ 9$^{th}$ of June 1683 to be / their free act & deed, & ordered to be / Recorded Test JOHN PITT Cl Cur

I y$^{e}$ subscribed do by consent of my wife ELLENOR assigns over unto THO: JOYNER Jun$^{r}$ / & his heires & for ever, all my Right title & Interest of this w$^{th}$in specified / Conveyance for one hundred & fifty acres of land Wittnesse my hand & seal this 6$^{th}$ day / of October 1685

THOMAS LAMIFE — Signum
ROB$^{T}$ STURDY — THEOPHILUS + JOYNER O seale
his **O** Mark — her
ELLENOR **YV** JOYNER
mark

Acknowledged in open Co$^{rt}$ held / for y$^{e}$ Isle of County [*sic*] Aug$^{t}$. y$^{e}$ 13$^{th}$ 1687 / by THEOPHILUS JOYNER & ELLENOR his / wife to be their free act & deed & / Ordered to be recorded

Test JNO PITT C$^{l}$ C$^{ur}$

I y$^{e}$ subscribed doe by Consent of my wife ELIZABETH Assigne over unto / BRIDGEMAN JOYNER & his heires & for ever all my right title & Intrest / of the w$^{th}$in specified Conveyance for one hundred & fifty acres of land / As Wittness my [*sic*] o$^{r}$. Hands this 15$^{th}$. of December, 1699

W$^{M}$. CRUMPLER — THOMAS JOYNER
SAM$^{LL}$ WARD — her
JENKIN DORMAN — ELIZABETH **E** JOYNER
mark

Acknowledged in open Co$^{rt}$. held / for y$^{e}$ Isle of Wight County y$^{e}$ 15$^{th}$ / 10$^{br}$. 1699 by y$^{e}$ s$^{d}$ THOMAS JOYNER / & ELIZABETH his wife to be their / free act & deed & ordered to be / Recorded

Test CHA CHAPMAN C$^{l}$C$^{ur}$

**[305]**

Know all men by these p$^{r}$sents y$^{t}$ I BRIDGEMAN JOYNER of y$^{e}$ Isle of Wight / County & ANN my wife for & Consideration of two Thous$^{d}$ five hundred p$^{ds}$ of / good Mercht$^{ble}$: Tob$^{o}$ & Cask to us in hand p$^{d}$ before y$^{e}$ sealing hereof by HENRY TURNER / of y$^{e}$ County afores$^{d}$ have bargained & sold, & doe by these p$^{r}$sents for us & our / heires for ever bargain sell & deliver, enfeoff & confirme unto y$^{e}$ s$^{d}$ TURNER / his heires & assignes for ever, A certain peice or ꝑcell of land containing fifty / acres be it more or less lying on y$^{e}$ North side of y$^{e}$ Branch called y$^{e}$ beaver / Dam Branch begining att y$^{e}$ mouth of y$^{e}$ Branch & running up y$^{e}$ sd / Branch to y$^{e}$ Land of THOMAS JOYNER Sen$^{r}$. & soe along his Line to a line y$^{t}$ / ꝑts. his Land, & land of W$^{M}$. BODDY being alsoe y$^{e}$ s$^{d}$ TURNERs own line of / his own Land & soe along y$^{e}$ sd TURNERs Line to White Oake A Corner / tree of M$^{r}$. BODDYEs, on y$^{e}$ South side of y$^{e}$ Beaver dam Branch, & soe along / y$^{e}$ sd Line to y$^{e}$ Cyprus Swamp to a Spanis Oake a corner tree of y$^{e}$ sd BODDYs / & soe down y$^{e}$ Cyprus Swamp to y$^{e}$ first station. To have & to hold y$^{e}$ / sd land w$^{th}$ his due share of all mines & minerall therein contained, w$^{th}$: / all Rights & priviledges of hunting, hawking, fishing & fowling, w$^{th}$ all / woods, waters & Rivers, & other profitts, commodityes, & hereditam$^{ts}$ w$^{t}$soever / to y$^{e}$ sd land belonging or in anywise appertaining to him y$^{e}$ s$^{d}$ HENRY / TURNER his heires & assignes for ever, in as full & ample manner to all / intents & purposes, as I my self might or could enjoy y$^{e}$ same, by / vertue of a deed of gift made me by my father THOMAS JOYNER bearing / date January y$^{e}$ 5$^{th}$ 1683, & I doe hereby oblidge my self my Ex$^{rs}$, & / Adm$^{rs}$. to warr$^{t}$ & defend this my sale of & singular y$^{e}$ ꝑmises ag$^{st}$. / all manner of ꝑsons w$^{t}$soever, & to acknowledge this Deed together w$^{th}$ / my wife in open Co$^{rt}$. held for y$^{e}$ Isle of Wight, & if thereto required to / give y$^{e}$ s$^{d}$ TURNER his heires & Assignes such further assurance of y$^{e}$ ꝑmises / as by his Councell learned in y$^{e}$ Lawes shall be thought fitt, in Wittness / whereof we have put hands & seale y$^{e}$ 9$^{th}$ of 10$^{br}$. 99

signum<br>
BRIDGEMAN **B** JOYNER Seal<br>
her<br>
ANN + JOYNER Seal<br>
mark

Signed sealed<br>
& delivered in<br>
y$^{e}$ p$^{r}$sence of us<br>
his mark<br>
W$^{M}$ **W** THOMAS<br>
JENKIN DORMAN<br>
W$^{M}$. CRUMPLER

Acknowledged in open Co$^{rt}$. held / for y$^{e}$ Isle of Wight County y$^{e}$ 15$^{th}$ / of 10$^{br}$. 99 by y$^{e}$ s$^{d}$ BRIDGEMAN JOYNER & ANN his wife

Recorded ꝑ CHA CHAPMAN C$^{l}$C$^{ur}$

**[306]**

This Indenture made the 6$^{th}$. day of Aprill in y$^{e}$ year of o$^{r}$ Lord God / 1700 & in y$^{e}$ 12$^{th}$ year of y$^{e}$ Reigne of our Sov$^{r}$ainge Lord y$^{e}$ William by y$^{e}$ / Grace of God King of England, Scotland ffrance & Ireland &c: betweene / GEORGE WILLIAMS of y$^{e}$ Isle of Wight County of y$^{e}$ one p$^{ty}$ And RICHARD / REYNOLDS Jun$^{r}$ & ELIZABETH his wife of y$^{e}$ sd County on y$^{e}$ other ꝑt Wittnesseth / y$^{t}$ y$^{e}$ sd GEORGE WILLIAMS for & in

Consideration of y^e^ sum of four thousd / p^ds^ of Tob^o^ in Caske to him in hand att & before y^e^ sealing & delivery / of these p^r^sents by y^e^ sd RICH^D^ REYNOLDS & ELIZABETH his wife well & truly / paid y^e^ Receipt whereof he y^e^ said GEORGE WILLIAMS doth hereby acknowledge / & himself therewith satisfied & paid, & thereof every part & / parcell thereof doth Clearely acquit, Exonerate & discharge y^e^ RICHARD / REYNOLDS & ELIZABETH his wife & their heires, Ex^rs^. Adm^rs^. & Assg^n^ for Ever / By these p^r^sents hath given, granted Alien'd, Bargained, sold enfeoffed and / confirmed, & by these p^r^sents doth fully, clearely, & absolutely, give grant / bargaine, sell, alien, Enfeoff, & confirme unto y^e^ said RICHARD REYNOLDS and / ELIZABETH his wife, & theire heires, and Ass^gs^ for ever: one parcell or tract / of Land containing by Estimation one hundred Acres be itt more or less / Scituate lyeing & being in y^e^ Lower Parrish of y^e^ foresaid County. / contained in a deed beareing date y^e^ 10^th^ of Aprill in y^e^ yeare of our / 1671 [*sic*] w^ch^ deed was made by PHAROAH COBB & ANNE his wife unto GEORGE / WILLIAMS Taylor father of y^e^ forsd GEORGE WILLIAMS: which land did / descend unto W^M^. WILLIAMS Elder Brother of y^e^ first named GEORGE / WILLIAMS who is dead and from y^e^ said W^M^. WILLIAMS did descend unto / y^e^ first named GEORGE WILLIAMS: now in y^e^ tenure & occupation of / MATHEW LOWERY: And bounded according to y^e^ foresd deed & now more / sett forth & specified: that is to say begining att y^e^ Mouth of a Branch / or Marsh: to a mnrked White oake Saplin w^ch^. Marsh or Branch runs out / of y^e^ maine Creek to y^e^ said White Oake Saplin thence to a Cedar Post / fixed in y^e^ roome of a great Poplar stump: in PHAROAH COBBs old corner / field from thence to a Pockickory standing by a great Poplar being / a Corner tree wich are both gone, & now to a small m^r^ked Maple / Tree standing in y^e^ Roome of a small Spainish Oake neare a / small Gum by a pond side; from thence through y^e^ sd pond to a / m^r^ked Pockickiry & from thence downe a valley to a m^r^ked Red Oake / Saplin in or neare to y^e^ sd PHAROAH COBBs line of m^r^ked trees parting / y^e^ sd PHAROAH COBBs Land & M^r^. ARTHUR SMITHs land: & soe from thence / downe y^e^ sd parting line of m^r^ked trees to a m^r^ked Cedar standing / close on or near to a Marsh neare on y^e^ Maine Creeke side, from / thence up y^e^ sd maine Creeke to y^e^ 1^st^ menconed Branch of Markt & White / Oake Saplin

**[307]**

To have & to hold the foresd Parcell, of land according to y^e^ / foresd bounds with all & Singular its members, Jurisdictions & appurtinances / together with all houses, edifices, buildings, Barnes, stables, orchards, gardens / yards, backsides, trees, waters, hereditaments & appurtinances w^t^soever to y^e^ said / messuages or tenements & Premises, or to any part or parcell of them belonging / or in any wise appertaining thereunto: unto y^e^ said RICH^D^ REYNOLDS & ELIZABETH / his wife & theire heires or Assgs to y^e^ only proper use & behoofe of y^e^ sd RICH^D^ / REYNOLDS & ELIZABETH his wife, & theire heires or Assgs for Ever against him / y^e^ sd GEORGE WILLIAMS, his heires & Assgs & all & every other person & persons / Whatsoever Lawfully claiming by from or under him, them or any of them shall / & will warrant & for Ever defend by these p^r^sents, and y^t y^e sd GEORGE WILLIAMS / for himselfe, his heires, Ex^rs. Adm^rs, or Assgs doe Covenant, promise, grant and / agree to & with y^e sd RICH^D REYNOLDS, & ELIZABETH his wife & theire heires, & Assgs / & Ev^ry of them: by these p^rsents that all & singular y^e aforesaid premisses & / parcell of land according to it's recited bounds with all marshes, & Marsh / ground & w^th all y^e appurtinances thereunto belonging. Now be & Ever here / often shall be stand & continue to y^e sd RICHARD REYNOLDS & ELIZABETH his wife / & theire heires, & Assgs for Ever, & y^t the said RICH^D REYNOLDS & ELIZABETH his / wife & theire heires or Assgs be freely acquited, Exonerated & discharged / & from time to time well & suficiently kept harmeless by y^e sd GEORGE WILLAIMS, his heires / Ex^rs, or Adm^rs of & from all manner of former & other gifts grants bargaines / sales leases, Mortgages, Joyntures, Dowers of & from all & singular / other titles, troubles, charges, demands, & incumbrances whatsoever / had made, committed, suffered, omitted or done, by y^e sd GEORGE WILLIAMS, his / heires, or Assgs: and y^t the said GEORGE WILLIAMS, his heires or Assgs for / & dureing y^e space of seven yeares next ensueing y^e date of these p^rsents / shall & Will at & upon y^e reasonable request, & att y^e Cost & Charges in / y^e Law, of y^e sd RICH^D REYNOLDS & ELIZABETH his wife, theire heires or / Assgs, make such further lawfull & Reasonable asurance or / assureances or Conveyances in y^e Law for y^e more better & Perfect / assurance or assurances of y^e foresaid p^rmises as by y^e sd RICHARD / REYNOLDS, & ELIZABETH his wife, or theire heires, or Assgs, or by them or / theires Councell learned in y^e lawes shall be Reasonably advised or / required, & y^t y^e aforesaid prmnises with all y^e appurtinances thereunto / belonging shall be esteemed & adjudged & taken to be, & Ennure to y^e onley / proper use & behoofe of y^e sd RICH^D REYNOLDS Jun^r, & ELIZABETH his / Wife, & theire heires, & Assgs for Ever: & to none other use, intent or / purposes w^tsoever. In wittness hereof I have hereunto sett my hand and / Seal y^e day, yeare, & Reigne, 1^st above=written

Signed sealed & deliv^red in y^e p^rsence of us whose names are here under written
AR SMITH
THOMAS SMITH
MATH^W. LOWRY

his m^rke
GEO: **W**: WILLIAMS seal

Acknowledged in open Co^rt held for y^e / Isle of Wight County y^e 9^th of Aprill 1700 / by GEORGE WILLIAMS & SARAH his wife

GEO: WILLIAMS [ ]ing in possession

p CHA CHAPMAN C^l C^ur

**[308]**

This Indenture made y^e 9^th day of Aprill in y^e year of o^r L^d 1700 betweene PHILLIP PARDOE / planter of y^e Isle of Wight County of y^e p^ty & THOMAS WOOD [ ] of y^e / said County of y^e other p^ty Wittness. y^t the sd PHILLIP PARDOE for a / valuable consideration of four Thousand twenty / five pound of Tob^o already rec^d. of y^e sd

THOMAS WOOD, before y^e^ / signing of these p^r^sents have therefore doth absolutely acquit and / discharge y^e^ said THOMAS WOOD, his heires, Ex^rs^, & Adm^rs^. for ever of y^e^ / foresaid Tob^o^. By these p^r^sents have granted, assigned, sold, conveyed / confered, & sett over & by these p^r^sents, doe fully, freely, & absolutly, / grant, assigne, sell, confirme, Convey'd & sett over, unto y^e^ said THOMAS WOOD, his / heires, and Assgs for ever, a certaine plantation or tract, of Land / lying and being in upper Parrish of y^e^ Isle of Wight County on y^e^ head / of Lawnes Creek being part of a patent of 200 acres of land granted / to ROBERT LAURENCE beareing date 20 Aug^st^. 1642; & now in y^e^ / possession of y^e^ sd PHILLLIP PARDOE, y^e^ said plant. or tract of land is bounded / as follow^th^. (Viz^t^) begining att a Ash stand in y^e^ Swamp, from / thence N by E to a m^r^kd hickory it being a line made by PHILLIP BRANTLY / betweene y^e^ sd PARDOE & WOOD, & from thence, NNE to a m^r^ked Red oake / standing in Maj^r^. BURNIELLs line by a pond side, & from then S by W / to y^e^ sd PARDOE's corner tree, from then W142 pole, from thence / eighty pole N to y^e^ Creeke, from thence along y^e^ Creeke to y^e^ mouth of y^e^ / Swamp, & soe up y^e^ said Swamp to y^e^ first Station or Ash there / being by esteemation fifty acres of land within y^e^ said bounds / with y^e^ houses & appartinances whatsoever to y^e^ same or any p^t^. / thereof belonging or in any wayes appertaining, or thereof / used, occupied, or enjoyed, or accounted, reputed or taken as p^t^ / or ꝑcell of y^e^ same withall priviledges, profitt & commodities / w^t^soever to y^e^ same granted, together w^th^ all y^e^ right & title, intres't / use, possession, reversion, property, claime & demand w^t^soever, / of him y^e^ sd PHILLIP PARDOE, his heires or Assigs, or in or to the / same, or which he now have or claime, or hereafter shall or / may claime to y^e^ sd Land w^th^ y^e^ appurtinances. To have & to Hold / y^e^ said land accordeing y^e^ foresaid bounds, with houseing & appurtinances / To y^e^ sd THOMAS WOOD, his heires, and Assgs for Ever, to y^e^ only use of / y^e^ sd THOMAS WOOD, his heires, and Assgs for evermore, & y^e^ sd PHILLIP / PARDOE for himself his heires & Assigns Covenant, promise & agree, / with y^e^ sd THOMAS WOOD, his heires & Assgs y^t^ he the sd PHILLIP PARDOE / his heires, and Assignes y^e^ sd Plantation or tract of land beforemencon'd / with y^e^ appurtinances to y^e^ sd THOMAS WOOD, his heires & Assignes / ag^st^. all person or persons whatsoever, claiming under them shall & / will warrant & for Ever defend by these p^r^sents & y^t^ the sd THOMAS / WOOD, his heires, & assgs shall & may from henceforth for Ever

**[309]**
Lawfully & peaceably & quietly have, hold possess & enjoy y^e^ / said plantacon or tract of Land with y^e^ appurtinances without / y^e^ lett, suit, trouble, molestation or interruption of any person / or persons w^t^soever claime or to claime under y^e^ sd PHILLIP / PARDOE free & cleare & freely acquited & discharged or / otherwayes discharged & save harmless from all former or / other gifts, grants, leases Assignements, title, charges & imcumbran= / =ces whatsoever, & lastly y^e^ sd PARDOE, his heires, or any person / claimeing or to claime under him shall & will hereafter upon / y^e^ reasonable request of y^e^ sd THOMAS WOOD, his heires or assignes / make such farther assurance & confirmation of y^e^ said Land to / y^e^ said WOOD & his heires as by y^e^ THOMAS WOOD his heires or / assgs, or

his or their coucell learned in y^e^ Law shall reasonable / Devised, advised or required, in Wittness whereof he the said PHILL= / PARDOE have to this Deed of bargaine, & sale y^e^ day & year above / =written.

Signed seale & deliver in y^e^ p^r^sence of

AR: SMITH
RICH^D^ REYNOLDS
JOHN WHETSTONE
THO'S PIDDINGTON

his
PHILLIP ? PARDOE
m^r^ke

Acknowledged in open Co^rt^ / held for y^e^ Isle of Wight County / Aprill y^e^ 9^th^. 1700 by y^e^ sd PHILLIP PARDOE to be his reall act & deed / & ordered to be Recorded

Per CHA CHAPMAN C^l^C^ur^

Know all men by these p^r^sents y^t^ I RICHARD REYNOLDS of y^e^ Isle / of Wight County send greeting, know yee y^t^ I the sd RICHARD / REYNOLDS for divers good causes & considerations to me in hand / p^d^. before y^e^ signing hereof have given, granted, alienated, effeofed, [*sic*] / bargained, sold, & confirme'd and soe by these ~~of ye County of Nanzimond~~ / p^r^sents freely and absolutly, bargaine, sell & Confirme unto / WILLIAM BUTLER of y^e^ County of Nanzimond a parcell of land containing / two hundred & twenty Acres, being part of a patent of seven hundred / & twenty acres of land scituate, lying, & being in y^e^ County of Nancimond / on y^e^ Cabbin Branch, y^e^ sd land begining att a m^r^ked Oake being a Corner / tree of y^e^ sd pattent, running thence North Westerly sixty degrees, three / hundred & twenty pole to a lightwood stake, thence North Easterly thirty / degrees one hundred & tenn pole for breadth, thence South Easterly / sixty degrees, three hundred & twenty pole, thence South Westerly thirty / degrees, one hundred & ten pole to y^e^ first Station. To have & To / hold all y^e^ sd ꝑcell of land, together with all houses & edifices and / buildings, w^th^ all benefitts, priviledges, Hereditaments, thereunto

**[310]**

belonging or appurtayning to him y^e^ sd W^M^. BUTLER, his heires, / Ex^rs^, Adm^rs^, or Assgs for ever, without lett, hinderance, molestation / or hinderances, eviction, ejection of me y^e^ sd RICHD REYNOLDS, my heires / Ex^rs^, Adm^rs^, or Assgs for Ever, free & freely acquited of & from all mann / manner [*sic*] of former grants & Bases, deed or incumbrances whatsoever / & of & from all manner of persons claimeing or pretending to claime / any Right, title or Interest to y^e^ demised premises or any part or / parcell thereof, & shall warrant, & defend for Ever, & doe oblidge my / self & JOYCE my wife to acknowledge y^e^ same in open Co^rt^. when / required In Wittness whereof we have hereunto sett o^r^ hands & seales / this 9^th^ day of June 1697

Signed & sealed
in prsence of us
JOHN COUNCELL
WILLIAM BROWNE

RICH^D^ REYNOLDS seal
her
JOYCE **J** REYNOLDS seal
marke

ROBERT DRYVER

Acknowledged in Open Court held / For y^e^ Isle Wight County 9^th^ June 1697 & / Recorded by me CHA CHAPMAN C^l^C^ur^

Know all men by these p^r^sents y^t^ I PHILLIP BURROW of Surry County / doe hereby nominate & appoint JN^O^ CHRISTOPHER FFYREABANT my / true & Lawfull attorny in my name & in my stead to prosecute an / action in y^e^ Isle of Wight County depending betweene me, & / THOMAS PRESTON, as wittness my hand

Testes

signum

JN^O^ **I:P:** PRIME

JO^S^ CHAPMAN

his

PHILLIP **PB** BURROW

m^r^ke

Test CHA CHAPMAN C^l^C^ur^

These are to Authorise you JOHN GILES for to appeare for me & / in my stead & name to prosecute a suite I have depending in the / Isle of Wight County Co^rt^. against Maj^r^. THOMAS GODWIN, & this / shlal be yo^r^. suficient warrant as wittness my hand this 9^th^ day / of October 1699

JOHN PITT

Test CHA CHAPMAN C^l^C^ur^

**[311]**

Know all men by these p^r^sents y^t^ I HUMPHREY MARSHALL of y^e^ / Isle of Wight County Com: doe oblidge my self to pay unto JOHN / EDMONSON when he cometh to y^e^ age of 21, i feather Bed & / furniture thereunto belonging, & also two thousand pounds of / good sound Tobaccoe to y^e^ which payment well & truely to be made, / I doe hereby bind my self firmely p these p^r^sents, sealed with my / Seal dated y^e^ 3^d^ day of Aprill in y^e^ 8^th^ year of y^e^ Reigne of o^r^. / Soveraigne Lord William y^e^ 3^d^. King of England, France &c: & in y^e^ / yeare of o^r^ Lord 1696

Signed Sealed & delivered

in y^e^ p^r^sence of us

THOMAS HILL

JOHN GILES

HUM MARSHALL seal

Know all men by these p^r^sents y^t^ I HUMPHRY MARSHALL of y^e^ / Isle of Wight County Com. doe oblidge my self to pay unto WILLIAM / EDMONSON when he cometh to y^e^ age of one & twenty one ffeather / bed & furniture, & also two Thousand pounds of good sound Tob^o^ / to y^e^ w^ch^ payment I doe hereby bind my self firmely by these / p^r^sents, Sealed w^th^ my Seal dated y^e^ 3^d^. day of Aprill in y^e^ 8^th^ year / of y^e^ Reigne of o^r^. Soveraigne Lord William y^e^ 3^d^ King of England / France &c: & in y^e^ yeare of our Lord 1696

Signed, Sealed & delivered in y$^{e}$ p$^{r}$sence of us
THOMAS HILL
JOHN GILES

HUM: MARSHALL seal

Know all men by these p$^{r}$sents y$^{t}$ I WILLIAM STRICKLAND and / MATHEW my Brother both jointly & severally of y$^{e}$ Isle of Wight / County in Virginia have bargained, sold & delivered from us our / heires, Ex$^{rs}$ Adm$^{rs}$, or Assgs, To ARTHUR WHITEHEAD, him, his heires / Ex$^{rs}$, Adm$^{rs}$, or Assignes, y$^{e}$ full quantity of two hundred Acres / of land lyeing & being in y$^{e}$ foresaid County & bounded as / followeth, begining att y$^{e}$ mouth of a Branch called y$^{e}$ White / Oake Branch, & soe running up y$^{e}$ said Branch to y$^{e}$ Branch / called y$^{e}$ Watry Branch, & Running up y$^{e}$ sd Branch to / Corawoak Line, & soe Running up y$^{e}$ aforesaid Line then / bearing to y$^{e}$ head of y$^{e}$ Horse Swamp, & soe running downe / y$^{e}$ sd Swamp to y$^{e}$ first Station. alsoe I y$^{e}$ W$^{M}$. STRICKLAND

**[312]**
& MATHEW STRICKLAND my Brother have sold another / parcell of land bounded fifty Acres more or less, begining att y$^{e}$ first / Stationed branch att y$^{e}$ foot of y$^{e}$ first Station on y$^{e}$ Lowermost side / of y$^{e}$ Branch & running down y$^{e}$ aforesaid Horse Swamp to y$^{e}$ first / Branch Called y$^{e}$ Popular Branch, & soe Running up the Branch to / Carawoak Line, & soe running along y$^{e}$ sd Line, to y$^{e}$ Watery Branch / aforesaid those Injoyned. To have, hold, occupy quietly Injoy y$^{e}$ / sd parcell of land with all Rights & Priviledges whatsoever there / belonging unto for Ever without any Letts, hinderances molesta= / =tions, Incumbrances or trouble further more I y$^{e}$ sd W$^{M}$ STRICKLAND / & MATHEW STRICK my Brother jointly & severally we say we bind our / selves o$^{r}$ heires, Ex$^{rs}$ Adm$^{rs}$, or Assignes to ARTHUR WHITEHEAD, to him / his heires, Ex$^{rs}$ Adm$^{rs}$ & Assgs in y$^{e}$ sum & penalty of twelve thousd / pounds of good Merchantable Tobaccos and Caske / whereof paym$^{t}$ true & faithfully to be made upon y$^{e}$ unperformance / we y$^{e}$ said W$^{M}$. STRICKLAND, & MATHEW STRICKLAND doe acknowledge / o$^{r}$selves both of full age to dispose of anything y$^{t}$ doth belong / unto us. as Wittness o$^{r}$. hands & Seales y$^{e}$ 30$^{th}$. day of July in the / yeare of o$^{r}$ Lord 1699

Tetes [*sic*]
BARNABY MACKQUINNY
JN$^{O}$ + BARRETT
JOHN **I** WORRELL
his m$^{r}$ke

his
WILLIAM **W** STRICKLAND
hir m$^{r}$ke
MATHEW **E** STRICKLAND

Acknowledged in open Co$^{rt}$. held for y$^{e}$ Isle / of Wight County 9$^{th}$ of August 1697 M$^{r}$ / DAVIS then Clerke & Recorded

p CHA CHAPMAN C$^{l}$C$^{ur}$

This Indenture made y^e^ 1^st^ day of May in y^e^ year of o^r^ Lord 1700 betweene / JOHN JOHNSON Docter of Nanzimond County of y^e^ one party & JOHN NEVILL / Jun^r^. of y^e^ Isle of Wight County planter of y^e^ other party Wittnesseth that / y^e^ said JOHN JOHNSON for a valueable Consideration of eight Thousand / pounds of Tob^o^ already receive of y^e^ sd JOHN NEVILL before y^e^ Signing of / these presents & therefore doe Absolutely acquit & Discharge y^e^ sd. JOHN NEVILL / his heires Ex^rs^. & Adm^rs^. for Ever, of y^e^ foresd eight Thousand pounds of Tob^o^ / By these p^r^sents have bargained, assigned, sold, conveyed / confirmed & sett over, & by these p^r^sents doe fully freely, & absolutely / grant, assigne, sell convey confirme, & sett over unto y^e^ sd JOHN NEVILL / Jun^r^. his heires, & assignes for Ever a certaine plantation or tract of / Land lying & being in y^e^ Isle of Wight County of y^e^ Western Branch of / Nanzimond River formerly called y^e^ Indian Town being one hundred acres / of Land according to y^e^ bounds Laid downe in y^e^ pattent which was / granted to HENERY BRADLY beareing date y^e^ 6^th^. day of March 1662

**[313]**

Wich was and since conveyed to M^r^. JOHN NEVILL Sen^r^ & by him / conveyed to me with all priviledges, proffitts or appurtinances / thereunto belonging or any way appertaining to y^e^ same Land or / plantation, together with all rights, title, interest, use, profession / revertions, property & demands whatsoever of him y^e^ sd JOHN / JOHNSON; his heires, or Assignes, of in or to y^e^ Same or wich have or / may have to y^e^ Land with y^e^ appurtinances. To have & to hold y^e^ / said Land, with all y^e^ appurtinances to y^e^ sd JOHN NEVILL Jun^r^ his / heires & Assignes for evermore, to be held to y^e^ only proper use / of y^e^ said JOHN NEVILL Jun^r^. his heires and Asssignes for Ever, & y^e^ said / JOHN JOHNSON for himself, his heires & Assignes for Ever, & y^e^ said / JOHN JOHNSON for himself, his heires & Assignes doth hereby / Covenant, promise & agree with y^e^ said JOHN NEVILL Jun^r^ his heires & / Assignes that he y^e^ sd JOHN JOHNSON, his heires y^e^ plantation / or track of Land, before mentioned with y^e^ appurtinances to y^e^ sd JN^O^ / NEVILL Jun^r^, his heires & assignes against, all person or persons / whatsoever claiming under him shall & Will ever warrant & / defend by these presents, that y^e^ sd JOHN NEVILL jun^r^. his heires and / Assignes shall & from henceforth for Ever Lawfully peaceably & quietly / have, hold, possess & enjoy y^e^ sd Plantation or tract of Land with / y^e^ appurtinances without lett, suit, trouble, molestation or inter= / ruption of any person or persons w^t^soever claiming or to claim / under y^e^ said JOHN JOHNSON & Lastly y^e^ said JOHN JOHNSON doe for / himself, his heires, Ex^rs^, & Adm^rs^, covenant to and with y^e^ said JOHN / NEVILL Jun^r^. his heires, & Assignes she he or them shall make, what / further assurance shall be devise by y^e^ sd JOHN NEVILL Jun^r^. his heires / Ex^rs^. & Assgs, or councell Learned in y^e^ Lawe wittness o^r^. hands this 10^th^ / day of June 1700

| | |
|---|---|
| Test THO: GILES | JOHN JOHNSON |
| TRUSTRUM NORSWORTHY | ELIZABETH **E** JOHNSON |
| ROBERT SMELLY | m^r^ke |

Acknowledged in open Co[rt]. held for / the Isle of Wight County y[e] 10[th]. day of / June 1700 by y[e] sd JOHN JOHNSON & ELIZABETH / his wife & then Recorded

p CHA CHAPMAN C[l]C[ur]

Know all men by these presents y[t] I JESPER ELIXON Sailer, doe by / vertue of these presents constitute, ordain & appoint PETER DE BERRY / of Isle of Wight County in Virginia to be my true & Lawfull Attorney for

**[314]**

Me & in my name to ask sue for & Recover all & singular such debts / & dues, as are or shall become due to me in this his Majesties Collony & / Diminion of Virg[a]. Giveing & granting to my said Attorny full power & / Authority upon receipt of any sum [or sums] to acquit & discharge all / & every person or psons of whome my sd Attorny shall receive them / & farther know y[e] y[t] I y[e] sd JESPER ELIXON doe hereby hold firm, and / stable all & every such thing or things whastsoever, y[t] my sd attorny / shall doe or Cause to be done in & about y[e] p[r]mises, as full & amply to all / Intents, Constructions & purposes as I my self might or could doe if / personally present. In Wittness whereof I have hereunto sett my hand / this 4[th] day of May 1700

his
JESPER **J** ELIXON
m[r]ke

Signed in p[r]sence of
WILLIAM BROWNE
his
PHILLIP **P** BRANTLY
m[r]ke

Proved in open Co[rt] held for / y[e] Isle of Wight y[e] 10[th]. day / of June 1700 by y[e] oathes of both Wittnesses

Recorded p CHA CHAPMAN C[l]C[ur]

This Indenture made y[e] 9[th] Day of May Anno Dom 1700 & in y[e] / twelfth year of y[e] Reign of o[r] Lord Willilam by y[e] Grace of God of / England, Scotland, ffrance, & Ireland King Defender of y[e] faith &c / Betweene PHILLIP SHELLY & SARAH his Wife of County of Surry, / Daughter of JOHN WAKEFEILD of y[e] one part & FFRANCIS LEE of y[e] / Isle of Wight County of y[e] other part. Wittnesseth y[t] y[e] sd PHILLIP / SHELLY & SARAH his Wife for & in Consideration of y[e] sum of four / Thousand, five hundred pounds of Tob[o]. to them in hand paid & / secured by y[e] said FFRANCIS LEE att & before y[e] ensealing & delivery / of these p[r]sents, y[e] receipt whereof y[e] said PHILLIP & SARAH doe / hereby acknowledge, & thereof & thereby are fully satisfied, have / bargained, sold, aliened, enfeoffed & Confirmed, & by these p[r]sents / doe for themselves, their Heires, Ex[rs] & Adm[rs] bargaine sell, alien / Enfeoff & Confirme unto y[e] said FFRANCIS LEE, his Ex[rs], Adm[rs], & Assgs / all that tract, peice or parcell of land containing by Estimacon / fifty acres be y[e] same more or less, adjoyning to y[e] land whereon / y[e] said FFRANCIS LEE now lives, scituate, lying & being in Warrisquaik /

Bay in y$^{e}$ Upper Parish of y$^{e}$ isle of Wight County. To have, & / To hold y$^{e}$ said bargained P$^{r}$mises & every part thereof / together with all wayes, water courses, all Mines & Mineralls / Royalties, Easmen$^{ts}$, Emoluments, rights, priviledges, Commodities, / & appurtinances to y$^{e}$ same belonging, or in any wayes appertaining

**[315]**

Unto ye said FFRANCIS LEE, his heires, & Assignes for Ever he paying his / Majesties Rents for y$^{e}$ same. Warranting y$^{e}$ said Bargained p$^{r}$mises / & every part thereof unto the said FFRANCIS, his heires & Assignes, / for Ever. against all person or persons w$^{ch}$ may or Can lay claime / to y$^{e}$ same, & the said PHILLIP SHELLY & SARAH his Wife doe by these p$^{r}$sents / for themselves, their Ex$^{rs}$, & Adm$^{rs}$ promise & Covenant to & with y$^{e}$ / said FFRANCIS LEE, his heires, Ex$^{rs}$, Adm$^{rs}$ & Assgs that they PHILLIP & / SARAH have att y$^{e}$ time of y$^{e}$ ensealing & delivery hereof / a full & Indefeazable right & Estate of Inheritance in ffee, in / y$^{e}$ said bargained p$^{r}$mises, & Every part thereof, In Wittness where / of y$^{e}$ said PHILLIP SHELLY & SARAH his Wife have hereunto sett / their hands & Seales y$^{e}$ day & year abovewritten.

Sealed & delivered in<br>the presence of<br>CHA CHAPMAN (1700)<br>JO$^{S}$ CHAPMAN (1700)

PHILLIP SHELLY seal<br>her<br>SARAH **4** SHELLY seal<br>mke

Acknowledged in Open Co$^{rt}$ held for / y$^{e}$ Isle of Wight County 10$^{th}$ of June 1700 by PHILLIP SHELLY & / SARAH his Wife to be their act & deed & Ordered to be / Recorded

Test CHA CHAPMAN C$^{l}$C$^{ur}$

Know all men by these p$^{r}$sents y$^{t}$ I y$^{e}$ within named SARAH / SHELLY doe hereby remise, release & relinquish unto y$^{e}$ sd FFRANCIS / LEE party to these p$^{r}$sents all Dower & right of Dower y$^{t}$ I may or / can claime in y$^{e}$ said Land or any part thereof by y$^{e}$ Lawes of / England or this County or any other wayes howsoever, wittness / my hand & Seal y$^{e}$ day & year abovewritten

her seal<br>SARAH **S** SHELLY<br>mke

Acknowledged in Open Co$^{rt}$ the same / day by SARAH SHELLY & Recorded ꝑ CHA CHAPMAN C$^{l}$C$^{ur}$

Know all men By these p$^{r}$sents that I HENERY APPLEWHAITE of the / Isle of Wight County, Virginia Doe for severall Reasons, & for / Naturall afections thereunto moveing me. Doe by These presents / Give unto son THOMAS APPLEWHAITE & to his heires Male lawfully / begotten y$^{e}$ one half of a dividend parcell of land scituate &

lying near the / Blackwater Branches w[ch] plantation he my sd son formly lived upon. / I Give to my son THOMAS APPLEWHAITE, to him, & his Heires / Male Lawfully begotten to possess after my decease, y[e] said Plant: with / all houseing shall be thereon with the one half of that track / or Dividend of land Nominated as in that Patent for that land

**[316]**

To Equally divided as nere as may both for quantity, quallity & Conven= / enency for both partyes, & for want of Male heires I give y[e] sd plant: / and y[e] sd Land to my son WILLIAM APPLEWHAITE, & to his heires / Male Lawfully begotten of his Body, and for want of such heires / to the next Male heire of Right.

I Give unto my son WILLIAM APPLEWHAITE the other half of y[e] abovesd / Land to possess after my decease to him, & his heires Male Lawfully / begotten of his Body for Ever. but for want of such heires Male / I Give the aforesaid Land all to my son JOHN, and to his heires / Male as aforesaid. In Wittness where to I have sett my hand & / Seale this eighth Day of August 1700 HEN: APPLEWHAITE seal

Signed, Sealed & deliv[r]ed
in y[e] presence of us
THO: PITT
HENERY PITT
NICHOLAS **N:** CASEY
his m[r]ke

Acknowledged in open Co[rt] held for y[e] Isle of Wight County y[e] 9[th] day of August 1700 by Cap[t] HENRY APPLEWHAITE & Ordered to be Recorded Test CHA CHAPMAN C[l]C[ur]

To all people to whome this p[r]sent writeing shall Come PETER VASSER / of Isle of Wight County in Virg[a]. Planter y[e] onely son & heire of his late / father JOHN VASSER of y[e] sd County of Isle of Wight Dece[d] send Greeting / in o[r]. Lord God Everlasting. Whereas y[e] sd JN[O] VASSER was in his lifetime / possessed in his demesne, as of fee; of a certaine plantation or tract of / Land now in y[e] possession of JN[O]. BELL: Containing one hundred & fifty / Acres of Land; Scituated & being in y[e] Isle of Wight County; being call'd / in y[e] Pattent Warrisquaike County bounded as followeth. being a Neck / of Land Lyeing upon y[e] Maine Creeke of Warrisquaike Bay, lying next / behind y[e] Land of NATHANIELL FFLOYD, on a Back Creeke parting them / two w[ch] Creeke runs up N:W: nere y[e] maine Creeke, & y[e] sd Maine / Creeke :W: on y[e] other side y[e] Land, w[ch] sd Tract of Land was Granted / unto my foresd father JN[O] VASSER by Patent beareing Date y[e] 18[tenth]: / day of Nov[r]. 1635. & y[e] sd JN[O]. VASSER being soe seized in fee, dyeing / & makeing noe devise by Will of y[e] sd Land; And Leaveing two Sonnes / JN[O] VASSER Jun[r]. & I y[e] sd PETER VASSER. And y[e] sd Land discending by Law / to my Brother JN[O]. VASSER Jun[r]. and he dyeing leaveing one Child / W[M]. VASSER, & he dyeing without heires, or makeing any devise of / y[e] sd Land, soe it discended to me Lawfully. Know yee therefore y[t] / y[e] sd PETER VASSER for a very valuable Consideration of six thousand / pounds of Tob[o]. & twenty five shillings of Lawfull money w[th]. w[ch]. y[e] sd / PETER VASSER acknowledge my self full satisfied, Contented, & paid / by JN[O]. BELL of y^e^ foresd County of y^e^ Isle of y^e^ Wight County Planter / And thereof doe acquit & discharge him for Ever. by these P^r^sents / have Granted, Assigned, sold, Conveyed, Confirmed & sett over. And

**[317]**

By these p^r^sents Doe fully, freely and Absolutly grant, Assigne / sell, Confirme, Convey & sett Over unto y^e^ sd JN^O^. BELL, his heires / & Assignes for Ever, y^e^ foresaid tract of land, w^th^ y^e^ houses, Orchards / & Appurtinances whatsoever to y^e^ same or any part thereof / belonging, or in any wise appertaining, or therewith used, occupied / or enjoyed, or accounted, reputed or taken as p^t^ or parcell / of y^e^ same: w^th^ all priviledges, Proffitts and Commodities whatsoever / to y^e^ same granted, together w^th^ all y^e^ Rights titles, interest, use / possession, reversion, property, claimes & demands what= / soever of him y^e^ sd PETER VASSER, his heires, or Assignes, of, in or to the / same, or w^ch^. he now have or claime, or hereafter shall or may have or Claime / to y^e^ sd Land, w^th^. the appurtinances, by force, vertue or meanes as being / son to y^e^ sd JOHN VASSER y^e^ first taker up of the Land, or by any other / rights or titles whatsoever or howsoever. To Have & to Hold y^e^ sd / 150 acres of land according to y^e^ foresd Bounds, w^th^ houses & appurtinances / to y^e^ sd JN^O^. BELL; his heires & Assgs for Ever, to y^e^ only use of y^e^ sd JN^O^ BELL / his heires & Assgs for Ever. And y^e^ sd PETER VASSER for himself, his heires / & Assgs doth hereby Covenant, promise & Agree w^th^ y^e^ sd JOHN BELL, his / heires & Assgs. That he the sd PETER VASSER, and his heires y^e^ sd Plantacon / or tract of y^e^ before menconed land w^th^ y^e^ appurtinances to y^e^ sd JOHN / BELL, his heires & Assgs, ag^st^ all person or persons w^t^soever claimeing / under y^e^ foresaid JN^O^ VASSER, my father, & he being y^e^ first taker up of y^e^ sd / land by any meanes whatsoever, that shall Claime under him, shall & / will warrant & for Ever defend by these p^r^sents and y^t^ y^e^ said / JN^O^. BELL, his heires & Assgs, shall & may from to hence forth for / Ever Lawfully, peaceably & quietly have, hold, possess, & enjoy y^e^ sd plantacon / or tract of Land; w^th^ y^e^ appurtinances, with^t^. y^e^ lett, suite, trouble, molestacon / or Interuption of any person or persons whatsoever, claimeing or to claime / under my father JN^O^. VASSER, my Brother JN^O^. VASSER Jun^r^. my self any / other person or persons whatsoever, by or under any VASSER, either by / devise, Conveyance, Discent by law, or any other wayes, or meanes / whatsoever, free & cleare, & free acquitted, exonerated & Discharge, or / otherwise discharged & saved harmless, from all former & other Gifts, grants, / Leases, assignements, titles, Charges, & Incumbrances w^t^soever made by / my sd father JN^O^. VASSER or any person or persons under him. And / further y^t^ I PETER VASSER, & his heires or any claiming or to / claime under him, shall & will att any time hereafter upon y^e^ Reasonable / request of y^e^ sd JN^O^ BELL, his heires or Assignes, make such further / assurance and Confirmation of y^e^ sd Land, to y^e^ sd JN^O^ BELL, & his heires / as by y^e^ said JOHN BELL, his heires or Assgs, or his or their Councell / Learned in y^e^ law shall be reasonably advised, Devised or Required. / In Wittness whereof y^e^ sd PETER VASSER and MARGERETT his wife have to / this Deed of Bargaine and Sale put their hands & Seales. And that / y^e^ sd PETER VASSER and his Wife will acknowledge this deed att the / next Co[rt] held for this County of Isle of Wight: Relinquish all Rights / w[t]soever y[e] 9[th] Day of October 1700

AR SMITH
EDRD CHITTY

PETER VASSER O
her
MARGARET + VASSER O
mke

Acknowledged in open / Co[rt]. held for Isle Wight County / y[e] 9[th]. day of 8[br]. 1700 by PETER VASSER

Acknowledged in open Co[rt] held For y[e] Isle Wight the 9[th]. 10[br] 1700 by MARGARET / VASSER her right of Dower Relinquished & Recorded ꝑ CHA CHAPMAN C[l]C[ur]

**[318]**

To all to whome these p[r]sents shall Come, I S[r]. EDMOND ANDROS K[nt]. His / Maties L[t]. & Govern[r]. Gen[r]all of Virg[a]. and Greeting: Whereas his late Matie / King Charles y[e] 2[d] hath been Graciously pleased by his Royall Letters Patents / Under y[e] Great Seal of England beareing Date att Westminster y[e] 10[enth]: / day Octob[r]. in y[e] 28[th] yeare of his Reigne, Amongst other things in y[e] said / Letters Patents Contained to Continue & Confirme y[e] Antient Priviledges / & Power of granting fifty Acres of land for every person Imported into / this Collony of Virginia. Now know yee y[t]. I y[e] sd S[r]. EDMOND ANROSS / K[nt]. Gov[r]n[r]. &c: doe with y[e] Advice & Consent of y[e] Councell of State / accordingly Give & grant unto W[M]. CARVER forty five Acres of Land in y[e] / Lower Parrish of y[e] Isle of Wight County bounded (Viz[t]) begining att a / Black Oake THOMAS MANDUEs Corner Three, & Running South Seventy / five degrees, East two hundred thirty six poles, to PHILLIP WRAYFORDs line, then / one [*sic*] his line North West one hundred twenty two poles to a White Oake / WRAYFORDs Corner Tree, thence South Seventy nine degrees, West one / hundred forty three pole to y[e] first Station. The sd forty five Acres of / land being due unto y[e] sd W[M]. CARVER by & for y[e] Importation of one / ꝑson into this Collony, whose names is to be in y[e] Records menconed under / this patent. To Have & To hold y[e] sd land w[th] his due share of all Mines / & Mineralls therein Contained, w[th] all Rights & priviledges of Hunting / Hawking, fishing, & fowling, w[th] all woods, Waters & Rivers, w[th] all profitts / Commodities & Heriditaments w[t]soever, belonging to y[e] sd Land to him y[e] sd / W[M]. CARVER, his heires & Assignes for Ever. In as large & ample manner / to all intents & purposes as hath been used & allowed since y[e] forsd / plantacon. To be held of o[r]. Sov[r]aigne Lord y[e] King, his heires & Successors / as of his Mannor of East Greenwich in free & Common Soccage, & not / *in Capite*, nor, by Knights Service Yeilding & paying unto o[r]. Sov[r]aigne / Lord y[e] King, his heires & Successors for every fifty Acres Land hereby / granted att y[e] feast of S[t]. Michael y[e] Arch Angell y[e] fee Rent of one Shilling / wich payment is to be made yearely from year to year provided that if / y[e] sd WILL CARVER his heires or Assgs doe not seat or plant nor cause / to be seated or planted thereon within three yeares next endueing the / Date hereof y[t] then it shall & may be lawfull for any Adventurer / or planter to make Choice thereof, & seat thereon, Given Under my / hand & y[e] Seal of the Collony this 25[th]. day of October in y[e] 7[th] year / year [*sic*] of his Maties Reigne Annoq[u] Dom. 1695

WILLIAM CAVER his patent for 45 Acres of Land in Isle of Wight County

ANDROS
H WORMELEY Sec[r].

*Vera Copia* Test CHA CHAPMAN C[l]C[ur]

**[319]**

Know all men by these p[r]sents y[t] WILL CARVER doth sell unto / W[M]. CRUMPLER all my whole Right of y[e] land within this patent from / me, my heires, Ex[rs]. Adm[rs]. or Assgs w[th] warrant of y[e] same unto WILL / CRUMPLER, his heires or Assgs for Ever. As Wittness my hand

february – 19[th] – 169$^7/_8$ WILLIAM **WC** CARVER
his m[r]ke

W[M] **W** STRICKLING
JN[O] **HH** STRICKLING
his mark

Acknowledged in Open Co[rt] held For y[e] Isle Wight County 9[th] October 1700 & Recorded

p CHA CHAPMAN C[l]C[ur]

To all X[pian] People Where three p[r]sents may appear I WILL CARVER / planter, & JANE my wife of y[e] Isle of Wight in y[e] Lower pish of Virginia / both holding & greeting in one Lord God Ever lasting. for sundry good / causes & Conveniences, & Especially for a Consideration & pcell of land / that I have of WILL CRUMPLER of y[e] same County & Parrish aforesaid Doe for us, o[r] / heires, Ex[rs], Adm[rs] or Assgs for Ever bargaine, alienate, sell, deliver make over, / and Acknowledge all o[r]. whole Right and title of a pcell of land lyeing, being, / & bounding as follow[th], wich is y[e] including of y[e] whole Patent. only one / hundred Acres w[ch]. was & is bargained & sold to PHILLIP RAFFORD; out of y[e] said / Patent, formerly taken up by JN[O]. MORE y[e] Shooemaker, & being given & granted / unto him by patent for three hundred & fifty Acres as also y[e] aforesd MORE deced / without Will or Testament, Child or Children saveing JANE his Daughter. it / being therefore found y[t]. y[e]. aforesd JANE MORE is y[e] lawfull heiress to her / father JOHN MOREs land. & alsoe Greeting & joyning in lawfull Marriage & / Matrimony WILL: & JANE CARVER, & furthermore I y[e] aforesd WILLIAM CARVER / & JANE my Wife, Doe for us, o[r]. heires, Ex[rs] Adm[rs]. or Assgs for Ever bargaine / sell, make over, alienate, deliver, & Acknowledge o[r] whole Right & title / & interest unto y[e] aforesd W[M]. CRUMPLER, to him, his heires, Ex[rs]. Adm[rs]. / or Assgs for Ever. To have & to hold w[th] all priviledges & appurtinances, & / emoluments thereunto belonging, w[th]. all lands timbers, houses, Orchards, fences, / woods & Water thereunto belonging To have & To hold without any letts, / hindrances, or Incumbrances, or trouble y[t] may now or hereafter / appear or Ever. we therefore Ingage o$^{r}$.selves, o$^{r}$. heires, Ex$^{rs}$. Adm$^{rs}$. or / Assgs to defend, maintaine & uphold y$^{e}$ Right of y$^{e}$ aforesd Land to WILL / CRUMPLER, to him, his heires, Ex$^{rs}$. Adm$^{rs}$. or Assgs. These P$^{r}$sents I WILL / CARVER & JANE my Wife doe bind o$^{r}$.selves o$^{r}$. heires, Ex$^{rs}$. Adm$^{rs}$. or Assgs / to Maintaine y$^{e}$ aforesd Right as far as any Councell in y$^{e}$ Law shall / require. And further we y$^{e}$ aforesd W$^{M}$. CARVER & JANE my Wife, Doe / Oblidge o$^{r}$selves o$^{r}$ heires. Ex$^{rs}$. Adm$^{rs}$. or Assgs entering into Covent & / Bond of forfeit, or one hundred pound sterling upon unperformance / of y$^{e}$ articles aforesd; to be p$^{d}$ well and truely to WILL CRUMPLER his / heires, Ex$^{rs}$. Adm$^{rs}$. or Assgs. As Wittness o$^{r}$ hands & Seales this 11$^{th}$. day of / September 1700

Signed, sealed & delivred
in p$^{r}$sence of us.
Test: BARNABY MACKQUINNY
his
WILL **M** WILLIAMS
m$^{r}$ke
WILL **W** JOHNSON
his mke

his m$^{r}$ke seal
WILL **W** CARVER
her seal
JANE **J** CARVER
m$^{r}$ke

Acknowledged in open / Co$^{rt}$ held for y$^{e}$ Isle Wight / County y$^{e}$ 9$^{th}$ day of October 1700 / by W$^{M}$. CARVER & JANE his Wife to be their / Act & Deed &

Recorded p CHA CHAPMAN C$^{l}$C$^{ur}$

**[320]**

To all X$^{pian}$. People where these P$^{r}$sents may appeare I WILLIAM / CRUMPLER Joyner & ELIZABETH my wife both of y$^{e}$ Isle of Wight County in / y$^{e}$ Lower Parrish in Virginia. both holding & Greeting in one Lord God / Everlasting. for sundry good Causes & Consideracons, especially for a / Parcell of land y$^{t}$ I have of WILL CARVER of y$^{e}$ same County & Parrish / aforesd wee doe for us, o$^{r}$. heires, Ex$^{rs}$. Adm$^{rs}$. or Assgs. for Ever we doe / bargaine, alienate, & sell, & acknowledge, and make over a good and / suficient Right unto WILL CARVER, to him, his heires, Ex$^{rs}$, Adm$^{rs}$. or Assgs / for Ever. it lyeing, & being & bounded as followeth. Wich parcell of land being / by computation fifty Acres be it more or less, it lyeing on y$^{e}$ Southside of y$^{e}$ / Blackwater Swamp; it being part of a trackt of land granted to M$^{r}$. GEO: / WILLIAMSON; & by grant of it being one Thousand Acres by Computation / of Patent. y$^{e}$ bounds as followeth. Begining att Lowermost Markt trees / of M$^{r}$. GEORGE WILLIAMSON begining att Blackwater and runing up one y$^{e}$ said / line unto a Division Line made betweene y$^{e}$ sd CRUMPLER & y$^{e}$ sd CARVER, / & Running on this Deviding Line unto y$^{e}$ Blackwater Swamp, & running / downe y$^{e}$ aforesd Swamp to y$^{e}$ first Station. wich land I y$^{e}$ sd W$^{M}$ CRUMPLER / & ELIZABETH my wife we give & grant, sell and make over & acknow= / ledge from us o$^{r}$. heires, Ex$^{rs}$, Adm$^{rs}$, or Assgs to WILL CARVER to / him, his heires, Ex$^{rs}$, Adm$^{rs}$. or Assgs for Ever. w$^{th}$. all priviledges / & appurtinances & emoluments thereunto belonging; with all lands, / Timbers, Woods & Water with all other priviledges whatsoever, & further / we doe confirme y[e] Articles above. I y[e] sd W[M]. CRUMPLER & ELIZABETH my wife / doth bind o[r]selves & o[r] Heires in y[e] penall Bond, & forfeit of five Thousd pounds of / Tob[o] & Cask; paym[t] well & truely to be made upon unperformance / of Articles aforesd, to be paid unto WILL CARVER, or his heires aforesd / as Wittness & Seales this 11[enth]. day of September 1700.

Signed & Sealed & deliv[r]ed
Test BARNABY MACKQUINY
his
WILL **W** WILLIAMS
m[r]ke
WILL **W** JOHNSON
his m[r]ke

WILL CRUMPLER seal
his [*sic*]
ELIZA: **E** CRUMPLER seal
m[r]ke

Acknowledged in open Co[rt] / held for y[e] Isle of Wight County / y[e] 9[th]. day of October 1700 by WILL / CRUMPLER & ELIZABETH his Wife to be their act & Deed &

Recorded p / CHA CHAPMAN C[l]C[ur]

This Indenture made y[e] 18[th]. day of December in y[e] yeare of O[r]. Lord god / 1700 & in the 12[th]. yeare of y[e] Reigne of o[r] Sov[r]aigne Lord William the 3[d]. / By y[e] Grace of God of England, Scotland, France & Ireland King &c / Betweene THOMAS PRICE, planter & RACHAEL his Wife (Eldest daught[r]. / of HENERY HERN deced, & Coparcenor with her two Sisters DEBORAH / HERN, & ELIZABETH HERN) of Chuckatuck Parrish in y[e] County of / Nanzimond of y[e] one p[t]. And THOMAS JORDAN of y[e] sd Parrish and / County Gent. of y[e] other part Wittnesseth y[t]. y[e] sd THOMAS PRICE & RACHAEL his wife

**[321]**

For and in Consideration of y[e] sum of one Thousd pounds of Tob[o]. to / him in hand att & before y[e] sealing & delivery of these p[r]sents by y[e] said / THOMAS JORDAN Gen[t]. well & truely paid y[e] receit whereof y[e] sd THOMAS / PRICE & RACHAEL his wife doth hereby acknowledge, & themselves therew[th] / fully satisfied & paid, & thereof & of every part & pcell thereof doth / clearely acquit, exonerate & discharge y[e] sd THOMAS JORDAN Gen[t]. his / Ex[rs], Adm[rs]. for ever. By these p[r]sents hath given, granted, Aliened, / Bargained, sold, Enfeoffed & Confirmed. And by these p[r]sents doth fully / clearly & absolutely Give, Grant, Bargaine, sell, Alien, enfeoff and / Confirme unto y[e] sd THOMAS JORDAN Gen[t]. his heires, & Assgs for Ever / one parcell of land Containing one hundred & seven Acres, scituate, lying / & being in y[e] County of Isle of Wight Contained in patent for three hundred / & twenty Acres granted unto THOMAS MANDUE, by patent dated y[e] 20[tieth]. / day of Aprill 1682 w[ch] sd three hundred & twenty Acres of land contained / in y[e] sd Patent was sold & made over by y[e] sd THOMAS MANDUE unto / y[e] sd HENERY HERN of Nanzimond County by deed beareing date y[e] 16[th] / day of May 1691 w[ch] sd trackt of land contained in y[e] sd Deed granted by / y[e] sd

THOMAS MANDUE unto y$^{e}$ sd HENERY HERN did descend from / y$^{e}$ sd HENERY HERN unto his foresd three Daughters RACHAEL, DEBORAH / and ELIZABETH soe y$^{t}$ y$^{e}$ land herein Conveyed is y$^{e}$ third part of y$^{e}$ fore / sd Patent, it being y$^{e}$ parcell or proportion w$^{ch}$ doth belong, or / did discend unto y$^{e}$ sd RACHAEL from her foresd father HENERY HERN / To have & to hold y$^{e}$ aforesd quantity or pcell of land w$^{th}$. all & / singular its Rights, members, Jurisdictions, & appurtinances: / togeth w$^{th}$ all houses, Edifices, buildings, Barnes, Stables, Or= / =chards, Gardens, yards, backsides, Easem$^{ts}$, Common of pastutre, heri= / =ditaments & Appurtinances w$^{t}$soever to y$^{e}$ sd Messuages, or / tenements, & p$^{r}$mises, or to any part or parcell of them belong / =ing, or in any=wise appertaining thereto unto unto [*sic*] y$^{e}$ sd THOMAS / JORDAN Gen$^{t}$: his heires or Assgs; to y$^{e}$ onely proper use & behoofe / of y$^{e}$ sd THOMAS JORDAN Gen$^{t}$. his heires, & Assgs for Ever. Against / them y$^{e}$ sd THOMAS PRICE & RACHAEL his Wife, their heires, & Assgs, / & all & every other person or persons, w$^{t}$soever lawfully Claiming by / from, or under them or any of them shall & will warrant & for / Ever defend by these p$^{r}$sents And y$^{t}$ y$^{e}$ sd THOMAS PRICE & RACHAEL / his Wife for themselves, their heires, Ex$^{rs}$, & Adm$^{rs}$. doe Covenant / promise grant, & agree to & w$^{th}$ y$^{e}$ sd THOMAS JORDAN Gen$^{t}$. his / heires & Assgs & every of them by these p$^{r}$sents y$^{t}$ all & singular / y$^{e}$ foresaid parcell of land w$^{th}$ all y$^{e}$ appurtinances thereunto / belonging now be & 8 [*sic*] Ever hereafter shall be, stand & Continue / to y$^{e}$ sd THOMAS JORDAN Gen$^{t}$: & his heires & Assgs for Ever / & y$^{t}$ y$^{e}$ sd THOMAS JORDAN Gen$^{t}$. his heires & Assgs be freely & / clearely acquit, exonerated, & discharged & form time to time well / & suficiently keept harmless by y$^{e}$ sd THOMAS PRICE & RACHAEL / his wife, their heires, Ex$^{rs}$ or Adm$^{rs}$, of & from all & all manner of form$^{r}$,

**[322]**
And other gifts, grants, bargaines, sailes, Leases, Mortgages, Joyntures / dowers, of & from all and singular other titles, troubles, charges, demands / & incumbrances w$^{t}$soever, had made commited, suffered, omitted or done by / y$^{e}$ said THOMPAS PRICE & RACHAEL his wife their heires, or Assgs for [ ] / any other person or persons w$^{t}$soever. And y$^{t}$ y$^{e}$ sd THOMAS PRICE / & RACHAEL his wife theire heires or Assgs for and dureing y$^{e}$ space of / seven yeares next ensueing y$^{e}$ date of these p$^{r}$sents shall & will att and / upon y$^{e}$ reasonable request of & att y$^{e}$ Cost & Charges in y$^{e}$ Law of y$^{e}$ said / THOMAS JORDAN Gen$^{t}$. his heires or Assgs make such further lawfull / & reasonable Assurance or Assurances or Conveyances in y$^{e}$ Law for y$^{e}$ more / better & perfect assurance of y$^{e}$ aforesaid p$^{r}$mises as by y$^{e}$ sd THOMAS JORDAN / Gen$^{t}$. his heires or Assgs or by his or their Councell learned in y$^{e}$ laws / shall be reasonably devised, advised, or required, & y$^{t}$ y$^{e}$ aforesd p$^{r}$mises with / all y$^{e}$ appurtinances thereunto belonging shall be esteemed & Judged & / taken to be & ennure to y$^{e}$ onely proper use & behoofe of y$^{e}$ sd THOMAS / JORDAN Gen$^{t}$. his heires & Assgs for ever. and to none other use, intent / or purpose w$^{t}$soever. In Witness hereof wee have hereunto sett o$^{r}$. / hands & Seales y$^{e}$ day year & Reigne first above written.
Signed, sealed & delivered in y$^{e}$ p$^{r}$sence his m$^{r}$ke seal

of us whose Names are hereunder= THOMAS **X** PRICE
=written her m$^{r}$ke seal
GEO: MOORE RACHAEL + PRICE
RICH$^{D}$ WILKINSON Jun$^{r}$.
RICH$^{D}$. REYNOLDS

Acknowledged in open Court held For y$^{e}$ / Isle Wight County y$^{e}$ 18$^{th}$ day of 10$^{br}$ / 1700 by THOMAS PRICE & RACHAEL his / Wife & Ordered to be Recorded Test

CHA CHAPMAN C$^{l}$C$^{ur}$

To all to whome these p$^{r}$sents may or shall Come, Know yee / that I JOHN LUTHER & MARY my Wife of y$^{e}$ Isle of Wight County / For diverse good causes & consideracons us thereunto moveing / more especially. For & in Consideracon of Three Thousand five / hundred & ffifty of Tobaccoe for us in hand paid, the Receipt / whereof wee acknowledge, Have bargained Sould, Enfeoffed / From us o$^{r}$ Heires Ex$^{rs}$ Adm$^{rs}$ & Assignes unto TRISTRAM NORSWORTHY / his Heires Ex$^{rs}$ Adm$^{rs}$. & Assignes For ever, a Certeyn ꝑcell of Land / & plantacon (whereon wee now Live) lying & being in y$^{e}$ Isle / Wight County & given to my Wife MARY Daughter of BENJ$^{N}$ BEAL / By AMBROSS BENNETT as by the said BENNETTs last Will & Testam$^{t}$ / will appear & y$^{e}$ bounds of y$^{e}$ Land & plantacon to be according

**[323]**
to y$^{e}$ Bounds as BENJAMIN BEAL held when he lived on it, being / by estimacon about Eighty Acres, be it more or less, and the said / & parcell of Land. I the abovesaid JOHN LUTHER & MARY my Wife doe / acknowledge to have Soaled, unto TRUSTRAM NOSWORTHY his / Heires Ex$^{rs}$ Adm$^{rs}$ & Assignes For ever w$^{th}$ all manner of Priveledges and / appertenances, thereunto belonging of Hawking hunting ffishing / & ffowling; Waies Waters Mineralls, Housings Orchards Gardens / Woods Underwoods, To have & to hould, y$^{e}$ said Land w$^{th}$ all / appertences thereto belonging For ever, From us O$^{r}$ Heires / Ex$^{rs}$ Adm$^{rs}$ or assignes, layeing any Clayme, Right Tytle or interest / to any ꝑte or ꝑcell of y$^{e}$ said Land, or any ꝑson or ꝑsons w$^{t}$soever / from by or under us or them laying any Clayme thereunto, as / witness o$^{r}$ hands & Seales this 9$^{th}$ day of December 1700

JN$^{O}$ LUTHER seal
MARY + LUTHER seal

Signed Sealed & delivered
JOSEPH BRIDG
ELIZ$^{A}$ HARRIS **E** mark
EDWARD MYLES

Acknowledged in Open Co$^{rt}$. held For y$^{e}$ Isle Wight County by M$^{r}$ RICHARD REYNOLDS attorney For JN$^{O}$ & by MARY LUTHER p$^{r}$sent in Co$^{rt}$. / this 10$^{th}$ day of ffeb$^{r}$ 170$^{0}$/$_{1}$ & Recorded

CHA CHAPMAN C$^{l}$C$^{ur}$

Know all men by these p$^{r}$sents y$^{t}$ I JOHN LUTHER doe hereby make / ordaine & appoint my Lov: friend M$^{r}$ RICHD REYNOLDS sen$^{r}$. my true & / Lawfull attorny, for me, & in my name, & to my use, to acknowledge / my plantacon I now Liveth on, in open Co$^{rt}$. unto TRISTRUM NORSWORTHY / & his heires for Ever Ratifieing, allowing, & Confirming all w$^{ch}$ my / sd Attorny shall Lawfully doe in y$^{e}$ sd prmises, as if I myself were then / & there p$^{r}$sonally p$^{r}$sent, As Wittness my hand & Seal this 8$^{th}$. day of / february 1700

Signed & Sealed in p$^{r}$sents of us — JOHN LUTHER seal
CHRISTOPHER REYNOLDS
his m$^{r}$ke — Recorded ꝑ CHA CHAPMAN C$^{l}$C$^{ur}$
JOHN + BUTLER

**[324]**

This Indenture made y$^{e}$ 30$^{th}$. day of December Anno Dom 1700 / & in y$^{e}$ 12$^{th}$. year of y$^{e}$ Reigne of o$^{r}$ Sov$^{r}$aigne L$^{d}$. W$^{m}$. y$^{e}$ 3$^{d}$. by y$^{e}$ Grace of / God of England, Scotland, ffrance & Ireland King, Defender of y$^{e}$ / faith &c: Betweene THOMAS CARTER & MAGDALEN his wife of y$^{e}$ Upper / ꝑish of y$^{e}$ Isle of Wight County in Virg$^{a}$. Planter of y$^{e}$ one ꝑt. & / GEORGE CARTER son of y$^{e}$ said THOMAS & MAGDALEN of y$^{e}$ p$^{te}$. / Witnesseth y$^{t}$ Whereas GEORGE MOORE of y$^{e}$ sd ꝑish & County Gent / father of y$^{e}$ sd MAGDALEN, by deed beareing date y$^{e}$ 11$^{enth}$. day of / Aug$^{t}$. 1673 did (in Consideraiton of Marriage) Convey unto the / sd THO: CARTER & MAGDALEN his Wife, four hundred Acres of land / being ꝑt. of a dividend or tract containing fourteen hundred / Acres Scituate on or near y$^{e}$ second ~~Blackwater~~ Swamp of y$^{e}$ / Blackwater in y$^{e}$ sd ꝑish & County granted to him, by Patent / dated y$^{e}$ twelfth day of May 1669 w$^{ch}$. sd four hundred Acres, begun / att a White Oake upon y$^{e}$ head of y$^{e}$ Beaver Dam Branch, & soe downe / y$^{e}$ said Branch to a take in y$^{e}$ sd quantity According to Bounds men= / =tioned in y$^{e}$ sd Patent. Now Know yee y$^{t}$ y$^{e}$. sd THOMAS CARTER & / MAGDALEN his Wife for & in Consideration of Naturall love and / affection, & for divers other good Causes then thereunto moveing / have bargained, sold, aliened, Enfeoffed & Confirmed, & by these / p$^{r}$sents doe for themselves, their Heires, Ex$^{rs}$ & Adm$^{rs}$, bargain / sell, Alien, Enfeoff & Confirme unto y$^{e}$ sd GEO: CARTER, his heires / & Assignes for Ever, two hundred Acres of Land part of y$^{e}$ four / hundred Acres, begining att a Sickamore or White Wood Tree / att or near y$^{e}$ Mouth of a Branch Called y$^{e}$ Red Root Point, & soe / downe y$^{e}$ Beaver Dam Branch to y$^{e}$ full quantity. To have and / hold y$^{e}$ sd two hundred acres of land, w$^{th}$. all woods, Waters, Mines / Mineralls, Royalties, proffitts, Emoluments, Comodities & appurtinan / =ces to y$^{e}$ same belonging, or in anywise appertaining unto y$^{e}$ said / GEORGE CARTER, his heires & Assgs for Ever, Covenanting & hereby / granting y$^{t}$ y$^{e}$ Land, & p$^{r}$mises hereby Conveyed is free & Clear of all / incumbrance w$^{t}$soever, and that the said THOMAS CARTER and / MAGDALEN his Wife have att y$^{e}$ time of y$^{e}$ sealing & delivery of these / p$^{r}$sents a free, clear & Indefeazable Estate in fee of y^e sd Land; & / in & to every part thereof. In Wittness whereof y^e sd THOMAS / CARTER & MAGDALEN his wife have hereunto sett their hands & / Seales y^e day & year abovewritten.

Signed, Sealed & delivered in p^r sence of
W^M. BROWNE
[ ]IND GRIFFEN

THO: CARTER O
her
MARDALEN **MC** CARTER O
m^r ke

Acknowledged in open Co^rt. / held for y^e Isle of Wight / County y^e 10^th of feb: 1700 by / y^e sd THO: CARTER & his Wife & / Recorded

p CHA CHAPMAN C^l C^ur

**[325]**

This Indenture made y^e 4^th: day of June 1696 Betweene HENERY BAKER / of y^e Isle of Wight County Gen^t. of y^e one part & EDMOND WICKINS of Nanzimond / County planter of y^e other part Wittnesseth. That y^e said BAKER for & in / Consideration of y^e sum of fyfteen hundred pounds of Tob^o. to him before / the sealing & Delivering of y^e sd p^r sents by y^e sd WICKINS well & truely paid / y^e Receipt he y^e said BAKER doe acknowledge & himself therewith fully satisfied / & paid, & thereof doe clearly, Acquit & Discharge y^e sd WICKINS, his heires, Ex^rs / & Adm^rs. for Ever. Have Bargained, sold & Confirmed, by these p^r sents doe / Bargaine, sell, Enfeoff & Confirme unto y^e said WICKINS, his heires & Assgs for / Ever. one hundred Acres of Land Scituate, lyeing & being att a place, / Comonly Called, or Knowne by y^e Name of y^e HENERY POTTS in y^e aforesaid / County of Nanzimond, w^th all its Rights, Members, Jurisdictions & Appurtinan / =ces thereunto belonging, as haveing, Orchards, Gardens, Wayes, Waters / &c: to y^e said p^r mises, or any ꝑt. or ꝑcell thereof belonging or any wayes / appertaining, & alsoe all y^e Estate, Right, Title, Interest, use, possession, / property, Claime & Demand whatsoever of him y^e sd BAKER, of in or to y^e / same. To have & to Hold y^e said one hundred Acres of land, & all, and / singular y^e p^r mises, hereby Bargained & sold; w^th their & every their Rights / Members & Appurtinances whatsoever, to y^e sd WICKINS his heires & Assgs / for Ever, & to y^e onely proper use & behoofe of y^e sd WICKINS, his heires, & / Assgs for Ever. And y^t sd BAKER for himself his heires, Ex^rs, Adm^rs, y^e / sd one hundred Acres of land & all & Singular y^e p^r mises, before granted, / Bargained & sold w^th y^e Appurtinances, unto y^e sd WICKINS, his heires, Ex^rs, / Adm^rs & Assgs for Ever, ag^st. him y^e sd BAKER his heires, Ex^rs, Adm^rs, & Assgs / & all, & every other ꝑ^r son or ꝑsons whatsoever, Claiming, by, from / or under him, them, or any of them, or any other ꝑson w^t soever. / Wittness whereof the party first abovenamed, unto this p^r sent / Indenture have put his hand & Seal y^e day & year first abovewritten / Anno Dom: 1696

Signed, Sealed, & Deliv^r ed in y^e p^r sence of
his

HEN BAKER seal

EDWARD **:EF:** FFLOYD
m$^r$ke
THO: **H:** HAIREBOTTLE
his / m$^r$ke

Acknowledged in open Co$^{rt}$ / held for y$^e$ Isle of Wight County y$^e$ 10$^{th}$. / of ffeb$^r$: $^{1700}/_{1701}$ by y$^e$ sd HENRY BAKER / to be his Act & Deed & Recorded

ꝑ CHA CHAPMAN C$^l$C$^{ur}$

**[326]**

This Indenture made y$^e$ 3$^d$. day of June 1696 Betweene EDM$^D$ WICKINS / of y$^e$ County of Nanzimond of y$^e$ one ꝑ$^t$. & HENERY BAKER of y$^e$ County of y$^e$ / Isle of Wight Gent of y$^e$ other ꝑ$^t$. Wittnesseth, y$^t$ y$^e$ sd WICKINS for & in Consid= / eration of y$^e$ sum of five Thous$^d$ pounds of Tob$^o$ to him before y$^e$ seal= / =ing & delivering of y$^e$ s$^d$ p$^r$sents, by s$^d$ BAKER well & truely p$^d$, y$^e$ receipt / whereof he y$^e$ sd WICKINS doe acknowledge, & himself therew$^{th}$ fully satisfied / & paid, & thereof doe Clearly Acquit & discharge y$^e$ sd BAKER his heires, / Ex$^{rs}$, & Adm$^{rs}$ for Ever, have Bargained, sold & Confirmed & by these / p$^r$sents doe Alien, bargain, sell & Enfeoff & Confirme, unto y$^e$ sd HENERY / BAKER, his heires & Assgs for Ever, one hundred Acres of land, Scituate / lyeing & being, att a Place Called y$^e$ head of y$^e$ Runns in y$^e$ aforesaid / County of y$^e$ Isle of Wight, & Bought by y$^e$ sd WICKINS father of SION / HILL as by as Conveyance may appeare, with all it's Rights, Members, / Jurisdictions & appurtinances thereunto belonging, as housing, Orchards / Gardens, Wayes, Waters &c: to y$^e$ sd p$^r$mises or any ꝑ$^t$. or ꝑcell thereof / belonging or any wayes appertaining & alsoe all y$^e$ Estate, Right / Title, Interest, use, possession, property, Claime & demand Whatsoever / of him y$^e$ sd WICKINS, of, in , or to y$^e$ same. To have & to hold y$^e$ sd / one hundred Acres of land & all & singular y$^e$ p$^r$mises hereby bargained / & sold, with their, and every of their Rights, Members & Appurtinan= / =ces whatsoever unto y$^e$ sd BAKER, his heires & Assgs for Ever, & to y$^e$ / only proper use & behoofe of y$^e$ sd BAKER, his heires & assgs for Ever, & y$^e$ / sd WICKINS for himself, his heirs, Ex$^{rs}$, & Adm$^{rs}$, y$^e$ sd one hundred Acres / of land & all & singular y$^e$ p$^r$mises before granted bargained & sold w$^{th}$ y$^e$ Appurtin= / nances unto y$^e$ sd BAKER, his heires, Ex$^{rs}$, Adm$^{rs}$ & Assgs for Ever against / him y$^e$ sd WICKINS, his heires, Ex$^{rs}$, Adm$^{rs}$. & Assgs & all & every other / =person & persons w$^t$soever Claiming by from or under him, y$^m$. / or any of them or any other ꝑson w$^t$soever, shall & will warr$^t$. / & for ever defend, by these p$^r$sents & further y$^e$ sd WICKINS for himself / his heires, Ex$^{rs}$, & Adm$^{rs}$ doe Covenant, promise, grant, & agree to & / & w$^{th}$ y$^e$ sd BAKER. his heires, & Assgs & every of them by these p$^r$sents / y$^t$ he y$^e$ sd WICKINS shall & will, from time to time & all times / hereafter, att & upon y$^e$ Reasonable request, & att y$^e$ Cost & Charges / in y$^e$ Law of y$^e$ sd BAKER, his heires, & Assgs, make & Cause to be made / such further assurance in y$^e$ Law, for y$^e$ further / better & more perfect assurance, Surely & sure makeing & Conveying / all & singular, y$^e$ before hereby granted or mentioned, to be granted / p$^r$mises w$^{th}$. all & every of their Rights, Members & Appurtinances / unto y$^e$ sd BAKER, his heires, & Assgs, as by y$^e$ sd BAKER his heires & / Assgs, or by his or their Councell Learned in y$^e$ Law shall be / Reasonably, devised,

Advised or Required. In Wittness where / of y^e party first above mentioned unto these p^r sents / Indenture Interchaneably have put their hands & Seales

**[327]**

The day & year first above written Anno^q Dom 1696

(y^e words five Thousand was Interlined / before sealing)

Signed, Sealed, & Delivered in y^e p^r sence of us

his
EDWARD **EF** FFLOYD
m^r ke

his
THOMAS **H** HAREBOTTLE
m^r ke

his
EDMOND **M** WICKINS O
m^r ke

Acknowledged in open Co^rt. held for y^e / Isle of Wight County y^e 10^th. day of ffeb 1700/1701 by y^e sd EDMOND WICKINS to be his Act & deed & Recorded ꝑ

CHA CHAPMAN C^l C^ur

Knowe all men by these p^r sents y^t I JOHN WILLE of y^e Isle of / Wight County planter for & in Consideration of Thousd Weight of / Tob^o to me in hand paid or secured to be p^d by NATHANIELL WHITBY / of y^e sd County. Have granted, bargained & sold & by these presents for me & my heires / doe grant, bargaine, & sell, Infeoff & Confirme unto y^e sd NATHAN^LL. / WHITBY, his heires, & Assgs for ever a certaine peice or ꝑcell of land / Containing one hundred & seventy Acres scituate, lyeing & being between / y^e lands of THOMAS TOOKE, Cap^t. ENGLAND, THOMAS BLAKE, & EDW^D / BRANTLY in y^e Upper Parrish of y^e Isle of Wight County formerly purchased of / of [*sic*] ROB^T. FFLAKE y^e said one hundred & seventy Acres of land being formerly / granted, to Maj^r. ARTHUR ALLEN by Pattent dated y^e 20^th. day of / October 1691 And thus bounded begining att a Red Oake THOMAS / BLAKEs Corner Tree in M^r. TOOKEs line thence by BLAKE: South / seventy three degrees, West two hundred sixty Pole to a Small Red Oake / North seventy four degrees, West sixty Pole to a Pine, & North thirty / four degrees, West one hundred & two Pole to a Pine in M^r. NEWMANs / Line, Thence by his line North, North East twenty nine Pole to a / stooping Red Oake in, or near Cap^t. ENGLANDs line, thence by his line / South sixty nine degrees, East one hundred & eight Pole to a small / Wight Oake marked marked [*sic*] by Consent of GEORGE CRIPPS late possess^r / of y^e sd land, then North thirty one degrees, East an hundred & seven / Pole to two Pines, EDW^D BRANTLYs Corner Trees near y^e dancing / place then by y^e sd BRANTLY's lines South East fifty two poles to / a Pine & North East twenty Pole to M^r. TOOKEs line & soe by his / line South East an hundred thirty six pole to y^e first station. / To have & to hold y^e sd one hundred & seventy Acres of Land w^th. his / due share of all Mines & Mineralls therein Contained, w^th free / priviledge of hunting, hawking, fishing & fowling, w^th all Woods

**[328]**

Wayes & Waters, & all priviledges other Royalty's, prviledges, / proffitts, Commodities & Hereditam[ts]. w[t]soever to y[e] sd land belonging or / in any wise appertaining to him y[e] sd NATH[LL]. WHITBY his heires & Assgs / for Ever: in as full & ample manner to all intents & purposes, as I myself / might or could have enjoyed y[e] same And I doe hereby Covenant & promise / declare & agree, to & w[th]. y[e] sd NATHAN[LL]. WHITBY his heires & Assgs y[t] y[e] sd land / & every part thereof is free & cleare from all manner of Incumbrances / by me Committed, or any person claimeing from or under me. I hereby / Oblidge my self, my heires, Ex[rs], & Adm[rs] to warrant & defend this my sale / of y[e] p[r]mises to y[e] sd NATH[LL]. WHITBY, his heires, & Assgs for Ever. In / Wittness whereof I have hereunto sett my hand & Seal this Eighth day / of ffeb[r]. 1700

Signed & Sealed
in y[e] p[r]sents of
REUBEN PROCTER
JONE PROCTER

the m[r]ke of
JOHN **W** WILLE O

Acknowledged in open Co[rt]. / held for y[e] Isle of Wight County y[e] ffeb[r]. y[e] 10[th]. 1700 by / JN[O] WILLE to be his Act & Deed / Recorded ꝑ / CHA CHAPMAN C[l]C[ur]

I doe hereby freely and / Absolutely give up & Relinquish / unto y[e] sd NATH[LL]. WHITBY all my / Right & Dower to y[e] abovemen= / tioned land & ev[r]y ꝑt thereof

MARY **W** WILLE O
the m[r]ke of

Recorded ꝑ CHA CHAPMAN C[l]C[ur]

Memorandum that seizen & possession of y[e] within mentioned / p[r]mises was given by y[e] w[th]in named JN[O]. WILLE to y[e] w[th]in named NATH[LL]. / WHITBY by deliv[r]y of a Turf & Twigg on y[e] w[th]in said Land this 8[th]. / day of ffebruary 1700 in y[e] p[r]sence of

REUBEN PROCTTER

Recorded ꝑ CHA CHAPMAN C[l]C[ur]

To all to whome these p[r]sents shall Come I S[r]. W[M] BERKELEY K[nt] / Gov[r]nour & Cap[t]. Gen[r]all of Virg[a]. send Greeting in o[r] Lord God Ev[r]lasting / whereas by Instructions from y[e] Kings most Excellent Matie directed / to me & y[e] Councell of State his Ma[tie]. was graciously pleased to / Authorize me y[e] sd Gov[r]nour & Councell to grant Patts & to Assg / such ꝑportions of land to all Adventurers & planters as have bin / heretofore usuall in y[e] like Cases, either for Adventu[rs]. of money or

**[329]**

Transportations of people into this Collony, according to a Charter / of Orders from y^e^ late Treas: & Company. & y^t^ y^e^ same ꝑportions of fifty / acres of land be granted or Assgd for ev^r^y p^r^son transported hither since / Midsummer 1665 And y^t^. y^e^ same Course be Continued to all Adventurers / & planters untill itt shall be otherwise determined by his Ma^tis^. / Now know yee y^t^. I y^e^ sd S^r^. W^M^. BERKELEY K^nt^. Gov^r^nour &c: doe / w^th^ y^e^ Consent of y^e^ Councell of State accordingly give & grant unto / JN^O^. WAKEFIELD & JN^O^: SHERRER one Thousd & fifty acres of land / lyeing in y^e^ Isle of Wight County on y^e^ Branches of y^e^ first Swamp / of y^e^ Blackwater begining att a Red Oake & Runing E:S:E: one / hundred & sixty pole to a Red Oake in COOKEs line, then S:S:W: / seventy pole to COOKEs Corner tree, then SE a hundred & twenty / pole to a White Oake, then :S: a hundred & sixty two pole to a White / Oake, then W a hundred & twelve pole to their owne old markt trees / then S one hundred & fifty four Pole to a White Oake, then SW / Eighty Eight pole to a Red Oake, then W:NW: two hundred & forty / two Pole to a Pine, then N:NE: five hundred & thirty two pole / to y^e^ first Station. Whereof Seven hundred Acres part / thereof being formrly granted to X^FER^. LEWIS by patt^n^ dated y^e^ / 26^th^ day of July 1662: & by y^e^ said LEWIS, sold to y^e^ sd WAKEFIELD & / SHERRER & three hundred & fifty Acres y^e^ residue being due by and / for y^e^ Transportation of seven ꝑsons into this Collony whose names / are on y^e^ Records menconed und^r^neath this patt: To have, & to hold / y^e^ sd land w^th^ his due share of all Mines & Mineralls therein / contained, w^th^ all Rights & priviledges of hunting, hawking, / fishing & fowling, w^th^ all Woods, Waters, & Rivers, w^th^ all profitts / Commodities & heriditam^ts^ to y^e^ said land belonging to them y^e^ / them y^e^ [*sic*] sd JN^O^. WAKEFIELD & JN^O^. SHERRER their heires & Assgs for Ever / in as large & ample manner to all intents & purposes as is exprest in a / Charter of orders from y^e^ late Treas: & Comp^a^: Dated y^e^ 18^th^. day of Novem^br^ / 1618 or by Consequence may be Justly Collected out of y^e^ same, or out / of y^e^ Lett^rs^. patts whereon they are grounded to be held of O^r^ Sov^r^aigne / Lord y^e^ King, his heires or Success^rs^. for Ever, as of his Mannor / of East Greenwich in free & Comon Soccage & not *in Capite* / nor by Kn^ts^. Service yeilding & paying to o^r^ Sov^r^aigne Lord / y^e^ King, his heires & Success^rs^. for every fifty acres of Land / hereby granted yearely att y^e^ Feast of S^t^. Michael y^e^ Arch / Angell y^e^ fee Rent of one shilling w^ch^. paym^t^ is to be made yearly / from year to year according to his Maties Instructions of y^e^ 12^th^.

**[330]**
Of September: 1662 provided that if y^e^ said JN^O^ WAKEFIELD or JOHN / SHERRER their heires, or Assgs doe not seat or plant or cause to be / seated or planted upon y^e^ sd land w^th^in three yeares next ensueing / then it shall be lawfull for any Adventurer or planter to make / Choice thereof & Seat thereupon. Given under my hand, & y^e^ Seal of / y^e^ Collony this 5^th^. day of Aprill. In y^e^ year of O^r^. Lord 1668 Anno / Regis Caroli 2^d^. 20^o^.
JN^O^. WAKEFIELD & JN^O^ SHERRER their WILLIAM BERKELEY
Patt for 1050 Acres of Land in Isle
Wight County
Recordatur Teste

PHILL LUDWELL C^l Off: Recorded ꝑ CHA CHAPMAN C^lC^ur

Know all men by these p^rsents that I ROB^T THOMAS of y^e Isle Wight County / in y^e Collony of Virginia Gent For and in Consideracon of y^e sume of ffifty / pounds sterling money to me in hand p^d. by CHARLES [--] of y^e County planter / y^e rec^t. whereof I doe hereby acknowledge and therew^th am Fully sattisffied doe / by these p^rsents For me my Heires &c bargaine, Sell, alien, Assigne, & Sett / over unto y^e sd CHARLES EDWARDS, y^e w^thin menconed pattent & all & every the / Lands to me belonging in y^e same granted, Conteyning by Divident / Three hundred & Seventy Acres of Land more or less, as by the sd / Division may appear; To have & to hold the said land & every ꝑte / thereof w^th all houseings & appertences to y^e same belonging: unto / y^e said CHARLES EDWARDS his Heires & assignes For ever, Warranting the / said bargained p^rmises, & every ꝑte thereof to be Free From all & all / manner of incumbrances whatsoever, In witness whereof I have / hereunto sett my hand & Seal this 31^th day of March 1701

Signed Sealed & delivered in y^e p^rsence of
JOHN DAVIS
CHA CHAPMAN

ROB^T THOMAS seal

By vertue of a power of Attorney proved / Court, Acknowledged y^e 9^th day of Aprill in / open Co^rt by CHARLES CHAPMAN & Recorded ꝑ / CHA CHAPMAN C^lC^ur

**[331]**

Know all men by thee p^rsents that I ROB^T THOMAS of y^e Isle Wight County / in y^e Collony of Virginia gent doe by these p^rsents make Ordeyne & Constitute / CHARLES CHAPMAN of the same County gent my true & lawfull Attorny / For me & in my name to appear att y^e next Co^rt to be held For y^e said / County, then & there to acknowledge one assigem^t or Conveyance by / me made bearing even date w^th these p^rsents unto CHARLES EDWARDS / of y^e sd County For w^ch have reced A Valluable Consideracon, Ratifiing / & by these p^rsents Confirmeing whatsoever my said Attorney shall / lawfully doe For y^e Further & more safe Conveyance y^e Land by me sould / to y^e sd EDWARDS In witness whereof I have hereunto sett my hand & / Seal this 31^st day of March 1701

Signed Sealed & delivered in p^rsence of
JN^O DAVIS
CHA CHAPMAN

ROB^T. THOMAS seal

Proved in open Co^rt held For y^e Isle Wight / County y^e 9^th day of Aprill 1701, by y^e Oaths / of both y^e witnesses & Recorded

ꝑ CHA CHAPMAN C^lC^ur

This Indenture made y^e 6^th. of October in y^e year of O^r Lord God / 1681 & in y^e 33^d. yeare of y^e Reigne of o^r Sov^raigne Lord King / Charles y^e 2^d. of Great Brittaine,

France & Ireland Defender of / y^e^ faith. Betweene PHILLIP RAYFORD of y^e^ Isle of Wight County of y^e^ / one ꝑt. & THOMAS MANDUE of y^e^ aforesd Isle of Wight County of y^e^ / ꝑt. Wittnesseth y^t^ y^e^ sd PHILLIP RAYFORD for & in Consideration of a / good & valueable Consideracon to him already made, & in hand paid / by y^e^ sd THO: MANDUE before y^e^ ensealing & deliv^r^y of these p^r^sents / wherein he acknowledgeth himself fully Contented, satisfied & paid / have granted, demised & sold, Alienate, Confirme & made over unto / y^e^ sd THOMAS MANDUE, his heires, Ex^rs^, Adm^rs^, & Assgs for Ever two hundred / Acres of land more or less lyeing & being in y^e^ aforesd Isle of Wight / County being part of a Pattent of three hundred And fifty acres of / land Granted unto y^e^ sd PHILLIP RAYFORD beareing date y^e^ 23^d^. of Aprill 1681 / y^e^ sd two hundred Acres of land being bounded as followeth (Viz^t^) / bounded upon a Corner Pine of y^e^ sd RAFFORDs unto a Corner Red / Oake from y^e^ Red Oake along y^e^ line to a Reedy Branch & soe down y^e^ / Reedy Branch to y^e^ sd RAFFORDs line & soe along y^e^ line to y^e^ aforesd Corner / Pine. Wich y^e^ sd PHILLIP RAYFFORD doth for himself his heires, Ex^rs^, Adm^rs^

**[332]**

Or Assgs & to & ev^r^y of them y^t^ he y^e^ sd THOMAS MANDUE his heires, Ex^rs^, Adm^rs^. & / Assgs shall from y^e^ day of y^e^ date for Ev^r^. hereafter have, hold, occupy, possess / & quietly Enjoy y^e^ sd two hundred Acres of Land before demised with all rights / proffitts, Commodities & heriditam^ts^ w^t^soever thereunto belonging or in any / wise appertaining w^th^out any lett or hinderance, or molestation, or Contradiction / of y^e^ sd PHILLIP RAFFORD, or his heires Ex^rs^, Adm^rs^. of Assgs or by any other ꝑson / or ꝑsons w^t^soever by his knowledge, Consent or procureation w^th^out any / manner of Condition, or limitation of use, or uses, Rent or Rents (y^e^ Kings / only excepted) & for y^e^ better & more Authenticke Confirmation of y^e^ before / demises ꝑmises y^e^ aforesd PHILLIP RAYFORD doth hereby Oblige himself to / Acknowledge this deed of sale in open Co^rt^. w^n^. thereunto Required to be his free / Act & Voluntary deed. In Wittness whereof I y^e^ sd PHILLIP RAYFORD have / hereunto sett my hand & seal y^e^ day & year first abovewritten

Signed, Sealed, & delivered — PHILLIP **R** RAYFORD seal
in y^e^ p^r^sence — hes m^r^ke
JOHN BROWNE
GEORGE **G** PEIRCE
his m^r^ke

Acknowledged in Co^rt^. held for y^e^ Isle / of Wight County y^e^ 9^th^. of June 1682 by / PHILLIP RAYFORD to be his Act & deed and / Ordered to be recorded

Test JOHN PITT C^l^ C^ur^:

Be it knowne unto all men by these p^r^sents y^t^ I THOMAS MANDUE / sen^r^. & SARAH MANDUE his wife, or heires, Ex^rs^. Adm^rs^ or Assgs for good / Consideration in hand reced have fully by these p^r^sents Assged over unto ABRAHAM RICKES, his heires, Ex^rs^, Adm^rs^. or Assgs all o^r^. Right title / & Interest of this within specified deed of

Conveyance for Ev$^{r}$. / In Wittness hereof we have hereunto sett o$^{r}$. hands this 4$^{th}$. / day of Jan$^{ry}$ 1699

And for further Confirmacon y$^{e}$ p$^{ties}$. abovemenonced together / w$^{th}$ their son THOMAS MANDUE Jun$^{r}$. have obliged themselves to / acknowledged this same said deed before o$^{r}$. Court held for y$^{e}$ Isle / of Wight which being Aprill Co$^{rt}$. next after y$^{e}$ date hereof in y$^{e}$ year / 1700

| | his m$^{r}$ke | signum |
|---|---|---|
| ISAAC RICKES | THOMAS **T** MANDUE | O |
| THOMAS MANDUE Jun$^{r}$ | SARAH **W** MANDUE | O |
| ROB$^{T}$ RICKES | her m$^{r}$ke | |

Acknowledged in open Co$^{rt}$. held for Isle / of Wight County y$^{e}$ 9$^{th}$ day of Decem$^{br}$ / 1700 by THO: MANDUE & SARAH his wife to / be their Voluntary Act & Deed & Ordered / to be Recorded

Test CHA CHAPMAN C$^{l}$C$^{ur}$

**[333]**

This Indenture made y$^{e}$ 9$^{th}$ day of Aprill Anno Dom 1701 and in y$^{e}$ Thirteenth year of the / Reigne of o$^{r}$ Soveraigne Lord William y$^{e}$ third by y$^{e}$ grace of God of England Scotland / ffrance & Ireland King defender of y$^{e}$ faith &c Between JOHN MACKMIHILL & SARAH his / Wife of y$^{e}$ Lower ꝑish of y$^{e}$ Isle of Wight County in y$^{e}$ Collony of Virginia planter of y$^{e}$ one / part & JOHN COTTON of y$^{e}$ same ꝑish & County planter of y$^{e}$ other ꝑte Witnesseth / that y$^{e}$ said JOHN MACKMIHILL For & in Consideracon of y$^{e}$ sume of Two Thousand pound / of Tob to him & hand p$^{d}$ or secured before y$^{e}$ ensealing & delivery of these p$^{r}$sents, the / receipt whereof he doth hereby acknowledge, & himselfe thereby & therewith Fully / Contented sattisfied & p$^{d}$ Hath bargained sould aliened enfeoffed confirmed & sett over / and by these p$^{r}$sents For himselfe his hieres Ex$^{rs}$ & Adm$^{rs}$ doth Firmely & absolutely / bargain sell alien Enfeoff confirme assigne & sett over unto y$^{e}$ sd JOHN COTTON / his Heires & assignes For ever, all that ꝑcell & Tract of Land, scituate w$^{th}$in y$^{e}$ County / & ꝑish abovesaid, conteyning by estimacon two Hundred acres, granted to y$^{e}$ sd / JOHN MACKMIHILL, by pattent dated y$^{e}$ 28$^{th}$ of October Anno Dom 1697 under / the hand of S$^{r}$ EDMOND ANDROS K$^{t}$ his Ma$^{ties}$ then L$^{t}$ & Governr generall of / Virginia and under y$^{e}$ Seal of y$^{e}$ Collony being For y$^{e}$ Importacon of Four ꝑsons / into this Collony, Togeather w$^{th}$ all Buildings Houses Orchards & appertences, to y$^{e}$ / same belonging or in any wise apperteyning, togeather w$^{th}$ all Royaltyes & / priviledges, by y$^{e}$ said pattent granted, being butted & bounded as in y$^{e}$ said pat$^{t}$ / is sett Forth, As by y$^{e}$ said pattent relacon being thereunto had may more att large appear, To have & to hould the said pattent & y$^{e}$ said two hundred / acres of Land by y$^{e}$ same granted, w$^{th}$ all & singuler y$^{e}$ appertences thereunto / belonging to y$^{e}$ said JOHN COTTON hes Heires & assignes For ever, And the said / JOHN MACKMIHILL For himselfe his Heires Ex$^{rs}$ & Adm$^{rs}$ doth Coven$^{t}$ promise / and grant to & w$^{th}$ the said JOHN COTTON, his Heires Ex$^{rs}$ Adm$^{rs}$ & assignes / that y$^{e}$

said bargained p^r^mises & every ꝑte thereof is att y^e^ tyme of y^e^ sealing / & delivery hereof Free & clear of & From all & all manner of / incumbrances by him y^e^ sd JOHN MACKMIHILL had made suffered Comitted or / done, in any manner howsoever, And that he has an absolute & indefeazable / right in fee to y^e^ said bargained p^r^mises, And that he y^e^ said JOHN MACKMIHILL / his Heires Ex^rs^ Adm^rs^ & assignes y^e^ said bargained p^r^mises ag^t^ all ꝑsons clayming / y^e^ same shall & will warr^t^ & Forever defend by thes p^r^sents In witness / whereof y^e^ said JOHN MICKMIHILL & SARAH his Wife have hereunto Sett their / hands & Seales y^e^ day & year First above written

hes
Signed Sealed & delivered in y^e^ p^r^sence of — JN^O^ **J** MACKMIHILL Seal
JN^O^ BATLEY — m^r^ke
W^M^ GREEN — SARAH + MACKMIHILL Seal
m^r^ke

Acknowledged in open Co^rt^ held For y^e^ Isle Wight / County by JN^O^ MACKMIHILL & hes Wife y^e^ 9^th^ Aprill 1701 / & Recorded
ꝑ CHA CHAPMAN C^l^C^ur^

Know all men by these p^r^sents y^t^ I y^e^ w^th^in named SARAH MACKMIHILL doe by these p^rnts^ Freely & / absolutely, relinquish all my right of Dower, w^ch^ I may any waies clayme to y^e^ w^th^in bargained / p^r^mises, or any ꝑte thereof, or w^ch^ I may or might clayme by any Law usage or Custome / whatsoever, witness my hand & seal y^e^ day & year w^th^in named

her
Signed Sealed & delivered in p^r^sents of — SARAH + MACKMIHILL
JN^O^ BATLY — m^r^ke seal
W^M^ GREEN

Acknowledged in Open Co^rt^ y^e^ Same day by y^e^ sd / SARAH MACKMIHILL / Recorded ꝑ CHA CHAPMAN C^l^ C^ur^

**[334]**

This Indenture made y^e^ Ninth Day of Aprill in y^e^ year of o^r^ Lord God One Thousand / Seaven hundered One & in y^e^ thirteenth year of y^e^ Reign of o^r^ Soveraigne Lord W^m^ / y^e^ third by y^e^ grace of God of England Scotland ffrance & Ireland King &c Between JN^O^ / GYLES & PHILARETE his Wife of y^e^ Isle of Wight County in Virginia of y^e^ One ꝑte and / LEWIS WILLIAMS of North Carolina of y^e^ other ꝑte Witnesseth y^t^ y^e^ said JOHN GILES / & PHILARETE his Wife For divers good causes & Consideracons them thereunto / moveing, but more especially For y^e^ sume of Fifteen hundred pounds of Tob to y^m^ / in hand p^d^ before y^e^ sealing & delivery of these p^r^sents y^e^ receipt whereof y^e^ sd / JOHN GILES & PHILARETE his Wife doth hereby acknowledge and For ever Exonerate / & discharge y^e^ said LEWES WILLAIMS his Heires Ex^rs^ Adm^rs^ & assignes Doth give grant, / Enfeoff & Confirme and by these p^r^sents doth Fully clearly & absolutely Enfeoff and / Confirme, unto y^e^ said LEWIS WILLIAMS hes Heires &

Assignes For ever all or right / Title & Interest, in and to a Certeyn ꝑcell of Land Conteyning ffive hundred Acres / scituate lying & being in North Carolina upon Choanock Rever Conteyned in a / pattent For Two Thousand Acres granted by y^e Right hono^ble S^r W^M BARTLETT / unto M^r THOMAS WOODWARD Sen^r and THOMAS WOODWARD Jun^r bearing date y^e 20^th / day of Sept^r 1668 y^e said Five hundred Acres of Land being bounded as followeth / it lying upon y^e Upper Side of y^e said pattent, begining on y^e mouth of a Creek / & soe runing to y^e head Lyne of y^e said pattent For length and soe along y^e / said Lyne untill it doth make Five hundred Acres & soe downe to y^e River and / soe up y^e River to y^e said Creek, w^ch Tract is on y^e Upper side of y^e High land / It being y^e next Creek above y^e said High land To have & hould y^e Foresaid / ffive hundred acres of Land, w^th all itts rights priveledges Jurisdiccons and / appertences, whatsoever to y^e said LEWIS WILLIAMS his Heires & assignes Forever / ag^t y^e said JOHN GILES & PHILLARETE his wife their Heires & Assignes or any / clayming From by or under them to y^e only proper use & behoof of the / said LEWES WILLIAMS his Heires & Assignes For ever In witness whereof wee / have hereunto sett o^r hands & seales y^e Day year & Reign First above / written

Signed Sealed & delivered in y^e
p^rsence of us whose names are underwitten
THOMAS GILES
PENELLOPE GILES
PHILLARETE GILES

JOHN GILES seal
PHILARETE GILES seal

Acknowledged in Open Co^rt held For y^e Isle / of Wight County y^e 9^th of Aprill 1701 / by Mr JOHN GILES & PHILLARETE his Wife / to be their Acts & Deed & Recorded / ꝑ CHA CHAPMAN C^lC^ur

**[335]**

This shall oblidge me WILLIAM MACKIE of y^e Isle of Wight County m^rchant, to assigne & / make over unto JAMES FFOWLER (merchant of Nanzimond County, all manner of / debts dues & demands, w^ch may any wayes concerne me by reason of my ꝑtenership / w^th y^e said JAMES FFOWLER, and doe acknowledge that all y^e right Title & interest of any / Debts dues & demands, w^ch are due or what is now remainining of o^r said Stock by / reason of o^r ꝑtenershipp (w^ch is this day made void) doe remain unto y^e said JAMES / FFOWLER his Ex^rs & Adm^rs the said FFOWLER haveing this day made Full sattisfaccon to / me For y^e same by Co[ ]^r passed, as witness my hand & Seal this Fifteenth day of / December 1698

WILLIAM MACKIE seal

Delivered & Signed Sealed in y^e
p^rsence of us whose names are underwritten
HEN: APPLEWHAITE
JOHN PITT

Proved in open Court held For y^e Isle of Wight County 9^th Aprill 1701 to be y^e Act & Deed of Mr W^M MACKIE, by y^e Oaths of Capt: HENRY

JOHN GILES APPLEWHAIT & Mr JOHN GILES
Recorded ꝑ CHA CHAPMAN C[l] C[ur]

June y[e] 6[th] 1701

Articles of Agreement made & agreed upon betwixt M[rs] SILVESTRA / HILL of y[e] Upper ꝑish of Isle of Wight County of y[e] one p[ty]. & W[M]. THOMAS of / y[e] same ꝑish & County of y[e] other p[ty]. Wittness y[t] y[e] sd M[rs] SILVESTRA / HILL hath Lett a certain ꝑcell of land unto y[e] sd. W[M]. THOMAS Lyinge / bounding as follow[th]. Joyning upon Mr. DAYs Line from y[e] River / Side Southerly, & on y[e] other side as y[e] Run goes from y[e] River Side / to a markt White Oake, being Marked four wayes, & a corner / Tree & East to Mr DAYEs line againe. The sd Land I y[e] sd SILVESTRA / HILL doe bind me, my Heires Ex[rs] & Adm[rs] or Assgs y[t] sd WILL / THOMAS shall quietly & peaceably enjoy y[e] sd Land w[th]out any Lett / Molestation or hinderance dureing y[e] time he shall [ ] / for a valueable Consideration already Reced in Hand, & w[n]. / y[e] said W[M]. THOMAS shall Depart this world then y[e] sd Land / shall Returne to y[e] sd M[rs]. HILL Her heires, Ex[rs], Adm[rs], or Assg / Againe W[M]. THOMAS paying A Ear of Corne every / day of New year for Acknowledgem[t]

Signed, Sealed & deliv[r]ed
in y[e] p[r]sence of us
CHARLES EDWARDS
MARTHA THROPP

SILL HILL O

Acknowledged in open Co[rt]. / held for y[e] Isle of Wight County / y[e] 9[th] of June 1701 to be her Act
Test CHA CHAPMAN C[l]C[ur]

**[336]**

Know all men by these p[r]sents y[t] I RICHD HOLLYMAN of y[e] Upper ꝑish of y[e] Isle of / Wight County for a valueable Consideracon to me in hand p[d] by / X[OFER]. HOLLYMAN of y[e] same ꝑish & County w[th] w[ch]. I acknowledge my / self fully satisfied, have Bargained & sold & doe hereby for my & my heires / for Ever, Bargaine, sell, & deliver, Infeoff, transfer, Release & Confirme / unto y[e] sd X[POFER] HOLLYMAN, & to his heires & Assgs for Ever two hundred / & ten Acres of Land or thereabout scituate on y[e] main Blackwater / in y[e] ꝑish & County aforesaid it being y[e] middle p[t]. of a Pattent of / one Thousd & twenty Acres granted to X[POFER]. HOLLEMAN deced / by a patent beareing date att James Citty Aprill y[e] 20[th]. 1684 since given / to me y[e] sd RICHD HOLLEMAN by y[e] last Will & Testamt of y[e] sd X[POFER] / HOLLEMAN deced as aforesd w[ch]. Land y[e] sd X[POFER]. HALLEMAN is in p[r]sent / possession of. To have & to hold y[e] sd two hundred & ten Acres / of Land together w[th] all the houses, Orchards, Gardens, Woods. Wayes & / Waters, & other priviledges, proffitts, Commodities & Heriditamts / w[t]soever to y[e] sd Land belonging or in any wis App[r]taining. To him y[e] / sd X[POFER] HALLEMAN & unto his heires & Assgs for Ever in as free & ample / manner to all Intents & purposes as I y[e] sd RICHD HOLLYMAN might or / Could have enjoyed y[e] same by vertue of y[e] before recited gift & I doe / hereby declare & Afirme, Covenant & Agree to & w[th] y[e] sd X[POFER]: HALLEMAN / his heires & Assgs y[t] y[e] aforesd Land & ev[r]y part & ꝑcell thereof is cleare / & free from all & all manner of Bargaines & sales, Mortgages, Joyntures / Dowers, Judgments & Ex$^{rs}$ & all other manner of Incumbrances / w$^{t}$soever & y$^{t}$ I have att y$^{e}$ time of y$^{e}$ sealing & deliv$^{r}$y hereof to all & / singular y$^{e}$ p$^{r}$mises a good, pure & Indefeazable estate of Inheritance / in fee Simple w$^{ch}$. I hereby transfer & oblige myself my heires, Ex$^{rs}$ / & Adm$^{rs}$. to warrant & defend this my sail of all & singular y$^{e}$ p$^{r}$mises / w$^{th}$ their Appurtinances to him y$^{e}$ sd X$^{POFER}$ HOLLEMAN & to his heires / & Assgs for Ever, ag$^{st}$. All & All manner of ꝑsons w$^{t}$soever by, from, / or under me deriveing or pretending any Claime, tittle or Interest / thereunto w$^{n}$. thereunto required will give to him or any of them / all such other & further lawfull Assurance & Confirmacon of y$^{e}$ / same as his or their learned Councell well read in y$^{e}$ law shall think fitt / & will acknowledge this Instrum$^{t}$ of Conveyance to be my Reall / Act & deed in open Co$^{rt}$. next to be held for y$^{e}$ Isle of Wight County / abovesd. In Testimony of all w$^{ch}$. I have hereunto putt my hand / & Seal this 6$^{th}$. Day of December y$^{e}$ year 1700

Signed Sealed & deliv$^{r}$ed in y$^{e}$ p$^{r}$sence — RICHARD HALLEMAN Sign$^{u}$

JOHN **Ɨ M** MORRIS

RICHARD **R C** CLERK
Signum

Acknowledged in Open Co$^{rt}$ held For y$^{e}$ Isle of Wight County 9$^{th}$ 10$^{ber}$ 1700 by RICHARD HOLLYMAN

Test CHA CHAPMAN C$^{l}$C$^{ur}$

**[337]**

This Indenture made y$^{e}$ 9$^{th}$. day of Jan$^{r}$y in y$^{e}$ year of o$^{r}$ Lord God 1700 / & in y$^{e}$ 12$^{th}$ year of y$^{e}$ Reigne of o$^{r}$. Sov$^{r}$aigne Lord W$^{m}$. y$^{e}$ 3$^{d}$. by y$^{e}$ Grace of God / of England, Scotland, France & Ireland King &c: Between JN$^{O}$ POWELL / of Nanzimond County planter & DEBORAH his Wife 2$^{d}$. Daughter of / HENERY HERN deced (& Coparcener w$^{th}$. her two sisters RACHAELL HERN / & ELIZABET HERN) of y$^{e}$ one part, & THOMAS JORDAN of y$^{e}$ sd County / Gen$^{t}$: of y$^{e}$ other part Wittnesseth That y$^{e}$ sd JN$^{O}$ POWELL & DEBORAH his / wife for & in Consideracon of y$^{e}$ sum of one Thousand pounds of Tob$^{o}$ / to them in hand all & before y$^{e}$ sealing &deliv$^{r}$y of these p$^{r}$sents by y$^{e}$ said / THOMAS JORDAN Gen$^{t}$. well & truely p$^{d}$ y$^{e}$ rec$^{t}$. whereof they the sd JOHN / POWELL & DEBORAH hsi wife doth hereby acknowledge & themselves / therewith fully satisfied, & p$^{d}$. & thereof & ev$^{r}$y p$^{t}$. & ꝑcell thereof / doth clearly acquit, exonerate & discharge y$^{e}$ sd THOMAS JORDAN Gen$^{t}$. / his heires, Ex$^{rs}$, & Adm$^{rs}$. for ever, by these p$^{r}$sents hath Given granted / Alliened, Bargained sold enffeoffed & Confirmed, & by these p$^{r}$sents / doth fully clearly & absolutely give, grant bargaine, sell, alien, / enfeoff & Confirme unto y$^{e}$ sd THOMAS PITT Gen$^{t}$. his heires & Assgs / for Ever one ꝑ$^{t}$. & ꝑcell of land Containing one hundred & seven / Acres scituate, lyeing & being in y$^{e}$ County of y$^{e}$ Isle of Wight Con / =tained in a pattent for three hundred & twenty acres granted / unto THOMAS MANDUE of y$^{e}$ Isle of Wight County by pattent dated / y$^{e}$ 20$^{th}$ day of Aprill 1682 w$^{ch}$ sd three hundred & twenty Acres of / land contained in y$^{e}$ sd pattent was sold & made over by y$^{e}$ sd THOMAS / MANDUE unto y$^{e}$ foresd HENERY HERN of Nanzimond County planter / by deed bearing date y$^{e}$ 16$^{th}$. day of May in y$^{e}$ year of o$^{r}$ Lord God 1691 / w$^{ch}$. sd tract of Land contained in y$^{e}$ sd Deed granted by y$^{e}$ sd THOMAS / MANDUE unto y$^{e}$ sd HENERY HERN did discend from y$^{e}$ sd HENERY / unto his foresd three daughters RACHAEL HERN, DEBORAH HERN / & ELIZABETH HERN soe y$^{t}$: y$^{e}$ land herein conveyed is y$^{t}$ ꝑcell of y$^{e}$ porcon / w$^{ch}$. did decend & doth belong unto y$^{e}$ foresd DEBORAH quallified as / aforesd. To have & to hold y$^{e}$ foresd ꝑcell or tract of land w$^{th}$. all / & singular it's Rights, Members & Jursidictions & Appertinances / w$^{t}$soever to y$^{e}$ sd land belonging, together w$^{th}$ all houses, edifices / buildings, barnes, stables, orchards, gradens, yards, backsides, easmts / Common of pasture, heriditamts & Appurtinances whatsoever / to y$^{e}$ sd Land or tenemts & ꝑmises or to any ꝑ$^{t}$. or ꝑcell of them / belonging or in any wise appertaining thereunto y$^{e}$ sd / THOMAS JORDAN Gen$^{t}$. his heires, or Assgs to y$^{e}$ only proper use / & behoof of y$^{e}$ sd THOMAS JORDAN Gen$^{t}$. his heires & Assgs for ever / Ag$^{st}$. them y$^{e}$ sd JN$^{O}$. POWELL & DEBORAH his wife, their heires & Assgs / & all & ev$^{r}$y other ꝑson or ꝑsons w$^{t}$soever lawfully claimeing by / from or under them or any of them & will warr$^{t}$ & for ev$^{r}$ / defend by these p$^{r}$sents & y$^{t}$. y$^{e}$ sd JN$^{O}$. POWELL & DEBORAH his Wife

**[338]**

For themselves their heires, Ex$^{rs}$, & Adm$^{rs}$ doe Covenant, promise, & agree / to & w$^{th}$ y$^{e}$ sd THOMAS JORDAN Gen$^{t}$. his heires & assgs & ev$^{r}$y of them by these / p$^{r}$sents that all & singular y$^{e}$ aforesd parcell or quantity of Land w$^{th}$ all / y$^{e}$ appurtinances thereunto belonging now be & ever hereafter shallbe / stand & Continue to y$^{e}$ sd THOMAS JORDAN JORDAN [*sic*] Gen$^{t}$. & his heires & Assgs / forever. And y$^{t}$ y$^{e}$ sd THOMAS JORDAN Gen$^{t}$. his heires or assgs be freely & clearly / acquitted, exonerated & discharged & from time to time well & suficiently kept / harmeless by y$^{e}$ sd JN$^{O}$ POWELL & DEBORAH his wife their heires, Ex$^{rs}$, & Adm$^{rs}$ of / & from all & all manner of former & other gifts, grants, bargaines, sailes, / Leases, mortgages, Joynters, dowers of & from all & singular other titles / troubles, charges, demands & incumbrances w$^{t}$soever had made committed / suffered omitted or done by y$^{e}$ sd JN$^{O}$. POWELL & DEBORAH his wife their / heires or Assgs or by any other ꝑson or ꝑsons w$^{t}$soever, & y$^{t}$ y$^{e}$ sd JN$^{O}$. POWELL / & DEBORAH his wife their heires or assgs for & dureing y$^{e}$ space of seven / yeares next ensueing y$^{e}$ date of these p$^{r}$sents shall & will at & upon the / Reasonable request, & at the Cost & charges in y$^{e}$ Law of y$^{e}$ sd THO: JORDAN / Gen$^{t}$. his heires or Assgs make such further lawfull & reasonable / Assurance or Assurances or Conveyances in y$^{e}$ Law for y$^{e}$ more better & / perfect assurance of y$^{e}$ aforesd ꝑmises as by y$^{e}$ aforesd THOMAS JORDAN / gen$^{t}$. or by his or their Councell Learned in y$^{e}$ Lawes shall be reasonably / devised, advised or required shall be esteemed & Judged & taken to be & ennured / to y$^{e}$ only proper use & behoof of sd THOMAS JORDAN Gen$^{t}$. his heires & Assgs / forever & to none other use intent or purpose w$^{t}$soever. In Wittness / hereof, we have hereunto sett o$^{r}$ hands & seales y$^{e}$ day, year & Reigne / first above written

Signed, sealed & deliv$^{r}$ed in y$^{e}$ p$^{r}$sence — JOHN POWELL
of us whose names are underwritten — DEBORAH § POWELL
HUM: MARSHALL

ANDREW WOODLY

Acknowledged in Open Co$^{rt}$ held For the / Isle of Wight County the 9$^{th}$ of December / 1701 by JOHN POWELL & DEBORAH his Wife / to be their act & Deed and Ordered to be / Recorded

Test CHA CHAPMAN C$^{l}$C$^{ur}$

**[339]**

Know all men by these p$^{r}$sents y$^{t}$ I JN$^{O}$. POWELL of Nanzimond County planter / doe stand & am firmly obliged & bounden to THOMAS JORDAN of y$^{e}$ sd County Gen$^{t}$. / in y$^{e}$ sum of one hundred pounds of good & lawfull money of England, to be p$^{d}$. to y$^{e}$ sd / THOMAS JORDAN Gen$^{t}$. or to his true & lawfull Att$^{o}$. Ex$^{rs}$. or Adm$^{rs}$. to y$^{e}$ wich payment / well, faithfully & truly to be p$^{d}$. I doe bind me, my heires, Ex$^{rs}$. & Adm$^{rs}$ firmly / by these p$^{r}$sents, Sealed w$^{th}$. my Seal, dated y$^{e}$ 9$^{th}$ day Jan$^{r}$y in y$^{e}$ year of o$^{r}$. Lord / God 1700

The Condition of this Obligation is such, y$^{t}$ if y$^{e}$ w$^{th}$in named THOMAS / JORDAN Gen$^{t}$., his heires & Assgs & ev$^{r}$y of them shall & may for ever / from henceforth peaceably & quietly have, hold, occupy, possess & enjoy all those / lands & tennements scituate, lyeing & being in y$^{e}$ County of the Isle of Wight, / & every part & parcell thereof mentioned to be bargained & sold by y$^{e}$ within / bound JOHN POWELL, to y$^{e}$ sd THOMAS JORDAN Gentleman, in & by a certained / Indenture of bargaine & sail, bearing date, y$^{e}$ of y$^{e}$ date within written, / made between y$^{e}$ within bound JOHN POWELL & DEBORAH his wife on y$^{e}$ one part / & y$^{e}$ abovenamed THOMAS JORDAN Gen$^{t}$. on y$^{e}$ other p$^{t}$, clearly discharged or / otherwise suficiently saved & kept harmless, of & from all & all manner of / Estates, titles, troubles, charges & Incumbrances w$^{t}$soever or all any time hereto / =fore had made committed, suffered, permitted or done, by y$^{e}$ sd JN$^{O}$ POWELL and / DEBORAH his wife or either of them, or by his or their means or procuremt / y$^{t}$ then this Obligation to be void & of noe effect, or otherwise to stand & / remaine in full force, power, & Virtue

Signed Sealed & delivered
in y$^{e}$ p$^{r}$sence of us
HUM: MARSHALL
AND$^{W}$. WOODLY

JN$^{O}$. POWELL Seal

Acknowledged in open Co$^{rt}$ held for y$^{e}$ Isle of Wight County y$^{e}$ 9$^{th}$ of December 1701 by JN$^{O}$. POWELL & Recorded

Isle of Wight County

The Dep$^{o}$ of THOMAS REEVES aged about 52 yeares or thereabouts Sheweth / That yo$^{r}$ depon$^{t}$ knoweth that MICHAELL MACKQUINY was possesed w$^{th}$ a ꝑcell of / Land in his life tyme: & by his last Will & Testamt, he gave his Mann$^{r}$ plantacon / to his Younger Sonne BARNABY MACQUINEY, but after his decease the Land / was Found to be Escheat & I haveing the Land in my Custody, Holding of / by my Wife

ELIZABETHs right, & possession w$^{ch}$ her aforesaid Husband MICHAELL / MACKQUINY gave he [*sic*] for her life tyme, but there was agreemt made between / yo$^{r}$ depon$^{t}$ & JN$^{O}$ MACQUINEY, that he should enter and Escheat upon his Broth$^{rs}$ / Land in his name, in behalfe of his Brother BARNABY because y$^{t}$ y$^{e}$ aforesaid / BARNABY MACQUINY was not of Age And yo$^{r}$ Depon$^{t}$ hath p$^{d}$ y$^{e}$ Full ꝑte of y$^{e}$ / Composicon for y$^{e}$ Escheat in BARNABY MACKQUINYs behalfe & this Further yo$^{r}$ Depon$^{t}$ will / Certifie & declair upon Oath in Open Co$^{rt}$ & Further saith not.

THOS **T** REEVES
his m$^{r}$ke

Jur in Cur 9$^{o}$ 10$^{br}$ 1701 CHA CHAPMAN C$^{l}$C$^{ur}$
Recorded ꝑ CHA CHAPMAN C$^{l}$ C$^{ur}$

**[340]**

The dep$^{o}$ of ELIZ$^{A}$ REEVES aged about Sixty yeares or thereabouts sheweth / That yo$^{r}$ Depon$^{t}$ Knoweth, that my afore husband MICHAEL MACQUINY / was possed w$^{th}$ a parcell of Land, w$^{ch}$ by his Last will & Testam$^{t}$, he gave / his Mannor plantacon, to his younger Sonne BARNABY MACQUINY but / after my Husbands decease, the Land was Found to Escheat, wherefore / my Sonne JOHN MACKQUINEY, enter an Escheat upon his Brother / BARNABYs ~~Land~~ MACQUINYS Land in his owne name being in y$^{e}$ behalfe / of his Brother BARNABY MACQUINY, because that y$^{e}$ abovesd BARNABY / was not of Age, and this Farr yo$^{r}$ Depon$^{t}$ knowes, that my Husband / THOMAS REEVES hath p$^{d}$ Composition in my BARNABYs behalfe this / yo$^{r}$ Depon$^{t}$ is willing to Testifie upon Oath in Open Co$^{rt}$ & Futher / saith not

ELIZABETH **I** REEVES
her m$^{r}$ke

Sworne in Open Co$^{rt}$ y$^{e}$ 9$^{th}$
December 1701
Test CHA CHAPMAN C$^{l}$ C$^{ur}$

Recorded ꝑ CHA CHAPMAN C$^{l}$C$^{ur}$

To all xpian people to whome these p$^{r}$sents shall Come BARNABY / MACKQUINY & MARY his Wife sends greeting in o$^{r}$ Lord God / everlasting. Know yee that I the said BARNABY MACKQUINY / & MARY my Wife, of y$^{e}$ County of the Isle of Wight For / diverse good Causes & Consideracons us hereunto moveing but / now especially for & in Consideracon of A Certeyn sume of Tob / to us in hand p$^{d}$ or secured to be p$^{d}$ before the Sealing & deliv$^{r}$y / hereof, the receipt whereof wee doe hereby acknowledge & / Confess have given grated [*sic*] Bargained sould aliened Conveyed & / Confirmed, and doe by these p$^{r}$sents, For us o$^{r}$ Heires Ex$^{rs}$ / &

**[341]**

And Adm$^{rs}$ give grant bargain sell alien Convey Enfeoff & Confirme / unto RICHARD EXUM of the aforesd County his Heires Ex$^{rs}$ Adm$^{rs}$ & / Assignes, a parcell of Land to say, my ffather MICHAELL / MACKQUINEYs mannor plantacon beginning att y$^{e}$ Foot of the / Spring Branch, & soe Runing on the South East side of y^e^ Spring / Branch to the Head Lyne & soe along y^e^ head Lyne to the / Corner to HENRY GAYEs Lyne, & soe down along the sd Lyne / to y^e^ Main Swamp & soe up the maine Swamp to y^e^ First / Station, To say All the Land given to me by my ffathers / last Will & Testam^t^ scituated lying & being in the County of / the Isle of Wight afforesaid, And is part of an Escheat / pattent of Four hundred & Fifty acres of Land granted to my / Brother JN^O^ MACQUINY deceased bearing date the 20^th^ day of / Aprill 1694 To have & to hould the sd Land according to y^e^ / demencons abovewritten unto him the said RICHARD EXUM his / Heires Ex^rs^ & Adm^rs^ For ever Free & clear & Freeely / & clearly acquitted exonerated & discharged, of & From all / manner of Former & other guifts grants bargaines Sales / Dowers Judgem^ts^ Extents or Execucons whatsoever had made / done or suffered to be done From by or under us, or either / of us, And the said BARNABY MACKQUINY & MARY his Wife / doth Further Coven^t^ promise & grant For us Our heires Ex^rs^ / & Adm^rs^ by & w^th^ the said RICHARD EXUM his heires & assignes / to warr^t^ & defend & keep harmeless the said RICHARD EXUM / From & ag^t^ any ꝑson or ꝑsons that shall or may lawfully / clayme or p^r^tend any right Tytle or Interest to y^e^ sd Land / And that y^e^ sd RICHARD EXUM, & hes heires, shall & may From / tyme & att all tymes quietly enjoy the said Land w^th^ all / profetts Comoditys priveledges & advantages to the same / belonging

**[342]**

Or any wayes apperteyning, without the [ ] interrupcon / molestacon or Eviccon, of us or either of us or any other / ꝑson or ꝑsons whatsoever In witness whereof wee have / hereunto sett o^r^ hands & seales this 9^th^ of December / in y^e^ year of o^r^ Lord God One Thousand Seaven hundred / & One

BARNABE MACKINNE seal
MARY M MACKINNE seal
her marke

Signed sealed & delivered
in y^e^ p^r^sence of us
JAMES WEBB
JN^O^ COUNCILL

Acknowledged in Open Court held for y^e^ / Isle of Wight County 9^th^ 10^br^ 1701 by y^e^ / said MACKQUINY & his Wife to Capt RICHARD / EXUM as their Act & Deed &c
Recorded ꝑ CHA CHAPMAN C^l^C^ur^

Know all men by these p^r^sents that I BARNABY MACKENNY of / the Isle of Wight County in Virginia planter is held & Firmely / Bound unto RICHARD EXUM, of y^e^ aforesd place his heires Ex^rs^ / Adm^rs^ or assignes in the Full & Just sume of Twelve Thousand / pounds of every way well quallified Tob & Cask Convenient / in the afforesd County of Isle of Wight to y^e^ w^ch^ paym^t^ well / & truly to be made I bind my selfe my heires Ex^rs^ & Adm^rs^ & / Fermely by these p^r^sents In witness whereof I have / hereunto sertt my hand & seal this 9^th^ day of December / 1701

BARNABY MACKINNY Sigill

**[343]**

The Condicon of this Obligacon is such that whereas JOHN / MACKINEY Brother to y$^{e}$ aforesd BARNAY MACKINEY, did Obteyn an / Escheat pattent for Four hundred & Fifty acres of Land in y$^{e}$ County / aforesd bearing date the 20$^{th}$ day of Aprill 1694 whoe afterward / Conveyed a part thereof to the said BARNABY his Brother, by / an Instrum$^{t}$ of writeing bearing date the 13$^{th}$ day of Jan$^{rij}$ / 1694 but before y$^{e}$ sd JN$^{O}$ MACKQUINY could make a lawfull / Conveyance of y$^{e}$ same to y$^{e}$ sd BARNABY, his Brother dyed / But notwithstanding the said BARNABY has made a Conveyance / to y$^{e}$ sd RICHARD EXUM, Now if y$^{e}$ Heires of the sd JOHN / MACKENNY, when they come to y$^{e}$ age of Twenty One Yeares / shall make a goode & Lawfull Conveyance of y$^{e}$ aforesd Land / as the Learned in the Law shall think fitt, to the sd RICHARD / EXUM & his Heires Then the above obligacon to be voyd and / of noe effect, otherwise to remain & Continue in Full Force / power & vertue

Signed sealed & delivered
in y$^{e}$ presence of
HENRY PITT
JN$^{O}$ COUNCILL

BARNABY MACKENNY seal

Acknowledged in Open Co$^{rt}$ held For y$^{e}$ Isle Wight County y$^{e}$ 9$^{th}$ 10$^{br}$ 1701 by BARNABY MACKENNY to be his Act & Deed

Test CHA CHAPMAN C$^{l}$C$^{ur}$

**[344]**

Virginia

Know all men by these p$^{r}$sents that I NATHANIELL WILLIAMSON / m$^{r}$chant For divers good causes & Consideracons me hereunto moving / have made, Ordeyned, deputed & appointed & in my stead and / place putt, my Trusty & welbeloved Frenids [*sic*], M$^{r}$. NATH$^{LL}$ RIDLEY & / M$^{r}$ DAN$^{LL}$ SULEVAN Joyntly & sev$^{r}$ally to be my true & lawfull / attorney For me & in my name & to & For my use, to ask / demand sue For, Levy require recover & receive all & such every / sume & sumes of money Tobacco or any other Goods and / Comodities whatsoever, w$^{ch}$ now are or hereafter may be / due & oweing unto me, From amy ꝑson or ꝑsons whatsoever / in Virginia by any manner of wayes or meanes whatsoever / And upon my sd Attorneys recovery & rec$^{t}$ of any sume or / sumes of money whatsoever, or any other goods or / Comodities From any ꝑson or ꝑsons one or more discharge / or discharges, or other sufficient release or releases For me / & in my name to signe seal & deliver & alsoe to / Compound referr & agree to & w$^{th}$ the said ꝑsons indebted / me, otherwise to prosecute them to y$^{e}$ utmost extent of y$^{e}$ / Law, For y$^{e}$ speedy recovery of my Just right, Giveing & / by these p$^{r}$sents granting, unto my sd Attorneys all my / whole power, strength & authority in the p$^{r}$mises to Act / & doe all such act & Acts thing & things devise & devises in / the Law, as to my sd Attorneys shall seem necessary and / Convenient, rattifieing & by these p$^{r}$sents alloweing and / Confermeing For good & sufficient in the Law all and / whatsoever

**[345]**

Whatsoever my said Attorneys shall lawfully doe or cause to be / done in the p$^{r}$mises, as punctually & really & absolutely to all intents / Construccons & purposes whatsoever, as if I my selfe were might or / could be then & there ꝑsonally p$^{r}$sent, as witness my hand & Seal / this 6$^{th}$ day of March 1700

sealed & delivered in the p$^{r}$sencs of — NATH WM$^{SON}$ sigill

AND: WOODLEY
his
W$^{M}$ **W** SMYTH
m$^{r}$ke

Proved in Open Co$^{rt}$ held For y$^{e}$ Isle of Wight County 15$^{th}$ December 1701 to be the Act & Deed of M$^{r}$ NATH$^{LL}$ WILLIAMSON, by the Oaths of both y$^{e}$ Witnesses & Recorded

ꝑ CHA CHAPMAN C$^{l}$C$^{ur}$

Know all men by these p$^{r}$sents y$^{t}$ I ROB$^{T}$. MOORE of y$^{e}$ Island of Barbados Merch$^{t}$ / doe Constitute make & appoint my trusty & good friend Maj$^{r}$. HEN BAKER / of Warricks Creeke Bay in James River in Virg$^{a}$ Merchant my true & / lawfull Attorny for me & in my name to & for my use to ask for / & demand, Receive from every ꝑson or ꝑsons inhabiting within y$^{e}$ / sd Collony & Dominion of Virg$^{a}$. all goods & Merchandise, bonds, Bills / of Exchange or Accounts, or any Debts w$^{t}$soever y$^{t}$ shall come due to / me by Bond, Bill of Exchange or account giveing & granting to my said / Att$^{o}$ full power & Lawfully Authority, to sue for prosecute, implead & recover / all & singular y$^{e}$ Goods, Bonds, Bills of exchange & acco$^{ts}$. of all ꝑsons what / soever, & upon non payment of y$^{e}$ sd Goods, Bonds, Bills of Exch$^{a}$ & [ ] / abovesaid to Cast into prison, & att his reill pleasure on rec$^{t}$. / of y$^{e}$ sd Bill Exch$^{a}$. &c as is abovesd forth of prison to release, & Rec$^{ts}$ or / other discharges, & I y$^{e}$ sd ROB$^{T}$ MOORE doe give & grant unto my sd Att$^{o}$. full power / & authority to one or more Attorneys under him to substitute quallify / & impower as need may require For y$^{e}$ more effectuall managem$^{t}$ of my / affaires in these parts & firmly doe hereby give unto y$^{e}$ sd HENERY / BAKER & such as he shall substitute to act & doe all & ev$^{r}$y lawfull / thing & things in my name & stead to all intents & purposes w$^{t}$soever / as fully, amply & Largly as if I were or could be there ꝑsonally p$^{r}$sent / ratifieing & Confirmeing w$^{t}$soever my sd Att$^{o}$. shall Lawfully doe or cause / to be done in y$^{e}$ ꝑmises. In Witness whereof I have hereunto sett my hand & / Seal this y$^{e}$. day of Septemb$^{r}$. 1701 & in y$^{e}$ 13$^{th}$. year of his Maties Reigne &c$^{a}$:

Signed, sealed, & deliv$^{r}$ed in p$^{r}$sence of — ROB$^{T}$: MOORE seal

JN$^{O}$. SKELTON
CHA. EDWARDS

Proved in open Co$^{rt}$. held for y$^{e}$ / Isle of Wight County 15$^{th}$. Decemb$^{r}$ / 1701 to be y$^{e}$ Act & deed of M$^{r}$. ROB$^{T}$ MOORE

Test CHA CHAPMAN C$^{l}$C$^{ur}$

**[346]**

This Indenture Made y^e^ 6^th^. day Septemb^r^. Anno Dom 1701& in y^e^ 13^eenth^ year / of y^e^ Reigne of O^r^. Sov^r^aigne Lord W^m^. y^e^ 3^d^. by y^e^ Grace of God of England / Scottland ffrance & Ireland King Defender of y^e^ faith &^c^: Betweene / JUDITH EDWARDS of y^e^ Isle of Wight County in Virg^a^ Spinster of y^e^ one ꝑ^t^ / & JAMES BRAGG of y^e^ same County, planter, of y^e^ other ꝑ^t^. Witnesseth / y^t^ y^e^ sd JUDITH being one of y^e^ daughters & Coheires of ROB^T^ EDWDS deced for dv^es^. / good Causes & Considerations her thereunto moveing but more Especially / for a sum of Tob^o^. to her in hand p^d^ y^e^ rec^t^ whereof she doth hereby acknow / =ledge; & herself thereby fully Contented, sattisfied & p^d^. Hath bargained, / sold, aliened, enfeoffed, & Confirmed, & by these p^r^sents for her self, her heires / Ex^rs^. & Adm^rs^. doth bargaine, sell, alien, Enfeoff & for ever Confirme unto y^e^ sd JAMES / BRAGG His heires, & Assgs for Ev^r^. all y^t^ her third ꝑ^t^. or ꝑportion of a cirtaine / tract or parcell of land containing by Estimaticon one hundred Acres or / thereabouts purchased by her father ROB^T^. EDWARDS aforesd of EDMOND / PALMER & lying in y^e^ County aforesaid bounding upon y^e^ Lands of Capt. HEN: / APPLEWHAITE & W^M^. FRIZELL together with all share of mines & Mineralls, Woods, / Waters, Watercourses, Royalties, & apputtinances to y^e^ same belonging / or in any wise Appertaining, as Likewise liberty of Fishing, fowling / & Hunting & all other priveldges accustomed. To have & To hold y^e^ said / Land & ꝑmises above Conveyed, & every part & ꝑcell thereof with y^e^ / appurtinances unto y^e^ sd JAMES BRAGG his heires & Assgs for Ev^r^. with / warranty y^t^ y^e^ same is free from all and all manner of Incumbrances / & y^t^ y^e^ sd JUDITH hath att y^e^ time of y^e^ ensealing & deliv^r^y thereof / a free, & clear & defeazable Estate of inheritance in fee simple of / in & to y^e^ sd Bargained p^r^mises and every part & ꝑcell of y^e^ same / & y^e^ sd JAMES BRAGG his heires, Ex^rs^, Adm^rs^, & Assgs shall & may have / hold, occupy possess & Enjoy y^e^ sd bargained p^r^mises & ev^r^y ꝑ^t^. thereof / w^th^ y^e^ appurtinances clear & free from all and every person or / persons Clayming y^e^ same by from or under her in any manner / howsoev^r^. In Wittness hereunto y^e^ sd JUDITH EDWARDS hath hereunto / sett her hand & Seal y^e^ day & year above written

her
JUDITH **m** EDWARDS O
m^r^ke

Signed, sealed & deliv^r^ed
in y^e^ p^r^sence of us
Tes HENRY PITT
EDWARD **N** BROWNE
his marke

Acknowledged in open Co^rt^. held for
y^e^ Isle of Wight County y^e^ Ninth day of
Septemb^r^ by JUDITH EDWARDS to be her
Act & Deed & Recorded 1701

Test CHA CHAPMAN C^l^C^ur^

**[347]**

Know all by these presents y^t^. I WILLIAM JOHNSON of y^e^ / Lower ꝑish of y^e^ Isle of Wight County Blacksmith doe Assg^e^ / my whole Right, tittle & Interest of this Conveyance, & I / y^e^ Aforesd W^M^. JOHNSON & SARAH JOHNSON my wife do hereby wee / o^r^. heires, Ex^rs^. Adm^rs^. doe Assge o^r^. whole Right & tittle unto JOHN / BARDIN of y^e^ ꝑish & County aforesaid he his heires, Ex^rs^. Adm^rs^ or / Assgs for Ever as Wittness o^r^ hands & seals this 8^th^. day of Septemb^r^. / Anno Dom 1701

Test WILLI: CRUMPLER
WILLIAM WILLIAMS

W^M^ **M** JOHNSON O
his mark
SARAH **H** JOHNSON O

Acknowledged in open Co^rt^ held for y^e^ Isle / of Wigh [*sic*] County 9^o^ October 1701

Teste CHA CHAPMAN C^l^C^ur^

This Indenture made y^e^ 26^th^. day of March Anno Dom: 1702 / & in y^e^ 14^eenth^. year of y^e^ Reigne of o^r^. Sov^r^aigne L^d^. W^m^. y^e^ 3^d^. by grace of / God of England. Scotland ffrance & Ireland King Defender of y^e^ / faith &^c^: Whereas a Marriage is by Gods Will shortly intended / to be made & Solemnized betweene me SUSANAH BRESSY of y^e^ Isle / of Wight County in Virginia Widdow, & MATTHEW JORDAN of Nanzi= / =mond County. Now for y^e^ more sure & better settling & Establishmt / of all y^t^ my freehould land & Plantation w^th^. y^e^ Appurtinances / whereon I now Live, scituate, lyeing & being in y^e^ ꝑish & County / of y^e^ Isle of Wight in Virg^a^. aforesd, Have alienated, transferred, / enfeoffed, Confirmed & made over. And by these p^r^sents doe alienate / transfer, enfeoff. Confirme & make over unto y^e^ sd MATTHEW JORDAN, the / abovemenconed p^r^mises w^th^. y^e^ appurtinances to y^e^ uses hereafter / menconed, as followeth (Viz^t^) to me y^e^ sd SUSANAH & MATTHEW for & dure= / =ing y^e^ terme of o^r^. Naturall lives & y^e^ Longest liver of us, And after y^e^ / decease of us y^e^ sd SUSANAH & MATTHEW & y^e^ longest liver of us, To y^e^ / sd MATTHEW JORDAN & y^e^ Heires of his Boddy lawfully to be begotten / either Male or female, & Heires for ever, & for want of such / Issue lawfully to be begotten of the boddy of y^e^ sd MATTHEW JORDAN then / y^e^ same to remaine to y^e^ right Heires of me y^e^ sd SUSANAH & their / Heires in ffee Simple for ever; to all intents & purposes, in Law as / if this deed had never been made. In Testimony whereof I have / hereunto sett my hand & seal y^e^ day & year first abovewritten

Sealed & delivered
in p^r^sence of
W^M^ WILSON
CHA CHAPMAN

SUSANA BRESSIE O seal

Acknowledged in open Co^rt^ held for y^e^ / Isle of Wight County y^e^ 9^th^ day of Aprill Anno / Dom: 1702 by M^rs^ SUSANAH BRESSY to be her Act / & Deed & Recorded

ꝑ me CHA CHAPMAN C^l^C^ur^

**[348]**

To all to whom these p^r^sents shall Come greeting this 12^th^ day of March / Anno Dom: 170$^1/_2$, & In y^e^ 14^th^ year of y^e^ Raigne of o^r^ Sov^r^aigne L^d^ W^m^ y^e^ 3^d^ by / by [*sic*] y^e^ Grace of God of England, Scotland, ffrance & Ireland King defender / of y^e^ faith &c: Know yee y^t^ I SUSANAH BRESSY of y^e^ Isle of Wight County / in Virginia Widdow, for in Consideration of y[e] Naturall love & great afection / I bear unto my dear & loveing Nephew WILLIAM JONES of York County, & for / other Consideracons me hereunto Moveing, have given & freely made over; / & by these p[r]sents doe Voluntarily, spontaniously & of my own free & good / Will & afection give unto my said loveing Nephew, y[e] full & Just sum of Eight / Thousand pounds of Tob[o], or y[e] value thereof in manner as followeth (Viz[t]) / That it shall be att my Will & pleasure, to pay to him y[e] p[t]. or y[e] whole / thereof att y[e] time or Times (during my naturall Life) / as to me shall seem most Convenient & requisite, & in such Comodities / of this my Gift or y[e] whole shall be behind & unpaid att y[e] time of my decease / I doe hereby for y[e] more sure paym[t] of w[t]: shall be soe behind & unpaid / Alienate, Assigne & make over unto my sd Loveing Nephew all y[t] my / land & plantation w[th]. y[e] appurtinances whereon I now live, to have, hold / & enjoy y[e] same & every pte thereof, unto him my sd Nephew, untill / y[e] whole so behind or such pte of y[e] gift by me given as abovesaid shall be / fully p[d] & satisfied; And upon, paym[t] of y[e] same y[e] sd Land plantation & / p[r]mises, to returne, be & revert to such person or psons, or to such uses; / as by any writeing under my hand & seal, or by my last will & Testamt / in writeing, I shall give & bequeath or devise y[e] same; Anything in these / p[r]sents conteine to y[e] Contrary notwithstanding: & further I declare, & it is my / true, intent, will & meanining [*sic*], y[t] in Case my sd Nephew shall dye & depart / this life before all or any of y[e] sd gift be pd, y[t] then y[e] same or such pte / thereof, as shall be behind & unpaid att y[e] time of such his death, shall not / of Right belong, or in any wise become due, to his Ex[rs], or Administrat[rs]. / or any person to whome he shall give or bequeath y[e] same, But / shall remaine revert & be to me y[e] said SUSANAH to all intents / & purposes as fully as if this Deed of Gift had not been made any thing / herein Contained to be Contrary notwtithstanding. In Wittness whereof / I have hereunto sett my hand & Seal y[e] day & year first abovewritten

Selaed & delivered in p[r]sence of us SUSANA BRESSIE O

ANN CHAPMAN

CHA CHAPMAN

Acknowledged in open Co[rt]. held for Isle of Wight County y[e] 9[th]. of Aprill 1702 to be her Act & deed & recorded

p me CHA CHAPMAN C[l]C[ur]

**[349]**

This be itt knowne to all whome itt may concerne y[t] I JOHN SHERRER senior / doth of my owne free will, voluntarily give unto my Loving son THOMAS SHERRER / & my Loving Grandaughter ELIZ[A]. SHERRER A peice of Land Joyntly and / severaly; bounded thus begining att y[e] Mouth of A small Branch att y[e] Maine Branch whereon THOMAS SHERRER died live / & up y[e] said Branch too JOHN BRETTs Line & along y[e] sd BRETTs Line to y[e] Corner / tree, Being A white Oake & Running from y[e] sd white Oake along a Line of trees / to y[e] head of y[e] Main branch & downe y[e] Maine Branch to y[e] first Station / to hold, peaceably & quietly they & their heires for Ever lawfully begotten / of their owne boddyes without any molestation of any pson or psons / whatsoever, & this

I doe owne my free deed of Gift, & will Acknowledge / y$^{e}$ same in open Court held y$^{e}$ 9$^{th}$. of Aprill in y$^{e}$ year of o$^{r}$. Lord 1701 As / Wittness my hand this 16$^{th}$. day of March

JOHN **B** SHERRER O seal

Testes
CHA CHAPMAN
ROB$^{T}$ BROCKE

Acknowledged in open / Co$^{rt}$. for y$^{e}$ Isle of Wight / County y$^{e}$ 1$^{st}$ of May 1702 by / JOHN SHERRER sen$^{r}$ &

Recorded ꝑ me CHA CHAPMAN C$^{l}$C$^{ur}$

To all Xpian people to whome these p$^{r}$sents shall come I ARTHUR / SMITH of y$^{e}$ Isle of Wight County send Greeting in o$^{r}$ Lord God / Ev$^{r}$lasting. Know y$^{e}$ y$^{t}$ I y$^{e}$ sd ARTHUR SMITH for y$^{e}$ Love & in Consid / eration of a Gift made by my father Coll$^{o}$ AR: SMITH in his last / Will & Testament of a certaine tract of Land Containing one / hundred Acres (being ꝑt. of a patten of three hundred & ten Acres / of Land being formerly Granted to W$^{M}$ OLDIS by patten) unto / JEREMIY FFLY have Given, granted & Confirmed & by this my p$^{r}$sent / p$^{r}$sent [*sic*] writeing doe fully, freely & Absolutely Give, grant & Confirm / unto y$^{e}$ sd JEREMIAH FFLY & his heires for Ev$^{r}$. & I doe hereby for me, my / heires, Give, & grant unto y$^{e}$ sd JEREMIAH FFLY his heir or his Boddy for / Ever. y$^{e}$ sd trackt of Land itt being bounded as y$^{e}$ patten is on y$^{e}$ ꝑt / next to y$^{e}$ Cyprus Mill: & soe y$^{e}$ breadth of y$^{e}$ Land till y$^{e}$ hundred acres / Compleated y$^{e}$ said land is in y$^{e}$ Isle of Wight County. To have & to / hold y$^{e}$ sd Land for evermore unto y$^{e}$ sd JEREMIAH FFLY his heires of his / Boddy forever & I y$^{e}$ aforessd AR: SMITH doe by this my Deed of Gift for me, my heires, Give, & grant unto y$^{e}$ sd JEREMIAH FFLY & his heires of his Boddy / for ever y$^{e}$ sd tract of land w$^{th}$. all woods, waters, priviledges & profitts / thereunto belonging: only reserving y$^{e}$ third ꝑt of y$^{e}$ sd Land unto / MARY TYLER for her Naturall Life, with what profitts there= / unto belonging; & after her life to y$^{e}$ sd JEREMIAH FFLY, & his / heires, for Ev$^{r}$. further I y$^{e}$ said ARTHUR SMITH, Doe by this / p$^{r}$sent wrighting for me, my heires warrant y$^{e}$ sd tract of land

**[350]**

Before menconed unto y$^{e}$ sd JEREMIAH FFLY, & his heires of his boddy / for Ever; against any ꝑson or ꝑsons y$^{t}$ shall Lay any Just Right by / or under me, or my heires unto y$^{e}$ sd Land, As Wittness my hand & seale / this 9$^{th}$. Day of Aprill 1702

Signed, sealed & Delivered in y$^{e}$ p$^{r}$sents of
RICH$^{D}$ REYNOLDS
THO: GILES

AR: SMITH seal

Acknowledged in open Co$^{rt}$ held / for y$^{e}$ Isle of Wight County y$^{e}$ / 9$^{th}$. day of Aprill 1702 by Cap$^{t}$. AR: SMITH to be his free Act & / deed & Recorded

Test CHA CHAPMAN C$^{l}$C$^{ur}$

This Indenture made y^e^ 2^d^. day of Aprill Anno Domini 1701 betweene / REBECKA MACKRISTY of one pty & W^M^. JOLLY of y^e^ Other part Witness / That I y^e^ foresaid REBECKAH MACKRISTOE doe sell, demise & firmly make / over from me, my heires, Ex^rs^. Adm^rs^. or Assgs a certaine pcell of Land / Containing one hundred Acres, or theireabout, scittuate, Lyeing & / being att y^e^ Cyprus, in y^e^ Lower pish of y^e^ Isle of Wight County wich / lands was given to y^e^ foresd REBECKAH by one M^r^. W^M^. RUFFIN & I y^e^ / foresd REBECKAH doe make over all my Right, title & Interest of y^e^ / foresd Lands to W^M^ JOLLY, his heires, Ex^rs^, Adm^rs^. or Assgs, / w^th^ all priviledges of hawking, hunting & fishing with all woods, wat^rs^: / & heriditaments w^t^soever to me belonging, & will warrant y^e^ foresd Land / to y^e^ foresd W^M^. JOLLY his heires, Ex^rs^, Adm^rs^. of Assgs from any Clayme / whatsoever^r^. & I y^e^ foresd REBECKAH MACKRISTY Doe acknowledge I have / Received a Consideracon already in hand for y^e^ same: as Wittness my hand & Seal y^e^ year abovewritten

Signed, Sealed & delivered in y^e^ p^r^sents of us
JAMES BAGNALL:
THOS PITT

her
RECEBKAH **W** MACKRISTOE O
m^r^ke

Acknowledged in open Co^rt^ held for / y^e^ Isle of Wight County y^e^ 9^th^. day Aprill / Anno 1702 by REBECKAH MACKRISTOE to / be her Reall Act & deed
Test CHA CHAPMAN C^l^C^ur^

**[351]**

Know all men by These presents y^t^. I OWEN BOURNE of Isle of / Wight County, & HANNAH my wife for & in Consideration of two thousd / pounds of good M^r^chantable Tob^o^. & Caske to us in hand paid before y^e^ / sealing hereof by THOMAS MANDUE Jun^r^. of y^e^ County Aforesd: have / bargained & sold & Doe by these p^r^sents for us & one heires for ever bar / =gaine, sell, & deliver, enfeoff & Confirme unto y^e^ said MANDUE his / heires & Assgs for Ever, a certaine peice or pcell of Land Containing one / hundred acres, scituate on y^e^ Maine Blackwater River in y^e^ County / aforesaid: being y^e^ one half of a Conveyance to me granted by Cap^t^ / HUGH CAMPBELL for two hundred acres bearing Date ffeb^r^. y^e^ 10^th^ 1698: / Bounded thus (Viz^t^) begining In y^e^ fork of A Branch Called Richard / Bracewells Branch; & soe up along y^e^ Maine Branch to y^e^ head line; & soe / along y^e^ head Line South y^e^ Breadth of y^e^ two hundred Acres, & from / thence to y^e^ head of Small Branch y^t^ makes y^e^ fork & soe to y^e^ 1^st^ / Station. To have & to hold y^e^ sd land w^th^ his due share of all Mines / & Mineralls therein Contained w^th^ all Rights, & priviledges, of hunting / hawking, fishing & fowling: With all Woods, Waters, & Rivers, & all other / profitts, Commodities, & heriditaments, what soever to y^e^ sd Land / belonging, or in any wise Appertaining to him y^e^ said THO MANDUE / his heires & Assgs for ever in as full & Ample manner to all In / tents & purposes as I my self might or Could enjoy y^e^ same by / Virtue of y^e^ before recited Conveyance, & I doe hereby Oblige / my self, my Ex^rs^, & Adm^rs^. to Warrant & Defend this my sale of all / & Singular y^e^ premises against all & all manner of ꝑsons what / Soever, to acknowledge this deed together with my Wife in open / Co^rt^. held for y^e^ Isle of Wight County, & if thereto Required to give y^e^ / said MANDUE his heires & Assgs such further Lawfull Assurances / of y^e^ ꝑmises as by his Councell Learned in y^e^ Law shallbe thought / fitt In Wittness whereoff Wee have hereunto putt o^r^ hands & seales / this 28^th^. Day of ffeb^r^. 170^1^/~2~

his m^r^ke seal

Signed, sealed & Delivered OWEN **X** BOURNE O

in y^e^ ꝑsence of us HANNAH **X** BOURNE seal O

ROBERT BRACEWELL

JENKIN DORMAN

Acknowledged in open Co^rt^. / held for y^e^ Isle of Wight County / y^e^ 1^st^ day of May 1702 by OWEN / BOURNE & HANNAH his Wife to be / their free Act & deed

Test CHA CHAPMAN C^l^C^ur^

**[352]**

This Indenture made y^e^ 16^eenth^. day of May Anno / Domini 1702 & in y^e^ 14^eenth^. year of y^e^ Reigne of o^r^. Sov^r^aign / Lord Willliam y^e^ 3^d^. of England, Scotland, France & Ireland / King Defender of y^e^ faith &c: Betweene Cap^t^. LUKE HAVIELD / of y^e^ County of Nanzimond in y^e^ Collony of Virginia of y^e^ one ꝑ^t^. / And NATH^A^. RIDLY of y^e^ Isle of Wight County in y^e^ Collony / aforesd of y^e^ other ꝑ^t^. Witnesseth y^t^. y^e^ sd LUKE HAVIELD for / & in Consideration of y^e^ Just sume of one hundred & fifty pounds / sterling mony to him att or before y^e^ unsealing & delivery of these / p^r^sents well & truly paid or otherwise well & suficiently secured to be / paid by y^e^ said NATH^A^. RIDLY whereof & wherewith he y^e^ sd LUKE HAVIELD / doth hereby acknowledge himself fully satisfied contented & paid, / Hath granted, bargained sold, aliened, enfeoffed & Confirmed, & by / these p^r^sents doth grant, bargaine, sell, alien, enfeoffe, & Confirme, / unto y^e^ said NATHANIELL RIDLY his heires, Ex^rs^, Adm^rs^ & Assgs all that / tract or parcell of land scituate, lying & being in y^e^ Upper Parrish / of y^e^ Isle of Wight County, & now in y^e^ possession of CHARLES CHAPMAN / & Containing by Estimation two hundred Acres more or less w^th^ all / & singular its Rights, members, Jurisdictions & appurtinances, together / w^th^ all houses, out houses, buildings Gardens, Orchards, Woods, Underwoods / Wayes, Waterwayes, easments, proffitts, Commodities, & Appurtinances / w^t^osever thereunto belonging,or therewith Commonly held. occuppyed / & enjoyed, or accompts or part of or belonging to y^e^ said Land, wich said / plantation & other y^e^ Appurtinances before menconed, were by y^e^ sd LUKE / HAVIELD Parchased of PETER BAYNTON, & by him held by Pattent granted / by Escheat beareing date y^e^ 16^eenth^. day of Aprill Anno Dom: 1683: as / (Relation being had thereunto) may more fully & att Large appear)

**[353]**

To have And to hold y$^{e}$ above recited said premises, w$^{th}$ & singular y$^{e}$ / Appurtinances before by these p$^{r}$sents granted, bargained & sold or menconed / or intended to be hereby granted, bargained, sold, aliened, enfeoffed & Confirmed / & every part & parcell thereof unto y$^{e}$ said NATHANIELL RIDLY his heires & / Assignes, to y$^{e}$ only use & behoofe of y$^{e}$ sd NATH$^{A}$. RIDLY his heires & Assgs for Ev$^{r}$: / And y$^{e}$ said LUKE HAVIELD for himself, his heires, and Assgs y$^{e}$ said land & / and [*sic*] all & singular other y$^{e}$ premises before granted, bargained, & sold with / y$^{e}$ appurtinances unto y$^{e}$ said NATHANIELL RIDLEY & his heires to y$^{e}$ only proper use and behoof of y$^{e}$ said NATHANIELL RIDLEY, his heires & Assgs for Ever / against him y$^{e}$ said LUKE HAVEILD, his heires & Assgs & all & every other person / and persons Whatsoever Lawfully claiming by from or under him them or / any of them, shall & will Warrant & for ever defend by these presents. And / y$^{t}$ he y$^{e}$ said NATHANIELL RIDLY, his heires, & Assgs & every of them shall or / may by Vertue of these p$^{r}$sents from time to time, & att all times forever / hereafter lawfully, peaceably, & quietly have, hold, use, Occupy, possess and / enjoy y$^{e}$ said land, & all & singular y$^{e}$ before granted p$^{r}$mises w$^{th}$ them & every / of their rights, members & appurtinances, & have received & take [*sic*] y$^{e}$ Rents, Issues / & Proffitts thereof, to his & their owne proper Use & behoof for Ever, without / any lawfull lett, suit, Trouble, denyall, interruption, Eviction or Disturbance / of y$^{e}$ said LUKE HAVIELD, his heires, or Assgs, or of any other person / or persons whatsoever lawfully claiming, by from or under him, y$^{m}$. / or any of them, or by his, or their meanes, act, consent, title, interest, / privity or procurement, & that, & free & clear & freely & clearly acquit / [ ], exonerated & discharged, or otherwise well & suficiently saved / & kept harmless by y$^{e}$ sd LUKE HAVIELD, his heires, Ex$^{rs}$: & Adm$^{rs}$: of and from / all & all manner of former and other gifts, grants, bargaines, sales, / bases, mortgages, Joyntures, dowers, titles of Dower & of & from all / other titles, Troubles, charges, demands & incumbrances whatsoever had, / made, suffered, committed or done by sd LUKE HAVIELD, his heires or / Assgs or by any other person or ꝑsons whatsoever Lawfully claiming / by from or under him, them or any of them, or by or from or under / his or their meanes, act, consent, title, Interest, privity or procurement / (y$^{e}$ Cheife rent to his Matie only excepted & forepassed) And further y$^{e}$ / said LUKE HAVIELD for himself, his heires, Ex$^{rs}$, & Adm$^{rs}$. Doth hereby

**[354]**

Covenant. promise, grant & agree to and with y$^{e}$ said NATH$^{A}$: RIDLY / his heires & Assgs y$^{t}$ he y$^{e}$ said LUKE HAVIELD his heires & Assigns / shall & will from time to time & att all times hereafter att & upon / y$^{e}$ Reasonable request & att y$^{e}$ proper Cost & Charges of y$^{e}$ Law / of y$^{e}$ said NATH$^{A}$. RIDLEY, his heires, or Assigns make, doe perform / Acknowledge, Levy execute & suffer or cause to be made done performed / acknowledged, levied, executed & suffered all & every such further / Lawfull, Act & acts thing & things, Devise & Devises Assurance & / Assurances in y$^{e}$ Law whatsoever for y$^{e}$ further better & more perfect / Assurances & Conveying of all & singular y$^{e}$ premises before hereby / granted or menconed to [ ] granted premises with their & every of / their rights, members & appurtinances, unto y^e^ sd NATHANIELL RIDLY / his heires or Assigns as by y^e^ said NATHA^LL^: RIDLY, his heires or Assignes / or by his or their Councell Learned in y^e^ Law shall be Reasonably devis / =ed advised or required. In Wittness whereof y^e^ sd LUKE HAVIELD have / thereunto putt his hand & seal y^e^ day & year first abovewritten.

Signed sealed & delivered
in y^e^ p^r^sence of
THO: SWANN
JAMES WHEDON
JAMES HAMILTON

LU: HAVIELD
O seal

Acknowledged in open Co^rt^. held for / y^e^ Isle of Wight County y^e^ 9^th^. day of June / Anno Dom 1702 by Cap^t^. LUKE HAVIELD / to be his Act & Deed & Recorded

ꝑ me CHA CHAPMAN C^l^C^ur^

**[355]**

Know all men by these presents y^e^ I ISABELLA HAVEILD wife of y^e^ abovenamed LUKE HAVEILD for divers / good causes & Considerations me hereunto moveing. Have Remised / Released & for ever quit claime, & by these p^r^sents doe Remise, Release / & for ever quit claime unto y^e^ abovenamed NATHANIELL RIDLY, his / heires and Assignes, & to every of them, all & all manner of Dower / Title of Right & Title of Dower w^ch^. I y^e^ said ISABELLA / now have, may, might, should, or of Right ought to have or claime / of, in, or out of all and singular, & every y^e^ abovemenconed messuages / lands, Tennements & hereditaments Whatsoever or in any or either / of them, & all & all manner of Actions & Writts of Dower, whatsoever / soe y^t^ neither I y^e^ sd ISABLLE HAVEILD nor any for me, / or in ny name any manner of Dower or Action / or Writt of Dower, or any manner of Right ot title of Dower / of or in y^e^ sd Messuages, Lands, tenements & heriditaments, or of or / in any part or ꝑcell thereof att any time hereafter shall or may / have or claime or prosecute against y^e^ sd NATH^A^. RIDLY, his heires, or / Assignes, nor any or either of them but of and from y^e^ same shall / be utterly debarred, & for Ever Excluded by these presents. In Witness / whereof I have hereunto put my hand & Seal this 16^th^ Day of May 1702

Signed, Sealed & Delivered
in y^e^ presents of
THO: SWANN
JAMES WHEDON
JAMES HAMILTON

ISSABELLA HAVEILD
O seal

This Relinquishmt of Dower / was Acknowledged Open Co^rt^ / held for y^e^ Isle of Wight County / y^e^ 9^th^. day of June Anno Domini / 1702 by M^rs^ ISABELLA HAVEILD to / be her Reall, Act & Deed & Recorded

ꝑ me CHA CHAPMAN C^l^C^ur^

**[356]**

To all to whome this deed Indented of bargaine & sale shall Come, Know / yee that I WM EDWARDS of James Citty County in Virginia Gent. for & / Consideration of ye Just sume of twenty pounds sterling to me in hand paid / or otherwise well & suficiently secured to be paid by WILLIAM KINCHIN / of the County of ye Isle of Wight, with which I here=by acknowledge, / my self fully sattisfied Contented & paid. Have granted bargained / sold & aliened enfeoffed and Confirmed, And doe by these prsents for / me my heires, Exrs, & Admrs for Ever Grant, bargaine, sell, alien, enfeoff / & Confirme unto ye sd WM. KINCHIN his heires & Assignes a certaine / tract or parcell of land containing by estimation four hundred Acres / ye same being ye one Full half part or proportion of eight hundred acres / granted by pattent to me ye sd WM. EDWARDS & Majr. AR. ALLEN dated / ye 25th: day of Aprill 1701 & scituate lyeing & being on ye South Side / of ye Maine Blackwater Swamp & bounded by ye: Various courses / in ye sd pattent mentioned & expressed To Have & to Hold ye sd four hundred / Acres of Land together wth. all houses, out houses, gardens, Orchards / woods, underwoods, wayes, watercourses, easmts, proffitts, commodities / and appurtinances whatsoever thereto belonging: or therewith Commonly / held, occupyed & enjoyed to him ye sd WILL KINCHIN & his heires. to ye only / proper use & behoof of him ye sd WM. KINCHEN, his heires & Assgs for Ever / & I ye sd WM. EDWARDS doe hereby oblige my self, my heires, Exrs & Admrs / to warrant & defend this my sale of all & singular ye before recited / prmises wth: their appurtinances to ye sd WM. KINCHEN, his heires and / Assgs for ever, against me, my heires Exrs, & Assgs or from any / person or persons lawfully claiming by from or under me my / heires, Exrs. Admrs or Assgs. as alsoe to acknowledge this present / Instrument to be my reall Act & deed att ye next Cort to be held

**[357]**

For ye County of Surry [*sic*] aforesaid. In Wittnes whereof I / have hereunto putt my hand & Seal this 9th. day of June 1702

Signed, Sealed, & delivered WM. EDWARDS O seal
in ye prsence of
JNO. CHAPMAN
JOS. CHAPMAN
1702

Acknowledged in open Cort held / for ye Isle of Wight County ye 9th. day of June 1702 by Mr. WM. EDWARDS to be his Real Act & Deed & Recorded
p me CHA CHAPMAN ClCur

This Indenture made ye 12th: day December in ye year / of or Lord God 1701 & in ye 13th. year of ye Reigne of / or. Soveraigne Lord Wm. by ye Grace of God King of England, Scot= / =land ffrance & Ireland &c: Betweene WILL: FFOWLER of ye Isle of / Wight County of ye one Part: & BENJAMIN BEAL of ye sd County on / ye other part Wittnesseth: That ye sd WM FFOWLER for & in Consider / =acon of ye sume of three Thousand pounds of Tobo. in Caske to him / in hand att and before ye sealing & delivery of these prsents by ye sd / BENJAMIN BEAL, well & true paid ye Receipt whereof he ye sd W$^{M}$. FFOWLER doth / hereby acknowledge & himselfe therewith satisfied & p$^{d}$ & thereof & / of every ꝑt. & ꝑcell thereof doth clearly acquit Exonerate & discharg / y$^{e}$ sd BENJ$^{A}$. BEALE, his heires, Ex$^{rs}$ & Adm$^{rs}$. for Ev$^{r}$. by these P$^{r}$sents / hath given, granted, Aliened, Bargained, sould, Enfeoffed & Confirmed / & By these p$^{r}$sents doe fully Clearly & absolutly Give, grant, bargain, sell, alien, enfeoff and / Confirme unto y$^{e}$ sd BENJ$^{A}$. BEAL, his heires & Assgs for Ever one Parcell / or tract of land Containing one hundred Acres scituate, lying & being / in y$^{e}$ Lower Parrish of y$^{e}$ Isle of Wight County, on y$^{e}$ South West Side /of Currawock swamp w$^{ch}$. sd Land came & is bounded as hereafter

**[358]**

Shall be Expressed Which foresaid hundred Acres of land was / formerly granted to JN$^{O}$. DRAKE late of this County deced: by patent / bnearing date y$^{e}$ 22$^{d}$. day of Septemb$^{r}$. 1682 & by him deserted = & is since / granted to WILL: FFOLWER late of y$^{e}$ foresd County deced. by Order of y$^{e}$ Gen$^{r}$all Co$^{rt}$. dated att James Citty y$^{e}$ 21$^{st}$: day of October 1690. wich / said land soe granted to my father W$^{M}$. FFOWLER was by him reentered / taken up & pattented, by Patent beareing date y$^{e}$ 28$^{th}$. of Aprill / Anno Dom: 1691 w$^{ch}$. land doth discend to me y$^{e}$ first abovemenconed WILL / FOWLER son & lawfull Inheritor of y$^{e}$ sd WM. FFOWLER my father w$^{ch}$. is / now dead; & now is in y$^{e}$ tenure & occupation of me W$^{M}$. FFOWLER son and / lawfull Inheritor of my father W$^{M}$. FFOWLER w$^{ch}$ is now dead. And is bounded / as by Pattent aforemenconed doth direct: (Viz$^{t}$:) Begining att y$^{e}$ / Mouth of a Branch y$^{t}$ Devides it from y$^{e}$ Land of THOMAS MANN thence / up y$^{e}$ sd Branch S:W: one hundred, ninty eight Pole to a Pine in HODGES / COUNCELLs line; thence by his line North seventy four degrees West / Eighty Pole to a Red Oake THOMAS PARNELLs Corner tree, thence by & / PARNELLs line North North East one hundred pole: South East fifty pole / & North East one hundred & twenty Pole to a Red Oake a markt Tree / of Coll$^{o}$. BRIDGERs land; And soe by Coll$^{o}$ / BRIDGERs y$^{e}$ same Course / continued sixty Pole further to Currawough Swamp, & then up y$^{e}$ sd Swamp S: twenty degrees E sixty pole to y$^{e}$ first Station. To have & to Hold y$^{e}$ foresaid one / hundred acres of land according to y$^{e}$ foresaid Bounds w$^{th}$. all & singular / its members, jurisdictions & Appurtinances together w$^{th}$. all houses / Edifices, Buildings, Barnes, Stables, Orchards, Gardens, yards, back sides

**[359]**

Heriditaments & Appurtinacnes w$^{t}$soever to y$^{e}$ sd land & p$^{r}$mises / or to any ꝑt or ꝑcell of them belonging, or in any wise appertaning, / thereunto. unto y$^{e}$ sd BENJ$^{A}$: BEAL his heires, or Assgs to y$^{e}$ only proper / use & behoofe of y$^{e}$ sd BENJ$^{A}$: BEAL his heires & Assgs for Ever against / him y$^{e}$ sd WILL FFOWLER, his heires Assgs for Ev$^{r}$, & all; & every person / & Persons w$^{t}$soever, lawfully Claiming by, from, or under him, them, or / any of them, shall and will warrant & For Ever defend by these / p$^{r}$sents; And y$^{t}$ y$^{e}$ sd WILL FFOWLER, for himself, his heires, Ex$^{rs}$. and / Adm$^{rs}$ doe Covenant, promise, grant & agree to & w$^{th}$. y$^{e}$ BENJ$^{A}$. BEAL / his heires & Assignes & every of them by these p$^{r}$sents, that all & singular y$^{e}$ / aforesd ꝑcell of land according to y$^{e}$ forerecited bounds:

with all y$^{e}$ / appurtinances thereunto belonging Now bee & Ev$^{r}$. hereafter shall be / stand & Continue to y$^{e}$ sd BENJ$^{A}$. BEAL & his heires & Assgs for Ever / & y$^{t}$ y$^{e}$ sd BENJ$^{A}$. BEAL his heires of Assgs be freely acquitted, / Exonerated & discharged. & from time to time well & suficiently / kept harmless by y$^{e}$ sd W$^{M}$. FFOWLER, his heires, Ex$^{rs}$ Adm$^{rs}$ of Assgs / of and from all & all manner of former & other gifts, grants, / Bargaines, sales, bases, mortgages, joyntures dowers of and from / all & singular other titles, troubles, charges, demands & incum= / =brances w$^{t}$soever had made, committed, suffered, omitted or done by / y$^{e}$ sd W$^{M}$. FFOWLER, his heires, or Assgs. And y$^{t}$ y$^{e}$ sd W$^{M}$. FFOWLER, his / heires, Ex$^{rs}$, Adm$^{rs}$, or Assgs for & dureing y$^{e}$ sapce of seven yeares / next ensueing y$^{e}$ date of these p$^{r}$sents, shall & will att & upon the / Reasonable Request, & att y$^{e}$ Cost & Charges in y$^{e}$ law of y$^{e}$ sd BENJ$^{A}$.

**[360]**
BEALE, his heires, or Assgs make such further Lawfull & Reasonable / Assurance or Assurances or Conveyances in y$^{e}$ Law for y$^{e}$ more better & / & ꝑfect assurance or assurances of y$^{e}$ aforesd p$^{r}$mises as by y$^{e}$ sd BENJ$^{A}$. BEAL / his heires, or Assignes, or by his, or their Councell learned in y$^{e}$ Law shallbe / Reasonable devised, advised, or Required. And y$^{t}$ y$^{e}$ aforesd land & ꝑmises / w$^{th}$. all woods & waters, & all y$^{e}$ appurtinances thereunto belonging shall / shall be & Esteemed, & ajudged, & taken to be & Ennure, to y$^{e}$ only proper use & / behoofe of y$^{e}$ sd BENJ$^{A}$. BEAL, his heires, Executors, Adm$^{rs}$, & Assgs for ever, / And to no other use, intent, or purposes Whatsoever. In wittness / hereof I have hereunto sett my hnad and Seale y$^{e}$ day, year & Reigne / first above written & Specified: And further by these p$^{r}$esents / I do Oblidge my self, my heires &c: to Come to y$^{e}$ next Co$^{rt}$. to be held for / this County, & there in open Co$^{rt}$. Acknowledge this foresd Conveyance to / be my Voluntary act & deed, & alsoe then & there to bring ANNE my wife / to acknowledge y$^{e}$. same to be her Act & Deed alsoe

his seale
Signed, sealed & Delivered in y$^{e}$ p$^{r}$esence of WILLIAM **F** FFOWLER O
Us whose Names are hereunder Written m$^{r}$ke

his her seale
ARTHUR **A** WHITEHEAD ANNE **N** FFOWLER O
m$^{r}$ke m$^{r}$ke
CHRISTOPHER REYNOLDS
RICHARD REYNOLDS Signed & sealed by W$^{M}$. FFOWLER / & his wife & Dower Relinquist / Teste CHA CHAPMAN

Acknowledged in open Co$^{rt}$. held for y$^{e}$ Isle of / Wight County y$^{e}$ 15$^{th}$. day of Decemb$^{r}$. 1701 by W$^{M}$ / FFOWLER to be his Act & Deed & ordered to be Recorded / & Acknowledged by his wife y$^{e}$ 9$^{th}$. of Aprill 1702

Test CHA CHAPMAN C$^{l}$C$^{ur}$

**[361]**

This Indenture made y^e^ first day of May in y^e^: yeare / of o^r^. Lord 1702 & in y^e^ yeare of y^e^ Reigne of o^r^. Sov^r^aigne Lord / Will y^e^ 3^d^ by y^e^ Grace of God King of England, Scotland, / ffrance & Ireland &c: Betweene W^M^. EVANS of y^e^ Isle of / Wight County, one ꝑty: & GEORGE BENN of y^e^ other ꝑty Wittness / that I y^e^ sd W^M^. EVANS for a valueable Consideration of / [--] already received & most especialy in Consideration / y^t^ my father W^M^. EVANS deced did receive of JAMES BENN / deced y^e^ father of y^e^ sd GEORGE BENN full payment for y^e^ / said Land hereafter menconed, & Dyeing before he made any / Right to y^e^ sd BENN. therefore, I doe hereby these p^r^sents / hath given, granted, alienated, bargained, sold, enfeoffed and / Confirmed. And I y^e^. foresaid W^M^. EVANS doe by these p^r^sents / fully, clearly & absolutely Give, grant, bargaine, sell, alien / enfeoff & Confirme unto y^e^ sd GEORGE BENN, his heires & Assgs / for Ever. a ꝑcell, or tract of land, being y^e^ half of eight hundred / Acres more or less bought of MATTHEW STRICKLAND by my / father W^M^. EVANS Deced, w^ch^. half is four hundred more / or less, & y^t^ part of y^e^ land y^t^ now is bounded & mark & Esteeme / & Called Cap^t^. BENNS Land y^e^ said Land lyeing & being in y^e^ / Isle of Wight County on y^e^ Beaver Dam Swamp. To have & / To hold y^e^ foresd four hundred acres of Land be it more or Less / being y^e^ half of y^t^. Land bought by my father W^M^. / EVANS of MATTHEW STRICKLAND w^th^ all woods, underwoods, / priviledges & appurtinances, w^t^soever unto y^e^ sd GEORGE BENN / his heires & Assgs for ever. to y^e^ sole use & behoofe of y^e^ said / GEORGE BENN, & to his heires & Assgs for Ever against y^e^ sd W^M^.

**[362]**

EVANS, his heires, Ex^rs^, Adm^rs^. & Assgs, & all & every other ꝑson or / ꝑsons w^t^soever claiming by from or under him and y^t^ he / shall & will warrant & for Ever defend by these p^r^sents & y^t^. / y^e^ sd WILL: EVANS doth Covenant & agree to & w^th^ y^e^ sd GEORGE / BENN, his heires, Ex^rs^. & Adm^rs^, & every of them y^t^ att any time or / times will give any further assurance to y^e^ sd GEORGE BENN, his / heires, Ex^rs^. & Adm^rs^. or Assgs, as they shall advise or desire from / me y^e^ sd W^M^. EVANS or my heires & further Covenant to & / w^th^. y^e^ sd GEORGE BENN y^t^. I will acknowledge this to be my deed / in open Co^rt^. to JANE BENN for y^e^ proper use, & behalf of y^e^ sd GEORGE / BENN, as Wittness my hand & seale

his
WILL W EVANS
m^r^ke

Signed, sealed & delivered
in y^e^ p^r^sence of
A^R^. SMITH
W^M^ KERLE

Acknowledged in open Co^rt^. held / for y^e^ Isle of Wight County y^e^ 9^th^. day / of June 1702 by W^M^ EVANS to be / his act & deed

Test CHA CHAPMAN C^l^C^ur^

This Indenture made y^e^ 9^th^. day of June in y^e^ yeare of o^r^. Lord / God 1702 Betweene THOMAS BLAKE of y^e^ Isle of Wight County of y^e^ one / ꝑty & JOHN PRIME of same County y^e^ other party Wittnesseth, y^t^ I / y^e^ sd: THO: BLAKE for & in

Consideration of y$^{e}$ sum of three thousand / pounds of Tob$^{o}$ already paid by y$^{e}$ sd JN$^{O}$: PRIME. Know yee therefore y$^{t}$ I / aforesd THO: BLAKE doe hereby acknowledge my self fully satisfied & paid / & every part & pcell thereof doth barly acquit exonerate & discharge y$^{e}$ / sd JN$^{O}$ PRIME, his heires, Ex$^{rs}$ & Adm$^{rs}$ for Ev$^{r}$. & by these p$^{r}$sents hath Given

**[363]**

Hath given, granted, assigned, bargained, sold, enfeoffed & Confirmed, & / by these p$^{r}$sents doth fully, clearly & absolute, give, grant, bargaine, sell, / alien, enfeoff & Confirme unto y$^{e}$ sd JN$^{O}$. PRIME, his heires & Assignes his / heires & Assignes for ever, a certaine tract of land being one hundred / acres scituated in y$^{e}$ Isle of Wight County being part of a patten of four / acres, Granted to y$^{e}$ sd BLAKE, bearing date y$^{e}$ 20$^{th}$ day of Octobr 1670 being / bounded (Viz$^{t}$) begining att a white Oak standing in y$^{e}$ head of a Branch of / y$^{e}$: Blackwater being a Corner Tree betweene y$^{e}$ sd THOMAS BLAKE & THOMAS / TOOKE, & Running along y$^{e}$ sd Line y$^{t}$ part or devide y$^{e}$ sd BLAKE & TOOKE as / by Course of Pattent is: South West & by West, one hundred & forty eight / pole to a White Oake standing by a Cart path side & from thence North / fifty five degrees, West along or near y$^{e}$ Cart path one hundred & twenty / pole to a Red Oake, & from thence South Westerly to y$^{e}$ head of A / Small Branch, & soe downe y$^{e}$ sd Branch to y$^{e}$ first mentioned Branch of / Blackwater, & soe up y$^{e}$ sd Branch to y$^{e}$ first Station To Have & To Hold / y$^{e}$ said one hunderd acres of Land (except thirty foot square y$^{e}$ sd THOMAS / BLAKE Reserves in y$^{e}$ Old Orchard for a Buriall place) unto y$^{e}$ sd JOHN / PRIME, his heires & Assignes for Ev$^{r}$. to y$^{e}$ sole & only use & behoofe of / y$^{e}$ sd JOHN PRIME, his heires, & assignes for Ever with all woods, under / =woods, ways, waters, houses, orchards, profitts, Commodities or appurtinances / thereunto belonging or any wayes appertaining unto y$^{e}$ sd one hundred / acres of Land. & y$^{e}$ sd THO: BLAKE doth for himself, his heires, Ex$^{rs}$. & Adm$^{rs}$ / Covenant to & with y$^{e}$ sd JN$^{O}$. PRIME, his heires, Ex$^{rs}$, & Assignes to warr$^{t}$. / & Ever defend against all p$^{r}$sons or persons [*sic*] w$^{t}$soever, y$^{t}$ shall lay any / claime, right, Tittle, or Interest to y$^{e}$ sd one hundred acres of land by / or under me. And by these p$^{r}$sents doe hereby warrant y$^{e}$ sd Land to / y$^{e}$ sd JN$^{O}$. PRIME, & his heires & assgs for Ever: against y$^{e}$ sd THOMAS BLAKE / his heires, Ex$^{rs}$ & Adm$^{rs}$ & all & every other person or persons whatsoever / y$^{t}$. shall claime by, or under y$^{e}$ sd THO: BLAKE, by any means. & further / y$^{e}$ sd THO: BLAKE, doth for self, his heires, Ex$^{rs}$, Adm$^{rs}$, Covenant to and w$^{th}$

**[364]**

The sd JOHN PRIME, y$^{t}$ he his heires, Ex$^{rs}$. Adm$^{rs}$, and Assignes & every of / them shall stand seis'd of y$^{e}$ said one hundred acres of Land with the / appurtinances thereunto belonging, & saved harmless from all bargaines / formerly made & y$^{e}$ sd THO BLAKE, doth by these p$^{r}$sents Covenant y$^{t}$ his / heires, Ex$^{rs}$, Adm$^{rs}$, & either of them shall & will be ready to give y$^{e}$ / said JN$^{O}$ PRIME, his heires, Executo$^{rs}$. or Assgs, or either of them any / further lawfull assurance of y$^{e}$ sd Land & appurtinances as the said / PRIME, his heires, or Assignes, or theirs learned Councell in $y^{e}$ Law / shall devise, or think fitt & for further $y^{e}$ said BALKE doth agree $y^{t}$: $y^{e}$: sd BLAKE / & ALICE his wife shall & will acknowledge these $p^{r}$sents to be their free Act / & Deed in open $Co^{rt}$. next $y^{t}$ is to be held for $y^{e}$ Isle of Wight County in / Wittness hereof have sett my hand & seal ye day & year above written.

| | his |
|---|---|
| Signed, sealed & delivered | THOMAS **B** BLAKE O seal |
| in $y^{e}$ $p^{r}$sence of | her $m^{r}$ke |
| AR: SMITH | ALICE **A** BLAKE O seal |
| JOHN BROWN | $m^{r}$ke |

Acknowledged in open $Co^{rt}$ / held for $y^{e}$ Isle of Wight County $y^{e}$ $9^{th}$ / day of June 1702, by THOMAS / BLAKE, ALICE his wife, she relinquishing / all her right of Dower att $y^{e}$ Bar & / owning it to be their free Act & deed

Test CHA CHAPMAN $C^{l}C^{ur}$

Know all men by these $p^{r}$sents $y^{t}$ I WILLIAM BODDY, have bargained / & sold unto JAMES MERCER $y^{t}$. plantation $w^{ch}$. JAMES BARNES now dwelleth / on, & $y^{e}$ old feild & Woodland gound thereunto belonging, & $y^{e}$ sd plantation / ould feild & Woodland ground is bounded $y^{t}$. it begineth, att a Red Oake / Corner Tree $w^{ch}$. standeth between THOMAS JOYNERs land & my land / & from thence along a parcell of marked trees haveing eight Notches

**[365]**

In each Tree four on one side & four on $y^{e}$ other side, along to a white Oake / standing near to $y^{e}$ head of a Branch, & $y^{n}$. downe $y^{e}$ sd Branch to $y^{e}$ Mouth / thereof to a marked Ash Tree, & it standing in or near $y^{e}$ Cypress Swamp and / from thence downe $y^{t}$. side of $y^{e}$ Cyprus Swamp $w^{ch}$. $y^{e}$ Ash tree standeth / on soe far as to a little Red Oake marked $w^{th}$. eight notches, & standeth in $y^{e}$ sd / Cyprus Swamp. And then from $y^{e}$ sd little Red Oake along a parcell of $m^{r}$ked / trees haveing eight notches in each tree, every tree of them to $y^{e}$ first / Station, or first mentioned Red Oake Corner nere $w^{ch}$. standeth / betweene THOMAS JOYNERs land & my land. Now how many acres / of land lieth within these bounds we do not certainly know, but / we doe suppose it to be one hundred acres of land or thereabouts but / now wither $y^{e}$ land within these bounds be more / or less then one hundred acres of land, all $y^{e}$ land $y^{t}$ lieth within / these bounds here beforementioned. I WILLIAM BODDY have sold itt all / to him $y^{e}$ foresaid JAMES MERCER, to him & his heires for ever and / I doe hereby warrant $y^{e}$ sale of this foresaid land, to be good, & law= / =full to him $y^{e}$ sd JAMES MERCER, & to his heires for ever. alwayes / provided $y^{t}$. all $y^{e}$ Kings Rents of this foresaid land be all honestly / paid yearly, & every year for ever paid by him $y^{e}$ sd JAMES MERCER & / by them $y^{t}$. shall come after him. And further I $y^{e}$ foresd $W^{M}$. BODDY / doe give him $y^{e}$ foresaid JAMES MERCER free leave to take pine from / any of my land in $y^{e}$ great pocososon [*sic*] from any of my land there / $w^{ch}$. I have not already letten, for him to make use of on this /

foresaid plantation. And further I y$^{e}$ sd W$^{M}$. BODDY doe promise / him y$^{e}$ sd JAMES MERCER y$^{t}$. both I and my wife will acknowledge / this writinge in open Co$^{rt}$. And to y$^{e}$ true & honest performance of

**[366]**

What is here abovewritten I y$^{e}$ said W$^{M}$. BODDY have hereunto / sett my hand & seale this 22$^{d}$. day of June Anno 1702

In y$^{e}$ p$^{r}$sence of us

his<br>
JAMES **B** BARNES<br>
m$^{r}$ke<br>
her<br>
SARAH **M** BARNES<br>
m$^{r}$ke<br>
her<br>
DIANA + BARNES<br>
m$^{r}$ke

WILLIAM BODDY seal<br>
her<br>
MARY **MB** BODDY<br>
m$^{r}$ke

Acknowledged in open Co$^{rt}$ / held for y$^{e}$ Isle of Wight County / y$^{e}$ 9$^{th}$. day of July 1702 by M$^{r}$. W$^{M}$. / BODDY & MARY his wife she relin= / quishing her Dower att Bar

Test CHA CHAPMAN C$^{l}$C$^{ur}$

Know all men by these p$^{r}$nts that I WILLIAM BODDIE have bargained & sowld / to JOHN MICKMIHILL a plantacon & the Ould Ffeild & Woodland ground thereunto / belonging, and it lyeth on y$^{e}$ Southwestside of y$^{e}$ Sipress Swamp Betweene / JAMES MERCERs Land, & CHARLES BECKETTs ground, and y$^{e}$ Cipress Swamp is / att one end of it, & THOMAS JOYNERs Land, lyeth by y$^{e}$ other end of it / And the bounds of it is thus, It beginneth att a marked swamp Gum / Standing in or near y$^{e}$ Supross Swamp, in y$^{e}$ mouth of a Branch Then / up the sd Branch to a marked white Oak & From thence to a marked / pine, & From y$^{e}$ sd pine straight away to y$^{e}$ nearest part of THOMAS / JOYNERs Land, & then along by y$^{e}$ side of THOMAS JOYNERs Land to A / Redd Oak a Corner Tree w$^{ch}$ standeth betweene THOMAS JOYNER Land & / my Land, And From thence downe along a ꝑcell of marked Trees to A / Saplin White Oak marked & Standing in the sd Sepres Swamp and / From thence downe y$^{e}$ sd Sepress Swamp to y$^{e}$ First station or First / menconed Swamp Gum Now how many acres of Land there[ ] w$^{th}$in / w$^{th}$in [*sic*] these Fore menconed bounds wee doe not sertainly Know but

**[367]**

Wee doe suppose it to be One hundred Acres of Land. but now whither it be / more then one hundred Acres of Land, or whither it be less All y$^{e}$ Land lying / w$^{th}$in y$^{e}$ bounds herebefore menconed, I y$^{e}$ sd WM BODDIE have sould it all to him y$^{e}$ / Foresd JOHN MIKMIALL, and I doe warr$^{t}$ y$^{e}$ sale of it all to be good & Lawfull to / him the Foresd JOHN MACKMIALL, to him his heires Ex$^{rs}$ Adm$^{rs}$ & A*f*s For ever he or / they well & freely paying the Kings Rent thereof yearly & every year For ever / And Further I y$^{e}$ Foresd W$^{M}$ BODDIE doe give him the Foresd JN$^{O}$ MACKMIALL / Free leave to take pine From any of my Land in y^e great pocosson, any of / my Land there w^th I have not already letten For him & his heires For ever / to make use of on this Foresd Plantacon. If y^e any pine soe long [ ] there / And further I doe promise him y^e sd JOHN MICKMEALL, that I & my / Wife well acknowledge this writing in Open Co^rt be o^r Act & deed / whensoever he shall desire us soe to doe And this I doe acknowledge / to be my Act & Deed, as witness my hand & seal 24^th. day of Augt 1702 / And Further I y^e Foresd W^M BODY doe oblidge my heires Ex^rs Adm^rs to this / above Ritting to JN^O MACKMIALL his heires Ex^rs Adm^rs & Afs as / Witness my hand & seal y^e day & year above written

Tes THO: PIT — WILLIAM BODDIE seal
his — MARY **MB** BODDIE seal
THO **A** HUTCHINS
marke
JAMES **B** BARNES
his m^rke

Acknowledged in Open Co^rt held For y^e Isle of Wight County y^e 9^th of Sept^r 1702 by M^r W^M BODDIE & MARY his Wife (whoe relinquished her Dower in Co^rt) to JOHN MICKMIALL as their voluntary Act & Deed & Ordered to be Recorded

Teste CHA CHAPMAN C^lC^ur

**[368]**

Be it knowne unto all men by these p^rsents y^t wee THOMAS / HAYES & PRUDENCE HAYES his wife of Northumberland County in / Virg^a doe hereby assigne, ordaine authorize, Constitute, & in o^r / names & steads putt appoint & depute Cap^t. ARTHUR SMITH & / RICHARD WILKINSON Jun^r. both of y^e Isle of Wight County in / Virginia they or either of them our true & lawfull attorney / & attornyes Irrevoccable for us & in o^r. names, & to our owne propr / use & behoofe to deliver peaceable possession of a parcell of / land lyeing, & being in y^e Isle of Wight County contained in a de= / [=ed] of sale bearing date y^e 12^th. of October 1702 unto THOMAS BEVAN / his heires, Ex^rs: Adm^rs: or Assignes for ever. & further wee THOMAS / HAYES & PRUDENCE, his wife doth depute authorize & appoint in / o^r. steads y^e sd Cap^t. ARTHUR SMITH & RICHARD WILKINSON Jun^r / they or either of them to acknowledge y^e foresaid ꝑcell of Land / in open Co^rt. held for y^e Isle of Wight County in as full force & / vertue as if wee were present rattifyeing & allowing w^tsoever / our said Attornyes or either of them shall doe in y^e foresaid ꝑmices / In Wittness we have sett o^r. hands & seales this 12^th: day of Octob^r: / in y^e yeare of o^r. Lord 1702

Interlined & word put out before / Assigned

Signed, Sealed & deliv^red — THO: HAYES seal
in y^e p^rsence of us — PRUDENCE **H** HAYES seal
WILLIAM SMITH
his ^M marke
his
THOMAS **R** ROBINSON

Proved in open Court held for y^e / Isle of Wight y^e 9^th. day / of Novemb^r 1702 by y^e Oathes of both y^e wittness & / Recorded ꝑ m[r]ke CHA CHAPMAN C[l]C[ur]

**[369]**

Know all men by these p[r]sents y[t] I THOMAS HAYES of North= / umberland County i[n]: Vig[a]: have for a valueable Consideration / to me in hand paid befor y[e] sealing & deliv[r]y of this / Indenture it being three thousand pounds of Tob[o]. have / bargained, sold, enfeoffed & Confirmed unto THOMAS BEVAN of y[e] / Isle of Wight County in Virg[a]: & to his heires & Assgs for Ever, A / Certaine, parcell of Land lying in y[e] Isle of Wight County / whereon he y[e] sd THOMAS BEVAN now liveth it being a Patten / Containing 350 Acres formerly pattent p[d] by PETER HAYES / Grandfather to y[e] foresd THOMAS BEVAN. Excepting one hundred / Acres of y[e] foresaid patten y[e] said 350 acres of land being bounded / to y[e] North by y[e] back Bay Creeke, & Easterly upon Verger Creeke / & soe begining & Running as y[e] aforesaid pattetn of 350 Acres / direct To have & to hold y[e] foresaid Land w[th] all houses / Orchards, ffences, priveledges, Royalties & Immunities w[t]soever / To him y[e] sd THOMAS BEVAN & to his heires & Assignes for: Ever / w[th]. wearranty ag[st] me y[e] sd THOMAS HAYES my heires or Assgs / for Ev[r]: as Wittness my hand & seal this 12[th]: day of Octob[r], in y[e] year / of O[r]. Lord 1702

Further I y[e] sd PRUDENCE HAYES wife to y[e] foresd THOMAS HAYES / doth Relinquish my Dower of this w[th]in menconed deed of sale / for Ev[r]: as Wittness

Signed, sealed & d~~dd~~ THO: HAYES sigellum
in y[e] p[r]sence of us her
WILLIAM **V** SMITH PRUDENCE **H** HAYES seal
his m[r]ke m[r]ke
THOMAS ROBARTSON
his **R** m[r]ke Endorsed on y[e] Back of y[e] Deed / Novemb[r]. y[e] 25[th] 1702

The peaceable & quiett Possession & seizen of y[e] lands & heriditam[ts]. / within menconed to be granted was had & Taken by Cap[t]. ARTHUR SMITH / & RICHARD WILKINSON y[e] Atto[r]. withinmenconed THOMAS HAYES & by y[m]. / was deliv[r]ed to y[e] w[th]in named THOMAS BEVAN y[e] Bargainee in his owne proper ꝑson / to hold to him y[e] sd THO: BEVAN & his heires, to y[e] use of him y[e] sd THOMAS / BEVAN & of his heires & Assgs for Ev[r]: according to y[e] tenour form & / effect of y[e] within written deed in p[r]sence of us

RICHARD REYNOLDS
RICH[D]. FFULGHAM
LAURENCE STORY
JN[O]. LUCK
THO **R** ROBERTSON
his m[r]ke

Acknowledged in open Co[rt]. by Cap[t]. AR: SMITH & Mr. RICH[D] WILKINSON / by Vertue of y[e] foregoeing L[re] of Att[o]. held for y[e] Isle of Wight County / y[e] 9[th]. of Decemb[r]. 1702 to y[e] sd THOMAS BEVAN & Recorded ꝑ / CHA CHAPMAN C[l]C[ur]

**[370]**

This Indenture made y$^{e}$ Twenty Sixth day of Novemb$^{r}$ in y$^{e}$ year of o$^{r}$ L$^{d}$ God one / Thousand Seaven hundred & Two, and in y$^{e}$ First year of y$^{e}$ Reigne of our / Sovereigne Lady Anne, by the grace of God of England Scotland ffrance & / Ireland Queen &c: Between THOMAS HAYES of Northumberland County of y$^{e}$ / one part & WILLIAM CLERKE & MARY his Wife of y$^{e}$ Isle of Wight County of y$^{e}$ / other part, Witnesseth, that y$^{e}$ said THOMAS HAYES For & in consideracon of y$^{e}$ / sume of three Thousand pounds of good Tob, to him in hand p$^{d}$ att and / before the sealing & delivery of these p$^{r}$sents. by the sd W$^{M}$ CLERKE well & / truely p$^{d}$, the receipt whereof he the sd THOMAS HAYES, doth hereby acknowledge / and himselfe therew$^{th}$ Fully sattisfied & p$^{d}$. and doth Freely acquitt / exonerate & discharge the sd WILLIAM CLERKE & MARY CLERKE their heires Ex$^{rs}$ / & Adm$^{rs}$, For ever, by these p$^{r}$nts, Hath given granted alined bargained sowld / enfeoffed & confirmed, unto the sd W$^{M}$. CLERKE & MARY his Wife their heires / & assignes For ever, one plantacon or ꝑcell of Land lyeing in Newport ꝑish / in y$^{e}$ County of Isle of Wight, now in the tenure & Occupacon of JOHN / PILKINGTON, being part of a pattent of Three hundred & Fifty Acres Form$^{r}$ly / pattented by PETER HAYES, being bounded on the South East by / Vergos Creek, on y$^{e}$ North by y$^{e}$ Back Bay Creek, on y$^{e}$ West by a Lyne / of m$^{r}$ked Trees, w$^{ch}$ parts this part of the sd patten, From y$^{e}$ ꝑt. whereon / THOMAS BIVAN doth now dwell, y$^{e}$ sd parcell of Land conteyning / above One hundred Acres, To have & to hold the Foresaid quanty of Land / accordeing to y$^{e}$ aforesd Bounds, w$^{th}$ all & singuler itts right members / Jurisdiccons, & aptences togeather w$^{th}$ all houses Edifices buildings / hereditam$^{ts}$ & apptences, w$^{t}$soever, or to any part of ꝑcell of them / belonging or in any wise apperteining thereunto unto y$^{e}$ sd WILLIAM / CLERKE & MARY his Wife their heires &A*f*s to y$^{e}$ Onely proper use and / behoofe, of y$^{e}$ sd W$^{M}$ CLERKE & MARY his Wife their Heires & Assignes For / ever, ag$^{t}$ him the sd THOMAS HAYES his heires & A*f*s, and all & every other / ꝑson & ꝑsons w$^{t}$soever lawfully cleyming From, by, or under him them / or any of y$^{m}$ shall & will warr$^{t}$ & For ever defend by these p$^{r}$sents & that / y$^{e}$ sd THOMAS HAYES, For himselfe his heires Ex$^{rs}$ & Adm$^{rs}$ doe Covent promise / grant & agree to & w$^{th}$ y$^{e}$ sd W$^{M}$ CLERKE & MARY his Wife their heires & A*f*s & every / of y$^{m}$ by these p$^{r}$nts that all & singuler the Foresd One hundred Acres of Land

**[371]**

According to y$^{e}$ before recited bounds w$^{th}$ all the appertences thereunto / belonging, now be & ever hereafter shall be, stand & continue to the sd W$^{M}$ / CLERKE & MARY his Wife, their heires & Assignes For ever, And that y$^{e}$ said / W$^{M}$ CLERKE & MARY his Wife their heires & A*f*s be Freely acquitted & discharged / & From tyme to tyme well & sufficiently kept harmeless by the sd THOMAS / HAYES his heires Ex$^{rs}$ or Adm$^{rs}$, of & From all manner of Former & other / Guifts, grants, sales, Leases, Dowers, & From all other demands and / incumbrances w$^{t}$soever, had or made by the sd THOMAS HAYES, or by any other / ꝑson or ꝑsons w$^{t}$soever, and the aforesd p$^{r}$mises, w$^{th}$ all thapptences thereunto / belonging, shall be esteemed, & Judged & taken to be, & enure to y$^{e}$ onely / proper use & behoofe of y$^{e}$ sd WM CLERKE & MARY his Wife and to their heirs / &

A*f*s For ever, & to noe other use intent or purpose w[t]soever, In Witness / whereof I have hereunto sett my hand & seal, the Year day & Reigne / First abovewritten
Signed sealed & delivded [*sic*] in y[e] p[r]sence of us
whose names are underwritten [ ] THO: HAYES seal
JOHN PILKINGTON PRUDENCE HAYES seal
sign
WM **8** SMYTH

This Deed was proved in Open Co[rt] held for the Isle of Wight / County y[e] 9[th] of 10[br] 1702 by the Oathes of both y[e] Witnesses / To be y[e] Act & deed of THOMAS HAYES & PRUDENCE his Wife and / Acknowledged by Mr JOHN GILES & Mr GEORGE GREEN attorneys of / the sd HAYES

Test CHA CHAPMAN C[l]C[ur]

Know all men by these p[r]nts that I PRUDENCE HAYES Wife of THOMAS HAYES of / Northumberland County, doe Constitute & appoint in my stead & place, JN[O] GILES / & GEORGE GREEN, both of y[e] Isle of Wight County or either of them, to be my lawfull / attorney or Attorneys, & in my name to relinquish my right of Dower, in & / to a certain parcell of Land lying in the Isle of Wight County conteined in A / Deed made by my abovesd Husband unto W[M] CLERKE & MARY his Wife dated y[e] / 26[th] day of November 1702 and y[t] my right of Dower being by my said / attorney or attorneys relinquished in y[e] Isle of Wight County Co[rt] I y[e] said / PRUDENCE HAYES, doe promise by these p[r]sents shall be as effectuall in Law / to all intents & construccons, as if I were personally p[r]sent, to doe y[e] same / my selfe In witness whereof I have hereunto sett my hand & sela this 26[th] day / of Novemb[r] 1702
sign PRUDENCE HAYES
Test WM **V** SMYTH
JN[O] PILKINGTON

Proved in Open Co[rt] held For y[e] Isle of Wight / County 9[th] 10[br] 1702 by Oaths of both y[e] witnesses / Ordered to be Recorded, the sd Attorneys haveing in Co[rt] relinquish / y[e] sd Dower

Test CHA CHAPMAN C[l]C[ur]

**[372]**

To all to whome thes p[r]sent writeing shall Come I THOMAS HAYES of Northumberland / County Whereas I the sd THOMAS HAYES have subscribed & sealed one writeing / bearing date w[th] these p[r]sents & hereunto annexed purporting, a ffeoffm[t] or / Sale of Land, unto WILLIAM CLERKE of the Isle of Wight County & to MARY / his Wife of a certein plantacon conteining one hundred Acres of Land / w[th] thappertences in Newport Parrish, in the Isle of Wight County now / in the Tenure & occupacion of JOHN PILKINGTON, To have & to hould the said / Land & Plantacon & all other y[e] appertences, to y$^e$ sd WILLIAM CLERKE & MARY his Wife, and to their / Heires & A*f*s For ever, As by the sd Deed Indented may more att large appear / Now know yee that I the sd THOMAS HAYES, For diverse good Causes and / consideracons me hereunto espetially moveing, Have made ordeyned / Constituted & Authorized, and in my pace & stead, by these p$^r$sents have / nominated & putt, JOHN GILES & GEORGE GREEN, both of y$^e$ Isle of Wight / County, Jointly or sev$^r$ally, to be my sufficient Attorney or Attorneys / For me & in my name, to deliver as my Act & Deed unto y$^e$ sd W$^M$ CLERK & / to MARY his Wife, The abovesd Recited Indenture w$^{th}$ Livery of Seizen / of y$^e$ Land therein conteined, And y$^e$ same to acknowledge in y$^e$ Isle of / Wight County Co$^{rt}$, as my Voluntary Act & Deed, In Order y$^t$ y$^e$ same may / be putt upon y$^e$ Records, of y$^e$ sd County Which Indenture after y$^e$ same / shall be soe deliv$^r$ed & acknowledged, by my sd Attorney or Attorneys / I the sd THOMAS HAYES doe promise by these p$^r$sents shall be my / effectuall Deed In Law, to all intents construccons & purposes, as if I y$^e$ said / THOMAS HAYES had been there my selfe to ꝑforme the same In / Witness whereof I have hereunto sett my hand & seal the Twenty Sixth / day of Novemb$^r$. One Thousand Seaven hundred & One.

Signed sealed & deliv$^r$ed in y$^e$ p$^r$sence of us whose names are underwritten
W$^M$ S SMYTH
JOHN PILKINGTON

THO: HAYES seal
PRUDENCE HAYES seal

Livery & seizen of the Land above Entred in Fol 395

This L$^{re}$ of Attorney was proved in Open Co$^{rt}$ Held For y$^e$ Isle Wight County y$^e$ / 9$^{th}$ 10$^{br}$ 1702 by y$^e$ Oaths of W$^M$ SMYTH & JOHN PILKINGTON / and ordered to be Recorded

Test CHA CHAPMAN C$^l$C$^{ur}$

**[373]**

Know all men by these p$^r$sents y$^t$ I THOMAS CUTCHIN have bargained / sold & deliv$^r$ed to WILLIAM BODDY one young Negroe Maid or Woman of / eighteene or twenty yeares of age or thereabouts. And I y$^e$ sd THOMAS / CUTCHIN have sold this foresd Negroe Woman, to him y$^e$ foresaid W$^M$. / BODDY, to be a servant or slave, to him y$^e$ sd W$^M$. BODDY, his heires, Ex$^{rs}$, / Adm$^{rs}$. or Assgs. all y$^t$ time y$^t$ She hath yett here to live, in this p$^r$sent / World; even, all y$^e$ time of her Naturall Life, w$^{ch}$ is yett to Come, & I y$^e$ / aforesaid THOMAS CUTCHIN, doe hereby Warrant y$^e$ sale of this foresaid / Negroe woman, & of all her Increase, to be good & Lawfull, to him the / foresaid WILL BODDY, his heires, Executors, Adm$^{rs}$. & Assgs, against the / claime & claimes, of all person or persons whatsoever, & further I y$^e$ / foresaid THOMAS CUTCHIN doe hereby acknowledge y$^t$ y$^e$ he foresaid / WILLIAM BODDY hath fully paid, & sattisfied me, for this foresd Negroe / woman, before y$^e$ signing & delivering hereof w$^{th}$ a good lawfull and / valueable Consideration, of eight Thousand pounds of good Tobaccos / or y$^e$ worth of itt, ready downe pay; And further I y$^e$ foresd THOMAS / CUTCHIN, doe hereby promise & oblidge my self to him y$^e$ sd WILLIAM / BODDY y$^t$ I will acknowledge this Bill of sale, in open Co[rt], when he y[e] / said W[M]. BODDY shall intreate me to doe it, & to y[e] true & honest / performance, of what is here abovewritten, I have hereunto sett my / hand & seale, Decemb[r]. y[e] 5[th]. in y[e] year 1702

Signed, sealed, & delivered THO: CUTCHIN seal
in y[e] presence of us
HEN: APPLEWHAITE Jun[r] The herein / mentioned Negroe / Woman called by y[e]
JAMES E BRAGG Name of Hanah

Acknowledged in open Co[rt]. held for y[e] / Isle of Wight County 9[th]. of Decemb[r]. / 1702 by THO: CUTCHIN & ordered to be / Recorded

Test CHA CHAPMAN C[l]C[ur]

Know all men by these p[r]sents y[t] I W[M]. BODDY of y[e] Isle of Wight / County, & MARY my wife, doe for us, o[r]. heires, Ex[rs] bargaine, sell, make / over alienate, & deliver unto THOMAS CUTCHIN of Nanzimond County / to him, his heires: Ex[rs]: or Assgs, to say a parcell of lands lyeing on y[e] / South side of y[e] Westerne Branch w[ch]. wee doe esteeme to be two / hundred Acres of Lands or thereabouts, scituated & lyeing & Binding / on y[e] sd Westerne Branch Runn, to a great Pine tree w[ch]. is a Corner / tree, betweene this pcell of Lands & M[r] HUGH BRESSYs land, w[ch] was formerly taken / up By M[r] W[M]. BRESSY, & from thence there along a line of m[r]ked trees y[e] / trees are herein menconed as they stand in y[e] sd line from y[e] aforesaid / Corner tree (itt being a Pine) to another Pine, & from thence to a old pine Being

**[374]**

Being much Burnt w[th]. fire, from thence to a stooping Red Oak & from / thence to a stooping Red Oake, & from thence to a Pine wich Pine is / A Corner tree for this herein mentioned parcell of Land, & M[r] / HUGH BRESSY, formerly M[r]. W[M]. BRESSYs land, from thence along / y[e] old line of m[r]ked trees, these following named trees a pine / & from thence to a small red Oake, att y[e] Road side, & from thence / to a Old Black Pine stump, & from thence to Pine marked for A / Corner tree, & from thence to a thriveing Red Oake Sapling, & / from thence to Red Oake standing by a pond side, & from thence / to Pine tree, & from thence to a Red Oake, & from thence to White / Oake, & from thence to Red Oake, w[ch] stands by a path, called M[r]. / BODDYEs Path, & from thence to a White Oake upon a Branch / y[t] is Called y[e] Red Branch Betweene ALLEXANDER MATTHEWS & / this same parcell of Land, & plantation where now WILLIAM / ARRINGTON now dwelleth on w[ch] plantation & lands; I y[e] abovesd / WILL BODDY, & MARY BODDY my wife, doe as aforementoned, Bargaine / sell, make over, & alienate, & deliver up all our Rights, titles, & intrest, / y[t] wee ever had, or ever shall have, in plantation & lands herein / mentioned, from us, our heires, Ex[rs], Adm[rs], or Assignes for Ever to y[e] / abovenamed to him, to his heires, Ex[rs], Adm[rs], or Assgs for Ev[r] & doe alsoe / warrant y[e] sale of y[e] land & plantation for to be good sale form any / person or persons y[t] shall lay any Claime or Right in any p[t]. or pcell / of plantation or land herein mentioned,

& w[th] all y[e] benefitts thereunto / belonging, & priviledges soever, is of houses, orchards, pasture, grounds & / woodland ground; w[th] all Royalties w[t]soever. To have & to hold y[e] p[r]mises / to him y[e] sd THOMAS CUTCHIN, his heires, Ex[rs], or Assgs for Ever. for and / alsoe I WILLIAM BODDY & MARY my wife, doe oblidge our selves for to Come / to y[e] next Co[rt]. held in this County of Isle of Wight County, & acknowledge / this our Voluntary act & deed; as wittness o[r]. hands & seales this 5[th]. day / of December Anno 1702.

Sealed, signed & delivered
in y[e] presence of
HEN: APPLEWHAITE J[r]:`
JAMES **E** BRAGG
his m[r]ke

WILLIAM BODDY O seal
her
MARY **M** BODDY O seal
m[r]ke

The herein menconed THOMAS / CUTCHIN paying y[e] quitrents yearly / & every year for Ev[r]. of this / Abovementioned Lands

Acknowledged in open Co[rt]. held for y[e] Isle of Wight County y[e] 9[th] / of Decemb[r]. 1702 by W[M]. BODDY to be his deed & Recorded / ꝑ CHA CHAPMAN C[l]C[ur]

Acknowledged in y[e] same Co[rt]. y[e] same day & year by MARY BODDY / to be her deed she relinquishing her dow[r]. att y[e] Barr, & owning it / to be her Voluntary act & deed w[th]out any Compulsion w[ch]. was ordred / to be Recorded

Test CHA CHAPMAN C[l]C[ur]

**[375]**

To all to whome these presents shall Come I FFRANCIS NICOLSON / Esq[r]. his Ma[ties] L[t]: & Governour Generall of Virg[a] send Greeting. Whereas / his late Matie King Charles y[e] second hath been Graciously pleased by his / Royall Letters Patents under y[e]. Great Seal of England beareing date att / Westminster y[e] tenth Day of October in y[e] eight & twenttieth year of his Reigne / amongst other things in y[e] sd Letters Pattents Contained to continue & Confirm / y[e] antient power & priviledge of Granting fifty acres of Land for every ꝑson / Imported into this Collony & Dominion of Virg[a]. Now know yee that I y[e]. said / FFRANCIS NICHOLSON Esq[r]. Governour &c: Doe with y[e] advice & Consent of / the Councell of State accordingly Give & grant unto ROBERT SMELLY, THO: / GILES, JOSEPH BRIDGER, LEWIS SMELLY & WILLIAM SMELLY six hundred seventy / eight acres of Land on y[e] South Side of y[e] Maine Blackwater on y[e] Cyprus / Swamp Comonly knowne by y[e] Name of Quin Quan begining att y[e] mouth of / a Branch, & soe Runing up y[e] Various Corses of y[e] sd Branch to a m[r]ked / white Oake thence Runing North Eighty five degrees, West one hundred & / sixty pole to a great Pine, thence North sixty one degrees, West / ninety pole to a white Oake, thence South West one hundred Eighty two / pole to a great Pine on y[e] South Side of y[e] sd Swamp thence up y[e] said / Swamp North thirty seven degrees & a half, West Ninty six pole to an Arme / of the Swamp, thence West five Degrees, North seventy pole to a white / Oake standing in y[e] fork of a Branch, thence South thirty Degrees, west two / hundred twenty seven pole to a pine, thence South sixty five degrees; East Eighty two pole to a Black Oake, thence North fifty Degrees; / East one hundred, & one pole, to two Black Oakes; thence / East two degrees, South one hundred thirty eight pole to a pine. / thence South fifty five Degrees, East two hundred thirty eight / pole to a live Oake standing in y[e] head of a Branch, thence North / twenty nine degrees, East one hundred & eight pole to a Pine by y[e] side / of a Meadow; thence downe y[e] sd Meadow; & Crossing y[e]: aforesd Swamp / to y[e] first Station. The sd land being due up to y[e] sd ROBERT SMELLY, / THOMAS GILES, JOSEPH BRIDGER, LEWIS SMELLY & WILLIAM SMELLY by, & for the / transportation of fourteen persons unto this Collony whose names are to be in the / Records mentioned under this patent. To have and to Hold the said / land with his due share of all mines, & Mineralls therein Contained, with all / Rights & Priviledges of hunting, Hawking, fishing & fowling, with all woods, / Waters, & Rivers, with all profitts, Commodities & hereditaments w[t]soever / belonging to y[e] said land, to them y[e] sd ROBERT SMELLY, THOMAS GILES, JOSEPH / BRIDGER, LEWIS SMELLY, & WILLIAM SMELLY Their heires & assignes for Ever. in as large & ample manner to all intents & purposes as hath been used & allowed since / y[e] first plantation, To be held of Our Sovereigne Lord y[e] King his heires & Successo[rs]. / as of his Mannor of East Greenwich in free & Common Soccage & not *in Capite* nor / by knights service

**[376]**
Yeilding and paying unto o[r]: sd soveraigne Lord y[e] King his heires and / Successors for every fifty acres hereby granted att y[e] feast of Saint Michael / the Arch Angell y[e] fee Rent of one shilling w[ch]. payment is to be made yearly / from yeare to yeare Provided y[t]. if y[e] sd ROB[T]: SMELLY, THOMAS GILES, JOSEPH / BRIDGER, LEWIS SMELLY & WILLIAM SMELLY their heires or assignes Doe not / seat or plant nor Cause to be seated or planted thereon within three years / next ensueing three [*sic*] Date hereof that then It shall, & may be lawfull / for any adventurer or planter to make Choice thereof & seat thereon / Given under my hand & y[e] seale of y[e] Collony this 24[th]: day of October / in y[e] thirteenth year of y[e] Reigne of o[r]. Sov[r]aigne Lord William y[e] / third by y[e] Grace of God of England, Scotland, France & Ireland / King Defender of y[e] faith Annoq[u] Dom: 1701

ROBERT SMELLY, THOMAS GILES, } FFRA: NICHOLSON
JOSEPH BRIDGER, LEWIS SMELLY & W[M] }
SMELLY ther Pattent for 678 Acres }
of Land on y[e] South side of y[e] Main }
blackwater }
E: JENINGS

Be it knowne unto all men by these p[r]sents, that wee ROBT SMELLY / THOMAS GILES JOSEPH BRIDGER LEWIS SMELLY & W[M] SMELLY w[th]in menconed / For diverse good causes & consideracons, wee thereunto moveing but / more especially For the good & Valluable consideracon of y$^{e}$ sume of Tenne Thousand pounds of good Tobaccoe in Cask, to us in hand p$^{d}$ by / THOMAS SWANN, of Nansemond County gent, the rec$^{t}$ whereof wee doe / hereby acknowledge, & o$^{r}$selves therew$^{th}$ Fully sattisfied contented & paid / have given granted assigned made over, & sell unto / the sd THOMAS SWAN his heires Ex$^{rs}$ Adm$^{rs}$ & A*f*s For ever, all or right / Title interest clayme, & demand aforesd, to y$^{e}$ w$^{th}$in menconed tract / of Land menconed in y$^{e}$ w$^{th}$in pattent conteinedig [*sic*] Six hundred / Seaventy Eight Acres, according to y$^{e}$ Meets & bounds menconed & / expressed in the w$^{th}$in pattent aforesd as Fully & effectually in as large / & ample a manner, as it is to us y$^{e}$ partys to these p$^{r}$sents granted / and wee doe hereby warr$^{t}$ save harmless & For ever keep indemnified

**[377]**
The aforesd THOMAS SWAN his heires & A*f*s From y$^{e}$ Clayme & Title the [ ] / the sd. ROBT SMELLY THOMAS GILES JOSEPH BRIDGER, ~~W$^{M}$ SMELLY~~ & LEWIS SMELLY & / W$^{M}$ SMELLY, or any of us, o$^{r}$ or any of o$^{r}$ heires, Ex$^{rs}$ or Adm$^{rs}$ or From by us or / From any one of o$^{r}$ procurem$^{t}$ by any means w$^{t}$soever but that the same / shall For ever hereafter be deemed & taken to be the onely Free and / absolute right of inheritance in Fee Simple, Revert & be in the aforesd / THOMAS SWAN his heires & A*f*s For ever, as Fully & effectrually as it is to us / granted, by the w$^{th}$in pattent & noe otherwise In witness wherof wee / have hereunto sett o$^{r}$ hands & Seales, this Ninth day of October Anno / Dom: 1702, in the 14$^{th}$ year of his Ma$^{ties}$ Reigne &c

Sealed & dd in y$^{e}$ p$^{r}$sence of us & y$^{e}$ words is to in y$^{e}$ Eleaventh Line of this assignem$^{t}$ was interlined before signed in p$^{r}$sence of AND WOODLEY<br>RICH$^{D}$ HOLLYMAN

ROBT SMELLY seal THO: GILES seal<br>J$^{O}$. BRIDGER seal

This Assignem$^{t}$ was acknowledged in Open Co$^{rt}$ held / For y$^{e}$ Isle Wight County y$^{e}$ 9$^{th}$ of Octob$^{r}$ 1702 by the / ꝑsons whoe have Signed & sealed the same and / Ordered to be Recorded

Test CHA CHAPMAN C$^{l}$C$^{ur}$

Know all men by these p$^{r}$sents that I W$^{M}$ COOKE of the Upper Parish of / y$^{e}$ Isle of Wight County, For a valluable consideracon to me in hand p$^{d}$ / by JOHN PROCTOR of y$^{e}$ same Parish & County & w$^{th}$ w$^{ch}$ I acknowledged my / selfe Fully sattisfied bargained & sold, & doe hereby For me & my / heires For ever, bargaine sell & deliver, enfeoff transferr & confirme / unto the sd JOHN PROCTOR, & to his heires & A*f*s For ever, One hundred / Twenty five Acres of Land, Scituate near the main Blackwater, in y$^{e}$ / parresh & County afforesd being y$^{e}$ Westward part of a Pattent For Two / hundred Acres of Land to me granted the Ninth day of Aprill last past / To have & to hold the sd

One hundred Twenty Feve Acres togeather w^th^ all / y^e^ houses Orchards Gardens Woods Waies & Waters & all other Royalties

**[378]**

Priviledges proffitts Comodities, & hereditam^ts^ w^t^soever, to y^e^ sd Land belonging / or in any wise apperteining, to him y^e^ sd JOHN PROCTER & to his heires and / A*f*s For ever in as Full & ample manner to all intents & purposes, as I my / self might or could have, enjoyed y^e^ same by vertue of y^e^ Foremenconed / pattent And I doe hereby declare & affirme Coven^t^ & agree to & w^th^ the sd / JOHN PROCTER, his heires & A*f*s, that y^e^ aforesd Land & every part and / parcell thereof, is clear & Free From all & all mannor, of Former and / other bargaines & sales Mortgages Jointures Dowries, Indyements [*sic*] and / Execucons, and all other manner of incumbrances w^t^soever, And I / have att y^e^ time of y^e^ sealing & delivery hereof, to all & singular y^e^ p^r^mises / A good sure & indefeazable Estate of Inheritance in Fee Simple w^ch^ I / hereby transferr & oblidge my selfe or Adm^rs^ to warr^t^ & defend this my / sale of all & singuler the p^r^mises w^th^ ther appertences to him the sd / JOHN PROCTER, & to his heires & A*f*s For ever, ag^t^ all & all manner of / ꝑsons w^t^soever, by From or under me dureing or p^r^tending any clayme / Title or interest thereto, When thereto required, will give to him or any / of them, all such Further or other lawfull assurance, & confirmacon of y^e^ / same, as his or their learned Councell shall think Fitt and will alsoe / acknowledge this assignem^t^ of Conveyance to be my reall Act & deed / in Open Co^rt^ next to be held For y^e^ Isle of Wight County abovesd togeather / w^th^ JOAN my Wifes Relinquishm^t^ of her right of Dower, to y^e^ Land / herein abovemenconed, In Testimony of all w^ch^, I have togeather w^th^ / JOAN my Wife hereunto putt my hand & Seal, y^e^ 9^th^ day of ffeb^rij^ 1694
Signed Sealed & dd in y^e^ the p^r^sence of us

| | |
|---|---|
| THO: MORE | W^M^ **W** COOK seal |
| Isle Wight County | her m^r^ke |
| ffeb^rij^ 9^th^ 1694 | JOAN **I** COOKE seal |
| | her m^r^ke |

Acknowledged in Open Co^rt^ by the sd W^M^ COOKE and / JOAN his Wife to be their Free & Voluntary Act and / Deed

Test HUGH DAVIS C^l^C^ur^

Recorded ꝑ HD

**[379]**

Know all men by these p^r^nts that I JOHN PROCTOR, of the Upper Parrish / of the Isle of Wight County doe w^th^ the Consent of MARY my Wife Assigne / over all my right & Title of all the sd Land heremenconed in the Conveyance / From me my heires Ex^rs^ Adm^rs^ & A*f*s, to JOHN DOLE his heires Ex^rs^ Adm^rs^ & A*f*s / For ever, quietly & peaceably to enjoy. And doe oblidge o^r^ soever to acknowledge / this Sale, in Open Co^rt^

held next in this County after the date hereof In / Witness o[r] hands the 18[th] day of October in the year of o[r] Lord 1702

Witness — JOHN **P** PROCTOR Seal
hes m[r]ke
EDWARD CHITTY — MARY § PROCTOR Seal
her m[r]ke
THO **T** DOLE
his m[r]ke

Thes Deed was acknowledged in Open Co[rt] held For / y[e] Isle of Wight County 9[th] 10[br] 1702 by JOHN PROCTOR / & MARY his Wife to be their Free Act & Deed and / Ordered to be Recorded

Test CHA CHAPMAN

MARY the Wife of y[e] sd JOHN PROCTOR Relinquished her / right of Dower in the above sd Land in Open Co[rt] y[e] / same day

Test CHA CHAPMAN C[l] C[ur]

Know all men by these p[r]sents that Whereas W[M] SCOTT FRANC / BRIDLE JOHN DENSON, THOMAS HAMPTON, JAMES DENSON, JOHN SIKES / ISACK ROOKES, have desired to purchase and [*sic*] Acre of Land of us FFRANCES / HUTCHINS & RICHARD HUTCHINS his sonne, o[r] Heires Ex[rs], Now this is to / certifie unto all people that Wee the afore FFRANCES HUTCHINS / togeather w[th] RICHARD HUTCHINS the sonne o[r] heires Ex[rs] For a / valluable consideracon already in hand reced have have [*sic*] bargained / sold & made over & delivered unto y[e] abovesd parties their heires Ex[rs] / the quantity of and Acre of Land or thereabouts scituated lying & / being w[th]in the County of the Isle of Wight & lying upon an Arme / of a Branch called the Westerne Branch of Nanzemond River geven / & granted unto me by Pattent by S[r] W[M] BERKLY K[t] & Governr of Virginia / bearing date y[e] Eleaventh day of March in the Year 1664

**[380]**

The abovesd Acre of Land begining att a marked pine in the ould Feild by the / Highway side, & running From y[e] aforesd marked Pine due North, to y[e] second / Station & soe running From thence, due West & from thence due South and / From thence due East along the Road to the first Station

Wee the abovesd FFRANCES HUTCHINS & RICHARD HUTCHINS his sonne o[r] Heires / Ex[rs] doe say To have & to hold the aforesd Acre of Land For ever togeather / w[th] all the appertences & p[r]viledges w[t]soever thereunto belonging by the / abovemenconed pattent, in as strong & Ferme a manner as may or can be / expressed, by word or writeing notw[th]standing any thing of y[e] p[r]mises abovesd / to the contrary w[th] Free priviledge to come & goe Carry & recarry to & From / the sd Acres or parcell of Land above expressed and as the aforesd ꝑties / their heires or A*ſ*s shall ahve occasion, And Further wee the sd FFRANCES / HUTCHINS & RICHARD HUTCHINS his Sonne o[r] heires Ex^rs doe bind o^rselves in the / penalty of Teane Thousand pounds of good Tob, to acknowledge this our / Act & Deed before the Co^rt held For y^e County of the Isle of Wight to be our reall / Act & Deed and to be or Free consent, that it may be Recorded, And For Further / confirmacon & holding of the aforesd Acres of Land in refference to the / aforesd ptıes, & their heires & Successo^rs For ever according as is above / expressed, And alsoe Wee & o^rselves o^r heires Ex^rs in y^e penalty abovesd / never to disturb the aforesd parties their heires & Successo^rs in the / right & Title of the aforesd Acre of Land in case we should never be / required to make or acknowledge this in Co^rt, For the Recordeing of y^e free / resignem^t of the aforesd Ac[--] of Land, And For the true pformance hereof / according to the true intent & meaning hereof Wee have hereunto sett / o^r hands & seales this

Interlined before assignem^t — FFRANCIS **H** HUTCHINS seal
his marke

This 8^th day of June 1702 — RICHARD **AR** HUTCHINS seal
his marke

ABRAHAM RICKS
ROBT RICKS
GEORGE **V** WATKINS
his m^rke

Acknowledged in Open Co^rt held For the Isle of / Wight County 9^th Octob^r 1702, by RICH^D HUTCHINS / Attorney of FFRANCES HUTCHINS, and by RICH^D HUTCHINS / in his owne pson to be their Free & voluntary Act / & deed and Ordered to be Recorded

Test CHA CHAPMANC^lC^ur

**[381]**

Know all men by these p^rsents, that I FFRANCIS HUTCHINS of the Isle of Wight / doe make constitute & appoint my loveing sonne RICHARD HUTCHINS my lawfull / attorney to acknowledge A Deed of Sale For One Acre of Land made to ISACK / REEKS & W^M SCOTT & some others bearing date 1702 and to conFerme y^e same / in my stead w^th a Full & lawfull power as if I was there in parson Given under my / hand and Seal this 9^th day of Octob^r 1702

Test JACOB DARDEN — FRAN: **IH** HUTCHINS Seal
JOHN SCOTT — his m^rke

Thes L^re of attorney was proved in Open Co^rt held For y^e Isle of / Wight County 9^th Octob^r 1702 by the Oathes of both witnesses / and Ordered to be Recorded

Test CHA CHAPMAN C^lC^ur

Know all men by these p^rsents, y^t I ARTHUR ALLEN of Lawnes Creek pesh / in the County of Surry For & in consideracon of Twenty Five pounds, of good Curr^t / money, to be in hand p^d & well & sufficiently secured to be p^d by EDW^D BOYKIN, of / y^e upper pish of y^e Isle of Wight Planter, have bargained & sold, & doe hereby / For me

& my heires, For ever bargain sell & deliver, enfeoffe transfer and / confirme, unto y$^{e}$ sd EDWARD his heires and Afs For ever, all y$^{t}$ my Estate Right / Title & interest, that I have in & to one Moiety or half of Eight hundred / Acres of Land, granted to me y$^{e}$ subscribed, and M$^{r}$ W$^{M}$ EDWARD late of / James Citty County by pattent dat$^{d}$ the 25$^{th}$ day of Aprill 1701 scituate / lyeing & being on Turkey Swamp on y$^{e}$ South side y$^{e}$ Main Blackwater / in y$^{e}$ Isle of Wight County aforesd To have & to hold y$^{e}$ sd ꝑcell of Land / w$^{th}$ his due shares of all Mines & Mineralls, therein conteined, w$^{th}$ all Rights / & priviledges, of hunting, Hawking, ffishing, & Fowling, w$^{th}$ all Woods / Waters & Rivers, & all other Royalties, prviledges, proffitts Comodities and / Hereditam$^{ts}$ w$^{t}$soever, to y$^{e}$ sd Land belonging, or in any wise / apperteining, to him y$^{e}$ sd EDW$^{D}$, & to his heires & Afs For ever, in as Full and / ample manner, to all intents & purposes, as I my selfe might or could have / enjoyed y$^{e}$ same by vertue of y$^{e}$ before recited pattent or otherwise And I / doe hereby oblidge my selfe my Ex$^{rs}$ Adm$^{rs}$ to warr$^{t}$ & defend, this my Sale of all & / singuler y$^{e}$ prmises, w$^{th}$ their Apptences to him y$^{e}$ sd EDW$^{D}$ his heires & Afs For ever

**[382]**
Ag$^{t}$ all & all manner of ꝑsons w$^{t}$soever by From or under me, dewring or p$^{r}$tending / any clayme, Title or Interest thereto; And doe hereby alsoe Further oblidge my / selfe, att y$^{e}$ next Co$^{rt}$ to be held For the Isle of Wight County aforesd, to acknowledge / this Instrum$^{t}$ of Conveyance to be my reall Act & Deed / togeather w$^{th}$ my Wifes relinquishm$^{t}$ of her right of Dower to the Lands / herein abovemenconed In Testimony of all w$^{ch}$ I have togeather w$^{th}$ KATHERINE / my sd Wife hereunto putt o$^{r}$ hands & seales y$^{e}$ 5$^{th}$ day of ffebr A$^{o}$ Dom 170$^{2}$/$_{3}$

| | |
|---|---|
| Signed Sealed & dd in | AR ALLEN seal |
| p$^{r}$sence of | KATHARINE ALLEN seal |
| JO$^{S}$ JN$^{O}$: JACKMAN | |
| RALPH MARE | |

This Deed was acknowledge in Open Co$^{rt}$ held For / y$^{e}$ Isle of Wight County y$^{e}$ 9$^{th}$ of ffebr 170$^{2}$/$_{3}$ to be / his reall act & Deed by Majo$^{r}$ ARTHUR ALLEN / And by vertue of a L$^{re}$ of Attorney Under the hand & seal of / M$^{rs}$ KATHARINE ALLEN Wife of the sd Majo$^{r}$ ARTHUR ALLEN / to Cap$^{t}$ W$^{M}$ BRIDGER, the sd Cap$^{t}$ BRIDGER did on her behalfe / Acknowledge the sd Deed in Open Co$^{rt}$ the same day / and Relinqish her right of Dower, to y$^{e}$ sd Lands above / Conveyed, w$^{ch}$ were Ordered to be Recorded

Test CHA CHAPMAN C$^{l}$C$^{ur}$

Know all men by these p$^{r}$sents, y$^{t}$ I KATHARINE the Wife of ARTHUR ALLEN / of Lawnes Creek parresh, in y$^{e}$ County of Surry, doe hereby apoint & Ordeine / Cap$^{t}$ W$^{M}$ BRIDGER of y$^{e}$ Isle of Wight County, to be my true & lawfull / Attorney For me & in my name, to acknowlegde my relinquishm$^{t}$ of / my right of Dower in & to Four hundred Acres of Land, scituate on Turkey / Swamp on y$^{e}$ South side y$^{e}$ Main Blackwater in y$^{e}$ Isle of Wight County / aforesd, & this day sould & conveyed, by my sd husband to

EDW$^{D}$ BOYKIN / of y$^{e}$ sd County of Isle of Wight, In Testimony of w$^{ch}$ I have hereunto sett my / hand & Seal y$^{e}$ 5$^{th}$ day of ffeb$^{rij}$ 170$^{2}$/$_{3}$

Test KATHARINE ALLEN seal

JO$^{S}$: JN$^{O}$: JACKMAN

RALPH MARE proved by both Witnesses in Open Co$^{rt}$ held For y$^{e}$ Isle Wight County 9$^{th}$ ffeb$^{rij}$ 170$^{2}$/$_{3}$

Test CHA CHAPMAN C$^{l}$C$^{ur}$

**[383]**

This Indenture made y$^{e}$ 17 day of ffeb$^{rij}$ Anno Dom, 1702, and in y$^{e}$ First year of y$^{e}$ Reign / of o$^{r}$ Lady Anne by the Grace of God of England Scotland ffrance & Ireland, Queen / Defender of the Faith and Between THOMAS COOKE & MARY his Wife, of y$^{e}$ County of y$^{e}$ / Isle of Wight, Dafter of ARTHUR JONES, of the one part & ROBERT SHERRER, of y$^{e}$ same / County of the other part Witnesseth That the sd THOMAS COOK & MARY his Wife / For & in consideracon of the sume of Twelve hundred pounds of Tob, to them in hand / p$^{d}$ & secured by the sd ROBERT SHERRER, att & before the ensealing & delivery, of these / p$^{r}$sents, the receipt whereof the sd THOMAS & MARY doe hereby acknowledge, and thereof & thereby are Fully sattisfied, have bargained sould aliened, enfeoffed and / confirmed, and by these p$^{r}$sent doe For themselves their, heires Ex$^{rs}$ & Adm$^{rs}$, bargaine / sell unto the sd ROBERT SHERRER, his Ex$^{rs}$ Adm$^{rs}$ & Assignes, all the tract peice or / parcell of Land, conteining by Estimacon Fifty acres, be the same more or / less, adjoining to the Land, whereon the sd ROB$^{T}$ SHERRER now lives, scituate / lying & being on the west side, of the First Swamp of y$^{e}$ main Blackwater / in the Upper Parrish of the Isle of Wight County. To have & to hold the said / Bargained & every part thereof togeather w$^{th}$ all Woods Waters all Mines and / Mineralls, Royalties, Easm$^{ts}$ rights, priveledges Comodities, to y$^{e}$ same belonging / or in any wayes apperteining unto the sd ROBERT SHERRER, his heires and / A*f*s For ever, he paying his Ma$^{ties}$ Rent For y$^{e}$ same warranting y$^{e}$ sd bargained / p$^{r}$mises, & every part thereof unto y$^{e}$ sd ROB$^{T}$. his heires & a*f*s For ever, From / themselves their heires Ex$^{rs}$ Adm$^{rs}$ or A*f*s For ever, And the sd THOMAS COOK & MARY / his Wife doe by these p$^{r}$sents For themselves, their Ex$^{rs}$ & Adm$^{rs}$ promise & Coven$^{t}$ / to & w$^{th}$ the sd ROBERT SHERRER his heires Ex$^{rs}$ Adm$^{rs}$ & A*f*s That they y$^{e}$ said / THOMAS & MARY have att the time of sealing & delivery hereof. A Full / & indefeazable Estate of Inheritance in Full in the sd Bargained p$^{r}$mises & / every part thereof. In Witness whereof the sd THOMAS COOK & MARY his Wife / have hereunto sett their hands & seales, the day & Year abovewritten

Sealed & ~~dd~~ in y$^{e}$ p$^{r}$sence of us THOMAS COOK Seal

JN$^{O}$ BRETT MARY COOK his hand **M** her marke Seal

RICH$^{D}$ HALLOMAN

THO: HARRIS

Ackn$^{o}$ in Open Co$^{rt}$ held For y$^{e}$ Isle of Wight County 19$^{th}$ ffeb$^{rij}$ / 170$^{2}$/$_{3}$ by THOMAS COOKE & MARY his Wife to be their Act & Deed / & Ordered to be Recorded

Test CHA CHAPMAN C$^{l}$C$^{ur}$

**[384]**

Know all men by these p$^{r}$sents that I the w$^{th}$in named MARY COOKE doe hereby / remise, Release & Relinquish, unto the sd ROBT SHERRER, partie to these p$^{r}$sents all / Dower & right of Dower, that I may or can clayme in the sd Land or any pte / thereof by the Lawes of England or this County or any other waies / howsoever, Witness my hand & Seal the day & Year w$^{th}$in written

her
MARY **M** COOKE Seal
marke

Sealed & ~~dd~~ in y$^{e}$ p$^{r}$sence of
JOHN BRETT
RICH$^{D}$ HALLOMAN
THO HARRIS

This Relinquishm$^{t}$ of Dower was acknowled in Open Co$^{rt}$ / held For y$^{e}$ Isle of Wight County 19$^{o}$ ffeb$^{rij}$ 170$^{2}$/$_{3}$ by MARY COOK / to be her Free & Voluntary Act & Deed & Recorded p me

CHA CHAPMAN C$^{l}$C$^{ur}$

Know all men by these p$^{r}$sents that Wee THOMAS COOKE & MARY COOK are / held & Fermely bound unto ROB$^{T}$ SHERRER of the Isle Wight County his Ex$^{rs}$ Adm$^{rs}$ & / A*f*s in y$^{e}$ sume of Three Thousand pounds of Tbb$^{o}$ For y$^{e}$ pFormance as / Witness o$^{r}$ hands & Seales this 17$^{th}$ day [*sic*] of 1702

Whereas the above bound THOMAS COOKE & MARY his Wife by Deed bearing / date w$^{th}$ these p$^{r}$sents have conveighed A certain Tract of land conteining / Fifty Acres, nmore or less lyeing in the Upper Parresh of y$^{e}$ Isle of Wight / County. If therefore the sd W$^{M}$ [*sic*] COOK & MARY his Wife, their heires Ex$^{rs}$ & / Adm$^{rs}$ shall well & truely pForme, the Coven$^{t}$ Article & Agreem$^{ts}$ in y$^{e}$ sd / Bargain & Sale menconed & conteined, and indemnifie save & keep / harmeless, the sd ROB$^{T}$ SHERR his heires Ex$^{rs}$ Adm$^{rs}$ & A*f*s, From himselfe his / heires Ex$^{rs}$ Adm$^{rs}$ soe that y$^{e}$ sd ROB$^{T}$ SHERRER his Heires & A*f*s peaceably & / quietly enjoy the same, Then this Obligacon to be void or else to / remaine in Full Force & Vertue

Sealed & ~~dd~~ in y$^{e}$ p$^{r}$sence of us
JN$^{O}$ BRETT
RICH$^{D}$ HALLOMAN
THO HARRIS

THOMAS COOK
his hand Seal
MARY **M** COOK her hand Seal

Acknowledged in y$^{e}$ Isle of Wight Co$^{rt}$ by THO COOK / & MARY his Wife 19$^{o}$ ffeb$^{rij}$ 1702

Test CHA CHAPMAN C$^{l}$C$^{ur}$

**[385]**

To all X$^{pian}$ people, to whome these p$^{r}$sent Deed shall Come Wee Cap$^{t}$: HENRY / APPLEWHAIT Sen$^{r}$ & M$^{r}$ GEORGE MOOR, of y$^{e}$ Isle of Wight County send Greeting / Whereas by order of Co$^{rt}$ dated the 14$^{th}$ ffeb$^{rij}$ 1699 Wee the sd HENRY APPELWHAIT / & GEORGE MOORE, were Ordered & appointed feeofees in trust, For the disposeing / & passing of Deeds, For the Towne Land accordeing: as is p$^{r}$sented in the Act / of Assembly began att James Citty the 16$^{th}$ day of Aprill Anno Dom, 1691 / Now know Yee that Wee the sd HENRY APPLEWHAIT & GEORGE MOORE For the / Consideracon of One hundred Sexty Seaven pounds of Tob, & an halfe, & Cask / by us already reced ꝑ Rate, For one Left, doe For & in behalfe of the Co$^{rt}$ & County / give, grant, Alien, Sell & Conferme, & by these p$^{r}$sents, doe geve grant, alsoe / sell & Conferme, unto M$^{r}$ W$^{M}$ SMITH Sen$^{r}$, of the sd County his heires Ex$^{rs}$ / Adm$^{rs}$ & Assignes For ever, one halfe Acres of Land scituate lyeing & being / in the Towne of Newport, Knowne by the name of the Sixth Lott / or N$^{o}$ Six, beginning att a Stake on the Front that Devides, this From N$^{o}$ 7 / thence South Eighty Five degrees, Easterly Six poles to y$^{e}$ Street, thence South / Twenty two degrees, Westerly Fourteen pole to A Stake, & Southerly Sixty / One degrees, Westerly Four pole to a Lane to be made, Soe by the Lane / North Four degrees Easterly, Tenne pole & North Twenty two degrees / Easterly, Six pole $^{8}/_{10}$ to the First station Warranting, y$^{e}$ sale of the sd Lands / to be good, lawfull & authentick, & Ferme in Law to the sd W$^{M}$ SMITH Sen$^{r}$ / his heires Ex$^{rs}$ Adm$^{rs}$ & A*f*s For ever, in as large & ample manmner, as is / made to us; The sd W$^{M}$ SMITH Sen$^{r}$ haveing ꝑFormed according to y$^{e}$ Act / In Witness whereof Wee have hereunto sett o$^{r}$ hands & Seales this 19$^{th}$ / of ffeb$^{rij}$ 170$^{2}$/$_{3}$

Signed Sealed ~~dd~~ in y$^{e}$ p$^{r}$sence of
HUMPHRY MARSHALL
CHA CHAPMAN

HENRY APPLEWHAITE Seal
GEO: MOORE Seal

Acknowledged in Open Co$^{rt}$ held For the Isle Wight / County by Cap$^{t}$ HENRY APPLEWHAITE & M$^{r}$ GEORGE / MOORE ffeoffees in Trust the 19$^{th}$ of ffeb$^{rij}$ / 170$^{2}$/$_{3}$ & Ordered to be Recorded

Test CHA CHAPMAN C$^{l}$C$^{ur}$

**[386]**

Bee, it knowen [*sic*] unto all X$^{pian}$ ~~people~~ persons, where thes p$^{r}$sent / may appear, That I WILLIAM STRICKLAND, & OLLIFFE STRICKLAND my / Wife, of the Isle of Wight County, of Virginia, have bargained / sould, & delivered For me my heires, Ex$^{rs}$ Adm$^{rs}$ or A*f*s, a parcell of Land / by Computacon One hundred & Fifty Acres of Land, be it more or less, / unto ARTHUR WHITEHEAD, & his heires, Adm$^{rs}$ or A*f*s Forever, lying & / being as Followeth, Beginning att the head of the Horse Swampe, att / GEORGE PEARCE's Lyne, Runing Northerly along the sd Lyne unto A / marked Pine,

& soe Runing Westward, unto the Black Pond / and soe runing downe the Black Pond, branch unto a marke / Pine Soe runing a Corse of m$^{r}$ked Trees, unto the Horse Swamp, / & soe runing up the Horse Swamp to the Ferst station, Now I / the sd W$^{M}$ STRICKLAND & OLLIFF my Wife, doe warr$^{t}$ the Sale of y$^{e}$ / aforesd Land, From us o$^{r}$ heires Ex$^{rs}$ Adm$^{rs}$ or A*f*s For ever To have / & to hould & peaceable, possess, w$^{th}$ all p$^{r}$viledges & appertinances / thereunto belonging, Wood, & Water, Land, & Timber, w$^{th}$ all p$^{r}$veledges / appteining, to y$^{e}$ aforesd land, unto him the aforesd ARTHUR / WHITEHEAD, or his heires or A*f*s For ever, Whereunto, ConFirmacon / of y$^{e}$ aforesd Sale, & y$^{e}$ aforesd W$^{M}$ STRICKLAND, doe bind my selfe / my heires, Ex$^{rs}$ Adm$^{rs}$ or A*f*s, in the Speciall Bond, and For ForFeit of / Ffive Thousand pounds of Tob, & Cask, paym$^{t}$ well & truely to be / made, upon, unperformance of Articles hereof, unto ARTHUR / WHITEHEAD, or his heires, as Witnesseth my hand & Seal the 15$^{th}$ / day of ffeb$^{rij}$ 1699

Test JOHN GILES — W$^{M}$ **W** STRICKLAND Seal
JN$^{O}$ CHAPMAN — OLIVE **O** STRICKLAND Seal
AND$^{REW}$ WOODLEY

Ackn$^{o}$ by W$^{M}$ STRICKLAND & OLLIVE his Wife in / Open Co$^{rt}$ held For the Isle Wight County 15$^{th}$ ffeb$^{rij}$ / 1699 to be their reall Act & Deed, & Dower / relinquished att the Barr w$^{ch}$ is Ordered to be / Recorded

Test CHA CHAPMAN C$^{l}$C$^{ur}$

**[387]**

To All X$^{pian}$ people to whome the p$^{r}$sent Deed or writeing shall Come I POOL HALL / of the Lower paresh of y$^{e}$ Isle of Wight County send greeting in o$^{r}$ L$^{d}$ God Everlasting / Now Know yee, y$^{t}$ I y$^{e}$ sd POOL HALL For diverse good causes me hereunto moveing / & More especially For & in consideracon, of y$^{e}$ sume of Five Thousand Five hundred / pounds of good Tob to me in hand p$^{d}$ before thensealing & deliv$^{r}$ing of these p$^{r}$sents / by JOHN WATTS of y$^{e}$ aforesd County y$^{e}$ rec$^{t}$ whereof I doe herew$^{th}$ acknowledge & thereof / & of every pte doe Fully acquitt, exon$^{r}$ate & discharge y$^{e}$ sd JN$^{O}$ WATTS his heires Ex$^{rs}$ / Adm$^{rs}$ & A*f*s For ever, have granted bargained, sould, Aliened, Enfeoffed Assigned & / confirmed, & sett over & by these p$^{r}$nts doe For me my heires, Ex$^{rs}$. Adm$^{rs}$, grant / bargaine, sell alien Enfeoff, assigne confirme & sett over, unto y$^{e}$ sd JN$^{O}$ WATT his / heires Ex$^{rs}$, Adm$^{rs}$, & A*f*s For ever, Seaventy Seaven Acres of Land lying & being in y$^{e}$ / Foresd County being pte of a pattent granted to my Grandfather, THOMAS POOL / Joining unto on One side, the Land that I Formerly sould to y$^{e}$ sd WATTS begining / att a Gum in a Swamp y$^{t}$ was a deviding tree of WATTS, & soe runing downe y$^{t}$ sd / Swamp to a small Branch y$^{t}$ a great poplar stood, & soe runing up the said / Branch, & soe along a Line of m$^{r}$ked trees, to my head Line, & soe along y$^{t}$ / sd Line till it meet y$^{e}$ sd WATTS Corner Tree, & soe downe y$^{e}$ sd WATTS Line / to y$^{e}$ First Station To have & to hold y$^{e}$ sd Seaventy Seaven Acres of Land / w$^{th}$ all & Singuler y$^{e}$ houses, Orchards ffences proffitts, Comodities, p$^{r}$viledges / Emminities [*sic*] thereunto belonging or in any wise appteining to him y$^{e}$ sd / JN$^{O}$ WATTS his heires Ex$^{rs}$ Adm$^{rs}$ &

A*f*s For ever, in as Full large & ample manner / as I my selfe might or could doe, by vertue of my Deed or other writing w$^{t}$soever / And Further I y$^{e}$ sd POOL HALL doe For my selfe, my Heires Ex$^{rs}$, Adm$^{rs}$ & Assignes / Coven$^{t}$ ꝑmise & grant to & w$^{th}$ y$^{e}$ sd JOHN WATTS his heires Ex$^{rs}$ Adm$^{rs}$ & A*f*s / & w$^{th}$ every of y$^{m}$ by these p$^{r}$sents, y$^{t}$ he y$^{e}$ sd JN$^{O}$ WATTS his heires Ex$^{rs}$ Adm$^{rs}$ & / A*f*s, shall have hold occupy possess quietly & peaceably enjoy y$^{e}$ sd Seaventy / seaven Acres of Land, w$^{th}$ all houses Orchards ffences proffitts, Comodities / priveledges & immunities thereto belonging or in any wise apꝑteining w$^{th}$out / y$^{e}$ lett trouble molestacon, or incumbrance w$^{t}$soever, of me y$^{e}$ sd POOL / HALL, my heires Ex$^{rs}$ or Adm$^{rs}$ or of or by any other ꝑson or ꝑsons w$^{t}$soever, / w$^{ch}$ shall or may clayme any Title or Interest thereunto, or of any part / thereof, And Further y$^{e}$ sd POOL HALL doth hereby Coven$^{t}$ to & w$^{th}$ y$^{e}$ said / JOHN WATTS, his heires Ex$^{rs}$ & A*f*s that y$^{e}$ sd Seaventy seaven acres of Land / & every ꝑte thereof w$^{th}$ all & singuler y$^{e}$ p$^{r}$mises above menconed, the day of y$^{e}$ / date hereof, & att y$^{e}$ ensealing & delivery hereof, Free & clear & soe shall / be & continue unto y$^{e}$ sd JOHN WATTS his heires Ex$^{rs}$ Adm$^{rs}$ & a*f*s, sufficiently / kept harmeless of & From, all Former, bargaines Sales Guifts, Leases / Joyntures Mortgages, Deeds writeings or Conveyances, w$^{t}$soever Formerly / made or passed of For or concerning the aforemenconed p$^{r}$mises, & Likewise / doe

**[388]**

Doe herewith oblidge my selfe, my heires Ex$^{rs}$ & Adm$^{rs}$ to make such Further assurance / in wrighting, of all & singuler y$^{e}$ above menconed p$^{r}$mises as he y$^{e}$ sd JN$^{O}$ WATTS / or his Councell learned in y$^{e}$ Law shall att any time advise or desire, And / Lastly I doe oblidge my selfe, & my Wife ANNE to acknowledge y$^{e}$ above Deed / att y$^{e}$ next Co$^{rt}$ to be held For this County. In Wittness whereof I the above / menconed POOL HALL have hereunto sett my hand & Seal this 9$^{th}$ day of / of March In y$^{e}$ year of o$^{r}$ Lord One Thousand seaven hundred two three

POOL HALL Seal

Signed Sealed & delivered in<br>the p$^{r}$sence of us<br>JO$^{N}$ WALKER<br>JO$^{S}$: CHAPMAN

her<br>ANNE **B** HALL Seal<br>m$^{r}$ke

Acknowledged in Open Co$^{rt}$ held For y$^{e}$ Isle of Wight / County 9$^{o}$ Marcij $170^{2}/_{3}$ by POOL HALL & ANNE his / Wife, to be their Free, Act & Deed & Ordered to be / Recorded

Test CHA CHAPMAN C$^{l}$C$^{ur}$

The sd ANNE HALL did likewise then in Co$^{rt}$ all her right of / Dower, of the Land above Conveyed, voluntary relinquish / to y$^{e}$ sd JN$^{O}$ WATTS

Test CHA CHAPMAN C$^{l}$C$^{ur}$

This is to all X^pian^ people to whome it shall Come For that I ANNE LEWES / Wife of JOHN LEWES deced doth make my Lawfull Sonne W^M^ MACKONE / a Letter of Attorney to receive all my lawfull debts & pay all my / debts legall & Just as witness my hand the third of ffeb^rij^ 170²/₃

Test WILL WILLIAMS — ANNE N LEWES her m^r^ke

JOHN I LEGG hes m^r^ke

proved in Open Co^rt^ held For the Isle Wight County / 9^th^ Aprill 1703 by the Oathes of both y^e^ Witnesses / & Ordered to be Recorded

Test CHA CHAPMAN C^l^C^ur^

Isle Wight County

In the difference between W^M^ WEST & JN^O^ DRAKE wherein it appeares y^t^ y^e^. sd JN^O^ DRAKE / hath most grossly abused him y^e^ sd W^M^ WEST & his daughter ANNE WEST being proved / by y^e^ Oaths of sev^r^all evidences, For these reasons y^e^ sd JN^O^ DRAKE hath acknowledged y^t^ he / hath soe done, & begged Forgiveness of y^e^ sd W^M^ WEST, & ANNE upon his knees, For w^t^ is past / & promised For y^e^ Future, to refraine such doings, & desire this Order may be Recorded on / y^e^ County Records Aprill y^e^ 11^th^ 1703

Recorded p CHA CHAPMAN C^l^C^ur^

to M^r^ CHARLES CHAPMAN Clerk for Record

& DRAKE to pay

10° April 1703

**[389]**

To all people before whome the present deed or writeing Shall come to be seen or read / Know yee, that I GEORGE WILLIAMSON of the County of Isle of Wight in Virginia & HESTER / my Wife, For a valluable consideracon to us in hand alreadly p^d^ & satisfied att & / before the sealing signing & delivering hereof, For w^ch^ we acknowledged o^r^ selves / to be Fully sattisfied & p^d^ by PHILLIP RAYFORD of y^e^ County aforesd doe For us & our / heires Ex^rs^ Adm^rs^ & A*f*s, make over bargaine sell alienate & conFirme to the sd / PHILLIP RAYFORD & to his Heires Ex^rs^ Adm^rs^ & A*f*s For ever, Two hundred Acres of Land / bounded thus, Begining att a Redd Oake a Corner Tree, of W^M^ CRUMPLER and / runing North three degrees East 130 poles to a redd Oak thence South Seaventy Five degrees East Two hundred Eighty Four pole to y^e^ Maine Runne of the / Blackwater Swamp, thence downe y^e^ sd Runn to a Line of WILLIAM CRUMPLER / thence on his Line to y^e^ First station, be the same more or less To have & to / hold, in as large & ample manner as I have enjoyed or might have enjoy'd / the same, by reason of the pattent For y^e^ sd Land w^th^out y^e^ lett molestacon or / desturbance, of us or either of us, O^r^ or either of o^r^ heires Ex^rs^ Adm^rs^ or A*f*s / to PHILLIP RAYFORD his heires Ex^rs^ Adm^rs^ or A*f*s, To ye Confirmacon whereof Wee / have sett o^r^ hands & seales this 29^th^ day of March in y^e^ year 1703

FFRANCIS WILLIAMSON GEO: WILLIAMSON Seal
WILLIAM CRUMPLER HESTER **H** WILLIAMSON Seal

Acknowledged in Open Co$^{rt}$ held For y$^{e}$ Isle of Wight County 9$^{th}$ / Aprill 1703 by M$^{r}$ GEORGE WILLIAMSON & HESTER his Wife to be / their Free & Voluntary Act & Deed & Ordered to be Recorded

Test CHA CHAPMAN C$^{l}$C$^{ur}$

M$^{rs}$ HESTER WILLIAMSON did then likewise voluntarily relinquish / her right of Dower in the Lands above conveyed, att y$^{e}$ Barr / w$^{ch}$ was ordered to be Recorded

Test CHA CHAPMAN C$^{l}$C$^{ur}$

To all people before whome this p$^{r}$sent Deed or writeing shall coem to be seen / Know yee y$^{t}$ I GEORGE WILLIAMSON of y$^{e}$ County of Isle of Wight in Virginia & / HESTER my Wife doe For a valluable consideracon to us in hand paid and / sattisfied, att & before the sealing signeing & delivery hereof w$^{ch}$ wee / acknowledge o$^{r}$selves to be Fully sattisfied contented & p$^{d}$ by WILLIAM / CRUMPLER of y$^{e}$ County aforesd doe For us & o$^{r}$ heires Ex$^{rs}$ Adm$^{rs}$ & A*fs* make / over bargaine sell alienate & conFerme to y$^{e}$ sd W$^{M}$ CRUMPLER & his heires / Ex$^{rs}$ Adm$^{rs}$ & A*fs* For ever Two hundred Acres of Land bounding this / begining

**[390]**

Beginning att a Pine by y$^{e}$ main runne of y$^{e}$ Blackwater Swamp & runing North / ffifty six degrees West thirty Four Pole to a White Oake, then North twenty / Five degrees, Two hundred Pole to a White oake, then North Seaventy Five / degrees West Sixty Six pole, to a poplar, thence North three degrees East / Seaventy pole to a Redd / Oake, then South Sixty Two degrees East Two hundred & Thirty Pole to y$^{e}$ Maine Runn / of the Blackwater Swamp & downe the Runne to y$^{e}$ First station, to y$^{e}$ Same more or / less To have & to hould in as large & ample mannor as I have or might have enjoyed y$^{e}$ / same by vertue of y$^{e}$ pattent For y$^{e}$ sd Land w$^{th}$out y$^{e}$ lett molestacon or disturbance of us or / either of us O$^{r}$ or either of O$^{r}$ heires Ex$^{rs}$ Adm$^{rs}$ or A*fs*, to W$^{M}$ CRUMPLER & to his heires Adm$^{rs}$ / & A*fs*, To y$^{e}$ ConFermacon hereof Wee have sett o$^{r}$ hands & Seales this Twenty Ninth day / of March in y$^{e}$ Year 1703

FFRA: WILLIAMSON GEO: WILLIAMSON Seal
his HESTER **H** WILLIAMSON Seal
PHILLIP **R** RAYFORD
m$^{r}$ke

Acknowledged in Open Co$^{rt}$ held For y$^{e}$ Isle of Wight County y$^{e}$ 9$^{th}$ of Aprill / 1703 by M$^{r}$ GEO: WILLIAMSON & HESTER his Wife to be their ffree and / Voluntary Act & Deed & Ordered to be Recorded

Test CHA CHAPMAN C$^{l}$C$^{ur}$

M$^{rs}$ HESTER WILLIAMSON did then likewise att the barr relinquish all her right / of Dower, to y$^{e}$ Land menconed in y$^{e}$ above Conveyance w$^{ch}$ was Ordered to be / Recorded

Test CHA CHAPMAN C$^{l}$C$^{ur}$

To all to whome these p$^{r}$sents shall come Know yee that I JOHN PORTIS of y$^{e}$ / Lower parrish of y$^{e}$ Isle of Wight County in Virginia planter, For & in consideracon / of the sume of Eight hundred & Fifty pounds of Tob to me in hand p$^{d}$ before the / sealing & delivery of these p$^{r}$sents, by JOHN PORTIS Jun$^{r}$ of y$^{e}$ sd parrish & County / in Virginia, the receipt whereof I doe hereby acknowledge & my self Fully / contented sattisfied & p$^{d}$ & every ꝑte & parcell thereof doe hereby acquitt / exonerate & discharge y$^{e}$ sd JOHN PORTIS Jun$^{r}$ his heires & Afs For ever, Have / given granted bargained sould, aliened Enfeoffed & confirmed & by these / p$^{r}$sents doe Fully Freely & absolutely give grant bargaine sell, alien / enfeoff & conFerme unto the sd JOHN PORTIS Jun$^{r}$ his heires Ex$^{rs}$ Adm$^{rs}$ & / Afs For ever, A Certein tract or parcell of Land scituate lying & being in y$^{e}$ / Isle of Wight County, beginning att a Red Oak & Runing S:S:E: along a Line / of New m$^{r}$ked Trees, to a Redd Oak Standing in a Branch & downe y$^{e}$ sd Branch / E:N:E, to y$^{e}$ Maine Swamp & up y$^{e}$ Main Swamp, to a Line of m$^{r}$ked Trees w$^{ch}$ / parts y$^{e}$ Land From a certein tract of Land w$^{ch}$ I the sd JN$^{O}$ PORTIS Form$^{r}$ly gave / unto y$^{e}$ sd JOHN PORTIS Jun$^{r}$ & up y$^{e}$ sd Line to y$^{e}$ First station, the sd track of / Land

**[391]**

Land conteining by estimacon Five & Twenty Acres be it more or less To have & to hould / the sd Land w$^{th}$ his due shares of all Mines & Mineralls, w$^{th}$ all Rights & priveledges, of / hunting hawking Fishing & Fowling, togeather w$^{th}$ all proffitts Comodities & Hereditam$^{ts}$ / whatsoever to the sd Land belonging or in any Wise appteining to him y$^{e}$ sd JOHN / PORTIS Jun$^{r}$ his heires & Afs For ever, in as Full & ample manner to all intents & purposes / as I my selfe might or could have enjoyed the same by vertue of these p$^{r}$sents / I the sd JOHN PORTIS Sen$^{r}$. doe Further Coven$^{t}$ & oblidge my selfe, to & w$^{th}$ y$^{e}$ sd JOHN / PORTIS Jun$^{r}$ his heires Ex$^{rs}$ Adm$^{rs}$ & Afs, to save indempniFied & Keep harmeless y$^{e}$ said / JOHN PORTIS Jun$^{r}$ his heires &c of & From all manner of Former Guifts Grants, / Bargaines seales, Leases Jointures Dowers Mortgages or other incumbrances / whatsoever, as likewise to give the sd JOHN PORTIS Jun$^{r}$ his heires &c such Further / lawfull assurance or assurances. Conveyance, or Conveyances, as him y$^{e}$ sd JOHN / PORTIS Jun$^{r}$ his heires &c or to him or his Councell learned in the Law shall seem / necessary And I the sd JOHN PORTIS Sen$^{r}$, doe oblidge my heires Ex$^{rs}$ Adm$^{rs}$ & Assignes / to the true ꝑFormance of y$^{e}$ p$^{r}$mises, And that I togeather w$^{th}$ my Wife will / acknowledge this att y$^{e}$ next Co$^{rt}$ to be held For this County to be o$^{r}$ Reall Act / & Deed As Witness my hand & seal this Eighth day of March Anno Dom 170$^{2}$/$_{3}$

Signed Sealed & delivered in his

the p<sup>r</sup>sence of us JOHN **P** PORTIS Seal
THOMAS CLARKE marke
JO<sup>S</sup>: CHAPMAN

Acknowledged in Open Co<sup>rt</sup> held For the Isle of Wight County / 9° Marcij 170²/₃ by JOHN PORTIS & Ordered / to be Recorded
Test CHA CHAPMANC C<sup>l</sup>C<sup>ur</sup>

I JANE PORTIS Wife of JOHN PORTIS Sen<sup>r</sup> abovemenconed doe by these presents / relinquish & make over, all y<sup>e</sup> Right Title & interest that I have or by y<sup>e</sup> Lawes / of England or Virginia, might, Could, should or ought to have, to y<sup>e</sup> third of the / Land abovemenconed, to y<sup>e</sup> sd JOHN PORTIS Jun<sup>r</sup> his heires Ex<sup>rs</sup> Adm<sup>rs</sup> or A*f*s / For ever, & doe promise & oblidge my selfe to acknowledge this my Relinquishm<sup>t</sup> / of Dower att y<sup>e</sup> next Co<sup>rt</sup> to be held For this County As Witness my hand & seal / this Eighth day of March, Anno Dom: 170²/₃ her
Signed Sealed & ~~dd~~ in y<sup>e</sup> p<sup>r</sup>sence of us JANE **I** PORTIS Seal
THOMAS CLARKE m<sup>r</sup>ke
JO<sup>S</sup>: CHAPMAN

The above JANE PORTIS Wife of JN<sup>O</sup> PORTIS Sen<sup>r</sup> did in Open Co<sup>rt</sup> / held for y<sup>e</sup> Isle of Wight County 9° Marcij 170²/₃ Freely and / voluntarily acknowledge this her Relinquishm<sup>t</sup> of Dower to / y<sup>e</sup> Lands above menconed & / Recorded
ꝑ CHA CHAPMAN C<sup>l</sup>C<sup>ur</sup>

**[392]**

Wee WILLIAM ARRINGTON & my now Wife ELIZABETH ARRINGTON wee doe both of us / hereby acknowledge, that on the Tenth day of September in y<sup>e</sup> year One Thousand / Six hundred Eighty & three, that then W<sup>M</sup> BODY did grant a Lease to o<sup>r</sup> ffather JAMES / PEDDEN, For that plantacon w<sup>ch</sup> wee doe now dwell on, and that the sd W<sup>M</sup> BODDY / did lett to him, w<sup>th</sup> y<sup>e</sup> sd Plantacon Woodland ground & Cattell & other things Now / soe it is, that W<sup>M</sup> BODDY hath sould this Foresd Plantacon & some of y<sup>e</sup> Woodland / gound w<sup>ch</sup> did belong, to y<sup>e</sup> sd Plantacon, by & w<sup>th</sup> the consent of me y<sup>e</sup> sd W<sup>M</sup> ARRINTGON / & alsoe of my Wife, And as For y<sup>e</sup> other ꝑcell of Woodland grounde w<sup>ch</sup> was letten with / this Foresd Plantacon, I W<sup>M</sup> ARRINGTON & my now Wife ELIZABETH ARRINGTON Wee / doe, both of us agree & consent, to it that he the sd W<sup>M</sup> BODY may sell, Lett or any / way dispose of it w<sup>ch</sup> way he y<sup>e</sup> sd W<sup>M</sup> BODY pleaseth himselfe, For wee doe both / of us acknowledge, that Wee have nothing to doe with that Land nor w<sup>th</sup> nothing nor / w<sup>th</sup> anything menconed in y<sup>e</sup> Foresd Lease, neither w<sup>th</sup> Cattle nor w<sup>th</sup> anything else / therein menconed, This Foresd Lease was recorded in Co<sup>rt</sup> y<sup>e</sup> day & year above menconed / But wee both us revoak & make void that Lease & all things therein menconed / and wee doe both of us acknowledge that wee have noe thing to doe w<sup>th</sup> y<sup>t</sup> Lease / nor w<sup>th</sup> anything menconed in that Lease And wee doe acquitt & discharge the sd / W$^{M}$ BODY of that Lease & of all things therein menconed, And Further wee doe both / of us acquitt him the sd W$^{M}$ BODY his heires Ex$^{rs}$ Adm$^{rs}$, Wee doe acquitt clear and / dischardge y$^{m}$ all not onely of all things menconed in this Foresd Lease, but alsoe / of all manner of accons, trespasses, Recknonings, acco$^{ts}$. suits of Law & of & From all / debts di[ ]s & demands w$^{t}$soever, and From all things & every thing, that are or / can by any lawfull meanes be made to appear between him y$^{e}$ sd W$^{M}$ BODY & / me or my Wife From y$^{e}$ begining of y$^{e}$ World unto y$^{e}$ day of y$^{e}$ date hereof And / Further I y$^{e}$ Foresd W$^{M}$ ARRINGTON & my now Wife ELIZABETH ARRINGTON, doe both / of us promise & bind, & oblidge o$^{r}$selves, to W$^{M}$ BODY to acknowledge this writeing / in Open Co$^{rt}$ to be o$^{r}$ Act & Deed, w$^{n}$soever he y$^{e}$ sd W$^{M}$ BODY shall desire us soe to / doe, And in witness hereof wee have both of us hereunto sett o$^{r}$ hands & Seales / this 24$^{th}$ day of May 1703

Signed Sealed & ~~dd~~ in y$^{e}$ p$^{r}$sence of us his

JOSHUA TURNER WM **W** ARRINGTON Seal

FRANCIS WILLIAMSON m$^{r}$ke

This hereunder written, concerneing the Deed of Guift / was written before y$^{e}$ signeing sealing & delivring hereof her

ELIZABETH **X** ARRINGTON Seal

m$^{r}$ke

The Foresd W$^{M}$ ARRINGTON & his Wife ELIZABETH doth discharge the Foresd W$^{M}$ BODY of A / Deed of Guift, y$^{t}$ W$^{M}$ BODY did give to JAMES PEDDEN his ffather in Law, about 20 yeares / agoe & Recorded in Co$^{rt}$

Acknowledged in Open Co$^{rt}$ held For the Isle of Wight Counthy y$^{e}$ 9$^{th}$ of / June 1703 by W$^{M}$ ARRINGTON & ELIZABETH his Wife to be their Free / & Voluntary Act & Deed, & Ordered to be Recorded

Teste CHA CHAPMAN C$^{l}$C$^{ur}$

**[393]**

Know all men by these p$^{r}$sents, that I WILLIAM BODDIE of y$^{e}$ Isle of Wight County in Virg$^{a}$ / have by & w$^{th}$ y$^{e}$ good Will & concent of my Wife MARY BODDIE, bargained, sould & deliv$^{r}$ed to / NICHOLAS CASEY, that plantacon w$^{th}$ y$^{e}$ Widow Woman MARTHA DARSON now dwelleth, on, w$^{th}$ y$^{e}$ / Woodland gound therewith belonging, and y$^{e}$ sd plantacon & Woodland ground as bounded / thus, It begineth att a great pine tree m$^{r}$ked, & it standeth by the Easterne side, of y$^{e}$ Cipruss / Swamp, and From y$^{e}$ sd pine Tree along a ꝑcell of m$^{r}$ked Trees, to a little Red Oak standing / by y$^{e}$ side of a little Branch, and then downe y$^{e}$ Run of y$^{e}$ sd little Branch to A greater / Branch, And then downe y$^{e}$ Run of that greater Branch, to y$^{e}$ Cypres Swamp Runne / And then up the Cyprus Swamp Run, soe Farr as y$^{e}$ First Station or First menconed / marked Pine Tree How wee deoe not certainly know how many Acres of Land this / Foresd plantacon & Woodland ground is, but wee doe suppose it is One hundred Acres / of Land, Now if it be more than One hundred Acres of Land, I will take none From it / And if it be les then One hundred Acres of Land, I will add none to it, Now I have sould / this sd Plantacon & Land, to NICHOLAS CASEY For one hundred Acres of Land be it more or / less, and NICHOLAS CASEY hath bought this plantacon & land of me For One hundred Acres of / Land be it more or less, And soe the bargainers to stand betweene us One hundred / Acres be it more or less Now I doe in the behalfe of my selfe my heires Ex[rs] & Adm[rs] / Warr[t] the sale of the Foresd Plantacon of Land, to be good & lawfull to him y[e] said / NICHOLAS CASEY his Heires Ex[rs] Adm[rs] & A*f*s For ever, ag[t] the Clayme & claymes of all ꝑsons / w[t]soever, Excepting onely the Foresd Weddow woman MARTHA DARSON, and her three / Sonnes HENRY DARSON, JOHN DARSON, & MARTIN DARSON, I doe Except these Four / persons, For I have a long tyme suite letten this Foresd plantacon & Woodland to / these Four ꝑsons For soe long time as them Four ꝑsons or any or either of them / shall live in thes p[r]sent world, Therefore I cannot sell away their rights, of / this plantacon & Land, but they are all Four of them, To have & to hold this Foresd / plantacon & Land, peaceably & quietly w[th]out y[e] lett or trouble or hindrance of / him the sd NICHOLAS CASEY, his Heires or Succossors, But after those Foresd Four / ꝑsons are all deced, then he the sd NICHOLAS CASEY his heires & Successo[rs] may / have y[e] Full proffitts, & p[r]viledges of this Foresd palntacon & Land For ever, he y[e] / sd NICHOLAS, his heires & Successo[rs] yeilding & payeing Yearly & every Year For ever / y[e] Quitrent of thes one hundred Acres of Land, and to begin now thes p[r]sent year / 1703 And I the Foresd W[M] BODDIE doe hereby promise him y[e] Foresd NICHOLAS CASEY / that I y[e] sd W[M] BODDIE & my Wife well acknowledge this writeing in Co[rt] w[n] he y[e] / sd NIC[O] CASEY shall desire us soe to doe And in Witness hereof, wee have hereunto / sett o[r] hands & seales this 9[th] day of June 1703

Signed Sealed & delivered in y[e] p[r]sence of us ADAM MURRAY
HEN: BEST
RALPH FFUZELL

WILLIAM BODDIE Seal
MARY **M** BODDIE Seal
her m[r]ke

Acknowledged in Open Co[rt] held For the Isle of Wight County / June y[e] 9[th] 1703 by M[r] W[M] BODDIE & MARY his Wife, whoe / Relinquished her right of Dower att y[e] Barr, and Ordered to be / Recorded

Teste CHA CHAPMAN C[l]C[ur]

**[394]**

Know all men by these p[r]sents that I WILLIAM BODDIE of Isle of Wight County in / Virginia, have by & w[th] y[e] good will & consent of my now Wife MARY BODDIE bargained / sould & delivered unto JAMES BRAGG A certain ꝑcell of Land, scituate lying and / being in y[e] Foresd County, and it lyeth by y[e] side of y[e] Westerne Branch Meadow, and / it is bounded thus, It begineth att a marked White Oak A Corner / Tree, And From thence streight away to another corner Tree, and it is a great Ould / pine Tree, & that pine Tree is a Corner Tree of THOMAS ROBERTS's ꝑcell of ground, &

From / thence along a parcell of m$^{r}$ked Trees, to a great pine marked & standing In a Pond / and From thence along a parcell of marked Trees, to a little White Oak, a Corner Tree / & it standeth by a path side, that goeth toward y$^{e}$ Westerne Branch Meadow and / From thence downe along a parcell of marked Trees, along by y$^{e}$ right hand of the sd / path, goeing toward y$^{e}$ Westerne Branch meadow, and then along that path & / marked Trees, by it, through the pocoson, and then along y$^{e}$ path & marked / Trees by it, through the pocoson, and then along y$^{e}$ path & marked / Trees by it, beyond y$^{e}$ pocoson, and then along y$^{e}$ path & marked / Trees by it, beyond y$^{e}$ pocoson, soe Farr as to the head of a Branch, that cometh / out of y$^{e}$ Westerne Branch, Meadow, & then downe y$^{e}$ side of y$^{e}$ head of y$^{t}$ Branch / a little way & y$^{n}$ Cross, to y$^{e}$ other side of y$^{t}$ Branch, to a Redd Oak a m$^{r}$ked Tree / & a Corner Tree of that ꝑcell of Land w$^{ch}$ I Formerly sould to GEORGE WILLIAMS / and downe by y$^{e}$ side of the sd Branch & Cross y$^{e}$ Mouth of another Branch, to / another m$^{r}$ked Red Oak, and it standeth by y$^{e}$ side of y$^{e}$ Foresd Westerne Branch / Meadow and from thence straight away, to y$^{e}$ nearer ꝑte of y$^{e}$ Foresaid / Westerne Branch Meadow Runne, And then up the sd Runne to the First / Station, or First menconed marked White Oak & Corner Tree of W$^{M}$ BACKONs / parcell of gound, Now how many Acres of Land there is w$^{th}$in y$^{e}$ Bounds here / before menconed, Wee doe not certainly know, but wee doe suppose it to be / Four hundred Acres of Land, now it if be more y$^{n}$ Four hundred Acres of Land / I will take none From it, and it if be less then Four hundred Acres of Land / I will add none to it, Now JAMES BRAGG hath bought this ꝑcell of Land of me / For Four hundred Acres of Land being more or less, and I have sould it to him / For Four hundred Acres be it more or less, and soe y$^{e}$ bargaine is to stand / between us For Four hundred Acres of Land whither it be more or whither it / be less Now I y$^{e}$ sd W$^{M}$ BODDIE doe in y$^{e}$ behalfe of my selfe my heires Ex$^{rs}$ & Adm$^{rs}$ / warr$^{t}$ y$^{e}$ sale of this Foresd Land, to be good & lawfull to him y$^{e}$ Foresd JAMES / BRAGG, his Heires Ex$^{rs}$ & Adm$^{rs}$ For ever, He y$^{e}$ sd JAMES BRAGG, his heires and / Successo$^{rs}$, Yeilding & payeing yearly & every Year, Forever y$^{e}$ Quit Rent of this Foresd Four hundred Acres of Land, And I y$^{e}$ Foresd W$^{M}$ BODDIE & my / Foresd, Wife MARY BODDIE, doe acknowledge that this Deed of Sale is or Act & / Deed, As Witness o$^{r}$ hands & Seales this 29$^{th}$ day of May 1703

Sealed Signed & deliv$^{r}$ed in the p$^{r}$sence of us

his
OWEN **O** GRIFFEN
m$^{r}$ke

her
ANNE **A** DRAKE
m$^{r}$ke

WILLIAM BODDIE Seal

her
MARY **M** BODDIE Seal
m$^{r}$ke

Acknowledged in Open Co$^{rt}$ held For y$^{e}$ / Isle of Wight County y$^{e}$ 9$^{o}$ Junij 1703 by M$^{r}$ W$^{M}$ / BODDIE & MARY his Wife, whoe relînqed her Dower / att y$^{e}$ Barr & Ordered to be Recorded

Test CHA CHAPMAN C$^{l}$C$^{ur}$

**[395]**

Leases, Joyntures Mortgages, Deeds, Writeings, or Conveyances, w[t]soever Form[r]ly made or / passed, of For or concerneing the abovemenconed p[r]mises, And likewise doe herew[th] oblidge / my selfe, my heires Ex[rs] & Adm[rs], to make such Further assurance in writeing, of all & singuler / the abovemenconed p[r]mises, as by y[e] sd ROB[T] KAE or his Councell learned in the Law, shall / att any tyme, Advise or desire, And doe oblidge my selfe to acknowledge the above Deed / att y[e] next Co[rt] to be held For this County In Witness whereof I the abovemenconed PHILLIP / PARDOE, have hereunto sett my hand & seal this Ninth Day of Aprill 1703

his
PHILLIP + PARDOE Seal
mrke

Signed Sealed & delivered in the p[r]sence of
W[M] THOMAS
JOHN BRANTLY

Acknowledged in Open Co[rt] held For the Isle of Wight / County y[e] 9[th] of June 1703 by PHILLIP PARDOE to be his / reall & Free Act & Deed & Ordered to be Recorded

Teste CHA CHAPMAN C[l]C[ur]

To y[e] Worp[Full] y[e] Isle Wight Co[rt]

This to sattisfie y[e] Worp[Full] Co[rt] that I EDWARD BRANTLY, the last of July last, heard HUPP / the Taylor say, that two Young men, and JANE JONES lay upon A Bedd, And before and y[e] / other behind, and he that lay behind ffuckt her, & Further saith not

Ju[r] in Cu[r] 15° ffeb[rij] 1699 & Recorded ꝑ / CHA CHAPMAN C[l]C[ur]

To all to whome these p[r]nts shall came Wee S[r] SAM[LL] DASHWOOD K[t] L[d]: Mayor and / the Aldermen of the Citty of London, Send greeting, Know yee that on y[e] day of y[e] / date hereof, in y[e] Queens Ma[ties] Co[rt], houlden before us in the Chamber of the Guildhall, of the sd Citty ꝑsonally came, & appeared HUMPHRY SPURWAY WILLIAM / FFRAZER, & ROBERT HUNTER, of London M[r]chants, being ꝑsons well Knowne & worthy of / good Creditt, & did by solemne Oath which they sev[r]ally tooke, upon the holly / Evangelects of Almighty God, before us, Then & there solemnely declare Testfie & / depose to be true in manner followeing (vez[t]) And Ferst the sd WILLIAM FFRAZER & / ROBERT HUNTER, depose & say, that they verily beleive, that y[e] names ALEXANDER / CLARKE principall, W[M] BLACKWOOD ROB[T] BLACKWOOD & HARRIE BAIRD as witnesses to / a certeine Deed in writeing now produced, unto them y[e] sd Depon[ts] bearing date / att Edingbrough the Sixteenth day of Janr[j] 1703 yeares purporting and being / & assignem[t] made, by the sd ALEXANDER CLARKE as Adm[r] of y[e] goods & Estate / of JN[O] SOMERVELL, late of the Citty of Edingbrough, M[r]ch[t] but since deced in Virg[a] / to the sd HUMPHRY SPURWAY of Sixty Five Hogsheads of Tob & other Estate w[ch] / belonged, to y[e] sd SOMERVELL, & sev[r]ally writt w$^{th}$ y$^{e}$ proper hands of ALEXANDER CLARK / M$^{r}$ch$^{t}$ in Edingbrough W$^{M}$ BLACKWOOD ROB$^{T}$ BLACKWOOD HARIE BAIRD also M$^{r}$ch$^{ts}$ / there, There Depon$^{ts}$ being ꝑsonally acquainted, w$^{th}$ y$^{m}$ (Viz$^{t}$) the sd HUNTER w$^{th}$ all / three of y$^{m}$ & y$^{e}$ sd FFREZOR w$^{th}$ the two Ferst the sd HUNTER haveing often seen them & write & signe their names, & y$^{e}$ sd FFRAZER being also very well acquainted w$^{th}$

**[396]**

Their hand writeing, And they Further depose, that they were p$^{r}$sent & saw the sd HUMPHRY / SPURWAY, Seal & as his Act & Deed deliver the power, L$^{re}$ of Attorney by Deputacon now / alsoe produced, & Shewe unto them bearing date, the Six & Twentieth day of ffebrij last for / the purposes therein conteyned, And that they as witnesses did thereunto subscribe their / names, as thereby doth & [ ] appear, And the sd HUMPHRY SPURWAY by himselfe maketh / Oath, that he never reced, either directly or indirectly, nor does he know or belive that y$^{e}$ / sd ALEXANDER CLARKE ever reced all or any of the Tobaccoes, & other Estate w$^{ch}$ belonged to / the sd Late JOHN SOMERVELL, and w$^{ch}$ are by the sd ALEXANDR CLARKE assigned & transfered / to him the sd Depon$^{t}$, in & by the before menconed Deed of Assignm$^{t}$ or any the least / returnes, For the same, and doth not know or beleive, that the sd ALEXANDER CLERKE / was in the last indebted to the sd late JOHN SOMERVELL, or that he has released or / discharged all or any of the Tobaccoes or other Estate by him as Adm$^{r}$ of the sd SOMERVELLs / Estate, assigned and transfered, to the sd Depon$^{t}$ as aforesd In Faith & Testimony / whereby wee the sd Lord Mayer & Aldermen, have caused the seal of the Office of / Mayoralty of this sd Citty to be hereunto putt & assised, (and the sd Deed of Assngem$^{t}$ / & Letter of Attorney to be hereunto annexed) Dated in London the Eleaventh day / of the Month of March, 1702 and in the Ferst year of y$^{e}$ Reigne of o$^{r}$ Sovereigne / Lady Anne Queen of England &c

GIBSON seal

These p$^{r}$sents doe witness that I HUMPHRY SPURWAY of London M$^{r}$ch$^{t}$ by vertue of / an assignem$^{t}$, & Transferr, (Dated at Edingbrough the Sixteenth day of January last) / granted & made to me & my Heires & Donators For the consideracon therein menconed / by ALEXANDER CLARKE of Gladreik Iun$^{r}$ M$^{r}$cnt in Edingbrough, aforesd, of in & to an / Adtracon upon y$^{e}$ Effects of JN$^{O}$ SOMERVAIL (late of Gladstaines) who died in Mary= / Land in the County of Somersett, & ꝑticularly Sixty Five hh~~ds~~ of tobaccoe, as by y$^{e}$ sd / Assignem$^{t}$ (relacon being thereun to had) more att large it doth & nigh appear Doe / hereby Nominate constitute & appoint GEORGE FFRAZER of Nansimun in James / River in Virginia M$^{r}$chant JAMES FFOWLER & ROBERT TUCKER of Pagan Creek in y$^{e}$ / same River M$^{r}$chants, or any one or two of them, my true & lawfull Attorneys & Attorney / giveing unto them & to any or more of them, Full power & authority, For me, in my / name & to my use, to demand, recover, & recover the sd Tobaccoes & all other, y$^{e}$ goods & / Marchandizes, effects & concernes, whatsoever as are to me belonging & apperteining by / Force & vertue, of y$^{e}$ sd recited assignem^t, and that From & out of the hands & Custody of M^r BENJAIN WALLES of the County aforesd M^rchant & From & out of y^e hands and / custody of all & every such other ꝑson or ꝑsons whome it doth or may concerne, togeather / w^th all Costs, damages & interests, upon recoveries & rec^ts. to make & give doe & sufficient / acquittances, & discharges, alsoe to acc^t, Compromise compound conclude & agree, in the / p^rmises as occasson shall require, & one Attorney or in or under them or any of them / to make & substitute, & him or y^m againe att pleasure to revoak, Giveing & by these / p^rsents granting to my sd Attorneys & every of y^m my Full & whole power & authority in y^e / p^rmises, as well Judicall as Extrajudiciall promises to hould & rattifie For good & Vallue / w^tsoever

**[397]**
Whatsoever my sd Attorneys or any of them of their Substitutes shall lawfully p^d / or cause to be deuely by vertue of these p^rsents, In Witness whereof I have hereunto putt / my hand & Seal, Dated in London, this Six & Twentieth day of ffebrij Anno 1702 and / in in Fert [*sic*] Year of y^e Reigne of o^r Soveraigne Lady Anne Queen of England &c
Sealed & delivered in HUMPHREY SPURWAY Seal
y^e p^rsence of us
RO: HUNTER JN^O WRIGHT
WILL^M FRASER DAVID REED
GUILL SCOREY Not Pub / 170^2/_3

Be It Kend to all men by these p^rnts L^ts MOBLE & CLERKE of Glandrich Jun^r M^rcts in / Edingbrough, For one Certeine sume of money advanced p^d & delivered by M^r HUMPHREY SPURWAY M^rcht in London to me, wherw^th I hold me weel satisfied, & discharge him of / the same, Renncering all excepcons in y^e Contrarie, Therefore to have made Constitute & / Ordeined, Lyke as I be these p^rnts made Constitute & Ordine the sd M^r HUMPHRY / SPURRAWAY his Aeres & Donat^rs my very lawfull Cossion^r & assignees, In & to one / Administrations upon y^e Effects of JOHN SOMERVAIL, late of Gladstaines, in MareeLand in / the County of Somersett & perticularly to Sixty ffive Hogesheads of Tobaccoe / purchased by my serv^t in Rapahanuck Cap^t PATRICK SIMONS & ZEBENEZAR ROBERTSONE / Captaines & supracargoes For the sd serv^ts. and also upon my acco^t there was Six / sent over the Bay, and Three w^ch went along w^th M^r SOMERVAIL And in & to some / goodes in the sd JOHN SOMERVAILES hand w^ch was sould to M^r ALEX BROWNE in the / sd County of Somersedd And also in & to my ffactorie that I have Formerly given / to FFRAZOR FFOWLER & TENCTEOR, and y^e sd M^r ALEX BROUNE / all deteyned in the fforesd ffactorie Surrogating & substituteing the sd M^r / HUMPHREY SPURRAWAY in my Full right Title & place of y^e p^rmises w^th Full power to / him & his Foresds, to ask Crave & interactt w^th & upLift, the Foresd haill affects Sixty Five / hoggsheads ot Tobaccoe & goods in the sd JOHN SOMERVAILEs hands, and ffactorie / [ ] due to me Compone transact & agree grant acquittances & discharges upon y^e / receipt thereof in haile or in part to grant subscrive & delyver, &

genrally all other / things to doe grant w^ch^ I might have done my selfe before the granting hereof / w^th^ Assignane @ wrine I bind & oblidge me my aeres & Ex^rs^ to warr^tt^ & be good and / sufficient to y^e^ sd M^r^ HUMPERY SPURRAWAY & his foressds From my owne proper Fact & / deed allowably consenting these p^r^nts be insert & regular in the bookes of Councill / & sessione or any other Judges Books Competent therein to remaine For Conservatione / and if need bees that l^rs^ & others needful pass hereupon in Forme as affor and / Constitute my powers by, In Witness hereof I have subscribed these p^r^sents / [ ] be THOMAS WILSONE Servitor to the said ALEXANDER CLARKE att / Edingborough Mer^cht^ the sixteenth day of January [--] and three / yeares before these Witnesses S^r^ WILLIAM MEINZES M^r^chant in Edingbrough

**[398]**

ROBERT BLACKWOOD p^r^sent Bayly of Edinborough WILLIAM BLACKWOOD & HAIRIE BAIRD / M^r^chants there ALEX^R^ J 1703

WILLIAM BLACKWOOD witness

RO: BLACKWOOD witness

W^M^ MEINZEIS witness

HAIRIE BAIRD Witnes

The w^th^in L^tr^ of Attorney was proved in Open Co^rt^ held for the Isle / of Wight County to be the the [*sic*] Act & Deed of HUMPHRY SPURWAY / Aug^t^ the 9^th^ 1703 by the Oaths of Cap^t^ JOHN WRIGHT & M^r^ DAVID / REED & Ordered to be Comitted to Record

Teste CHA CHAPMAN C^l^C^ur^

This Indenture made y^e^ Eighth day of December in y^e^ Year of o^r^ Lord God One Thousand / Seaven hundred & Two & in the First year of y^e^ Reigne of o^r^ Sovereigne Lady, Anne / by y^e^ Grace of God of England Scotland ffrance & Ireland Queen Defender of y^e^ ffaith & / Between MATHEW STRICKLAND of the Isle of Wight County of y^e^ one ꝑte & THOMAS BOON / of the sd County of y^e^ other ꝑte Witnesseth That y^e^ sd MATHEW STRICKLAND For and in / Consideracon, of y^e^ sume of Twelve Thousand pounds of Tob in Cask to him in hand / att & before the sealing & delivery of these p^r^sents, by y^e^ sd THOMAS BOONE well and / truely p^d^ the rec^t^ whereof he y^e^ sd MATHEW STRICKLAND doth hereby acknowledge & / himselfe therew^th^ sattisfied & p^d^ & thereof & of every ꝑte & ꝑcell thereof doth Freely / acquitt Exonerate & discharge, the sd THOMAS BOON his Heires Ex^rs^ & Adm^rs^ For Ever / by these p^r^sents Hath given granted, aliened bargained sould, Enfeoffed, & ConFermed & / by these p^r^sents, doth Fully, clearly & absolutely, Give, grant, bargaine, Sell, alien / Enfeoff & conFerme, unto y^e^ sd THOMAS BOONE his Heires & A*f*s For ever, a ꝑcell or / Tract of Land conteining by Estimacon, Three hundred Acres or thereabouts, scituate / lying & being in the Lower ꝑish of the Isle of Wight County, in Virg^a^, which ꝑcell or / Tract of Land is bounded as Followeth Viz^t^ Begining att y^e^ Mouth of a Swamp called / y^e^ Horse Swamp, Runing out of y^e^ Blackwater, From thence, up y^e^ Run of the said / Blackwater, to y^e^ mouth of y^e^ First

Branch, Thence up y^e^ sd Branch to a m^r^ked popler / A Corner Tree, Thence along A Lyne of m^r^ked Trees A Cross A Branch called the / Gum Branch , To a Pine a Corner Tree Thence along a Line of m^r^ked Trees to a Pine / A Corner Tree, of ARTHUR WHITEHEADs Lyne standing in A Branch, Thence along A / Lyne of m^r^ked Trees, parting y^e^ aforesd ꝑcell of Land & the Land of ARTHUR WHITEHEAD / to y^e^ Foresd Horse Swamp, Thence downe the Runn of the sd Horse Swamp to the / Ferst Station, To Have & to hould y^e^ sd ꝑcell or Tract of Land accordeing to y^e^ Foresaid / bounds w^th^ all & singuler its members Jurisdiccons & appertences, togeather w^th^ all houses / Edifeces buildings, Barnes Stables Orchards Gardens, Yards, backsides Woods Waters pastures / Feedings Meadowes, Swamps marsh or Marsh grounds, Hereditam^ts^ & appertences / whatsoever to y^e^ sd Messuages or Tract of ꝑcell or Land & p^r^mises or to any ꝑte or ꝑcell / of them belonging or in any wise apperteining thereunto, unto y^e^ sd THOMAS BOON / his Heires or A*f*s to y^e^ onely proper use & behoof of y^e^ sd THOMAS BOON his Heires & / assignes

**[399]**
Assignes For Ever, ag^t^ him the sd MATHEW STRICKLAND his Heires & A*f*s & all & every other / ꝑson or ꝑsons whatsoever, lawfully clayming by From or under him them or any / of them shall & will warr^t^ & For ever defend by these p^r^sents, And that y^e^ sd MATHEW / STRICKLAND, For himselfe his heires Ex^rs^ & Adm^rs^ doe Coven^t^ promise grant & agree to & / w^th^ y^e^ sd THOMAS BOONE his Heires & A*f*s & every of them by these p^r^sents, That all & / singuler the aforesd ꝑcell of Land according to y^e^ recited bounds w^th^all thappertences / thereunto belonging, Now be & ever hereafter shall be stand & Continue to y^e^ sd / THOMAS BOONE & his heires & A*f*s For ever, And that y^e^ sd THOMAS BOON his heires / or A*f*s be Freely acquitted Exonerated & discharged & From tyme to tyme well and / sufficiently kept harmeless, By the sd MATHEW STRICKLAND his heires Ex^rs^ or Adm^rs^ / of & From all & all manner of Former & other, Guifts Grants, bargaines Sales, Mortgages / Jointures Dowers, of & From all & singuler other Titles, troubles charges demands and / Incumbrances whatsoever, had made comitted suffered omitted or done by y^e^ sd / sd [*sic*] MATHEW STRICKLAND his Heires or A*f*s, And that y^e^ sd MATHEW STRICKLAND his / heires or A*f*s For & dureing the space of Seaven Yeares next ensueing y^e^ date of / these p^r^nts shall & will & att & upon y^e^ reasonable request & att y^e^ Cost and / charges, in y^e^ Law of the sd THOMAS BOON, his heires or A*f*s make such Further / lawfull & reasonable Assurance or Assurances or Conveyances, on y^e^ Law For / the more better & ꝑfect assurance or assurances, of y^e^ aforesd p^r^mises, as by y^e^ sd / THOMAS BOON his heires or A*f*s, or by his or their Councell learned in y^e^ Law shall / be reasonable devised advised or required, And that y^e^ aforesd p^r^mises w^th^ all the / appertences thereunto belonging, shall be esteemed & adjudged & taken to be / & more to y^e^ onely proper use & behoofe of y^e^ sd THOMAS BOON his heires & A*f*s / For ever & to none other use intent or purpose whatsoever In witness / hereof I have hereunto sett my hand & seal the Day year & Reigne First above / written mark

Signed Sealed & delivered in y$^{e}$ p$^{r}$sence of us whose names are underwritten
WILL JOLLY
JAMES JOLLY
ADAM MURRAY

MATHEW ┌┬┐ STRICKLAND
his

Acknowledged in Open Co$^{rt}$ held For y$^{e}$ Isle Wight County y$^{e}$ 9$^{th}$ of Aug$^{t}$. 1703 by MATHEW STRICKLAND to be his Act & Deed & Ordered to be Recorded
Test CHA CHAPMAN C$^{l}$C$^{ur}$

To all X$^{pian}$ people to whome thes p$^{r}$sent Writeing shall come I THOMAS NOSWORTHY / of Newport Parish in y$^{e}$ County of y$^{e}$ Isle of Wight Send greeting Know yee that I / y$^{e}$ sd THO: NOSWORTHY For diverse good Causes & consideracons me thereunto / moveing have have given granted remised released & For ever quit claymed And / by these p$^{r}$sents For me & my Heires grant Remise Release & For ever quit / clayme unto JOHN GILES & PHILLARITEE his Wife of y$^{e}$ sd Parish & County in / their Full peaceable & quiett possession & Seizen & to their Heires & A*f*s For ever / all

**[400]**
All such Right Estate, Tytle Interest & demand whatsoever w$^{ch}$ I the sd THOMAS NOSWORTHY may / have or hath or w$^{ch}$ my heires Ex$^{rs}$ or Adm$^{rs}$ att any tyme hereafter shall or may have or / Clayme of in or to all y$^{e}$ Lands or Tenem$^{ts}$ or plantacons scituate lying or being in the / parris [*sic*] & County aforesd Conteyning two hundred Acres more or less, the greatest ꝑte of / which lyeth w$^{th}$in a pattent of ffour hundred Acres, granted to JOHN MOON Gent by S$^{r}$ / JOHN HARVY K$^{t}$ then Govern$^{r}$ dated the second day of November, 1638 the other part / called or Knowne by y$^{e}$ name of y$^{e}$ wast Land, the whole being butted as Followeth / Begining att a marked White Oak, standing by WILLIAM HUNTERs CorneFeild in ROBERT / CLARKE Lyne, and From thence Runing West North West along A Lyne of Marked Trees / by the sd THOMAS NOSWORTHY now made, to A Great stooping White Oak w$^{th}$ a Small / Gum tree & groweing out of the Rent thereof they being both antient marked Trees / standing in an antient Lyne of marked Trees, thence North & by East along the said / antient Lyne unto A great White Oak standing att the head of a Branch by THOMAS / OWENs plantacon, an Ould marked Tree, & now now [*sic*] marked, thence From y$^{e}$ said / Oak (Northerly) as the sd Branch Runneth, into the Creek thence downe y$^{e}$ Creek / to a place called Joneses Landing, From thence West along A Lyne of m$^{r}$ked Trees / into a White Oak, an antient Corner Tree Sanding by Nantzimond path Side / on y$^{e}$ West side thereof It being in M$^{r}$ NICHOLAS FFULGHAMs Lyne, From thence / Runing South along an antient Lyne of m$^{r}$ked Trees standing on y$^{e}$ West side of / the aforesd path of Nanzimond unto a Corner Tree in M$^{r}$ RICHARD WILKINSON Jun$^{r}$ / / Lyne From thence runing East & by South along the sd Lyne of m$^{r}$ked Trees unto / an antient marked White Oake, It being a Corner Tree of y$^{e}$ sd ffour hundred / Acres patten, From thence Runing East North East Along A Lyne of m$^{r}$ked / trees unto the First Station, To have & to hould all the sd Land & Tenem$^{ts}$ / accordeing to y$^{e}$ Forerecited bounds, unto the sd JOHN GILES & PHILLARITEE his /

wife ther heires & A*f*s to y[e] onely use & behoofe of sd JOHN GILES & PHILARETE / his Wife their Heires & A*f*s For ever, Soe that neither he y[e] sd THOMAS / NOSWORTHY nor his heires nor any other ꝑson or ꝑsons For him or them or / or [*sic*] in his or their names, or in the name right or stead of any of them, shall / or will by any way or meanes hereafter, Have Clayme Challenge or demand / any Estate, Right Tytle or Interest, of in or to y[e] p[r]mises or any ꝑte or ꝑcell / thereof But From all & every Accon Right Estate Tytle Interest or demand / of in or to y[e] p[r]mises or any ꝑte or ꝑcell thereof, they & either of them, shall / be utterly excluded & barred For ever by these p[r]nts In witness whereof I have / hereunto put my hand & seal this Sixth day of October One Thousand Seaven / hundred & three THO: NORWORTHY Seal

Signed Sealed & delivered in y[e] p[r]sence of us
whose names are underwitten
NICHOLAS FFULGEHAM
ADAM MURRAY
THOMAS OWEN

Acknowledged in Open Co[rt] held For y[e] Isle Wight / County 9[th] Octob[r] 1703 by M[r] THO[S]: NOSWORTHY / to be his Act & Deed & Ordered to be Recorded
Test CHA CHAPMAN C[l]C[ur]

**[401]**

To all X[pian] people to whome these p[r]n[ts] Shall Come be it knowne that I WILLIAM BROWNE / & my Wife of the Lower parrish of the Isle of Wight County, send greeting in o[r] Lord God / Everlasting hereunto, [ ]eed, by A certeyn sume of money reced down in hand, dwoe [*sic*] For, / us or heires Ex[rs] Adm[rs] or A*f*s For ever, doe hereby Confirme, bargaine, alienate make over sell / & deliver all, in o[r] hole rights, Tytle & in trust of a ꝑcell of Land as Followeth to RICHARD / BRACEWELL Jun[r], to him his heires Ex[rs] Adm[rs] or A*f*s For ever, It being ꝑte of a pattent of / One hundred Fifty Six Acres, of Land granted unto WILLIAM BROWNE bearing date y[e] 29[th] / day of Octob[r] in the year of 1702 It being on the South side of y[e] maine Blackwater / in the County & ꝑish aforesd, Wherefore I the sd W[M] BROWNE, me my heires Ex[rs] Adm[rs] or / A*f*s doe warr[t] the Sale of Thirty Five Acres of Land, more or less w[th]in the Foresd pattent to RICHARD / BRACEWELL aforesd, to him his heires Ex[rs] Adm[rs] or A*f*s lying & begining att the Mouth of y[e] / afforesd W[M] BROWNEs Spring Branch, soe runing up the North West Side of the aforesd Spring / Branch, to a Red Oak marked w[th] two Notches, And thence to a small White Oak Sapling, thence / to a Pine marked w[th] three Notches att y[e] aforesd W[M] BROWNEs Side Lyne, all y[e] Land on the / Northwest Side of this aforesd Bounds to the Foresd RICHARD BRACEWELL To have & to hould / to him, his heires Ex[rs] Adm[rs] & A*f*s, w[th] all p[r]viledges & appertences & amedments thereunto berlonging / w[th] ꝑte of all Woods & Waters Lands & Timber Mines & Minerins [*sic*] [ ]olking, hunting, Fowling / & Feshing, w[th] all other Rights, that the land hereby Covenanted shall aford, And Furthermore / I the sd W[M] BROWNE & MARTHA BROWNE doe For o[r] Heires Ex[rs] or A*f*s, stand bounded and / oblidged to keep keep harmless the aforesd RICHARD BRACEWELL, his heires Ex[rs] or A*f*s, to defend & / keep harmless in as Full & ample mannor to all intents & purposes as I my selfe might / or could Enjoy the same by vertue of the Foresd pattent, I doe hearby & my Wife MARTHA / BROWNE, hereunto sett o^r^ hands & seales y^e^ 9^th^ day of Octob^r^ 1703

THOMAS MANDEW — WILLIAM BROWNE Seal

his — her

W^M^ **W** BRACEWELL — MARTHEA ┌┬┐ BROWNE Seal

m^r^ke — m^r^ke

Acknowledged in Open Co^rt^ held For the Isle of Wight County by W^M^ / BROWNE & MARTHEA his Wife the 9^th^ of Octob^r^ 1703 to be their Free & / Voluntary Act & Deed, & Relinquisht of Dower Confer by the / sd MARTHEA & Ordered to be Recorded

Test CHA CHAPMAN C^l^C^ur^

To all X^pian^ people to whome these p^r^nts shall come W^M^ BROWNE & MARTHA his Wife send / greeting in o^r^ L^d^ God Everlasting, Know yee that I y^e^ sd W^M^ BROWNE & MARTHA my Wife of y^e^ County of / y^e^ Isle of Wight For Diverse good causes & consideracons us hereunto moveing, but more especially / For & in consideracon of a certein Sume of Tob to us in hand p^d^ or secured to be p^d^ before the / sealing & delivery hereof, The Rec^t^ whereof Wee doe hereby acknowledge & Confesse Have / given granted, bargained, Sold, aliened, sould Conveyed & Confermed, And doe by these p^r^nts / For us o^r^ Heires Ex^rs^ & Adm^rs^, give grant, bargaine, sell, alien Convey, Enfeoff & confirme, unto / THOMAS BROWNE of y^e^ County of Nanzimond his heires Ex^rs^ Adm^rs^ & A*f*s Ffifty Acres of Land / more or less be it what it will, w^th^in the bounds hereafter menconed, scituated lying & being / in the County of the Isle of Wight & is ꝑte of a pattent of One hundred Fifty Six Acres of / Land granted unto W^M^ BROWN bearing date y^e^ 28^th^ day of Octob^r^ in y^e^ Year of o^r^ L^d^ 1702 / being on y^e^ South side of y^e^ Maine Blackwater Swamp, Begining att y^e^ Mouth of a Branch / called Anthonys Selight Branch, & soe runing up the sd Branch, to A m^r^ked Pine a / Corner tree, thence runing along the Lyne Trees, to a Red Oak saplin A Corner Tree / standing on y^e^ side of a pocoson, called Anthonys Selight Pocoson thence along the / pocoson side to the Ferst Station To have & to hold unto him y^e^ sd THOMAS / BROWNE

**[402]**

BROWNE his heires Ex^rs^ & Adm^rs^ For ever Free & Clear & Freely & Clearly acquitted Exonerated & discharged / of and From all & all manner, of Former & other Suits grants bargaines Sales, Dower Judgem^ts^ / Extents, or Execucons whatsoever, had made done or suffered to be done From or under us or either / of us, And the sd W^M^ BROWNE & MARTHA his Wife doth Further Coven^t^ Promise & grant For us o^r^ / heires Ex^rs^ & Adm^rs^ to & w^th^ the sd THOMAS BROWNE his heires Ex^rs^ & A*f*s to warr^t^ save defend & keep / harmeless the sd THOMAS BROWNE From & ag^t^ any ꝑson or ꝑsons that shall or may lawfully / clayme or p^r^tend to Clayme any right Title or interest to y^e^ sd Land And that y^e^ sd THOMAS / BROWNE & his heires, shall & may From tyme to tyme & att all tymes quietly enjoy the sd Land w$^{th}$ all / proffetts p$^{r}$viledges Comodities & advantages to the same belonging or in any wayes / app$^{r}$teining, w$^{th}$out any the least interrupcon molestacon or Eviccon of us or either of us or / any other ꝑson or ꝑsons whatsoever; In witness whereof wee have hereunto sett o$^{r}$ hands & / seales this 11$^{th}$ Day of Octob$^{r}$ in y$^{e}$ year of o$^{r}$ L God One Thousand seaven hundred & Three

Signed Sealed & ~~dd~~ in y$^{e}$ p$^{r}$sence of us
RICHARD EXUM
ROBERT **R** SIMES [?]

WILLIAM BROWN Seal
MARTHAY ┌┬┐ BROWN Seal
her m$^{r}$k

Enterlined before Signed & sealed

Acknowledged in Open Co$^{rt}$ held For the Isle of Wight County y$^{e}$ 9$^{th}$ of / Octob$^{r}$ 1703 by WILLIAM BROWNE & MARTHA his Wife to be their / Free & Voluntary Act & Deed, and Relinquishm$^{t}$ of Dower Conferred / att y$^{e}$ Barr & Ordered to be Recorded
Test CHA CHAPMAN C$^{l}$C$^{ur}$

This Indenture made y$^{e}$ eighth Day of December Anno Dom 1703 Betweene / RICHD WOOTTEN & LUCY his wife of y$^{e}$ one part, & Majer HENERY BAKER of y$^{e}$ Other part / Wittnesseth, y$^{t}$ y$^{e}$ sd RICHARD WOOTTEN & LUCY his wife for & in Consideration of y$^{e}$ same / of Six Thousand pounds of Tob$^{o}$. in Cask to y$^{m}$. before y$^{e}$ sealing & deliv$^{r}$y of these p$^{r}$sents / By y$^{e}$ sd HENERY BAKER, Well & Truely p$^{d}$, y$^{e}$ Receipt whereof, they y$^{e}$ sd RICHD WOOTTEN / & LUCY his Wife doe Acknowledge, & themselves therewith contented, sattisfied & / p$^{d}$ & thereof doe clearly Acquitt & discharge y$^{e}$ sd HENERY BAKER his heires Ex$^{rs}$, & / Adm$^{rs}$, for Ev$^{r}$. have bargained sold & Confirmd, & by these p$^{r}$sents do alien, bargaine / sell Enfeoff & Confirme unto y$^{e}$ sd HEN: BAKR, his heires & Assgs for Ev$^{r}$. one hundred / & fifty acres of Land, Lying & being in y$^{e}$ Upper ꝑish of y$^{e}$ Isle of Wight County, being / y$^{e}$ Southwardly, & otuwardmost Bounds, of ROB$^{T}$. EALES patten w$^{th}$: all its Right, memb$^{res}$ / Jurisdictions & appurtinances, together w$^{th}$ all Woods, und$^{r}$woods, feedings, wayes, wat$^{rs}$. / proffitts, Commodities & appurtinances, to y$^{e}$ sd premises, or any part or ꝑcell thereof / belonging, or in any wise appertaining, & alsoe all y$^{e}$ Estate, Rights, title, Intrest / use, possession, property, Claime & demand w$^{t}$soever, of them y$^{e}$ sd RICHD WOOTTEN / & LUCY his Wife, of in or to y$^{e}$ same, To have & To Hold y$^{e}$ sd Hundred & fifty acres / of Land and all & singular other y$^{e}$ premises, hereby bargain'd & sold; with their / & every of Rights, members and Appurtenances, whatsoever unto y$^{e}$ sd HENERY / BAKER his heires, & Assignes for Ever. To y$^{e}$ only & behoof of him y$^{e}$ sd HENERY / BAKER his heires & Assgs for Ever, & y$^{e}$ sd RICHD WOOTTEN, & LUCY his wife, for y$^{m}$. selves / & their heires, y$^{e}$ sd hundred & fifty acres of Land and all & singular y$^{e}$ premises / before granted, bargained & sold w$^{th}$ y$^{e}$ appurtinances, unto y$^{e}$ sd HENERY BAKER

**[403]**

His heires and Assgs to y$^{e}$ only proper Use & behoof of him y$^{e}$ sd HEN BAKER / his heires & assgs for ever ag$^{st}$ them y$^{e}$ sd RICHD WOOTTEN & LUCY his Wife their heires & Assgs and / all & ev$^{r}$y person or persons w$^{t}$soever lawfully claiming by from or under them or any of y$^{m}$. or any other ꝑson w$^{t}$soever shall & Will warrant & for Ever defend by these p$^{r}$nts / and further y$^{e}$ sd RICH$^{D}$ WOTTEN & LUCY his wife for themselves their heires, Ex$^{rs}$ & Adm$^{rs}$ doe forev$^{r}$ / promise, grant & agree to & w$^{th}$ y$^{e}$ sd HENERY BAKER, his heires & Assgs, & ev$^{r}$y of y$^{m}$. by these / presents that they y$^{e}$ sd RICH$^{D}$ WOOTTEN & LUCY his wife shall make from time to time and Att all / times hereafter att & upon y$^{e}$ Reasonable request, & att y$^{e}$ Cost & charges in y$^{e}$ Law of y$^{e}$ sd / HENERY BAKER, his heires & Assgs for Ever make or Cause to be made such further / assurance and Assurances, In y$^{e}$ Law for y$^{e}$ further Better & more ꝑfect assurance, surety & / sure makeing & Conveying all & singular y$^{e}$ before hereby granted or mentioned to be granted / premises w$^{th}$ their & every of their Rights memb$^{res}$ & appurtinances unto y$^{e}$ sd HENERY / BAKER, his heires & Assgs or by His or their Councell Learned in y$^{e}$ Laws shall be reason= / =ably devised, advised or required, In Wittness whereof y$^{e}$ parties first abovenamed unto / these p$^{r}$sents Indentures, interchangeably have put their hands & Seales y$^{e}$ day & year / first abovewritten Anno: Dom: 1703

Signed sealed & delivered<br>in y$^{e}$ p$^{r}$sence of us<br>THO: THROPP<br>W$^{M}$. BUTLER

his<br>RICHARD **R** WOOTTEN Seal<br>m$^{r}$ke<br>LUCY **X** WOOTTEN Seale<br>her m$^{r}$ke

Acknowledged in open Co$^{rt}$. held for y$^{e}$ / Isle of Wight County y$^{e}$ 9$^{o}$ ffeb$^{ris}$ 1703 / Teste CHA CHAPMAN C$^{l}$C$^{ur}$

LUCY WOOTTEN did y$^{n}$. Likewise att y$^{e}$ Barr / Relinquish all her Right of Dower to y$^{e}$ land / mentioned in y$^{e}$ aforesd Conveyance Which / was ordred to be Recorded

Test CHA CHAPMAN C$^{l}$C$^{ur}$

To all Christian people to Whome this p$^{r}$sent deed or writeing shall / Come, to be seen I JOHN HALL of y$^{e}$ Low$^{r}$. ꝑish of y$^{e}$ Isle of Wight County / send greeting in o$^{r}$. Lord God Everlasting, Now know yee that I y$^{e}$ said / JOHN HALL for divers, good, Causes me hereunto moveing, more / especially for & In Consideration of y$^{e}$ sume of Three thousand pounds of / good Tob$^{o}$ to me in hand p$^{d}$ before y$^{e}$ ensealing, & deliv$^{r}$y of these p$^{r}$sents, by / JOSEPH BURCK of y$^{e}$ aforesd County y$^{e}$ receipt whereof, I doe acknowledge / & thereof & every part doe fully acquitt & discharge y$^{e}$ sd JOSEPH / BUCK; his heires, Ex$^{rs}$, Adm$^{rs}$. or Assgs for Ev$^{r}$: have bargained, sold, alienated, / Enfeoffed, assigned, confirmed, & sett over, & by these p$^{r}$sents, doe for me, my heires, Ex$^{rs}$ & Adm$^{rs}$. grant, bargaine, sell, alien, Enfeoff assgs & Confirme unto y$^{e}$ sd JOSEPH / BURK, his heires, Ex$^{rs}$, Adm$^{rs}$, & Assgs for Ev$^{r}$. a ꝑcell of Land y$^{t}$ lyes on y$^{e}$ Westside of / Main freshitt being all y$^{e}$ Land y$^{t}$. I have on y$^{e}$ side y$^{e}$ sd Swamp, bounded as / followeth, between y$^{e}$ Swampe & WILL: GREEN, & soe till it meet w$^{th}$. POOL HALLs /

Line, & then along & betweene POOLL HALL & W$^{M}$. GREEN's Line to y$^{e}$ head / Line itt being all y$^{e}$ Land y$^{t}$. I have of y$^{e}$ West side of y$^{e}$ Swamp, called y$^{e}$ Main / freshitt lyeing, & being In y$^{e}$ Isle of Wight County itt being part of a Pattent of / one hundred acres of Land, that my Grandfather THO: POOLL gave me y$^{e}$ sd JN$^{O}$. / HALL

**[404]**

HALL, by & in his Last Will & Testament, being by Estimation forty acres be / itt more or Less, To have & to Hold y$^{e}$ sd parcell of land of forty acres, be / itt more or less, with all itt rights, privildedges proffitts Commodities thereunto / belonging, or in wise appertaining to him y$^{e}$ sd JOSEPH BURK, his heires, Ex$^{rs}$ Adm$^{rs}$ / & Assignes for Ev$^{r}$. in as large & ample manner as I my self might or could / doe, by vertue of any gift deed or writeing whatsoever, & further I y$^{e}$ sd JN$^{O}$ / HALL, doe for my self, my heires, Ex$^{rs}$. Adm$^{rs}$ & Assgs Covenant / promise, & Grant to & w$^{th}$. y$^{e}$ sd JOSEPH BURK, his heires, Ex$^{rs}$, Adm$^{rs}$ & Assgs / & w$^{th}$ every of them by these p$^{r}$sents y$^{t}$. he y$^{e}$ sd JOSEPH BURK his heires, Ex$^{rs}$, / Adm$^{rs}$ & Assgs, shall have, hold, occupy, possess, quietly & peaceably Enjoy / y$^{e}$ sd parcell of Land of forty acres be it more or less, w$^{th}$. all woods, und$^{r}$woods / wayes proffitts, Commodities, priviledges & immunities thereunto belonging / or in any wise appertaining, without y$^{e}$ lett, trouble, molestation or incumbrance / whatsoever, of me y$^{e}$ sd JOHN HALL, my heires, Ex$^{rs}$, Adm$^{rs}$, or any other ꝑson or / ꝑsons whatsoever, y$^{t}$ shall lay any claime, Right, tittle or Interest under me / unto y$^{e}$ sd ꝑcell of Land of forty acres be itt more or less, & I y$^{e}$ sd JOHN HALL / doe hereby, Covenant, for my self, my heires, Ex$^{rs}$, Adm$^{rs}$, & Assgs, to with y$^{e}$ sd / JOSEPH BURK his heires, Ex$^{rs}$, Adm$^{rs}$ & Assgs to warrant, & ever defend y$^{e}$ / heires, Ex$^{rs}$, Adm$^{rs}$, & Assgs against any ꝑson or ꝑsons whatsoever, y$^{t}$ shall / Lay any claime, right, tittle or Interest by or und$^{r}$ me: unto y$^{e}$ sd ꝑcell of / Land of forty acres be itt more or less, & I y$^{e}$ sd JOHN HALL doe promise to / and with, y$^{e}$ sd JOSEPH BURK, his heires &c: y$^{t}$ I y$^{e}$ sd JOHN HALL & ANNE my / Wife shall & will acknowledge this deed in open Co$^{rt}$. next held for this / County to be our free act, & deed. In Wittness whereof; have sett hands, / & seales, this eighty of ffeb$^{rij}$ 170$^{3}$/$_{4}$

Signed, sealed & deliv$^{r}$ed
in y$^{e}$ p$^{r}$sence of of [*sic*]
AR: SMITH
JOHN WATTS

JOHN **I** HALL seal
his m$^{r}$ke
ANNE **X** HALL Seal
her m$^{r}$ke

Acknowledged in open Co$^{rt}$ held for y$^{e}$ / Isle of Wight County y$^{e}$ 9$^{th}$. day ffeb$^{rij}$ 170$^{3}$/$_{4}$ / by JOHN HALL to be his Act & deed & ordered / to be Recorded

Test CHA CHAPMAN C$^{l}$C$^{ur}$

ANNE HALL att y$^{e}$ sd Co$^{rt}$. did appear, & / att y$^{e}$ Barr did Relinquish, all her Right / of Dower to y$^{e}$ land mentioned in y$^{e}$ sd / foresaid Conveyance w$^{ch}$: was ordered to / be Recorded

Test CHA CHAPMAN C$^{l}$C$^{ur}$

**[405]**

To all Christian people to whome this p$^{r}$sent deed or writeing shall come / to be seen I ARTHUR SMITH of y$^{e}$ Isle of Wight County send / Greeting in o$^{r}$. Lord God Everlasting. Now Know yee y$^{t}$. I y$^{e}$ sd ARTHUR SMITH / for divers good causes me hereunto moveing, & more especially for; and in / Consideration of the sume of two thousand five hundred pounds of good / sound Tob$^{o}$: to me in hand, paid before ensealing & delivery of these p$^{r}$sent by / ROB$^{T}$. EDWARDS of y$^{e}$ foresaid County y$^{e}$ receipt whereof I doe hereby acknowledge / & thereof & of ev$^{r}$y part doe fully acquitt & discharge y$^{e}$ sd ROB$^{T}$. EDWARDS, his heires / Adm$^{rs}$, & Assgs for Ever; have granted, bargained, sold, aliened, Enfeoffed, Assigned / Confirmed, & sett over: And by these p$^{r}$sents doe for me my heires, Ex$^{rs}$, Adm$^{rs}$ & / Assgs for Ever, one hundred & fifty Acres of Land lyeing & being in y$^{e}$ Isle of Wight / County, being part of a patten of five hundred acres, grant to me y$^{e}$ sd ARTHUR / SMITH by ord$^{r}$. of Aprill Generall Co$^{rt}$ in year 1702 being relapst by my father / Coll$^{o}$ ARTHUR SMITH being bounded as followeth begining att a forked Small Red / Oake standing hard by a pond in y$^{e}$ N or S Line y$^{t}$. parts this Land, & y$^{t}$ land y$^{t}$ my / father & JOSIAH HARRISON took up from thence Easterly to a spreading topt Pine / & thence y$^{e}$ same Course through y$^{e}$ Pocoson to y$^{e}$ Eastermost line of y$^{e}$ land & / soe Southerly according as y$^{e}$ Line Runns for bright [*sic*] on y$^{e}$ Deviding Line of JAMES / TULLAGHs Land, & this five hundred acres of Land, & from thence across y$^{e}$ Land Mostly / to y$^{e}$ North or South Line y$^{t}$ y$^{e}$ first tree stands in, & thence along y$^{e}$ line North / to y$^{e}$ first station y$^{e}$ sd bounds including one hundred & fifty acres of Land / To have & To hold y$^{e}$ sd one hundred & fifty acres of land with all & singuler / y$^{e}$ woods, houses, proffitts, Comodities, Priviledges immunities thereunto belong= / =ing, or any wise appertaining, to him y$^{e}$ sd ROB$^{T}$. EDWARDS, his heires, Ex$^{rs}$, Adm$^{rs}$ / Assgs for ever in as full & large a manner as I y$^{e}$ sd ARTHUR SMITH could / or might doe by any deed, patten, or any other writeing w$^{t}$soever & further I y$^{e}$ sd / ARTHUR SMITH doe for my self, my heires, Ex$^{rs}$, Adm$^{rs}$, & Assgs Covenant promise / & agree to & With y$^{e}$ sd ROB$^{T}$. EDWARDS, his heires, Ex$^{rs}$, Adm$^{rs}$, & Assgs & every of / them, & by these p$^{r}$sents y$^{t}$. he y$^{e}$ sd ROB$^{T}$. EDWARDS his heires, Ex$^{rs}$ Adm$^{rs}$ & Assgs / shall have, hold, occupy, possess, quietly & peaceably enjoy y$^{e}$ sd one hundred / & fifty acres of land, w$^{th}$. all woods, houses, proffitts, Commodities, priviledges / & Immunities thereunto belonging, or anywise appertaining w$^{th}$out y$^{e}$ lett, / trouble, molestation, or incumbrance whatsoever of me y$^{e}$ sd ARTHUR SMITH / my heires, Ex$^{rs}$, Adm$^{rs}$ or of, or by any other ꝑson or ꝑsons whatsoever ~~of~~ / ~~me ye sd ARTHUR SMITH my heires, Exrs, Admrs~~ w$^{ch}$. shall or may claime any / title or Interest thereunto, or any part thereof, by or under me y$^{e}$ sd ARTHUR / SMITH, my heires, Ex$^{rs}$, Adm$^{rs}$ & Assgs & further, I y$^{e}$ sd ARTHUR SMITH / doe hereby Covenant to & with y$^{e}$ sd ROB$^{T}$. EDWARDS, his heires, Ex$^{rs}$ Adm$^{rs}$ / Assgs y$^{t}$. the sd one hundred, & fifty acres of Land & every part thereof with / all & singular y$^{e}$ premises abovementioned, is y$^{e}$ day of y$^{e}$ date hereof, & att / y$^{e}$ Ensealing & delivering hereof free & clear, & soe shall be & Continue unto / y$^{e}$ sd ROB$^{T}$ EDWARDS, his heires, Ex$^{rs}$, Adm$^{rs}$ & Assgs suficiently freed & clear'd / defended &

kept harmless of & from all former bargaines, sales, gifts, Leases / Joyntures, Mortgages, Deeds, writeings, or Conveyances whatsoever formerly

**[406]**

Made or passed of for or concerning y$^{e}$ aforemenconed premises, & likewise / doe herewith oblige my self, my heires, Ex$^{rs}$, Adm$^{rs}$, to make such farther / assurance in writeing of all & Singular y$^{e}$ abovementioned premises, as he y$^{e}$ sd / ROB$^{T}$ EDWARDS, or his Councell Learned in y$^{e}$ Law shall att any time advise or / devise, & Lastly I doe oblige my selfe & MARY my wife to acknowledge y$^{e}$ above / deed att y$^{e}$ next Co$^{rt}$. to be held for this County In wittness whereof I y$^{e}$ / abovenamed ARTHUR SMITH & MARY my Wife have hereunto sett o$^{r}$ hands & / Seales this 9$^{th}$. day [*sic*] 1703

Signed, sealed & delivered, AR: SMITH O
in y$^{e}$ p$^{r}$sence of MARY SMTIH O
WILLIAM GREEN
THO: SUMMERVELL Acknowledged

Isle of Wight County be itt known p$^{r}$: these p$^{r}$sents y$^{t}$ I MARY SMITH y$^{e}$ wife / ARTH$^{R}$: SMITH: doe hereby constitute appoint and ordaine my Loveing ffreind M$^{r}$. CHA$^{RLS}$: CHAPMAN / to be my lawfull Attorney to Acknowledge all my right title or intrest y$^{t}$ I have to our / hundred and fifty acres of Land y$^{t}$ My husband ARTH$^{R}$: SMITH Sould Unto ROB$^{T}$: EDWARDS and / his heires p$^{r}$: conveyance beareing date w$^{th}$ this p$^{r}$sent Righting and I doe hereby impow$^{r}$: / my Sd Attorney to Acknowledge and relinquish my right of Dowery y$^{t}$ I have to y$^{e}$ aforesd / one hundred and Fifty acres of Land Unto y$^{e}$ aforesd ROB$^{T}$: EDWARDS and his heires Rattyfying / and allowing w$^{t}$: my sd att$^{o}$: doth in as Large and Ample Mann$^{r}$: as If I y$^{e}$ Said MARY SMITH / was there my Self as wittness my hand and Seal this 9$^{th}$ day of ffeb$^{rij}$ 1703

Testis MARY SMITH Seal
WILLIAM GREEN
THOMAS SUMERVELL

Acknowledged in Open Co$^{rt}$: held for Isle of Wight / County y$^{e}$ 9$^{th}$ of ffeb$^{rij}$ 170$^{3}$/$_{4}$ p$^{r}$: Cap$^{t}$: ARTH$^{R}$: SMITH to be / his act and deed and M$^{rs}$: MARY SMITH did likewise / acknowledge y$^{e}$ Same and relinquish her dow$^{r}$: p$^{r}$: M$^{r}$. / CHA$^{RLS}$: CHAPMAN her attorney p$^{r}$: Vertue of a Lett$^{r}$: / of Attorney to him granted

Teste CHA CHAPMAN C$^{l}$C$^{ur}$

**[407]**

Know all men by these p$^{r}$sents that Wee SAM$^{LL}$ BRIDGER & W$^{M}$ BRIDGER / of the Isle of Wight County For & in consideracon of o$^{r}$ love & good Will / wee bear to JN$^{O}$ MACKMIHILL, Have Given granted bargained & sould / and by these p$^{r}$sents doe absolutely give & grant unto him y$^{e}$ sd JOHN / MACKMIHILL his Heires Ex$^{rs}$ Adm$^{rs}$ &c Two hundred Acres of Land / lying & being in a Divident of seaven Thousand Acres, of

Land att / Currawaugh, w[th] all houses Orchards Woods &Waters, w[th] all profitts / & benifitts & priviledges whatsoever unto him the said JOHN / MACKMIHILL his Heires Ex[rs] & Assignes For ever w[th] a Full warranty / From the clayme of all & every pson whatsoever, In Witness whereof / Wee have hereunto sett o[r] hands & Seales the 27[th] day of December / 1701 Anno Dom SAM[LL]: BRIDGER seal
Signed Sealed & delivered ELIZ[A] BRIDGER
in y[e] prsence of us W[M]. BRIDGER Seal
[--] ELIZ A BRIDGER

Wee ELIZ[A] BRIDGER Wife of Coll SAM[LL] BRIDGER & ELIZ[A] BRIDGER Wife of / Cap[t]. W[M] BRIDGER, doe hereby Voluntarily & of o[r] owne Free Will / remise & relinquish, all o[r] right or Dower w[ch] wee may att any / tyme clayme in y[e] Land above Conveyed, Witness o[r] hands & Seales / y[e] day & year abovesd
Sealed & delivered in y[e] ELIZ[A] BRIDGER
p[r]sence HEN: BAKER ELIZ[A] BRIDGER

Ackn[o] in Open Co[rt] held For y[e] Isle Wight County 9[th] / March 170³/₄ by Co[ll] SAM[LL] BRIDGER & Cap[t] WM BRIDGER / and Relinquishm[t] of Dower acknowledged by M[rs] / ELIZ[A] BRIDGER y[e] Wife of Cap[t] W[M] BRIDGER by M[r] CHARLES / CHAPMAN her Attorney by vertue of a power to him / given
M[r] CHARLES CHAPMAN Teste CHA CHAPMAN C[l]C[ur]

I hereby impower you my true & lawfull Attorney to acknowledge / & relinquish my right of Dower, w[ch] may att any tyme be claymed in / a pte or pcell of Land out of Currawaugh pattent being two hundred / Acres to JN[O] MACKMIHILL & his heires For ever accordeing to a Deed / bearing dated y[e] 27[th] day of Sept[r] 1701 Witness my hand this 9[th] day of / March 170³/₄ ELIZ[A]: BRIDGER
Witness HEN: BAKER

**[408]**

This Indenture made y[e] third day of ffeb[rij] One Thousand Seaven hundred & three Between / HENRY PLUMPTON of Nanzimond County of the one part, and FFRANCES BRIDLE of the Isle of / Wight County on y[e] other part Witnesseth, that y[e] sd HENRY PLUMPTON For & in Consideracon / of Four hundred & Fifty pounds of Tob, & Four Bushells of Wheat, w[ch] have been paid / Yearly rent this Twenty Yeares, For w[ch] I the sd HENRY PLUMPTON am Fully paid and / sattisfied before the Insealing & delivery of these p[r]sents, And also that y[e] sd / FFRANCES BRIDLE his Ex[rs] or A*f*s due well & truely pay the same yearly Rent of Four / hundred & Fifty pounds of Tob & Four Bushells of Wheat yearly rent dureing y[e] / naturall life of the sd HENRY PLUMPTON & ISABELL his Wife, and upon y[e] Consideracon / aForesd Reced, & the same to come For o[r] naturall lives, Whereof & Wherew[th] y[e] said / HENRY PLUMPTON doth acknowledge himselfe Hath granted aliened bargained and / confirmed, and by these p[r]sents doth Fully clearly & absolutely, alien, bargaine / & conFirme, unto FFRANCES BRIDLE & MARY his Wife all that Messuage or Tenem$^{t}$ / scituate or being in the Isle of Wight County, now in the tenure or occupacon of / the sd FFRANCES BRIDLE & MARY his Wife, being by estimacon Fifty Acres be y$^{e}$ same / now or less lying & being on the head of the Westerne Branch, begining att a / Branch that is on the North side of ROGER TARLTONs house, & soe runing down / the sd Branch includeing the same to a marked Ash of THOMAS MARKs Lyne / standing in the Swamp soe runing up the Lyne that devides y$^{e}$ sd MARKEs and / PLUMPTON to A Stake, deviding W$^{M}$ SMELLY & the sd PLUMPTON, soe along the / head Line to A marked pokikory being the First station, The aforesd Land and / Tenem$^{t}$. to him the sd FFRANCES BRIDLE & MARY his Wife To have & to hould w$^{th}$ / all houseing, Orchards, Gardens, building & other Hereditam$^{ts}$, to y$^{e}$ same / belonging or apperteining w$^{th}$ these appertences bargained, granted, aliened and / confermed, & every part & parcell thereof, unto the sd FFRANCES BRIDLE & MARY / his Wife, & their Heires & A*f*s For ever, And the sd HENRY PLUMPTON For himselfe / his Heires &c that he the sd HENRY PLUMPTON, For & notwithstanding any Act done / by him, to y$^{e}$ Contrary att y$^{e}$ tyme of the Insealing & delivery of these p$^{r}$sents, is and / standeth lawfully & rightfully seized, Domesne as of Fee Simple in his owne / right & to his owne use, w$^{th}$out any condicon or Limitacon or other use or / trust to alter change or determine, the same estate of & in the said / Messuages, Lands Tenem$^{ts}$ & p$^{r}$mises before menconed, but doe hereby warr$^{t}$ y$^{e}$ / sd Land, as aforesd From all & all manner of ꝑson or ꝑsons whatsoever Clayming / For by or under me my heires Ex$^{rs}$ or A*f*s or any of us, unto y$^{e}$ sd FFRANCES / BRIDLE & MARY his Wife, & their Heires For ever, And For Further ConFirmacon / whereof I doe by these p$^{r}$sents Authorize nominate & appoint, my trusty & / well beloved Freind, JOSEPH MEREDETH, my true & lawfull Attorney For me & in my / name & stead, to my use, to acknowledge this above instrum$^{t}$, or writeing in y$^{e}$ Isle of / Wight County Co$^{rt}$, sattifieing [*sic*] & holding For Firme & Stable all & w$^{t}$soever my sd Attorney / shall doe by vertue of these p$^{r}$sents, as I my selfe were ꝑsonally p$^{r}$sent, As Witness whereof / I have hereunto sett my hand & Fixt my seal y$^{e}$ day & year above written HENRY PLUMPTON seal

Signed Sealed & deliv$^{r}$ed in
y$^{e}$ p$^{r}$sence of
ROBERT SMELLY
JN$^{O}$: **J:H:** HOOKER
m$^{r}$ke

Acknowledged in Open Co$^{rt}$ held for y$^{e}$ Isle Wight County y$^{e}$ 9$^{th}$ March 170$^{3}$/$_{4}$ by M$^{r}$ JOSEPH MERIDETH Attorny for HENRY PLUMPTON / & Ordered to be Recorded
Teste CHA CHAPMAN C$^{l}$C$^{ur}$

**[409]**

Know all men by these p$^{r}$sents that I GEORGE PEIRCE of y$^{e}$ Isle of Wight County w$^{th}$ the Consent of / ANNE my Wife, doe For the love wee bear to o$^{r}$ Grandson W$^{M}$ JONES & o$^{r}$ Coz: ANNE WOOLCE, Give grant / & bequeath unto them A ꝑcell of Land granted to me by pattent in y$^{e}$ year 1701 It being Two / hundred Acres of Land, lyeing & being on A Swamp, upon y$^{e}$ Southside of the Maine / Blackwater Called Seacock Swamp, Wee say to them & their Heires To Have & to Hold / Forever, And For it to be equally divided between them when they see Fitt, The uppermost / part where the plantacon is, to y[e] sd W[M] JONES, & the Lower ꝑte next Blackwater for y[e] sd / WOOLCE, togeather w[th] all its p[r]viledges, thereunto belonging, In as large & ample mannor / as is expressed in the aForesd pattent, And I the sd GEORGE PERICE doe maintaine y[e] sd Guift / ag[t] any that shall lay clayme thereunto, by any p[r]tence of right discending From me / my heires Ex[rs] Adm[rs] & A*f*s. and For the ꝑFormance hereof according to true intent and / meaning of the sd PEIRCE, & alsoe my Wife in ConFermacon of her consent have hereunto / sett o[r] hands & seales this [--]

y[e] m[r]ke of
GEORGE **G** PEERCE Seal
the m[r]ke of
ANNE **A** PEERCE Seal

Testes
CHA CHAPMAN
W[M] BROWNE

Acknowledged in Open Co[rt] held For the Isle / of Wight County 9[th] March 170$^3/_4$ by GEORGE / PEIRCE & ANNE his Wife to be their Act & Deed / & Recorded

ꝑ me CHA CHAPMAN C[l]C[ur]

This Indenture made the Sixth day of March in the second Year of the / Reigne of o[r] Sovereigne Anne of England Scotland ffrance &c Queen &c[a] and in / the year of o[r] Lord God One Thousand Seaven hundred & Four Between MADDISON / STREET of Isle of Wight County in the Collony of Virginia planter of y[e] one ꝑty, / & W[M] HUNTER of the Collony & County aforesd of the other ꝑte Witnesseth that / I the sd MADDISON STREET For divers Causes me hereunto moveing and more / Especially For & in consideracon of the sume of Five Thousand pounds of Tob / to me in hand p[d] before the Ensealing & delivery of these p[r]sents by y[e] sd W[M] / HUNTER, the rec[t] whereof I doe acknowledge, and thereof & of every ꝑte thereof / doe Fully acquitt & Exon[r]ate the sd W[M] HUNTER his Heires Ex[rs] Adm[rs] & A*f*s For ever / Have granted bargained, sould, aliened, Enfeoffed, & Assigned, Confirmed & sett over / and by these p[r]sents doe For me my Heires Ex[rs] & Adm[rs], Grant bargaine, Sell / Enfeoff, A*f*s, Confirme & sett over, unto the sd W[M] HUNTER his Heires, Ex[rs] Adm[rs] / and A*f*s Forever, A Certein Tract or ꝑcell of Land of ffifty Acres be it more or / less lyeing & being in the Isle of Wight County, being the Upper ꝑte of y[e] pattent / of Two hundred Acres, of Land granted to RICHARD MADDISON by an Escheat / bearing date the 16[th] of Aprill Anno Dom 1670 and y[e] pattent bearing date / the Fourteenth day of September, when he made his Composicon, For y[e] paym[t] / of the Fees due thereupon, accordeing to Act of Assembly being bounded as / Followeth, begining att a small pine in y[e] Sandy point Vally, & Running up a Lyne / of marked trees to Nanzemond Road, to a Red Oak Standing Just by y[e] Road / side, & soe runing up the Road to y[e] Creek & soe downe the Creek to y[e] First Station / To have & to hold y[e] sd ꝑcell or Tract of Land of Fifty Acres be it more or less If soe / be there should happen A Survey hereafter, w[ch] should take away any of y[e] ꝑcell or / or [*sic*] Tract of Land, butted, & bounded as afforesd, That he the sd MADDISON STREET his Heirs / Ex[rs]

**[410]**

Ex$^{rs}$ Adm$^{rs}$ Shall make the same good out of any remaining ꝑte of y$^{e}$ Two hundred Acres / of Land adjoyning to the Line of him the sd W$^{M}$ HUNTER) w$^{th}$ all & Singuler Houses Orchards / ffences proffitts Comodities priveledges & Imunities thereunto belonging, or in any wise / apperteyning, to him the sd W$^{M}$ HUNTER his Heires Ex$^{rs}$ Adm$^{rs}$ For ever, in as Full and / ample manner as I my selfe might or could dooe by vertue of any Deed or any other / writeings whatsoever, And Further I the sd MADDISON STREET doe For me my Heires / Ex$^{rs}$ Adm$^{rs}$ & A*fs* Coven$^{t}$ promise & agree to & w$^{th}$ the sd W$^{M}$ HUNTER his Heires Ex$^{rs}$ / Adm$^{rs}$ & A*fs*, shall have & occupy, possess peaceably & quietly enjoy, the sd ꝑcell or / Tract of Land of ffifty Acres, be it more or less, w$^{th}$ all houses Orchards fences, proffitts / Woods, Underwoods, Comodities priveledges, & Imunities thereunto belonging, or in / any wise apperteining, w$^{th}$out the lett trouble or molestacon or incumbraces of / whatosever of me the sd MADDESON STREET My Heires Ex$^{rs}$ Adm$^{rs}$, or A*fs*, or by any / other ꝑson or ꝑsons whatsoever, that shall lay any clayme right, Title, or interest thereunto / or any ꝑte thereof, by or under me the sd MADDESON STREET, my heires Ex$^{rs}$ Adm$^{rs}$ / or Assignes And I the sd MADDISON STREET doe Further Coven$^{t}$ w$^{th}$ him y$^{e}$ sd W$^{M}$ HUNTER / that I my Heires Ex$^{rs}$ & Adm$^{rs}$ shall For ever warr$^{t}$ & defend, the afore menconed Tract, / or ꝑcell of Land butted & bounded as aforesd to him the sd W$^{M}$ HUNTER his heires / Ex$^{rs}$ Adm$^{rs}$ & A*fs* For ever From all ꝑsons claymning, or who hereafter shall Clayme / any right Title or interest in by or From of in or From the abovemenconed Lands / p$^{r}$mises & Further assurance thereof to give (if required) arriseing by the Co[ ] / of him the sd W$^{M}$ HUNTER, his Heires Ex$^{rs}$ Adm$^{rs}$ or Assignes Learned in the Law to / be Devised, or advised thereunto, And Further I the sd MADDESON STREET, my Heires / Ex$^{rs}$ Adm$^{rs}$ of A*fs* doe Coven$^{t}$ & agree to & w$^{th}$ him the sd W$^{M}$ HUNTER his heires Ex$^{rs}$ / Adm$^{rs}$ & A*fs* in Consideracon that he the sd W$^{M}$ HUNTER his Heires Ex$^{rs}$ Adm$^{rs}$ A*fs* / will assist in the repairing of the pasture Fences and the Bridges For y$^{e}$ Cattles / safe goeing into the point of Marsh For their depastureing there. That he y$^{e}$ / sd W$^{M}$ HUNTER his heires Ex$^{rs}$ Adm$^{rs}$ or A*fs* shall have Free priveledge For / their Cattles depasturing there, & other Creatures Subject nevertheless to this p[ ] / that I MADDISON STREET my Heires Ex$^{rs}$ Adm$^{rs}$ or A*fs* shall hould this Marsh / From all ꝑsons Claymeing, or whoe hereafter shall Clayme any Title or right / hereunto sett my hand Seal the day & year & in my Reigne of o$^{r}$ Sovereigne / Lady that now is First above written

Signed Sealed & delivered in the p$^{r}$sence of us — MADDISON STREET seal

JAMES MELVIN<br>signum<br>THOMAS WHITLY<br>RICHARD WILKINSON Ju$^{r}$

Acknowledged in Open Co$^{rt}$ held For the Isle of Wight County 9$^{th}$ March 170$^{3}$/$_{4}$ by MADDISON STREET to be his Free act & Deed And Ordered to be Recorded

Test CHA CHAPMAN C$^{l}$C$^{ur}$

March y[e] 9[th] 170$^3/_4$ And Ordered to be Recorded
Test CHA CHAPMAN C[l]C[ur]

March ye 9[th] 170$^3/_4$

Then delivered by MADDISON STREET possession of y[e] pcell of Land knowne by y[e] name of y[e] King of / all places by Turfe & Twigg to W[M] HUNTER accordeing to the bounds menconed in this / Indenture in the p[r]sence of us

Testes
RICH: WILKINSON
THO **T** WHITLEY his m[r]ke
JN[O] STREET **J** hes mrke

This was indorsed on y[e] Indenture & ackn[o] by MADDISON STREET y[e] same day / in Open Co[rt] & Recorded / by Order
Test CHA CHAPMAN C[l]C[ur]

**[411]**

To all to whome these p[r]nts shall come I FFRANCIS NICHOLSON Esq[r] their Ma[ties] L[t] Govern[r] / of Virginia of Virginia [*sic*] send greeting Whereas his Ma[tie] King Charles y[e] second hath / been gratiously pleased, by his Royall L[res] pattents under y[e] great Seal of England / bearing date att Westm[r] y[e] 10[th] day of October in the Eight & Twentieth year of his / Reigne, amongst other things in y[e] sd L[rs] pattents conteined to continue & conferm / the antient priviledge & power of granting Fifty acres of Land For every person / imported into this Collony of Virginia Now know yee, That I the sd FFRANCIS / NICHOLSON Esq[r] L[t] Gov[r] &c doe w[th] y[e] advice & consent of the Councill of Estate / accordingly Give & grant unto JAMES CURLEE One hundred Eighty Seaven Acres of / Land, lying in Isle of Wight County, beginning att a Stake where A Red Oak [ ] / RIVES Corner Tree Formerly stood, thence by y[e] sd RIVES Line west by South Thirty / Two pole to White Oak, thence North by East, Forty Nine pole to a White Oak, / Thence North Forty Three degrees East One hunder [*sic*] Thirty two pole, to a pine then / South East One hundred Eighty Four pole to a pine, Then Southwest Two hundred / twenty & Five pole, to a pine in sd RIVES Lyne, then along y[e] sd RIVES Lyne of / markt Trees to the First Station, The sd Land being due unto y[e] sd JAMES CURLEE / by & Forty [*sic*] by Importacon of Four persons into this Collony, whose names are in y[e] / Records menconed under this pattent To have & to hould the sd One hundred / Eighty Seaven acres of Land, w[th] his due share of all Mines Mineralls thereon / conteined w[th] all right & priveledges, as Hunting Hawking Fishing & Fowling / w[th] all woods Waters & Rivers, w[th] all proffett Comodities & Hereditam[ts] whatsoever / belonging to y[e] sd Land to him the sd JAMES CURLEE his Heires & A*f*s For ever / in as large & ample manner to all intents & purposes as hath been used and / allowed since the First plantacon To be held of o[r] Sovergien Lord & Lady the / King & Queen their heires & Successo[rs] as of their Manno[r] of East Greenwitch in Free / & Common Soccage & not *in Capite* or by Knights Service Yeilding & payeing unto / o[r] Sd Sovreigne L[d] & Lady the King & Queen their Heires & Successo[rs] For ever For / every Fifty acres of Land hereby granted att the Feast of S[t] Michaell the / Archangell, the Fee Rent of One Shilling w[th] paym[t] is to be made yearly

From / year to year according to his Ma$^{ties}$ instruccons of y$^{e}$ 12$^{th}$ of Sept$^{r}$ 1662 provided / that if the sd JAMES CURLEE his Heires or A*f*s doe not Seat or plant or cause to be / Seated or planted on y$^{e}$ sd Land w$^{th}$in these three yeares next ensueing y$^{e}$ date / hereof, That then it shall & may be Lawfull For any other adventurer or / planter to make Choice thereof & Seat thereon. Given under my hand & Seal / of y$^{e}$ Collony thes 23$^{d}$ day of Octobr 1690 FR: NICHOLSON

Recorded WILLIAM COLE Sec$^{r}$

Indorsed on the Back of y$^{e}$ pattent as Followeth

Underwritten JAMES CURLEE w$^{th}$ consent of my Wife ELIZ$^{A}$ doe a*f*s & make over whole / right Title & interest in y$^{e}$ w$^{th}$in To THOMAS KERBY his heires & A*f*s Witness my / hand this 9$^{th}$ day of ffeb$^{rij}$ 1694

his<br>
JAMES **I** CURLEE<br>
mrke<br>
ELIZ$^{A}$ **&** CURLEE her m$^{r}$ke

Test RICH$^{D}$ **A** BRACEWELL<br>
his m$^{r}$k<br>
his<br>
W$^{M}$ **W** WEST

Ackn$^{o}$ in Open Co$^{rt}$ y$^{e}$ word THO: KIRBY interlined & to be Recorded by JAMES CURLEE & his Wife ELIZ

Test ARTHUR SMYTH Jun$^{r}$ Dep C$^{l}$C$^{ur}$<br>
on y$^{e}$ other side

**[412]**

Isle Wight May the 1$^{st}$ ackn$^{o}$ in open Co$^{rt}$ by y$^{e}$ sd JAMES CURLEE & ELIZ$^{A}$ his Wife / to bee their Free & Voluntary Act & Deed

Test HUGH DAVIS C$^{l}$

Know all men by these p$^{r}$sents that I THOMAS KIRBY w$^{th}$ y$^{e}$ Consent of RUTH my / Wife doe assigne & make over all o$^{r}$ whole right title & interest in the w$^{th}$in pattent / to JOHN UNDERWOOD his heires & A*f*s For ever, Witness my hand this 1$^{st}$ day of Jan$^{rij}$ / 1703

THOMAS KIRBY<br>
her<br>
RUTH **R** KIRBY

Ackn$^{o}$ in Open Co$^{rt}$ held For the Isle Wight County the 10$^{th}$ / day of Aprill 1704 by THOMAS KIRBY & RUTH his Wife to / be their Voluntary Act & Deed & Ordered to be Recorded

Teste CHA CHAPMAN C$^{l}$C$^{ur}$

Know all men by these p$^{r}$nts, That Whereas I the Subscriber hereof W$^{M}$ WILLIAMS / of the Lower parish of y$^{e}$ Isle of Wight County haveing a pattent granted to me by / S[r] FFRANCIS NICHOLSON Esq[r] her ma[ties] L[t] & Govern[r] Gen[r]all of Virginia, For 600 Acres / of Land granted by Pattent bearing date y[e] 28[th] day of October 1702 & in y[e] First / year of o[r] Sov[r]eigne Lady Anne by y[e] grace of God Queen of England Scotland / ffrance & Ireland Defender of y[e] Faith &c Lying & being in y[e] above County of / Isle of Wight, on y[e] South side of Blackwater, Now know yee that I y[e] above said / W[M] WILLIAMS & w[th] the Consent of MARY his Wife doe[th] by these p[r]nts / give grant demise & Fully & absolutely lett & sett over unto THOMAS KERBY of the / abovesd County his heires or A*fs* For ever one ꝑte or ꝑcell of y[e] abovesd Pattent / of Land being by estimacon about 250 acres be it more or less, the sd ꝑte or ꝑcell / of Lande being due to y[e] sd KERBY by agreem[t] in right of paying & disburseing [ ] / proporconable ꝑte of charge & expences in taking up the sd Lands, Lying and / bounding as Followeth, begining att y[e] mouth of y[e] sd W[M] WILLIAMS Spring Branch / where it runneth into y[e] Blackwater Swamp y[e] sd Branch to [ ] / thence by Corse of m[r]ked Trees beareing Southwestwardly to y[e] head Lyne as Followeth / Ferst to a Hickory, thence to a pine in a pond, then to a Red Oak on y[e] South Side / of the sd Pond, thence to a Pine, thence to a Red Oak, thence to a White Oake / Thence to a Red Oak, thence to a pine by Boones Branch thence to y[e] head Lyne / see along y[e] sd Lyne to a Gum marked w[th] three Notches on A side a Corner tree / standing in the naturall bounds, Soe by a Lyne of m[r]ked Trees bearing Northwestwardly / to y[e] First Station, To have & to hold the aforesd parcell or Tract of Land, according / to the aforesd Bounds, w[th] all & singuler its members & Jurisdiccons & appertences, / togeather thereunto belonging, w[th] all houses Edifices buildings, w[th] all Woods Waters / & pastures, Feedings Meadowes: Swamps Marsh, or Marsh grounds hereditam[ts] / appertences, thereunto belonging to the sd Messuage or tract or parcell of Land or / Lands & p[r]mises or to any part or ꝑcell of y[m] belonging or in any wayes apꝑteining / thereunto unto [*sic*] y[e] sd THOMAS KERBY his heires or a*fs* to y[e] onely proper use and / behoof of the sd THOMAS KERBY his heires & A*fs* For ever ag[t] him the said / WILLIAM

**[413]**
W[M]. WILLIAMS his heires Ex[rs] Adm[rs] & A*fs* & all & every ꝑson or ꝑsons whatsoever lawfully / clayming by From or under him them or any of them, shall & Forever will warrant, & / defend by these p[r]sents, and that y[e] sd W[M] WILLIAMS doth For himselfe his heires Ex[rs] / & Adm[rs] doe Covent promise grant & agree, to & w[th] the sd THOMAS KERBY by his heires & / A*fs*, & every of y[m] by these p[r]nts, that all & singuler the aforesd parcell of Land according / to the aforesd recited bounds, w[th] all the apꝑtences thereunto belonging, now be & For / ever shall be stand & continue unto y[e] sd THOMAS KERBY his heires & A*fs* For ever / And that y[e] sd THOMAS KERBY his heires & A*fs* to be Freely acquitted Exonerated and / discharged, and From tyme to tyme well & sufficieably [*sic*] kept harmless by the said / W[M] WILLIAMS his heires Ex[rs] & Adm[rs], and From all & all manner, troubles charges demands / & incumbrances, w[t]soever of any ꝑson or ꝑsons, claymin [*sic*] or to clayme by From or / under him y[e] sd W[M] WILLIAMS, his heires Ex[rs] Adm[rs] & a*fs*, and that y[e] Foresd Land and / p[r]mises w[th] all its rights &

Jurisdiccons & appertences doe & be and For ever hereafter / shall be, stand good & Indure to him the sd KERBY his heires & A*f*s For ever In / confirmacon whereof wee have hereutno sett o[r] hands & seales this 10[th] day / of Aprill in the year of o[r] Lord God 1704

Signed Sealed & delivered in the p[r]esnce of us
JOHN WILLIAMS
NICHOLAS WILLIAMS
JOHN **B** BARNES
his m[r]ke

WILLIAM WILLIAMS Sigill
**M**
MARY WILLIAMS Sigill

Acknowledged in Open Co[rt] held For y[e] Isle of Wight / County y[e] 10[th] of Aprill 1704 by W[M] WILLIAMS and / MARY his Wife to be their Free & Voluntary Act / & deed & Ordered to be Recorded
Dower Relinquished by the sd MARY, att the Barr / after Examinacon of her Free consent

Teste CHA CHAPMAN C[l]C[ur]

To all to whome this Deed Indented of Bargaine & Sale shall come Know yee y[t] I WILLIAM / WILLIAMS of Isle of Wight County For & in consideracon of y[e] Just quantity of ffive Thousand / pounds of good sound M[r]chantable Tob & Cask to me in hand p[d] or / otherwise well and / sufficiently secured to be p[d] by NICHOLAS WILLIAMS, of the same County w[th] w[ch] I acknowledge / my selfe Fully sattisfied contented & p[d]. Have granted bargained sold aliened Enfeoffed & / confirmed and doe by these p[r]sents For me my heires Ex[rs] & Adm[rs] For ever Grant bargaine / sell Aliene Enfeoff & Confirme unto NICHOLAS WILLIAMS his heires Ex[rs] Adm[rs] & A*f*s A / certein Tract or ꝑcell of Land, conteining by Estimacon One hundred Acres / more or less scituate lyeing & being on the Southside of the Blackwater Swamp Beginning / att a Gum att y[e] / side of y[e] Run, w[ch] is a Corner Tree of JN[O] WILLIAMS Lyne, & soe running / up his Lyne to y[e] head Lyne of y[e] pattent & soe running along, y[e] sd Lyne to a Meadow / Branch, & soe runing downe the sd Branch, to A Black Oak standing by y[e] Branch / side, & soe runing downe a Lyne of m[r]ked tree to a Gum, w[ch] stands by y[e] Run side / w[ch] is made a Corner Tree, of y[e] natturall bounds of y[e] sd pattent, & soe running the / Run to y[e] Sd begining Gum To have & to

**[414]**
Hould y[e] sd hundred Acres of Land, togeather w[th] all houses Outhouses, Gardens Orchards / Woods, Underwoods, Waies Watercourses Easm[ts] proffitts, Comodities, & apꝑtences, / whatsoever, thereunto belonging or therew[th] comonly held occupied & enjoyed, to him / the sd JOHN BARNES & his Heires, to y[e] onely proper use, & behoof of him the said JOHN / BARNES his Heires & A*f*s For ever. And I the sd WILLIAM WILLIAMS doe hereby Oblidge my / selfe my heires Ex[rs] Adm[rs] to warr[t] & defend this my sale, of all & singuler the before / recited p[r]mises, w[th] their appertences to the sd

JOHN BARNES his Heires & A*f*s For ever, / ag^t^ me my heires & A*f*s, or From any ꝑson or ꝑsons claymeing lawfully by From or / under me, my heires Ex^rs^ Adm^rs^ & A*f*s, as alsoe to acknowledge thes p^r^sent instrum^t^ to be / my reall act & deed att y^e^ next Co^rt^ to be held For y^e^ Isle of Wight County afforesaid / In Witness, whereof I have hereunto putt my hand & Seal This Tenth day of Aprill / Anno Dom: 1704

Signed Sealed & delivered in y^e^ p^r^sence of<br>JOHN WILLIAMS<br>RICHARD WILLIAMS<br>JOHN UNDERWOOD

W^M^ WILLIAMS<br>**M** seal<br>MARY WILLIAMS

Acknowledged in Open Co^rt^ held For y^e^ Isle Wight County / y^e^ 10^th^ Aprill 1704 by W^M^ WILLIAMS & MARY his Wife to be / their Free Act & Deed, And the sd Dower, w^ch^ is Ordered to be Recorded

Test CHA CHAPMAN C^l^C^ur^

To all to whome this Deed Indented, of Bargaine & Sale shall come Know yee y^t^ I / WILLIAM WILLIAMS, of Isle Wight County For & in consideracon of y^e^ Just quantity of [ ] / Thousand / pounds of good sound M^r^chantable Tob & cask, to me in hand p^d^ or otherwise well and / sufficiently secured, by JOHN WILLIAMS of y^e^ sd County, w^th^ w^ch^ I acknowledge my selfe Fully / sattisfied, contented & p^d^., have granted bargained sold aliened Enfeoffed & confirmed and doe / by these p^r^sents For me, my heires Ex^rs^ & Adm^rs^ For ever Grant bargaine sell aliene Enfeoff & / confirme, unto JOHN WILLIAMS, his heires Ex^rs^ Adm^rs^ & A*f*s a certein Tract or ꝑcell of Land / conteining One hundred & twenty Five Acres of Land, be it more or less scituate lyeing & / being on y^e^ South side of Blackwater Swamp, beginning upon the Upper [ ] of Notaway / Swamp, Att a marked corner Tree of JN^O^ BARNES, being a Gum, standing by y^e^ Runn side / From thence up y^e^ deviding lyne to a Pine, standing by the side of a Branch From / thence up y^e^ sd Branch to a Pine tree standing in y^e^ Branch being a Corner Tree, up to / a lyne of m^r^ked Trees, to y^e^ pattent Lyne, & soe according to pattent to a marked Red Oake / being made a Corner Tree of y^e^ divideing Lyne between JN^O^ WILLIAMS & NIC WILLIAMS / from thence downe a Line of marked Trees to a Gum standing in y^e^ Run of a Branch / soe downe y^e^ Branch to a Gum, soe downe a lyne of m^r^ked Trees to a Gum Standing / in Notaway Swamp, by y^e^ Run side being a Corner Tree, from thence downe y^e^ Runn to / a Gum being a Corner Tree standing in y^e^ side of y^e^ Runn, being a corner Tree betwixt JN^O^ / BARNES & JN^O^ WILLIAMS To have & to hold y^e^ sd Hundred & Twenty Five acres of Land / togeather, w^th^ all houses Gardens Orchards Woods Waies, Watercourses Easm^t^ proffitts / Comodities & appertences whatsoever thereunto belonging or therew^th^ conveniently held / Occupied

**[415]**

Occupied & enjoyed, to him y^e^ sd JOHN WILLIAMS & his heires, to the onely proper use & behoof of / him y^e^ said JOHN WILLIAMS his heires & Ass For ever, And I the sd

W$^{M}$ WILLIAMS, doe hereby oblidge / my selfe my heires & Ex$^{rs}$ or Adm$^{rs}$ / to warr$^{t}$ & defend this my sale of all & singuler the beforecited / p$^{r}$mises, w$^{th}$ their appertences to y$^{e}$ sd JOHN WILLIAMS his heires & A*fs* For ever, ag$^{t}$ me my / heires Ex$^{rs}$ Adm$^{rs}$ & Ass From any ꝑson or ꝑsons clayming lawfully by From or under me my heirs / Ex$^{rs}$ Adm$^{rs}$ & A*fs*, as alsoe to acknowledge this p$^{r}$sent Instrumt be my reall act & Deed, att y$^{e}$ / next Co$^{rt}$ to be held For the Isle of Wight County aForesd In witness whereof I have hereunto / putt my hand & Seal / this Tenth day of Aprill Anno Dom: 1704

Signed Sealed & delivered in p$^{r}$sence of us
JOHN **B** BARNES
his m$^{r}$ke
RICHARD WILLIAMS
NICHOLAS WILLIAMS

WILLIAM WILLIAMS
**M** seal
MARY WILLIAMS

Ackn$^{o}$ in Open Co$^{rt}$ held For y$^{e}$ Isle of Wight County y$^{e}$ 10$^{th}$ Aprill / 1704 by W$^{M}$ WILLIAMS & MARY his Wife to be their Free Act / & Deed, and the sd MARY haveing been examined of her / voluntary consent by the Co$^{rt}$ relinquished her right of / Dower w$^{ch}$ is Ordered to be Recorded
Teste CHA CHAPMAN C$^{l}$C$^{ur}$

To all to whome this Deed Indented of Bargaine & Sale shall come Know yee y$^{t}$ I WILLIAM / WILLIAMS of Isle of Wight County For & in consideracon of y$^{e}$ Just quantity of ffive Thousand / pounds of good sound M$^{r}$chantable Tob & Cask to me in hand p$^{d}$ or / otherwise well and / sufficiently secured to be p$^{d}$ by NICHOLAS WILLIAMS, of the same County w$^{th}$ w$^{ch}$ I acknowledge / my selfe Fully sattisfied contented & p$^{d}$. Have granted bargained sold aliened Enfeoffed & / confirmed and doe by these p$^{r}$sents For me my heires Ex$^{rs}$ & Adm$^{rs}$ For ever Grant bargaine / sell Aliene Enfeoff & Confirme unto NICHOLAS WILLIAMS his heires Ex$^{rs}$ Adm$^{rs}$ & A*fs* A / certein Tract or ꝑcell of Land, conteining by Estimacon One hundred & Tenne Acres / more or less scituate lyeing & being on the Southside of the Blackwater Swamp Beginning / att a Gum att y$^{e}$ / side of y$^{e}$ Run, w$^{ch}$ is a Corner Tree of JN$^{O}$ WILLIAMS Lyne, & soe running / up his Lyne to y$^{e}$ head Lyne of y$^{e}$ pattent & soe running along, y$^{e}$ sd Lyne to a Meadow / Branch, & soe runing downe the sd Branch, to A Black Oak standing by y$^{e}$ Branch / side, & soe runing downe a Lyne of m$^{r}$ked tree to a Gum, w$^{ch}$ stands by y$^{e}$ Run side / w$^{ch}$ is made a Corner Tree, of y$^{e}$ natturall bounds of y$^{e}$ sd pattent, & soe running the / Run to y$^{e}$ Sd begining Gum To have & to hold the said Hundred & Tenn Acres of / Land, togeather / w$^{th}$ all Houses, & Gardens Woods & Underwoods, wayes, Water courses / Easm$^{t}$ proffitts Comodities & appertences whatsoever thereunto belonging or / therew$^{th}$ conveniently held occupied & enjoyed to him the said NICHOLAS WILLIAMS / & his heires to the onely proper use & behoof of him y$^{e}$ said NICHOLAS WILLIAMS his heires / & A*fs* For ever And I y$^{e}$ sd W$^{M}$ WILLIAMS doe hereby oblidge my selfe my heires & Ex$^{rs}$ or Adm$^{rs}$ / to warr$^{t}$ & defend this my sale of all & singuler the aboverecited p$^{r}$mises w$^{th}$ ther appertences / to y$^{e}$ sd NICHOLAS /

WILLIAMS his heires & A*f*s For ever, ag[t] me my heires Ex[rs] Adm[rs] and / A*f*s as alsoe to acknowledge this p[r]sent Instant be my reall act & Deed att y[e] next / Co[rt] to be held For the Isle of Wight County aForesd In witness whereunto I my hand & Seal / y[e] 10[th] of Aprill Anno Dom: 1704

Signed Sealed and delivered
in the presence of
THO: KIRBY
RICH[D] WILLIAMS
JOHN WILLIAMS

W[M] WILLIAMS
**M** Seal
MARY WILLIAMS

Acknowledged in Open Co[rt] held For y[e] Isle of Wight 10[th] Aprill 1704 by / W[M] WILLIAMS & MARY his Wife to be their Free act & Deed and / Dower relinquished att y[e] Barr & Ordered to be Recorded

Teste CHA CHAPMAN C[l]C[ur]

**[416]**

To all to whome this Deed indented of Bargaine & Sale shall come Know yee that I W[M] / WILLIAMS of Isle of Wight County, For & in consideracon of y[e] Just quantity of ffive / Thousand pounds of good sound M[r]chantable Tobacco & Cask to me in hand p[d]. or / otherwise well & sufficiently secured to be p[d] have granted by RICHARD WILLIAMS of the / same County, by w[ch] I acknowledge my selfe Fully sattisfied conted & paid have / granted, bargained, sould, aliened, Enfeoffed, & confirmed, and doe by these p[r]sents For / me my heires Ex[rs] & Adm[rs] For ever, Grant, bargaine, sell, Alien Enfeoff, & Confirme / unto RICHARD WILLIAMS his heires Ex[rs] Adm[rs] & A*f*s A certein Tract of ꝑcell of Land / conteining by Estimacon One hundred & Thirty acres more or less scituate lyeing & / being on the south side of the Blackwater Swamp Beginning att a Hickory att the / side of a Swamp the Run by m[r]ked [*sic*], soe running up y[e] Run at the sd Swamp to a Cyprus in y[e] / sd Run of the Swamp a Corner Tree soe along a Course of marked Trees, to a Lyne / of y[e] pattent southwesterly soe along the Lyne accordeing to pattent, to the said / Hickory To have & to hould the said Hundred & Thirty Acres of Land togeather / with all Houses, & Gardens, Orchards, & Woods, Underwoods, wayes, Water courses / Easm[ts], proffitts, Comodities, & appertences whatsoever, thereunto belonging or / therewith comonly held, occupied, & enjoyed, to him the said RICHARD WILLIAMS & / his heires, to the onely proper use & behoof of him the said RICHARD WILLIAMS / his heires & Assignes For ever, And I the said WILLIAM WILLIAMS doe hereby / oblidge my selfe my heires & Ex[rs] or Adm[rs] to warr[t] & defend this my sale of all / & singuler, the beforerecited prmises w[th] their appertences to the said RICHARD / WILLIAMS his heires & Assignes For ever, ag[t] me me [*sic*] my heires Ex[rs] and Assignes / of From any person or persons clayming lawfully by From or under me my / heires, Ex[rs] Adm[rs] & Assignes, as alsoe to acknowledge this p[r]sent Instrument / be my reall Act & Deed att the next Co[rt] to be held For the Isle of Wight / County aforesaid In witness whereunto I sett my hand & Seal this Tenth day / of Aprill Anno Dom: 1704

Signed Sealed and delivered

W[M] WILLIAMS

in the presence of us **M** Seal
[--] MARY WILLIAMS

Acknowledged in open Co[rt] held for the Isle of / Wight County the 10[th] day of Aprill 1704 / by WILLIAM WILLIAMS & MARY his Wife to be / their Free & Voluntary Act & Deed, And the said / MARY haveing been examined by the Court of / her Free consent. Acknowledged her Relinquishm[t] / of Dower in the said Land which was Ordered / to be Recorded

Teste CHA CHAPMAN C[l]C[ur]

**[417]**

This Indenture made the Third day of Aprill in the Year of o[r] Lord One Thousand / seaven hundred & Four, and in the third year of the Reigne of o[r] Sovereigne Lady / Anne by the Grace of God, Queen of England, Scotland ffrance & Ireland, Defender / of the faith &c Betweeen WILLIAM WILLIAMS of the Isle of Wight County of y[e] one / part, and THOMAS BOONE of the same County of the other part Witnesseth / that for & consideracon of the sume of Six Thousand pounds of Tob in Cask to / him the said WILLIAM WILLIAMS in hand att & before the sealing & delivery of these / p[r]sents, by the s[d] THOMAS BOON well & truely p[d], the receipt whereof he the said / WILLIAM WILLIAMS doth hereby acknowledge and himselfe therew[th] Fully sattisfied and / paid, and thereof and every part & parcell thereof doth clearly acquit Exonerate and / discharge the said THOMAS his Heires Ex[rs] & Adm[rs]. For ever, By these p[r]sents hath / given, granted, bargained, aliened, Sould, Enfeoffed & confirmed And by these / p[r]sents, doth fully clearly, & absolutely, Give grant, bargaine, Sell, Alien, Enfeoffe & / Confirme, unto the s[d] THOMAS BOONE, his heires & A[s]s For ever, a Parcell or Tract / of Land conteining by Estimacon, One hundred & Fifty Acres, it being more or less / scituate lying & being in the Lower Parrish of the Isle of Wight County in Virginia / on the South side of the Blackwater Swamp. It being part of a pattent of Six hundred / Acres of Land bearing date the 28[th] day of October in the year of o[r] Lord One Thousand / Seaven hundred & Two, granted unto the said WILLIAM WILLIAMS, of w[ch] part or parcell of / Land & conveyed by him the sd W[M] WILLIAMS To him the sd THOMAS BOONE Is bounded as / Followeth, (Viz[t]) Begining att a Live Oak Standing on the side of the Blackwater swamp / afores[d], It being a Corner Tree of THOMAS KERBYs Land, From thence along a Lyne of m[r]ked / trees, parting this Land & KERBYs Land, to a Gum a Corner Tree of the s[d] KERBYs Land / standing in the head lyne of the afores[d] pattent, in a Branch From thence downe the s[d] / Branch or natturall bounds to y[e] maine Runn of the s[d] Blackwater Swamp, thence / downe the s[d] Runn of the Blackwater Swamp to y[e] ferst menconed live Oak To have / And to hould, the Fores[d] parcell or Tract of Land according to y[e] Fores[d] Bounds, with / all & Singuler its members Jurisdiccons, & appertences, Togeather w[th] all houses / Edifices, & buildings, w[th] all Woods, Waters, pastures, Feedings, Meadows, Swamps / Marsh or marsh grounds, hereditam[ts], & appertences whatsoever, to the s[d] Messuage or / Tract or parcell of Land or lands, & premises, or to any part or parcell of y$^{m}$ belonging / or in any wise apperteining thereunto, unto the said THOMAS BOONE his Heires &c / to y$^{e}$ onely proper use & behoof of the s$^{d}$ THOMAS BOONE, his heires & a$^{s}$s Forever, ag$^{t}$ / him the s$^{d}$ WILLIAM WILLIAMS, his heires Ex$^{rs}$ Adm$^{rs}$ & A$^{s}$s. and all & every other person or / persons, whatsoever, lawfully clayming, by From or under him them or any of them / shall & For ever will warr$^{t}$ & defend by these p$^{r}$sents, And that the s$^{d}$ WILLIAM WILLIAMS / For himselfe his heires Ex$^{rs}$ & Adm$^{rs}$ doe Coevn$^{t}$. promise grant & agree to and w$^{th}$ the s$^{d}$ / THOMAS BOONE, his heires & A$^{s}$s & every of y$^{m}$ by these p$^{r}$sents that all & Singuler the / afores$^{d}$ parcell of Land according to the Forerecited bounds w$^{th}$ all thappertences / thereunto belonging, now be & ever hereafter shall be stand & continue to the s$^{d}$ / THOMAS BOONE & his heires &c For ever, And that the s$^{d}$ THOMAS BOONE his heires &c / be Freely acquittted Exonerated & discharged, & From tyme to tyme well & sufficiently / kept harmeless, by the s$^{d}$ WILLIAM WILLIAMS his heires Ex$^{rs}$ & Adm$^{rs}$, of & From all & / all manner of troubles charges demands & incumbrances whatsoever of any / person or persons lawfully clayming or to clayme by From or under him the / said WILLIAM WILLIAMS his heires &c and that y$^{e}$ Fores$^{d}$ Land & p$^{r}$mises wth all / Its

**[418]**
Its Rights & pertinances, now be & For ever hereafter shall be, stand good & Enure to him / the s$^{d}$ THOMAS BOON his Heires & A$^{s}$s Forever, And I the said WILLIAM WILLIAMS doe / Further promise, or reasonable request to bring MARY my Wife to the next Co$^{rt}$ held For / this County, there w$^{th}$ me to acknowledge this above specified writeing, to be o$^{r}$ lawfull / Act & Deed, In witness whereof I have hereunto sett my hand & Seal, this day Year / and Reigne abovewritten

WILLIAM WILLIAMS
**W** Seal
MARY WILLIAMS

Signed Sealed & delivered in the p$^{r}$sence of us
RICHARD WILLIAMS
JOHN UNDERWOOD
JOHN WILLIAMS

Acknowledged in Open Co$^{rt}$ held For the Isle Wigtht County / 10$^{th}$ Aprill 1704 by WILLIAM WILLIAMS & MARY his Wife / to be their Free & Voluntary Act & Deed, and the s$^{d}$ / MARY haveinge been examined by the Co$^{rt}$ of her Free / consent relinquished her right of Dower, w$^{ch}$ is / Ordered to be Recorded

Test CHA CHAPMAN C$^{l}$C$^{ur}$

Know all men by these p$^{r}$sents, that I THOMAS BLAKE of the Upper Parrish of y$^{e}$ Isle / of Wight County in Virginia, For & in consideracon of naturall love & affeccon, y$^{t}$ I bear / to my Sonne WILLIAM BLAKE, & MARY his Wife, and For diverse other good, Causes and / Consideracons hereunto moveing have given granted aliened, Enfeoffed & confirmed / And doe For me my heires Ex$^{rs}$ & Adm$^{rs}$ Fully Freely & absolutely give grant alien / Enfoeff & confirme, unto my s$^{d}$ Sonne W$^{M}$ BLAKE &

MARY his Wife, and the heires / of their bodys lawfully begotten, For ever, One tract or parcell of Land to contein / One hundred Acres scituate lyeing & being in the Upper Parrish of the Isle of / Wight County, and bounded as followeth (viz[t]) begining att a small White Oak A / Corner Tree, of a parcell of Land formerly belonging to me y[e] s[d] THOMAS BLAKE / & sould to JOHN PRIME and running From thence For length Northerly along a Line / of marked trees, w[ch] parteth my Land & THOMAS TOOKES, along the s[d] Lyne to y[e] & [ ] out / of my Bounds, and For breadth along PRIMEs, North West Lyne To have & to hold the s[d] Land & every part & parcell thereof, to him the s[d] W[M] BLAKE & MARY his Wife & / the heires of their bodys lawfully begotten For ever, And the s[d] THOMAS doth Further / Covent & agree to & w[th] the s[d] W[M] BLAKE & MARY his Wife their heires &c that the said / Land is Free From all & all manner of Former Guifts, grants, bargaines, Sales, Joyntures / Dowers, Tytles of Dower, and other troubles, & Incumbrances whatsoever, And that y[e] / said THOMAS BLAKE, has an undoubted & underfeazable Estate of Inheritance in ffee / of in & to all & Singular the p[r]mises abovegranted, and the same ag[t] all & all manner / of persons, shall & will warr[t] & defend by these p[r]sents, And the s[d] THOMAS BLAKE doth / Further oblidge himselfe, to acknowlege thes my Deed of Guift att the next Co[rt] to be / held For this County, Witness my hand & Seal this 10[th] day of Aprill 1704

Testes | y[e] m[r]ke of **TB** THOMAS BLAKE Seal
THOMAS TOOKE
JOHN SMITH

Ackn[o] in Open Co[rt] held For y[e] Isle of / Wight County by THOMAS BLAKE to be his reall / Act & Deed & Ordered to be Recorded Aprill y[e] 10[th] 1704

Test CHA CHAPMAN C[l]C[ur]

Turne Over

**[419]**

I ALICE BLAKE Wife of THOMAS BLAKE doe hereby relinquish all my Right & Title / of Dower, that I have or ought to have, to all & singuler the p[r]mises afore given, to / the s[d] W[M] BLAKE & MARY his Wife to uses w[th]in menconed, and doe obledge my selfe to / acknowledge this my relinquishm[t] of Dower att y[e] next Co[rt] to be held For this / County Witness my hand & Seal this Tenth day of Aprill Anno Dom 1704

Test | The m[r]ke **AB** of ALICE BLAKE Seal
THOMAS TOOKE
JOHN SMITH

Ackn[o] in Open Co[rt] held For y[e] Isle Wight County y[e] 10[th] / Aprill 1704 by ALICE BLAKE & Ordered to be Recorded

Test CHA CHAPMAN C[l]C[ur]

Surry County S[C]

Depositions taken by vertue of a *Dedimus potestatem*, granted by / L[t] Co[ll] SAM[LL] BRIDGER returnable to y[e] Isle Wight County Co[rt] in a Suit / there depending between PETER DEBERRY pl[t] & W[M] THOMAS defd[t] in a / 2 Plea in *Ejecione Firmae*

MARY y[e] Wife of Mr SAM[ELL] THOMPSON aged 41 yeares or thereabouts / Sworne & Examined saith:

That shee this Depon[t] was well acquainted w[th] MARTHA SPILTIMBER, the reputed / Daughter of ANTHONY SPILTIMBER & Wife of ROB[T] HOUSE Jun[r] w[ch] s[d] MARTHA about / Twenty yeares since or upwards, very much importuned the depon[t] to be / Godmother to a Daughter w[ch] she this depon[t] supposed was borne of her body / by the sd ROB[T] HOUSE, att whose request shee this depon[t] did stand For her and / accordingly gave her y[e] name of MARY by w[ch] name she hath ever since been / Knowne, & now is the Wife of THOMAS CARRELL & Further sayth not.

7[th] June 1704 MARY THOMPSON
Sworne & examined before
A[R] ALLEN
SAM[LL] THOMPSON

Surry County / JANE PLOW aged 74 yeares or thereabouts Sworne / & Examined saith: / That shee this depon[t] very well knew MARY HARRIS afterwards y[e] Wife of ANTHONY / SPILTIMBER who had Issue one Daughter called MARTHA w[ch] sd MARTHA intermarried / w[th] ROBERT HOUSE Jun[r] and by assistance of y[e] depon[t] (w[th] others) was delivered of / a Daughter, afterwards named MARY now the wife of THOMAS CARROLL & Further saith not. JANE **O** PLOW sign[u]

7[th] June 1704
Sworne & Examined before us
A[R] ALLEN
SAM[LL] THOMPSON

**[420]**

Surry County / ELLINOR the wife of JOHN HICKES aged 46 yeares or thereabouts / Sworne & Examined saith:

That shee this Depon[t] well knew MARTHA SPILTIMER y[e] reputed Daughter of ANTHONY / SPILTIMBER the wife of ROBERT HOUSE Jun[r], w[ch] sd MARTHA by the sd ROBERT had Issue / one Daughter named MARY now the wife of THOMAS CARROLL, att whose Birth this Depon[t] was / p[r]sent & assisting & Further saith not

7[th] June 1704 ELLINOR HICKS
Sworne & Examined before us
A[R] ALLEN
SAM[LL] THOMPSON

Recorded ꝑ CH[A] CHAPMAN C[l] C[ur]

To all Christian people to whome thes p^r^sent writeing Shall Come, that MARKE / ALESBURY of Nansemond County sendeth greeting in o^r^ Lord God everlasting Know that I y^e^ / s^d^ MARKE ALESBURY, have bargained & sould & For ever made sale unto THOMAS PAGE Sen^r^ / of the Isle of Wight County, One ꝑcell of Land conteining One hundred & Seaventy Acres / more or less lying upon the South side of Currawock Swamp begining att y^e^ maine Run / & soe Runing up the Spring Branch Joining upon ROB^T^ CARRs Lyne, From thence to A / markt Tree, & From thence straight to the head Lyne, & soe along the head Lyne to / a Corner Tree, standing in THOMAS MANNs Lyne, and soe along that Lyne to y^e^ Maine / Swamp & From thence to y^e^ Ferst Station, Which s^d^ Land I the s^d^ ALESBURY, For a / valluable consideracon already in hand reced, doth acknowledge to have sould unto / y^e^ s^d^ PAGE & his heires For ever, From me my heires Ex^rs^ adm^rs^ quietly & peaceably to Enjoy / the s^d^ Land w^th^ all proffitts: prviledges, Hereditam^ts^, Emolum^ts^ w^t^soever, thereunto belonging / w^th^out any Suits, letts or troubles or disturbances, as may or shall arrise by me my heirs / or any other ꝑson or ꝑsons w^t^soevr that shall lay any clayme, Title or interest, to the s^d^ / Land farthermore, I the s^d^ ALESBURY doth bind my selfe my Heires Ex^rs^ Adm^rs^ & A^s^s, For to / warr^t^ & Insure the sale of the s^d^ Land, From tyme to tyme & attt all times, to the said / PAGE & his Heires For ever, In witness whereof I the s^d^ ALESBURY have hereutno sett / my hand & Seal, this Twenty Sixth day of ffeb^rij^ in the year of o^r^ Lord God One Thousand / Seaven hundred & ¾

Assigned Sealed & ddd<br>in y^e^ presents of us<br>WILLIAM PARKER<br>JOHN GAY<br>MARY **m** PARKER

MARKE **M** ALESBURY Seal<br>his mark

Acknowledged in Open Co^rt^ held For y^e^ Isle of Wight / County June y^e^ 9^th^ 1704 by MARKE ALESBURY to / to be his reall Act & Deed & Ordered to be / Recorded

Teste CHA CHAPMAN C^l^C^ur^

**[421]**

Know all men by these prsents, that I THOMAS MANDEW of the Lower Parish of the / Isle of Wight County For & in Consideracon of 322 pounds of tobaccoe, to me / already in hand p^d^ before the Sealing hereof by PETER PARKER of y^e^ Western Branch / of Nansemond County have bargained & Sould, and doe by these p^r^sents For me my / heires For ever, bargaine sell & deliver Enfeoff & Confirme to the s^d^ PETER PARKER / his heires & a^s^s For ever a Certeine ꝑcell of Land Conteining One hundred Acres / more or less being scituated & lying on the South side of the Maine Blackwater / River It being part of a pattent of Three hundred & ninety Acres to me granted the / 28^th^ of October 1702 Begining att a m^r^ked Hickory standing in or near y^e^ Lyne / From thence to a marked Gum, a Lyne tree of the pattent, and soe along y^e^ s^d^ Lyne / to a marked White oake: a

Corner Tree of y^e pattent, standing by y^e side of a Branch called the / Indian Feild Branch, & soe downe y^e s^d Branch to the Swamp & soe alon [*sic*] y^e various / Courses of y^e Run of y^e Swamp, to a m^rked Gum, standing in the side of the Runn, and / From thence, by a Lyne of marked Trees to the Ferst station, the s^d Land being bounded / upon Nottoway Swamp, To have & to hould, the s^d Land w^th his due share, of all / mines & Mineralls, therein conteyning w^th all rights & p^rviledges of hunting hawking / Fishing & Fowling, w^th all Woods Waters, & Rivers & all other proffitts & Comodities / w^tsoever, to y^e s^d Land belonging or in any wise apperteining, to him y^e s^d PETER PARKER / his heires & A^ss For ever, in as Full & ample manner to all intents & purposes, As I my / selfe might or Could enjoy the same by the vertue of y^e afores^d pattent, I doe hereby / oblidge my selfe my heires Ex^rs & Assignes, to warr^t & defend this my Sale, ag^t all / & all manner of persons whatsoever, to acknowledge this my Deed, in Open Co^rt / held For the Isle of Wight County, and if thereto required, to give the s^d PETER / PARKER his heires or Assignes, such Further Lawfull assurance, as by his Councell / Learned in Law, shall be thought Fitt, In Witness whereof I putt my hand / & Seal

his m^rke

W^M C CAHN — THOMAS MANDEW Seal

JACOB -|-|- LEWIS

Acknowledged in Open Co^rt For the Isle / of Wight County June y^e 9^th 1704 by / THOMAS MANDEW to be his Reall / Act & Deed & Ordered to be / recorded

Test CHA CHAPMAN C^lC^ur

**[422]**

Know all mnen by these p^rsents that I SUSANNAH SKELTON, of the Upper parrish of Isle of Wight / County Widdow, for & in Consideracon: of that naturall love & affeccon w^ch I bear unto my Two / Children JAMES & WILLIAM have hereby Freely given & granted, and doe by these p^rsents / freely give & grant, unto Them my sd Children four Thousand pounds of good sound / M^rchantable tobaccoe, w^ch I hereby promise to pay to them, when they shall severally attaine / to y^e age of Fourteen yeares or be Capable of choosing their Guardians, but in Case that / either of them dye before they attaine their severall ages of fourteen yeares, that then / the sd Tobaccoe to remaine & be to me my Ex^rs adm^rs or a^ss but if it should happen that / one of my sd Children should survive the other, that then his share that dyes, shall remain / & be to y^e Surviv^r of my sd Children, I alsoe for the Consideracon above menconed, doe / Freely give & grant unto my daughter SARAH a ffeatherbed & Furniture w^ch I promise to / deliver to my sd Child when she comes to the age of One & Twenty yeares or is married / w^ch shall Ferst happen and in Case my Daughter shall dye before Shee Comes to y^e age / aforesd or before marriage that then such Daughters proporcon shall remaine & be / to me my Ex^rs & adm^rs In witness whereof I have hereunto sett my hand this Ninth / day of June 1704

SUSANNAH S SKELTON
her mark

Acknowledged in Open Co[rt] held for y[e] Isle of / Wight County June y[e] 9[th] 1704 by M[rs] / SUSANAH SKELTON to be her free & Voluntary / Act & Guift and Ordered to be Recorded

Test CHA CHAPMAN C[l]C[ur]

To all people to whome these p[r]sents shall Come know yee y[t] I W[M] BODDY of y[e] Isle of Wight County / in Virg[a] have bargained & sold & doe by these p[r]sents acknowledge w[th] y[e] free Consent of ELIZ[A]: BODDY / my wife to have bargained sold & deliv[r]ed unto GEORGE WILLIAMS of y[e] fores[d] County for y[e] Con= / =sideracon of six thousand pounds of Tob & Cask in hand paid by y[e] s[d] GEORGE WILLIAMS a pcell of / Land by Estimacon one hundred acres (more or less) lyeing & being in y[e] foresd County & on y[e] / North East side of y[e] Western branch side swamp & near unto y[e] head Thereof & where JAMES / BRAGG now dwelleth: And y[e] fores[d] tract or pcell of Land is bounded thus = The first marked / tree is a white oake as Corner tree m[r]ked two wayes, & standing on y[e] South west side of the / great pocoson & in a skirt thereof had by a pond; from thence sttraight to a white oake a / former m[r]ked tree standing by y[e] old horsepath; from thence straight down to a m[r]ked Pine, / thence to a m[r]ked red oake a former m[r]ked tree standing on a branch side, parting this land & / y[e] plantation JOSHUA TURNER now dwelleth upon: thence downe y[e] run of y[e] sd branch, to a marked / poplar standing near, in y[e] side of y[e] sd Branch; and near to y[e] side of y[e] sd Western branch Swampe / y[nce] from y[e] foresd Poplar down y[e] run of y[e] sd Branch, to y[e] maine Run of y[e] foresd Western / Branch Swamp: thence up y[e] maine Run of y[e] Western Branch Swampe, soe farr as to y[e] mouth of y[e] / Western Branch meadow Runn: thence up y[e] sd Meadow Runn, oposite ag[t] a form[r] m[r]ked red / Oake: y[nce] to y[e] sd m[r]ked red Oake standing close, on y[e] foresd Meadow Side from thence / straight along

**[423]**

Straight along a line of m[r]ked trees to a former m[r]ked Red oake standing on y[e] side of a / branch & near y[e] mouth thereof w[ch]: branch parteth this land & y[e] land belonging to y[e] plantation W[M] / ARRINGTON now dwelleth on: thence up y[e] run of y[e] sd Branch soe farr as to a m[r]ked Red oake a former m[r]ked / tree, & standing close on y[e] side of y[e] sd Branch by y[e] side of y[e] Old horsepath: from thence straight / by or near y[e] foresd Branch, about two hundred yards or thereabouts toward y[e] great pocoson side / to a m[r]ked white oake a Corner Tree m[r]ked two wayes: & then from this last menconed white oake / a Corner tree, straight by or near y[e] great pocoson side to y[e] first station: or first menconed m[r]ked / white Oake. To have, & To Hold y[e] foresd tract, or pcell of Land together w[th] all houces / Edifices, orchards, gardens, woods, underwoods, waters, marshes, marsh grounds, pastures, fencings / proffitts, priviledges & appartinances thereunto belonging, to him y[e] foresd GEORGE WILLIAMS, his heires, / Ex[rs] Adm[rs] & A[s]s: for Ever. And I y[e] foresd W[M] BODDY, doe for my self, my heires, Ex[rs] Admn[rs] & As[sg]s / Covent & agree to & w[th] y[e] foresd GEORGE WILLIAMS, hee his heires Ex[rs] Adm[rs] & As[sg]s y[t] I y[e] foresd / W[M] BODDY, will for my self, my heires, Ex[rs] Adm[rs] & A[si]gs for Ever hereafter warrant

& defend / him y$^{e}$ foresd GEO: WILLIAMS, he, his heires &c in y$^{e}$ peaceable & quiett possession of y$^{e}$ ꝑmises / w$^{th}$ y$^{e}$ appurtinances free & clear from any Lawfull Claime, molestation or disturbance / from me y$^{e}$ foresd W$^{M}$ BODDY, my self, my heires, Ex$^{rs}$ Adm$^{rs}$ & As$^{sg}$s to him y$^{e}$ foresaid GEORGE / WILLIAMS, his heires, &c for Ever or from any ꝑson or ꝑsons Lawfull claiming / or to claime by, from or under me, y$^{m}$, any or either of y$^{m}$ & I y$^{e}$ foresd W$^{M}$ BODDY & together / doe w$^{th}$ ELIZ$^{A}$: BODDY my wife freely acknowledge this p$^{r}$sent Conveyance to be our voluntary / Act & deed; And to y$^{e}$ true ꝑformance of all y$^{e}$ ꝑmises here beforemenconed we doe here= / -unto sett o$^{r}$ hands & seales this 25$^{th}$ day of June Anno dom 1697

WILLIAM BODDIE Seal
ELIZA + BODDY seal
signum

Acknowledged in open Co$^{rt}$ held / for y$^{e}$ Isle of Wight County y$^{e}$ 9$^{th}$ / day of Aug$^{st}$ 1697 by M$^{r}$ W$^{M}$ BODDY / to be his act & deed & by vertue of an / Order of y$^{e}$ 9$^{th}$ June 1698 Recorded

ꝑ CHA$^{R}$ CHAPMAN C$^{l}$C$^{ur}$

Att a Co$^{rt}$ helden for y$^{e}$ Isle of Wight County Aug$^{st}$ y$^{e}$ 9$^{th}$ 1697 / by M$^{rs}$ ELIZ$^{A}$: BODDY came into Co$^{rt}$ & relinquished her right of / Dower w$^{ch}$ was ordered to be Recorded & by vertue of / an ord$^{r}$ of y$^{e}$ 9$^{th}$ of June 1689

Recorded / ꝑ CHA CHAPMAN C$^{l}$C$^{ur}$

## Name Index

Proper names are indexed according to the page numbers and in the beginning (the original grantor index) in letters, in bars, of the original document. Numbers at the bottom of the page (of this *book*) have not been used as guides, only as pagination for the table of contents. Names may appear more than once on a page. An effort has been made to index females by their maiden and married names, and to distinguish males by their relationships to other persons or by their titles. The following items have not been indexed:

[1] Deities, names of monarchs and the countries over which they preside, or saints.

[2] Any information contained in the introduction

[3] Maiden names of most women which were not revealed by information from this text.

[4] Names beginning with "ff-" as such; they are indexed under "F."

A word of explanation: where I have distinguished between, for instance, John Smith, Sr., and John Smith, Jr., there will be a time (within the temporal scope of the transcribed text) at which John Smith, Jr., will acquire his father's title. Therefore, not all the persons indexed as John Smith, Sr., are the same person. In the same way, persons with military titles ascended the ladder of success, supposedly; Lt. Colonels and Colonels as titles may refer to the same persons.

**NO LAST NAME**
Charles, 330

**AARON/ARON**
Ann, 82-83,212-213

**ADAMS**
Elizabeth (--), 37
Gilbert, a,37

**ADKINS**
James, 36

**ALESBURY**
(--), a
Marke, 420

**ALLEN**
(--), p
(--) [Major], 57,68
Arthur, a,19-20,37,44-45,48,76,94,116,
127,151-152,195246a,298,
300-301,327,356,381,419-420
Henry, p,66a,166,193-194
Katherine (--), 382
James, 50,74-75,181
Mary [d/o Mary (--) Powell], 66a

**ALTMAN**
(--), a,d
Elizabeth, 84
John, 62,120
Thomas, 62

**ANDROS**
Edmond [Gov.], 151,258-259,265,270, 278-279,287,289,318,333

**APPLEWHAITE**
(--), a,d,m,p
Henry [Capt.], 13,39,43,52,124-126, 179,190-191,250-251,264,268, 274,292-295,315,316,335,346, 385
Henry, Jr., 52,255,373-374
Thomas, 202,315
William, 316

**ARCHER**
George, 97
William, 113,125,142-143,161,176

**ARRINGTON**
(--), a
Elizabeth (--), 392
William, 374,392,423

**ARTHER**
(--), j,w

**ASHELLEY**
John, 150

**ASKEW**
(--), a
Bridget (--), 13
John, 131-132,220
Nicholas, 131-132
Sarah (--), 132

**ASTENG**
Samuel, 23

**ATKISSON/ADCHISON**
John, 200
James, 32,145

**BACON/BACKON**
Anne (--) Bacon [m2 Mathews], 48
James, m,48
Nathaniel, 23,32
William, 394

**BAGNAL/BAGNALL**
(--), d
James, 14,62,204-205,217,219,350
Mary (--), 205

**BAIRD**
Harrie, 395,398

**BAKER**
(--), b,l-m,s,w
(--) [wife of], b
Henry, b,w,1,13,34-35,66,69,90,97-101, 128,153,160,186,208-209,221, 244,246a,264,269,325-326, 345,402-403,407
Mary (--), 99-101

**BALDWIN/BALDING**
(--), b
Benjamin, 265
Elizabeth (--), 59
William, 58-59,158,268

**BALLARD**
Robert, 162

**BARAN/BARON**
(--), b
James, 108-110

**BARDEN/BARDING/BARDIN**
John, 190,347

**BAREFOOT**
Noah, 192

**BARLOW**
George, 145,268,294-295

**BARNES/BARNS**
(--), w
Diana, 366
Jacob, 56,84,208
James, 40,364,366-367
John, m,40,413-415
Sarah, 366

**BARNFIELD**
(--), b
William, 66

**BARR**
Edmund, 255

**BARRETT**
John, 312

**BARTLETT**
William, Sr., 334

**BASS**
Charles, 227

**BATEMAN**
(--), b
Christopher, 118

**BATLER**
(--), r

**BATLEY**
John, 333

**BAYNTON**
(--), b
Elizabeth (Bourchier), 104
Peter, 104-105,150-153,352

**BEAL/BEALLE/BEEL**
(--), b,l
Benjamin, f,n,41,144,174,322-323,357, 359-360
Benjamin, Sr., 205
Benjamin, Jr., 22,210
Martha (--), 22
Mary [m Luther], 80,88,172-173,322-323
Mary (--), 174,229
Richard, 25,172-173,210,229

**BEAMIS**
James, 69

**BECKETT**
Charles, 366

**BEIGHTON/BYTON/ BUIGHTON**
Lucie, 2-4
Richard, 2-4
Rosamund, 2-4

**BELANGE/BELLANCE/ BALLANGE**
(--), b-c
Eve, 212-214

**BELL**
(--), b
John, v,59,66,113,316-317

**BENBRIDGE/BEMBRIDGE**
Thomas, 25,220

**BENN/BEN/BINNS/BENNE**
(--), e,h
George, 361-362
James, p,24-25,28,35,37-39,43,51,63, 83,110,118,126-127,133,213,

217,219,241,361-362
Thomas, 11

**BENNETT**
(--), b
Ambrose, 43,80,172,174,258
James, 27,29
Richard, 292,295
Richard, Sr., 268,292
Richard, Jr., 268,292
Silvestra [m Hill], 24,335

**BENSON**
James, 215

**BERKLEY**
William [Gov.], 15,21-22,30,104,151, 225-226,230-231,285,328-330, 379

**BEST**
Christopher, 147,272
Henry, 393
John, 148
Martha (Hill), 148-149
Mary (--), 147
Peter, b,147
Peter, Jr., 147
Thomas, 147
William, 147

**BETTEN**
Daniel, Sr., 219

**BEVAN/BEVANS/BIVEN**
Thomas, b,h,w,19-20,144,158,368-370

**BLACKWOOD**
Robert, 395,398
William, 395,398

**BLAKE**
(--), b
Alice (--) [wife of Thos.], b,364,419
Mary (--), 418-419
Thomas, b,44,298,300,327,362-364, 418-419
William, b,418-419

**BLUNT**
(--), c
Richard, 158,267
Richard, Sr., 267
Richard, Jr., 267
Susan (--), 158

**BOAZMAN/BOOZMAN**
(--), h
Elizabeth, 97 275
Henry
Mary (--) [m2 Hooker], 222
Ralph, 222

**BODDIE/BODY**
(--), a-b
(--) [wife of Wm], b
Elizabeth (--), 21,65,111-112,422-423
Mary (--), 366-367,373-374,393-394
William, b,21,64-65,87,111-112,190, 232,281,305,364-367,373-374, 392-394,422-423

**BOND**
(--) [Maj.], 41-42

**BONFELL**
George, 23

**BOONE**
(--), s
Nicholas, 95
Thomas, w,182,398-399,417-418

**BOOTH**

(--), b,49
Elizabeth (--), 169-170
Richard, 26,48,53-54,169-170,218,304

**BOSEMAN**
Ralph, 30

**BOSSE**
(--) [Capt.], 192

**BOTTUST**
John, 25

**BOURCHIER**
Elizabeth [m Baynton], 104

**BOURNE**
Owen, b

**BOYKIN**
(--), a
Edward, a,32,45,381-382

**BRACEWELL/BROISEWELL/ BRASELL**
(--), 258
Richard, b,103,262,411
Richard, Jr., 401
Robert, 202,351
Robert [Rev.], 21,204,238
Susanna (--), 202
William, 401

**BRADLEY/BRADLY**
Henry, 78,139,253,312
Richard, 275

**BRADSHAW**
Elizabeth (--), 173,178
William, 25,128,132,144,173,205,210

**BRAGG**
(--), b,e
James, e,250-251,274,346,373-374,394, 422

**BRANCH/BRANSH**
Anne, b,11-12
Anne (--), 10
Anthony, 5,66a,222
Francis, b,2-5
George, b,2-8,10-12
John, b,2-5,11-12,145
Katherine (--), 12
Sarah (--), 12
Susannah (--), b,2-8,12

**BRANTLEY**
Edward, b,44,298-300,327,395
John, 114,145,395
Phillip, 43,308,314

**BRASHUR**
Mary, 197

**BREAD**
Anne, 49
Richard, 66

**BREED**
Richard, b

**BRESSY/BRESSIE/BRACY**
(--), 280
Hugh, 281,373-374
Susannah (--), b,347-348
William, 52,199,373-374

**BRETT**
John, p,277-278,349,383-384
Susannah (--), 277-278

**BREWER**
John, Sr., 16

John, Jr., 16
Thomas, b,16

**BRIAN** [ses **BRYAN**]

**BRIDGER**
(--) [Col.], b,77,120,358
Elizabeth (--), 407
Hester (Pitt), b,127,160-161,276
Joseph, r,229,238-241-242,250,252, 271,276,301,323,375-377
Samuel, 69,162,407,419
William, 191,382,407

**BRIDLE/BRIDDLE**
Francis/Franses, b,6,23,66a,166,194, 206,379,408
Mary (--), 23,408

**BRIGGS/BRIGS**
Edward, 186-187
James, 99,145,186-187,268
Richard, 186

**BRITT**
John, b,s,27,198

**BROCK**
(--), s
Robert, m,67,244,255,261,281-282,349

**BROMFIELD**
John, 30

**BRONSDON**
Robert, b,9

**BROOKHOUSE**
William, 246

**BROWNE/BROWN/BROUN**
Alexander, 397
Edward, 127,186,208,241,346
Elizabell, 182
James, 15,130
John, b,14,22,31,33-35,40,94-95,99, 101,114,187,332,364
John, Sr., 33,187
[ ]11, 66
Martha (--), 401-402
Mary (--), 33-35,187
Thomas, b,60,401-402
William, b,169,192,310,314,324,401-402,409

**BRUCE**
Abraham, 83,213
Walter, 83,213

**BRYAN/BRIAN/BRYON**
Edmund, 122
Edward, 123,246a,248
James, 24,50,74
John, 16-17, 288
John, Sr., 17
Lewis, b,g,16-17

**BUCK**
Joseph, h

**BUCKNELL**
(--), b
Samuell, 55

**BULLARD**
Henry, 253

**BULLMANT**
(--), 220

**BULLOCK**
Mary (--), 167
Thomas, 167,194

**BUNKLEY/BUNCLY**
(--) [d/o Jno], 182
(--) [wife of Jno], 182
John, 58,182

**BURCK**
Joseph, 403-404

**BURNE/BURN/BOURNE**
(--), c
Hannah (--), 351
Owen, 262-263,351

**BURNELL/BURNIELL**
(--), 308
John, 230

**BURNETT**
John, d,25

**BURROWS**
(--), b
Phillip, 310

**BURNELL**
Ellis [m Shipley], 23
John, 23

**BURWELL**
Lewis, 180-181

**BUSH**
Martha (--), 39
William, j,39-40,48-49,122-123

**BUTLER**
(--), m
Dorothy, 88
John, 80,255,257,323
William, 235,309-310,403

**CAHAN/CAHN**
John, 54
William, 421

**CAMPBELL**
(--), c,j,t,w,110
Hugh, c,15,19,57-58,62,66,79,94,110-111,160,162,187,253,258-260,262-263,280,351
John, c,l,15,57
William, c

**CARR**
Robert, 420

**CARRELL**
(--), b
John, 200-201
John, Jr., 59
Mary (House), 419
Thomas, 419

**CARTER**
(--), c
Elizabeth, 245
George, 324
Magdalen (Moore), 324
Thomas, 145,324
Will, 79

**CARVER**
(--), c
Jane (Moore), 46-47,89,319
William, c,46-47,57,89,318-320

**CASEY/KASEY/SCASIE**
(--), b-c,r
Anne (--), 82-83,212-213
Nicholas, b,h,16,64-65,81-83,111-112,141,178,211-213,219,226,231,316,393

**CAUFFIELD**

Elizabeth, 158-159
James, 295

**CAVENOE**
John, 233

**CHAMBER/CHAMBERS**
(--), c
Rosamond (--), 94,114,116
William, 92,94,114-117

**CHAMPION**
(--), c
Edward, 202
John, 268

**CHAPMAN**
Ann, 348
Charles, 105,138,149,153,167,183,187, 192,206,209,212,214-216,218, 220,222,224,226-229,231-233, 235-236,238-239,241-244,246-246a,249-253,255,257,260-261,263-271,273-280,282-283, 287,289,291-295,297-298,301, 303-305,307,309,312-315,317, 319-320,322-324,327-328,330-336,338-340,342-343,345,347-352,354-355,357,360,362,364, 366-369,371,373-374,377,379-386,388-392,394-395,398-404, 406-410,412-416,418-423
John, 260,267,310,357,386
Joseph, 315,357,391

**CHESNUTT**
Alexander, 51

**CHESTER**
(--), 81,211

**CHICHLEY**
Henry [Gov.], 36-37,49,234-235,254

**CHILTON**
E., 6

**CHITTY/CHITTEE**
Edward, 27,58,294,317,379
Margery, 27

**CLARKE**
Alexander, 395-397
John, 4,28,63,69,144,165,186,210
Thomas, 1,82,211,391
William, 400

**CLERKE**
(--), h
(--) [Lt.], 397
Mary (--), 370-372
Richard, 336
Thomas, c,264,268
William, 370-372

**C(--)LTON**
Edword, 125

**COB/COBB**
(--), 86
Ann (--), 90,306
Dorothy (--), 42-43,298
Edward, c,41-43,158,296-298
Elizabeth [m Hutchins], 85,90-92
Elizabeth (--), 90
Joseph, Sr., 85,90
Joseph, Jr., 85,90
Nicholas, c,37,42,44,296-297
Nicholas, Sr., 41
Nicholas, Jr., 41
Pharoah, c,8-9,86,90-91,306

**COCKRELL**
Edward, 66

**CODIN**
(--) [Mr.], g
Mary (--) Greene, 17
Phillip, c,17

**COGAN/COGGON**
John, 39,275
John, Sr., 185

**COHOON**
(--), d
Samuel, 112,128-130,160,167,170-171

**COKER**
(--), 285

**COLE**
Alexander, 10
Bethiall (Hill), c.10
William, 40,50,74,77,103,299,411

**COLEMAN/COLLMAN**
(--), c,51,188-189
Robert, 87,111,118,127,144,163,167,
182

**COLLINS/COLLINGS**
James, 278
John, 145
John, Sr., 58,200
John, Jr., 58

**COOK/COOKE/COOCK**
(--), 329
(--) [wife of Thos.], c
Elizabeth, 164
Jane/Joane (--), 2-4,136,378
John, 280
Mary (Jones), 383-384
Thomas, c,383-384
William, 2-4,81,135-136,199,377

**COOPER**
(--), s
Julian "Indian," 269
Thomas, 289

**COOPES**
Elizabeth (Powell), 193
John, 193

**COPELAND/COPLAND**
(--) [Mr.], 178
Joseph, 222

**COREN**
Joseph, 197

**CORLE/CORLEY**
(--), c
Elizabeth (--), 103
James, 103

**COTTON**
(--), m
John, 333

**COUNCELL/COWNCELL**
Hodges, c,k,w,30,45-46,78,139,218,
303,358
Hodges, Jr., 26,40-41,139
John, 310,342-343
Lucy (--), 45

**COX**
James, 9-10

**CRAINE**
John, 106

**CRANAGE**
(--), 108

**CRAWFORD**
Hugh, 224

**CREWES**
(--), c
John, 206,264,267

**CRIPPS/CRIPS**
George, 7,10-11,44,327

**CROAKER**
Henry, 142

**CROWE**
John, 296

**CRUMPLER/CRUMPLAR/ CRUMPLER/CRUMPLOE**
(--), w
Elizabeth (--), 320
William, c,h,31,46-47,183-184,304-305,319-320,346,389-309

**CULPEPPER**
Thomas, Lord, 104

**CULLY/SKULLY**
Cornelius, c,43

**CURLEY/CURLEE**
(--), m
Eliza (--), 411-412
James, 121-123,411-412

**CURTIS**
Francis, 60

**CUTCHIN**
Thomas, b,373-374

**DAILE**
Thomas, 289

**DANIELL**
William, 12

**DARDEN**
Jacob, d,h,48,102,233,381

**DARKE**
John, b

**DASHWOOD**
Samuel, 395

**DAVIS**
(--), 4,7,312
(--) [wife of], m
Anthony, 21
Francis, d,26,120-121
Hugh, d,50-52,54-60,62-63,65-66a,68-71,73-76,78-84,87-90,92,94-95,99,101-103,105-107,110-114,116-118,120-133,138,162,197,211-213,215,218,221-222,224,243,378,412
John, 32,36,54,79,145,160,168,176,195,222,267,294,330-331
Sarah (Mann), 26,120-121
Thomas, 110
William, 183-184

**DAWSON/DARSON**
(--), d
Henry, 64,235,393
John, 393
Martha (--), 235-236,393
Martin, 393

**DAY**
(--), 335
James, 13,18,39,153,158-159,222,225
John, 244

**DEBERRY**
(--), d
Peter, 294-295,313,419

**DELK**
John, 125

**DENSON**
Frances (--) [widow], 159,208,210
James, 159,206,208,379
John, 379
William, 137,184

**DICKSON**
Mary (Phillips), 269

**DINFORD**
James, 125

**DOLL/DOLE**
John, s,32,379
Thomas, 379

**DORMAN**
Jenkin, 304-305,351

**DOUGHTIE**
(--), d,e
Elizabeth (--), 279
James, 6,16-17,23,37,48,66a,246a,248, 278-279

**DRAKE**
Anne, 394
Jemima (--), 128
John, 358,388

**DRIVER**
(--), g
Charles, d,47,230,256,261
Elizabeth (--), 47
Giles, 48,138,172,174,224,258,270-271
Prudence (--), 261
Robert, d,47,132,310

**DUCHER/DUCK**
Melchezidec, 197,223

**DUCKE/DUCK**
(--), m
Margaret (--), 121
William, 49,121-123

**DUKE**
Bridgett (--), 25
Elizabeth (--) [m2 Mercer], 25,88
John, d,21,25,64,111
John, Sr., 25

**DUNN**
John, 215

**DUNSTAN**
(--), Rev., 269

**DURDEN/DURDING**
(--), d
Ann (--), 265
Jacob, 25,193-194,265

**DURHAM/DIRHAM/DURRIM/ DERROM**
Charles, 60,127,166,168,176,186

**EALES**
Robert, 402

**EDMONSON**
John, 311
William, 311

**EDWARD**
William [of James City], 381

**EDWARDS**
(--), e,l
Charles, 330-331,335,345
Elizabeth (--), 119
Judith, e,346
Margaret, 274
Robert, s,131,274,346,405-406
William, e,15,79,356-357

**EFFINGHAM**
Francis, Lord, 5-6,26,34,51,58

**ELIXON**
(--), e
Jesper, 313-314

**ELLIS**
Jeremiah, 263

**ELLY**
(--), d
Robert, 279

**ELMES**
Thomas, 192,200

**ENGLAND**
(--) [Capt.], 44,298,300,327
Francis, 7,10,252
Joyce (--), 10

**ENGLISH**
Elianor (--), 15,18
James, 184
Thomas, e,15,18,183

**ENNIS**
James, 28

**EVANS**
Charles, 56
John [Capt.], 150
William, e,1-5,8,12,38-39
Thomas, 38
William, 361-362
William, Sr., 361

**EVERETT/EVERITT**
Simon, 66a,193-194

**EXUM**
(--), m
Jeremiah, 137,159,169,182,208
Richard, 341-343,402
Thomas, 13
William, 198
William, Jr., 36,59

**FAUKNER**
(--), Rev., 269

**FEBUARY**
(--), b
Edmund [Capt], 9

**FENNERYEARE/FEBERYEAR**
(--), k
Edmond, f,9-10,1,12,19n,55-56
John, c

**FIREBANT/ FYRABENT/ FURABANT**
(--), b,f
John Christopher, 261,265-266,310

**FISHER**
William, 119,141

**FITZGERRARD**
Thomas, 60-61

**FLAKE**
(--), f,221
Margaret (--), 301

Robert, a,f,38,44-45,249,299-301,327
Robert, Sr., 227

**FLEARE**
Theophilus, 48

**FLOID/FLOYD**
Edward, 34,325,327
Francis, 255,257
Nathaniel, 316
Thomas, 267

**FLY**
George, s
Jeremiah, 349-350

**FORD**
(--), t
Joseph, 31,252

**FOULES**
James, 35

**FOWLER**
(--), j,m,379
(--) [wife of Wm], f
Anne (--), 360
Bartholomew, 92
James, 335,396
William, f,21,218,357-360

**FRANKLIN**
Marable, 130
Peter, 95

**FRAZER**
(--), s,397
George, 396
William, 395,397

**FRISSELL/FRIZZELL**
John, 29
Ralfe, 16,179
Susannah (Portis) [m2 Thomas], 65
William, 65,274,346

**FULGHAM**
(--), p
Anthony, 52
John, 191,282
Michaell, 28
Nicholas, 19-20,28,69,113,127,179,186, 400
Richard, 369

**FULLERTON**
(--), e
Ellioner (--), 28
Robert, f,18,28

**FUZZELL**
Ralph, 393

**GADSBY**
Richard, 216

**GALE/GAILE**
Thomas, 18,23,28,193

**GANY**
William, 210

**GARDNER**
(--), g
Elizabeth (--), 51
James, g,51
Margaret, 90

**GARLAND**
John, 130

**GARNER**
Susanah, 182

**GAWEN**
John, 31

**GAWLER**
Henry, 110

**GAY**
Henry, b,g,16-17,341
John, 420

**GEORGE**
Hester (--), 196-197
Isaac, 196-197
John, 79,196

**GIBS**
Dorothy, 210
Thomas, s

**GILES/GYLES**
(--), c,g-h,l,p,r,w,79
(--) [wife of Jno], g
John, g,n,9,41,43,52,63,94-95,110-113, 118,125,138,156-157,159-160, 162-163,165,186,212,214,220-221,224-225,253,261,267,270-271,310-311,334-335,371-372, 386,399-400
Penelope, 334
Philarete (Woodward), 156-157,334, 399-400
Thomas, 22,35,39,48,52,68,126-127, 167,174,190,194,202,238, 246a,248,279,313,350,375-377

**GLOVER**
Richard, 276

**GODERD**
William, w

**GODWIN/GODWINE.GODDIN**
(--), g,r
Edmond, 13-14
Thomas, 13-14,127,242-243,250,310
William, 25,52,178

**GOODMAN**
(--), s
William, 249-250

**GOODRICH**
(--), g
Ann (--) [m2 Kae], 243
Charles, g,252
John, a-b,37,57,75,117,119,133,141, 149,151-153,222-223,243,268-269,293-295
John, Sr., 252
John, Jr., 6,8
Rebecah (--), 252

**GOODSON**
Edward, 12,133,254

**GOODWIN**
John, 252

**GORDON**
(--), 199

**GORINGE**
Charles,79

**GOSELING**
John, 25

**GOUGH**
Hugh, 279

**GOULDSBOROUGH**
Ann (Powell?, gr/d/o Nich Smith), 214-215
Nicholas, 214-215

Robert, 214-215

**GREENE/GREEN/GREANE**
(--), g,p,107
Bartholomew, g,18
Elizabeth, 125,162
George, g,69,94-95,112,154-158,210, 251,371-372
Jacob, s,23
John, 268
Mary (Green), 154-155
Mary (--), 107,182
Mary (--) [m2 Greene],17
Sarah, 168
Thomas, c,f,,69,95,155
Thomas, Sr., 17
Thomas, Jr., 17
William, h,81,107,112,144,166,182, 210,251,333,403.406

**GRIFFIN/GRIFING**
(--), g
Andrew, 90,117,223-224
Edward, 271-273
[--]ind, 324
John, g,52,62,133
Mary (Mumford), 271-273
Owen, 131,394
Thomas, 133

**GROSSE/GROSS/GROSE**
(--), g
Jane [m Rigane], 226,231
Richard, 225-226,230-231
Thomas, 124-125,127,263

**GWIN**
Boaz, 218

**HADLEY**
Ambrose, 190

**HALL**
(--) [wife of Jno], h
Ann (--), 287,388,404
John, h,251,403-404
Pool, h,285-287,387-388,403
Thomas, 285

**HALLOMAN** [see **HOLLIMAN**]

**HAMILTON**
James, 354-355

**HAMPTON/HAMTON**
(--), h
Elizabeth (--), 23
Mary, 23
Richard, 57 -58
Thomas, b,23,28,206,379

**HANSCOME**
Richard, 268

**HANSFORD**
John, 245

**HARDEN/HARDIN**
(--) (--), 8,86

**HARDY**
George, h,187
George, Jr., 188
Jacob, 229
Richard, 188
Thomas, 230

**HAREBOTTLE/HAIREBOTTLE**
Thomas, 325,327

**HARRIS**
Elizabeth, 323
John, 32,58
Mary [m Spiltimber], 419

Thomas, h,46,52,383-384

**HARRISON**
Josiah, 405

**HARTWELL**
Henry, 138

**HARVEY**
John, 400

**HASWELL**
Samuel, 90

**HAVIELD/HAVILD**
(--), b
Isabella (--), 355
Luke [Capt.], h,104-105,148-150,202, 352-355

**HAWKINS**
(--), h
Henry, 233
Thomas, 82-83,147,212-213

**HAWLY/HAWLEY/HALEY**
(--), c,h
Mallacke, 17,95,111,118,144,167

**HAYES**
(--) [wife of Thos.], h
Peter, 20,369
Prudence (--), 368-369,371-372
Thomas, h,368-372

**HAYWOOD**
Nicholas, 245

**HEARNE/HERN**
(--), m
Deborah [m Powell], 320-321,337-338
Elizabeth, 320-321,337
Elizabeth (--), 6,32
Henry, h,m,5-6,24,32,37,320-321,337
Rachel [m Price], 320-322,337

**HEATHFIELD**
Thomas, 202

**HERRING**
(--), w
Anthony, 96

**HICKES**
Ellinor (--), 420
John, 420

**HILL**
Bethiall [m Cole], c,10
Martha [m Best], 148-149
Mary [m Jennings], 149
Nicholas, 180
Robert, 97
Silvestra (Bennett), h,24,148,180-181, 202,335
Sion, 326
Thomas, 51-52,75,311

**HILMOTH**
Tristrum, 61,73

**HINSON**
(--), 95

**HOBBY**
Thomas, 223

**HODGES/HOGGES**
Robert, 4,145

**HOLE**
John, c,8-9,86

**HOLLAND**

Anthony, 209

**HOLLIDAY/HOLLADAY**
(--), b,h,69
Anthony, 16,68,175,217,219,244,250

**HOLLIMAN/HALLOMAN/ HOLLYMAN**
Christopher, 40,336
Richard, 200,292-293,336,377,383-384
William, 292

**HOLMES**
Christopher, h,81-83,211-213
Mary (--), 82,211-212

**HOLT**
Thomas, 246a

**HOOKER**
John, 408
Mary (--) Boazman, 222
Robert, 222

**HOOKES/HOOKS**
(--), h
Robert, h,48
William, 49

**HORNEING**
Robert, 246a,248

**HORSNELL**
James, 224

**HOULDER**
Thomas, 49

**HOUSE**
Martha (Spiltimber), 419-420
Mary [m Carrell], 419-420
Robert, Jr., 419-420

**HOWARD**
Francis Lord Effingham, 188-189,240-241

**HOWELL**
Thomas, 89
Walter, 21

**HUNT**
Godfrey, 13
Sarah (--), 92
William, 92

**HUNTER**
(--), s
Robert, 395,397
William, 400,409-410

**HUPP**
(--) [tailor], 395

**HUTCHINS/HUTCHIN/HUCHINS**
(--), h
Elizabeth (Cobb), 85-87,90-92
Francis, 18,28,379-381
Mary (--), 18
Richard, 25,85-87,90-92,193,379-381
Thomas, 367

**HYINGTON**
(--), h
Cuthbert, 110

**INGLES** [see **ENGLISH**]
Thomas, w

**IRBY**
(--), j
Edmund, 92,125

**IZARD/ISERD/ISEARD**

John, 239
Martha [m Rutter], 240-242
Mary, 240,242
Richard, 238-240,242

**JACKMAN**
Joseph John, 382

**JACKSON**
John, 21,64,112
Mary, 132
Richard, 132

**JENKINS**
Henry, 245

**JENNINGS**
E., 258,289,376
George, 201
John, j,148-149,181,201-202,225,230
Mary (Hill), 149
Sarah [m Lucks], 201

**JOHNSON**
(--), j
(--) [Dr.], 127
Eliner, 49
Elizabeth (--), 313
James, 24,49,121
John, j,n,50,72,73-74,95,253,280
John, Dr., 312-313
Katherine (--), 48-49
Mary (--), 49,72,74
Robert, j,48-49
Sarah (--), 346
Walter, 44
William, j,p,31,48,127,129,266,319-320,347

**JOLIFE**
John, 182

**JOLLY/JOLLEY**
(--), j,m
James, 58,90,132,138,179,270,399
Will, c
William, 58,118,139,182,259-260,270,350,399

**JONES/JOANES**
(--), m,t,42
Ann (--), 273
Arthur, 81,383
Jane, 395
John, c,41,44,64,114,117,198,273-274
John, Sr., 40,134-135,228,232
John, Jr., 40
Margaret, 30
Mary [m Cooke], 383-384
Richard, 113,192
Sarah [m Tyrrell], 266
Thomas, 39,208
William, b,83,138,140,213
William [of York Co.], 348
William [grands/o Peirce], 409

**JORDAN**
(--), p
Christian, 223-224
Christian (Taberer), 223-224
James, 168,223-224
John, 135
Joseph, 166
Matthew, b,347
Robert, 223-224
Thomas, p,15,320-322,337-339

**JOYNER**
(--), j
Ann (--), 305
Bridgman, 24,26,41,46-47,50,74,178,283,303-305
Ellenor (--), 304
Elizabeth (--), 283,304

Francis, 202
John, 164
Theophilus, 164,173,303-304
Thomas, j,164,176,191,203,210,282, 364-366
Thomas, Sr., 164,282-283,305

**KAE**
(--), k
Ann (--) Goodrich, 243
Robert, p,105,124,141,145,186,243. 292-293,395

**KAR**
Robert, 119

**KASEY** [see **CASEY**]

**KEEBEL**
Ann, 160-161

**KEELL**
William, k,41

**KENT**
(--), j-k
Hannah (--), 75
Luke, j-k,50,72-75

**KERBY**
(--), c,k,w
Thomas, 103

**KERLE/KERLOR**
William, 41,46-47,50,74,89,96,107,192, 362

**KINCHIN**
William, e,89,356

**KINDER**
Thomas, 37

**KING/KINGE**
(--), k
Henry, 21,199
John, 77
Robert, 81,83,120,213,217

**KIRBY**
Ruth (--), 412
Thomas, 411-413,415,417

**KIRKMAN**
Francis, 22

**KITCHIN**
Robert, k,9

**LACY**
Mary (--), 199
Robert, 199

**LAMIFE**
Thomas, 304

**LANE**
Ann, 164
Thomas, 199

**LASWELL/LYSEWELL**
(--), 237

**LAWRENCE/LAURENCE**
Giles, 209
John, 1,77
Robert, 16,22,308
Robert, Jr., 26,30,45

**LAWSON**
Epaphroditus, 81,83,211,213

**LEACH**
Joseph, 79

**LEAR**
John [Col.], 47,79,166

**LEE/LEES**
(--), s
Francis, 228,232,314-315
John, 246a

**LEGG**
John, 388

**LEIGH**
Daniel, 187

**LEWERD**
William, 151

**LEWIS/LEWES**
(--), m
Anne, l
Anne (--) Macon, 388
Christopher, 329
Jacob, 421
John, 388
Richard, 15,66,77-78,139,228,232
Thomas, 77-78,139
William, 238

**LEYBURN**
Samuel, 56

**LINKIN**
John, 17

**LINSCOTT/LYNSCOTE**
Giles, l,1,26,77

**[--]LINT**
John, 289

**LITTLEBOY**
Robert, 131,160

**LONG/LONGE**
(--), l
Daniel, r,14,25,28,69,285
James, Sr., 233
James, Jr., 233

**LOPER**
James, 145

**LOVEDAY**
(--), 47
George, 57-58

**LOVEGROVE/LOVEGRAVE**
(--), Mr., 275
Richard, 68

**LOWERY**
Mathew, 306-307

**LOWTER**
John, 58

**LOYDE**
Richard, 128

**LUCAS**
Thomas, 32,164

**LUCKE/LUCKS**
(--), l
John, 57,369
Samuel, 197
Sarah (Jennings), 201
William, 79

**LUDWELL**
Phillip, 15,226,231,235,330
Thomas, 239
Thomas, Sr., 22

**LUPO/LUPOE**
James, b,2-5,8,11-12

**LUTEN** [see **LUTHER**]
John, 132

**LUTHER/LUTER**
(--), l
John, l,80,88,127,138,172-174,273,322
Mary (Beal), 80,88,172-173,322

**MACFADDEN**
James, 147

**MACKCLAM**
Brian, 159

**MACKDOWELL**
James, 179
Mary (--) [m2 Whitley], 179
Olive, 179

**MACKLOUD**
John, 29

**MACKMIALL** [see **MICKMIHILL**]

**MACKON/MACON**
Ann (--) [m2 Lewis], 388
William, 388

**MACKQUINNY/MACKINNEY**
(--), m,r
Elizabeth (--) [m2 Reeves], 339-340
Barnabe, 303,312,319-320,339-343
John, 339-341,343
Mary (--), 340-342
Michael, 339-341

**MACKRISTY**
Rebecka, m,350

**MACKUNHILL**
(--), m

**MACKY/MACKIE**
(--), m
William, 276-277,335

**MACODINE/MACKCODDING**
Phillip, 113,183

**MADISON**
Richard, 409

**MAINALL**
John, 191

**MAN/MANN**
(--), b,h,k,m
Charles, 53,120,122
Elizabeth (--), 53-54,303-304
Sarah [m Davis], 26,120-121
Thomas, 120-123,234-235,303-304,
358,420
Thomas, Sr., m,24,32,40-41,53-54,218
Thomas, Jr., 53-54,218

**MANDUE/MANDEW/MADUS**
Sarah (--), 37,332
Thomas, b,m,36-37,46,283,318,321,
331-332,337,401,421
Thomas, Jr., 332,351

**MANGUM**
John, 200

**MARE**
Ralph, 382

**MARKS/MARK**
Thomas, 303,408

**MARKUM**
John, b

**MARSHALL/MERSHALL**
(--), h,m,69
Anne (--) (Smith), 22,195,214
Humphrey, m,69,79,83,126,141,168,
213-214,21,311,338-339,385
Humphrey, Jr., 71
John, 81,126,211,290-291
Robert, 175,179

**MARTYN/MARTIN**
(--), m,p
(--) [wife of], m
Henry, 190-191,228,232,273,280-282
Henry, Sr., 281
Mary (--), 190-191,228,232,273,281-
282

**MASON**
(--), 68

**MATHER**
Thomas, 2-5

**MATTHEWS**
(--) [widow], 131
Alexander, 178,273,374
Anne, m
Anne (--) Bacon-Matthews,48
Anthony, 59,108
Edward, 50
Richard, r,49

**MAYO**
(--), m
(--) [wife of], m
Isabell (--), 78,139
William, m,50,74,77-78,139,297-298,
303-304

**MEAKHOM/MEACOM**
(--), l
Frances, 128-129

**MEINZES**
William, 397-398

**MELVIN**
James, 410

**MELYM**
Isaac, 66

**MERCER/MERSER**
(--), l-m
Elizabeth (--) Duke, 25,88
James, 236,364-366
Robert, 1,80,88

**MEREDETH**
Joseph, 170,210,408

**MERRICK**
Giles, 79

**MICE**
James/Jacobus, 293

**MICKMIHALL/MICHNIELL**
John, s,22,237,333,366-367,407
Sarah (--), 333

**MILES/MYLES**
(--), m,15
Daniel, 84
Edward, 323
William, 2-4,11,199,269

**MILLER**
Edward, 195
Nicholas, 195

**MINERD/MINARD**
Kingsman, 276,282

**MOBLE**
(--) [Lt.], 397

**MOMFORD**
Thomas, 209-210

**MOON**
John [Capt.], 154,400
Mary [m Green], 154-155

**MOORE/MOOR**
(--), c,m
(--) [wife of], m
Elizabeth (--), 117
George, 10-11,13,66,99,101,105,117, 156-157,159,179,200-201,222-223,250,264,269,292-293,322, 324,385
Jane [m Carver], 46-47,89,319
John, b,m,25,28,46-47,57-58,79,185, 275,319
Magdalen [m Carter], 324
Margaret (--), 275
Robert, m,345
Thomas, 1,11,31,38,41,43,45,92-94, 114-117,124-125,128,133,136, 158,162,181,186,202,206,209, 221-223,378

**MORELL/MARRELL/MEARIL**
George, 199-200
George, Sr., 199

**MORGAN**
James, 246

**MORRIS**
John, 336
John, Jr., 40
Morgan, 40
William, 40

**MORRISON/MORYSON**
Francis [Gov.], 238-239

**MOSTYN/MESTYN**
Thomas, 17

**MOUNTFORT**
Thomas, 245

**MUMFORD**
Mary [m Griffen], 271-273
Thomas, 271

**MURFREY/MURFREA**
(--), m
Francis (--), 216,220
Michael, 216,220
William, 25,49,66a,193-194,216,220, 246a,248

**MURRAY**
Adam, 40,393,399-400

**NEVILL/NEVELL**
(--), h
(--), Jr., j
Benjamin, 22
Elizabeth (--), 22,25,253
John, n,r,22,25,144,188-190,216,233, 253
John, Sr., 190,313
John, Jr., 22,312-313
William, 166,168,109

**NEWMAN**
(--), 44,298,300,327
John, 222-224
Richard, 223
Thomas, 206

**NICHOLSON**
Francis [Gov.], 29,40-41,50,74,77,103, 283,298,300,375-376,411-412
Jeffray [Gov.], 50

**NOLIBOY/NOLOBOY**
(--), m
Daniel, Jr., 216,220

**NORSWORTHY/NASWORTHY**
(--), b,d,l,s,96
George, 22,212-214,226,231,236-238, 272-273
Thomas, n,118,128-130,144,170-171, 261,265-266,399-400
Tristram, 205,229,239,241-242,265, 313,322-323

**OGBORNE**
Nicholas, 223

**OGLETHORPE**
Thomas, 13,49,102,131

**OISER**
(--), Rev., 269

**OLDIS**
William, 22,96,236,349

**OLEHAM**
Henry, 145

**OLTMAN**
(--), o

**OWEN**
Thomas, 81,179,239,241,400

**PAGE**
(--), a
Thomas, h,6
Thomas, Sr., 420

**PALIN**
(--), 281

**PALMER/PALLMER**
(--), p
Alice (--), 280
Edmund, 108,190,232,273-274,280-281,346

**PARDOE**
(--), p
Phillip, 308-309,395

**PARK/PARKE**
Robert, 268

**PARKER**
(--), m,p
Francis, 84,217,219
John, 62,84
Mary (--), 62,84,420
Peter, 421
Thomas, 84,287
William, 233,420

**PARNELL**
John, 210
Thomas, 358

**PARSON**
John, 199

**PARTRIDGE**
James, 182

**PASFIELD**
Nicholas, 252

**PEASLEY**
J., 30

**PEDDEN**
James, 392

**PENNY/PENNE**
(--), 68
Elizabeth, 174-175
Frances, 175
John, 127
Mary, 16,175
William, p,127,174

**PETERS**
James, 012

**PIERCE/PEARCE/PEERCE**
(--) [Capt.], 7
Anne (--), 30-31,409
George, p,30-31,36,46,332,386,409
Katherine (--), p,38,124,144
Thomas, p,38,221

**PERMENTOR/PERMENTO**
John, 58
Nathaniell, 167,176

**PERSIE/PERCE**
George, 40,89

**PHILLIPS**
Mary [m Dickson], 269
William, 202,269

**PIDDINGTON**
Thomas, 309

**PILKINGTON/PILKINSON**
John, 13-14,94,370-372

**PITT**
(--), d,p,w,302
(--) [widow], 179
Henry, 316,343,346
Hester [m Bridger], 276
John, p,1-2,4,8-19n,20-41,43-49,51, 54-55,57-58,68,82-83,111,113, 125,127,131,199,213,216,220, 238,240,301,304,310,332,335, 367
John, Sr., 27
Olive (--), 125
Robert, 24
Thomas, 16,94,116,124-125,265,271, 275,316,337,350

**PLOW**
Jane, 419

**PLUMPTON**
Henry, 30,248,408
Isable (--), 408

**POLEGREEN**
(--), p
Frances (--), 229
George, 229
John, 229-230

**POOLE**
Thomas, p,14,21-22,238,240,387,403

**POPE**
(--), d
Henry, 170,265
John, p,29
Richard, 29
Thomas, 210

**PORTEN**
William, 15

**PORTIS/PORTEOUS**

(--), b,p
(--), Sr., p
Jane (--), 110,134-135,198,391
John, p,43-44,59,62,65-66,110,198,273, 277-278,390-391
John, Sr., 134-135,198,232,277,391
John, Jr., p,59,236,277,390-391
Susannah [m1 Frizell, 2 Thomas], 65

**POTTS**
Henry, 325

**POWELL**
(--), p
Ann [m Gouldsborough], 214-215
Anne (--) [wife of Js, m2 Randolph], 75-76,95,268
(--) [wife of Jno], p
(--) [wife of St], p
(--) (Smith) [w/o Thos], 195,214
Deborah (Hern), 337-339
Elizabeth [m Coopes], 193
Elizabeth (--), 193
James [Col.], 24,75-76,114,127,196-197,268
John, p,193,337-339
Mary [d/o Mary (--) Powell, m Allen], 66a
Mary (--), 66a
Stephen, p,66a
Thomas, 18,28,167,193-195
William, 25,193
William, Jr., 193

**POWER**
Anthony, p

**PRESTON**
Thomas, 310

**PRICE**
(--) [wife of Thos.], p
Daivd, 107
Rachel (Hern), 320-322
Thomas, p,320-322

**PRIME**
Edmund, 66
Edward, 48,59
John, b,59,66,310,362-364,418

**PROCTER/PROCKTOR**
John, 135-136,377-379
Jone (--), 136,328
Mary (--), 379
Reuben, 328

**PUDDINATT**
William, 104

**PUGH/PEUGH**
Daniel/Danuel, 141

**PURSELL/PURSLEY/PURSILL**
(--), j
Arthur, 107,178,203,282-283

**PURVIS**
(--), p
John [Capt.], 245-246

**PYLAND/PILAND**
(--) [5 children], 162
Elinor (--), 161-162
James, 7
Richard, 161-162,268

**RAND**
(--), w

**RANDALL** [see **RANDOLPH**]
(--), r
Ann (--), 197
Robert, r,197,246-246a

**RANDOLPH/RANDALL**
(--), d,r
Anne (--) Powell, 75-76,95,268
Robert, 75-76,95,268
William, 243-244

**RATLIFFE**
Richard, 209,272

**RAWLINS**
Edward, 66
Roger, b,49,66

**RAYFORD/REYFORD/ WRAYFORD/RAFFORD**
(--), c,w
Phillip, 36,46,89,95,210,218,318-319, 331-332,389

**RAYNARD/RAYNER**
Francis, 145,252

**REED**
David, 397-398

**REEVE/REEVES/RIVES**
(--), r,411
Elizabeth (--) Mackinne, 206,339-340
Henry, r
Henry, Sr., 13
Henry, Jr., 13-14
Thomas, b,33-35,206,339-340

**REGAN/RIGANE**
(--), r
Jane (Gross), 226,231

**RENN**
Francis, 294

**REYNOLDS/RANALDS**
(--), h,r,w
Christopher, 323,360
Elizabeth (Williams), 90-91,216,306-307
Joyce (--), 80,88,235,310
Richard, r,25,46,48,80,88,138-139,167, 172,174,176,191,203,210,212, 214,216,220,224,226,231,235, 238,243,252,254-257,273,293-295,297,306-307,309-310,322-323,350,360,369
Richard, Sr., 160,254-257
Richard, Jr., 48,90-91,144

**RICHARD**
Lewis, 1

**RICHARDS**
George, 245
Robert, 27,127
Thomas, 27

**RICHARDSON**
(--), r
John, 128

**RICKS/REEKS/RICKSIS/RISE**
(--), m
Abraham, 380
Isaac, 169-170,332,381
Jack, 103
Jacob, 275
James, 18
John, 206,265
Katherine (--), 18
Robert, 275,332,380

**RIDLEY**
(--), w
Nathaniel, h,344,352-355

**RIGHT** [see **WRIGHT**]

**RIVERS**
George, 90

**ROADS**
Anne (--), 49,102
Charles, 233
John, r,49,102

**ROBERT/ROBERTS**
John, 288
Thomas, 394

**ROBINSON/ROBARTSON/ ROBERTSON**
Thomas, 368-369
Zebenezar, 397

**ROCHFORD**
George, 51

**ROGERS**
John, 32,53,169
William, 84

**ROOKES**
Isaac, 379

**ROSSER**
John, 95

**ROYALL**
Elizabeth, 182
Henry, 245
Richard, 117

**RUCK**
John, 246
Joseph, 246

**RUFFIN**
Robert, 22,236
William, 350

**RUTTER**
(--), r
Jeremiah, 25
Jeremy, 15
Martha, 107
Martha (Izard), 14,107,239-242
Walter, r,14,25,28,107,127,239-243

**SAMPSON**
James, 224

**SANBORNE**
(--), g
Daniel, 82-83,209,211,213,271-272
Elizabeth, 210
Sarah (--), 82,211

**SANDERS/SANDEOR**
(--), s
Henry, 287-289
Lawrence, 15
Margaret (--), 289

**SANFORD**
James, 215

**SAVIDGE**
Charles, 2-5,249-250

**SAYOR/SAWER**
Thomas, 141,210

**SAYWELL**
William, 158,251

**SCOREY**
William, 245-246,397

**SCOTSCOTT/RIGANE**
(--), l

John, 381
Richard, 28,33,35
Robert, 33-35,61,135,208,210,233
William, b,f,28,33,35,379,381
William, Jr., 30

**SCREWS/SCRUES/SKRUSE**
John, 43,158

**SEAGRAVE**
Francis, 132

**SELLAWAY**
John, 39

**SELLER**
John, 81

**SENIOR**
Joseph, s,19-19n,24

**SESSUM**
Nicholas, 249-250

**SEWARD**
(--), 240

**SHARPE**
Richard, 12

**SHELLY**
Sarah (Wakefield) [wife of Ph], s,314-315
Phillip, s,301,314-315

**SHEPPARD**
Margary, 235

**SHERRER/SHERER/SHEARER SERER**
(--), c,r
Aleck, 198
Elizabeth, 349
Elizabeth (--), 27
John, s,128,198,277-278,329-330
John, Sr., s,27,349
Robert, 383-384
Thomas, s,278,349

**SHERWOOD**
William, 11

**SHEWELL/SHOWELL**
Richard, b,33-35,206

**SHEWMACKE**
Ann (--) Williams, 106-107
Arnold, 107

**SHIPLY/SHIPLEY**
Ellis (Burnell), 23
Jonathan, s,23

**SHIRLEY**
Ralph, 2685

**SIKES/SYKES**
John, 27,379

**SIMONS**
Patrick, 397

**SKELTON**
(--), s,132
(--) [wife of], s
James, 422
John, 58,99,168,181,186,197,260,345
Sarah, 422
Susannah (--), 422
William, 422

**SLAUGHTER**
Oliver, 270

**SMELLY**
(--), s
John, 246a,248
Lewis, s,246a,248,375-377
Robert, s,246a,248,313,375-377,408
William, 246a,248,375-377,408

**SMITH/SMYTH**
(--), s
(--) [Col.], h,8,179,182,228
(--) [wife of Capt.], s
(--) [m Thos Powell], 195,214
Anne (--) [m2 Marshall], 22,195,214
Arthur, 70-71,75,85-87,91,106,124-126,
131,254-256,271,280,282,291,
297,306-307,309,317,349-350,
362,364,368,404-406
Arthur, Sr., s,8-9,13,23,54-56,349,405
Arthur, Jr., 56,106,133,411
Elizabeth (--), 249-250
George, 210,212,214,222
Hannah (--), 215
Joane (--), 8
John, s,22,96,191,236-238,418-419
Mary (--), 56-57,406
Nathan, 277
Nicholas, s,27-28,35,44,125,195,214,
277,296
Peter, 15
Thomas, f,6,8,178,227,249-250,307
William, f,1,56-57,95,120,143,179,197,
215,345,368-369,371-372
William, Sr., 385

**SOJORNER/SORJOURNER**
(--), w
John, s,32,36,58
Mary (--), 32

**SOMERVELL**
Francis (--), 29
John, s,26,29,395-397

**SPENCER**
Nicholas, 37

**SPILTIMBER**
Anthony, 419-420
Martha [m House], 419-420
Mary (Harris), 419

**SPURWAY**
(--), s
Humphrey, 395-398

**STANTON**
Christian, 287
Thomas, 240

**STAPLES**
Richard, 22,25

**STEVENS/STEPHENS**
Robert, 43,209
Roger, 42-43,59,90

**STEVENSON**
John, 27

**STOCKES**
Robert, 233

**STONE**
Richard, 36,94,197,206

**STORY**
Laurence, 369

**STREETE**
John, 61,410
Madison, 409-410

**STREETER**
(--), s

Edward, 242-243

**STRICKLAND/STRICKLING**
(--), s
John, 302-303,319
Joseph, 302
Matthew, 38-39,124,210,302,311-312, 361,398-399
Matthew, Jr., 208-209,302-303
Olive (--), 386
Samuel, 302
William, 302-303,311-312,319,386

**STURDY**
(--), d
(--) [Goody] (--), 52
Robert, 52,210,304

**STYLES**
(--), 56

**SULEVAN**
Daniel, 344

**SUMMERELL**
John, 131

**SUMMERVELL**
Thomas, 406

**SURBER**
John, p,40

**SWANN**
(--) [Capt.], 59
Samuell, 25,221,224
Thomas, s,354-355,376-377

**SYMES**
(--), s
George, 260
Robert, 402

**SYMONDS**
(--), 5

**TABERER**
Christian [m Jordan], 223-224
Mary [m Webb], 223
Thomas, 18-19n,24,28,54-55,70-71, 105,222-223

**TALL**
(--) [illeg. child x Williamson], 160-161
Martha, 160

**TARLETON**
Roger, 6,248,408

**TAYLER**
Caleb, 187
Thomas, 62

**TELWELL**
Edward, 287

**TENCTEOR**
(--), 397

**TETHER/TEATHER**
Anne, 2-4
George, 2-4,199-200

**THACKER**
C[--], 284

**THOMAS**
(--), d,h,m
John, 65,224,228,232,273,281
Robert, t,13,19-19n,29,31,224,273,330-331
Susan/Susanna (Portis) Frizell, p,65
William, 141,201-202,305,335,395,419

**THOMPSON/THOMSON**
John, 19n
Mary (--), 419
Samuel, 419-420
William, 22,25

**THORNE**
(--) [wife of Wa], t
Grace (--), 1
Wa:, t
William, 1

**THORNEHILL**
John, 50,66

**THORNETON**
John, 23,181

**THROPP**
(--), e
Martha (--), 150-153,201,335
Thomas, 117,119,133,143,150-153,200-202,268,403

**TIBBOT/TIBBOTT**
(--) [Capt.], 160
Richard, 159,246

**TINNER**
Nicholas, 15

**TOCKER/TOOKER**
(--), 4
Henry, 142-143, 161,221,246

**TOMLIN/TOMBLIN**
Mary (--), 192
Mathew, 22,191,192,227

**TONAY**
Nathaniel, 30

**TOOKE/TOOKES**
(--), 42,298-299
Abraham, 230
Thomas, 37,41,44,59,65,300,327,363,418-419

**TOWELL/TOWLE**
(--), t
Richard, 133

**TUCKER**
(--), m
Robert, 276,396

**TULLAGH/TULLOUGH/TALLOCH**
(--), d,k
Anne, 133
Elizabeth (--), 73
James, c,k,23,25,28,37,39,42-43,60-61,69,72-73,75,111,118,139,163,165,186,204,226,231,285,405
Sarah, 133

**TURNER**
(--), b,j
Henry, 144,305
John, 27-28,81,110,293
Joshua, 280,392,422

**TYLERR/TYLER**
John, 81.254
Mary, 349

**TYNER**
(--), m
Nicholas, 218

**TYRELL**
Blackaby, t,266
Sarah (Jones), 266

**UNDERWOOD**
(--), k
John, 412,414,419

**UPTON**
John [Capt.], 238,252

**VALLENTINE/VOLLINGTINE**
James, 175
John, 16,175

**VANCLORE**
(--), 272

**VASSER**
(--) [wife of Ptr], t
John, 316-317
Margaret (--), 317
Peter, v,145,292,316-317

**VERY**
Jonathan, 9-10

**VICKS/VICKE**
Joseph, w, 45-46

**VOLINTINE** [see **VALLENTINE**]

**WADE**
(--), w
Christopher, 51,128,188-189
Samuel, 190
Susana (--), 127-128,190

**WAKEFIELD**
John, 27,314,329-330
Sarah [m Shelly], 314-415

**WAKLY**
Mathew, 280

**WALKER**
John, 388
Timothy, 127

**WALLER**
Thomas, 227

**WALLIS/WALLES**
Benjamin, 396
John, 301

**WALTER/WALTERS**
(--), d,g
Walter, g,51

**WARD**
(--), w
Mary (--), 94
Samuel, 304
Thomas, b,w,19-20,28,94

**WATKINS/WOCKINS**
George, 380
James, 184
John, w,15,183,203
John, Sr., 183-184
John, Jr., 183-184
Mary (--), 15,183-184,203

**WATTERS**
John, 102,216,220
Mary (--), 102
Walter, 210

**WATTS**
(--), c
John, h,127,130,285-286,387,388,404
John, Jr., 130

**WEBB/WEBES**
James, 342
Mary (Taberer), 223

Richard, 216
Thomas, 43,195
William, 223

**WEBSTER**
Allexander, 27

**WEST**
(--), d,m,w
Anne, 388
Henry, 26,50,74,198,277
Rebecca/Rebecha (--), 96-97
Robert, 97
William, 25,60-61,103,127,254,274, 290-291,388,411
William, Sr., 96-97,204-205
William, Jr., 14,60-61

**WESTOWREY**
William, 96

**WHARTON**
Michael, 75

**WHEDON**
James, 354-355

**WHETSTONE**
John, 95,113,294,309

**WHITBY**
(--), w
Nathaniel, 327-328

**WHITE**
Henry, 162

**WHITEHEAD**
(--), s
Arthur, 302-303,311-312,360,386,389

**WHITFIELD**
(--), w
William, 111

**WHITLEY/WHITLY/WHETLEY**
John, 28,52,118,162,165,178-179,186
John, Jr., 186
Margarett, 27
Mary (--) Macdowell, 163,178-179,186
Thomas, w,28,52,127,186,266,410
William, 186

**WICKINS/WICKINGS**
(--), b,w
Edmond, b,w,325-327
Thomas, 34,97-101

**WILKINSON/WILKISSON**
(--), d,g,p,w
Ann, 167
Richard, w,19-20,27-28,68,144,155-156,170-171,210,410
Richard, Sr., 56-58
Richard, Jr., 57,70,127,154,157,226, 231,322,368,400,410

**WILLE**
John, 327-328
Mary (--), 328

**WILLIAMS**
(--), b,g,w
(--) [wife of], w
Ann (--) [m2 Shewmacke], 105-107
Dennis, 62
Elizabeth [m Reynolds], 90-91,306-307
Elizabeth (--), 223
George, b,l,90,158,250-251,306-307, 394,422-423
Jane, 106
John, w,60,94.105,167,223,413-415,418
John [minister], 132
John, Jr., 105

Lewis, 334
Mary, 106
Mary (--), 412-416,418
Nicholas, 106,413-415
Richard, w,106,414-416,418
Sarah (--), 307
Thomas, 106
William, w,105,112,131,141.250,306, 319-320,347,388,412-418

**WILLIAMSON**
(--), w,160
(--) [wife of Geo], w
Francis, 389,392
George, w,36,45,93,115,117,144,151-152,217,219,320,389-390
Hester (--), 389-390
Nathaniel, 344-345
Robert, 32,36
Thomas, 1,113-114,202

**WILLIFORD**
John, 47

**WILLS**
Jonathan, 141

**WILLY**
John, w

**WILSON**
(--), b,d,w,114
(--) [wife of], w,113
Anne, 76
James, 76,143,264
John, 224
Margaret (--), 75-76,95,142-143,161, 176
Nicholas, r,75-76,95,113,142-143,161, 264,268
Sampson, 142-143
Thomas, 114,397
William, 347

**WINN** [**see WYNN**]

**WOKINS** [see **WATKINS**]

**WOOD**
Thomas, p,308-309

**WOODLEY/WOODLY**
(--), b
Andrew, c,42-43,90,108-110,150,160, 229-230,296-298,338-339,345, 377,386
Henry, 297

**WOODWARD**
(--), Mr., 302
Philarete [m Giles], 334,399-400
Thomas, Sr., 334
Thomas, Jr., 334

**WOOLCE**
Anne, 409

**WOORY**
(--) [Mrs.], 95
Joseph, 23-25,27,35,127
Robert, 35

**WOOTEN**
(--) [wife of Rcd], w
Lucy (--), 402-403
Richard, w,255,257,402-403

**WORD**
Mary (--), 125

**WORGAR**
Robert, 15

**WORMELEY**

H., 318

**WORRELL**
John, 312
Richard, 192
William, 192

**WRAYFORD** [see **RAYFORD**]

**WRENN/WREN**
(--), k
Francis, 243
John, 243

**WRIGHT/RIGHT**
(--), w
Elizabeth (--), 106
George, 28,63,144,210,293-294
James, 270
John, 397-398
Thomas, 63,144,210

**WYATT**
John, 35

**WYNN/WINN**
(--), p
Richard, 245
Thomas, 124

## Locations

"Isle of Wight" County has not been indexed
Whenever "Blackwater" was mentioned by itself, I have indexed it as a river.

**ENGLAND**,56
**COUNTIES**
Devon, 8

**PARISHES/CITIES**
Bristol, 79,150,244
Dawlish, 29
London, 245,395-397

**SCOTLAND**
Edinbrough, 395-398

**POSSESSIONS**
Barbados, 19,229
Bridge Town, 23

**US COLONIES**
**STATES**

**MARYLAND**, 10,397
**COUNTIES**
Somerset, 397
Talbot, 214-215

**MASSACHUSETTS**
New England, 56
**COUNTIES**
Essex, 9-10,12

**TOWNS**
Boston, 9
Charlestown, 18
Salem, 9-10,12

**NORTH CAROLINA**, 233
**COUNTIES**
Perquimans, 221

**VIRGINIA**
**COUNTIES**
Charles City, 125,161
Henrico, 243
James City, 138,356,381
[Lower] Norfolk, 15,259
Nansemond, 5-6 ,15-17,22,24-25,30,37, 85,90,100,104,212,214,236, 253,279,309,312,320-321,325-326,337,339,373,376,401,408, 420-421
Northumberland, 368-372
Rappahannock, 13-14,397
Surry, 2-6,10,44-45,115,117,142,199-200,246,249-250,310,381-382
Warrick, 235
Warrisqueake, 12,316
York, 180,348

**PARISHES**
Chuckatuck, 14,35,320
Lawnes Creek, 44-45,199,300,381-382
Lower in Isle of Wight, 20-21,28,31,37-38,40,45-48,50-51,53,59,72, 90,96,131,134,157,168,188, 209,211,216,228,231,235,241, 254,256,273,275,277-278,287, 296,306,318-320,333,350,357, 390,398,401,403,417,421
Nansemond, 23
Newport, 27,372,399
Southwarke, 10
Upper in Isle of Wight, 1,3-6,11,27,38, 41-42,44-45,58,65,108,135,

148,168,191,196,199,206,227-228,231,267,273,277,292,296, 298,300,308,314,324,327,352, 379,383-384,418,422
Upper in Surry, 2-6,11
Upper in Nansemond, 5,102
Western Branch, 85,90

**TOWNS**, etc.
Chuckatuck, 13-14
Indian, 312
James City, 54,336,358
Newport, 54,70-71,385

**LAND**

**BRIDGE**
Horse, 41

**PATH**, 174
Cart, 8,37,81,211,227,241,249
Cobb's, 8

**FIELD**
Major Bond's, 41-42

**HILL**
Turkey, 240

**MEADOW**
Western Branch, 394

**MILL**, 60-61,227,249
Cypress, 349
Flake's, 227
Path, 107

**NAMED LOCATIONS**
Broandecke, 33
Buckland, 100
Capt. Benn's Land, 361
Cart way, 241
Carawoak Line, 312
Coblers line, 36
Herring's Plantation, 241
Hickory Vally, 292
High Street, 54
Hugh's Island, 84
John Jones plantation, 41-42
Jones Landing, 400
King of all places, 410
Low meadow ground, 277
Miles End, 258
Mill, 43,266
Mill neck, 43
Nansemond Path side, 400
Old corner field, 306
Old horsepath, 422-423
Poke Courte Necke, 15
Poplar Neck, 155
Quin Quan, 375
Timber purcotion, 255
Town land, 70-71
West's freshett, 254,256
The head of the runs, 326

**NECK**
Broad, 193
Chinkapin, 252
Corasid, 271
Little, 296,298
Oyster shell, 65

**ROADS**
Blackwater, 64
Lane, 62
Nansmond, 409
Nansemond path, 155
Side, 241

**VALLEY**, 8,111
Sandy Point, 409
Stone, 107

**WOODS**, 7,151-152,252,262

**WATER**

**BAY**
Lawson's, 83,213
Warrisqueake/Orisqueake, 201,269,314, 316

**BRANCH**, 1-2,8,29,32,41,53,59,64, 66a,77,86,111,115,174,211, 217,227,234,241,262,275,292, 306
Anthony's Delight, 401
Beaver Dam, 2,39,199,305,324
Blackwater, 36,40,198,302,315
Boiling Spring, 14
Boones, 412
Burnt House, 16
Cabbin, 309
Cypress, 64
Davis, 7
Deep, 275
Doctors, 32,36
First of Blackwater, 252
Great, 123,218
Greater, 21
Gum, 302
Herrings, 241
Indian Field, 421
Knave Tree, 3
Little, 21,112,123,172,393
Long, 49,96,248
Main, 31,41,349,351
Meadow, 413,415
Northwest, 222
Pipe Clay, 33,206
Popular, 312
Porters, 227,249
Ready/Reedy, 241,331
Red, 374
Richard Bracewell's, 351
Small, 27,41-42,49,100,206,213,220, 349,351
Spring, 13,65,341,401,412,420
Watery, 302,311
Western, 18,25,28,51,233,253,312,373, 408,421
White Oak, 311
Wight Marsh, 248
Wolf pitt, 33

**COVE**, 234

**CREEK**, 8,16,41-42,86,241
Back, 316
Back Bay, 155,370
Bay, 369
Beverly, 272
Castle, 196
Chuckatuck, 13
Indian, 275
Laien [Lawnes], 180
Lawns, 201,308
Lower bay, 254
Main, 91,306,316
Mount Lawson's Bay, 81,211
Pagan, 55,155,296
Small, 83
Timber Neck, 209,272
Virgoes/Vergers, 19-20,369-370
Warrisqueake Back bay, 19-20

**DAM**
Beaver, 13
Mill, 60-61,107,204
Piney Point, 3
Tullaugh's, 204

**POCOSIN**, 51,275,277
Anthony's Delight, 401
Great, 422

**POND**, 91,111,306

Black, 303,386
Bushy, 14
Fish, 277
Island, 14

**RIVERS**
Blackwater, 2-3,6-7,10,27,363,377,398, 412
Choanock [in NC], 334
Chowan, 234
James, 12,19n
Main Blackwater, 1,351,375,381-382, 401,409,421
Nansemond, 25,51,222,233,245,253, 312
Side, 151

**RUN**, 115,120,191
Fresh, 100
Main, 417,420
Meadow, 422
Western Branch, 373

**SPRING**
Mrs. Harden's, 86
Webbs, 43

**SWAMP**, 25,44,193,206,277,285,308
Beaver Dam, 29,38,45,50,74,208,361
Blackwater, 11,45-46,96,169,192,246, 262,320,389-390,412-416,417
Bowes and arrows, 15,193
Clam, 16
Currawaugh/Corawake, 39,48-49,53, 120-123,218,407,420
Cypress, 64,111,305,365-366,375,393
Dirty, 248
First of Blackwater, 6-7,329,383
Freshett, 256
Gualkine, 296
Horse, 302-303,312,386,398
Indian Branch, 13
Kingsale, 33-34,37,40,50,74,208,278, 287
Locker line, 48
Maine, 33,36,59,65,233,262,341,390, 420
Maine Blackwater, 36,77 ,92-93,115, 282,303,336,356,401
Meadow, 220
Mill, 249
Nottoway, 414,421
Powell, 18,28
Seacock, 409
Second of Blackwater, 2-4,11,324
Third, 45
Turkey, 381-382
Western Branch side, 422

## Slaves

Anne, 76
Doll, 76
Franck, 267
Francke [fem.], 76
Hanah, 373
Rachell, 267
Siscoe, 182
Tom, 182
Willy, 229

## Approximate Ages as Indicated by Depositions in the Records

| Name | age | date of deposition | approximate year of birth | Record |
|---|---|---|---|---|
| John Altman | 30 | 11 Apr 1693 | 1663 | [62] |
| Benjamin Baldwin | 27 | 10 Oct 1698 | 1671 | [265] |
| Jacob Barnes | 43½ | 9 Feb 1692 | $164^{8}/_{9}$ | [56] |
| Benjamin Beale | 62 | 7 June 1690 | 1628 | [174] |
| Elizabeth Browne | 56 | 7 Oct 1695 | 1639 | [182] |
| Thomas Browne | 34 | 11 Apr 1693 | 1659 | [60] |
| Elizabeth Cookes | 47 | 8 June 1695 | 1648 | [164] |
| Francis Curtis | 30 | 11 Apr 1693 | 1663 | [60] |
| Jemima Drake | 43 | 11 Dec 1694 | 1651 | [128] |
| Giles Driver | 34 | 5 Jan $169^{4}/_{5}$ | $166^{0}/_{1}$ | [138] |
| Charles Durham | 38 | 11 Apr 1693 | 1655 | [60] |
| Thomas Fitzgerald | 20 | 11 Apr 1693 | 1673 | [60] |
| Robert Flake | 70 | 10 Aug 1691 | 1621 | [38] |
| Marable Franklin | 44 | 11 Dec 1694 | 1650 | [130] |
| John Garland | 23 | 11 Dec 1694 | 1671 | [130] |
| John Goodrich | 80 | 5 Mar $169^{7}/_{8}$ | $161^{7}/_{8}$ | [269] |
| John Griffin | 23 | 11 Apr 1693 | 1670 | [62] |
| Ellinor Hickes | 46 | 7 June 1704 | 1658 | [420] |
| Tristram Hilmoth | 30 | 11 Apr 1693 | 1663 | [61] |
| William Johnson | 44 | 11 Dec 1694 | 1650 | [129] |
| William Johnson | 50 | 10 Oct 1698 | 1648 | [266] |
| John Jolife | 39 | 7 Oct 1695 | 1656 | [182] |
| Richard Jones | 22 | 9 Apr 1694 | 1672 | [113] |
| Joseph Jordan | 23 | 8 Aug 1695 | 1672 | [165] |
| Theophilus Joyner | 35 | 8 June 1695 | 1660 | [164] |
| Ann Keebel | 50 | 10 June 1695 | 1645 | [160] |
| Ann Lane | 50 | 8 June 1695 | 1645 | [163] |
| Thomas Lucas | 34 | 8 June 1695 | 1661 | [164] |
| John Lucke | 22 | 2 Jan 1692 | 1670 | [57] |
| John Luther | 39 | 5 Jan $169^{4}/_{5}$ | $165^{5}/_{6}$ | [138] |
| William Miles | 75 | 5 Mar $169^{7}/_{8}$ | $162^{2}/_{3}$ | [269] |
| Thomas Norsworthy | 30 | 29 June 1695 | 1665 | [170] |
| John Parker | 27 | 11 Apr 1693 | 1666 | [62] |
| Mary Parker | 21 | 11 Apr 1693 | 1672 | [62] |
| Katherine Pierce | 25 | 10 Aug 1691 | 1666 | [38] |
| Jane Plow | 74 | 7 June 1704 | 1630 | [419] |
| Margarett Whitley | 36 | *ca.* 2 July 1690 | 1654 | [27] |

| | | | | |
|---|---|---|---|---|
| Elizabeth Reeves | 60 | 9 Dec 1701 | 1641 | [340] |
| Thomas Reeves | 52 | 9 Oct 1701 | 1649 | [339] |
| Thomas Richards | 28 | *ca.* 2 July 1690 | 1662 | [27] |
| Arthur Smith, Sr. | 55 | 9 Feb $169^{2}/_{3}$ | $163^{7}/_{8}$ | [55] |
| Arthur Smith, Jr. | 23 | Feb 1692 | 1669 | [55] |
| Mary Smith | 58 | 9 Feb 1692 | 1634 | [57] |
| William Smith | 58 | 9 Feb 1692 | 1634 | [56] |
| John Streete | 41 | 11 Apr 1693 | 1652 | [61] |
| Robert Sturdy | 56 | 24 Sept 1696 | 1640 | [210] |
| Mary Thompson | 41 | 7 June 1704 | 1663 | [419] |
| Henry Tooker | 40 | 10 June 1695 | 1650 | [161] |
| James Tullagh | 46 | 5 Jan $169^{4}/_{5}$ | $164^{8}/_{9}$ | [139] |
| Thomas Whitley | 40 | 10 Oct 1698 | 1658 | [266] |
| Ann Wilkinson | 23 | 2 Aug 1695 | 1672 | [167] |
| Richard Wilkinson | 28 | 2 Jan 1692 | 1664 | [57] |
| Dennis Williams | 26 | 11 Apr 1693 | 1667 | [62] |
| John Williams | 18 | 11 Apr 1693 | 1675 | [60] |
| Nicholas Williams | 7 | 21 May 1694 | 1687 | [106] |
| Thomas Willson | 28 | 9 June 1694 | 1666 | [114] |

## Previous Publications

"The Maternal Ancestry of Gov. Augustus Hill Garland," in *The Arkansas Family Historian*, vol. 17, no. 1 [Jan-Mar 1979], pp. 25-27.[1]

"Wilkinsons of Virginia and Yazoo County, Mississippi," in *The Virginia Genealogist*, vol. 24, no. 4 [Oct-Dec 1980], pp. 178-80.

"Almost *Mayflower* Descendants in the Carolinas," in *Nexus*, vol. 8, no. 1 [Feb-Mar 1991], pp. 24-25.

"Following the Clues: The Family of Dr. Joel Walker," in *Tennessee Ancestors*, vol. 7, no. 1 [Apr 1991], pp. 55-59.

"The Ancestry of Tennessee Williams," in *Nexus*, vol. 8, nos. 3 & 4 [June-Aug 1991], pp. 108-112.

"The Maternal Ancestry of Henry Soane," in *The Virginia Genealogist*, vol. 35, no. 3 [July-Sept 1991], pp. 163-72.

"The Ancestry of Tennessee Williams," in *Tennessee Ancestors*, vol. 7, no. 2 [Aug 1991], pp. 159-204.

"The Descendants of Moses White of Rowan Co., NC," in *Tennessee Ancestors*, vol. 7, no. 3 [Dec 1991], pp. 303-66.

"Carter, Helms, and Presley--A Foray into the Piedmont *Non-Plantation South*," in *Nexus*, vol. 8, no. 6 [Dec 1991], pp. 204-06.

"Using Middle Names To Establish a *Burned County* Pedigree," in *The Virginia Genealogist*, vol. 36, no. 3 [July-Sept 1992], pp. 163-72.

A series of articles (concerning the English ancestry of the following families: Castlyn, Fisher, Knapp, Lake, Lucas, Oldham, Sowter, Whitman), in John Brooks Threlfall, *Twenty-Six Great Migration Colonists to New England and Their Origins*. Madison, Wis., 1993.

"Hollywood Gothic and the Alabama Three," in *Nexus*, vol. 10, no. 4 [Aug-Sept 1993], pp. 110-15.

---

[1] A work of extreme youth which should be treated with extreme caution.

*The Complete Ancestry of Tennessee Williams.* Jackson, Miss., 1993.

"An Illegitimate and a 'Legitimate' Royal Descent for John Fisher of Virginia," in *The Virginia Genealogist*, vol. 38, no. 4 [Oct-Dec 1994], pp. 283-89.

*An Addendum to* The Complete Ancestry of Tennessee Williams: *The Ancestry of Gen. James Robertson, "Father of Tennessee."* Jackson, Miss., 1995.

*The Five Thomas Harrises of Isle of Wight County, Virginia.* Jackson, Miss., 1995.[2]

"A Royal Descent for Christopher Calthorpe of York Co., VA," in *The Virginia Genealogist*, vol. 40, no. 1 [Jan-Mar 1996], pp. 64-67.

*The Descendants of Cheney Boyce, "Ancient Planter," and of Richard Craven, for Seven Generations.* Jackson, Miss., 1996.

"Joseph Bridger of Dursley, Gloucestershire," in *The Virginia Genealogist*, vol. 41, no. 3 [July-Sept, 1997], pp. 183-84.

"Subtle Recognition in Seventeenth-Century Virginia," in *The American Genealogist*, vol. 73, no. 1 [Jan 1998], p. 10.

"The Batte Family of Birstall, Yorkshire, and Bristol Parish, Virginia," in *The Virginia Genealogist*, vol. 42, no. 3 [July-Sept, 1998], pp. 214-30.

"William[3] Tooke's Children: A Reinvestigation," in *The Virginia Genealogist*, vol. 42, no. 4 [Oct-Dec, 1998], pp. 291-99.

*Colonial Families of Surry and Isle of Wight Counties, Virginia.* Vol. 2. *The Descendants of Robert Harris.* Jackson, Miss., 1999.

"The Will of Arthur Jones of Bermuda," in *The Virginia Genealogist*, vol. 43, no. 3 [July-Sept, 1999], pp. 227-31.

---

[2] This is actually the first volume of *Colonial Families of Surry and of Isle of Wight Counties, Virginia.*

"Of Things Clerical," in *Friends of the Virginia State Archives, Archives News*, vol. 9, no. 2 [Fall 1999], pp. 1 and 12.

*Colonial Families of Surry and Isle of Wight Counties, Virginia.* Vol. 3. *Isle of Wight Co., VA, Court Orders, Oct 1693-May 1695.* Jackson, Miss., 1999.

In collaboration with Kenneth W. Kirkpatrick, "Cottoniana, or 'That Cotton-Pickin' Somerby!' ", in *The New Hampshire Genealogical Record*, vol. 16, no. 4 [Oct 1999], pp. 145-70.

*"By a Line of Marked Trees," Abstracts of Currituck Co., NC, Deed Books [1], 1-2, and 3, pp. 1-122.* Jackson, Miss., 2000.

"The Ancestry of Robert Batte," in *The Virginia Genealogist*, vol. 44, no. 3 [July-Sept, 2000], pp. 163-71.

"America's Best Southern Genealogical Libraries," in *Friends of the Virginia State Archives, Archives News*, vol. 10, no. 2 [Fall 2000], pp. 1, 4-7.

"The Ancestry of Robert Batte [concluded]" in *The Virginia Genealogist*, vol. 44, no. 4 [Oct-Dec 2000], pp. 301-08.

"Madam Ester Pollock and the Cullens," in *The North Carolina Genealogical Journal*, vol. 26, no. 4 [Nov 2000], pp. 363-75.

"The Ancestry of Thomas Cullen," in *The North Carolina Genealogical Journal*, vol. 26, no. 4 [Nov 2000], pp. 376-92.

"The Ancestry of Edward Jones of Isle of Wight County, Virginia," in *The Virginia Genealogist*, vol. 45, no. 1 [Jan-Mar, 2001], pp. 66-70.

*Colonial Families of Surry and Isle of Wight Counties, Virginia.* Vol. 4. *The Descendants of Capt. John Jennings of Isle of Wight County, Virginia.* Jackson, Miss., 2001.

*Colonial Families of Surry and Isle of Wight Counties, Virginia.* Vol. 5. *Isle of Wight County, Virginia, Book A, Deeds, Wills, Conveyances.* Jackson, Miss., 2001.

*Colonial Families of Surry and Isle of Wight Counties, Virginia.* Vol. 6. *Isle of Wight County, Virginia, Will & Deed Book 1, 1662-1688. Deed Abstracts, 1715.* Jackson, Miss., 2001.

"The English Ancestry of Benjamin Laker of Perquimans Co., NC," in *The North Carolina Genealogical Society Journal*, vol. 27, no. 3 [Aug 2001], pp. 291-94.

"The Weepings and Wailings of a Disappointed Genealogist: A Partisan Revue of Volume 1 of *The Dictionary of Virginia Biography*," in *Friends of the Virginia State Archives, Archives News*, vol. 11, no. 2 [Fall 2001], pp. 6-8.

"The Ancestry of Henry Applewight of Isle of Wight Co., VA," in *The Virginia Genealogist*, vol. 45, no. 4 [Oct-Dec, 2001], pp. 243-253.

*The Annotated Abstracts of Southampton County, Virginia, Deed Book One*. Jackson, Miss., 2001.

"The English Ancestry of Christopher Gale, Attorney General of North Carolina, for Four Generations," in *The North Carolina Genealogical Society Journal*, vol. 28, no. 1 [Feb 2002], pp. 44-69.

"The Ancestry of the Rev. Francis Doughty of Massachusetts, Long Island, New Amsterdam, Maryland, and Virginia," in *The American Genealogist*, vol. 77, no. 1 [Jan 2002], pp. 1-16.

"Notes on the Roper Family of Somerset and Isle of Wight Co., Va.," in *The Virginia Genealogist*, vol. 46, no. 1 [Jan-Mar 2002], pp. 66-67.

"Historical Records as Literature," in *Friends of the Virginia State Archives, Archives News*, vol. 12, no. 1 [Spring 2002], pp. 3-6.

"Check the Original! Two Lessons Learned the Hard Way: Hardy of South Carolina—A 'Discreet Omission to Hide an Indiscretion,' " in *The National Genealogical Society Quarterly*, vol. 90, no 1 [Mar 2002], pp. 69-71.

"The Ancestry of the Rev. Francis Doughty of Massachusetts, Long Island, New Amsterdam, Maryland, and Virginia [concluded]," in *The American Genealogist*, vol. 77, no. 2 [Apr 2002], pp. 127-36.

*Colonial Families of Surry and Isle of Wight Counties, Virginia*. Vol. 7. *The Ancestry of the Pitt Family of Bristol, Gloucester, Charlestown, Massachusetts, and Isle of Wight County, Virginia*. Jackson, Miss., 2002.

"Thomas Mallory (1566-1644), Rector of Davenham and Dean of Chester," in *The Virginia Genealogist*, vol. 46, no. 2 [Apr-June, 2002], pp. 83-90.

"Just What are They Doing Over There, Anyway? Differences in American and English Genealogical Research Methodology," in *Friends of the Virginia State Archives, Archives News*, vol. 12, no. 2 [Summer 2002], pp. 3, 6-7.

"A Tentative Royal Descent for Daniel Dobyns of Essex Co., Va.," in *The Virginia Genealogist*, vol. 46, no.3 [July-Sept 2002], pp. 163-66.

"A Tentative Reconstruction of the Crowder Family of Bristol Parish, Charles City, and Prince George, Counties, 1680," in *Tidewater Virginia Families*, vol. 11, no. 2 [Aug-Sept, 2002], pp. 74-78.

"Notes on the Ancestry of Valentia (Sparke) Branch, Mother of Christopher Branch," in *The Virginia Genealogist*, vol. 46, no. 4 [Oct-Dec 2002], pp. 282-92.

"Notes on the Ancestry of Mary (Addy) Branch, Wife of Christopher Branch," in *The Virginia Genealogist*, vol. 46, no. 4 [Oct-Dec 2002], pp. 293-98.

"Rolfe/Relfe-Jennings: The Unclosed Case of an Unclosed Case," in *The North Carolina Genealogical Society Journal*, vol. 29, no. 1 [Feb 2003], pp. 3-43.

"Genealogical Notes from Virginia Colonial Decisions by William Ronald Cocke, III—A Correction and Another 'Burned County Pedigree,' " in *The Virginia Genealogist*, vol. 47, no. 1 [Jan-Mar, 2002], pp. 38-50.

"Early Riveses of the Tidewater," in *The Virginia Genealogist*, vol. 47, no. 2 [Apr-June, 2003], pp. 83-92.

"Robert, William, and Thomas Hicks of Flushing, Long Island, NY, and Granville Co., NC," in *The North Carolina Genealogical Society Journal*, vol. 29, no. 3 [August 2003], pp. 238-309.

"The Warwick Family of Middlesex Co., VA" in *The Virginia Genealogist*, vol. 47, no. 3 [July-September, 2003], pp. 198-214.

*Transcriptions of Provincial North Carolina Wills, 1663-1729/30.* Vol. 1, *Testators A-K.* Jackson, Miss., 2003.

"Notes on the Taborer Family of Derby, Derbyshire, England, and Isle of Wight County, Virginia," in *Magazine of Virginia Genealogy*, vol. 41, no. 3 [August 2003], pp. 177-92.

"Good News and Bad News in Applewight Research," in *The Virginia Genealogist*, vol. 47, no. 4 [Oct-Dec, 2003], pp. 267-71.

"The Other Philacrista," in *The North Carolina Genealogical Society Journal*, vol. 30, no. 1 [February 2004], pp. 47-64.

"Did the Rev. John Farnefold Have Descendants?" in *The Virginia Genealogist*, vol. 48, no. 1 [January-March, 2004], pp. 28-37.

"Some English Descendants of a North Carolina Colonist," in *Friends of the Virginia State Archives, Archives News*, vol. 14, no. 1 [Winter 2004], pp. 1 and 7.

"Nicholson and Redknap Families of Massachusetts and North Carolina," in *The North Carolina Genealogical Society Journal*, vol. 30, no. 2 [May 2004], pp. 173-97.

"From One Boston to Another: Notes on the Ancestry of Mary (Jackson) Woodward," in *The New England Historical and Genealogical Register*, vol. 158, no. 631 [July 2004], pp. 213-27.

"The Ancestry of Frances (Baldwin) Townshend-Jones-Williams," in *The Virginia Genealogist*, vol. 48, no. 3 [July-September, 2004], pp. 170-84.

"The Early Whitakers of Middlesex County, Massachusetts," in *The Genealogist*, vol. 18, no. 2 [Fall 2004], pp. 232-54.

*Colonial Families of Surry and Isle of Wight Counties, Virginia.* Vol. 8. *Isle of Wight Co., VA, Will & Deed Book 2, 1666-1719.* Jackson, Miss., 2004.

"The Ancestry of Mrs. Anne (Thoroughgood) Chandler-Fowke," in *The Virginia Genealogist*, vol. 48, no. 4 [October-December, 2004], pp. 243-56.

*Transcriptions of Provincial North Carolina Wills, 1663-1729/30.* Vol. 2, *Testators L-Z.* Jackson, Miss., 2005.

Order of First Families of North Carolina. *Ancestor Registry*. Vol. 1. Jackson, Miss., 2005.

"The Pasquotank Descendants of John Scarborough of Middlesex Co., VA, for Four Generations," in *The North Carolina Genealogical Society Journal*, vol. 31, no. 3 [August 2005], pp. 234-47.

"The Hayman Family of Somerset Co., MD, and Pasquotank Co., NC," in *The North Carolina Genealogical Society Journal*, vol. 31, no. 3 [August 2005], pp. 248-54.

"The Ancestry of Frances (Baldwin) Townshend-Jones-Williams, Part II," in *The Virginia Genealogist*, vol. 49, no. 3 [July-September, 2005], pp. 210-14.

*Transcriptions of Provincial North Carolina Wills, 1663-1729/30*. Vol. 2, *Testators L-Z*. Jackson, Miss., 2005.

"The Wrong James and Alice (__) Ashton, Alas!" in *The New England Historical and Genealogical Register*, vol. 160 [2006], p, 60.

*Transcription of Norfolk Co., VA, Record Book D, 1655-1665*. Jackson, Miss., 2007.

"Additions to the Ancestry of Sarah (Hawkredd) (Story) (Cotton) Mather of Boston, Lincolnshire," in *The Genealogist*, vol. 20, no. 1 [Spring 2007] and vol. 21, no. 2 [Fall 2007], pp. 191-217 (conclusion).

*By a Line of Marked Trees*. Vol. 2. *Abstracts of Currituck County, North Carolina, Deed Books 3-4*. Baltimore, Md., 2007.

"Brayton Family Record, Herkimer County," in *The New York Genealogical and Biographical Record*, vol. 138 [2007], pp. 300-01.

*Order of First Families of North Carolina, Ancestor Registry*, vol. 2. *The Descendants of John and Thomas Williams of Isle of Wight Co., VA*. Baltimore, Md., 2008.

*Transcriptions of Provincial North Carolina Wills, 1663-1729/30*. Vol. 2, *Testators L-Z*. 2nd Edition. Baltimore, Md., 2008.

"An Annotated Pedigree of a Medlock Family from the Louisa County, Virginia Chancery Suits," in *Magazine of Virginia Genealogy*, vol. 46, no. 3 [August 2008], pp. 188-202.

*Colonial Families of Surry and Isle of Wight Counties, Virginia.* Vol. 9. *The Family of George Williams, died 1672, Isle of Wight Co., VA. With Corrections and Additions to* Adventurers of Purse and Person, *4th Ed. Including the Families of Reynolds, Hunt, and Parker.* Baltimore, Md., 2008.

*Abstracts of Pasquotank Co., NC, Deeds, 1750-1770.* Baltimore, Md., 2008.

"The Pumphrey Family of Gloucestershire, Maryland, and North Carolina," in *The North Carolina Genealogical Society Journal*, vol. 35, no. 3 [August 2009], pp. 217-54.

"Corrections and Additions to *Adventurers of Purse and Person*, 4th ed., Rookings-Watson," in *Magazine of Virginia Genealogy*, vol. 47, no. 3 [August 2009], pp. 249-52.

"Daniel Tanner of Norfolk, Virginia, and Canterbury, Kent," in *Magazine of Virginia Genealogy*, vol. 47, no. 4 [November 2009], pp 257-61.

*Colonial Families of Surry and Isle of Wight Counties, Virginia.* Vol. 10. *Bridger of Godalming, Surrey; Slimbridge, Gloucestershire; and Virginia.* Baltimore, Md., 2010.

*Transcription of Norfolk Co., VA, Record Book C, 1651-1655.* Baltimore, Md., 2010.

*Abstracts of Carteret County, NC, Deed Books A-F, 1713-1759.* Baltimore, Md., 2010.

*Abstracts of Beaufort County, NC, Deed Book 2, 1729-1748.* Baltimore, Md., 2011.